ANTENNAS: FUNDAMENTALS, DESIGN, MEASUREMENT

This book is dedicated to my wife Beverly Benson Long, for our enduring love and her world-wide work in the promotion of mental health and the prevention of mental disorders.

ANTENNAS: FUNDAMENTALS, DESIGN, MEASUREMENT

THIRD EDITION

LAMONT V. BLAKE
MAURICE W. LONG

Yes Dee Publishing Pvt Ltd
Publishing Par Excellence

ISBN: 978-93-80381-26-8

Indian Reprint, 2012

Lamont V. Blake, Maurice W. Long, *Antennas-Fundamentals, Design, Measurement*

Published by
Yes Dee Publishing Pvt Ltd
New No.16, Old No.18/A,
Govindan Street, Ayyavoo Colony,
Aminjikarai, Chennai – 600 029.
Tamil Nadu, INDIA.

+91 44 4508 2085
suresh@yesdee.com
www.yesdee.com

Printed at Chennai Micro Print Pvt. Ltd., Chennai.

Contents

	Dedication	**ii**
	Preface	**xv**
Chapter 1	**Electromagnetic Waves**	**1**
	1.1 Characteristics of Electromagnetic Waves	2
	1.1.1 Wave Velocity	2
	1.1.2 Frequency and Wavelength	3
	1.1.3 Space–Time Relationships	4
	1.1.4 Polarization	6
	1.1.5 Rays and Wavefronts	7
	1.1.6 Spherical Waves and the Inverse-Square Law	8
	1.1.7 Field Intensity and Power Density	10
	1.1.8 Decibel (Logarithmic) Expression of Attenuation	12
	1.1.9 Absorption	13
	1.2 Radio-Wave Optical Principles	15
	1.2.1 Refraction	15
	1.2.2 Reflection	18
	1.2.3 Principle of Images	21
	1.2.4 Interference	22
	1.2.5 Huygens' Principle: Diffraction	25
	1.3 Radiation and Reception	26
	1.3.1 Requirements for Radiation	28
	1.3.2 Reception and Reciprocity	30
	1.4 Environmental Wave-Propagation Effects	31
	1.4.1 The Earth Environment	31
	1.4.2 Beyond-the-Horizon Propagation	32
	1.4.3 Reflection from the Earth's Surface	35
	1.4.4 Variations in Earth's Reflection Coefficient	39
	1.4.5 Wave Nomenclature	40
	1.4.6 Transionospheric Propagation	41
	1.4.7 The Radio-Transmission Equation	42
	References	44
	Problems and Exercises	44

Chapter 2 Transmission Lines **47**
2.1 Basic Transmission-Line Concepts 47
2.1.1 Equivalent-Circuit Line Representation 48
2.1.2 The Lossless Infinite Line 50
2.1.3 Reflection and Standing Waves 52
2.2 Transmission-Line Equations 54
2.2.1 Steady-State Lossless Line Equations 54
2.2.2 Some Important Special Line Conditions 55
2.2.3 Impedance-Admittance Relationships 58
2.2.4 Reflection Coefficient and *VSWR* 60
2.2.5 Standing-Wave Patterns 62
2.2.6 Determination of Load Impedance by Standing-Wave Measurement 63
2.2.7 Attenuation 64
2.3 Impedance Matching and Power Division 65
2.3.1 The Matching Principle 65
2.3.2 Stub Transformers 66
2.3.3 Power Dividers 67
2.4 Forms of Transmission Lines 69
2.4.1 Characteristic Impedances 71
2.5 Waveguides 72
2.5.1 Phase and Group Velocities 72
2.5.2 Cutoff Frequency 74
2.5.3 Rectangular Waveguides 74
2.5.4 Modes of Propagation 75
2.5.5 Impedance in Waveguides 76
2.5.6 Impedance Matching in Waveguides 76
2.5.7 Transmission-Line-to-Waveguide Coupling 77
2.5.8 Waveguide Junctions 78
2.5.9 Other Forms of Waveguide 78
2.6 Hybrid and Directional Couplers 80
References 83
Problems and Exercises 84

Chapter 3 Antenna Parameters **87**
3.1 Antenna Structures 88
3.1.1 Size 88
3.1.2 Supports 88
3.1.3 Feed Lines 89
3.1.4 Conductors 89
3.1.5 Insulators 90
3.1.6 Weather Protection 90

	3.2	Radiation Pattern	91
		3.2.1 Coordinate Systems	91
		3.2.2 Definition of Pattern	93
		3.2.3 Patterns in a Plane	93
		3.2.4 Absolute and Relative Patterns	94
		3.2.5 Near-Field and Far-Field Patterns	95
		3.2.6 Free-Space and Earth-Reflection Patterns	97
	3.3	Directivity and Gain	98
		3.3.1 Definitions of Directivity and Gain	99
		3.3.2 Solid Angle	99
		3.3.3 Radiation Intensity	100
		3.3.4 Directivity	101
		3.3.5 Gain	102
	3.4	Effective Area and Friis Transmission Equation	103
	3.5	Beamwidth	105
		3.5.1 Practical Significance of Beamwidth	105
		3.5.2 Beamwidth Definition	106
		3.5.3 Principal-Plane Beamwidths	107
	3.6	Minor Lobes	107
	3.7	Radiation Resistance and Efficiency	108
	3.8	Input Impedance	110
	3.9	Bandwidth	111
	3.10	Polarization	112
	3.11	Interdependencies of Gain, Beamwidths, and Aperture Dimensions	113
	References		115
	Problems and Exercises		115
Chapter 4	**Basic Radiators and Feed Methods**		**119**
	4.1	Short Dipoles	119
		4.1.1 Dipole Radiation	120
		4.1.2 Pattern of an Elemental Dipole	123
		4.1.3 Radiation Resistance	125
		4.1.4 Directivity	125
		4.1.5 Beamwidth	126
		4.1.6 Input Impedance	126
		4.1.7 Short Dipole with Nonuniform Current Distribution	127
		4.1.8 Short Vertical Antenna with Ground Image	129
		4.1.9 Top-Loaded Antenna	130
	4.2	Current and Voltage in Longer Antennas	132
	4.3	The Half-Wave Dipole	136

4.4	Long-Wire Antennas		138
	4.4.1	Patterns of Resonant Antennas	139
	4.4.2	Radiation Resistance and Directivity	141
	4.4.3	Patterns of Nonresonant Antennas	142
	4.4.4	Polarization	142
	4.4.5	Effect of the Ground and Other Factors	143
	4.4.6	Uses of Long-Wire Antennas	143
4.5	Loop Antennas		144
	4.5.1	The Small Loop	144
	4.5.2	Other Loop Antennas	146
4.6	Helical Antennas		148
4.7	Horn Radiators		150
4.8	Slot Radiators		155
4.9	Patch or Microstrip Antennas		157
4.10	Surface-Wave and Leaky-Wave Antennas		159
4.11	Basic Feed Methods		159
References			164
Problems and Exercises			165
Chapter 5	**Arrays**		**169**
5.1	Basic Array Theory		169
	5.1.1	The Two-Isotropic-Element Array	170
	5.1.2	Pattern Versus θ and ϕ	174
	5.1.3	Parallel-Dipole Two-Element Array	174
	5.1.4	Mutual Coupling	177
	5.1.5	Input and Mutual Impedances, and Radiation Resistance	178
	5.1.6	Principle of Pattern Multiplication	179
	5.1.7	Effects of Element Directivity and Mutual Coupling	181
5.2	Multielement Uniform Linear Arrays		182
	5.2.1	Radiation Pattern	183
	5.2.2	Broadside Linear Arrays	183
	5.2.3	Endfire Arrays	186
5.3	Parasitically Excited Endfire Arrays		188
5.4	Planar and Volume Arrays with Uniform Aperture Distribution		190
	5.4.1	Planar Arrays	190
	5.4.2	Pattern Versus θ and ϕ	191
	5.4.3	Volume Arrays and Plane Reflectors	193
5.5	Linear Array Pattern Calculations		194
	5.5.1	General Equations for Array Patterns	194
	5.5.2	Linear Array Patterns	196

	5.5.3	Broadside Linear Array Patterns	197
	5.5.4	Grating Lobes	198
	5.5.5	Comparisons: Broadside Array and Continuous Aperture Antenna	198
	5.5.6	Endfire Array Patterns	199
5.6		Array Tapering for Side-Lobe Reduction	201
	5.6.1	Introduction	201
	5.6.2	Amplitude Tapering of Broadside Arrays: General	202
	5.6.3	Dolph-Chebyshev Synthesis	203
	5.6.4	Simplified Calculations for Dolph-Chebyshev Patterns	205
	5.6.5	The Taylor Distribution	206
	5.6.6	Other Low-Side-Lobe Array Distributions	208
5.7		Planar Arrays: Patterns, Directivity, and Gain	209
	5.7.1	Introduction	209
	5.7.2	Principal Plane Patterns: Equal Element Spacings	210
	5.7.3	Separable Aperture Distributions	211
	5.7.4	Patterns Versus θ and ϕ: Equal Amplitude, Separable Arrays	212
	5.7.5	Summary of Planar Array Patterns	213
	5.7.6	Beamwidth and Gain of Broadside Arrays	215
5.8		Some Other Array Types	218
	5.8.1	Long-Wire Arrays	218
	5.8.2	Horn and Slot Arrays	220
	5.8.3	Patch or Microstrip Arrays	220
	5.8.4	Phased Arrays for Scanning	221
5.9		General Remarks on Mutual Coupling	221
References			222
Problems and Exercises			223
Chapter 6		**Reflectors and Lenses**	**227**
6.1		Focusing and Collimation	228
	6.1.1	Focusing by a Parabolic Reflector	228
	6.1.2	Paraboloids and Parabolic Cylinders	230
	6.1.3	Space Attenuation for Point and Line Sources	230
6.2		Beamwidth and Directivity	233
	6.2.1	Shape of Aperture	233
	6.2.2	Primary and Secondary Patterns	233
	6.2.3	Beamwidth	234
	6.2.4	Directivity	234
6.3		Reflector Illumination	234
	6.3.1	Primary Pattern Requirements	235

6.3.2 Taper and Side Lobes for Elliptical Apertures 237
6.3.3 Optimum Illumination Taper 238
6.3.4 Line-Source Feeds 239
6.3.5 Feed-Positioning Requirements 241
6.3.6 Cassegrain Feeds 244
6.4 Radiation Patterns of Horn Antennas 245
6.4.1 Horn Patterns, in General 245
6.4.2 Shapes of Major Lobes 246
6.4.3 Measured Wide-Beamwidth Horn Patterns 247
6.4.4 Summary 248
6.5 Pattern Calculation and Reflector Antenna Design 248
6.5.1 General Remarks 248
6.5.2 Aperture Distribution and Pattern of a Half Parabolic Cylinder 250
6.5.3 Steps for Reflector Antenna Design 251
6.6 Reflector Construction 252
6.6.1 Fabrication Methods 253
6.6.2 Reflector Surface Accuracy Requirements 253
6.7 Corner-Reflector Antennas 255
6.8 Lens Antennas 257
6.8.1 Optical Lenses 257
6.8.2 Lens Surface Configurations 258
6.8.3 Lens Refracting Media 260
6.8.4 Variable-Index-of-Refraction Lenses 261
6.8.5 Focusing with Dielectric and Metal Plate Lenses 262
6.8.6 Dielectric Lenses 262
6.8.7 Metal Plate Lenses 264
6.8.8 Geodesic Luneberg Lenses 265
6.9 Beam Steering by Feed Offset 269
6.10 Pattern Calculations for Continuous Apertures 269
6.10.1 Historical Note on Aperture Analyses 270
6.10.2 Continuous Line Source 271
6.10.3 Aperture Analysis: General 274
6.10.4 Apertures Having Separable x and y Distributions 275
6.10.5 Equivalent Linear Apertures in Principal Planes 277
6.10.6 Circular Apertures 279
6.10.7 Patterns Versus θ and ϕ: A Summary 279
6.11 Comparison of Directive Antenna Types 281
References 282
Problems and Exercises 283

Chapter 7 Antennas with Special Properties **285**

7.1 Broad-Band Antennas 285

7.1.1 Basic Broad-Band Principles 286

7.1.2 Broad-Band Dipoles 288

7.1.3 Biconical Antennas 289

7.1.4 Monopoles 290

7.1.5 Folded Dipoles 291

7.1.6 Superturnstile Antenna 292

7.1.7 Miscellaneous Broad-Band Dipoles and Other Radiators 292

7.2 Frequency-Independent Antennas 293

7.2.1 The Log-Periodic Principle 294

7.2.2 Practical Log-Periodic Designs 297

7.2.3 Equiangular Log-Periodic Antennas 299

7.2.4 Self-Complementary Antennas 300

7.2.5 Spiral Antennas 301

7.3 Antennas for Multiple Polarizations 302

7.3.1 Antennas for Circular Polarization 302

7.3.2 Polarizers and Dual-Mode Transducers 305

7.3.3 Corrugated Horn Feeds 307

7.4 Omnidirectional Antennas 307

7.5 Electrically Small Antennas 308

7.6 Direction-Finding Antennas 310

7.6.1 Low-Frequency Null Systems 311

7.6.2 Beam-Maximum Systems 312

7.6.3 Lobing Antennas 312

7.7 Mechanical Scan Antennas 314

7.7.1 Introduction 314

7.7.2 Rapid Mechanical Scan Antennas 315

7.8 Low-Noise Receiving Antennas 320

7.9 Synthetic-Aperture Antennas 324

7.10 Antennas with Extremely Low Side Lobes 326

7.11 Geometrical Theory of Diffraction, Method of Moments, and Fractals 328

7.11.1 Geometric Theory of Diffraction 328

7.11.2 Method of Moments 329

7.11.3 Fractals and Fractal Antennas 330

References 332

Problems and Exercises 335

Chapter 8	**Electronically Steered Arrays**		**337**
	8.1	Phased Array Principles	338
	8.1.1	Time Delay and Phase Shift Requirements	339
	8.1.2	Effective Aperture Versus Scan Angle	340
	8.1.3	Frequency-Scan Antennas	341
	8.1.4	Array Bandwidth	342
	8.1.5	Phased Array Patterns	344
	8.1.6	Grating Lobes	346
	8.2	Beam-Steering Technology	347
	8.2.1	Phase Shifters	347
	8.2.2	Effects of Phase Quantization	349
	8.2.3	Effects of Element Mutual Coupling	350
	8.2.4	Time Delayers	351
	8.3	Phased Array Feed System Technology	351
	8.3.1	Feed Systems	352
	8.3.2	Active Arrays and T/R Modules	354
	8.3.3	Alternative Configurations, Including Subarrays	355
	8.3.4	Butler Matrix	355
	8.3.5	Array Sum and Difference Patterns	357
	8.3.6	Microstrip and Printed-Circuited Technology	357
	8.3.7	Conformal Arrays	357
	8.4	Adaptive Array Antennas	358
	8.4.1	Background System Developments	358
	8.4.2	Adaptive Beam-Forming Arrays	360
	8.4.3	Space-Time Adaptive Processing	362
	8.5	Examples of Electronically Steered Arrays	364
	References		368
	Problems and Exercises		370
Chapter 9	**Antenna Measurements**		**371**
	9.1	Antenna Patterns, General	371
	9.1.1	Radiating Near- and Far-Field Patterns	373
	9.1.2	Pattern Statistics: Near- and Far-Field Statistical Gain	376
	9.2	Far-Zone Pattern Measurements	377
	9.2.1	Low-Frequency Techniques	379
	9.2.2	High-Frequency Techniques	379
	9.2.3	Far-Field Ranges	381
	9.3	Compact Ranges	382
	9.4	Near-Field Antenna Measurements	385
	9.4.1	Planar Near-Field Measurements	386

9.4.2 Cylindrical Near-Field Measurements 387
9.4.3 Spherical Near-Field Measurements 387
9.5 Polarization Measurement 388
9.6 Scale-Model Measurements 389
9.7 Antenna Pattern Measurement Equipment 390
9.8 Directivity and Gain Measurements 393
9.8.1 Absolute-Field-Strength Method 394
9.8.2 Standard Gain Antennas 395
9.8.3 Power-Measurement Methods 396
9.8.4 Gain Measurement by Comparison 396
9.9 Antenna Efficiency 398
9.9.1 Radiation Efficiency 398
9.9.2 Aperture Efficiency 399
9.10 Radiation Resistance 399
9.11 Impedance Measurements 400
9.11.1 Standing-Wave Method 401
9.11.2 Network Analyzers 402
9.12 The Smith Chart 404
9.13 Antenna Noise Measurement 407
9.13.1 Elementary Noise Theory 407
9.13.2 Antenna Noise Temperature 409
9.13.3 Measurement Techniques 410
9.13.4 Low-Noise-Temperature Comparison Sources 413
9.13.5 Measurements Using Ambient Temperature Noise Sources 413
9.14 System Noise Calculations 414
9.14.1 Noise Figure 414
9.14.2 System Noise Temperature 415
References 417
Problems and Exercises 420

Answers to Problems **423**

Appendices

A. Maxwell's Equations 427
References 431
B. Polarization Theory 433
B.1 Elliptically Polarized Waves Resolved into Linearly Polarized Components 433
B.2 Elliptically Polarized Waves Resolved into Circularly Polarized Components 435

	B.3	Relationships between Linearly and Circularly Polarized Components	436
	References		437
C.	Review of Complex-Variable Algebra		439
D.	Complex Reflection Coefficients and Multipath Effects		445
	D.1	Fresnel's Equations	445
	D.2	Reflection Coefficients for Smooth Land and Sea	447
	D.3	Reflection Coefficients for Rough Surfaces	449
	D.4	Pattern-Propagation Factor *F*	450
	D.5	Flat Earth Geometry	451
	D.6	Multipath Dependencies on Frequency, Polarization, and Surface Roughness	453
	D.7	Spherical Earth Geometry	455
	D.8	Divergence Factor	459
	References		460
E.	Radomes		463
	References		466
F.	Far-Zone Range-Approximation and Phase Error		467
	References		468
G.	Radiating Near and Far Fields, and the Obliquity Factor		469
	G.1	The Radiating Fields	469
	G.2	Principal-Plane Patterns Versus Range	473
	References		474
H.	Path Length Differences from a Planar Aperture		475
I.	Effects of Random Aperture Phase Errors		479
	References		482

Index 483

About the Author 503

Supplemental Materials (SM)

The publisher has posted a list of supplemental materials (SM) to an accompanying website at:

www.scitechpub.com/blakelong3.htm

Within the text of the book you will find references to the specific SM sections that relate to the material being covered. A computer icon ( ) is used in the margin to further identify sections that refer to the SM.

SM Table of Contents

SM 1.0 Reflection Coefficients for Flat, Smooth Surfaces
- SM 1.1. Reflection Coefficients-Flat, Smooth Sea
- SM 1.2. Reflection Coefficients-Flat, Smooth Land

SM 2.0 Spherical Earth Geometry

SM 3.0 Earth Effects on Patterns and Multipath Propagation
- SM 3.1. Ground Effects on Elevation Patterns
- SM 3.2. Pattern Range Illumination Versus Observation Height
- SM 3.3. Multipath Versus Range, Flat Conducting Surface
- SM 3.4. Multipath Versus Range, Rough Flat Land
- SM 3.5. Multipath Versus Range, Spherical Earth
- SM 3.6. Divergence Factor Comparisons

SM 4.0 Antenna Radiation Analyses
- SM 4.1. Radiating Near and Far Fields, Uniform Aperture Approximation
- SM 4.2. Relative Gain Versus Range
- SM 4.3. Random Aperture Phase Errors
- SM 4.4. Radiating Near and Far Field Patterns of an Array
- SM 4.5. Radiating Near Field along an Aperture
- SM 4.6. Linear Array Pattern, Quadratic Phase Distribution
- SM 4.7. Steered Array Patterns Versus Phase
- SM 4.8. Steered Array Patterns at Two Frequencies
- SM 4.9. Pattern of Parabolic Cylinder with Offset Feed

SM 5.0 Three-Dimensional Pattern Construction, by Aaron Loggins

Preface

This is a senior undergraduate or first-year graduate level textbook on antenna fundamentals, design, performance analysis, and measurements. In addition to its use as a formal course textbook, it is well-suited for professional training and self-study by practicing engineers, scientists, and technologists who desire to expand their knowledge of antennas. The book provides a broad coverage of antenna types and phenomena, for operations at very low radio frequencies, as well as frequencies up to those of submillimeter wavelengths. Unlike most university-level antenna textbooks, reading it does not require prior skills in electromagnetic theory, sophisticated mathematics, or computer programming. An additional feature is the downloadable collection of computer solutions in both Mathcad® and MATLAB® to numerous antenna radiation examples, which can be easily implemented and revised by persons not having prior programming experience.

Evolution of the Third Edition

This new edition was prepared for use in a one-semester first-year graduate night class at the Southern Polytechnic State University located in Marietta, Georgia, where student backgrounds vary widely. At least half the students are from overseas and hold a bachelor's degree in electrical engineering or electronics. Of those from the United States, about half have degrees in electrical engineering, and the remainder hold degrees in electrical engineering technology. Generally, the students are older than a typical first-year graduate student, being 25 to 35 years of age. A few of the students have excellent backgrounds in vector calculus and the use of Maxwell's equations, while some of the older ones may need to refresh their abilities with the phasor calculations of electrical circuits.

The computer capabilities of the students also vary widely. Many of the entering graduate students are proficient in use of MATLAB or Mathcad software, but sometimes they are experienced with neither and rarely both. Additionally, some students who have been away from academics a few years may have little computer proficiency. Thus, to expedite the class learning on antennas with computer analyses, Mathcad, which is easily read without prior experience, is used in classroom lectures. For class assignments, students are allowed to use whatever computer software they choose. Mathcad software is used most often, with MATLAB being the second most popular choice. Often, original MATLAB users, after switching to Mathcad, have expressed appreciation for their introduction to Mathcad for its relative ease of use and intuitive qualities.

Because of the wide differences in student backgrounds, and after considering the available textbooks, Blake's *Antennas, Second Edition*, was selected for adoption because of its superior readability. Due to the book's age, the selection required preparing and distributing materials for updating and expanding the text and adding appendices. Consequently, the present book evolved into one that retains the benefits of Blake's second edition but expands the subject material suitably for a senior or graduate level textbook.

Background Assumed

Most antenna textbooks are written for students proficient with vector calculus and begin with the use of Maxwell's equations in the development of antenna theory. Such books often do not meet the needs of many students and practicing engineers who, because of their backgrounds or personal interests, desire a more direct path for assimilating antenna fundamentals and their connection to application topics of antenna engineering. Although antenna theory is founded on Maxwell's equations, understanding their concepts does not require advanced mathematics. At the beginning of each antenna course, the revising author (MWL) uses Appendix A, Maxwell's Equations, to address the key "postulates" of Maxwell and provide a brief introduction to, or review of, the essential equations. Thus, Maxwell equations are discussed with the goal of expressing their meaning in *words*. Then, the concepts of displacement current, interdependence of changing electric and magnetic fields, and wave propagation are described, and thus Maxwell's equations are underscored as "the ultimate truth" but thereafter considered outside the scopes of antenna design, performance analysis, and measurements.

Organization

This book was prepared with the intention of providing a comprehensive antenna text that can be readily understood by persons with undergraduate educations in engineering, science, or technology. The chapter titles follow:

Chapter 1. Electromagnetic Waves
Chapter 2. Transmission Lines
Chapter 3. Antenna Parameters
Chapter 4. Basic Radiators and Feed Methods
Chapter 5. Arrays
Chapter 6. Reflectors and Lenses
Chapter 7. Antennas with Special Properties
Chapter 8. Electronically Steered Arrays
Chapter 9. Antenna Measurements

Chapters 1 through 6 cover, generally, the physics and technology of antennas and include such subjects as wave propagation, reflection, refraction, diffraction, transmission and reception, basic radiators, antenna arrays, reflector antennas, and lenses.

Chapter 7 discusses antenna properties and analysis techniques not addressed in other chapters. Its range of topics is wide, and includes techniques for providing wide bandwidths, multiple polarizations, low receiver noise, and extremely low sidelobes. In addition, direction-finding antennas and mechanical beam scanners are addressed. Finally discussed are synthetic-aperture antennas, geometrical theory of diffraction (GTD), method of moments (MoM), and fractals.

Chapter 8 treats electronically steered arrays, whereas Chapter 5 is focused on fixed beam arrays. In other words, chapter 8 stresses array concepts specific to beam movement made possible with fast, wide-dynamic-range digital components and cheap computer memory, along with continued improvements in high-speed switches and phase shifters.

Chapter 9 includes a broad coverage of antenna measurement techniques and equipment. Subjects include radiating near fields as well as far field patterns and pattern statistics, compact ranges, and near-field measurements. Included also is a comprehensive treatment of antenna noise, noise temperature, noise figure, and system signal-to-noise ratios.

There are problems at the end of each chapter, and answers to the odd numbered problems are included in a section near the book's end. Appendices provide technical depth to the chapters, appropriate for a senior or first graduate level antenna course. The appendix titles follow:

Appendix A. Maxwell's Equations
Appendix B. Polarization Theory
Appendix C. Review of Complex-Variable Algebra
Appendix D. Complex Reflection Coefficients and Multipath Effects
Appendix E. Radomes
Appendix F. Far-Zone Range-Approximation and Phase Error
Appendix G. Radiating Near and Far Fields, and the Obliquity Factor
Appendix H. Path Length Differences from a Planar Aperture
Appendix I. Effects of Random Aperture Phase Errors

It is to be noted that Appendix C discusses complex-variable algebra. Although its contents will be familiar to most readers, it is included because some may find parts of it useful for review.

Data files of computer scripts

Where appropriate, the appendices and the downloadable data files are referenced in the chapters for providing a more complete treatment of antennas. In the Deluxe Edition, a full-featured copy of Mathcad 14.0 is included so that readers can easily create their own computer analyses. The downloadable data files provide computer solutions in both Mathcad and MATLAB to problems in the areas that follow:

– reflection coefficients for surfaces versus dielectric properties, conductivity, polarization, surface roughness, and incidence angle
– earth's multipath effects on antenna patterns versus surface properties, antenna and observation heights and separation distance, and polarization for flat and spherical earth models.
– radiating near and far fields from arrays and continuous aperture antennas, as functions of aperture phase and amplitude distributions and random aperture errors.

The files also include a supplemental chapter in PDF on the creation of antenna radiation field graphics using Mathcad. It was prepared by student Aaron Loggins as one of three project assignments in a one-semester antenna course.

Files can be downloaded from the publisher's web page for this book:

www.scitechpub.com/blakelong3.htm

Acknowledgements

Permissions to use the contents of *Antennas, 2nd Edition*, by Lamont V. Blake, now deceased, were provided by Barbara Blake, Lamont Blake's daughter, and other Blake family members and are gratefully appreciated. This third edition could not have been written otherwise because it was built upon an easily read, well-written text based on a solid technical foundation. Therefore, it could be readily expanded to provide a senior or graduate level textbook suitable for students with widely different academic backgrounds, including persons with limited or no computer programming experience.

Two important and closely related tasks were accomplished by Dr. Donald G. Bodnar in connection with "Chapter 9 – Measurements." First, he completed a technical review of an early version of the chapter, and he then wrote Sec. 9.4, a major section titled "Near Field Antenna Measurements." That section is copyrighted by MI Technologies, Inc., Don Bodnar's company.

Appreciation is acknowledged to Aaron Loggins for letting me use his classroom project paper as a PDF file that discusses the creation of 3-D graphics with Mathcad.

A major and generally thankless task of pursuing a penetrating technical edit of each chapter and appendix was accomplished by Dr. Edward B. Joy, and it was performed with record-breaking speed. Ed found and corrected not only accidental and careless errors, but he also underscored and made suggestions for correcting more substantive oversights.

Special thanks are due to Dr. Anatoliy Boryssenko of the University of Massachusetts for his expertise in checking the Mathcad files, offering helpful suggestions, and then rewriting them into MATLAB scripts. He did so under very tight deadlines. Dr. Boryssenko has also graciously offered additional files from his personal collection to further enhance the data set of the publisher's web page.

A major contribution to this book was made by Dr. Randy J. Jost of Utah State University, as an advisor to SciTech Publishing, by reviewing and suggesting additions to my early book writing plans. One of those suggestions was to include the files that contain a number of antenna radiation problems and their computer solutions. Inclusion of the CD in the Deluxe Edition that contains Mathcad, version 14, software results from the initiative of Dudley Kay, Founder of SciTech Publishing, and the cooperation of Parametric Technology Corporation, the owner of Mathcad. Permission by Parametric Technology Corporation to use screenshots of computer images from Mathcad software, included in the file on creating 3-D graphics is gratefully acknowledged.

There have been a number of persons who have made significant editorial improvements and others who have simply expressed an interest in an updated edition of Lamont Blake's *Antennas* becoming available. Some of these include Gerald Oortman of Lockheed Martin, Marietta, Georgia; Professor Charles Bachman of the Southern Polytechnic State University; Dr. Andrew Peterson of the School of Electrical and Computer Engineering, Georgia Institute of Technology; James Gitre of Motorola; Michael Havrilla of the Air Force Institute of Technology; and Rickey Cotton (deceased), Mark Mitchell, and Dr. Charles Ryan (retired) of Georgia Tech Research Institute.

I thank Phyllis Hinton of Georgia Tech Research Institute, who has, over the years, brightened my days when she sketches a figure I need or somehow helps me find my way through the ends and outs of Microsoft Word.

Appreciation is expressed here to Dudley Kay, Susan Manning, and Robert Lawless of SciTech Publishing who, during the preparation of this book, have demonstrated an enthusiasm for producing quality textbooks.

Maurice W. Long
Atlanta, Georgia
ML20@bellsouth.net

CHAPTER 1

Electromagnetic Waves

This book begins with an elementary discussion of electromagnetic wave theory, which is basic to an understanding of antennas. Readers who are quite familiar with the principles of electromagnetic waves may prefer to begin with the second (or third) chapter, but even they may find this introductory chapter a handy review of the subject and a useful reference source.

Electromagnetic waves in space are the basis of radio transmission over great distances without direct wire connection between the transmitting and receiving points. At the transmitting and receiving stations, radio signals exist in the form of high-frequency alternating currents in conductors and in electronic amplifying devices. Between the transmitter and receiver they exist as electromagnetic waves in space. Antennas, the subject of this book, are the devices that act as go-betweens.

At the transmitting station the antenna is energized by the electrical currents generated in the transmitter, and it converts the energy into the form of an electromagnetic field. It "launches" the waves into space. At the receiving station the antenna captures energy from the arriving field, and it converts the field variations into current and voltage replicas of those at the transmitter (though of much smaller amplitude).

Current and voltage in conductors are always accompanied by electric and magnetic fields in the adjoining region of space, and in a sense it is incorrect to speak of "converting" electrical energy from the form of current and voltage into the form of an electromagnetic field, and vice versa. In a practical sense, however, the distinction is made. In the one case the fields are bound to the conductors in which the current flows; in the other they are "free."

The picture of electromagnetic waves presented here is considerably simplified and necessarily leaves unanswered some questions that may be disturbing to the reader with an inquiring mind. Often these questions can be answered, but only through the use of rather sophisticated mathematical and physical concepts, based on James Maxwell's equations, which he published in 1873 (see Appendix A). Bear in mind that most of the ideas and principles to be discussed have this background, even though it is not necessary to look deeply into Maxwell's equations for the purposes of this book.

1.1. Characteristics of Electromagnetic Waves

A wave is an oscillatory motion of any kind, the most familiar being waves on the surface of water. Sound waves, another common example, are vibrations of the air or of various material substances. Both wave types involve mechanical motion. Electromagnetic waves are electric and magnetic field variations that can occur in empty space as well as in material substances.

All waves are characterized by the property called *propagation*. The vibrations at a particular point in space excite similar vibrations at neighboring points, and thus the wave travels or *propagates* itself. This concept is given more specific form as Huygens' principle, to be discussed later in this chapter. The particular substance or space in which a wave exists is the *propagation medium.*

1.1.1. Wave Velocity

Waves travel at characteristic speeds, depending on the type of wave and the nature of the propagation medium. For example, sound travels about 330 meters per second in the normal atmosphere, but in water the speed is 1,450 meters per second. In both media the figure varies with the temperature and other factors.

Free space is a term much used in discussion of electromagnetic waves. It implies not only empty space (a vacuum), but also remoteness from any material substances from which waves may be reflected. Electromagnetic waves travel exceptionally fast, approximately 300,000 kilometers per second (3×10^8 m/s) in free space. In other propagation media their speed may be less, but ordinarily it is very high compared with the speeds of things observable without special instruments. In the gases of the earth's normal atmosphere, in fact, the speed is only slightly less than in empty space (vacuum), and for practical purposes the difference is negligible except over very long paths. Even then it is ordinarily permissible to use the approximate free-space velocity figure for calculating how long it takes a radio wave to travel from one point to another in the atmosphere.

An important exception to this statement occurs when waves at certain radio frequencies travel in the ionosphere, a layer of charged particles (ions) lying above the earth between the heights of about 60 and 300 kilometers. At very low radio frequencies radio waves cannot penetrate the ionosphere; they are reflected from it. At very high frequencies waves pass through the ionosphere unimpeded at the same speed they would have in empty space. But in a critical intermediate frequency region, depending on ionospheric conditions (which vary considerably from day to night and with the season and other factors), the wave velocity in the ionosphere may be different than it is in vacuum.

The speed of electromagnetic propagation in a vacuum is of fundamental importance. This value, commonly called the "speed of light" in a vacuum, is designated by the symbol c. (Light waves are actually electromagnetic waves of very high frequency.) The value of c is 299,793 kilometers per second, rounded off for most purposes to 3×10^8 meters per second.

1.1.2. Frequency and Wavelength

The oscillations of waves are *periodic*, or repetitious. They are characterized by a *frequency*, the rate at which the periodic motion repeats itself, as observed at a particular point in the propagation medium. Complex waves may contain more than one frequency. The frequency is expressed in Hertz (*cycles per second*, a cycle being one full period of the wave). Hertz is abbreviated as Hz. A single-frequency wave motion has the form of a sinusoid.

The *wavelength* of an electromagnetic wave is the spatial separation of two successive "oscillations," which is equal to the distance that the wave travels during one sinusoidal cycle of oscillation. Therefore, if the wave velocity is v meters per second and the frequency is f cycles per second (Hertz), the wavelength in meters is

$$\lambda = \frac{v}{f} \tag{1–1}$$

As has been noted, v may have different values in different propagation media. When the wave velocity in free space (vacuum) c is used in (1–1), the resulting value of λ is the *free-space wavelength*, sometimes denoted by λ_0.

The electromagnetic spectrum covers an enormous range of frequencies, including cosmic-ray radiation with frequencies in excess of 10^{20} Hz. Radio frequencies, their designations, and free-space wavelengths are given in Table 1-1, that is derived from the reference IEEE Standard 211-1997. However, the radio waves that may be detected and amplified, from a practical point of view, are from about 10 kHz to 100 GHz (IEEE Standard 100–1992, p. 1059).

The International Telecommunications Union (ITU), an organization of the United Nations, makes the general guidelines for the assignment and use of frequencies.

TABLE 1-1 The Radio Frequency Spectrum

Designation	Frequency	Free-Space Wavelength
Ultra low frequency (ULF)	<3 Hz	>10^8 m
Extremely low frequency (ELF)	3 Hz–3 kHz	10^8–10^5 m
Very low frequency (VLF)	3–30 kHz	10^5–10^4 m
Low frequency (LF)	30–300 kHz	10^4–10^3 m
Medium frequency (MF)	300 kHz–3 MHz	10^3–10^2 m
High frequency (HF)	3–30 MHz	10^2–10 m
Very high frequency (VHF)	30–300 MHz	10–1 m
Ultra high frequency (UHF)	300 MHz to 3 GHz	1 m–10 cm
Super high frequency (SHF)	3–30 GHz	10–1 cm
Extremely high frequency (EHF)	30–300 GHz	1 cm–1 mm
Submillimeter	300 GHz–3 THz	1 mm–0.1 mm

Key to abbreviations. Hz = Hertz, kHz = kilohertz (10^3 Hz), MHz = megahertz (10^6 Hz), GHz = gigahertz (10^9 Hz), THz = terahertz (10^{12} Hz), m = meters, cm = 10^{-2} m, mm = 10^{-3} m.

Generally, the regulations of individual nations follow those of the ITU. For the United States, separate authorities for use by federal governmental and nonfederal governmental frequency usages are assigned to the National Telecommunications and Information Agency and the Federal Communications Commission, respectively. The ITU Radio Regulations allocates the frequencies between 9 kHz and 275 GHz into frequency bands, according to forty-two types of radio services usage—radio amateur, FM broadcast, television, and so on—and location within three regions of the world.

A governmental operating license, with restrictions on transmit power and waveform, is ordinarily required for radio transmit equipment, but there are some frequency bands where operations are permitted for low-power, short-range operations. Ah Yo and Emrick (2007) is a useful information source on frequency bands available for amateur ("ham"), commercial, and military.

Some of the better-known frequency allocations within the United States include:

- AM (amplitude modulation) broadcast: 535–1705 kHz
- FM (frequency modulation) broadcast: 88–108 MHz
- Television in 6 MHz bandwidth numbered channels:
  - 2–6, 54–60 MHz, . . . , 82–88 MHz
  - 7–13, 174–180 MHz, . . . , 210–216 MHz
  - 14–36, 470–476 MHz, . . . , 600–608 MHz

  Note: Following the current website on U.S. frequency allocations, www.ntia.doc.gov/osmhome/allocchrt.pdf, the region 614–698 MHz (without channel numbers) is allocated to TV. The frequencies 608–806 MHz were previously allocated for TV channels 37–69.
- GPS (global positioning satellite): 1227.6 MHz (military); 1575.42 MHz and 1227.6 (civilian); telemetry on 2227.5 MHz

Radar band designations following IEEE Standard 521-1984, page 8, are given in Table 1-2. Although standard for radar, these designations are used in a broader electronics community. The region 1 GHz (30 cm) to 30 GHz (1 cm) is usually called the microwave region; and, contrary to Table 1-2, the region 30 GHz (10 mm) to 300 GHz (1 mm) is usually called the millimeter wavelength region. Although millimeter-wave radars are becoming more widely used, most radars operate within the microwave region. Some operate at frequencies of a few MHz and a few even use infrared (8×10^{11}–4×10^{14} Hz) and visible light (4×10^{14}–7.5×10^{14} Hz) frequencies.

There are differences between Tables 1-1 and 1-2. In Table 1-1 (which is for nonradar usage), UHF is the frequency range 300 MHz–3 GHz, and the designations SHF and EHF cover the range 3–300 GHz. Although Table 1-2 is widely used, there is not universal agreement on its letter designations and frequencies.

1.1.3. Space–Time Relationships

An electromagnetic wave has two components, an electric field and a magnetic field. Each component varies sinusoidally in time at a fixed point of space, with time period $T = 1/f$ seconds, where f is the frequency in Hertz (cycles per second). Also at a fixed

TABLE 1-2 Standard Radar Band Designations

Designation	Frequency	Free-Space Wavelength
HF	3–30 MHz	100 m–10 m
VHF	30–300 MHz	10 m–1 m
UHF	300–1000 MHz	100 cm–30 cm
L Band	1–2 GHz	30 cm–15 cm
S Band	2–4 GHz	15 cm–7.5 cm
C Band	4–8 GHz	7.5 cm–3.75 cm
X Band	8–12 GHz	3.75 cm–2.50 cm
Ku Band	12–18 GHz	2.50 cm–1.67 cm
K Band	18–27 GHz	1.67 cm–1.11 cm
Ka Band	27–40 GHz	1.11 cm–.75 cm
V Band	40–75 GHz	7.5 mm–4.0 mm
W Band	75–110 GHz	4.0 mm–2.7 mm
mm Band	110–300 GHz	2.7 mm–1.0 mm

instant of time there is a sinusoidal variation in space along the direction of propagation, with spatial period (wavelength) $\lambda = v/f$ meters, where v is the velocity of propagation in meters per second [from (1–1)]. In terms of a cartesian coordinate system (rectangular coordinates x, y, z), if the electric field E of the wave is represented by vectors parallel to the x-axis and the wave is propagating in free space in a direction parallel to the z-axis, the magnetic field H will be represented by vectors parallel to the y-axis, as shown in Fig. 1–1. These space–time relationships for a *plane wave* are expressed by (1–2) and (1–3):

$$\boldsymbol{E}_x(z,t) = \boldsymbol{E}_0 \sin\left(2\pi ft - \frac{2\pi z}{\lambda} + \phi\right) \tag{1–2}$$

$$\boldsymbol{H}_y(z,t) = \boldsymbol{H}_0 \sin\left(2\pi ft - \frac{2\pi z}{\lambda} + \phi\right) \tag{1–3}$$

The notation $\boldsymbol{E}_x(z, t)$ indicates that $\boldsymbol{E}_x$ is a vector parallel to the x-axis and has a magnitude that depends on the values of the variables z and t. The parameter $\boldsymbol{E}_0$ is the maximum value, defined as the *amplitude* of the wave. Note that $\boldsymbol{E}_0$ is the value that $\boldsymbol{E}_x(z, t)$ attains when $|\sin(2\pi ft - 2\pi z/\pi + \phi)| = 1$, which in turn will occur periodically at time intervals of $T = 1/2f$ at a fixed point and at z-intervals of $\lambda/2$ (half-cycle and half-wavelength intervals). Sometimes the root-mean-squared (rms) value, rather than the peak value, is used to characterize the amplitude of a sinusoidal oscillation. The parameter ϕ is the initial phase angle of the wave; that is, at $t = 0$ and $z = 0$, $\boldsymbol{E}_x(z, t)$ has the value $\boldsymbol{E}_0 \sin \phi$. Similar statements apply to $\boldsymbol{H}_y(z, t)$. Figure 1–1 portrays these relationships schematically.

As shown, both the electric and magnetic components of the wave are "in phase" in space, that is, their maxima and minima occur for the same values of z. They are also in

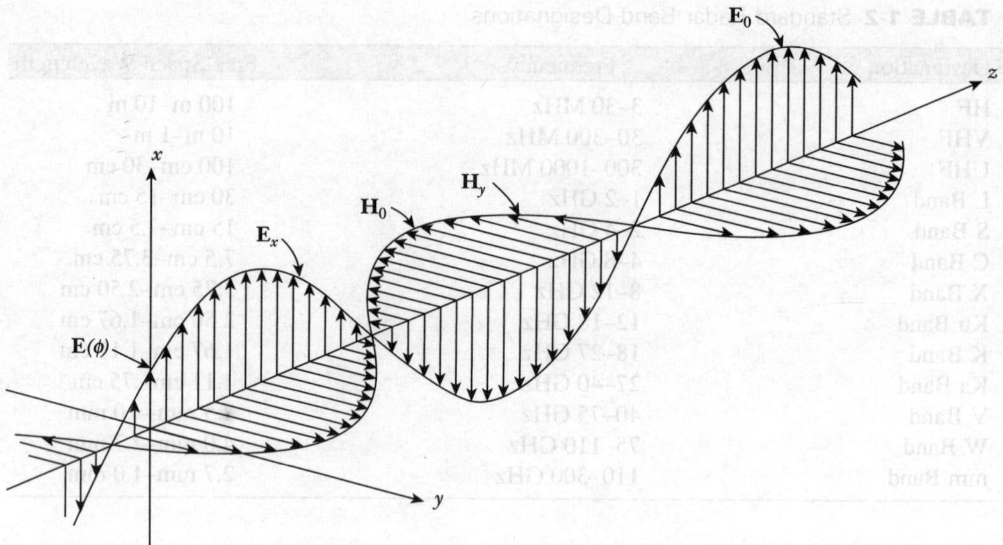

FIGURE 1–1.
Spatial relationships of a plane electromagnetic wave in free space.

phase in time, at a fixed value of z. However, they are both directed at right angles to each other and to the direction of propagation, a relationship that they always bear to each other in free-space propagation. The designation *plane wave* means that the pattern shown, although described as existing only along the z-axis, actually exists everywhere in space, the wave vectors at any point (x, y, z) being exactly like those at the point $(0, 0, z)$. At a fixed value of z there is no variation of the field in the x- and y-directions, that is, in an xy-plane at the point z; hence the name *plane wave*. (Not all electromagnetic waves are plane. A plane wave is an idealization never perfectly realized, but in practice waves may often be considered locally plane, with small error and with great simplification of mathematical description.)

The motion of the wave may be visualized by imagining that the entire set of field vectors, not only those shown but also those at all other values of x and y, is moving in unison in the positive z-direction at velocity $c = 3 \times 10^8$ meters per second. An observer at a fixed point would see a sinusoidal time variation of both E and H. On the other hand, if he could somehow (magically) "freeze" the motion and take measurements of E and H along the z-axis he would observe the pattern in Fig. 1–1.

1.1.4. Polarization

The plane wave shown in Fig. 1–1 is *linearly polarized*; that is, the electric vector has a particular direction in space for all values of z, in this case the x-axis direction. The wave is therefore said to be polarized in the x-direction. In actual space above the earth, if the electric vector is vertical or lies in a vertical plane, the wave is said to be vertically polarized; if the E-vector lies in a horizontal plane, the wave is said to be horizontally polarized. (It is conventional to describe polarization in terms of the E-vector.)

The initial polarization of a radio wave is determined by the antenna (and its orientation) that launches the waves into space. The polarization desired, therefore, is one of the factors entering into antenna design. In some applications a particular polarization is preferable; in others it makes little or no difference.

Electromagnetic waves are not always linearly polarized. In *circular polarization*, from the viewpoint of a *fixed observer*, the electric vector appears to be rotating with a screw motion about the z-axis (direction of propagation), making one full turn for each rf cycle. In further analogy with a screw thread the rotation may be clockwise or counterclockwise, corresponding to right-hand-circular and left-hand-circular polarizations. A circularly polarized wave results when two linearly polarized waves are combined—that is, if they are simultaneously launched in the same direction from the same antenna—provided that the two linear polarizations are at right angles to each other and their phase angles [the angle ϕ in (1–2) and (1–3) differ by 90 degrees or $\pi/2$ radians]. The right-hand or left-hand rotation depends on whether the phase difference is plus or minus. For truly circular polarization it is necessary also that the two linearly polarized components be of equal amplitude. If they are of different amplitudes, elliptical polarization results (see Figs. B-1 through B-4 of Appendix B).

The polarization is random when there is no fixed polarization or pattern of polarization-variation that is repetitive along the z-axis, an effect present in light waves emitted from an incandescent source (e.g., the sun or an electric light bulb). It is seldom observed in manmade radio emissions, but such would result if two independently random sources of radio noise (used in radio and radar military countermeasures, or "jamming") are connected to right-angle-polarized elements of a single antenna.

Linear polarization is the most commonly employed by far. One application for circular polarization is in communications between earth and space, to mitigate the effects of polarization rotation caused by the ionosphere (see sec. 7.3.1).

1.1.5. Rays and Wavefronts

Because the detailed structure of an electromagnetic wave is invisible, its nature can be determined only by indirect methods. Diagrams such as Fig. 1–1 are not truly pictorial; they are purely schematic, man-conceived schemes of representing certain aspects of the waves, namely, the magnitude variations of the E and H components. Another such scheme utilizes the concept of *rays* and *wavefronts* as an aid in illustrating the effect of variations in the propagation medium (including discontinuities) on the propagation of the waves.

A ray is a line drawn along the direction of propagation of a wave. The z-axis in Fig. 1–1 is an example of a ray. Any line drawn parallel to the z-axis in this diagram is also a ray, since the wave is plane and has the same direction everywhere. Therefore, if the wave is plane, there is no point in drawing more than one ray, for they are all alike.

A wavefront is a surface of constant phase of the wave. As mentioned in connection with Fig. 1–1, such surfaces are planes perpendicular to the direction of propagation when the wave is plane. As also mentioned, not all waves are plane. In fact, in the vicinity of the source from which waves are emanating (an antenna, for example), rather complicated wavefronts may exist. Of particular importance, and only slightly more complicated than a plane wave, is the spherical wave. Any "point" source of waves in free space will generate a spherical wave, as is readily deduced from the fact that if a certain part of the wave travels outward from a point, at the same speed in all directions, it will, after traveling a distance R, define the surface of a sphere of radius R, with its center at the point of origin of the waves.

If the distance from a source of electromagnetic waves is sufficiently large, compared to the physical size of the source, the source may be considered equivalent to a point source. Then, the wavefronts will be spherical. The system of rays and wavefronts generated by a point source is shown in Fig. 1–2.

It is apparent that the wavefronts here are spherical (appearing as circles in this two-dimensional drawing) and that all the rays are diverging from the common center or source. But if a small portion of a spherical wave, at a great distance from its source, is considered, this small portion will be approximately plane. For example, consider a cubic region of space, shown dashed in Fig. 1–2 near the midportion of the arc denoted wavefront D. This is a spherical wavefront. Within the dashed region, however, the small portion of the wavefront can hardly be distinguished from the plane surface of the cube to which it is tangent. Moreover, all the ray lines inside this cube are approximately parallel.

1.1.6. Spherical Waves and the Inverse-Square Law

One of the fundamental laws of physics is the Law of Conservation of Energy. An electromagnetic wave represents a flow of energy in the direction of propagation. The rate at which energy flows through a unit area of surface in space (energy per unit time per unit of area) is called the *power density* of the wave, usually expressed in watts per square meter. The principle of energy conservation can be applied to a uniform spherical wave in the following terms, with reference to Fig. 1–2. If the source radiates power at a constant rate uniformly in all directions, the total power flowing through any spherical surface centered at the source will be uniformly distributed over the surface and must equal the total power radiated. Such a source is called an isotropic radiator, or *isotrope*.

In Fig. 1–2 wavefront B, for example, constitutes a spherical surface. Although only a portion of it is shown, the complete sphere may be visualized as surrounding the source. If wavefront B is at a distance R_B meters from the source, the total surface area of this sphere is, from elementary geometry, $4\pi R_B{}^2$ square meters. If the source is radiating a total power P_t watts, since this total power is by hypothesis distributed uniformly over the spherical surface at distance R_B, the *power density* p_B must be

$$p_B = \frac{P_t}{4\pi R_B^2} \quad \text{watts per square meter} \tag{1–4}$$

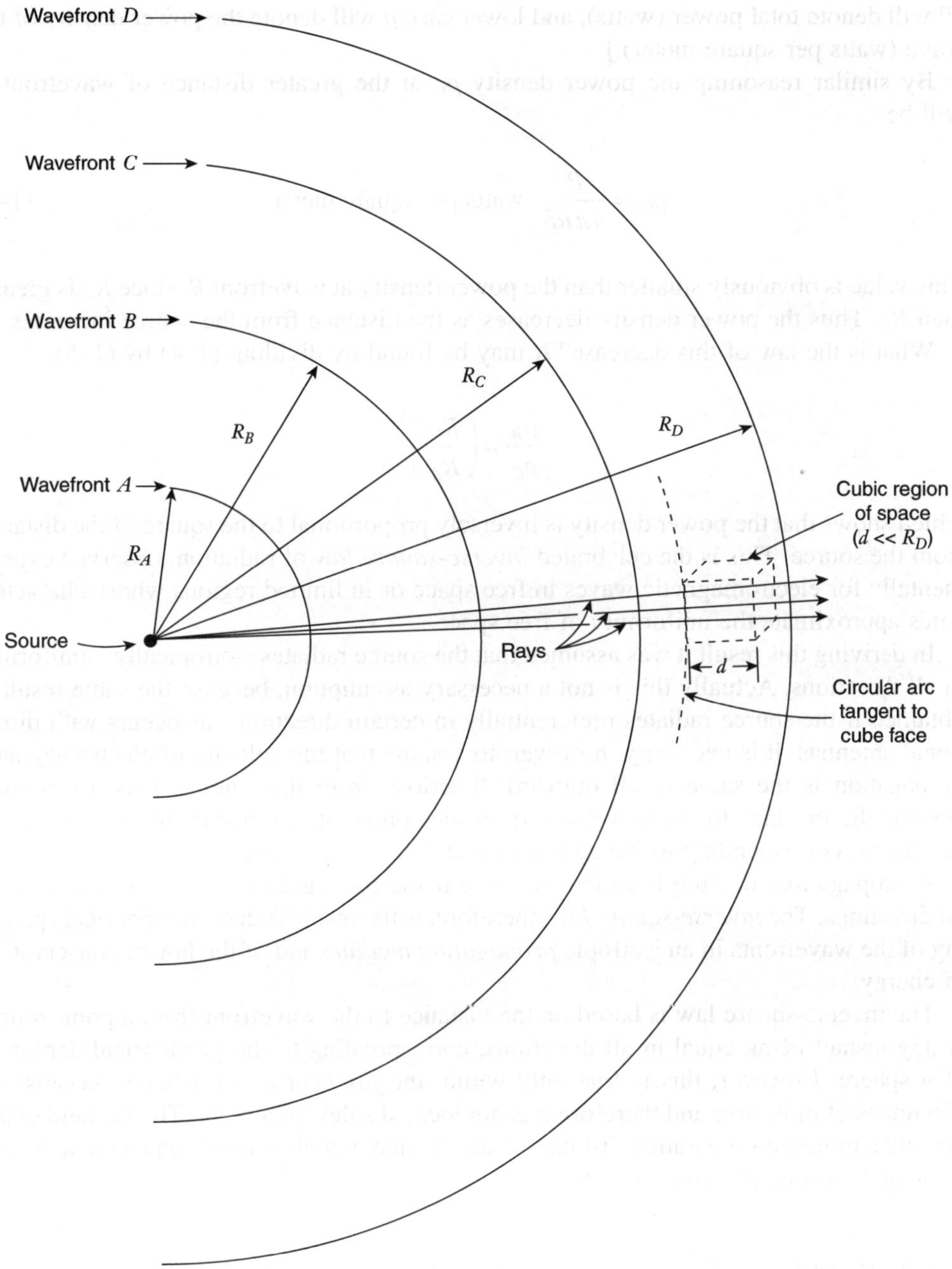

FIGURE 1–2.

Point-source wavefronts and rays in free space.

[P will denote total power (watts), and lower case p will denote the power density of the wave (watts per square meter).]

By similar reasoning the power density p_C at the greater distance of wavefront C will be

$$p_C = \frac{P_t}{4\pi R_C^2} \text{ watts per square meter} \tag{1–5}$$

This value is obviously smaller than the power density at wavefront B, since R_C is greater than R_B. Thus the power density decreases as the distance from the source increases.

What is the law of this decrease? It may be found by dividing (1–4) by (1–5),

$$\frac{p_B}{p_C} = \left(\frac{R_C}{R_B}\right)^2 \tag{1–6}$$

which shows that the power density is inversely proportional to the square of the distance from the source. This is the celebrated *inverse-square law* of radiation, observed experimentally for electromagnetic waves in free space or in limited regions whose characteristics approximate the uniformity of free space.

In deriving this result it was assumed that the source radiates isotropically—uniformly in all directions. Actually this is not a necessary assumption, because the same result is obtained if the source radiates preferentially in certain directions, as occurs with directional antennas. It is necessary, however, to assume that the velocity of electromagnetic propagation is the same in all outward directions from the source. This assumption permits the distance to the wavefront from the source at any instant to be equal in all directions, corresponding to the geometrical definition of a sphere.

A propagation medium is called isotropic if the propagation velocity is the same in all directions. The *inverse-square law*, therefore, is the result both of the spherical spreading of the wavefronts in an isotropic *propagation medium* and of the law of conservation of energy.

The inverse-square law is based on the distance to the wavefront from a point source at any instant being equal in all directions, corresponding to the geometrical definition of a sphere. However, this is true only within the *far field* of an antenna, because an antenna is of finite size and therefore it is not located solely at a point. The far field exists beyond a minimum separation distance of an antenna, which depends on antenna dimensions and wavelength. (sec. 3.2.5).

1.1.7. Field Intensity and Power Density

The power density of the field is related to the values of the electric and magnetic intensities in the same way that power in an electric circuit is related to voltage and current; it is the product of the two. (This assumes the free-space relationship of the field vectors depicted in Fig. 1–1.) The product of the instantaneous values gives the instantaneous power, but this quantity is usually of little interest. The average power density over an rf cycle is ordinarily desired, and, just as in computing power in a-c circuits, it is obtained by multiplying the *effective* values of E and H, equal to $1/\sqrt{2}$ times the amplitudes, or $0.707E_0$ and $0.707H_0$. Hence, the power density p may be expressed as (1–7) that follows:

$$p = (0.707E_0) \times (0.707H_0) = 0.5E_0H_0 \tag{1–7}$$

where E_0 and H_0 are the amplitudes as in (1–2) and (1–3). E_0 is expressed in volts per meter, H_0 in amperes per meter to give p in watts per square meter.

Just as voltage and current in circuits are related through the resistance by Ohm's law, the electric and magnetic intensities are related by the characteristic wave impedance of space. In a lossless propagation medium this impedance is equal to the square root of the ratio of its magnetic permeability μ to its electric permittivity ε, as given by (1–8) that follows:

$$Z_s = \sqrt{\mu/\varepsilon} \text{ ohms} \tag{1–8}$$

In a vacuum μ has the value 1.26×10^{-6} henrys per meter, and ε is 8.85×10^{-12} farad per meter. (These values are customarily denoted μ_0 and ε_0.) Consequently Z_s is about 377 ohms (actually 120π ohms) in free space, a value also applicable in air. Hence in these media

$$p = \frac{E^2}{377} = 377H^2 \text{ watts per square meter} \tag{1–9}$$

where E and H are the effective (rms) values, equal to $0.707E_0$ and $0.707H_0$, in volts per meter and amperes per meter, respectively. This also means that the magnetic intensity can be expressed by (1–10) that follows:

$$H = \frac{E}{377} \text{ amperes per meter} \tag{1–10}$$

for any wave propagating in free space or air; that is, E and H are related through this expression, and specifying one of them is equivalent to specifying both. Ordinarily, therefore, only the electric intensity is specified.

If (1–9) is applied to the inverse-square law, the result is

$$\frac{E_B}{E_C} = \frac{R_C}{R_B} \tag{1–11}$$

which states that the electric intensity is inversely proportional to the first power of the distance from the source (subject to the same stipulations that apply to the inverse-square law in its original form).

Equations (1–6) and (1–11) are different ways of showing how the electromagnetic wave is attenuated with increasing distance from the source. Equation (1–6) expresses the attenuation in terms of the power-density ratio, and (1–11) expresses attenuation in terms of the electric-intensity ratio.

1.1.8. Decibel (Logarithmic) Expression of Attenuation

Wave attenuation is expressed also in terms of the logarithms of the power-density or electric-intensity ratios, an alternative method widely used in describing signal amplification or attenuation in telephone and radio systems. The decibel attenuation is simply ten times the common (base 10) logarithm of the power-density ratio or twenty times the logarithm of the electric-intensity ratio. It may be readily verified that these definitions lead to the same decibel values for a given distance ratio R_C/R_B when applied to (1–6) and (1–11).

Example. Suppose that the field strengths are to be compared at two distances from a source, R_1 and R_2, such that $R_2 = 2R_1$. How much is the field strength reduced if the distance from the source is doubled? From equations (1–6) and (1–11) the question is answered as follows:

$$\frac{p_1}{p_2} = \left(\frac{R_2}{R_1}\right)^2 = \left(\frac{2R_1}{R_1}\right)^2 = 4$$

and

$$\frac{E_1}{E_2} = \frac{R_2}{R_1} = 2$$

In terms of decibels the attenuation is

$$10 \log \frac{p_1}{p_2} = 10 \log 4 = 10\,(0.60206) = 6 \text{ dB}$$

or

$$20 \log \frac{E_1}{E_2} = 20 \log 2 = 20\,(0.30103) = 6 \text{ dB}$$

Thus the same result is obtained for the attenuation in decibels from either the power-density or the electric-intensity ratio.

Attenuation due to the spherical spreading of the wave—that is, as expressed by the inverse-square law—is sometimes called the space attenuation of the wave. As can be shown from (1–6) or (1–11) by applying the definition of the decibel, the space attenuation in decibels is twenty times the logarithm of the distance ratio. As already shown, if the distance is doubled, the wave is attenuated by 6 dB ($20 \log 2$); if it is tripled, the attenuation is $20 \log 3$, or 9.5 dB; if the distance is increased by a factor of 10, the attenuation is 20 dB; and so on.

Since it is the distance *ratio* rather than the actual distance change that determines the space attenuation, a given distance change has a greater effect at points close to a source than it has far from the source. For example, two points differing by 1 km in distance from the source will show a 6-dB power-density ratio if they are 1 km and 2 km from the source, respectively; but if they are 100 km and 101 km from the source, the attenuation is only 0.09 dB, a negligible amount. This fact further supports the validity of regarding a spherical wave within a limited region of space at a considerable distance from the source, virtually as a plane wave; for it is a property of a plane wave that the power density and electric intensity do not change as the wave progresses.

In some antenna considerations, the ratios of the field intensities at different points in the vicinity of the antenna may be fairly large for relatively short separations of the points in question. However, at short distances from an antenna the fields may not obey the inverse-square law power relationship. Therefore, it is to be underscored that the inverse-square law relationship is applicable only to distances from an antenna that are large enough to be within the antenna far field (sec. 3.2.5).

1.1.9. Absorption

In addition to space attenuation, which is always present (even though it may be ignored over short distances far from the source of the waves), there may sometimes be attenuation due to absorption of power by the propagation medium. This does not occur in a vacuum, but it will occur in a medium that contains material particles that interact with the waves. At some frequencies, for example, certain gases of the earth's atmosphere (oxygen and water vapor) cause absorption. This occurs slightly in the VHF region and becomes significant over long transmission paths in the UHF region and above. Unlike space attenuation, attenuation due to absorption does not depend on the distance from the source but only on the total distance traveled by the wave. That is to say, attenuation due to absorption is the same over a one-kilometer path whether the path is 1 km or 100 km from the source of the waves.

Absorption in the atmosphere is significant only over appreciable distances, measured in kilometers, and so it is not a factor in antenna design, except in the very indirect sense that it may dictate what frequency or frequencies are chosen for a particular application. The earth's ionosphere also absorbs waves at some frequencies; this absorption may be significant in the high HF and low VHF regions. At frequencies above the low UHF the ionosphere is completely transparent to radio waves ordinarily, and below the HF region it acts like a reflecting barrier; that is, low-frequency waves do not penetrate the ionosphere appreciably.

Certain materials are capable of absorbing radio waves very strongly. Waves traveling in these materials will be attenuated greatly within a short distance, of the order of centimeters or meters. Sometimes such materials are used in antenna design to suppress radiation in undesired directions, or to prevent "leakage" of waves from one part of an antenna to another where they would have an undesirable effect.

Now let us assume a wave propagates in a homogeneous absorbing medium, that is, one that does not vary from point to point. Then, if the wave propagates in the x-direction, its amplitude will decrease as $e^{-\alpha x}$, where $e = 2.71828$. The term $e^{-\alpha x}$ is the *attenuation factor*, and α is the attenuation constant expressed in neper per meter (Np/m). Thus, if a wave of amplitude E_1 travels a distance x of 1 m and α is 1 Np/m, its new amplitude E_2 is E_1e^{-1}. Then, the attenuation in decibels is $20 \log (E_1/E_2) = 8.686$, and thus an attenuation of 1 Np/m equals 8.868 dB/m. In other words, if γ is the attenuation factor expressed in dB/m instead of Np/m as it is above for α, $\gamma = 8.868\ \alpha$. Similarly, in (1–12) attenuation in decibels A_{dB} is related to attenuation in nepers A_{NP} as

$$A_{dB} = 8.686 A_{Np} \tag{1–12}$$

Nowadays attenuation is commonly expressed in terms of decibels, not nepers.

Attenuation by absorption is now further explained. As before, let γ be the attenuation constant expressed in decibels per meter and R_1 and R_2 be two distances from the source of electromagnetic waves. Then, the total absorptive attenuation of the waves in traveling from R_1 to R_2 is $\gamma(R_2 - R_1)$ dB. This implies that the law of absorptive power loss is

$$\frac{p_1}{p_2} = 10^{0.1\gamma(R_2 - R_1)} \tag{1–13}$$

The factor 0.1 in the exponent is there because decibels are ten times the logarithm of the power ratio. Note that the mathematical form of (1–13) for attenuation due to absorption is different from (1–6), which is for space attenuation.

The total decibel attenuation A_{dB} over this path is the sum of the space attenuation and the absorption attenuation, which is

$$A_{dB} = \left[20 \log\left(\frac{R_2}{R_1}\right) + \gamma(R_2 - R_1)\right] \text{dB} \tag{1–14}$$

Thus the space attenuation depends on the *ratio* R_2/R_1, whereas the absorption attenuation depends on the *difference* $R_2 - R_1$. Therefore close to the source the space attenuation predominates, but at large distances from the source the absorption becomes more important, if γ has a nonzero constant value.

In the earth's atmosphere (troposphere and ionosphere), however, the situation is somewhat more complicated because γ does vary from point to point; it is a function of altitude (air density) in the atmosphere, and in the ionosphere it is a function of the electron density. In such cases the absorption attenuation of a wave over the propagation path from R_1 to R_2 is expressed mathematically by the following integral:

$$A_{dB} = \int_{R_1}^{R_2} \gamma(R)\, dR \text{ dB} \tag{1–15}$$

The evaluation of the variation of γ in the atmosphere is a complicated problem. Curves showing the results of calculations for typical paths in a standard troposphere have been published by Blake (1962).

1.2. Radio-Wave Optical Principles

So far the discussion has applied principally to electromagnetic waves in free space. The absorption effect is an exception, but it represents a relatively minor departure from "free space" because it does not alter the ray-wavefront behavior. The rays and wavefronts are the same in a uniformly absorbing (homogeneous, isotropic) medium as they are in free space.

In the environment of the earth, or in any "space" that is not empty, effects may occur that do alter the ray-wavefront behavior. Then Fig. 1–2 no longer represents the actual behavior. The effects that occur are referred to as optical effects because they were first observed and studied in connection with the science of optics—the behavior of light waves. It is, of course, not surprising that these optical phenomena also apply to radio-wave propagation, for light waves and radio waves are both electromagnetic waves, differing only in frequency (hence also in wavelength). It is also not surprising that some of these effects are most strongly observed at the shorter radio wavelengths (higher frequencies); however, they are generally important at all frequencies.

These effects are refraction, reflection, interference, and diffraction. The first two can be explained basically in terms of rays and wavefronts, the principles of geometric optics. The second two, however, can be explained only in terms of physical optics, which requires a more detailed consideration of the electric and magnetic fields. Geometric optics may be applied when the dimensions of all the significant elements of the situation are large compared with the wavelength and when no wavelength-dependent effects are involved; otherwise the problem comes within the purview of physical optics or, more generally, electromagnetic theory. The significance of these statements will become clearer in the ensuing discussion.

1.2.1. Refraction

When a wave passes from one region to another in which the wave speed is slower or faster, *refraction* occurs. Refraction takes place either when the two propagation regions are separated by a sharp boundary or when the wave velocity varies gradually and approximately linearly over a region that is large compared with the wavelength. Refraction at a plane boundary is illustrated in Fig. 1–3. It is to be noted that reflection also occurs at the boundary, and it is discussed in the section 1.2.2 that follows.

As shown, a plane wavefront *AB* in medium I is directed toward the boundary surface. The direction is defined by the angle of incidence θ_1, which the rays make with the normal (perpendicular) to the surface. This wavefront is shown at the exact instant that its lower edge *A* has reached the boundary surface.

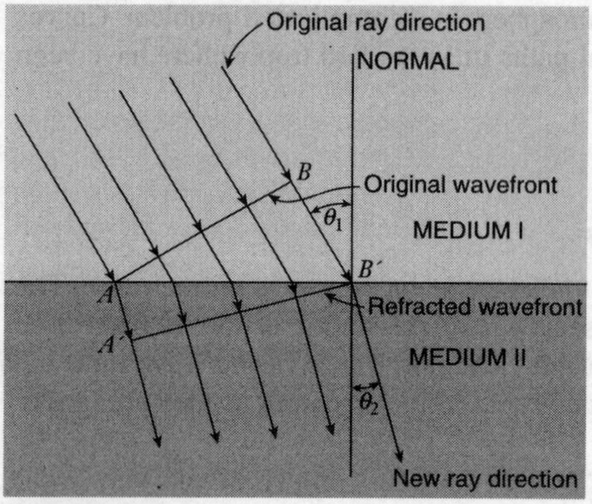

FIGURE 1–3.
Refraction at a plane boundary between two media.

It is assumed that the wave speed v_2 in medium II is slower than the speed v_1 in medium I. The wave proceeding downward from point A will now be traveling in medium II at the slower speed v_2, whereas that portion of the wavefront at B is still traveling in medium I at the faster speed v_1. Consequently, during the time that it takes the wave to go from B to B' in medium I the lower edge of the wave will go only from A to A' in medium II, the distances BB' and AA' being in the same ratio as the speeds v_1 and v_2. Consequently the wavefront is defined by the line $A'B'$, which is tilted with respect to AB. (This is the wavefront because it defines a surface of constant phase of the wave.)

Since rays are defined as being perpendicular to the wavefront at all points, the rays have now changed their directions. The direction of the wave has also been changed by the amount $\theta_1 - \theta_2$ to a direction defined by the angle θ_2, the angle of refraction.

By considering triangles ABB' and $B'A'A$ it can readily be shown, since the distances BB' and AA' have the same ratio as v_1 has to v_2, that the angles θ_1 and θ_2 are related by the expression

$$\frac{\sin\theta_1}{\sin\theta_2} = \frac{v_1}{v_2} \tag{1–16}$$

This ratio is also commonly expressed in terms of the *refractive indexes* of the two media. The refractive index is defined as the ratio of the speed of the wave in vacuum, $c = 3 \times 10^8$ meters per second, to the speed v in the actual medium. Thus the refractive index of medium I is $n_1 = c/v_1$ and that of medium II is $n_2 = c/v_2$. Consequently,

$$\frac{\sin\theta_1}{\sin\theta_2} = \frac{n_2}{n_1} \tag{1–17}$$

In an electrically nonconducting medium, the wave velocity is given by

$$v = \frac{1}{\sqrt{\mu\varepsilon}} \tag{1–18}$$

where μ is the magnetic permeability and ε is the electric permittivity. The index of refraction (i.e., refractive index), therefore, is given by

$$n = \frac{c}{v} = \frac{\sqrt{\mu\varepsilon}}{\sqrt{\mu_0\varepsilon_0}} \tag{1–19}$$

where μ_0 and ε_0 are the permeability and permittivity of a vacuum. These values are $\mu_0 = 1.26 \times 10^{-6}$ henry per meter and $\varepsilon_0 = 8.85 \times 10^{-12}$ farad per meter. Then, by using (1–18) and (1–19), and the numerical values of μ_0, and ε_0, c is attained as follows:

$$c = \frac{1}{\sqrt{(1.26\times10^{-6})(8.85\times10^{-12})}} \approx 3\times10^8 \text{ meters per second}$$

as previously stated. The permeability of most common dielectrics is the same as that of a vacuum (i.e., $\mu = \mu_0$). Thus, for most lossless dielectrics, the index of refraction n is the ratio $\sqrt{\varepsilon/\varepsilon_0}$, where $\varepsilon/\varepsilon_0$ is the relative permittivity ε_r. Therefore, from (1–16), one may usually write

$$\frac{\sin\theta_1}{\sin\theta_2} = \sqrt{\frac{\varepsilon_{r2}}{\varepsilon_{r1}}} \tag{1–20}$$

To account for the conduction current and ohmic losses in a nonideal dielectric, ε_r is expressed as $\varepsilon_r'' - j\varepsilon_r'$, where ε_r' is the relative permittivity related to the displacement current (Appendix A) and ε_r'' is the relative permittivity related to the conduction current. The reader may recognize that ε_r is a complex number (for a review, see Appendix C). Another name for ε_r' is dielectric constant, and for low-loss dielectrics (where $\varepsilon_r'' << \varepsilon_r'$) the dielectric constant (i.e., ε_r') is ordinarily assumed equal to ε_r. Thus, (1–20) is usually a valid approximation for most dielectrics used with antennas, but it is actually exact only if $\varepsilon_{r2}/\varepsilon_{r1}$ is replaced by $\varepsilon_{r2}'/\varepsilon_{r1}'$.

Dielectric constants of typical substances used at radio frequencies range from 1 to about 10, although a few special materials with higher values are available. Generally the low-loss materials (low absorption coefficients) tend also to have low dielectric constants. The value $\varepsilon_r = \varepsilon_r' - j\varepsilon_r'' = 1$ applies to air (approximately) and vacuum (exactly).

When the angle of incidence of a wave is zero ($\theta_1 = 0$), it is apparent from (1–16) to (1–18) that the angle of refraction must also be zero ($\theta_2 = 0$), regardless of the indexes of refraction. That is, an incident plane wave whose rays are normal to the plane surface between two propagation media will not be refracted (meaning that its direction of propagation will not be changed; however, its forward speed will of course be changed).

In Fig. 1–3 it is assumed that the wave goes from a medium of higher speed into one of slower speed. If the order of speeds is reversed, the behavior of the rays and wavefronts is reversed. That is, the directions of the rays in Fig. 1–3 may be reversed and everything else will remain unchanged, except that θ_2 becomes the angle of incidence and θ_1 the angle of refraction.

Refraction will also occur when a curved (e.g., spherical) wavefront is incident on a plane interface between two media, when a plane wavefront is incident on a curved

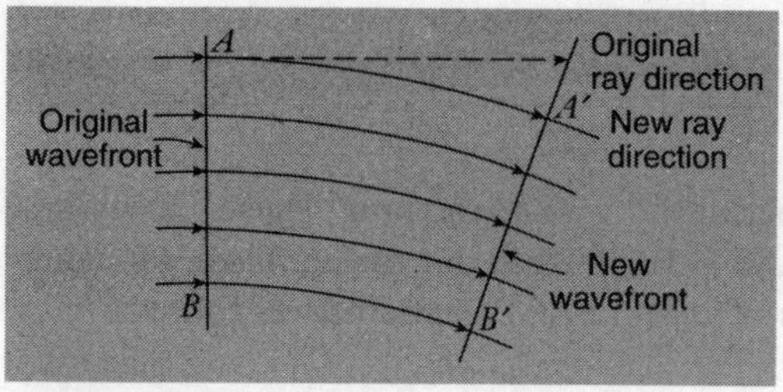

FIGURE 1–4.

Refraction in a medium having gradual variation of the refractive index.

boundary surface, and when curved wavefronts impinge on curved boundaries. The analysis of these cases, of course, is more complicated, but the principles are the same. In general, the curvature of the wavefront is changed by refraction. This is the basis of the design of lenses, both as used with light waves in telescopes, microscopes, spectacles, cameras, and so forth, and also as used with radio waves in some types of antenna at very short wavelengths.

Refraction may also occur when a wave travels in a medium that has a velocity gradient in the direction perpendicular to the direction of propagation (parallel to the wavefront); that is, when the index of refraction increases or decreases in a gradual manner rather than abruptly. Then the rays are bent gradually toward the direction of lower wave velocity (higher index of refraction), a result that may be deduced by reasoning similar to that employed for refraction at a plane boundary. In Fig. 1–4 a plane wavefront *AB* is traveling horizontally in a medium with a vertical index gradient. The wave velocity is assumed to be faster in the upper part of the medium than in the lower part; that is, the refractive index n is greater in the lower part of the medium. In the simplest case the variation is assumed to be linear. The upper part of the wavefront will travel the distance AA' in the same length of time that it takes the lower part to travel the shorter distance BB', so that the new wavefront $A'B'$ is tilted downward. This tilting occurs in a gradual fashion as the wave progresses, as indicated in Fig. 1–4 by the intermediate wavefronts shown by dashed lines.

This effect actually occurs for waves traveling approximately horizontally in the earth's atmosphere, because the refractive index of air is very slightly greater in the denser lower atmosphere than it is at very high altitudes, the variation being approximately linear over a restricted range of altitude. Because the refractive index of the lower atmosphere is only about 1.0003, compared to 1.0000 for a vacuum, the downward bending of the rays is very slight indeed, so small as to be unobservable over short propagation paths. It is significant over very long distances only. A similar type of bending occurs at some frequencies in the ionosphere, but there the ray curvature is in general more complicated because of the more complicated behavior of the refractive index variation.

1.2.2. Reflection

In the discussion of refraction at a plane boundary (Fig. 1–3) it was tacitly implied that the wave is totally refracted—that all the wave power incident on the surface in medium I passes into medium II. Actually this is not true. Some of the power is reflected. Reflection refers to the formation of an additional new wavefront that travels upward from the surface into medium I so that in general the incident wave is split up into two waves, one refracted (transmitted through the boundary surface) and one reflected. Figure 1–5 represents this situation. The reflected wave may be thought of, perhaps rather unscientifically, as one that bounces off the surface. The reflection of light waves (as from a mirror) is a familiar phenomenon that everyone has observed. Radio waves are similarly reflected. Because the reflected wave is traveling at the same speed as the incident wave, it may be deduced that the angle of reflection θ_3 is exactly equal to the angle of incidence θ_1.

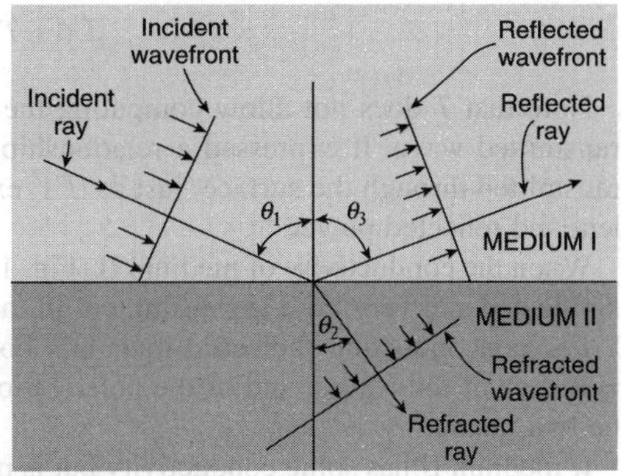

FIGURE 1–5.

Reflection and refraction at a plane boundary between two propagation media.

So far only the relationships between the relative *directions* of the incident, refracted, and reflected wavefronts have been considered. Equally important is determination of the relative amounts of the total *power* that are reflected and refracted (transmitted). Detailed analysis of this problem is quite complicated and requires a knowledge of advanced electromagnetic theory. Only a brief outline is given here.

The ratio of the reflected-wave electric intensity to that of the incident wave is called the *reflection coefficient* Γ (gamma). This coefficient expresses not only the relative amplitudes but also the phase shift that may occur in the reflection process; that is, Γ is a complex number (complex numbers reviewed in Appendix C):

$$\Gamma = |\Gamma| e^{j\phi_r} \tag{1–21}$$

where ϕ_r is the phase angle of the reflection coefficient. If the incident and reflected electric intensities are E_1 and E_3, with individual phase angles ϕ_1 and ϕ_3, then Γ is found as follows:

$$\Gamma = \frac{E_3}{E_1} = \frac{|E_3| e^{j\phi_3}}{|E_1| e^{j\phi_1}} = \frac{|E_3|}{|E_1|} e^{j(\phi_3 - \phi_1)} \tag{1–22}$$

Thus $|\Gamma|$ in (1–21) is given in (1–22) by the ratio of the amplitudes of the waves, and ϕ_r in (1–21) is given in (1–22) by the difference of their phase angles.

The ratio of the *power densities* of the reflected and incident waves is given by $|\Gamma|^2$, since the power density is proportional to the square of the electric intensity (1–9).

The fraction of the total incident power transmitted through the surface (refracted) is expressed by the *power transmission coefficient* T (usually called the transmission coefficient). Since the Law of Conservation of Energy requires that the total of the reflected and transmitted power shall equal the incident power, it is readily deduced that

$$|\Gamma|^2 + T = 1 \tag{1–23}$$

Note that T does not allow computing the electric intensity or power density of the transmitted wave. It expressed a relationship between the total power incident on and transmitted through the surface, just as $|\Gamma|^2$ expresses a similar relationship for the incident and reflected power.

When the conductivity of medium II (Fig. 1–5) is very high, most of the incident wave is reflected and very little is transmitted. In fact, for a perfect conductor $|\Gamma| = 1$ and $T = 0$. For nonconducting dielectric materials both Γ and T are functions of the angle of incidence of the waves, and of the polarization, as well as of the dielectric constants of the two media.

If medium II has some conductivity but is not an excellent conductor, waves penetrating the surface are *absorbed*, that is, they set up currents that are converted to heat in the resistance of the material. In this case it is customary to express the fraction of power that penetrates the surface in terms of an *absorption coefficient*, A, rather than a transmission coefficient. Equation (1–23) holds for this situation, with T replaced by A.

When the reflecting surface is curved rather than plane, the curvature of the reflected wave is different from that of the incident wave; however, when a curved wavefront is reflected from a plane surface, the curvature of the reflected wave is the same as that of the incident wave. Plane and curved metallic reflecting surfaces have important applications in the design of high-frequency antennas.

Reflection may also occur from a surface that is irregular or rough rather than smooth. Such a surface may destroy the shape of the wavefront. The reflected wave in this case is *scattered* in a random fashion, so that the reflected amplitude or power density in a given direction is not exactly predictable as it is for smooth surfaces. This phenomenon is called *diffuse* reflection, whereas reflection from a smooth surface is said to be *specular* (mirror-like).

Diffuse reflection is not characterized by a reflection coefficient containing a phase angle, as is specular reflection. The random nature of diffuse reflection results in a phase angle that varies unpredictably at different regions of the surface. Diffuse reflection, therefore, is expressible only in terms of a power reflection coefficient, R_d.

Surfaces may also be semi-rough. For such surfaces the degree of roughness is not sufficient to destroy the shape of the reflected wavefront completely; there is a mixture of diffuse reflection and specular reflection. In such cases a total power reflection coefficient, R, may be expressed in terms of the diffuse-power-reflection coefficient, R_d, and the specular-reflection coefficient $|\Gamma|$. Since the total reflected power must be the sum of the diffuse and specular components, the relation for R is

$$R = R_d + |\Gamma|^2 \tag{1–24}$$

When the incident wave is reflected partly specularly and partly diffusely and is also partly transmitted, R may be substituted for $|\Gamma|^2$ in (1–23).

For a given degree of actual roughness of a surface the values of R_d and $|\Gamma|$ vary with the angle of incidence θ_i of the wave before reflection. At normal incidence ($\theta_i = 0°$),

R_d has its maximum value and $|\Gamma|$ its minimum value. As θ_i increases, R_d decreases and $|\Gamma|$ increases, and for very large values of θ_i (near 90°) the semi-rough surface may reflect almost specularly, that is, with $R_d = 0$. This effect is described by the *Rayleigh criterion*, which states that a semi-rough surface will reflect *as if* it were a smooth surface (i.e., specularly) whenever θ_i is greater than the value defined by

$$\cos \theta_i = \frac{\lambda}{8d} \qquad (1\text{–}25)$$

where λ is the wavelength of the incident wave and d is the depth of the surface irregularities, as shown in Fig. 1–6. Here the specular component of the reflected wave appears to be reflected from a plane intermediate between the highest and lowest portions of the surface, whereas the diffuse reflection is indicated by ray lines going off in all directions from each point of the surface.

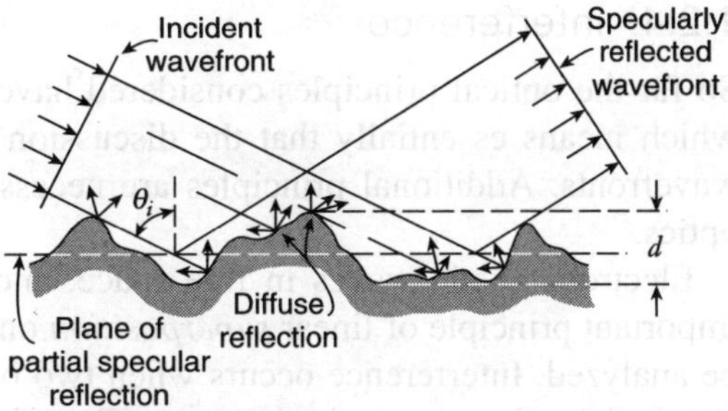

FIGURE 1–6.
Reflection from a semi-rough surface.

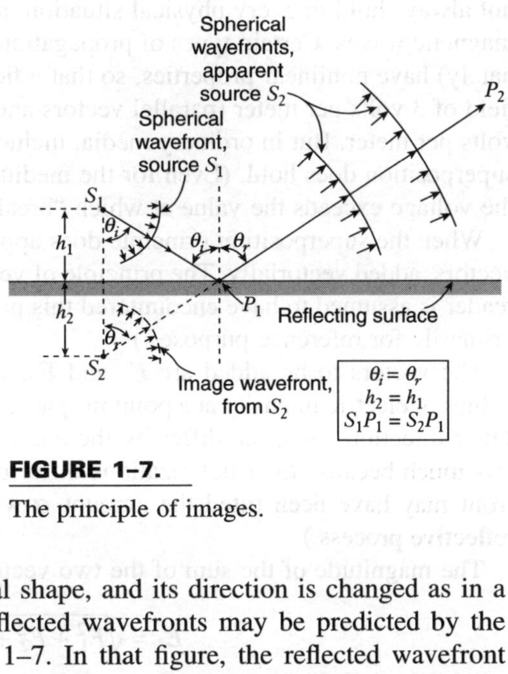

FIGURE 1–7.
The principle of images.

1.2.3. Principle of Images

When a spherical wavefront is reflected from a plane surface, it retains its spherical shape, and its direction is changed as in a plane wave. The exact behavior of the reflected wavefronts may be predicted by the principle of images, as illustrated in Fig. 1–7. In that figure, the reflected wavefront *appears* to be originating at S_2, although it actually originates at S_1 and is specularly reflected from the plane surface. The *virtual source* S_2 is located a distance h_2 below the reflecting surface equal to the actual height h_1 of the true source S_1 above the surface and on a line from S_1 perpendicular to the surface. Therefore the distance from the actual source to a point P_2, which is $S_1P_1 + P_1P_2$, is the same as the distance from the virtual source $S_2P_1 + P_1P_2$. The virtual source S_2 is called the *image* of the actual source S_1. This is the familiar optical principle of the mirror, according to which an observer at P_2, looking along the line P_2P_1, sees an image of an object located at S_1. The object *appears* to be at S_2, although the light waves are actually coming from S_1; they are reflected from the surface in such a way that they seem to be coming from S_2.

1.2.4. Interference

So far the optical principles considered have been in the category of geometric optics, which means essentially that the discussion has centered on the behavior of rays and wavefronts. Additional principles are necessary for problems in the realm of physical optics.

Electromagnetic waves in free space, and in many other media, are subject to the important principle of linear *superposition* on the basis of which *interference* effects can be analyzed. Interference occurs when two or more electromagnetic waves exist simultaneously at the same point in space. The principle of linear superposition states that the total electric and magnetic intensities at the point are the complex (amplitude and phase) vector sums of the individual complex wave vectors.

This may seem to be a simple and natural fact. However, linear superposition does not always hold in every physical situation, and sometimes it does not hold for electromagnetic waves. Certain types of propagation media (not commonly encountered, fortunately) have nonlinear properties, so that a field of 2 volts per meter superimposed on a field of 3 volts per meter (parallel vectors and instantaneous values) does not result in 5 volts per meter. But in ordinary media, including air and vacuum, the principle of linear superposition does hold. (Even for the medium of air an exception may be noted, when the voltage exceeds the value at which "breakdown" occurs.)

When the superposition principle does apply, it applies to the instantaneous values of vectors, added vectorially. The principle of vector addition is illustrated in Fig. 1–8. (The reader is assumed to have encountered this principle previously, and it is illustrated here primarily for reference purposes.)

The vectors to be added are $\boldsymbol{E}_1$ and $\boldsymbol{E}_2$, which may be thought of as instantaneous values of electric intensity at a point in space, described by equations of the type of (1–2). Their directions in space differ by the angle α, as shown. (Their directions may differ this much because their polarizations differ by this amount, for example; or one wavefront may have been tilted the amount α with respect to the other by a refractive or reflective process.)

The magnitude of the sum of the two vectors $\boldsymbol{E}_1$ and $\boldsymbol{E}_2$ is

$$E_3 = \sqrt{E_1^2 + E_2^2 + 2E_1E_2 \cos \alpha} \tag{1–26}$$

In this equation the letters E_1, E_2, E_3 denote the magnitudes (lengths) of the vectors $\boldsymbol{E}_1$, $\boldsymbol{E}_2$, $\boldsymbol{E}_3$. The equation gives no information concerning the direction of $\boldsymbol{E}_3$, which may be determined from Fig. 1–8 by measuring the angles γ (gamma) and δ (delta). It may also be determined by trigonometric analysis of Fig. 1–8, which yields

$$\tan \gamma = \frac{E_2 \sin \alpha}{E_1 + E_2 \cos \alpha} \tag{1–27}$$

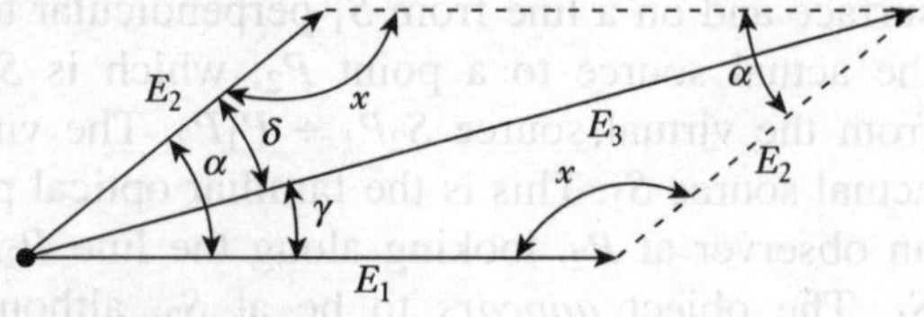

FIGURE 1–8.
Addition of vectors.

Some special cases are worth noting. Referring to Fig. 1–8, if $E_1 = E_2$, it may be seen that $\gamma = \alpha/2 = \delta$. In addition, if $E_1 = E_2$, and by using a standard trigonometric formula, (1–26) becomes

$$E_3 = E_1\sqrt{2+2\cos\alpha} = 2E_1\cos\left(\frac{\alpha}{2}\right) \tag{1–28}$$

The specialization $\alpha = 0$ results in $E_3 = E_1 + E_2$, and specialization $\alpha = 180°$ gives $E_3 = E_1 - E_2$, corresponding to the vector addition of parallel and antiparallel vectors.

This type of complex vector addition of two electric intensities solves the superposition (interference) problem in which $\boldsymbol{E}_1$ and $\boldsymbol{E}_2$ have the same frequency and the same time phase but different directions in space at the point under consideration. "The same time phase" means that the sinusoidal rf variations are perfectly synchronized, with their maxima and zero values occurring at exactly the same instants. As noted, the case in which the two intensity variations are exactly opposite in phase can also be handled by this kind of analysis, because two "parallel" vectors of opposite time phase correspond to the antiparallel case $\alpha = 180°$. If the time-phase difference is other than 0 or 180°, a more complicated analysis is required.

Complex vector addition of two vectors can be made fairly simply, if the spatial directions of the vectors are the same ($\alpha = 0$). This is so even if the time-phase difference is other than 0 or 180°. Now suppose, for example, that the two electric intensities are

$$E_1(r,t) = E_{01}\sin\left(2\pi ft - \frac{2\pi r}{\lambda} + \phi_1\right) \tag{1–29}$$

$$E_2(s,t) = E_{02}\sin\left(2\pi ft - \frac{2\pi s}{\lambda} + \phi_2\right) \tag{1–30}$$

in accordance with (1–2), except that the letters r and s are used here for distances measured along the propagation paths. This implies that the two waves may have traveled different distances before arriving at the point under consideration from the reference points at which $r = 0$ and $s = 0$ and at which the phase angles were ϕ_1 and ϕ_2. Moreover, the amplitudes of the two interfering waves E_{01} and E_{02} are not necessarily the same. The interference problem thus described has numerous antenna applications.

To avoid unnecessary complication of the equations in further discussion of this problem, the following standard abbreviations are used:

$$2\pi f = \omega \tag{1–31}$$

$$\frac{2\pi}{\lambda} = \beta \tag{1–32}$$

The quantity ω (omega) is known as the angular frequency, and β (beta) is the phase constant; ω expresses the angular rate (in radians) at which the phase angle of the wave at a fixed point in space changes in time, and β is the rate of phase change with distance at a fixed instant of time. The customary units for ω are radians per second, and for β, radians per meter; that is, t and λ are ordinarily measured in these units. Thus a time period $T = 1/f$ corresponds to 2π radians, or 360° of phase angle, as does also a distance $x = \lambda$. ($T = 1$ cycle and $\lambda = 1$ wavelength.)

If this notation is used and the principle of superposition is applied, it is apparent that when E_1 and E_2 are parallel vectors at the same point in space the resultant intensity is

$$E_3(t) = E_1(r, t) + E_2(s, t) = E_{01} \sin(\omega t - \beta r + \phi_1) + E_{02} \sin(\omega t - \beta s + \phi_2) \qquad (1\text{–}33)$$

No distance variable is indicated for E_3, since it expresses the intensity at a single point only. Therefore E_3 is a sinusoidally varying electric intensity with an amplitude and phase angle

$$E_3(t) = E_{03} \sin(\omega t + \phi_3) \qquad (1\text{–}34)$$

By algebraic manipulation it is found from (1–33) and (1–34) that

$$E_{03} = \sqrt{E_{01}^2 + E_{02}^2 + 2E_{01}E_{02} \cos[\phi_1 - \phi_2 - \beta(r - s)]} \qquad (1\text{–}35)$$

and

$$\tan\phi_3 = \frac{E_{01} \sin(\phi_1 - \beta r) + E_{02} \sin(\phi_2 - \beta s)}{E_{01} \cos(\phi_1 - \beta r) + E_{02} \cos(\phi_2 - \beta s)} \qquad (1\text{–}36)$$

Although these equations appear complicated, they are actually simple in the sense that if numerical values of all the quantities on the right-hand sides are known numerical values of E_{03} and ϕ_3 are easily calculated.

It is easily shown that (1–35) and (1–36) are essentially the same as (1–26) and (1–27), if α is equated to $[\phi_1 + \phi_2 - \beta(r - s)]$ and if the angle $(\phi_1 - \beta r)$ is arbitrarily taken to be zero, which is permissible, for it amounts only to choosing a particular origin for the coordinate system. Therefore, as is well known in a-c circuit theory, the same geometric construction (Fig. 1–8) can also be applied in this case.

When $\mathbf{E}_1$ and $\mathbf{E}_2$ are different both in direction and phase (other than 180°) the case is more complicated and is not treated in detail here. The resultant electric intensity is a space vector that undergoes an elliptical variation in its direction and amplitude in the general fashion described for an elliptically polarized wave (see Appendix B), except that the plane of the ellipse is not perpendicular to the direction of propagation unless $\mathbf{E}_1$ and $\mathbf{E}_2$ are propagating in the same direction.

The space–time relationships that have been described are often confusing to those who are encountering them for the first time. They become clear only after familiarity has been gained by working problems and by thinking about them at some length. Some helpful exercises are given at the end of the chapter. It is worthwhile to achieve familiarity with these ideas, because the interference phenomenon is the basic principle of most directional antennas, and it has other applications as well.

1.2.5. Huygens' Principle: Diffraction

The discussion of refraction and reflection in terms of rays and wavefronts assumed that the dimensions of the reflecting or refracting surfaces (or regions, in the case of gradual refraction) were large in relation to a wavelength. When a wavefront encounters an obstacle or discontinuity that is not large compared to the wavelength, the simple principles of geometric optics cannot be used to analyze the result. The correct analysis is obtained by application of Maxwell's equations, which are the basis of electromagnetic theory.

Huygens' principle, deducible from Maxwell's equations, is helpful in solving many problems of this type. According to the principle, every point on a given wavefront may be regarded as a radiating source, from which a spherical wavelet is propagated. At further points in space the resulting field intensity may be found by superposition of all of the fields due to these wavelets, taking into account their phases and the interference effects that have just been discussed. This superposition, regarded as the sum of an infinite number of wavelets, is expressed mathematically by an integral.

Diffraction is the process by which the direction of electromagnetic waves is changed by an obstacle, impediment, or blockage and not attributable to reflection and/or refraction. Shadowing by a building or focusing by an antenna are examples. Diffraction may be understood qualitatively with the aid of diagrams. In Fig. 1–9 it is supposed that a plane wavefront has reached position AA'. Spherical "wavelets" are shown originating from three arbitrarily chosen points on AA'. In actuality, of course, such wavelets are assumed by Huygens' principle to arise at every point on AA'. If now a new surface BB' is drawn tangent to all of the wavelets with equal radii, the field along BB' can be considered as the superposition of fields due to all the wavelets from AA'. For the situation shown, an exact mathematical solution of the interference integral would show that the field at a given point on BB' due to all wavelets originating on AA' would be exactly the same as the field at the nearest point of AA' with its phase retarded by $2\pi d/\lambda$ radians, where d is the distance between AA' and BB'. Thus the waves appear to propagate along straight ray paths perpendicular to the wavefronts, but this is actually because the interference of wavelets from all points on an existing wavefront produces this result. An analogous result is obtained for the propagation of spherical wavefronts.

This analysis applies exactly only if the plane wavefront extends infinitely in all directions of the plane. It applies practically if AA' is of large extent compared to a wavelength; then the ray-wavefront construction can be applied without appealing directly to Huygens' principle, although as indicated it is consistent with the principle.

Suppose, however, that the wavefront AA' encounters an obstacle that has an edge. At points beyond this obstacle it is apparent that the geometric-optics assumption is violated, and the wavefront is no longer of infinite extent, a situation described in Fig. 1–10. The "infinite" wavefront AA' is propagating to the right and encounters a barrier, or obstacle, which might be a sheet of metal, for example, or any other substance impenetrable to

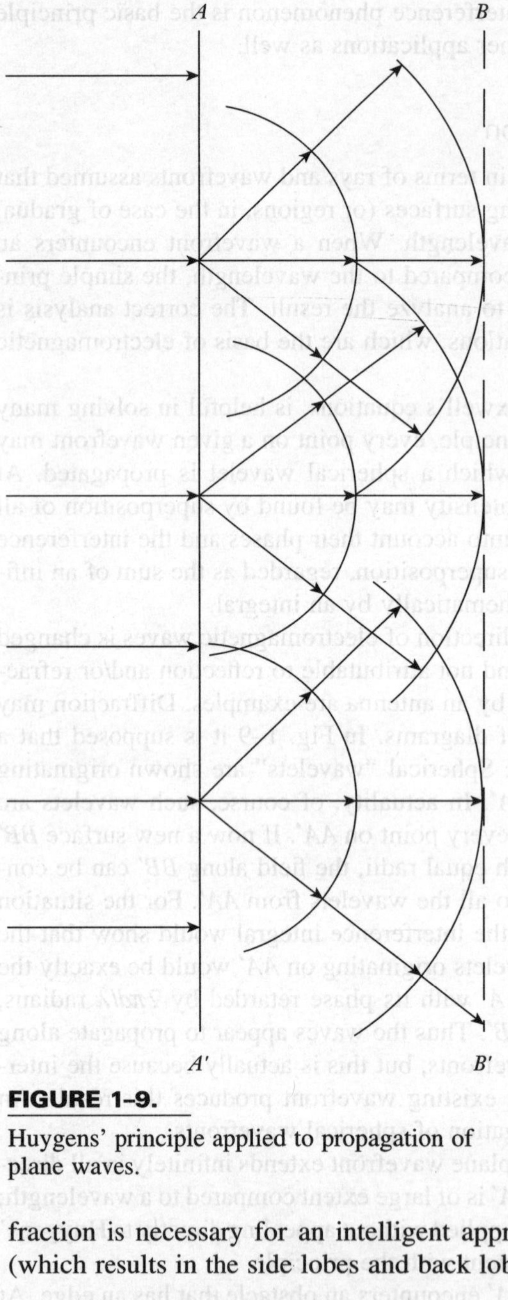

FIGURE 1–9.
Huygens' principle applied to propagation of plane waves.

electromagnetic waves. Therefore, when the wavefront is passing the edge of the obstacle, it extends in the upward direction only to the lower edge of the obstruction, at *B*. Beyond the obstacle (to the right) a semi-infinite wavefront *CC′* will be formed. According to the ray-wavefront concept, no electromagnetic field would exist in the "shadow region" above the dashed line *BC*. Huygens' principle, however, states that a wavelet originating, for example, at point *P* on the wavefront *BB′ will* propagate into the shadow region (and so also will wavelets from all other points on *BB′*). The existence or nonexistence of a field in the shadow region will then depend on the interference of all such wavelets in this region.

A detailed mathematical application of Huygens' principle to this problem shows that, in fact, the field is zero at *some* points in the shadow region and nonzero at other points. This diffraction effect, observable with light waves under laboratory conditions, is also observable with radio waves under suitable conditions. It is an important effect in analyzing the performance of some types of antennas—those for which it is desired to radiate a very narrow "beam" of waves in a preferred direction and to minimize radiation in all other directions. Ideally, it would often be desirable to have absolutely no radiation in undesired directions; but this result is never perfectly achievable because of the diffraction effect. Consequently, an understanding of the general principles of diffraction is necessary for an intelligent approach to minimizing the diffraction pattern (which results in the side lobes and back lobes of a directional antenna pattern).

1.3. Radiation and Reception

So far electromagnetic waves have been discussed as they propagate in space, and very little has been said about how they originate. The process by which this occurs is

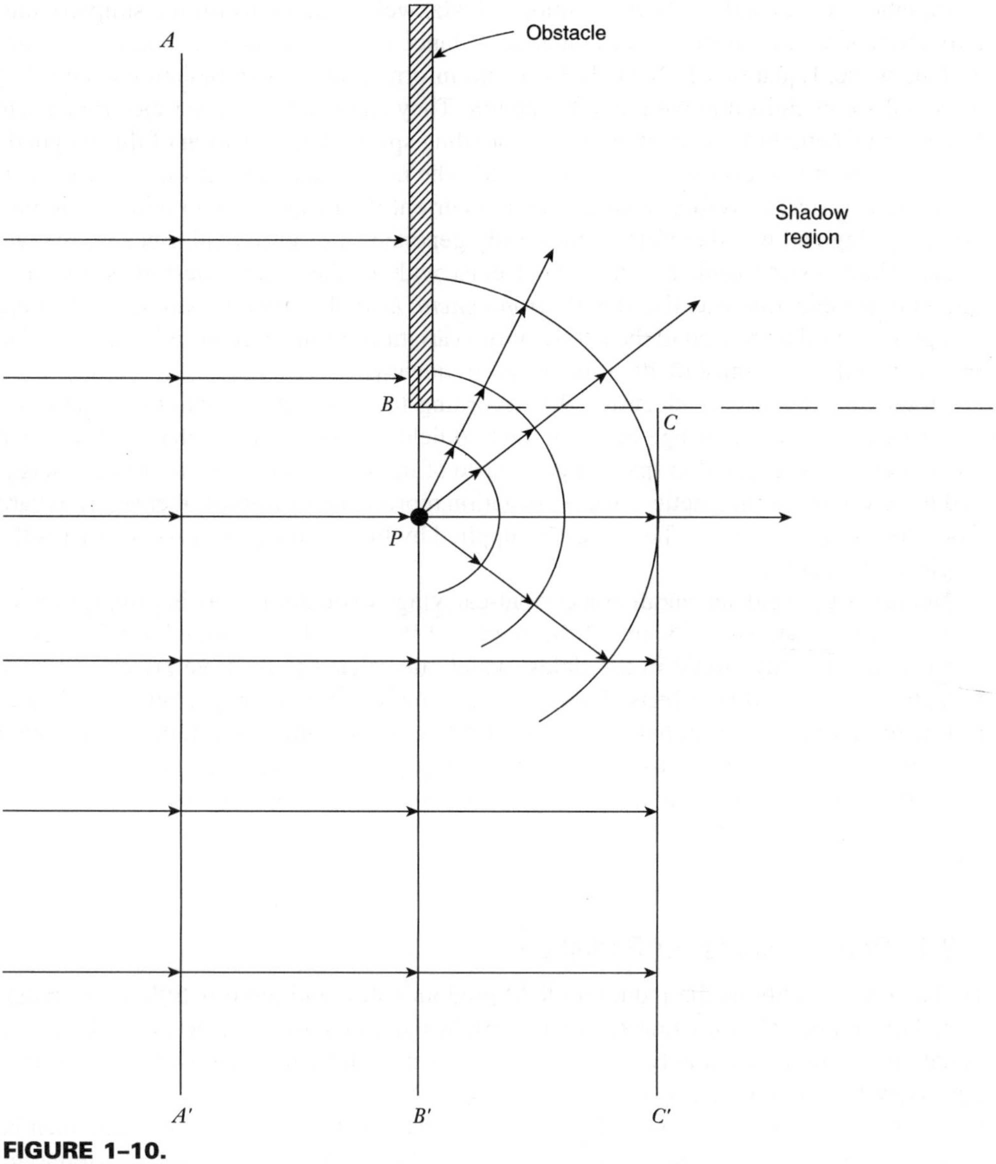

FIGURE 1–10.

Diffraction at the edge of an obstacle.

radiation. Radiation results when high-frequency electric currents flow under suitable conditions. The detailed mathematical description of the relationship between electric currents and their associated fields can be derived from Maxwell's equations. These are four partial differential equations (as usually formulated), and on them the whole structure of electromagnetic theory is based. The practical successes of this theory place it among the most impressive of man's scientific achievements.

Equations (1–2) and (1–3) are solutions of Maxwell's equations for the simplest situation, that of a wave in free space at a great distance from the radiating source—in short, a plane wave. Equations 1–2 and 1–3 give no information on how radiation occurs, but Maxwell's equations do give this information. They state that whenever electric current flows, a magnetic field is set up in the surrounding space. Any *variation* of this magnetic field will result in creation of an electric field. The magnetic field will vary, of course, if the current varies; therefore, with alternating current the magnetic field will be continuously varying and will therefore continuously generate an electric field. Because the two fields always exist together—one cannot exist without the other unless it is nonvarying—the combination is called the *electromagnetic field*. The time variations of the field components will be related to the nature of the variations of the current; if it is sinusoidal, the fields will vary sinusoidally at the same frequency.

Moreover, the varying electric field, according to Maxwell's equations, generates a magnetic field. This exchange between the two fields provides the mechanism by which waves may be propagated in space at the "speed of light." The fields are a form of energy, and therefore electromagnetic wave propagation represents a transport of energy outward from the radiating source. The energy is supplied by the electric power source that is the origin of the current.

Not all of the field surrounding a current-carrying conductor results in propagation of waves outward into space. Some of the energy of these fields is returned to the conductor; it is temporarily stored in the fields, which are related to reactive effects—that is, inductive and capacitive effects. The total field consists of two components—the induction field and the radiation field. The induction field is confined to a fairly local region near the conductors; the radiation field may propagate to great distances, although its strength will decrease with distance, both by spherical spreading of the wavefront (inverse-square law) and by absorption if there is any. This radiation process will be described in further detail for the case of a dipole radiator, in sec. 4.1.

1.3.1. Requirements for Radiation

Under some conditions the induction field predominates, and there is little or no radiation. For appreciable radiation to occur, certain requirements must be met. Maxwell's equations, or more accurately, conclusions derived from them, establish the conditions necessary for radiation to occur.

A fundamental requirement is that the current shall be time varying. As might then be supposed, the more rapid the variation, that is, the higher the frequency of an alternating current, the greater the amount of radiation that will occur for a given amount of current. It is not that radiation cannot occur at low frequencies. Instead, it is that conditions are more favorable for radiation at higher frequencies than at lower ones.

There are also some requirements on the configuration of the current flow. As is well known, at low frequencies current ordinarily flows in closed circuits, as indicated in Fig. 1–11. As shown, the current I in opposite sides of the circuit at an instant of time is in opposite directions. Because of this, although each leg of the circuit might *by itself* result in an appreciable radiated field, the radiation at distant points due to each leg separately will be exactly of opposite phase and will cancel—that is, destructive interference will occur with resultant zero field strength. Consequently, in effect, there will be no radiation.

This assertion tacitly assumes, however, that the physical separation of the opposite legs of the circuit, denoted by d_1 and d_2, is much smaller than a wavelength at the frequency of the current and also that the currents in opposite legs of the circuit are in phase but oppositely directed. If either of these assumptions is not correct, the fields will not cancel completely; in fact, it is readily seen that if phases and separations are just right the interference may be constructive rather than destructive, and appreciable radiation may result. However, at the low frequencies of a-c power circuits—60 Hz—and even at "audio" frequencies, the dimensions of any ordinary circuit will be such that these assumptions are correct. A wavelength in free space at 60 Hz, for example, is 5,000 km! Consequently, radiation is negligible, and is neglected in low-frequency a-c circuit theory.

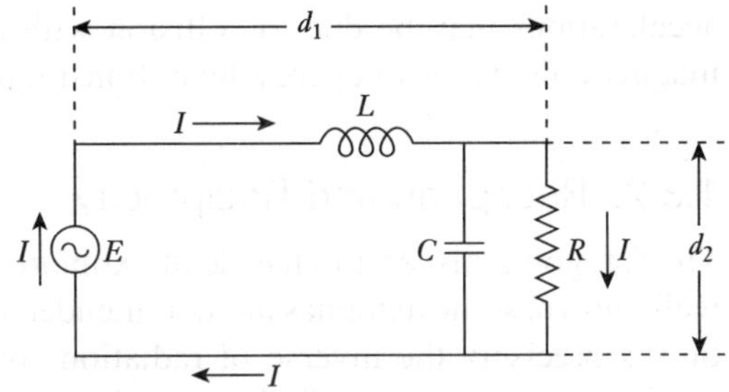

FIGURE 1–11.
Current in a closed-loop circuit.

But at radio frequencies it is entirely feasible to make the distances d_1 and d_2 appreciable compared with a wavelength, and it is also easily possible to produce phase shifts of the currents in opposite legs of the circuit. Also, it is possible to produce current flow in a "circuit" that is not (in the usual sense) a closed loop, that is, in a straight wire with an "open end" or ends. Then appreciable radiation results, and ordinary a-c (low-frequency) circuit theory is no longer applicable.

Finally, for radiation to occur, the conductor carrying the current must be reasonably "in the clear," that is, not enclosed by obstacles that are impenetrable to electromagnetic waves. This is a fairly obvious requirement, but worth mentioning. It means, for example, that radiation may be prevented, when desired, by placing circuits inside closed metallic enclosures; this is the principle of *shielding*.

A solid conductor carrying current is not necessary for radiation, although most antennas do employ metallic conductors. The element of electric current in conductors is the electron; the current consists of motion of electrons. Electrons can also exist and move in empty space (vacuum or near vacuum), as they do, for example, in vacuum tubes, in the earth's ionosphere, and in other regions of "outer space." When such "free electrons" undergo acceleration, radiation occurs, at a frequency depending on the acceleration. Radiation of this type from electrons in galactic space is one source of radio "noise" at high frequencies (and would be at low frequencies as well were it not for the shielding effect of the earth's ionosphere). Electrons accelerated in lightning discharges in the atmosphere also emit radio waves that are heard as noise of the type called "static," at frequencies of several MHz and below. (The radio waves radiated by a single lightning stroke cover a broad band of frequencies.)

Electromagnetic waves are radiated by individual electrons at frequencies in the range of visible and ultraviolet light and X-rays, when they undergo violent accelerations. Such accelerations may be due to collision with other particles, interaction with electric and magnetic fields, or to energy-level transitions of electrons in atomic orbits.

1.3.2. Reception and Reciprocity

The foregoing discussion has dealt explicitly with the radiation aspect of antennas. As is well known, some antennas are not intended to radiate; their function is to receive. Reception is precisely the inverse of radiation. Whereas an alternating current flowing in an antenna will produce radiation, an electromagnetic field impinging on an antenna will cause current to flow in it. A transmitting antenna "launches" electromagnetic waves into space. A receiving antenna captures energy from an incoming field and converts it into electric current. Maxwell's equations also predict this effect, stating that an electromagnetic field will cause alternating current to flow in any conductor exposed to it, of the same frequency and with proportional amplitude and phase variations. A medium or device is *reciprocal* if the response at point *n* to an excitation at point *m* is the same as the response at point *m* to the same excitation at point *n*. It therefore follows that, if the medium of wave propagation is reciprocal, the variations of the current in a receiving antenna will be proportional to the variations in the transmitting antenna that launched the waves.

Most metals and dielectrics used in making antennas are reciprocal, an exception being ferrites. Ferrites are used in circulators, some phase shifters, and isolators. An antenna constructed of only reciprocal materials is reciprocal, that is, its performance features are identical on transmission and reception. Therefore, any *reciprocal* antenna can be used for either transmitting or receiving, the only restriction being that a transmitting antenna may have to carry heavy currents and withstand high voltages. Antennas intended solely for receiving may not have heavy enough conductors or large enough insulators for transmitting. The currents and voltages in receiving antennas are ordinarily so small that they have to be electronically amplified.

In other respects, however, receiving and transmitting antennas are indistinguishable and will work equally well for either purpose. For this reason the properties of a particular antenna may be measured and discussed equally well on either a transmitting or a receiving basis. This is a very valuable bit of knowledge, because it is often easier to employ one form of operation than another in experimental work.

Receiving antennas, as sometimes designed, are inefficient. Such a design is acceptable for reception in a high-field strength region; for example, not very far from a transmitter. It is also permissible with high-gain receivers, at frequencies below a few MHz, when the noise level is determined primarily by external noise sources (e.g., atmospheric static). This statement, however, does not contradict what has been said concerning the interchangeability of the transmitting and receiving functions of an antenna; it merely stresses that inefficient operation may be acceptable in some receiving applications but that it is usually unacceptable for transmitting applications. At the higher frequencies, external noise is weaker and less limiting on reception performance. Then, without the limitations of receiving external noise, receiving antenna effectiveness is equally important as transmitting antenna effectiveness, in determining the overall performance of a complete communications system (see sec. 7.8).

The reciprocal relationships between radiation and reception and between the transmitting and receiving properties of antennas, developed mathematically in advanced texts, are examples of the reciprocity principle or reciprocity theorem.

1.4. Environmental Wave-Propagation Effects

The propagation of radio waves in free space has been considered in sec. 1.1, and certain nonfree-space effects such as refraction, reflection, and diffraction have been described in sec. 1.2. The actual environment in which radio waves are ordinarily propagated may contain obstacles, discontinuities, and propagation-medium variations that give rise to some or all of these effects, in ways that have important effects on radio system design, and thus indirectly at least on antenna design. Sometimes the effect on antenna design is more direct—for example, where the reflecting properties of the earth are utilized deliberately (as well as unavoidably perhaps) to produce a desired pattern of radiation and reception. (Hereafter, in view of the reciprocity relationship that has been described, properties of antennas may be referred to in terms of either radiation or reception, without the reciprocal property being expressly mentioned, but it will be assumed that the reader realizes the application of these properties to either function.)

1.4.1. The Earth Environment

In many respects the concept of free-space propagation is realized in space far from the earth or any other astronomical body, at least over a large portion of the total propagation path, to a degree unachievable in the earth's immediate environs. Even in the earth's atmosphere, however, essentially free-space conditions sometimes prevail—for example, over short paths between highly directional antennas. Such conditions usually exist only at rather high frequencies. Over long paths, and especially at lower frequencies, the effects of the earth's surface, the gases of the lower atmosphere (troposphere), and the charged particles (electrons) of the ionosphere play an important part.

The earth's surface produces two important effects. First, being solid and essentially impenetrable to electromagnetic waves, it represents an obstacle, in the sense of the discussion of diffraction (Fig. 1–10). Consequently, it "casts a shadow," as illustrated in Fig. 1–12. Thus, it is apparent that radio waves traveling in a straight line from the antenna cannot penetrate the shadow region. There will be some diffraction into the shadow

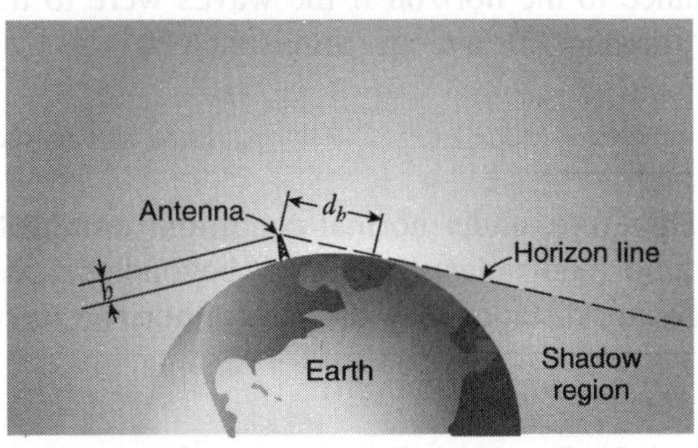

FIGURE 1–12.

Radio-horizon effect and earth's shadow.

region, but ordinarily the field strength from this effect is too small to be of practical value for radio communication. Thus, "line-of-sight" radio propagation from an antenna of height h, Fig. 1–12, would be limited to the horizon distance, dh, assuming that the receiving point is close to the earth's surface.

The spherical earth model is frequently used to estimate the propagation path of waves over the earth (Appendix D). With this model, the effects of the earth's curvature and refraction (bending) in the atmosphere are estimated by assuming the propagation is along straight lines and that the earth has an "effective" radius of a_E. For representing average or "typical" atmospheric effects, a_E is usually taken to be 8,493 km, which is 4/3 times the 6,370 km value geophysicists conventionally assume for the actual earth radius. With this model, the radar horizon d_h, that is, the distance from antenna at height h to the tangent point on a smooth earth of radius a_E, is

$$d_h = \sqrt{2a_E h + h^2} \quad (d_h, a_E, h \text{ in same units}) \qquad (1\text{–}37a)$$

From (1–37a), by neglecting the h^2 term (which is ordinarily much less than $2a_E h$) and letting a_E equal 8,494 km (the 4/3 earth radius), one gets (1–37b)

$$d_h(km) \approx 130\sqrt{h} \quad (d_h \text{ and } h \text{ in km}) \qquad (1\text{–}37b)$$

where both d_h and h are in km units.

Distance d_h of the equations above is, of course, the distance to the horizon as seen from height h. Further increase in distance not blocked by the earth is obtained if both transmitting and receiving antennas are elevated; the total horizon range is then the sum of the values of d, computed separately for the two antennas.

As already noted, atmospheric gases cause refraction, that is, a bending in the wave paths along the earth's surface. Interestingly, atmospheric gases affect the propagation on radio (or radar) and optical waves somewhat differently. Let d_h, d_o, and d_g denote distances to the radio, optical, and geometric horizons, respectively. Here d_g is the distance to the horizon if the waves were to travel in perfectly straight lines. Then, for a "standard" or average atmosphere,

$$d_h = 1.07d_o = 1.15d_g$$

Therefore, under normal conditions, atmospheric refraction extends the distance to the radio (and radar) horizon d_h beyond the geometric horizon d_g, and d_h is at a slightly greater distance than the optical horizon d_o (the one observed visually).

1.4.2. Beyond-the-Horizon Propagation

In 1903, Guglielmo Marconi began a regular transoceanic radio message service, then called wireless, operating at VLF frequencies (3–30 kHz). This service communicated between Poldhu, England, and stations he established in Nova Scotia and on Cape Cod (Kraus, 1988, p. 5). At VLF, the lower edge of the ionosphere behaves virtually like a perfect conducting surface, and vertically polarized waves at these frequencies may be propagated around the earth as if they were confined between two perfectly conducting spherical shells, the inner shell being the earth's surface. This is known as VLF waveguide-mode propagation; and it provides effective, narrow bandwidth, and reliable round-the-world communication. However, extremely high power and a large transmitting antenna are required.

By the early 1920s, the use of "wireless" had progressed into the present-day AM broadcast band (535–1605 kHz). At these higher frequencies vertically polarized waves may propagate to some distance beyond the line-of-sight horizon by means of a surface wave. However, this surface wave provides only a moderate extension of the line-of-sight limitation. Surface wave propagation depends on the fact that a conducting surface tends to "guide" a wave polarized perpendicularly to it, so that the wavefront remains approximately perpendicular and thus maintains a propagation direction parallel to the surface.

However, the guiding effect is only partial when there is but one guiding surface, rather than two as in the VLF waveguide mode. The surface wave partially escapes from the guiding surface as it progresses, so that the method is not effective beyond a distance that depends on the frequency. It also depends on the conductivity of the earth, being greater over the ocean, for example, than over dry land. Usable field strengths are attainable at distances ranging from about 150 kilometers (at the higher end of this frequency range to thousands of kilometers at the lower end, although here the VLF waveguide mode is probably partially operating. The surface wave is the principal mechanism of beyond-the-horizon broadcast-band propagation in the daytime and for propagation to moderate distances at night. The long-distance reception observed at night is due to ionospheric reflection.

The principal method of reaching a point around the curve of the earth consists of two steps, namely, propagation by a path that first goes upward to reach a point high above the earth and then downward into what would be the shadow region for direct-path propagation. This process is illustrated in Fig. 1–13. The transmission from point P_1 on the earth's surface reaches point P_3 by first going to P_2, high above the earth, then down again to P_3. As shown, it is possible to reach points well below the normal horizon line for direct-path propagation from P_1. Several means of accomplishing this result are now described.

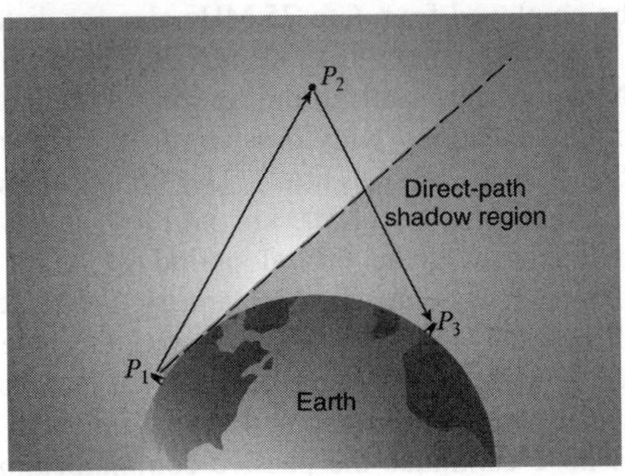

FIGURE 1–13.
Beyond-the-horizon propagation path.

The original method of long-distance radio propagation around the curve of the earth was by reflection from the ionosphere. This layer of electrically charged particles (actually, several layer-like regions at different altitudes) acts as a reflector of radio waves at the lower frequencies—generally from about 10 MHz downward, although the exact upper limit varies with time of day and other factors. The ionization is produced by the sun's radiation and so is most intense in the daytime; however, it persists to some degree through the night so that ionospheric propagation is possible throughout the twenty-four hours at some frequencies. For any particular path there is likely to be an approximately optimum frequency at a particular time of day. Round-the-world propagation is possible by means of multiple reflections. The ionosphere extends from about 60 to more than 300 kilometers above the earth. (It is a reflecting region rather than a reflecting surface; it is in fact more logical to regard the "reflection" as actually a refraction process, at least at the higher frequencies.)

The ionosphere continues to be a valuable means of long-distance radio propagation; but as it is subject to the vagaries of solar activity and is restricted to the lower frequencies, it has limited usefulness. Other means have therefore been sought, and found in the years following World War II.

Tropospheric scatter propagation is useful for distances up to a few hundred kilometers at frequencies in the VHF and UHF. In this method the waves are "scattered" downward from irregularities of the atmospheric dielectric constant. The exact nature of these scattering regions is a subject of some controversy. Scattering may be regarded as a diffraction process, semireflective in effect. Because the scattered field strength is not a very large percentage of the transmitted field, large antennas and high transmitter powers are required. Nevertheless, the scatter method has proved to be advantageous for fixed-point communication links, largely because of the freedom from ionospheric variability effects and because the distances involved are too short for good ionospheric reflection. It has the further important advantage of permitting the use of frequencies too high for ionospheric reflection, thus relieving the overcrowded conditions in the ionospheric-reflection portion of the radio spectrum.

Scattering from ionospheric irregularities and from the ionized trails of meteors have also been found to be practical methods. Ionospheric scatter is limited to the frequency region of about 25 to 60 MHz; it is effective up to about 1,500 km. Meteor scatter can be employed from 6 to 75 MHz also for distances up to about 1,500 km.

Because scatter methods are subject to limitations of distance and frequency useage, National Aeronautical and Space Administration (NASA) began investigating satellite communications with passive, metallized reflecting spheres (http://msl.jpl.nasa.gov/QuickLooks/echoQL.html). The first of these satellites, Echo 1, was placed in orbit at a height of about 1,500 km in 1960; it was a reflecting sphere 100 feet (30.5 m) in diameter, with an orbital period of about 2 hours. Echo 2, 135 feet (41.1 m) in diameter, was launched in January 1964. Reflection via these satellites required large directional antennas that followed the satellite in orbit. Echo 1 reflected 960 and 2,390 MHz signals; and Echo 2 reflected 162 MHz signals. Echo 1 successfully redirected transcontinental and intercontinental telephone, radio, and television signals. Echo 2 continued the passive communications experiments, and also investigated the dynamics of large spacecraft and was used for global geometric geodesy. Although NASA abandonded passive communications in favor of active satellites following Echo 2, the

Echo systems demonstrated several ground station and tracking technologies later used by active systems.

Active satellites receive signals from the earth, and then retransmit them at a different frequency to another location. These satellites contain receiving and transmitting equipment, including, of course, receiving and transmitting antennas. There are about 150 communications satellites operational today, and they use geostationary, Molnya, or low polar circular orbits (http://en.wikipedia.org/wiki/Communications_satellite).

Geostationary satellites appear stationary as viewed from the rotating earth; and they continue to operate above the equator, at an altitude of about 35,000 km. Although the path lengths are long, an important advantage is that the earth-based antennas do not have to track a rapidly moving satellite. However, since geostationary satellites remain over the equator, they are not well suited to high latitude (far North or far South) coverage. Molnya orbits are highly inclined, providing good Northern coverage. A major use of Molnya satellites is for telephony and TV over Russia.

A low earth orbit typically is circular and about 400 kilometers above the earth's surface, and time to revolve around the earth is about 90 minutes. Thus, they change their position relative to a fixed ground position quickly, and thus a large number of satellites are needed for uninterrupted connectivity. However, discontinuous coverage is possible by storing data received while passing over one part of earth and transmitting it later while passing over another part. Low earth orbiting satellites are closer to the ground than geostationary satellites and consequently their equipment costs are less. Thus, relative costs involve trades between the number of satellites and their individual costs.

For special purposes reflection from the moon's surface has been used as a communication method at VHF. This method has the disadvantage, of course, of being limited to the times that the moon is above the horizon; it also requires very high power and large antennas.

At some frequencies, usually VHF and higher, unusual atmospheric conditions sometimes result in abnormally great downward bending of ray paths, owing to an extreme effect of the type illustrated by Fig. 1–4. Under such circumstances waves may be propagated in a path that follows the curve of the earth, hence into the normal shadow region. This effect is called superrefraction or sometimes "trapping" or "ducting." It usually occurs in warm climates when unusual moisture and temperature conditions prevail and is not sufficiently reliable or predictable for most beyond-the-horizon propagation applications. However, under very unusual conditions propagation by this method beyond 1,500 km has been observed, and 150-km paths are not unusual.

1.4.3. Reflection from the Earth's Surface

Next to its role as a barrier, that is, creating a shadow region; the most important effect of the earth on the propagation of radio waves is its action as a reflector. Moist earth or a water surface will reflect electromagnetic waves in the lower part of the radio spectrum quite well. At the higher frequencies the surface may be too rough to reflect specularly. However, in accordance with Rayleigh's criterion, equation (1–25), a rough surface will reflect specularly at a sufficiently large angle of incidence (small angle between the ray direction and the surface, called the grazing angle). At larger grazing angles semispecular reflection may occur, as shown in Fig. 1–6. For smooth earth surfaces, effects of specular reflection may be observed at frequencies up to at least 35 GHz.

Reflection from a plane surface was illustrated in Fig. 1–5, and the principle of images for specular reflection was shown in Fig. 1–7. The reflection that occurs from the earth's surface may be understood in terms of these concepts. Although the earth is approximately spherical, the region of reflection may be regarded as virtually plane if the antenna is located within about a hundred meters of the earth's surface.

Waves reflected from the earth's surface are important because they interfere with waves propagated in a direct path, as illustrated in Fig. 1–14. A transmitting antenna is assumed to be located at S_1, at a height h above a perfectly reflecting plane surface; and therefore its image is located at S_2, a distance $2\,h$ from S_1. A direct wave travels to a receiving point at P_2 following a straight-line path (except for the slight downward curvature due to atmospheric refraction, which may be disregarded here). A reflected wave also arrives at P_2 via the path $S_1P_1 + P_1P_2$. However, in accordance with the image principle, the reflected wave may be regarded as originating at S_2 and proceeding to P_2 via the straight-line path $S_2P_1 + P_1P_2$. The *elevation angle* of point P_2 as viewed from S_1 is designated θ. Notice that the grazing angles ψ, whether entering or exiting point P_1, are equal in accordance with the principles of optics (Fig. 1–5).

Since the two waves arriving at P_2 are of exactly the same frequency, being from the same source, they will interfere in accordance with (1–35) and (1–36). Whether the interference is constructive or destructive depends on the phase difference. Since the lengths of the two wave paths are not the same, there will in general be a path difference δ and a consequent phase difference equal to $\beta\delta$ radians ($\beta = 2\pi/\lambda$). At some points in space the two waves will reinforce each other; at other points they will tend to cancel so that there will be regions of zero or near-zero field strength. This effect can have serious consequences; for example, it can create "blind" regions in space where signals cannot be detected.

Figure 1–14 is used to analyze a relatively simple multipath propagation problem that provides the results of Fig. 1–15. Applicable assumptions follow:

a. The wavelength is long enough that the surface is smooth, in accordance with the Rayleigh criterion [equation (1–25)]. Ordinarily, even in the presence of the earth's surface irregularities and undulations, this assumption is valid for VHF (30–300 MHz) and lower frequencies.
b. The distance S_1P_2 between antenna and the observation point is short enough that the earth's curvature is neglected.
c. The antenna elevation pattern is sufficiently broad that the amplitude and phase of the radiated waves are the same at every elevation angle θ.
d. The reflection coefficient amplitude and phase delay are constant, corresponding to $|\Gamma| = 1$ and $\phi = -\pi$ radians, respectively. This is a valid approximation for horizontal polarization and a reflecting surface that is sea water or another good conductor.
e. The paths S_1P_2 and S_2P_2 are long enough, relative to $2\,h$, so that they are effectively parallel.

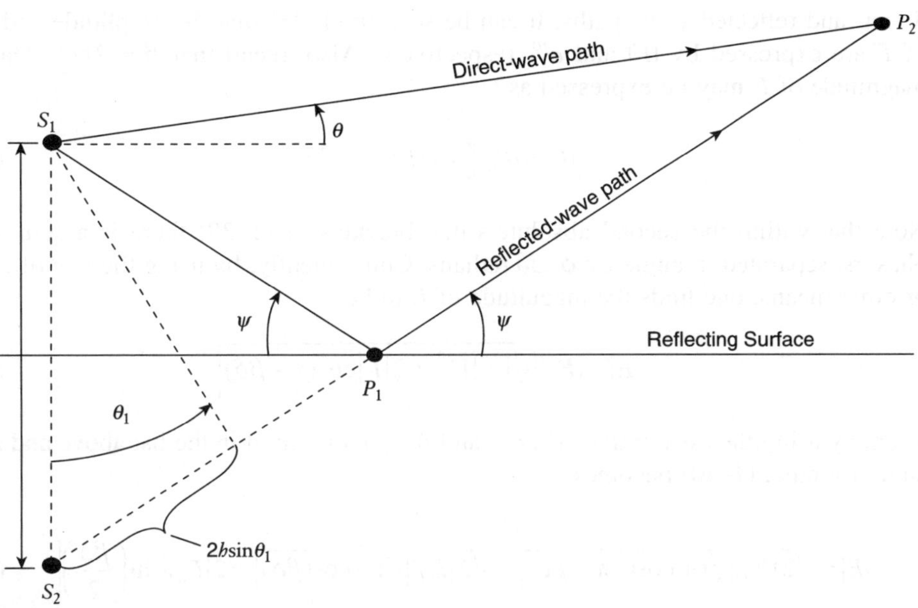

FIGURE 1–14.

Geometry of interference between direct-path and reflected-path waves.

In summary, the assumptions above require that the reflecting surface be a flat and smooth conductor, the polarization be horizontal, and the direct- and reflected-wave paths (S_1P_2 and S_2P_2) be effectively parallel.

For purposes of the analysis, we denote the electric intensity of the direct-wave as E_d and the reflected wave as E_r. Then, based on the above assumptions and Fig. 1–14, the electric field E resulting from the phasor sum of the direct-wave and the reflected-wave fields at P_2 follows:

$$E = E_d + E_r = E_d + E_d \Gamma e^{-j\beta\delta}$$
$$= E_d\left[1 + |\Gamma|^{j\phi} e^{-j\beta\delta}\right] \qquad (1\text{–}38)$$

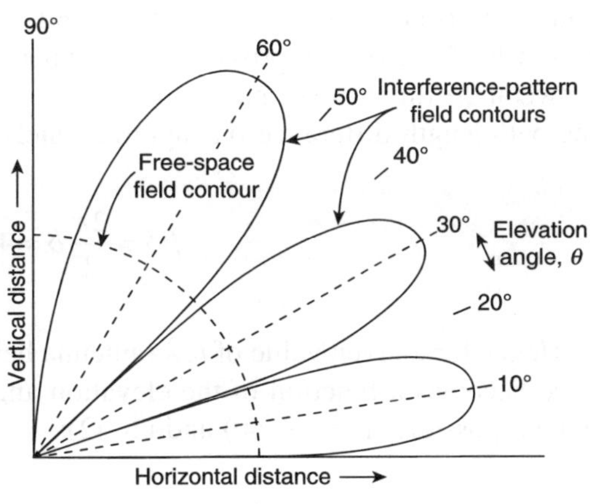

FIGURE 1–15.

Interference-pattern field-strength contours relative to free-space contour, for $h/\lambda = 1.44$ and $\Gamma = -1$.

Here Γ is the complex (amplitude and phase) reflection coefficient of the earth's surface, and $\beta\delta$ is the phase delay (in radians) caused by the difference δ of the lengths in the direct- and reflected-wave paths. It can be seen in (1–38) that the amplitude and phase of Γ are expressed by $|\Gamma|$ and $e^{j\phi}$, respectively. Also, recall that $\beta = 2\pi/\lambda$. Thus, the magnitude of E may be expressed as

$$|E| = |E_d|\left|\left[1+|\Gamma|e^{j\phi}e^{-j\beta\delta}\right]\right| \tag{1–39}$$

Note that within the second absolute-value brackets of (1–39) there is a sum of two phasors, separated in angle by $\phi-\beta\delta$ radians. Consequently, by using the law of cosines or other means, one finds the magnitude of E to be

$$|E| = |E_d|\left|\sqrt{1+|\Gamma|^2+2|\Gamma|\cos(\phi-\beta\delta)}\right| \tag{1–40}$$

Then, by using the assumptions $|\Gamma| = 1$ and $\phi = -\pi$ of item d in the list above and a half-angle formula, (1–40) becomes

$$|E| = \sqrt{2}|E_d|\left|\sqrt{1+\cos(-\pi-\beta\delta)}\right| = \sqrt{2}|E_d|\left|\sqrt{1-\cos(\beta\delta)}\right| = 2|E_d|\left|\sin\left(\frac{\beta\delta}{2}\right)\right| \tag{1–41}$$

where, as previously, $\beta = 2\pi/\lambda$. Note that changes in the path length difference δ cause $|E|$ to vary between $2|E_d|$ and zero.

From Fig. 1–14 it can be seen that δ equals $2h\sin\theta_1$ requires parallel S_1-P_2 and S_2-P_2 paths, but the angle θ_1 is generally not known. However, in many circumstances, the path S_2-P_2 is approximately parallel to path S_1-P_2 because S_1-P_2 is very much larger than height h. Then, θ_1 is approximately θ, where θ is the more likely known angle which is between the direct-wave path and the local horizontal at the antenna. Thus, when $\theta \approx \theta_1$, the path length difference δ is approximately $2h\sin\theta$ and then

$$\beta\delta = \frac{2\pi}{\lambda}\delta = 4\pi\left(\frac{h}{\lambda}\right)\sin\theta \tag{1–42}$$

Hence for a given value of h/λ (antenna height expressed in wavelengths) the interference becomes a function of the elevation angle θ only. A final simplification of (1–38) is then possible from (1–40) and (1–42):

$$E = 2E_d\left|\sin\left(\frac{2\pi h\sin\theta}{\lambda}\right)\right| \tag{1–43}$$

Application of this formula to the particular value of $h/\lambda = 1.44$ results in the field-strength pattern shown in Fig. 1–15.

The contours, or lobes, represent surfaces of constant field strength. The origin of the coordinate system is the location of the transmitting antenna. Elevation-angle markers are at 10-degree intervals up to 60 degrees. Field strength is compared to its strength if the antenna radiated uniformly in all elevation angles and there were no reflected wave (free-space contour). As shown, there are three lobe maxima between $\theta = 0°$ and $\theta = 90°$, for the particular h/λ assumed, namely, 1.44.

The number of lobes in an interference pattern is approximately $2\,h/\lambda$. Thus at very short wavelengths (very high frequencies) there may be many lobes and nulls; for example, at a frequency of 500 MHz (λ = 0.6 m) and with 30 m antenna height, there are approximately 100 lobes between $\theta = 0°$ and $\theta = 90°$. The pattern shown in Fig. 1–15 may occur with 30 m antenna height, 15 MHz frequency, and horizontal polarization.

Important assumptions in the calculation for Fig. 1–15 are that the reflection coefficient Γ is minus one, corresponding to $|\Gamma| = 1$ and $\phi = -\pi$ radians (180° delay). These assumptions are approximately correct for horizontal polarization at all angles of incidence. Thus, in accordance with (1–43), the field strength is zero at elevation angle $\theta =$ 0°, that is, the horizontal direction. Zero field strength at $\theta = 0°$ is, of course, undesirable in numerous applications. A remedy is to bring the first lobe maximum down to as low an angle as possible by increasing the ratio h/λ, by increasing the frequency and/or increasing the antenna height. (Parenthetically, the elevation angle of the first lobe maximum is approximately $\lambda/4\,h$ radians or about 15 λ/h degrees.) However, for long-distance ionospheric transmission, zero-angle radiation is of less importance than for non-ionospheric transmission. For long-distance ionospheric transmissions, horizontal polarization may be used if h/λ is equal to at least unity; although $h/\lambda = 2$ that gives a maximum field strength at about 7° elevation is better.

1.4.4. Variations in Earth's Reflection Coefficient

The present section discusses smooth planar surfaces, for which the reflections are specular. As discussed in Appendix D, these reflections may be reduced by either surface roughness or the earth's curvature. Additionally, the accompanying website includes Mathcad calculations of reflection coefficient and multipath effects versus their contributing factors.

Recall that, for the analysis pertaining to Fig. 1–15, the paths S_1P_2 and S_2P_2 are assumed parallel, and that causes the elevation angle θ and the grazing angle ψ to be equal. In fact, multipath propagation is strongly affected by both the amplitude and phase of the earth's reflection coefficient, which depend on the grazing angle ψ. The reflection coefficient Γ for dielectrics and conductors is different, and it depends strongly on whether the polarization is horizontal (H) or vertical (V). Land and sea have different dielectric properties: dry land is a poor conductor, water improves the conductivity of land, and seawater is a good conductor. For H and V polarizations, there are major differences between Γ versus grazing angle ψ. For a given land or sea surface, Γ also changes with frequency, but significant differences occur only with major changes in wavelength.

Land and sea surface reflections for H polarization (H POL) are easier to describe than those for V POL. This is because for H POL $|\Gamma| \approx 1$ and $\phi \approx -\pi$ radians, but $|\Gamma|$ and ϕ vary widely for V POL. More specifically, for H POL:

- Γ changes very little with changes in grazing angle, surface conductivity, or frequency and
- $|\Gamma|$ approaches unity as the grazing angle ψ approaches zero and it deviates the most from unity at angles that are near normal incidence, at the higher frequencies, and for the driest surfaces.

As now discussed, the Brewster angle effect causes large variations in $|\Gamma|$ and ϕ. The Brewster angle is the grazing angle at which the reflection coefficient is zero, and it occurs only for V POL and a lossless dielectric. Instead, for land and sea, which are imperfect dielectrics, $|\Gamma|$ for V POL has a non-zero minimum at the so-named pseudo-Brewster angle ψ_{pB}. Accordingly, $|\Gamma|$ is much larger for grazing angles both smaller and larger than ψ_{pB}. At grazing angles larger than ψ_{pB}, ϕ becomes close to 0°, ϕ is approximately −90° at ψ_{pB}, and ϕ approaches −180° as ψ approaches zero. Thus, ϕ will be very near −180° for very small grazing angles, even with V POL and poorly conducting ground. Additionally, $|\Gamma|$ increases and approaches unity for grazing angles ψ that approach zero. Therefore, an interference null exists at small grazing angles for both H and V polarizations—however, as now discussed, below 1 MHz, the V POL nulls near the horizontal direction will be increasingly filled as the frequency is reduced.

The pseudo-Brewster angle ψ_{pB} is at considerably smaller grazing angles for seawater than for land, and it becomes smaller for both land and sea with increasingly longer wavelengths. Interesting, the movement of ψ_{pB} closer to zero grazing permits acceptable V POL performance (without an interference null) down to very small grazing angles at low frequencies. For smooth planar surfaces at 1 MHz, ψ_{pB} is about 0.2° and 3° for sea and typical land, respectively. At 100 kHz, the corresponding ψ_{pB} values are about 0.07° and 1° for sea and land, respectively. Natural surface-slope undulations and other irregularities diminish the destructive interference and thereby further enhance signal amplitudes at the near-zero grazing angles. Therefore, at the lower frequencies it is possible to place a vertical-polarization radiator close to the ground and obtain acceptably strong radiation in the horizontal direction. This phenomenon permits the effective use of V POL for frequencies less than about 1 MHz.

Although the interference of direct and reflected waves creates undesirable minima in the radiation pattern, it also creates maxima in field strengths. Since the earth is not a perfect reflector, the amplitude of the reflected wave will be less than that of the direct wave, with the result that the field strength will be greater than zero at the minima and less than twice the free-space value at the maxima. As discussed in more detail in Appendix D, the earth's surface roughness and curvature reduces $|\Gamma|$, and thus the pattern nulls are partly filled and the maxima reduced. The reader will recall that, in accordance with the Rayleigh criterion, equation (1–25), surfaces become rougher (electromagnetically) with increases in the radio wave frequency.

1.4.5. Wave Nomenclature

The terms *sky wave* and *ground wave* were introduced many years ago when propagation at distances beyond the horizon was generally accomplished via ionospheric reflection, and at shorter distances by means of either a surface-guided wave or by direct line-of-sight transmission. These terms are still in use, and their meanings are illustrated in Fig. 1–16. As shown, the sky wave is propagated by an ionosphere-reflected path. The ground wave comprises the vector sum of (1) a direct-path (line-of-sight) wave; (2) a reflected-path wave; and (3) a surface-guided wave or, more simply, surface wave. In other words, the ground wave is the composite wave in the vicinity of the earth, that would exist in the absence of the ionosphere.

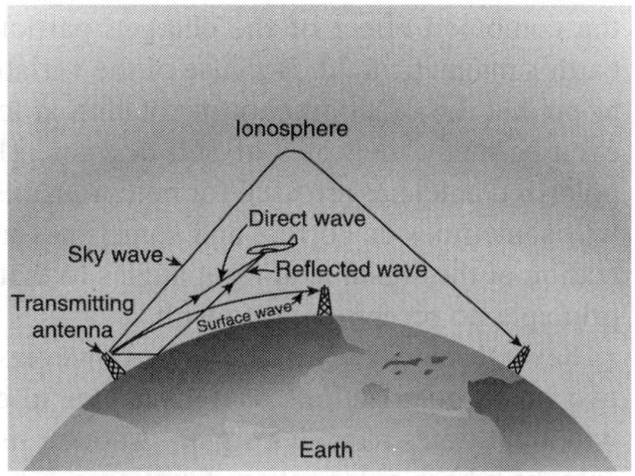

FIGURE 1–16.

Nomenclature of wave propagation (not to scale).

1.4.6. Transionospheric Propagation

Now that radio transmission to and from various outer-space locations is commonplace, the effect of the ionosphere on waves passing through it is of importance, whereas at one time the ionosphere was of interest primarily because of its ability to reflect radio waves back to earth. Naturally, transmission through the ionosphere requires the use of a frequency well above the frequencies that are reflected from it; generally, frequencies above 10 MHz are necessary.

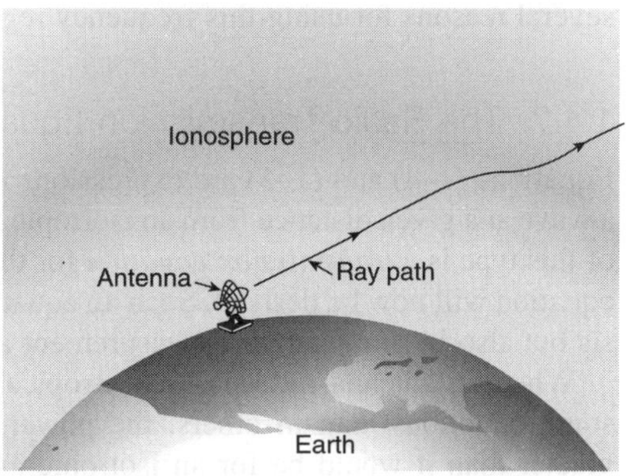

FIGURE 1–17.

Refraction in transionospheric propagation.

A wave that is above the critical reflection frequency may nevertheless be appreciably refracted in passing through the ionosphere, as illustrated in Fig. 1–17. As shown, the wave path is at first bent downward as it enters the ionosphere from below. Then, after reaching the region of densest ionization, it is bent back upward, and eventually emerges with nearly its original direction. If the direction of the antenna beam at the earth were used to determine the direction of a source of incoming waves, this bending effect would cause some error in the determination. Therefore it is important to be aware of the effect. If the ionosphere electron-density height profile is known, the magnitude of the effect can be calculated. Generally it is not an appreciable effect above 100 MHz and is less at night than in the daytime. A similar statement applies to the absorption losses that occur in the ionosphere.

A more important effect in transionospheric propagation below a few hundred MHz is the Faraday rotation of the polarization of a wave. This rotation occurs as a result of the combined effect of the charged particles (electrons) of the ionosphere and of the earth's magnetic field. Because of the variability of the effect, it is not feasible to attempt to predict the exact amount of rotation at low frequencies, where the total rotation may even be many multiples of 360 degrees. This rotation is important because, if linearly polarized antennas are used for both transmission and reception, the received polarization will sometimes be correct and sometimes incorrect for optimum reception. If the polarization of the signal is at right angles to that which the antenna is intended to receive, in principle no reception will result.

Several remedies are available, however. One is to use either circular polarization, or two linear polarizations at right angles to each other, so that one or the other of them will at all times receive a signal. Another remedy is to use a linearly polarized receiving antenna whose polarization direction can be varied to agree with the polarization of the incoming wave. The third remedy is to operate at a high enough frequency so that no appreciable rotation occurs—above 1,000 MHz, or possibly a bit lower. The present tendency for space communication and other space transmissions is to use frequencies between about 1 and 10 GHz, although avoidance of Faraday rotation is only one of several reasons for using this frequency region.

1.4.7. The Radio-Transmission Equation

Equations (1–4) and (1–5) are expressions for the far-field (sec. 3.2.5) power density of a wave at a given distance from an isotropic radiating source in free space. An expression of this type is a *transmission equation* for this special case. A more general transmission equation will now be derived. Such an equation is needed not only in radio system analysis but also in some antenna measurement applications.

When an antenna radiates nonisotropically, that is, when it radiates more power in some directions than in others, the power density in the preferred directions will be greater than it would be for an isotropic antenna. The *ratio* of the power density in a given direction to that which would be observed at the same distance if a lossless isotropic antenna were radiating the same total power is called the *gain* of the antenna, G. It follows that if a transmitting antenna has a gain G_t in a certain direction, the received power density p_r at a distance R in that direction will be

$$p_r = \frac{P_t G_t}{4\pi R^2} \qquad (1\text{–}44)$$

Equation (1–44) is a free-space radio-transmission equation. If the field strength (electric intensity) rather than the power density is desired, it can be obtained by applying (1–9) and noting that $377 = 120\pi$, which gives

$$E_r = \frac{\sqrt{30 P_t G_t}}{R} \qquad (1\text{–}45)$$

When the path between the transmitter and receiver is not in "free space," a modification of these equations is required. This is done through use of the *pattern-propagation factor F*. Following the IEEE definition (IEEE Standard 686–1997, p. 19), F is a scalar and it is the ratio of the field strength that is actually present at a point in space to that which would have been present if free-space propagation had occurred with the antenna beam directed toward the point in question. Accordingly,

$$F = \frac{E_{r(\text{actual})}}{E_{r(\text{free space})}} \tag{1–46}$$

By merely rearranging this definition, (1–45) which gives $E_{r(\text{free space})}$ can be converted to a nonfree-space equation, as follows:

$$E_{r(\text{actual})} = FE_{r(\text{free space})} = \frac{F\sqrt{30P_tG_t}}{R} \tag{1–47}$$

Similarly, the equation for power density p_r under nonfree-space conditions becomes

$$p_r = \frac{P_tG_tF^2}{4\pi R^2} \tag{1–48}$$

Ordinarily, the gain of an antenna varies with direction of radiation, but the gain G_t in (1–47) and (1–48) is the gain in a specific direction of observation. However, for use of the above IEEE definition of F, one is reminded that, in a nonfree-space environment, the actual field strength at a point may depend on gain in directions other than that toward the point in question. For example, in accordance with Fig. 1–14, waves radiated downward from an antenna may reflect from the earth and be summed at a point in space, both in phase and amplitude, with waves arriving directly from the antenna. Therefore, with the definition of F, antenna gain versus direction must be considered when more than one direction is involved, unless the antenna gain is the same in the various directions.

Effective receive aperture area A_r, and its relationships with maximum receive antenna gain G_r and received power P_r, is discussed in chapter 3, sec. 3.4. Received power P_r equals p_rA_r, assuming the receiving antenna and the incident wave are polarization matched, where p_r is the power density incident on the area A_r, and $A_r = G_r\lambda^2/4\pi$. Then, by using these relationships and (1–48), a useful relationship for received power follows:

$$P_r = \frac{P_tG_rG_t\lambda^2F^2}{(4\pi)^2 R^2} \tag{1–49}$$

The reflection-interference pattern calculation, exemplified by Fig. 1–15, can be used to determine F, for the case where the antenna gain is independent of the elevation angle. Accordingly,

$$F = \frac{E}{E_d} \tag{1–50}$$

since E_d is the free-space field strength. With E expressed in terms of (1–43), (1–50) becomes

$$F = 2\left|\sin\left(\frac{2\pi h \sin\theta}{\lambda}\right)\right| \tag{1–51}$$

In this case the maximum value of F is obviously 2 (when the sine function has its maximum numerical values ±1), and the minimum value is zero. In free space, of course, $F = 1$.

Appendix D and the accompanying website discuss calculations of the pattern-propagation factor for smooth and rough land and sea surfaces, under assumptions that the earth is either flat or spherical.

References

Ah Yo, D. M. K., and R. Emrick, "Frequency Bands for Military and Commercial Applications," ch. 2 in J. L. Volakis (ed.), *Antenna Engineering Handbook*, 4th ed., McGraw-Hill, 2007.

Blake, L. V., "Tropospheric Absorption Loss and Noise Temperature in the Frequency Range 100–10,000 Mc", *IRE Transactions on Antennas and Propagation*, AP-10, January 1962, p. 101.

IEEE Standard 100–1992, *The New IEEE Standard Dictionary of Electrical and Electronic Terms*, 1992.

IEEE Standard 211-1997, *The IEEE Standard Definitions of Terms for Radio Wave Propagation*, December 1997, p. 27.

IEEE Standard 686–1997, *IEEE Standard Radar Definitions*, 25 March 1998.

Kraus, J. D., *Antennas*, 2nd ed., 1988.

Problems and Exercises

1. A plane electromagnetic wave in free space has an electric-intensity amplitude of 10 volts per meter and initial phase angle ϕ of 15 degrees at the time $t = 0$ and the position $z = 0$. The frequency is $f = 5 \times 10^5$ Hz (500 kHz). What is the instantaneous electric intensity at the position $z = 3$ meters at time $t = 10^{-8}$ seconds? (*Note*: To work this problem in degrees rather than in radians, substitute the number 360 in place of 2π in Eq. 1–2.)

2. A wave propagating in free space is at a point 20 km from its source (assumed to be a point source), and the power density is $p = 2 \times 10^{-5}$ watts per square meter. What is the power density at a distance of 30 km?

3. The rms electric intensity of a wave in free space is 2.7×10^{-3} volt per meter. (a) What is its power density in watts per square meter? (b) What is the rms magnetic intensity in amperes per meter?

4. (a) The attenuation constant of a uniformly absorbing propagation medium is $\gamma = 0.01$ dB per kilometer. A plane wave propagating in this medium (assumed to be of infinite extent) has, at an initial point, a power density $p_1 = 1 \times 10^{-3}$ watt per square meter. What is the power density p_2 at a second point 300 km away in the direction of travel of the wave?

   (b) If the initial point in part (a) is at a distance $R_1 = 100$ km from the source of the waves, so that the wavefront must now be regarded as spherical (and spreading) rather than plane, and if a second point is at a distance $R_2 = 400$ km from the source in the same direction, what is the *total* attenuation in decibels due to both the spreading and the absorption? (*Note*: Because the medium is assumed to be of infinite extent, the wave propagation will follow free-space laws except for the absorption; Eq. 1–14 applies.)

5. A plane wave in free space is incident upon the plane surface of a dielectric material at an incidence angle of 30 degrees. The dielectric constant of the material $\varepsilon_r' = 4$. By what angle does the direction of propagation *change* as the wave passes into the dielectric medium? (That is, what is the *difference* between the angle of incidence and the angle of refraction?)

6. A boundary between two propagation media has a total power-reflection coefficient $R = 0.64$. (a) What is the power-transmission coefficient, T? (b) If the reflection is partly specular and partly diffuse, and the specular coefficient is of magnitude $|\Gamma| = 0.7$, what is the diffuse-power-reflection coefficient, R_d?

7. (a) A transmitting antenna is located on a mountain top at a height of 1,500 meters, overlooking the sea. A ship is steaming directly away from it. Assuming that the only signal that can be effectively received is the one that propagates via a direct (line-of-sight) path, at what maximum distance will the ship be able to receive signals from the mountain-top antenna? (Assume that the transmitting power is adequate for distances to the horizon. Neglect the height of the shipboard antenna.) (b) An airplane at an altitude of 300 meters is also flying out to sea, on the same course as the ship. At what maximum distance can it receive the signals?

8. A radio station has a total radiated power $P_t = 10{,}000$ watts, and an antenna gain $G_t = 30$. If free-space propagation is assumed, what is the rms electric intensity of the radiated field at a distance $R = 100$ km (10^5 meters), expressed in volts per meter?

9. A shipboard transmitting antenna radiates $P_t = 1{,}000$ watts and has a power gain $G_t = 100$. Its height above the sea surface is such that at a certain elevation angle the propagation factor is $F = 2$. An airplane at a range $R = 50$ km (5×10^4 meters) is at an altitude corresponding to this elevation angle. What power density exists at its receiving antenna due to the transmission from the ship?

10. An isotropic antenna is located at a height of 30.3 meters above a perfectly reflecting plane surface. The wavelength of the radiated signal is 3 meters. Assume the reflection coefficient $\Gamma = -1$. At a distant point whose elevation angle is 30 degrees, what is the propagation factor F? (*Note:* to use trigonometric functions in degrees rather than radians in Eq. 1–51, replace the factor 2π by the number 360.)

CHAPTER 2

Transmission Lines

This chapter discusses transmission lines. Transmission lines must be addressed in the study of antennas for three reasons: (1) A transmission line virtually always connects an antenna to a transmitter or receiver, and is often regarded as a part of the antenna system; (2) in some types of antennas transmission-line elements are integral parts of the antenna; and (3) the principles of transmission lines are applicable to understanding some aspects of antenna theory.

The material of this chapter, like that of chapter 1, is intended for review and reference. A complete treatise on transmission lines would provide material for an entire book. Therefore only the basic aspects of the subject will be covered here, with emphasis on antenna applications.

2.1. Basic Transmission-Line Concepts

A transmission line is a specific example of what is known in circuit theory as a linear passive four-terminal network or, in more modern terminology, a linear passive two-port. Its function is to convey electrical power or signals between two points appreciably separated in distance.

The simplest form of transmission line, a pair of parallel wires insulated from each other, is shown schematically in Fig. 2–1. It is called a two-wire balanced line. Basic transmission-line principles will be discussed in terms of this type of line, but most of them will be found to be applicable directly or with minor modifications to other forms of lines, such as coaxial lines and waveguides.

As indicated in Fig. 2–1, the spacing of the wires, *S*, their diameter, *d*, and their length, *l*, are important properties of the line. These are dimensional properties, but they are important electrically. Also important, naturally, are the electrical properties—the conductivity of the wires, and the permittivity, permeability, and loss characteristics of any material within the field of the line.

In operation, a load of impedance Z_L is connected to the load terminals of the line, and a sinusoidal voltage V_i is applied to the input terminals. Given these quantities, the

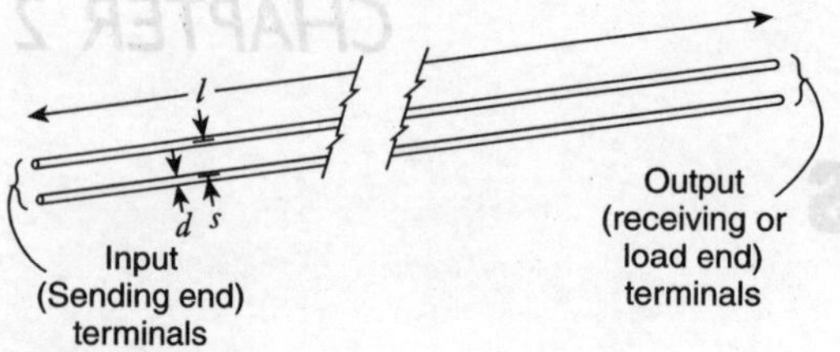

FIGURE 2–1.

Dimensional elements of a two-wire transmission line.

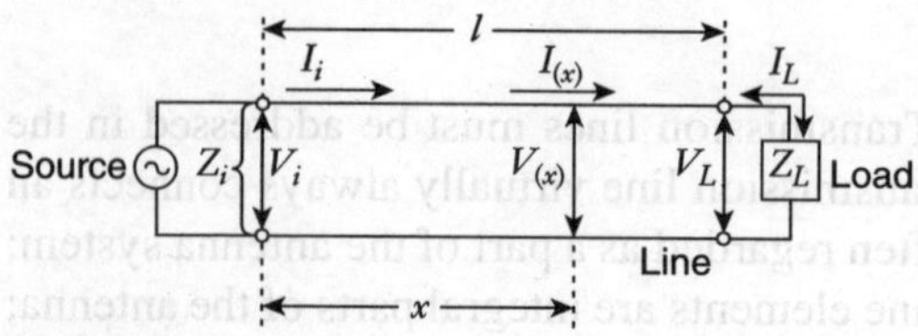

FIGURE 2–2.

Electrical elements of the transmission-line problem.

transmission-line problem is to find the current and voltage at points along the line and at the load. It is usually also of particular interest to know what impedance the line presents at its input terminals to the source (generator) of the input voltage. By definition this impedance, Z_i, is the ratio of the input voltage V_i to the input current I_i, so that finding Z_i is not a separate or additional problem.

Figure 2–2 indicates the nature of this electrical problem, which differs in an essential way from that of the simple four-terminal network of circuit theory. When the voltage V_i is applied at the input terminals, it does not result in the immediate appearance of a voltage V_L at the load terminals. A finite time is required for the voltage to travel the length of the line, in the same way that an electromagnetic wave has a finite velocity in space. In fact, voltage and current traveling along a transmission line are accompanied by an electromagnetic wave in the space between the conductors, and the transmission-line problem can be analyzed in terms of this field instead of in terms of the voltage and current. The line is then regarded as a means of guiding the field so that it is confined to a region near the line rather than spreading spherically in space. Because of this confinement, the waves do not suffer the inverse-square-law decrease of power-density with distance as do waves in free space.

Thus the transmission line may be considered either from the point of view of voltages, currents, and electrical circuit theory or from the point of view of a guided electromagnetic wave. It is more conventional to adopt the former approach, at least initially; and this will be done here. However, the wave concept cannot be avoided altogether; reference will be made to the propagation of voltage and current waves along the line, and the velocity of propagation will play an important part in the analysis. Eventually, in the discussion of waveguides as transmission lines, the electromagnetic-wave approach will necessarily be adopted.

2.1.1. Equivalent-Circuit Line Representation

A transmission line has inductance, capacitance, and resistance just as do "ordinary" four terminal networks. The essential difference is that these properties are distributed uniformly and continuously along the line, whereas in ordinary circuits they are "lumped." For purposes of analysis, however, the transmission line can be represented by an

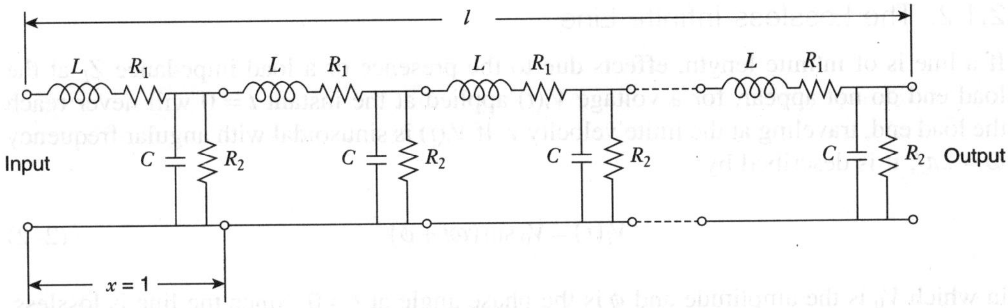

FIGURE 2–3.
Equivalent-circuit representation of a transmission line.

arrangement of many lumped-circuit elements (of short length) as shown in Fig. 2–3. In other words, small lumped circuit elements are used to connote the infinitesimally small amounts of inductance, capacitance and resistance that are distributed uniformly along a transmission line.

Each identical circuit section in this representation corresponds to a unit length of the line, that is, L is the inductance per unit length of the conductors, C is the capacitance between the conductors per unit length, R_1 is the series resistance of the conductors per unit length, and R_2 is the shunt or "leakage" resistance per unit length. For this representation of a line to be valid, it is necessary to assume that the "unit of length" is a very small fraction of the total line length, so that there will be very many of the identical lumped unit-length sections. More specifically, it is necessary that the unit of length be chosen small compared to a wavelength on the line, defined in the same way as for electromagnetic waves in space:

$$\lambda = \frac{v}{f} \text{ meters} \tag{2–1}$$

where v is the velocity of propagation of the voltage and current "waves" along the line, meters per second, and f is the frequency in Hertz of the applied voltage.

These assumptions are necessary to justify certain steps in the analysis; but after the analysis is made it is found that the results involve *ratios* of the unit-length circuit values. For this reason, in application of the results, L, C, R_1, and R_2 can be expressed as values for unit of length, for example, henrys per meter (H/m), farads per meter (F/m), ohms per meter (Ω/m).

To describe the behavior of a line in these terms, it is helpful to consider two special cases that are idealizations, that is, are never fully attainable in reality although they may be closely approximated. The first of these is the line of *infinite length* ($l \rightarrow \infty$ in Fig. 2–2) and is discussed in sec. 2.1.2. The second is the *lossless* line discussed in sec. 2.1.3, corresponding to $R_1 = 0$ and $R_2 \rightarrow \infty$ in Fig. 2–3.

2.1.2. The Lossless Infinite Line

If a line is of infinite length, effects due to the presence of a load impedance Z_L at the load end do not appear, for a voltage $V_i(t)$ applied at the instant $t = 0$ will never reach the load end, traveling at the finite velocity v. If $V_i(t)$ is sinusoidal with angular frequency $\omega = 2\pi f$, it is described by

$$V_i(t) = V_0 \sin(\omega t + \phi) \tag{2–2}$$

in which V_0 is the amplitude and ϕ is the phase angle at $t = 0$. Since the line is lossless, this voltage will travel down the line at velocity v with undiminished amplitude. If distance along the line is denoted by x, the voltage at the point x will be given by

$$V(x,t) = V_0 \sin(\omega t - \beta x + \phi) \tag{2–3}$$

provided that enough time has elapsed for the voltage wave to reach the point x, that is, at times t greater than $t = x/v$.

The quantity β, known as the *phase constant*, is defined as $2\pi/\lambda$. Equation (2–3) is identical to the equation of a plane electromagnetic wave of equation (1–2), ch. 1, with the substitution of a voltage V for the electric field intensity E.

The analysis of the transmission line of Fig. 2–3 leading to this result and to the further results that will be presented is made by writing and then solving second-order differential equations, based on the assumptions that the circuit sections of Fig. 2–3 represent infinitesimal lengths of the line. From the analysis, which will not be given here, it is also found that the velocity of the voltage waves is

$$v = \frac{1}{\sqrt{LC}} \tag{2–4}$$

for a lossless line, where L and C are the inductance and capacity per unit length of line. In this case if L and C are in henrys and farads per meter, v is obtained in meters per second.

Note the similarity of (2–4) to the equation for velocity of an electromagnetic wave in a lossless medium, equation (1–18), ch. 1. Moreover, it turns out that if the transmission line is primarily immersed in air or a vacuum (except perhaps for solid insulating supports of low loss at well-spaced intervals), the product of L and C will be a constant such that v is equal to 3×10^8 meters per second—exactly the velocity of an electromagnetic wave in space. Therefore the wavelength λ, as given by (2–1), will be the same on the line as for a wave in space.

These statements assume that the conductors are straight, smooth-surfaced, and are made of nonferrous metal having magnetic permeability of the same value as that of air or vacuum, that is, a relative permeability of unity. It may be noted in passing that copper-plated steel wire does not violate this assumption. This is because, at radio frequencies, the phenomenon called skin effect confines the current and fields to the surface of the wire and the external region of space; therefore the steel core does not affect the inductance.

But if a material having relative permittivity or relative permeability greater than one occupies the region between and surrounding the conductors, L and C will have a larger product. Then, v will be less than 3×10^8 meters per second, and is given by

$$v = \frac{c}{\sqrt{\mu_r \varepsilon_r}} \tag{2–5}$$

where $c = 3 \times 10^8$ meters per second, μ_r is the relative permeability, and ε_r is the relative permittivity. For most dielectric materials $\mu_r = 1$. A lossless line is being discussed here, where ε_r is a real number. For a lossy dielectric, ε_r is complex (see sec. 1.2.1), and then ε_r in (2–5) must be replaced by its real part (the dielectric constant).

When the voltage $V_i(t)$ is applied to the input terminals of the line, a current flows into the line. It is related to the input voltage by a quantity called the *characteristic impedance*, Z_0. That is,

$$I_i(t) = \frac{V_i(t)}{Z_0} \tag{2–6}$$

and Z_0 is found to be given by

$$Z_0 = \sqrt{\frac{L}{C}} \text{ ohms} \tag{2–7}$$

Equation 2–6 is of course Ohm's law, and (2–7) is analogous to the equation for the wave impedance of a propagation medium, equation (1–8), ch. 1. Therefore the current as a function of distance x along the line is given by

$$I(x,t) = \left(\frac{V_0}{Z_0}\right) \sin(\omega t - \beta x + \phi) \tag{2–8}$$

Or in other terms, as deduced from (2–2) and (2–6),

$$I_0 = \frac{V_0}{Z_0} \tag{2–9}$$

which is analogous to equation (1–10), ch. 1, for electromagnetic waves in space. Also, (2–8) is analogous to equation (1–3), ch. 1. In short, the voltage, current, and characteristic impedance of a lossless infinite transmission line correspond to the electric intensity, the magnetic intensity, and the impedance for a plane electromagnetic wave in free space.

2.1.3. Reflection and Standing Waves

When the line is of finite length l, as in Fig. 2–2, the voltage wave applied to the input terminals will reach the load end of the line in a time $t = l/v$, where the velocity v is given by (2–4). If it is assumed that the load impedance Z_L is at least partly resistive, the resulting current in Z_L will cause power to be delivered to the load. The power flowing down the line, since the voltage and current are in phase (as indicated by (2–3) and (2–8), is given by

$$P = V_{rms} I_{rms} \tag{2–10}$$

where the subscript *rms* stands for "root mean square" or effective value; it is related to the amplitudes by the well-known relations

$$V_{rms} = \frac{V_0}{\sqrt{2}} = 0.707 V_0 \tag{2–11}$$

and

$$I_{rms} = \frac{I_0}{\sqrt{2}} = 0.707 I_0 \tag{2–12}$$

From (2–9) through (2–12), it may be deduced that

$$P = \frac{V_{rms}^2}{Z_0} = I_{rms}^2 Z_0 \tag{2–13}$$

It is to be emphasized that this result applies to the power flow in terms of in-phase voltage and current in an infinite line, or in a finite line before the voltage wave reaches the load.

The load impedance Z_L may be purely resistive, purely reactive, or some combination of resistance and reactance. Suppose that it is purely resistive and of value R_L. Then the power delivered to the load will be

$$P_L = \frac{V_L^2}{R_L} = I_L^2 R_L \tag{2–14}$$

where V_L and I_L are the voltage and current at the load. Comparison of (2–13) and (2–14) shows that if $R_L = Z_0$, all the power flowing down the line will be delivered to the load. But if R_L does not have this value, the two powers cannot be equal if the voltage and current of (2–14) are assumed to be the same as the voltage and current of (2–13).

What actually happens is that some of the voltage and current are *reflected*. The reflected voltage and current then travel back toward the input end of the line, at the velocity v. Consequently, at every point x along the line, the voltage is that resulting from linear super-position of the original (incident) voltage wave, of amplitude $V_{0(i)}$, and a reflected wave, of amplitude $V_{0(r)}$. A similar statement applies to the current.

This situation is entirely analogous to the problem of interference between two electromagnetic waves at a point in space. The voltage and currents at various points on the line may either add or subtract from each other, depending on the difference in their phase angles, which in turn varies from point to point. The equation of the reflected voltage wave corresponding to (2–3) for the incident wave is obtained by substituting $V_{0(r)}$ in place of V_0, and $(2l - x)$ in place of x. The phase angle ϕ also will in general be changed in the process of reflection, depending on the phase angle of the impedance Z_L.

The result is that the voltage amplitude will vary along the line. There will be maxima at half-wavelength intervals, with minima at positions halfway between the maxima. The positions of these maxima and minima do not change with time, that is, they do not move along the line. The resulting pattern (actually, an interference pattern) is therefore a *standing wave*. A standing wave of current is also set up in the same way. The current maxima coincide with the voltage minima, and vice versa (see Fig. 2.5 of sec. 2.2.6).

The arrival of the reflected voltage and current waves at the line input terminals results in a changed voltage-current relationship at this point. Consequently, the effective input impedance of the line is no longer equal to the characteristic impedance Z_0, in general. It is by definition the resulting ratio of voltage to current.

Because the effective input impedance undergoes a sudden change when the reflected wave first reaches the input terminals, the applied voltage V_i may also undergo a change at that instant (since the output voltage of the usual source, or generator, will vary when the impedance presented to it varies). The voltage wave traveling down the line therefore takes on a new value at this instant, and so the reflected wave coming back $2l/v$ seconds later will also have a suddenly different value at that instant, resulting in a further readjustment of the input voltage, and still further adjustments at future intervals of $2l/v$ seconds. However, these readjustments become progressively smaller and gradually "die out." They are called *transients*. When they have died out, a *steady state* is said to exist. (Parenthetically, if the source impedance were Z_0, there would not be reflections at each end of the transmission line).

For some purposes it may be important to analyze the transient behavior of the line, but ordinarily only the steady-state behavior is important. This may be seen by considering a typical value of the time $2l/v$ required for a wave to travel down the line and be reflected back to the input. For a line 100 meters long (328 feet) this time is

$$t = \frac{2l}{v} = \frac{2\times100}{3\times10^8} = 6.7\times10^{-7} \text{ second}$$

or $\frac{2}{3}\mu$sec. The steady-state condition is practically achieved after a few of these reflection periods.

Nevertheless, in some very-short-pulse applications the transient effects would be important with this length of line, if an appreciable reflected wave occurred at the load end. Transient effects cannot be ignored if the time $2l/v$ is comparable to the reciprocal of the highest modulation frequency f_m of the rf applied voltage. For example, in television transmission the video modulation may contain frequencies up to several megahertz, so that $1/f_m$ may be less than a microsecond, and transient effects in a 100-meter line length would be of consequence. (The picture quality would be degraded. The remedy would be to eliminate the reflections at the load by methods that will be described in sec. 2–3.)

2.2. Transmission-Line Equations

2.2.1. Steady-State Lossless Line Equations

The equations of the steady-state case describe the standing waves of voltage and current along the line. The values of V and I in these equations may be interpreted as either the amplitudes or the *rms* values. Since the standing waves do not change with time, the time variable t does not appear in them; the radio frequency time variation $\sin(\omega t + \phi)$ has in effect been "factored out" of both sides of the equations. Moreover, the steady-state equations are customarily written in terms of *phasors*, as discussed in Appendix C.

The voltage equation is

$$V(x) = V_i \left[\frac{Z_L \cos\beta(l-x) + jZ_0 \sin\beta(l-x)}{Z_L \cos\beta l + jZ_0 \sin\beta l} \right] \tag{2–15}$$

and the current equation is

$$I(x) = \frac{V_i}{Z_0} \left[\frac{Z_0 \cos\beta(l-x) + jZ_L \sin\beta(l-x)}{Z_L \cos\beta l + jZ_0 \sin\beta l} \right] \tag{2–16}$$

The input impedance, Z_i, may be obtained dividing $V(0)$ by $I(0)$, as given by (2–15) and (2–16) for $x = 0$. The resulting equation is

$$Z_i = Z_0 \left[\frac{Z_L \cos\beta l + jZ_0 \sin\beta l}{Z_0 \cos\beta l + jZ_L \sin\beta l} \right] \tag{2–17}$$

This equation is often written in a modified form, obtained by dividing through both the numerator and denominator of (2–17) by $Z_0 \cos\beta l$, which gives

$$Z_i = Z_0 \left[\frac{(Z_L/Z_0) + j\tan\beta l}{1 + j(Z_L/Z_0)\tan\beta l} \right] \tag{2–18}$$

The definitions of the quantities in these equations are listed below for ready reference:

Z_i—impedance presented to a source (generator) at the transmission-line input terminals, ohms

Z_L—impedance connected at load end of line, ohms

Z_0—characteristic impedance of the (lossless) line, $= \sqrt{L/C}$ ohms (Eq. 2–7)

$V(x)$—voltage on line at distance x from the input terminals, volts

V_i—voltage applied to the input terminals, volts

$I(x)$—current in line at the point x, amperes

l—total length of line (Fig. 2–2)

β—$2\pi/\lambda$, where λ is the wavelength in the same units as l and x, e.g., meters

It is apparent that the quantities $V(x)$, $I(x)$, and Z_i are in general represented by *complex numbers*,* since the quantity $j = \sqrt{-1}$ appears in the equations. Even if j did not appear explicitly, it is implicit in the quantity Z_L, which is in general a complex impedance having a real (resistive) part R_L and an imaginary (reactive) part X_L.† That is,

$$Z_L = R_L + jX_L \tag{2–19}$$

2.2.2. Some Important Special Line Conditions

Lengths of transmission lines have certain properties that are of special interest for particular values of the length l or of the load impedance Z_L. As equation (2–18) indicates, a transmission line is in general an *impedance transformer*. That is, if an impedance Z_L is connected at the load end, a different impedance Z_i may be presented to a source at the input end. As will be shown, sections of transmission line may also exhibit the properties of *resonant circuits*. Therefore transmission-line sections are often used in lieu of more conventional circuits as transformers and as resonant circuits, especially at the higher frequencies where the equivalent coils and condensers become so small that their power-handling capabilities are limited, and losses may be high even at low powers. These properties of lines lead to results of special interest for particular cases.

(1) $Z_L = Z_0$. This condition, when applied to equation (2–18), gives

$$Z_i = Z_0\left[\frac{1 + j\tan\beta l}{1 + j\tan\beta l}\right] = Z_0 \tag{2–20}$$

That is, when the load impedance is equal to the characteristic impedance, the input impedance is also equal to this value. The line then acts as a one-to-one transformer. This equality of the load and characteristic impedances is called the *matched load* condition. The load impedance is said to be matched to the characteristic impedance of the line. The one-to-one transformation of impedance results regardless of the length of the line, l.

---

* The reader is assumed to have a basic familiarity with the concept of complex numbers and complex-number algebra. For reference and review, Appendix C covers the elements of this subject.

† The subscript L here stands for "load." The symbol X_L often stands for "inductive reactance," as opposed to capacitive reactance X_C. But here X_L denotes the *load* reactance, which may be either inductive or capacitive.

Moreover, if the condition $Z_L = Z_0$ is also substituted into (2–15) and (2–16), it is found that the amplitudes of $V(x)$ and $I(x)$ remain constant for all values of x, that is, everywhere on the line. Only the phases change, as would be expected from (2–3) and (2–8); in fact, these equations of the infinite line now apply to the finite line (if and only if $Z_L = Z_0$). This property is of great importance, for it provides a method of eliminating reflected waves and transient effects. Since there is no standing wave, with maxima and minima, such a line is called a *flat* line. It is important to note that since Z_0 for a lossless line is an entirely real (resistive) impedance, the matched-load condition requires that the load impedance be nonreactive (purely resistive) as well as have the magnitude of Z_0.

(2) $l = \lambda/2$. (Line length equal to one-half wavelength.) For this case, the angle βl that occurs in (2–18) becomes equal to π radians or 180 degrees. Since the tangent of this angle is zero, the equation becomes

$$Z_i = Z_0 \frac{Z_L}{Z_0} = Z_L \tag{2–21}$$

But there are two respects in which the half-wavelength one-to-one transformer is inferior to the matched line. First, there is a standing wave on the half-wavelength (or integral-half-wavelength) line, which means there are reflections and transient effects. Second, since the one-to-one transformation depends on the fact that l/λ has a particular value, the line will have this property only at one frequency and its integral multiples. If it is desired to operate over a wide range of frequency without readjustment of the line length, the matched-load line should be used. Nevertheless, the half-wavelength line is useful as a one-to-one impedance and voltage transformer when its limitations are not of concern.

(3) $l = \lambda/4$. (Line length equal to one-quarter wavelength.) In this case the angle βl in (2–17) becomes equal to $\pi/2$, or 90 degrees. Note that (2–17) rather than (2–18) is used because the tangent of 90 degrees is infinite, and consequently (2–18) leads to difficulties that require careful handling.) Since $\cos 90° = 0$ and $\sin 90° = 1$, (2–17) becomes

$$Z_i = Z_0\left(\frac{jZ_0}{jZ_L}\right) = \frac{Z_0^2}{Z_L} \tag{2–22}$$

The quarter-wavelength line transforms a load impedance Z_L that is smaller than Z_0 into a value Z_i that is larger than Z_0; and vice versa. It is sometimes called an impedance inverter for this reason. If Z_L is resistive, Z_i will also be resistive (real). Thus the quarter-wavelength transformer is useful when it is desired to transform a resistive impedance into a different resistive value, either larger or smaller. The desired transformation is accomplished by choosing the appropriate value of Z_0 in accordance with (2–22). The procedure for obtaining a desired value of Z_0 is described in sec. 2–4; it depends on the *ratio* of the spacing of the line conductors, s in Fig. 2–1, to their diameter d. Since these physical dimensions cannot practically have an infinite range of values, the transformation ratio of the quarter-wave transformer is subject to practical limitation. Nevertheless, it is a very useful device because of its simplicity and the ease with which its behavior is calculated. Lengths l equal to odd-number multiples of $\lambda/4$ will have the same transformation property, but as the length is made longer the sensitivity to a small change of frequency becomes greater.

The voltage transformation of the quarter-wave transformer is found from (2–15) by taking $x = l$, and as before $\beta l = 90°$. The result is

$$V_L = -jV_i \frac{Z_L}{Z_0} \tag{2–23}$$

which shows that when Z_L is real the amplitude is changed by the factor Z_L/Z_0 and the phase is changed by 90 degrees. (It should be noted here that (2–23) describes the transformation of input voltage to output voltage, whereas (2–22) describes the transformation of output impedance to input impedance, since these are the usual directions of interest.) A transformation of the current also takes place, but in the inverse ratio, so that the product of voltage and current is unchanged.

(4) *Open-circuited and short-circuited lines.* If a transmission line has no load connected at the load end (open-circuited), the load impedance Z_L is infinite (or nearly so). If Z_L in (2–17) becomes infinitely large, the terms $jZ_0 \sin\beta l$ in the numerator and $Z_0 \cos\beta l$ in the denominator are so much smaller that they can be ignored (considered equal to zero), and the equation becomes

$$Z_i = -jZ_0 \cot\beta l \quad (\text{for } Z_L \to \infty) \tag{2–24}$$

Similarly if the load end of the line is short-circuited, the result is

$$Z_i = jZ_0 \tan\beta l \quad (\text{for } Z_L = 0) \tag{2–25}$$

In both cases the input impedance Z_i is purely reactive (imaginary). This means that the input terminals of such lines "look like" the terminals of either an inductance or a capacitance, depending on the length of the line. If the length is between zero and a quarter wavelength, so that βl is an angle between zero and 90 degrees, the open-circuited line will be capacitive, a negative reactance in accordance with (2–24). In contrast, the short-circuited line of the same length will be inductive, following (2–25). For lengths between a quarter and a half wavelength, βl lies between 90 and 180 degrees, and both the tangent and cotangent are negative; therefore the open-circuited line becomes inductive, and the shorted line becomes capacitive. For each successive quarter wave increase of length, their behaviors interchange in this way. Such line sections may therefore be utilized as elements of inductance-capacitance circuits; and they are so used, especially at the higher frequencies (shorter wavelengths) where the required line lengths are not great.

Open-circuited and short-circuited lines can also behave like *resonant* circuits. This behavior occurs when the length of the line is an integral multiple of a quarter wavelength; then $\tan\beta l \to \infty$, and $\cot\beta l = 0$. The quarter-wave short-circuited line presents an infinite impedance at its input terminals, like a parallel-resonant LC circuit; and the quarter-wave open-end line presents a zero impedance at its input terminals, like a series-resonant LC circuit. These behaviors are interchanged for each successive quarter-wave increase of the line lengths. Transmission-line resonant circuits have many applications in high-frequency radio circuitry and in antenna design.

2.2.3. Impedance-Admittance Relationships

It is often convenient, in transmission-line calculations, to work with admittance (Y), conductance (G), and susceptance (B), which are respectively the reciprocals, in a somewhat restricted sense, of impedance (Z), resistance (R), and reactance (X). The restriction applies only to the conductance-resistance and susceptance-reactance relationships. The relationship of impedance and admittance is, without any restriction, given by

$$Z = \frac{1}{Y} \tag{2–26}$$

That is, they are reciprocals of each other. This equation holds when both Z and Y are complex, as well as for purely resistive or reactive cases. That is, in general,

$$Z = R + jX \tag{2–27}$$

and

$$Y = G + jB \tag{2–28}$$

with the understanding that R and X refer to resistance and reactance *in series*, and G and B refer to conductance and susceptance *in parallel*.

The restricted nature of the reciprocity between conductance and resistance, and between susceptance and reactance, may be understood in terms of the diagrams of Fig. 2–4. In Fig. 2–4a, it is evident that $Z = R + j0$. Substituting this value for Z in (2–26), and also applying (2–28), immediately gives $Y = 1/R = G + j0$. Thus in this simple case, $G = 1/R$. In other words, the reciprocal relationship between G and R holds for a purely resistive (conductive) circuit or branch of a circuit.

In Fig. 2–4b, the impedance is $Z = jX$ (purely reactive). (The reactance in this diagram is shown as a box, since for the purposes of this discussion it may be either an inductance or a capacitance, or any combination of the two.) If this value of Z is substituted in (2–26), the result is $Y = 1/jX = -j(1/X)$. If this result is compared with (2–28), it is evident that $B = -1/X$. Thus for a purely reactive circuit, or branch of a circuit, the susceptance is the *negative* reciprocal of the reactance.

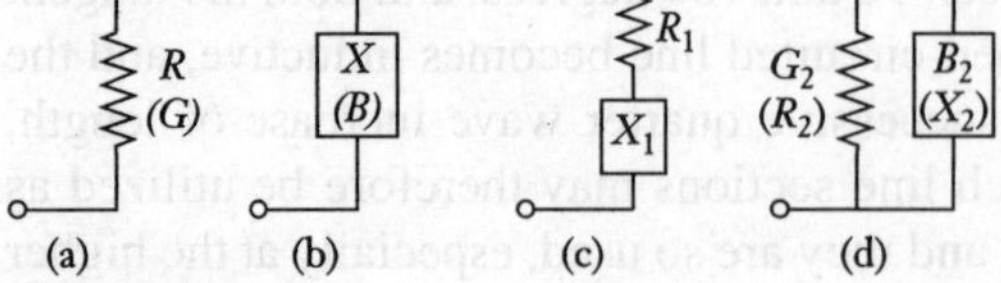

FIGURE 2–4.
Various two-terminal arrangements of resistance, reactance, conductance, and susceptance.

The restricted nature of the reciprocity relationships becomes evident when Fig. 2–4c is considered. The impedance Z_1 is of course simply $R_1 + jX_1$. Therefore the admittance is

$$Y_1 = \frac{1}{Z_1} = \frac{1}{R_1 + jX_1} = \frac{1}{R_1 + jX_1}\left(\frac{R_1 - jX_1}{R_1 - jX_1}\right) = \left(\frac{R_1}{R_1^2 + X_1^2}\right) - j\left(\frac{X_1}{R_1^2 + X_1^2}\right) \qquad (2\text{–}29)$$

Again comparison with (2–28) makes it evident that *for this circuit*:

$$G_1 = \frac{R_1}{R_1^2 + X_1^2} \qquad (2\text{–}30)$$

and

$$B_1 = \frac{-X_1}{R_1^2 + X_1^2} \qquad (2\text{–}31)$$

On the other hand, for the parallel circuit of Fig. 2–4d, the corresponding relations are simply $G_2 = 1/R_2$ and $B_2 = -1/X_2$. It is therefore apparent that the circuits of Fig. 2–4c and 2–4d are *equivalent* if

$$R_2 = \frac{R_1^2 + X_1^2}{R_1} = \frac{1}{G_2} \qquad (2\text{–}32)$$

and

$$X_2 = \frac{R_1^2 + X_1^2}{X_1} = \frac{1}{B_2} \qquad (2\text{–}33)$$

"Equivalent" means that if the same voltage is applied to the terminals of either circuit, the current that flows *at the terminals* will be exactly the same for both circuits. (Of course, this will in general hold—for fixed values of inductance and capacitance—at only one frequency.) This equivalence is of great importance and utility in impedance-matching calculations. It means that the impedance at the input terminals of a transmission line, for example, can be regarded as *either* a series combination *or* a parallel combination of resistance and reactance, whichever happens to be most convenient.

Equation (2–18) for the input impedance of a line can be converted, by applying (2–26) to it, into an equation for the input admittance, Y_i, of the line, where $Y_i = 1/Z_i$. The equation is

$$Y_i = Y_0\left[\frac{1 + j(Y_0/Y_L)\tan\beta l}{(Y_0/Y_L) + j\tan\beta l}\right] \qquad (2\text{–}34)$$

The symbol Y_0 denotes the *characteristic admittance* of the line, which is simply the reciprocal of the characteristic impedance; that is, $Y_0 = 1/Z_0$. The symbol Y_L denotes the load admittance, which is equal to $1/Z_L$.

The equations for open-circuited and short-circuited lines, (2–24) and (2–25), can also be expressed in terms of the input susceptances. For the open-circuit termination, the equation corresponding to (2–24) is

$$B_i = Y_0 \tan \beta l \tag{2–35}$$

and for the short-circuit termination, the equation corresponding to (2–25) is

$$B_i = -Y_0 \cot \beta l \tag{2–36}$$

Equations (2–35) and (2–36) can be obtained either by making the substitution $X_i = -1/B_i$ in (2–24) and (2–25), or by letting Y_L be zero for the open-circuit case and infinite for the short-circuit case in (2–34.)

2.2.4. Reflection Coefficient and *VSWR*

Just as in reflection of electromagnetic waves from a surface (sec. 1–2), the fraction of the incident wave voltage (or current) reflected from the load end of a line and the phase change that occurs in the reflection are described by a reflection coefficient, *r*. It is a complex number (see Appendix C), since it describes both a magnitude and a phase angle, and can therefore be expressed in the form

$$r = |r|e^{j\phi} = |r|\{\cos\phi + j\sin\phi\} \tag{2–37}$$

where $|r|$ is the magnitude (modulus) of the complex quantity and ϕ is the phase angle. The magnitude of the reflection coefficient is the ratio of the amplitudes (or *rms* values) of the reflected and incident voltage (or current):

$$|r| = \frac{V_{0(r)}}{V_{0(i)}} \tag{2–38}$$

The phase angle is the phase difference between the phases of the incident and reflected waves relative to an arbitrary reference phase:

$$\phi = \phi_i - \phi_r \tag{2–39}$$

(Since the phase of the incident wave is the usual reference, ordinarily $\phi_i = 0$, and $\phi = -\phi_r$.)

The reflection coefficient is determined entirely by the relationship of the load impedance, Z_L, to the characteristic impedance of the line, Z_0. Analysis shows that the relationship is

$$r = \frac{Z_L - Z_0}{Z_L + Z_0} = \frac{(Z_L/Z_0) - 1}{(Z_L/Z_0) + 1} \tag{2–40}$$

This is a complex-variable equation, in general, since Z_L may be complex, or reactive. If Z_L is real (resistive) and equal to or larger than Z_0 (assumed also to be real, as it will be for a lossless line), then r will be real and positive, which means that $r = |r|$, and $\phi = 0$. If Z_L is real and smaller than Z_0, r will of course again be real, but negative. It can be deduced from (2–37) that this means that ϕ is 180° (since $\cos 180° = -1$ and $\sin 180° = 0$). That is, in this case $r = -|r|$. But when Z_L is reactive, or complex, ϕ has values other than 0 or 180°, and r is complex.

The phase relations referred to in the foregoing discussion are those of the incident and reflected voltages *at the load* (i.e., immediately before and immediately after reflection). The phases of both of these voltages at other points along the line will have other values, since the phase of a wave (either in space or on a line or in a wave guide) changes with distance from a reference point in accordance with (2–2) and (2–3). In (2–3), the phase angle at an instant of time t_1 at a distance x from the reference point is $\omega t_1 - \beta x + \phi_1$ (where ϕ_1 is the phase angle when $t = 0$ and $x = 0$). (As previously given, $\omega = 2\pi f$, where f is the frequency, and $\beta = 2\pi/\lambda$, where λ is the wavelength.)

In computing the phase angle the distance x is always measured in the direction of travel of the wave, so that x increases in one direction for the incident wave and in the other direction for the reflected wave. The two phase angles therefore do not have a constant difference along the line (as they would if the two phases progressed in the same direction along the line). The result is that at some points on the line the incident and reflected voltages will be in phase and will add, resulting in a *voltage maximum* V_{max} given by

$$V_{max} = V_{0(i)} + V_{0(r)} \tag{2–41}$$

At other points the two voltage waves will be exactly out of phase and will therefore subtract, resulting in a voltage minimum V_{min} given by

$$V_{min} = V_{0(i)} - V_{0(r)} \tag{2–42}$$

the ratio of the maximum to the minimum voltage is called the *voltage standing wave ratio*, *VSWR*, that is

$$VSWR = \frac{V_{max}}{V_{min}} = \frac{V_{0(i)} + V_{0(r)}}{V_{0(i)} - V_{0(r)}} \tag{2–43}$$

Obviously the *VSWR* is a number equal to or greater than one. (It is equal to one when there is no reflected wave, or $V_{0(r)} = 0$. From (2–38) and (2–40) it is apparent that $VSWR = 1$ when $|r| = 0$ and therefore when $Z_L = Z_0$.)

2.2.5. Standing-Wave Patterns

The nature of the standing-wave voltage pattern may be found by plotting $V(x)$ as given by equation (2–15), for given values of Z_L and Z_0. However, for this purpose it is more convenient to obtain an equation for the voltage V relative to the voltage V_L existing at the load terminals, in terms of distance d measured back along the line from these terminals. In manipulating (2–15) to obtain such an expression in turns out that both V_i and l drop out, and a relatively simple formula is obtained:

$$V(d) = V_L\left(\cos\beta d + j\frac{Z_0}{Z_L}\sin\beta d\right) \tag{2–44}$$

The magnitude (modulus) of $V(d)$, in terms of $Z_L/Z_0 = R_L/Z_0 + jX_L/Z_0$, with R_L/Z_0 abbreviated to R and X_L/Z_0 abbreviated to X, is

$$|V(d)| = \left|V_L\sqrt{\left[\cos\beta d + \left(\frac{X}{R^2+X^2}\right)\sin\beta d\right]^2 + \left[\left(\frac{R}{R^2+X^2}\right)\sin\beta d\right]^2}\right| \tag{2–45}$$

Typical plots of $|V(d)|$ are shown in Fig. 2–5 for a number of values of R_L/Z_0 and X_L/Z_0.

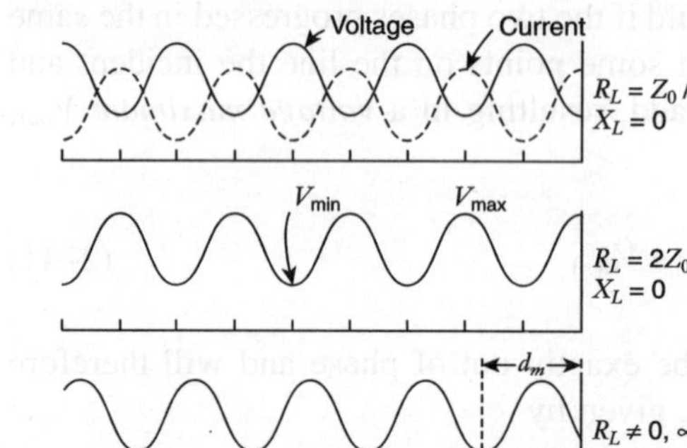

FIGURE 2–5.

Standing-wave voltage patterns for several Z_L/Z_0 conditions.

Noteworthy features of these plots are the following. (1) The maxima are separated by $\lambda/2$ and the minima are separated by $\lambda/2$; the distance from a minimum to a maximum is $\lambda/4$. (2) The minima are more sharply defined than the maxima; consequently, in making standing wave position measurements it is better to measure the position of a minimum than the position of a maximum (greater accuracy is possible). (3) When a resistive (nonreactive) load has a value less than Z_0, a voltage minimum is located at the load terminals. (4) When a purely resistive load has a value greater than Z_0, a voltage maximum is located at the load terminals. (5) When the load is complex (partially or wholly reactive), the voltage at the load is neither a minimum nor a maximum. (6) When the load is either zero or infinite, the standing-wave ratio is infinite (since $V_{min} = 0$) and the minima have the form of cusps.

2.2.6. Determination of Load Impedance by Standing-Wave Measurement

Equation 2–40 indicates that if the reflection coefficient is known, the load impedance Z_L can be determined. This is shown more explicitly by rearranging the equation as follows:

$$Z_L = Z_0\left(\frac{1+r}{1-r}\right) \tag{2–46}$$

The relationship of the *magnitude* of the reflection coefficient, $|r|$, to the standing-wave ratio *VSWR* has been shown indirectly through (2–38) and (2–43). From these equations it may be deduced that

$$|r| = \frac{VSWR-1}{VSWR+1} \tag{2–47}$$

Thus a *measurement* of the *VSWR* provides one ingredient necessary for determination of Z_L, in accordance with (2–46). The additional ingredient required is of course the phase angle ϕ of (2–37).

It can be shown that ϕ is related to the distance d_m, which as shown in Fig. 2–5 is *the distance from the load terminals to the first voltage minimum*. The relation is

$$\begin{aligned}\phi &= \pi - 2\beta d_m = \pi\left(1-\frac{4d_m}{\lambda}\right)\ \text{radians}\\ &= 180\left(1-\frac{4d_m}{\lambda}\right)\ \text{degrees}\end{aligned} \tag{2–48}$$

Therefore, if the two quantities *VSWR* and d_m are measured, Z_L can be calculated, through (2–46), (2–37), (2–47), and (2–48). Moreover, Z_i can also be calculated through (2–18), either by first calculating Z_L or directly by substituting (2–46) into (2–18), which gives

$$Z_i = Z_0\left[\frac{\left(\frac{1+r}{1-r}\right)+j\tan\beta l}{1+j\left(\frac{1+r}{1-r}\right)\tan\beta l}\right] \tag{2–49}$$

In practical work (2–46) and (2–49) are solved, including the intermediate steps of (2–47) and (2–48), by using a Smith Chart, as described in sec. 9.12.

2.2.7. Attenuation

The results presented thus far have all been based on the assumption that the line is lossless, which means that R_1 in Fig. 2–3 is zero and R_2 is infinite. In real transmission lines these assumptions are of course not perfectly justified; there are some losses. When the loss of a line is considerable, even the basic form of the transmission line equations is considerably modified. However, when the losses are fairly small, as is usually the case, the equations that have been given can be used for all purposes except computing the power ultimately delivered to the load. This power will be slightly less than the power delivered to the line at its input terminals. The power loss in decibels is given by multiplying the length of the line by a decibel attenuation constant. For most manufactured lines, the value of this constant is published in the manufacturer's sales literature. Additionally, a useful collection of data on transmission lines and waveguides is contained in Lowman and Simons (2007).

The attenuation constant (sec. 1.1.9) can also be expressed in terms of the conductor resistance R per unit length and the leakage conductance G per unit length. Ordinarily, transmission lines used with antennas are of the low-loss type. For these lines, the attenuation constant, when expressed in terms of decibels per meter (dB/m), is

$$\alpha_{dB} = 8.686\left(\frac{R}{2Z_0} + \frac{G}{2Y_0}\right) \text{dB/m} \tag{2–50}$$

Here Z_0 is, as usual, the characteristic impedance of the line and Y_0 is the characteristic admittance ($= 1/Z_0$). In terms of Fig. 2–3, $R = R_1$ and $G = 1/R_2$. When the line attenuation is appreciable, a more complicated formula must be used. "Appreciable attenuation," for practical purposes, may be taken to mean more than about one decibel per wavelength of the line, insofar as the validity of (2–50) is concerned.

The equations for transmission-line input impedance, voltage, and current, (2–15) through (2–18), and subsequent equations derived from them, are accurate for most antenna applications. However, this is not so if the total attenuation* of the line (α_{dBl}) is greater than about a decibel. Attenuation reduces the amplitude of the reflected wave as it travels back toward the line input, and the standing-wave ratio consequently diminishes toward the input. Thus, with large attenuation, the standing-wave ratio as calculated from equation 2–47 is valid only in the vicinity of the load end of the line. Additionally, if the attenuation is great enough the input impedance of the line will be essentially equal to the characteristic impedance regardless of the reflection coefficient of the load. More detailed treatments of transmission lines give equations for high attenuation, analogous to (2–15) through (2–18) (see, e.g., Lowman and Simons 2007, p. 51–5).

* Total attenuation from ohmic loss is α_{dBl} without a standing wave. However, e.g., with $VSWR = 2$, the attenuation is 1.25 times α_{dBl}, because of increased mean-squared voltage across the line (Ragan 1948, pp. 30–31).

2.3. Impedance Matching and Power Division

In their role as the connecting link between a transmitter and an antenna, or between an antenna and a receiver, transmission lines affect the efficiency of power transfer. In some cases they may be arranged to apportion a total amount of power among a number of loads. Methods of adjusting the line impedance relations to achieve optimum results in these functions will now be discussed.

2.3.1. The Matching Principle

A radio transmitter is in effect a generator possessing an internal electromotive force (emf) and an internal impedance, which may be complex, that is, $Z_g = R_g + jX_g$. A well-known theorem of a-c circuit theory states that such a generator will deliver the maximum possible power to a load whose impedance is the complex conjugate of Z_g, that is, equal to $R_g - jX_g$.

The ultimate load for the transmitter is the antenna, but the immediate load may be the input impedance of the transmission line, $Z_i = R_i + jX_i$. Consequently, in order for the transmitter to deliver its maximum power output it would seem necessary that $R_i = R_g$ and $X_i = -X_g$.

The value of Z_i, as shown by (2–18), depends on the values of Z_L, Z_0, and l. It would therefore seem possible to choose or adjust the values of these quantities to achieve the desired value of Z_i. But in practice the desired result is not usually accomplished in this way. The quantity l, for example, may be determined primarily by the necessary separation of the transmitter and antenna and will not be independently adjustable. The possible range of values of Z_0 is practically somewhat limited. Moreover, it is usually desired to eliminate or minimize standing waves on the line, and this means that Z_L must be at least approximately equal to Z_0.

Therefore the impedance usually presented at the input terminals of the line will be $Z_i = Z_0$. An impedance transformer is then inserted between the line input and the transmitter output to transform the impedance Z_0 into the value required for maximum transmitter power output, or optimum performance where best operation from some standpoint other than maximum power is required. The actual load impedance presented by the antenna to the transmission line output terminals may not be equal to the desired value, Z_0. Another impedance transformer may be required between the load end of the line and the antenna terminals, and this one must transform the antenna impedance, Z_a, into the value Z_0.

Sometimes these transformers may consist of coupled coils of wire or of coil-and-condenser circuits, especially likely at low frequencies. At frequencies in the multi-megaHertz region, however, these transformers often consist of sections of transmission lines in various arrangements. Some of the possible arrangements and their principles of operation will be described.

The quarter-wave impedance-inverting transformer has been described in sec. 2.2.2. Its principle of operation is given by (2–22). It is most useful when the desired transformation ratio is not great and can be predicted or determined to be stable, since this type of transformer is not easily adjustable.

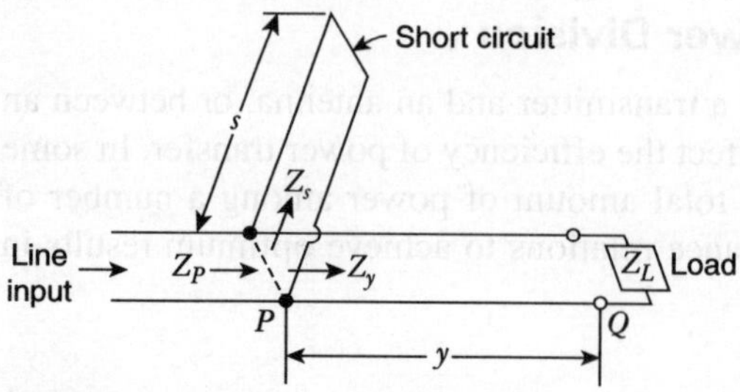

FIGURE 2–6.

Single-stub impedance transformer.

2.3.2. Stub Transformers

A type of transmission-line transformer frequently employed is diagrammed in Fig. 2–6. The principal element of this transformer is a short-circuited section of line whose open end is connected across the main line at a certain distance, y, from the load. This short-circuited branching section is called a *stub*, or sometimes a *tuning stub*. At its point of connection to the main line, P, it is equivalent to a pure reactance, in accordance with (2–25).

The operation of this transformer is analyzed by dissecting the line at the point P (figuratively speaking) and considering separately the dissected elements, then considering the result of putting them back together. As viewed from the point P, the section of the main line to the right (toward the load) will present an impedance given by (2–18) with l equal to y. The stub, as viewed from the point P, presents a reactance given by (2–25) with l equal to the stub length s. For simplicity it will be assumed that the characteristic impedances Z_0 are the same for all the line sections.

When these dissected elements are reconnected, they are in parallel, and they represent, in their combined effect, the load impedance Z_p of the main line *at the point P*. But because they are in parallel, it is advantageous to calculate their admittances. The sum of these admittances will then constitute a load admittance Y_p for the main line at point P, which can be inserted as Y_L into (2–34). If the objective is to present a matched load to the main line at point P, however, the requirement is simply to make the combined admittances of the stub and the load section PQ equal to $Y_0 = 1/Z_0$.

It can be shown that for some length y the admittance of the line section PQ will consist of a conductance G_y and a susceptance B_y such that $G_y = Y_0$. The necessary length to achieve this result may be calculated from (2–34), or it may be determined more speedily using a Smith Chart (sec. 9.12). The problem then is simply to eliminate the susceptance B_y without changing the conductance $G_y = Y_0$.

If the susceptance of the stub is B_s, the total admittance of the parallel combination at P is

$$Y_p = G_y + jB_y + jB_s \tag{2–51}$$

If now it can be arranged that $B_s = -B_y$, these two susceptances in (2–51) will cancel each other, leaving

$$Y_p = G_y = Y_0 \tag{2–52}$$

This admittance presents a matched load to the main line at point P, and so there will be no standing wave to the left of this point, that is, between point P and the line input. This is the desired result.

The susceptance of the stub, B_s, is computed from (2–36). By making s a suitable length, it is demonstrable that any needed value of B_s can be achieved. Therefore, if the two lengths y and s can be varied at will, the desired transformation of impedance can be achieved. In practice the position and length of the stub are roughly determined by Smith Chart calculations based on standing-wave measurements. Then the lengths are experimentally adjusted to minimize the standing wave ratio (*VSWR*) on the main line.

When it is not practical or advisable to provide a movable stub (one for which the distance y can be varied), the same result can be accomplished by means of two fixed-position stubs separated a suitable distance, usually between one-fourth and three-eighths of a wavelength. The analysis of the impedance transformation proceeds on the same principles, though it is of course somewhat more involved.

2.3.3. Power Dividers

For many purposes, particularly in array antennas, it is necessary to divide the power from a single transmitter among two or more loads. The simplest case of two loads will be considered first.

If the total transmitter power is first fed into a single transmission line, this line may then be "branched" into two lines, as shown in Fig. 2–7. Again, since the branches are in parallel, it is advantageous to work with the admittances. The net load admittance presented to the main line at the branch point will be the sum of the two branch-line admittances, Y_A and Y_B. It will usually be desired to make this sum equal to the characteristic admittance $Y_{0(M)}$ of the main line. The requirement is simply

$$Y_{0(M)} = Y_A + Y_B \tag{2–53}$$

If each branch line is terminated in its own characteristic admittance, $Y_{0(A)}$ and $Y_{0(B)}$, as will usually be true, then of course Y_A and Y_B will be equal to the characteristic values.

Since the branch lines are in parallel, the voltage applied to each of them at the junction point is the same and is equal to the voltage output of the main line, V_M. Therefore, the power delivered to each branch is

$$P_A = V_M^2 G_A \tag{2–54}$$

$$P_B = V_M^2 G_B \tag{2–55}$$

and the total power is

$$P_{total} = P_A + P_B = V_M^2 (G_A + G_B) \tag{2–56}$$

and G_A and G_B are the conductance components of the admittances Y_A and Y_B. These equations establish the power-

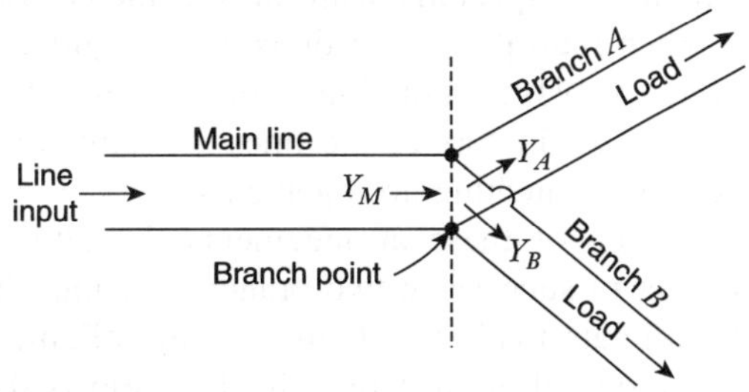

FIGURE 2–7.
Parallel branching transmission lines.

division property of the junction. That is, the fraction of the total power delivered to each branch will be

$$F_A = \frac{P_A}{P_{total}} = \frac{G_A}{G_A + G_B} \tag{2–57}$$

$$F_B = \frac{P_B}{P_{total}} = \frac{G_B}{G_A + G_B} \tag{2–58}$$

If each branch line is assumed to be terminated in its characteristic admittance, since these admittances are real for lossless lines, the conductances G_A and G_B will simply be equal to $Y_{0(A)}$ and $Y_{0(B)}$ respectively. If, in addition, it is desired that the main line be terminated in its characteristic admittance at the junction, the requirement is

$$Y_{0(M)} = Y_{0(A)} + Y_{0(B)} = G_A + G_B \tag{2–59}$$

For this case (2–57) and (2–58) become

$$F_A = \frac{Y_{0(A)}}{Y_{0(M)}} \tag{2–60}$$

$$F_B = \frac{Y_{0(B)}}{Y_{0(M)}} \tag{2–61}$$

It would be possible to divide the power at a junction among more than two branching lines. The analysis of the power division would be a simple extension of the foregoing analysis; the fraction of power delivered to each branch would be equal to the conductance component of the input admittance of that branch, divided by the sum of the conductances of all the branches. The conductances in the usual cases would be equal to the characteristic admittances of the branches. It is not customary to divide power in this way, however, partly because the required characteristic impedances of the branch lines become impractically large and partly because there are mechanical construction difficulties, especially with lines of the coaxial type.

When multiple power division is required, it is more common to employ one of the successively branching line structures shown schematically in Fig. 2–8. In these diagrams the two conductors of the lines are shown as single lines, for the purpose is solely to show the branching arrangements.

In each of these arrangements the ultimate power division is accomplished by a number of successive two-branch divisions. The required division of the total power to the ultimate loads results in a system of simple simultaneous equations for the division ratio required at each branch; this ratio is then achieved by the method that has been described. Although eight loads are shown in Fig. 2–8, the methods are not restricted to this number.

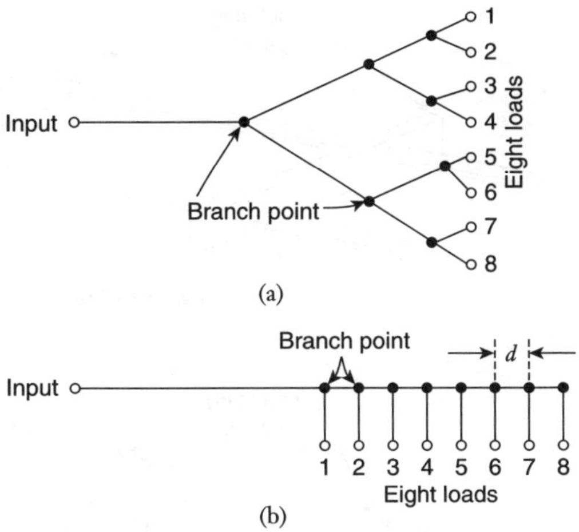

FIGURE 2–8.

Alternative arrangements for division of power among multiple loads.

In addition to the power-division requirement, it may also be required that the voltages and currents have the same phase at each load. This is readily achieved in the arrangement of Fig. 2–8a, by keeping the lengths of the parallel branches equal. In Fig. 2–8b it would be necessary to make the lengths denoted by *d* equal to a wavelength or an integral number of wavelengths; or *d* may be a half wavelength if the line is of the two-wire balanced type and if the line is "turned over" in each half-wavelength interval to reverse the polarity of the voltage. (This cannot be done, of course, with a coaxial or other unbalanced line type).

It may also be necessary to have stepdown impedance transformers in the branch lines to keep the characteristic impedances required in the successive branches from building up to too high a value; in short, there are numerous practical problems. Here the purpose has been primarily to present basic principles.

It is possible also to have two lines branching with a series connection instead of parallel, although such an arrangement is less common. The analysis would be made in a similar way, except that it would be more convenient to work with the impedances than with the admittances.

2.4. Forms of Transmission Lines

Two-conductor transmission lines of the type thus far discussed may take a number of physical forms. The principal forms are: (1) two-wire balanced lines; (2) coaxial (unbalanced) lines; (3) parallel-plate or "strip" lines (balanced or unbalanced). Examples of these forms are shown in Fig. 2–9.

Each of these forms has its advantages and disadvantages. The two-wire line, which is usually cheaper, may be fabricated from readily available components (e.g., ordinary wire). Also it is balanced with respect to the ground and may therefore be used to connect directly to balanced antennas. A disadvantage is that some radiation may occur, in the manner discussed in chapter 1 in connection with Fig. 1–11. As long as the spacing of the wires, *s*, is small compared to a wavelength, the radiation will be negligible; but at extremely high frequencies (short wavelengths) this condition may not be fulfilled, and appreciable radiation may result. This is of course undesirable, as radiation from the transmission line does not usually have the desired directional and polarization characteristics. It represents wasted power, at best, and at worst it may do harm by its presence in undesired locations.

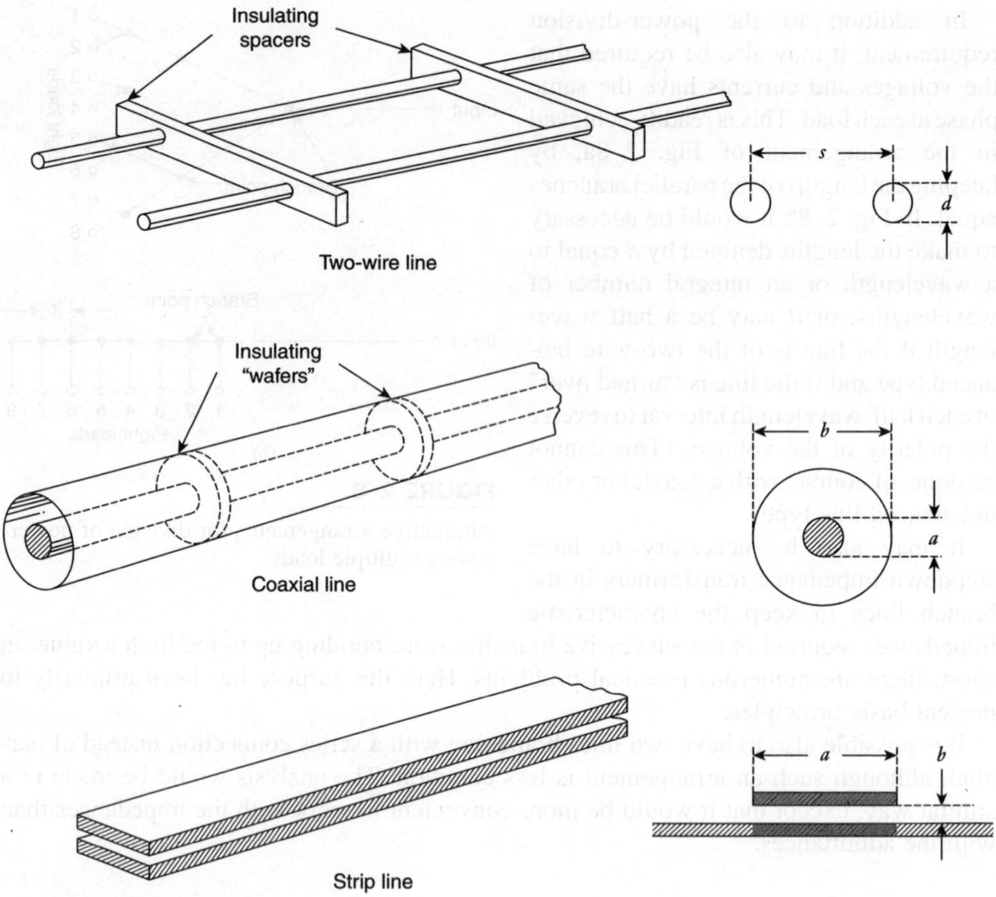

FIGURE 2–9.

Perspective sketches and transverse sections of two-wire, coaxial, and strip transmission lines.

Coaxial lines confine the fields entirely to the space between the inner and outer concentric conductors; therefore there is no radiation problem. Being unbalanced, these lines require special balanced-to-unbalanced transformers (called "baluns") to connect them to any balanced source or load. However, sources and loads are in some cases unbalanced, so that the unbalanced character of the line is as often an advantage as a disadvantage. Coaxial lines have the advantage of permitting the interior to be completely sealed against weather and contamination. The internal space may be pressurized to increase voltage breakdown and to resist intrusion of moisture. Some coaxial lines are made with a flexible braid outer conductor and flexible solid-dielectric material between the conductors. Such lines are flexible and compact and find many uses at low and intermediate power levels. For very high-power transmitting applications, coaxial lines employ solid copper pipe, with outer-conductor diameters up to 9 or more inches.

The strip line is a modification of the two-wire line in which the flat faces of the adjacent conductor surfaces are wider than the spacing between the conductors. Accordingly the field is virtually confined to the space between the conductors, and there is very little radiation. The two strips may be alike (balanced), or one of them may be a large flat (grounded) plate. Often a solid dielectric material is used as a spacing material. It is especially convenient for some purposes, usually at low power levels.

2.4.1. Characteristic Impedances

The characteristic impedances of these line types may be calculated from the transverse-section geometry. For the two-wire line the formula is

$$Z_0 = \frac{276}{\sqrt{\varepsilon_r}} \log\left(\frac{2s}{d}\right) \text{ ohms} \tag{2–62}$$

where s and d are the center-to-center conductor spacing and the conductor diameter respectively, as shown in Fig. 2–9. The relative permittivity ε_r is of the medium between and around the conductors ($\varepsilon_r = 1$ for air or vacuum). Typical values of Z_0 for two-wire lines range from about 200 to 800 ohms.

For a coaxial line the characteristic impedance is given by

$$Z_0 = \frac{138}{\sqrt{\varepsilon_r}} \log\left(\frac{b}{a}\right) \text{ ohms} \tag{2–63}$$

with b the inner diameter of the outer conductor and a the outer diameter of the inner conductor. The relative permittivity ε_r is for the material between the conductors. Typical values of Z_0 range from about 20 to 100 ohms.

For the strip line the following formula is good as long as the dimension b (Fig. 2–9) is much smaller than the dimension a:

$$Z_0 = \frac{377}{\sqrt{\varepsilon_r}} \left(\frac{b}{a}\right) \text{ ohms} \tag{2–64}$$

The typical range of characteristic impedances is about the same as for coaxial lines.

Numerous variations of these basic forms are sometimes used; however, there is a practical upper-frequency limit for any given type of line. Usually the limit is set either by the losses in dielectric material or by the spacing of the conductors in relation to the wavelength. When this spacing is an appreciable fraction of a wavelength, the open-wire lines will radiate excessively. Coaxial and strip lines will act like waveguides, as will be discussed in sec. 2–5, if the conductor spacing becomes comparable to or greater than a half wavelength.

A basic property assumed for all the lines discussed is uniformity, that is, constant spacings and conductor diameters. At joints, elbow turns, couplings, and so forth, there may be discontinuities that cause reflections that can be troublesome if care is not taken to minimize them. For broad-band impedance-transforming applications deliberately nonuniform tapered lines are used. These lines have a characteristic impedance that changes as the conductor diameters and spacings change, so that a gradual impedance transformation takes place.

2.5. Waveguides

At frequencies too high for successful operation of conventional transmission lines, rf power may be transmitted by means of waveguides. A waveguide in its commonest form is a hollow pipe, sometimes circular but more often rectangular in cross section, and occasionally of some other form. The dimensions of the cross section are such that an electromagnetic wave can propagate in the interior of the guide. Being confined by the walls of the guide, the field does not spread spherically as it would in free space, so there is no inverse-square-law decrease of the power density. There is some attenuation due to currents in the walls, but generally this loss is less than in a coaxial line of comparable size. Moreover, since no insulating supports are required, there is virtually no "leakage" loss and less tendency to flashover at high voltages.

Obviously the analysis of waveguide behavior must be made in terms of electromagnetic field concepts rather than in terms of an equivalent-circuit representation. The starting point is Maxwell's equations, and their solution requires advanced mathematical methods. Yet the results are that waveguides behave essentially like the conventional transmission lines that have been described, although there are some important differences.

2.5.1. Phase and Group Velocities

In transmission lines the wave velocity is independent of the frequency, and for air or vacuum dielectrics the velocity is equal to the velocity of free-space waves, 3×10^8 meters per second. But in wave guides the velocity varies with the frequency. Moreover, it is necessary to distinguish between two concepts of wave velocity, the *phase velocity* and the *group velocity*.

The phase velocity is the apparent velocity of a particular phase of the wave, for example, a crest, or electric-intensity maximum or minimum. The basic method of determining this velocity is to make a measurement of the wavelength, λ. This may be done, for example, by setting up a standing wave and measuring the separation of two minima (see Fig. 2–5). The frequency f being known, the phase velocity may then be calculated by an inversion of (2–1).

$$v_{ph} = f\lambda \tag{2–65}$$

The other concept of velocity may be understood by considering a pulse of radio waves, of the type used in radar. If such a pulse of waves is propagated in a waveguide, its velocity can be measured by standard radar timing techniques. For example, the pulse might be transmitted through a long guide of length l, then reflected back to the sending end, and the elapsed time t might be measured. The velocity of the pulse (group velocity) is given by the formula

$$v_{gr} = \frac{2l}{t} \tag{2–66}$$

(The factor 2 occurs because the total distance traveled is twice the length of the guide.)

If these two measurements are made at the same frequency in a waveguide, it will be found that in general the two velocities are not the same. At some frequencies they will be nearly the same; at others they will be considerably different. The distinction between these two velocities was not necessary for transmission lines because in conventional lines the group and the phase velocities are equal.

To explain why these velocities are different in waveguides requires a detailed analysis, which cannot be given here. It must suffice to define them and to state, at appropriate points, which velocity is meant. Unless otherwise stated, the phase velocity will always be meant; it is the one of importance whenever considerations of wavelength are involved. Yet obviously the group velocity is also of great importance in other applications—radar signal transmission, for example. In general it is the velocity at which signals of any kind—that is, intelligence—are propagated; it is also the velocity at which energy is propagated.

The phase velocity is always either equal to or greater than the group velocity. The following relationship holds between them in evacuated or gas-filled waveguides:

$$(v_{ph})(v_{gr}) = c^2 = 9 \times 10^{16} \text{ (meters per second)}^2 \tag{2–67}$$

That is, the product of the two velocities is equal to the square of the free-space propagation velocity, 3×10^8 meters per second. This means that V_{ph} is always *greater* than the free-space velocity and V_{gr} is always less, unless both are equal to c.

It is a principle of modern physics that no form of matter or energy can travel with a velocity greater than the free-space velocity of light (electromagnetic waves). However, this principle is not violated by phase velocities, because it is the group velocity that represents the velocity of propagation of energy.

Since the phase velocity in waveguide is greater than the velocity in free space, the wavelength at a given frequency will be *greater* in the guide than in free space. Using the conventional symbol c for the velocity in free space, the relationship of the wavelength in the guide, λ_g, to the wavelength in free space, λ_0, is:

$$\lambda_g = \lambda_0\left(\frac{v_{ph}}{c}\right) \tag{2–68}$$

The distinction between the guide wavelength and the free-space wavelength is an important principle of waveguide theory.

2.5.2. Cutoff Frequency

Whereas transmission lines of the conventional type cannot be operated practically above some maximum frequency, waveguides are characterized by a *minimum* frequency, the cutoff frequency f_c. This is an absolutely limiting frequency; frequencies below this value will not be propagated in the guide. It is determined by the cross-sectional dimensions of the guide in relation to the wavelength.

A relationship exists between the guide-wavelength λ_g at a particular frequency f and the cutoff frequency f_c:

$$\lambda_g = \frac{c}{\sqrt{f^2 - f_c^2}} \tag{2–69}$$

where c is the free-space propagation velocity. This can also be written in another form:

$$\lambda_g = \frac{\lambda_0}{\sqrt{1-(f_c/f)^2}} \tag{2–70}$$

Comparison of this equation with (2–68) shows that the phase velocity is given by

$$v_{ph} = c\left(\frac{\lambda_g}{\lambda_0}\right) = \frac{c}{\sqrt{1-(f_c/f)^2}} \tag{2–71}$$

It is evident from this expression that if f becomes less than f_c, the phase velocity becomes imaginary (in the complex-number sense); physically this means that the wave is not propagated. Equations (2–69) and (2–71) also show that as the frequency f approaches the cutoff frequency f_c, the phase velocity and the guide wavelength become infinite. Consequently, the group velocity tends to zero, according to (2–67).

The foregoing results have all presupposed that the waveguide is filled with air (or a vacuum) or any gas having virtual unity relative permittivity. Waveguides are seldom filled with solid material, but, if such a low-loss material were used, the foregoing equations still hold if c is replaced by $c/\sqrt{\varepsilon_r}$, where ε_r is the relative permittivity of the material in the guide.

2.5.3. Rectangular Waveguides

The commonest form of waveguide has a rectangular cross section, as illustrated in Fig. 2–10. The greater of the two transverse dimensions is customarily denoted by a, and the lesser dimension by b. The dimension a determines the cutoff frequency f_c, according to the relation:

$$f_c = \frac{c}{2a} \tag{2–72}$$

or

$$\lambda_c = 2a \qquad (2\text{–}73)$$

where λ_c is the cutoff wavelength. (It is to be noted that the cutoff wavelength is a free-space wavelength.) This relation states that cutoff occurs at the frequency for which the largest transverse dimension of the guide is exactly a half wavelength in free space.

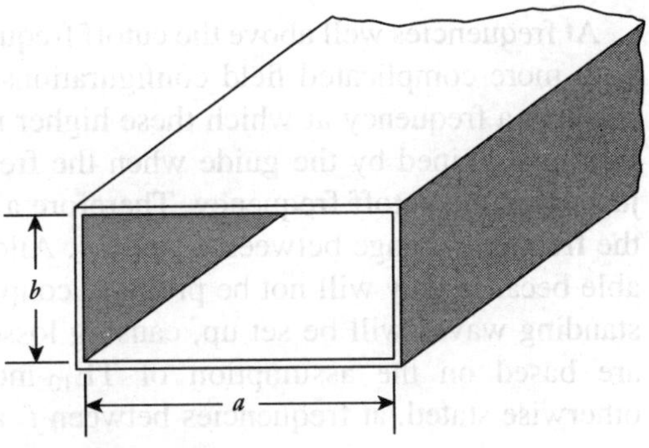

FIGURE 2–10.

Rectangular waveguide.

2.5.4. Modes of Propagation

At frequencies slightly above the cutoff frequency the configuration of the electromagnetic field is schematically represented in Fig. 2–11. The electric field (**E**) vectors, as shown, are parallel and are perpendicular to the wide face of the guide. Their amplitude is greatest midway between the narrow walls and decreases to zero at these walls, in a cosinusoidal fashion. The magnetic field (**H**) vectors, shown dashed, are also parallel to each other and perpendicular to the electric vectors. The magnetic intensity is constant in the vertical direction across the guide section. The wave is propagating in the longitudinal direction of the guide, perpendicular to the **E** and **H** vectors. This particular arrangement field, the only possible one *just above* the cutoff frequency, is called the TE_{10} mode of propagation. The letters stand for *transverse-electric,* meaning that the electric field lines are everywhere transverse (perpendicular to the guide walls). *Transverse-magnetic* (TM) modes and *transverse-electric-magnetic* (TEM) modes may also be propagated under certain conditions.

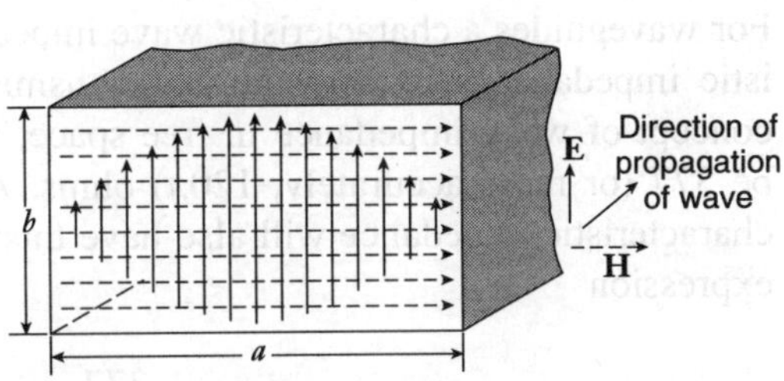

FIGURE 2–11.

Electric and magnetic field vectors in a transverse plane, TE_{10} propagation mode.

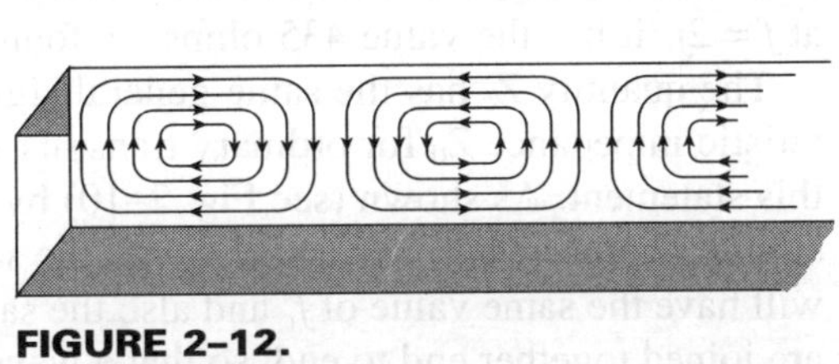

FIGURE 2–12.

Magnetic field configuration in a longitudinal section parallel to wide face, TE_{10} mode.

In this particular view of the TE_{10}, field, Fig. 2–11, the magnetic lines are also transverse; but this is not true for all views. As viewed in a longitudinal plane of the guide, the magnetic field is seen to have longitudinal components, but the electric field does not. Figure 2–12 shows a longitudinal section parallel to the wide guide wall, in which the magnetic field lines only are shown to illustrate this point.

The subscript numerals 10 refer to the number of half-sinusoid cycles in the transverse electric field pattern parallel to the *a* and *b* cross-section dimensions, respectively.

At frequencies well above the cutoff frequency, higher-order TE modes of propagation, with more complicated field configurations, are possible. It is undesirable to operate a guide at a frequency at which these higher modes can propagate. The next higher mode can be sustained by the guide when the free-space wavelength is equal to a, that is, at just twice the cutoff frequency. Therefore a rectangular guide is usually operated within the frequency range between f_c and $2f_c$. Allowing higher modes to propagate is undesirable because they will not be properly coupled to the load, and therefore reflections and standing waves will be set up, causing losses. The equations and discussion, therefore, are based on the assumption of TE_{10}-mode operation in rectangular guide unless otherwise stated, at frequencies between f_c and $2f_c$.

2.5.5. Impedance in Waveguides

For waveguides a characteristic wave impedance is defined, analogous to the characteristic impedance of a conventional transmission line. It is also closely related to the concept of wave impedance in free space, which was shown in chapter 1, Eq. 1–8, to be 377 (or more accurately, 120π) ohms. At frequencies well above cutoff, the guide characteristic impedance will also have this value, but more generally it is given by the expression

$$Z_c = \frac{377}{\sqrt{1-(f_c/f)^2}} = 377\left(\frac{\lambda_g}{\lambda_0}\right) \text{ ohms} \tag{2–74}$$

In general Z_c is greater than 377 ohms. At the cutoff frequency f_c it becomes infinite, and at $f = 2f_c$ it has the value 435 ohms, as found from (2–74).

The quantity Z_c has the same general significance for waveguide as does the characteristic impedance Z_0 for ordinary transmission lines, but there are certain exceptions to this statement. As shown (see Fig. 2–10) by (2–72), f_c is determined by only the dimension a. Therefore two waveguides with the same a dimension and different b dimensions will have the same value of f_c and also the same value of Z_c. But if these two waveguides are joined together end to end, so that a wave propagating in one of them passes through the junction into the other, a reflection will be set up at this point due to the disparity of dimensions, in spite of the impedances being "matched."

But for constant guide dimensions and a single mode of propagation, the characteristic wave impedance of the guide, Z_c, has the same significance as the characteristic impedance of a two-conductor transmission line, with respect to reflection and standing waves. The same principles of impedance matching and transformation apply, and the transmission-line equations, (2–15) through (2–18) and beyond, can be used provided that the guide wavelength, λ_g, is used in calculating β when using equation (1–32), ch. 1.

2.5.6. Impedance Matching in Waveguides

Just as reactive stubs are used for impedance transforming and matching in transmission lines, various reactive devices are used in waveguides. Short-circuited waveguide stubs

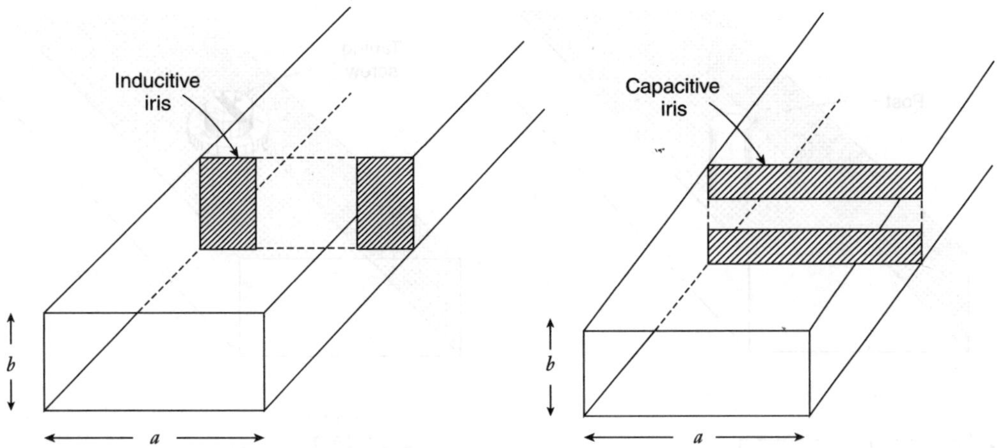

FIGURE 2–13.

Inductive and capacitive irises (as they would appear if the waveguide walls were transparent).

may be employed in the manner described for transmission-line stubs. Reactance may also be introduced into waveguides by means of *irises, posts*, and *tuning screws*. Their roles in impedance transformation and matching are the same as were described for the transmission-line tuning stub of Fig. 2–6; that is, the correct position of the reactance with respect to the load and the amount of reactance (susceptance) needed are determined in the same way.

Figure 2–13 illustrates capacitive and inductive irises in a rectangular waveguide. They behave like susceptances, that is, shunt reactances. As shown, they consist of thin metallic plates perpendicular to the guide walls and joined to them at the edges, with an opening between them. When the opening is parallel to the narrow walls of the guide, the susceptance is inductive; when it is parallel to the wide walls, it is capacitive. The amount of the susceptance is determined by the size of the opening. Many variations of these configurations may be used, for example, an unsymmetrical iris or a unilateral one.

A post placed across the narrow dimension of the guide acts as an inductive shunt susceptance, of a value depending on its diameter and its position in the transverse plane. A tuning screw projecting part way across the narrow guide dimension acts like a capacitive susceptance and may be made adjustable. These devices are illustrated in Fig. 2–14.

2.5.7. Transmission-Line-to-Waveguide Coupling

It is frequently necessary to transfer power from a coaxial transmission line into a waveguide, and vice versa. This is accomplished by means of any one of several coupling devices such as those illustrated in Fig. 2–15.

These couplers may be used as wave launchers at the input end of a waveguide, or as wave receptors at the load end, the operation in the one case being the reverse of the

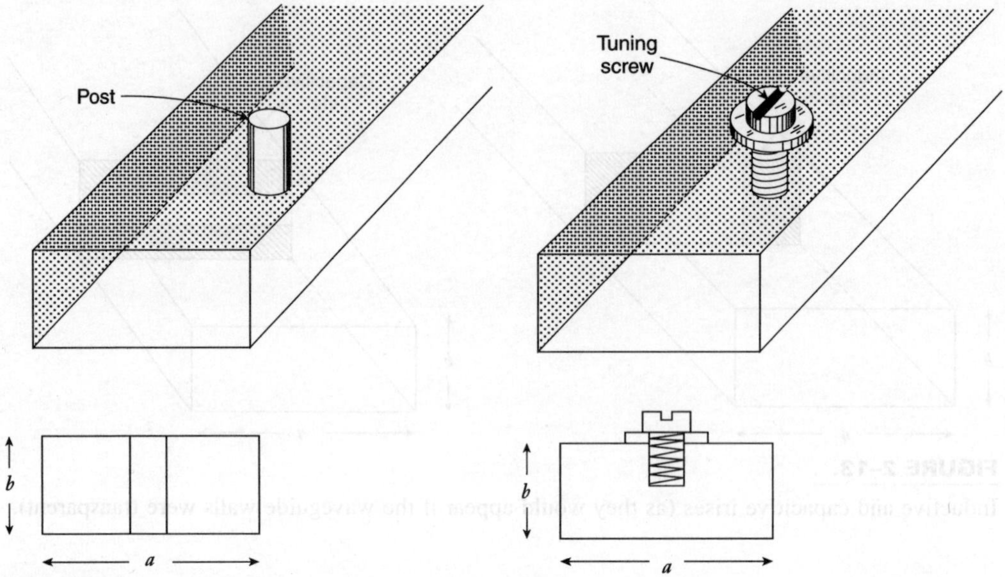

FIGURE 2–14.
Post and tuning screw in waveguide.

other. The various dimensions labeled $\lambda/4$ are approximate; in practice, they are experimentally adjusted for best operation. Note, however, that sometimes the approximate dimension is $\lambda_0/4$ and in others $\lambda_g/4$. The couplers illustrated are representative of the methods that may be employed; there are many variations of them in use.

2.5.8. Waveguide Junctions

Waveguides can be joined in various ways to result in power division among two or more branches. The two basic forms of junction are illustrated in Fig. 2–16. The analysis of the impedance relations for these junctions is complicated. In practice it is usual to employ manufactured junctions designed for a particular frequency range.

Numerous special forms of waveguide multiple-branching couplers for special purposes have been developed, too numerous to describe here. The magic-T is perhaps the best known of them.

2.5.9. Other Forms of Waveguide

Rectangular guide, as mentioned in this section (Fig. 2–10), is the most commonly used, but other forms are sometimes employed for special purposes. Circular guide, as the name implies, is simply a round pipe. As might be surmised, the field configurations are appreciably different from those in rectangular guide.

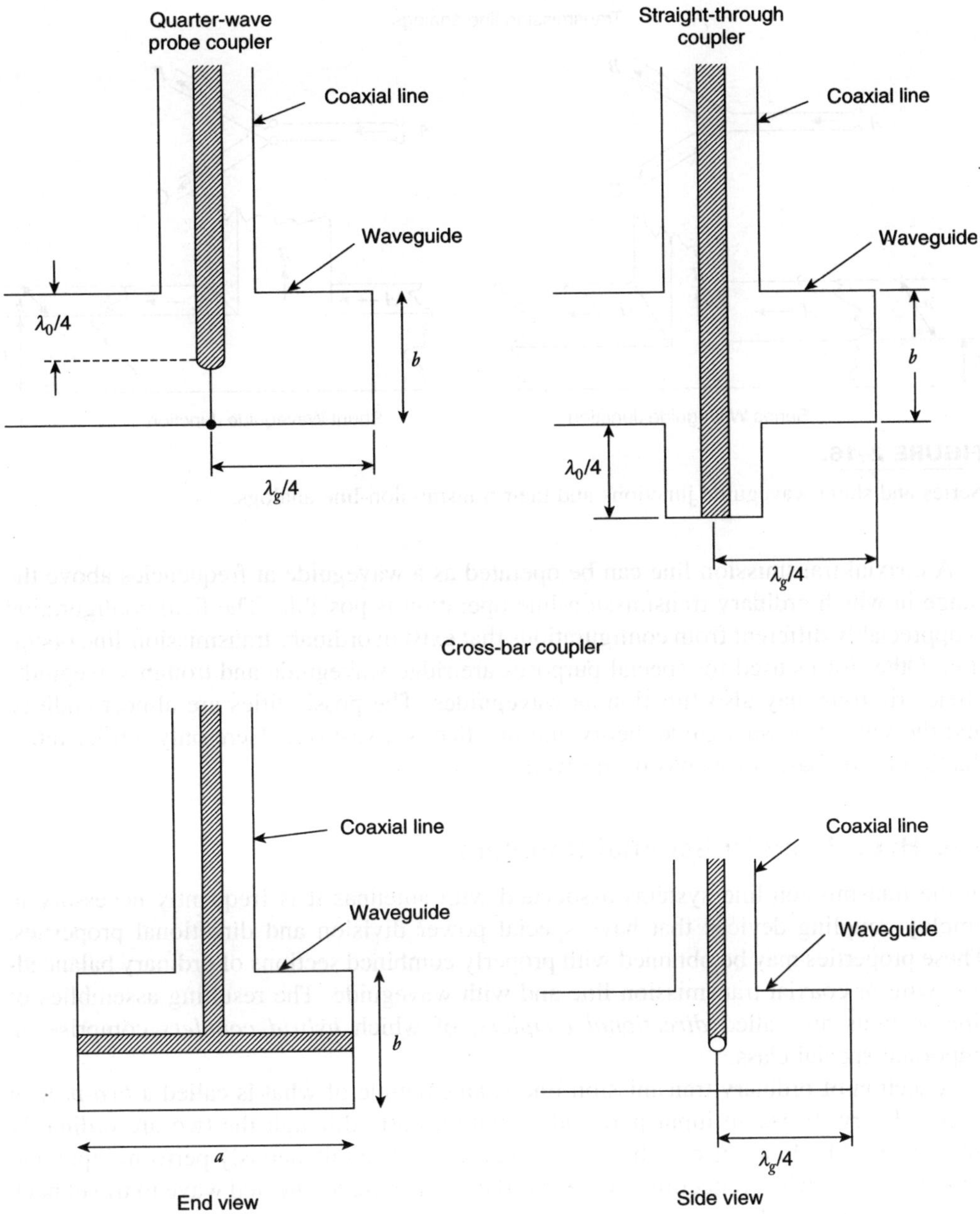

FIGURE 2–15.

Coaxial-line-to-waveguide couplers.

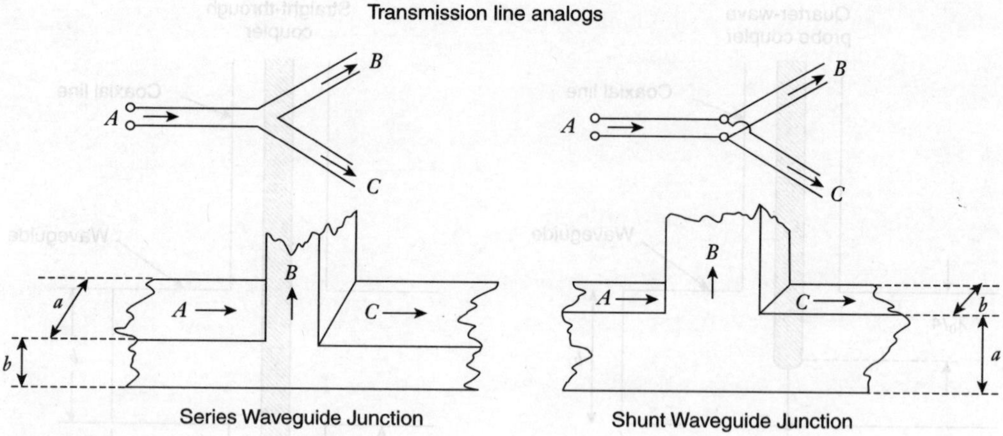

FIGURE 2–16.

Series and shunt waveguide junctions and their transmission-line analogs.

A coaxial transmission line can be operated as a waveguide at frequencies above the range in which ordinary transmission-line operation is possible. The field configuration is appreciably different from configurations that exist in ordinary transmission-line operation. Other forms used for special purposes are ridge waveguide and trough waveguide. Dielectric rods may also function as waveguides. The possibilities are almost endless, and the subject of waveguide theory and practice is a vast one. Here only a brief introduction to the basic ideas has been given.

2.6. Hybrid and Directional Couplers

In the transmission-line systems associated with antennas it is frequently necessary to employ coupling devices that have special power division and directional properties. These properties may be obtained with properly combined sections of ordinary balanced-two-wire or coaxial transmission line and with waveguide. The resulting assemblies of line sections are called *directional couplers,* of which *hybrid couplers* comprise an important special class.

A section of ordinary transmission line is an example of what is called a *two-port* in circuit theory. It has an input port and an output port, although the two are ordinarily interchangeable. In a sense each of the two ports may simultaneously perform input and output roles (as when reflections at the "output" end cause a reflected wave to travel back toward the input end).

A *port* in circuit theory is, speaking somewhat loosely, a physical place of access to a system or device. In ordinary low-frequency circuits it corresponds to a *pair of terminals*, as it does also in balanced-two-wire and coaxial transmission lines. In closed-wall waveguides and waveguide devices a port is often simply an opening through which electromagnetic fields may be introduced into or exit from the internal space of the guide. Sometimes a given port may serve as either an input port or an output port, at the will of the user, or it may serve simultaneously as both. (Additional qualifications on the definition of a port are necessary when it applies to multiple-frequency-response devices, such as heterodyne mixers, and to multimode devices, such as waveguides, but they are not of concern in the present discussion.)

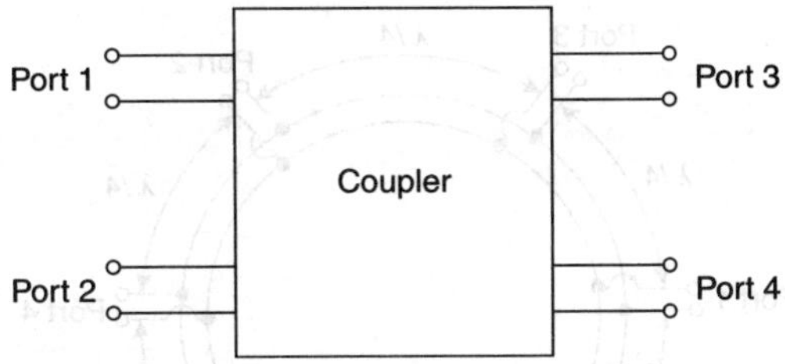

FIGURE 2–17.

A four-port coupler.

Hybrid and directional couplers are *four-port* devices. Figure 2–17 is a schematic representation of a four-port coupler, with the ports shown as terminal pairs, though restriction to this type of port is not implied. The essential feature of any four-port is that if power is fed into any one of the ports, some fraction of it may exit via each of the remaining three ports. If the device is passive and lossless, these fractions must of course add up to unity. ("Passive" means that the device does not contain any internal sources of power, such as oscillators or amplifiers.) The couplers to be discussed are passive, and for the purposes of discussion will be assumed lossless. (They are ordinarily nearly so.)

The feature of hybrid and directional couplers that distinguishes them from other four-ports is that one of the three "output" ports is *decoupled* from the input port, so that the fraction of input power available from it is virtually zero; moreover, the four ports are thus decoupled *in pairs*. For example, if port 1 of Fig. 2–17 is taken as the input port, all the output may appear at ports 3 and 4, and none at port 2. If then port 2 is taken as the input port, it will be found that again all the power appears at ports 3 and 4, with none going to port 1. Ports 1 and 2 thus comprise a pair of decoupled ports; ports 3 and 4 are similarly decoupled from each other.

In terms of this particular pairing, if port 1 is the input, a hybrid coupler divides the input power *equally* between ports 3 and 4, with none going to port 2. A directional coupler, on the other hand, divides the input power *unequally*, with (say) most of it going to port 3, a small fraction to port 4, and none to port 2. If, however, port 2 is taken as the input, the larger fraction will go to port 4, a small fraction to port 3, and none to port 1.

In the preceding example, if 1% (1/100) of the input power at port 1 goes to port 4, with 99% to port 3, the coupler is said to have a coupling factor of 20 dB (since $10 \log 1/100 = -20$). If the fractions are 0.1 and 99.9%, the coupling factor is 30 dB. A hybrid coupler is therefore actually a 3-dB directional coupler, but the term *directional coupler* is ordinarily reserved for couplers that divide the power unequally.

Hybrid couplers are used when power from a source is to be equally divided between two output ports, when these ports are required to be decoupled from each other. (The decoupling feature is not provided by the ordinary power dividers discussed in sec. 2–3.) They are also used when power from two sources is to be fed simultaneously to a load or loads and the sources must be decoupled from each other (so that there will not be an exchange of power between them). In this case the two sources are connected to a decoupled pair of ports, and the division of power between the remaining ports depends

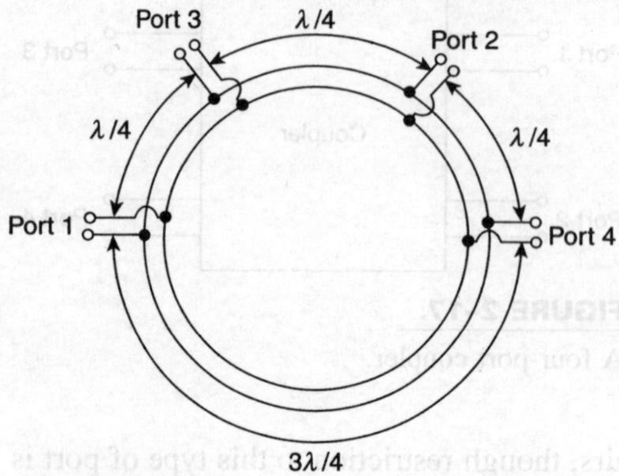

FIGURE 2–18.
Hybrid ring coupler.

on the relative phasing of the source voltages as well as on the design of the coupler. With proper coupler design the output voltage at one of the output ports will be proportional to the sum (in the phasor sense) of the two input voltages, and the output from the other will be proportional to their difference. This fact has an important application in *simultaneous lobing* antenna systems, which are discussed in sec. 7–6.

Figure 2–18 is a diagram of a ring type of hybrid coupler that exhibits the properties just described. The ports are numbered to conform to the description of behavior previously given, that is, ports 1 and 2 are a decoupled pair, as are also ports 3 and 4. If all the ports are properly impedance-matched, power fed into port 1 will provide equally divided outputs at ports 3 and 4, and none at port 2. This result is due to the lengths of the ring sections between the ports. The input at port 1 divides and goes both ways around the ring. The path differences of the two routes determine whether or not a voltage will exist across the terminal pair of a particular port. Since the path *differences* to ports 3 and 4 are respectively a full wavelength and zero, the voltage waves at these points are in phase and therefore add. At port 2, however, the path difference is a *half* wavelength; hence the oppositely traveling voltage waves are out of phase and cancel. This behavior occurs of course only at the frequency for which the ring sections have the lengths indicated, or odd-integer multiples of them. The ring couplers, however, will perform reasonably well over a small range of frequencies near the correct frequency. The ring may be two-wire balanced line, coaxial line, or waveguide. (The line sections need not actually form a ring as long as they are of the correct length.) Other methods of achieving this type of coupler action also exist, and some of them perform adequately over a broader frequency range than the ring coupler, at the expense of more complicated structure.

With input at port 1, the equal outputs at ports 3 and 4 will be out of phase with each other. If they are required to be in phase, as they may be in particular antenna applications, port 3 can be used as the input port; then equal in-phase outputs will be obtained at ports 1 and 2, with no output at port 4. Alternatively, port 2 can be used as the input port.

In a directional coupler there are in a sense two parallel *channels*, with "strong" bidirectional coupling between the ports of a given channel and weak unidirectional coupling between the channels. The description of directional-coupling behavior that has been given for Fig. 2–17 considers ports 1 and 3 to comprise one channel and ports 2 and 4 the other. The coupler is directional in the sense that if a particular port is considered an output port with respect to both ports of the *other channel* (main channel), it is apparent that output will occur when power flows one way in this main channel, but practically

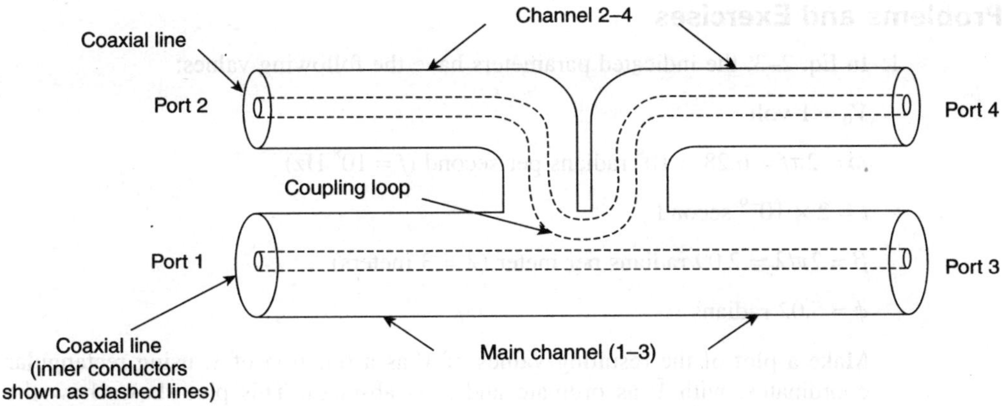

FIGURE 2–19.

Coaxial-line directional coupler.

no output will occur when it flows the other way. The ratio of these outputs for equal power flow in the two directions of the main channel is called the *directivity factor*. A typical value is 40 dB.

Figure 2–19 shows one form of directional coupler using coaxial line sections. The coupling between the two channels is by means by a short loop of the inner conductor of the 2–4 channel projecting into the interconductor space of the 1–3 channel. The plane of the loop is parallel to the inner conductor of the line into which it projects. It couples to both the electric and the magnetic field components in such a way that the currents that each type of field induces reinforce in the coupler branch leading to port 2 and cancel in the branch leading to port 4 (when the flow in the 1–3 channel is from port 1 to port 3). Many other coupling mechanisms exist for achieving a similar result.

In practice, directional couplers are often constructed with a matched-load termination on one port, such as port 4 in the above example, and only ports 1, 2, and 3 are made accessible. Then when there is a reflected wave in the 1–3 channel, which results in an output to port 4, the power thus received is absorbed in the load. (Otherwise it could be reflected and reach port 2, which would be harmful to the intended operation of the coupler.) Thus it might be considered that the coupler is not virtually lossless, as assumed. However, this load, though "built in," is not truly a part of the coupler itself, so that it does not invalidate the assumption of losslessness.

The principal uses of directional couplers in antenna applications are for measurement and monitoring of the power flow and the *VSWR*, as discussed in secs. 9.8.3 and 9.11.1.

References

Lowman, R. V., and R. N. Simons, "Transmission Lines and Waveguides," ch. 51 in *Antenna Engineering Handbook*, 4th ed., J. L. Volakis (ed.), McGraw-Hill, 2007.

Ragan, G. L. (ed.), *Microwave Transmission Circuits*, McGraw-Hill, 1948.

Problems and Exercises

1. In Eq. 2–3, the indicated parameters have the following values:

   $V_0 = 1$ volt

   $\omega = 2\pi f = 6.28 \times 10^8$ radians per second ($f = 10^8$ Hz)

   $t = 2 \times 10^{-9}$ second

   $\beta = 2\pi/\lambda = 2.09$ radians per meter ($\lambda = 3$ meters)

   $\phi = 5.02$ radians

   Make a plot of the resulting values of V as a function of x, using rectangular coordinates, with V as ordinate and x as abscissa. This plot shows how the instantaneous rf voltage varies with distance along the line at a particular instant of time.

2. A transmission line has an inductance $L = 9.99 \times 10^{-7}$ henry per meter of length and a capacitance between the conductors of $C = 1.11 \times 10^{-11}$ farad per meter. (a) What is the characteristic impedance, Z_0? (b) What is the velocity of propagation, v?

3. An air-dielectric transmission line has a characteristic impedance $Z_0 = 50$ ohms, and length $l = 25$ meters. It is being operated at a frequency $f = 7.5$ MHz (7.5×10^6 Hz). The wavelength is therefore $\lambda = 40$ meters, from equation (2–1). An impedance consisting of 25 ohms resistance in series with 30 ohms inductive reactance is connected at the load end of the line ($Z_L = 25 + j30$ ohms). A voltage $V_i = 100$ volts *rms* is applied at the input end of the line. (a) What is the *rms* current at a distance $x = 12$ meters from the line input terminals? (b) From equation (2–16), what is its phase angle relative to the phase of the input voltage?

4. An antenna is to be fed from a transmitter by a line of characteristic impedance $Z_0 = 500$ ohms. The line is several wavelengths long, and it is desired to have no standing waves (*VSWR* = 1). The impedance presented by the antenna at its input terminals is 80 ohms, purely resistive. Therefore a quarter-wavelength section of different characteristic impedance is inserted between the end of the 500-ohm line and the antenna terminals. What must the characteristic impedance of this quarter-wave-transformer section be in order to have no standing wave on the 500-ohm line?

5. A section of transmission line of length $l = 0.2\ \lambda$ and of characteristic impedance $Z_0 = 70$ ohms is short-circuited at the "load" end. (a) At its input end, what is the impedance? (b) If the frequency is 10^7 Hz, what inductance must a coil have in order to have this reactance value?

6. By measuring the rf voltage amplitude along a line with voltmeter, it is found that the voltage standing wave ratio (*VSWR*) is 4. (a) What is the magnitude of the reflection coefficient of the load, $|r|$? (b) If the characteristic impedance of the line is 600 ohms, and the load is known to be purely resistive and to have a value greater than 600 ohms, what is its resistance?

7. If in Problem 6 the load is not purely resistive, suppose that it is found (by sliding the voltmeter along the line) that a voltage minimum exists at a distance $d_m = (5/24)\lambda$ from the load terminals. (The *VSWR* is still 4.) (a) What is the (complex) reflection coefficient, r? (b) From equation (2–46), what is the value of the load impedance, Z_L?

8. The conductors of a transmission line have a series resistance of 0.01 ohm per meter of line and a leakage conductance of 10^{-5} mho per meter. (a) What is the attenuation, in decibels, of a 1,000-meter length of this line, assuming that $Z_0 = 50$ ohms and that the wavelength is less than 10 meters? (b) If a transmitter delivers 1,000 watts of rf power at the input terminals of this line, and if an antenna connected at the load terminals has a nonreactive impedance equal to the characteristic impedance of the line, how much power is delivered to the antenna?

9. A low-loss transmission line system connects a single source of power to eight loads in the manner of Fig. 2–8a. The loads are resistive (nonreactive) and are each 400 ohms in value. If the power divides equally at each branch point of the system, and if all line sections are completely free of standing waves, what must the characteristic impedance of the *input* line be? (Assume that no impedance transformers are used, so that the impedance [admittance] presented at each branch point depends solely on the characteristic impedances [admittances] of the branching lines.)

10. A rectangular air-filled waveguide has lateral dimensions $a = 7.2$ cm, $b = 3.4$ cm. (a) What is the cutoff frequency, f_c? (b) At an operating frequency of $f = 3 \times 10^9$ Hz, for which the free-space wavelength is $\lambda_0 = 10$ cm, what is the guide wavelength, λ_g?

CHAPTER 3

Antenna Parameters

An antenna is a device used to radiate or receive electromagnetic waves. To the layman, a rod or wire is probably the most familiar form of antenna. Antennas of this type are seen virtually everywhere—on rooftops, automobiles, boats and ships, aircraft, even on spacecraft. Another familiar type of antenna is the loop, made of wire formed into a large planar coil. Loop antennas are used on ships and aircraft for direction finding and are also commonly used as "built-in" receiving antennas for home radio and television. The layman also sees other forms of antennas, such as arrays, parabolic and corner reflectors, horns, slots, helixes, lenses, and log periodics that are discussed in chapters that follow. The increasing use of these more sophisticated forms of antennas reflects advances that have been made in antenna theory, the more demanding requirements of modern electronics systems, and the exploitation of higher frequencies where more exotic forms of antennas are feasible.

The ideal antenna is, in most applications, one that will radiate all the power delivered to it by a transmitter (usually via a transmission line) in the desired direction or directions and with the desired polarization. Practical antennas can never fully achieve this ideal performance, but their merit is conveniently described in terms of the degree to which they do so. For this purpose, certain parameters of antenna performance are defined. This chapter is primarily concerned with these definitions and related terminology, which will be needed in the later chapters for discussing the performance of specific forms of antennas.

The principal parameters of antennas are associated with the radiation pattern, the radiation efficiency, the input impedance, and the bandwidth. Parameters are defined under each of these categories such as the gain, beamwidth, beam polarization, minor lobe level, radiation efficiency, aperture efficiency, effective area, radiation resistance, various "bandwidths," and others that have specialized applications. Some of these parameters are interrelated or correlated. For example, if the beamwidth is given, the gain can thereby be estimated, though it cannot be calculated exactly from the beamwidth without additional information.

This book is primarily concerned with the electromagnetic design and performance of antennas. Often of almost equal practical importance are the mechanical design factors, some of which will be mentioned throughout the book in connection with related discussions of electromagnetic behavior. It is desirable, however, for the reader to have some general "feeling" for the structural factors in the design of antennas, as an aid in relating the somewhat abstruse electromagnetic concepts to real physical structures. A thumbnail sketch of some of these aspects of antenna design will be given here, before the definition of electromagnetic parameters is taken up.

3.1. Antenna Structures

3.1.1. Size

The sizes of antennas range from microminiature to gigantic. There is a general proportionality between antenna size and the wavelength at the frequency of operation, but this relationship is not hard and fast. Large antennas are sometimes used at short wavelengths (high frequencies) to obtain a highly directional radiation pattern (beam) and high gain in a preferred direction. However, there is a practical extreme beyond which further increase of size produces little or no additional gain because the required precision of construction or maintenance of phase relationships is not practically attainable. This limitation is in the size region of perhaps a few thousand wavelengths, but an antenna of as much as 100 wavelengths in any dimension is considered "electrically large."

Moreover, at long wavelengths (low frequencies) very small antennas may be used for reception when efficiency is not important. An antenna appreciably less than a half wavelength is termed "electrically small." Even a physically large antenna may be electrically small at very low frequencies.

In general, however, the largest antennas are those used at the very lowest frequencies (especially for transmitting, where radiation efficiency is important). An example of an extremely large VLF antenna is the navy's installation (actually two antennas) at Cutler, Maine, where wires supported by towers 1,000 feet high extend over an area of 2 square miles. In contrast, a half-wave dipole at the microwave frequencies may be considerably less than an inch long.

3.1.2. Supports

As mentioned in sec. 1–3, an antenna must be located "in the clear" for good results—away from large conducting or absorbing objects. Accordingly there must often be some supporting structure to place the radiating element or elements in a clear location (which often is synonymous with a high location). Antennas are supported by such devices as towers, masts, and pedestals. Towers are used when great height is required. Masts may be quite high, but they are often as short as a few feet. Pedestals are the base structures of antennas such as reflectors and lenses, for which height is not so important as strength. Sometimes an antenna may be mounted directly on a vehicle, such as an automobile, ship, aircraft, or spacecraft; no intermediate "support" is required. Moreover, towers and masts are sometimes themselves used as antennas rather than as supports. In the standard broadcast band (535–1,705 kHz), for example, vertical towers of heights up to several hundred feet are used as transmitting antennas.

3.1.3. Feed Lines

An important part of any antenna installation is the transmission line used to connect the transmitter or receiver to the antenna. In fact the design of a feed line and any necessary impedance-matching or power-dividing devices associated with it are usually considered part of antenna design. The line connects to the antenna at its *input terminals or input port.* At the very lowest frequencies, the earth (ground) is a part of the antenna electrical system, and one terminal of the antenna input is therefore a rod driven into the ground or a wire leading to a system of buried conductors (especially if the earth is dry in the vicinity of the antenna). The other terminal is then usually the base of a tower or other vertically rising conductor. Towers used in this way are usually supported at the base by a heavy insulator or insulators (series feed), but occasionally they are directly grounded and fed by connecting the feed wire a short distance up from the ground (shunt feed).

At somewhat higher frequencies, up to perhaps 30 MHz, the antenna may be a horizontal wire strung between towers or other supports (from which it is insulated). The feed line is then often a two-wire balanced line connected at the center of the antenna, either to the two terminals provided by a gap in the antenna wire (series feed) or to two points somewhat separated on the unbroken antenna wire (shunt feed). Sometimes the feed line is connected at the end of the horizontal span, or elsewhere off center, but center feed is preferred because it results in better balance of the currents in the feed wires. Two-wire-line spacings range from less than an inch to 12 inches or more.

At still higher frequencies, up to perhaps 1 GHz and occasionally somewhat higher, coaxial feed lines are commonly used. They are favored because the two-wire-line spacing becomes too great a fraction of the wavelength to prevent appreciable radiation and because waveguides below 1 GHz are quite large and expensive (though sometimes used). (Two-wire lines of small spacing may also be used in low-power applications.) Coaxial line diameters range from a fraction of an inch up to 9 inches or more. Above 1 GHz, waveguides are commonly used, with some use of small-diameter coaxial lines in low-power noncritical applications. In addition, microstrip constructed using printed circuit boards are used to reduce cost and bulk. When the antenna rotates on a pedestal, or has other motion with respect to its support, the feed line must contain flexing sections or rotating joints.

3.1.4. Conductors

Metals are the usual conducting materials of antennas. Metals of high conductivity, such as copper and aluminum (and its alloys), are naturally preferred. Brass may be used for machined parts. Magnesium is sometimes used where ultralight weight is important, usually in an alloy and with a protective coating or treatment. Where strength is of primary importance, steel may be used, either with or without a coating or plating of copper. The conductivity of unplated steel is adequate when it is used in the form of sheets or other large-surface-area forms (as for the surface of a paraboloidal reflector). Antenna wire is sometimes made with a steel core for strength and to minimize stretching, and with a copper coating to increase the conductivity. Such wire is virtually as good a conductor as solid copper, since rf currents are concentrated near the surfaces of conductors (skin effect). For this reason brass and other metals are sometimes silver plated when exceptionally high conductivity is required. For the same reason large-diameter conductors may be hollow tubes without loss of conductivity. At low radio frequencies the conductivity of large-diameter conductors may be increased, compared to a solid conductor, by interweaving strands of small-diameter insulated wires; the resulting conductor is called Litz wire. This technique is most effective below about 500 kHz. At higher frequencies it is not effective because the currents tend to flow only in the outer strands.

Conductor size in antenna design is determined by many factors, principally the permissible ohmic losses and resultant heating effects in some cases, mechanical strength requirements, permissible weight, electrical inductance and capacitance effects, and corona considerations in high-voltage portions of transmitting antennas. Corona is minimized by large-diameter conductors, by avoidance of sharp or highly curved edges, and by using insulators with metal end caps bonded to the insulating material, so that small air gaps between wires and insulators do not exist. Corona can occur on metal supports of the antenna as well as on the antenna conductor itself, as a result of induced voltages.

3.1.5. Insulators

The conducting portions of an antenna not only carry rf *currents* but also have rf *voltages* between their different parts and between the conductors and ground. To avoid "short circuiting" these voltage, insulators must sometimes be used between the antenna and its supports, or between different parts of the antenna. Insulators are also used as spacer supports for two-wire and coaxial lines and to "break up" guy wires used with masts and towers so that resonant or near-resonant lengths will not occur. The maximum permissible uninterrupted length of guy wire sections is about 1/8 wavelength. (A half-wavelength section would be resonant.) Insulators used to support long heavy spans of wire must be of high strength. Typical insulating materials for such insulators are glass and ceramics. Other "low-loss" materials such as polystyrene and other plastics are used where less strength is required. Very large and heavy insulators are necessary in high-power transmitting applications to prevent flashover. Coaxial lines and waveguides in high power applications may be filled with an inert gas, or dry air, at a pressure of several atmospheres, to increase the voltage-breakdown level. Printed circuit boards rely on low loss dielectric insulators.

3.1.6. Weather Protection

Since antennas are ordinarily "outdoors," they must withstand wind, rain, ice and snow, lightning, and sometimes corrosive gases or salt-laden air. Protection against wind and ice loads is primarily a matter of mechanical strength and bracing. Guy wires are used with tall structures or towers to prevent their overturning in high winds. At very low rf frequencies, where long spans of wire may be used, ice is sometimes melted from the wires by passing heavy 60-Hertz currents through them to produce heating.

Sometimes an antenna (such as a rotating paraboloidal reflector or lens) is totally enclosed in a protective housing of low-loss insulating material that is practically transparent to the electromagnetic radiation. Such a housing is called a *radome*. Radomes are commonly used on some types of aircraft antennas for aerodynamic reasons. They are also sometimes used on large microwave ground based antennas, permitting the antenna itself to be a lighter structure, at the cost of the expensive radome and some loss of rf power in the radome material. Electrical properties of radomes are addressed in Appendix E.

Protection against lightning-induced currents and static-charge buildup is necessary for some types of antennas, such as AM, FM and television broadcasting towers, or any structure that stands high above its surroundings if the conducting path to ground is not heavy and direct. Insulators may be protected by horn or ball gaps, and static may be drained by connecting high-ohmage resistors across insulators.

3.2. Radiation Pattern

The radiation pattern of an antenna is one of its most fundamental properties, and many of its performance parameters pertain to various aspects of the pattern. As mentioned in sec. 1.3, there is a reciprocal relationship between the processes of radiation and reception by an antenna. Although it is customary to speak of the antenna pattern as a radiation pattern, it is a "reception pattern" as well because it also describes the receiving properties of the antenna. However, it is perhaps somewhat easier to discuss the radiation pattern, which describes the relative strength of the radiated field in various directions from the antenna, at a far-field distance (sec. 3.2.5) that is fixed or constant.

3.2.1. Coordinate Systems

An antenna pattern is three dimensional, and therefore its description requires a three-dimensional coordinate system. Two possibilities are: (1) cartesian (rectangular) coordinates (x, y, z) and (2) spherical coordinates (r, θ, ϕ). The spherical coordinate system is more appropriate because the radiation pattern may be expressed in terms of the electric field intensity, for example, at some fixed distance r from the antenna, at all points on the spherical surface at that distance. Specific points on the surface are then defined by the direction angles θ and ϕ. The pattern then becomes a function of only two independent variables, since r is a constant, and this fact greatly simplifies matters.

It is sometimes convenient also to refer to the corresponding cartesian system. Figure 3–1 shows the relationships of these two coordinate systems, for some arbitrary point in space designated P. That is, the dashed lines parallel to the x-, y-, and z-axes define the cartesian coordinates of P, whereas the spherical coordinates are shown in terms of the line (of length r) going directly from the origin to the point P, and the projection of this

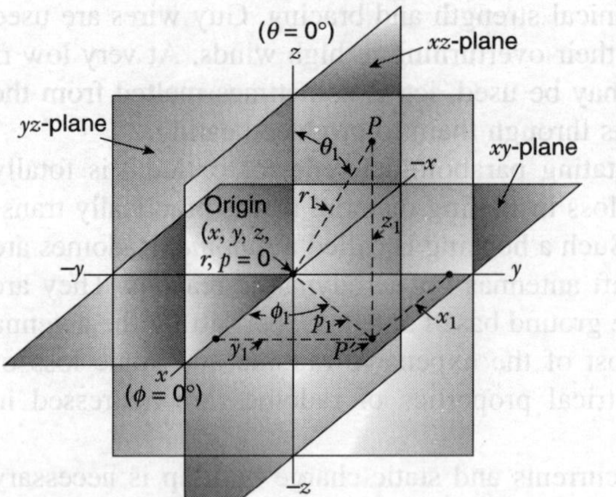

FIGURE 3–1.
Three-dimensional cartesian coordinate system. Coordinates of an arbitrary point P are shown as x_1, y_1, z_1. Corresponding spherical coordinates are also shown as r_1, θ_1, ϕ_1. Also, polar coordinates of projection of P (designated P') onto xy-plane are shown as ρ_1, ϕ_1.

line onto the xy-plane. This projection is designated ρ, and, as the reader may recognize, ρ and ϕ comprise a two-dimensional polar coordinate system in the xy-plane.

The following analytical relationships exist among the various coordinates:

$$r = \sqrt{x^2 + y^2 + z^2} \tag{3–1}$$

$$\cos\theta = \frac{z}{\sqrt{x^2 + y^2 + z^2}} = \frac{z}{r} \tag{3–2}$$

$$\tan\phi = \frac{y}{x} \tag{3–3}$$

$$x = r\sin\theta\cos\phi \tag{3–4}$$

$$y = r\sin\theta\sin\phi \tag{3–5}$$

$$z = r\cos\theta \tag{3–6}$$

$$\rho = \sqrt{x^2 + y^2} = r\sin\theta \tag{3–7}$$

$$x = \rho\cos\phi \tag{3–8}$$

$$y = \rho\sin\phi \tag{3–9}$$

The variables x, y, and z range from minus infinity to plus infinity, whereas r and ρ range from zero to infinity (always positive). The angle θ covers the range of 0 to 180 degrees (0 to π radians), and ϕ goes from 0 to 360 degrees (0 to 2π radians). The angle θ is called the angle of colatitude, or sometimes the polar angle, and ϕ is the angle of longitude. The system of angular coordinates used to describe positions on the surface of the earth (latitude and longitude) is essentially a spherical coordinate system with the radial coordinate fixed, except that the geographic latitude has the value zero at the equator where the colatitude is 90 degrees, and is +90 degrees at the north pole and –90 degrees at the south pole, where the corresponding values of colatitude are 0 and 180 degrees respectively.

It is in fact sometimes convenient to use the geographic system of coordinates in discussing antenna patterns that consist of a single main lobe of radiation. The axis of the lobe is assumed to lie in the xy-plane, so that its longitude angle is $\phi = 0°$. Then the angle θ is measured in the xz-plane and corresponds to the latitude angle of geographic coordinates. However, in this context θ is usually referred to as the *elevation angle*, and ϕ is called the *azimuth angle*. The value of θ corresponding to the beam axis is called the elevation angle of the beam. A positive elevation angle is equal to the complement of the colatitude angle in the corresponding system of true spherical coordinates.

3.2.2. Definition of Pattern

If an antenna is imagined to be located at the center of a spherical coordinate system, its radiation pattern is determined by measuring the electric field intensity over the surface of a sphere at some fixed distance, r. Since the field E is then a function of the two variable θ and ϕ, it is written $E(\theta, \phi)$ in functional notation.

A measurement of the electric field intensity $E(\theta, \phi)$ of an electromagnetic field in free space is equivalent to a measurement of the magnetic field intensity $H(\theta, \phi)$, since the magnitudes of the two quantities are directly related by $E = 377H$ in equation (1–10), ch. 1, for the far field. (Vectorially, of course, they are at right angles to each other; also, their phase angles are equal.) Therefore the pattern could equally well be given in terms of E or H. It is customary, however, to discuss patterns in terms of the electric field intensity, E.

The power density of the field, $p(\theta, \phi)$, can also be computed when $E(\theta, \phi)$ is known, the relation being: $p = E^2/377$ (equation [1–9]). Therefore a plot of the antenna pattern in terms of $p(\theta, \phi)$ conveys the same information as a plot of the magnitude of $E(\theta, \phi)$. In some circumstances, the phase of the field is of interest, and a plot may be made of the phase angle of $E(\theta, \phi)$ as well as its magnitude; this plot is called the *phase pattern* of the antenna. But ordinarily the term *antenna pattern* implies only the magnitude of E or p. Sometimes the polarization properties of E may also be plotted, thus forming a *polarization pattern*.

3.2.3. Patterns in a Plane

Although the total pattern of an antenna is a function of θ and ϕ, the pattern in a particular plane that passes through the peak of the main beam is often of interest. In fact, there is no satisfactory way of making a single plot of the entire pattern on a plane piece of paper. The θ versus ϕ pattern is usually represented in terms of pattern cuts in two planes that form 90 degree angles with each other, with the origin of a spherical coordinate system on their intersection line. The $\phi = 0°$ direction is taken to lie along the intersection line, and the $\theta = 0°$ direction is of course then perpendicular to this line and lies in one of the planes. This plane then becomes equivalent to the *xz*-plane of Fig. 3–1, the other being equivalent to the *xy*-plane. These are called *principal planes* of the coordinate system, and the patterns in them are the *principal-plane patterns* of the antenna.

The principal-plane pattern cuts do not, of course, convey the full θ and ϕ pattern information; this would require an infinity of plane patterns. For example, planes formed by rotating the *xy*-plane about the *x*-axis in small increments of the angle θ are appropriate for plotting additional plane patterns, which, in the aggregate, present a good picture of the total pattern. Alternatively, the planes may be formed by rotating the *xy*-plane about the *y*-axis or the *xz*-plane about the *z*-axis. Figures 6–32, 6–33, and 6–34 are examples of calculated patterns of amplitude versus θ and ϕ. Still another method of depicting three-dimensional pattern information is to plot contours of constant signal strength on the surface of a sphere containing the antenna at its center. But ordinarily only the principal-plane patterns are given, as they convey an adequate picture of the θ versus ϕ pattern for many purposes.

Patterns in a plane involve only one angle, and hence are polar-coordinate plots, except that the radial coordinate is the field strength or power density, rather than distance. However, because fortuitously in a given direction the field strength E is inversely proportional to the distance, *assuming far field free-space propagation*, equation (1–11), ch. 1, *a pattern that represents field strength as a function of angular direction at a fixed distance from the antenna is identical to a plot of distance for a constant field strength.* Therefore a field-strength pattern can be interpreted in either of these ways, by simply changing the labeling of the radial coordinate scale.

Although the pattern in a plane is thus appropriately represented by polar coordinates, it would be possible to employ cartesian coordinates, through the equations (3–7) to (3–9). If this were done, the shape of the pattern would be unchanged; but because interpretation of the meaning of the pattern in terms of the cartesian coordinates would be relatively difficult, this is never done. It is fairly common, however, to plot the pattern *on rectangular-coordinate graph paper* but *in terms of the direction angle as the abscissa and field strength or power density as the ordinate.* This type of plot distorts the appearance of the pattern geometrically but preserves the interpretability of an angle representation and makes the plotting and reading of the low-amplitude portions of the pattern easier. Figure 3–2 compares these two representations. Note that it is easier to locate the angular positions of nulls (zeros) of the pattern on the rectangular plot.

When the radiation of an antenna is polarized so that the E-vector lies in a plane (usually one of the principal planes), the pattern in this plane is sometimes referred to as the E-plane pattern; and the pattern in the plane perpendicular to it, in which the H-vector lies, is called the H-plane pattern.

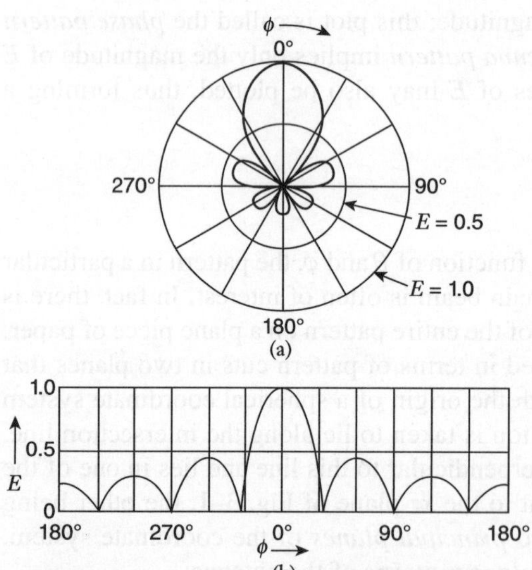

FIGURE 3–2.

Comparison of plane pattern plotted in polar and rectangular form. The same pattern is represented in both cases and the coordinates are the same. Only the *form* of the plot is different: (*a*) polar plot; (*b*) rectangular plot.

3.2.4. Absolute and Relative Patterns

If the radiation pattern is plotted in terms of the field strength in electrical units, such as volts per meter or the power density in watts per square meter, it is called an *absolute pattern*. An absolute pattern actually describes not only the characteristics of an antenna but also those of the associated transmitter, since the absolute field strength at a given point in space depends on the total amount of power radiated as well as on the directional properties of the antenna. An absolute pattern in terms of constant-field-strength contours plotted on a map is a most useful representation for a radio broadcast station, since it defines the geographic regions within which various received-signal levels are available to listeners.

Often, however, the pattern is plotted in relative terms, that is, the field strength or power density is represented in terms of its ratio to some reference value. The reference usually chosen is the field level in the maximum-field-strength direction. The field strength or power density is given the value unity in this direction and fractional values in other directions. This type of pattern provides as much information *about the antenna* as does an absolute pattern, and therefore relative patterns are usually plotted when it is desired to describe only the properties of the antenna, without reference to an associated transmitter (or receiver).

It is also fairly common to express the relative field strength E or power density p in decibels. This coordinate of the pattern is given as $20\log(E/E_{max})$ or $10\log(p/p_{max})$. The value at the maximum of the pattern is therefore zero decibels, and at other angles the decibel values are negative (since the logarithm of a fractional number is negative).

3.2.5. Near-Field and Far-Field Patterns

Antenna radiation patterns are graphical representations of the radiation, usually as a function of directional coordinates and in the far-field of the antenna. The far-field region is where the angular field distribution is essentially independent of the distance from the antenna (IEEE 1992, p. 482). For an out-of-doors pattern measurement, it is therefore important to choose a distance sufficiently large to be definitely in the far-field region. The minimum permissible distance, for a far-field measurement, depends on the dimensions of the antenna in relation to the wavelength. In free space, the general rule-of-thumb (see Appendix F) for the minimum separation distance r_{min} is

$$r_{min} = 2 \cdot \frac{D^2}{\lambda} \tag{3–10}$$

where D is the diameter of the smallest stationary sphere enclosing the radiating portions of the antenna as it is rotated for measurement and λ is the wavelength. The factor of 2 in (3–10) is sufficient for sidelobe levels higher than −20 dB, but a factor of 12 may be required for the measurement of −50 dB sidelobe levels (see sec. 7.10).

Sometimes, however, additional criteria are necessary for assurance that a measured pattern replicates a far-field measurement. While reviewing the manuscript, E. B. Joy added two additional criteria: (1) $r_{min} = 20\lambda$, that pertains to electrically small antennas and assures that the reactive near field is negligible at r_{min} and (2) $r_{min} = 20D$, that limits the relative down range far field decrease across the antenna under test to an acceptable value. As with the factor 2 in (3–10), choice of the factors 20 depends on the accuracy of measurement required. According to Hollis, Lyon, and Clayton (1970, sec. 14.2), the relevant effects are usually considered negligible if $r_{min} \geq 10\lambda$ and $r_{min} \geq 10D$.

Fields and patterns of an antenna are generally dependent on the distance from the antenna, broadly separated into near-field and far-field regions. The near-field region is further subdivided between the reactive near-field and radiating near-field regions. However, the total field present is actually the vector sum of the reactive (i.e., induction by time-varying electric and magnetic fields) and radiating fields. At distances from an antenna that are small compared to a wavelength (or small compared with the antenna dimensions if the antenna is large), field strengths within reactive near-field regions may greatly exceed the radiated fields. This is because the nonradiating electric and magnetic fields, caused by charges and currents on and within the antenna, decrease with range r as $1/r^2$ and $1/r^3$. As a consequence, these reactive fields decrease more rapidly with increased range than the radiation fields, which vary as $1/r$. At some range the reactive and radiating power densities are equal. This range may serve as a demarcation between the reactive and radiating near-fields. For a dipole that is electrically very short, or an equivalent radiator, the outer reactive field boundary is commonly taken to be at a distance $\lambda/2\pi$ from the antenna surface (IEEE 1992, p. 1080). Thus, for the VLF band and lower frequencies, having wavelengths of 10^4 meters and longer, antennas are electrically very short. Consequently, the reactive field extends to distances of 1.6 kilometer (about one mile) and farther. Thus, some of the original "wireless" communications were within the reactive near zone. Today, short-range communications between equipments is a developing application of reactive fields. Radio frequency identification (RFID) used for product inventory is another relatively new application of reactive fields. From near field measurements with antennas large compared to λ, it is known that the strengths of reactive fields are negligible compared to the radiating near fields at distances of 4 or 5λ (sec. 9.1.2). Like all varying fields, reactive fields can, at intense levels, be hazardous to people. For example, applications of reactive fields include RF heating of metals through induction and of insulating materials through dielectric loss. Unlike radiating fields, the magnitudes of electric and magnetic reactive fields are not generally predictable, one from the other. Thus, an unfamiliar reactive field environment may require monitoring, separately, the electric and magnetic fields.

The radiating near-field region is that portion of the near-field region between the reactive near-field and the far-field regions. As already noted, within the far-field the radiation pattern is essentially independent of the distance from the antenna. However, within radiating near-field regions, radiation patterns are dependent upon distance from the antenna. This is because the path length differences between various parts of the antenna and an observation point, in terms of phase differences, depend on distance from the antenna center. Consequently, for an antenna small compared to a wavelength, the radiating near-field region may not exist. Following optical terminology, the radiating near-field and far-field regions are sometimes called the Fresnel and Fraunhofer regions, respectively.

Pattern, gain, directivity, and polarization of an antenna are basically far field terms. Their definitions rely on the simplicity of the far field and do not include the complexities of reactive near fields. Accordingly, calculated radiating near and far fields of an antenna are meaningful for determining antenna patterns at different distances, only if there is assurance that the strength of the reactive near field is negligible.

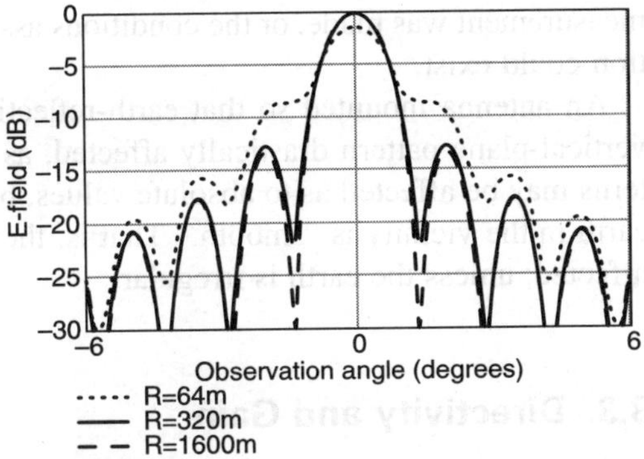

FIGURE 3–3.

Calculated patterns at different distances from an antenna, for which $2D^2/\lambda$ is 320 m.

The general methods for calculating radiation patterns versus distance are described in Appendix G, and radiating near-field Mathcad calculations for array and reflector antennas are included in the accompanying website. Figure 3–3 shows results of calculating radiation within the near- and far-field regions for a linear antenna, with constant amplitude and phase over its aperture. The antenna width D and wavelength λ are 4 m and 0.1 m, respectively, giving the calculated $2D^2/\lambda$ distance of 320 m to the boundary between the radiating near-field and far-field regions.

Figure 3–3 includes three patterns, corresponding to distances of $10D^2/\lambda$ (1,600 m), $2D^2/\lambda$ (320 m), and $0.4D^2/\lambda$ (60 m). Notice that the $2D^2/\lambda$ and $10D^2/\lambda$ patterns are nearly identical, except that the first nulls are much deeper for the larger distance. For the $0.4D^2/\lambda$ pattern, the first nulls are not apparent, the maximum field strength is reduced, and sidelobe levels are increased. Thus, it is seen that the $2D^2/\lambda$ rule-of-thumb provides useful approximate patterns if very accurate low-sidelobe measurements are not required.

3.2.6. Free-Space and Earth-Reflection Patterns

The antenna pattern calculated for an antenna in free space will obviously not be observed in the presence of the earth, which both absorbs and reflects, as described in sec. 1–4. Vertical-plane free-space and earth-reflection patterns of an isotropic radiator under certain conditions are compared in Fig. 1–15, which indicates how drastically the two patterns may differ.

Antenna patterns are usually given for the free-space condition, it being assumed that the user of the antenna will calculate the effect of ground reflection on this pattern for the particular antenna height and ground conditions that apply in the particular case. Some types of antennas, however, are basically dependent on the presence of the ground for their operation, for example, certain types of vertical antennas at low frequencies. The ground is in fact an integral part of these antenna systems. In these cases, the pattern *must* include the effect of the earth. Patterns of antennas intended for a specific environment or vehicle, such as a ship or aircraft, are usually measured so as to include the effects of reflections from the metallic surfaces of the deck, airplane wing, and so forth. It is always advisable to indicate clearly the conditions under which a pattern measurement was made, or the conditions assumed in calculating it, if any possible question could exist.

An antenna mounted so that earth-reflection interference effects occur will have its vertical-plane pattern drastically affected, as Fig. 1–15 indicates. Horizontal-plane patterns may be affected as to absolute values, but relative values will not be affected if the earth in the vicinity is "smooth." That is, the *shape* of the horizontal pattern will not be affected, unless the earth is irregular.

3.3. Directivity and Gain

In discussions of directivity and gain, the concept of an isotropic radiator, or isotrope, is fundamental. This concept was introduced briefly in sec. 1.1.4. Essentially an isotrope is an imaginary, lossless antenna that radiates uniformly in all directions. Its pattern is a perfect spherical surface in space; that is, if the electric intensity of the field radiated by an isotrope is measured at all points on an imaginary spherical surface with the isotrope at the center (in free space), the same value will be measured everywhere. Therefore, if an isotrope radiates a total power P_t in watts and is located at the center of a transparent (or imaginary) far field sphere of radius R meters, the power density over the spherical surface is

$$p_{isotrope} = \frac{P_t}{4\pi R^2} \text{ watts per square meter} \tag{3–11}$$

Equation (3–11) is true because P_t is distributed uniformly over the surface area of the sphere, which is $4\pi R^2$ square meters.

Actually an isotropic radiator is not physically realizable; all actual antennas have some degree of nonuniformity in their radiation patterns. A nonisotropic antenna will radiate more power in some directions than in others and therefore has a directional pattern. A directional antenna will radiate more power in its direction of maximum radiation than an isotrope would, with both radiating the same total power. Thus, since the directional antenna sends less power in some directions than an isotrope does, it follows that it must send more power in other directions, if the total powers radiated are the same.

Directivity D is a quantitative measure of an antenna's ability to concentrate radiated power per unit solid angle in a certain direction, and thus D is highly dependent on the three-dimensional pattern of an antenna. D will be explicitly defined in materials that follow. On the other hand, gain G is the ratio of the power radiated per unit solid angle to the power per unit solid angle radiated by a lossless isotrope, each having the same input power. Unless otherwise specified, the direction applicable to D and G is that for which maximum radiation occurs.

Over the years there have been several gain-related terms used. In fact, gain once was not defined in terms of signal strength relative to any specific antenna type (Terman 1943). Gain is sometimes specified relative to the gain of a one-half wavelength dipole, whose gain exceeds the isotrope by the factor 1.64 (2.15 dB). Then, gain is specified in

dB_d (gain above the gain of a lossless one-half wavelength dipole). However, almost universally, gain is expressed relative to the lossless isotrope and when specificity is desired, it is referred to as absolute gain or expressed in terms of dB_i.

3.3.1. Definitions of Directivity and Gain

The IEEE definitions of directivity and gain are expressed in terms of radiation intensity $U(\theta, \phi)$, which is a range-independent quantity that is the product of power density $p(\theta, \phi, r)$ and range squared r^2, that is, $U(\theta, \phi) = p(\theta, \phi, r)r^2$. Specifically,

- Directivity is the ratio of the radiation intensity in a given direction from the antenna to the radiation intensity averaged over all directions (IEEE 1993, p. 362). *Notes:* (1) The average radiation intensity is equal to the total power radiated by the antenna divided by 4π (area of sphere in steradians). (2) If the direction is not specified, the direction of maximum radiation intensity is implied.
- Gain is the ratio of the radiation intensity, in a given direction, to the radiation intensity that would be obtained if the power accepted by the antenna were radiated isotropically (IEEE 1993, p. 547). *Notes:* (1) Gain does not include losses arising from impedance and polarization mismatches. (2) If the antenna is without dissipative (I^2R) losses; then, in any given direction its gain is equal to its directivity. (3) If the direction is not specified, the direction of maximum radiation intensity is implied.

Sections 3.3.2 through 3.3.5 that follow discuss the mathematics of directivity and gain, and relationships between them. To accomplish this, the concepts of solid angle and radiation intensity are first introduced.

3.3.2. Solid Angle

Solid angle is the angle that, seen from the center of a sphere, includes a given area on the surface of the sphere. The value of the solid angle is numerically equal to the size of that area divided by the square the radius of the sphere (Jurgenson and Brown 2000). Mathematically the solid angle is unitless, but for practical reasons the steradian (s.r.) is assigned so that 1 steradian = 1 radian^2. Since radians are dimensionless, steradians are also dimensionless.

Figure 3–4 shows a cross-hatched area dA in spherical coordinates that is bisected by the solid angle $d\Omega$. Since $dA = r^2 \sin\theta \, d\theta \, d\phi = r^2 d\Omega$, the value of the cross-hatched solid angle in Fig. 3–4 is $d\Omega = \sin\theta \, d\theta \, d\phi$. In general, however, solid angles can have other shapes. The solid angle of area A/r^2 that subtends all of a sphere may be determined as follows:

$$\Omega = \frac{A}{r^2} = \int_0^{2\pi} \left[\int_0^{\pi} \sin\theta d\theta \right] d\phi = \int_0^{2\pi} 2d\phi = 4\pi \tag{3–12}$$

3.3.3. Radiation Intensity

The power P radiated by an antenna is equal to $p(\theta, \phi, r)dA$ integrated over a surface enclosing the antenna, where

- r = distance from origin to surface of sphere
- $p(\theta, \phi, r)$ = power density at θ, ϕ, and r
- $dA = r^2 \sin\theta\, d\theta\, d\phi$ = incremental area at θ, ϕ, and r normal to the propagation direction
- $p(\theta, \phi, r)dA$ = incremental power in area dA at θ, ϕ, and r

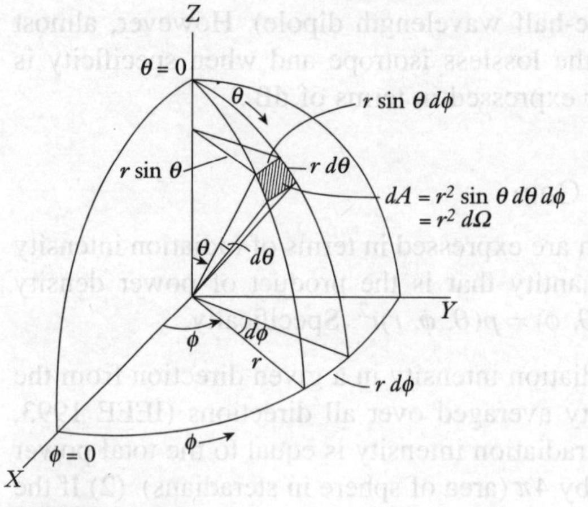

FIGURE 3–4.

The solid angle $d\Omega$ subtends area dA, and consequently the solid angle $d\Omega = r^2 \sin\theta\, d\theta$.

Now, using the coordinates of Fig. 3–4, let an antenna be at the center of the sphere. Then, the total radiated power P can be determined by summing the incremental power $p(\theta, \phi, r)dA$ over the surface, as follows:

$$P = \oint_{surface} p(\theta, \phi, r)dA = \int_0^{2\pi}\int_0^{\pi} p(\theta, \phi, r) r^2 \sin\theta\, d\theta\, d\phi \qquad (3\text{–}13)$$

The power density varies as $1/r^2$, and thus the product $p(\theta, \phi, r)r^2$ is independent of distance r from antenna. This range-independent product is defined as the radiation intensity U. Therefore

$$U(\theta, \phi) = p(\theta, \phi, r) r^2 \qquad (3\text{–}14)$$

and the incremental power that crosses surface area dA is

$$dP = p(\theta, \phi, r)dA = p(\theta, \phi, r) r^2 \sin\theta\, d\theta\, d\phi = U(\theta, \phi)\, d\Omega$$

where $d\Omega = \sin\theta\, d\theta\, d\phi$. Thus, the radiation intensity $U(\theta, \phi)$ is $dP/d\Omega$, that is, the incremental power per unit solid angle in direction (θ, ϕ). $U(\theta, \phi)$ is usually expressed in units of watts per steradian (i.e., watts per square radian). Then, from (3–13) and (3–14), total radiated power P is

$$P = \int_0^{2\pi}\int_0^{\pi} p(\theta, \phi, r) r^2 \sin\theta\, d\theta\, d\phi = \int_0^{2\pi}\int_0^{\pi} U(\theta, \phi)\, d\Omega \qquad (3\text{–}15)$$

In other words, total radiated power equals the sum of all radiation intensity that encloses the antenna.

3.3.4. Directivity

Directivity D is a quantitative measure of an antenna's ability to concentrate energy in a certain direction. Specifically, D is the ratio of the maximum radiation intensity U_{max} to the average radiation intensity U_{av}. Then

$$\text{Directivity} = U_{max}/U_{av} \quad \text{(dimensionless)} \tag{3–16}$$

If the radiation is isotropic, the radiation intensity in every direction is U_{av}. Thus, from (3–12) and (3–15), total radiated power P is a sphere's solid angle 4π times U_{av} and is given by (3–17)

$$P = 4\pi U_{av} \tag{3–17}$$

Now, by using (3–15), (3–16) and (3–17), directivity can be expressed as

$$\frac{U_{max}}{U_{av}} = \frac{4\pi U_{max}}{P} = \frac{4\pi U_{max}}{\int_0^{2\pi}\int_0^{\pi} U(\theta,\phi)\sin\theta\, d\theta\, d\phi} \tag{3–18}$$

Now, by shifting the constant U_{max} to the denominator, it is seen from (3–19) that D is a function the relative value on $U(\theta, \phi)$ (the bracketed term) that has a maximum of unity:

$$D = \frac{4\pi}{\int_0^{2\pi}\int_0^{\pi}\left[\frac{U(\theta,\phi)}{U_{max}}\right]\sin\theta\, d\theta\, d\phi} \tag{3–19}$$

The bracketed term of (3–19) can be replaced by functions, at a fixed distance, of power density $p(\theta, \phi, r)$ or electric field strength $E(\theta, \phi, r)$. This is because, with r constant,

$$U(\theta,\phi)/U_{max} = p(\theta,\phi,r)/p(\theta,\phi,r)_{max} = |E(\theta,\phi,r)/E(\theta,\phi,r)_{max}|^2 \tag{3–20}$$

Therefore, with r fixed, D can be determined with relative values of either $U(\theta, \phi)$, $p(\theta, \phi, r)$, or $|E(\theta, \phi, r)|^2$.

It is also to be noted that directivity D of (3–19) can be expressed as

$$D = \frac{4\pi}{\Omega_A} \tag{3–21}$$

where Ω_A is known as the beam solid angle. For the special case of an isotrope, since an isotrope radiates equally in all directions, $\Omega_A = 4\pi$ and $D = 1$. In general, however,

$$\Omega_A = \int_0^{2\pi}\int_0^{\pi}\left[\frac{U(\theta,\phi)}{U_{max}}\right]\sin\theta\, d\theta\, d\phi \tag{3–22}$$

and with r constant, $U(\theta, \phi)/U_{max}$ can be replaced with either $p(\theta, \phi, r)/p(\theta, \phi, r)_{max}$ or $|E(\theta, \phi, r)/E(\theta, \phi, r)_{max}|^2$. Use of the term Ω_A in (3–21) helps to emphasize that directivity is a measure of an antenna's ability to concentrate energy in a certain direction. Finally, it is important to again underscore that directivity is calculated by integrating relative values of an antenna's radiation pattern, and this does not require knowledge of an absolute value.

3.3.5. Gain

Gain, previously defined in sec. 3.3.1, is the ratio of the radiation intensity in a given direction to the radiation intensity that would be obtained if the power were radiated isotropically. If the direction is not specified, the direction of maximum radiation intensity U_{max} is implied. In addition, for isotropically radiated power, the radiation intensity is U_{av}. Therefore, for a lossless antenna, gain G equals directivity as defined previously by (3–16).

Gain is determined, in principle, by comparing the radiation intensity if both the actual test antenna and an isotrope have the same input power. The isotrope is assumed to radiate all of its input power, but some of the power delivered to the actual antenna may be dissipated in ohmic resistance (i.e., converted to heat). Thus, gain takes into account the antenna efficiency as well as its directional properties. The efficiency factor k is the ratio of the power radiated by the antenna to the total input power. Thus, the relationship between gain G and directivity D is

$$G = kD \tag{3–23}$$

where $0 \le k \le 1$ to account for dissipative (I^2R) losses.

It is apparent that the quantity of greatest significance to a system designer is gain. The antenna theorist, on the other hand, finds the concept of directivity convenient, for it depends only upon the pattern of the antenna. The theorist can compute the directive gain of a half-wave dipole, for example, by application of Maxwell's equations and the assumption that the dipole has no ohmic loss. The directivity of an isotrope, incidentally, is by definition unity, and the gain of an isotrope with efficiency factor k is (also by definition) equal to k.

Antenna gain is a power ratio. Values of gain of practical antennas may range from near zero (total loss) to as much as 10^6 or more. As with any power ratio, antenna gain may be expressed in decibels. The antenna gain G expressed in decibels is $G_{dB} = 10\log G$, where the word log denotes the common logarithm (base 10). Directivity in decibels is calculated using the same formula, with D substituted for G. Gain is expressed in decibels more commonly than as a power ratio.

3.4. Effective Area and Friis Transmission Equation

Although there is a reciprocal relationship between the transmitting and receiving properties of *reciprocal* antennas, it is sometimes more convenient to describe the receiving properties in a somewhat different way. Whereas the gain is the natural parameter to use for describing the increased power density of the transmitted signal due to the directional properties of the antenna, a related quantity called the *effective area*, is a more natural parameter for describing the reception properties of the antenna.

The effective area of an antenna A_e is defined as follows. Suppose that a distant transmitter radiates a signal that, at the receiving-antenna location, has a power density p_r. This is the amount of power incident on, or passing through, each *unit area* of any imaginary surface perpendicular to the direction of propagation of the waves.

A receiving antenna exposed to this field will have radio-frequency current and voltage induced in it, and at the antenna terminals this voltage and current represent radio-frequency power that can be delivered to a load (e.g., the input circuit of a receiver). In principle the power available at these terminals can be measured (although in practice it may be so small a power that amplifying equipment will be needed to measure it). This power, however small, is the *received signal power*, P_r. It can be deduced that in order for this amount of power to appear at the antenna output terminals, the antenna had to "capture" power from the field over a surface in space (oriented perpendicularly to the direction of the wave) of area A_e such that

$$P_r = p_r A_e \tag{3–24}$$

The area A_e, which bears this relationship to P_r and p_r, is the effective area of the antenna. (The conception of the capture process thus conveyed is a much oversimplified one, but it has validity for the present purposes.) Since received power depends on the antenna polarization, effective area is a function of the polarization of the incident field.

As might be supposed, there is a connection between the effective area of an antenna and its physical area as viewed from the direction of the incoming signal. The two areas are not equal, however, although for certain types of high-gain antennas they may be nearly equal. But some antennas of physically small cross section may have considerably larger effective areas. It is as though such an antenna has the ability to "reach out" and capture power from an area larger than its physical size, as in the case of a dipole antenna.

As is discussed in sec. 5.7.6, there is also a relationship between the gain of a lossless antenna and its physical size. This relationship suggests that there may also be a connection between the gain and the effective area, and this indeed turns out to be true. The equation relating the two quantities is

$$A_e = \frac{G\lambda^2}{4\pi} \tag{3–25}$$

where λ is the wavelength corresponding to the frequency of the signal. (This relationship may be proved theoretically and verified experimentally.)

Because of this connection between the effective area and the gain, (3–24) may be rewritten, with the right-hand side of (3–25) substituted for A_e. Thus:

$$P_r = \frac{p_r G\lambda^2}{4\pi} \tag{3–26}$$

Therefore the concept of the effective area of an antenna is not a necessary one. As (3–26) shows, it is possible to calculate the received-signal power without knowing A_e. As seen, the effective area definition has a conceptual value, however, and is a convenient quantity to employ in some types of problems. We now consider the relationship between transmit and receive powers with two antennas separated by far-field distance R. This relationship is highly useful, and it is known as the Friis Transmission Equation (Friis 1946). The following abbreviations are used:

P_r = received power
P_t = input power of transmit antenna
A_{et} = effective aperture of transmit antenna
A_{er} = effective aperture of receive antenna
G_t = gain of transmit antenna
G_r = gain of receive antenna

Now, from equation (3–11) for a lossless isotropic radiator and the definition of gain, the power density p_r at distance R from a transmit antenna may be expressed as $(P_t/4\pi R^2)G_t$. Recall that another antenna in the presence of p_r will receive power P_r that equals $p_r A_{er}$. Thus P_r becomes $(P_t/4\pi R^2)A_{er}G_t$. Finally, we use relationships, based on (3–25), between G_r and A_{er} and between G_t and A_{et} to express P_r as functions of $A_{et}A_{er}$ and of G_rG_t. The result is the Friis Transmission Equation which is given in (3–27) that follows.

$$P_r = \left(\frac{P_t}{4\pi R^2}\right) A_{er} G_t = P_t \frac{A_{et} A_{er}}{R^2 \lambda^2} = P_t \frac{G_t G_r \lambda^2}{(4\pi)^2 R^2} \tag{3–27}$$

When reciprocity applies, as is usually so, the effective transmit aperture area A_{et} of an antenna equals its effective receive aperture area A_{er}. Similarly, transmit gain G_t and receive gain G_r of an antenna are equal. Then, because of reciprocity, the transmitter and receiver locations can be interchanged. Thus, either antenna can be designated as the transmit antenna and the other as the receive antenna.

Equation (3–27) underscores the practical significance of gain. For example, a transmit power of 1,000 watts and a transmit antenna gain of 10 (10 dB) will provide the same received power as will a transmit power of 500 watts and a transmit antenna gain of 20

(13 dB). Obviously, this relationship has great economic significance. Sometimes it may be much less expensive to double antenna gain (add 3 dB) than it would be to double transmit power (though in other cases the converse may be true). Generally, it is desirable to use as much antenna gain as feasible, because it increases received signals.

3.5. Beamwidth

When the radiated power of an antenna is concentrated into a single major "lobe," as exemplified by the pattern of Fig. 3–2, the angular width of this lobe is the *beamwidth*. The term is applicable only to antennas whose patterns are of this general type. Some antennas have a pattern consisting of many lobes, for example, all of them more or less comparable in their maximum power density, or gain, and not necessarily all of the same angular width. One would not speak of the beamwidth of such an antenna, but a large class of antennas do have patterns to which the beamwidth parameter may be appropriately applied.

3.5.1. Practical Significance of Beamwidth

If an antenna has a narrow beam and is used for reception, it can be used to determine the direction from which the received signal is arriving, and consequently it provides information on the direction of the transmitter. To be useful for this purpose, the antenna beam must be "steerable," that is, capable of being pointed in various directions. It is intuitively apparent that for this direction-finding application, a narrow beam is desirable and the accuracy of direction determination will be inversely proportional to the beamwidth, assuming no errors in other parts of the system (although in practice this is not always a good assumption). Its relation to direction-finding accuracy is one significant aspect of the beamwidth parameter. This, however, is by no means its only practical significance.

In some applications a receiver may be unable to discriminate completely against an unwanted signal that is either at the same frequency as the desired signal or on nearly the same frequency. In such a case, pointing a narrow receiving-antenna beam in the direction of the desired signal is helpful; the resulting greater gain of the antenna for the desired signal, and reduced gain for the undesired one, may provide the necessary discrimination. If the directions of the desired and undesired signals are widely separated, even a relatively wide beam will suffice. But the closer the two signals are in direction, the narrower the beam must be to provide effective discrimination. (In radar systems the analogous problem is the ability to distinguish two targets that are close together in bearing, that is, in direction angle; this ability is called angular resolving power or resolution.)

Finally, as the foregoing discussion of gain and directivity (sec. 3.3) indicated, there is a relationship between the solid-angle width of an antenna beam and its directivity (also see sec. 3.11). Thus, with some exceptions, generally a narrower beam implies a greater gain. Since gain is usually a desirable property, this relationship constitutes an additional virtue of narrow beamwidth.

On the other hand, there are situations that call for a wide beam. For example, a broadcasting station must radiate a signal simultaneously to listeners in many different directions—typically, over a 360 degree azimuth sector. Any narrowing of the beam to obtain gain must therefore be done in the vertical plane. At the low frequencies of the AM broadcast band (535–1,705 kHz), and at lower frequencies, such vertical-plane beam narrowing is not feasible because it would require an impractically large (high) antenna. In television and FM broadcasting in the VHF and UHF bands, however, this means of obtaining gain while preserving 360 degree azimuthal coverage is much used. A situation in which an antenna beam must be moderately broad in the vertical plane is that of a search radar antenna on a ship that rolls and pitches. It is usually required that the beam of such antenna be directed at the horizon. But if the beam has, say, a 2-degree vertical beamwidth, and the ship rolls 20 degrees (which is not unusual), it is evident that at times no part of the beam will remain directed at the horizon. The vertical beamwidth in this case must be of size comparable to the maximum roll angle of the ship, unless some method of stabilizing the beam is employed (as is sometimes done).

3.5.2. Beamwidth Definition

As illustrated in Fig. 3–2, an antenna beam is typically round-nosed. Defining beamwidth, therefore, is a problem. As seen clearly in the rectangular plot, Fig. 3–2b, it would be possible in this case to cite the width of the beam between the two nulls (zero values) on either side of the maximum, since these are two definitely measurable points. Not all beams have such nulls, however, although they are present ordinarily. Moreover, it is logical to define the width of a beam in such a way that it indicates the angular range within which radiation of useful strength is obtained, or over which good reception may be expected. From this point of view the convention has been adopted of measuring beamwidth between the points on the beam pattern at which the power density is half the value at the maximum. (On a plot of the electric-intensity pattern, the corresponding points are those at which the intensity is equal to $1/\sqrt{2}$ or 0.707 of the maximum value.)

The angular width of the beam between these points is called the *half-power beamwidth*. When a beam pattern is plotted with the ordinate scale in decibels, as is frequently done, the half-power points correspond to the minus 3 dB points. For this reason the half-power beamwidth is often referred to as the 3 *dB beamwidth*. Figure 3–5 illustrates the procedure of determining the 3 dB beamwidth on a rectangular pattern plot. Only the nose region of the beam pattern is shown. As indicated, this beamwidth is approximately 10 degrees.

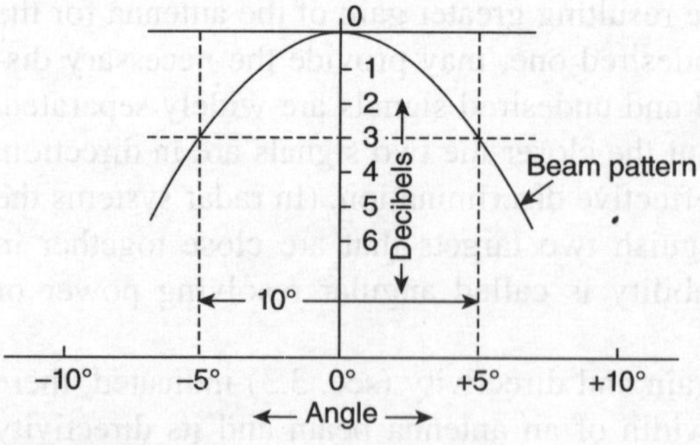

FIGURE 3–5.

Determination of half-power (3 dB down) beamwidth.

This criterion of beamwidth, although adequate and convenient in many situations, does not always provide a sufficient description of the beam characteristics. Beams have different shapes. An additional description may be given by measuring the width of the beam at several points, for example, at –3 dB, –10 dB, and at the nulls (if they are present). Some beams may have an asymmetric shape, for some special reason, and the specific nature of the asymmetry may be important. Special methods of describing such beams can be employed. In the final analysis the best description of a beam is a plot of its pattern.

3.5.3. Principal-Plane Beamwidths

An antenna beam occupies a solid angle, and a single beamwidth figure refers only to the pattern in a particular plane. It is apparent that the beam may have different widths in different planes through the beam axis. (The axis is the direction of maximum radiation, a line from the antenna passing through the nose of the beam.) Therefore it is customary to give the widths of the beam in two planes at right angles, usually the principal planes of the coordinate system. The beamwidths in planes at intermediate angles will generally have intermediate values, so that giving just these two beamwidth figures conveys considerable information concerning the solid-angular shape of the beam. When the beam is linearly polarized, the beamwidth in the plane containing the E-vector (plane of polarization) is sometimes called the E-plane beamwidth, and that in the perpendicular plane the H-plane beamwidth.

3.6. Minor Lobes

A directional antenna usually has, in addition to a main beam or major lobe of radiation, several smaller lobes in other directions; they are *minor lobes* of the pattern. Those adjacent to the main lobe are *sidelobes*, and those that occupy the hemisphere in the direction opposite to the main-beam direction are *back lobes*. Minor lobes ordinarily represent radiation (or reception) in undesired directions, and the antenna designer therefore attempts to minimize their level relative to that of the main beam. This level is expressed in terms of the ratio of the power densities in the mainbeam maximum and in the strongest minor lobe. This ratio is often expressed in decibels.

Since the sidelobes are usually the largest of the minor lobes, this ratio is often called the sidelobe ratio or sidelobe level. A typical sidelobe level, for an antenna in which some attempt has been made to reduce the sidelobe level, is 20 dB, which means that the power density in the strongest sidelobe is one percent of the power density in the main beam. Sidelobe levels of practical well-designed directional antennas typically range from about 13 dB (power-density ratio 20) to about 40 dB (power-density ratio 10^4). Attainment of a sidelobe level better than 30 dB requires very careful design and construction, but better than 50 dB (10^5) has sometimes been accomplished.

Figure 3–6 shows a typical antenna pattern with a main beam and minor lobes, plotted on a decibel scale to facilitate determination of the sidelobe level, which is here seen to be 25 dB.

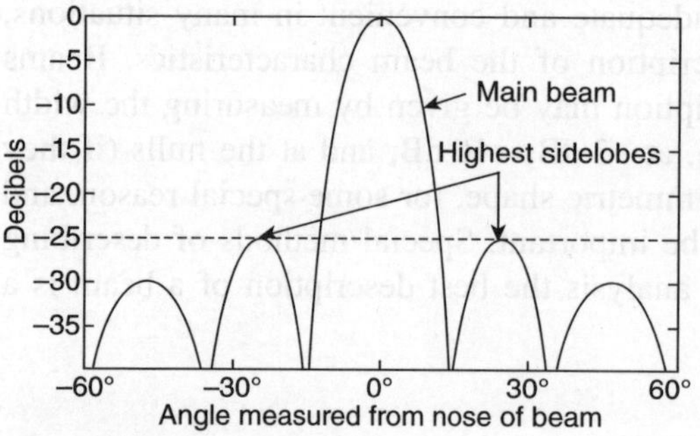

FIGURE 3–6.

Decibel pattern plot, indicating sidelobe level.

In some applications sidelobes are not especially harmful unless their level becomes comparable to the main-beam level; in other applications it may be important to hold the sidelobe level to an absolute minimum. In most radar systems, for example, a low sidelobe level is important. Since signals received in a sidelobe are ordinarily indistinguishable from signals received from the main beam, a large target located in the direction of one of the antenna sidelobes (or even a back lobe) may appear to the radar as though it were a target in the main beam. Such sidelobe echoes create "clutter" on the radar output that may mask main-beam echoes from smaller targets and overload the data-processing personnel or equipment. Therefore radar antennas are often designed for sidelobe levels of −25 dB or better in the horizontal-plane patterns. Sidelobes in the vertical-plane patterns may also be harmful in height finding radars but do no harm in search radars that provide angle information only in the azimuth plane, except to the extent that they represent wasted power.

3.7. Radiation Resistance and Efficiency

In a large class of antennas the radiation is associated with a flow of rf current in a conductor or conductors. Thus, when a current I flows in a resistance R, an amount of power $P = RI^2$ will be dissipated and converted into heat. In an antenna, even if there were no resistance in the conductors, the electrical energy supplied by the transmitter is radiated and it is in a sense "lost." It is customary to associate this "loss" of power through radiation with a fictitious "radiation resistance," that bears the same relationship to the current and the radiated power as an actual resistance bears to the current and dissipated power. If the power radiated by the antenna is P and the antenna rms current is I, the radiation resistance is

$$R_r = \frac{P}{I^2} \tag{3–28}$$

The concept of radiation resistance is applicable only to antennas in which the radiation is associated with a definite current in a single linear conductor. Even then, the definition of radiation resistance is ambiguous. This is because of standing waves, the current is not the same everywhere along a linear conductor. It is therefore necessary to specify the point along the conductor at which the current will be measured. Two points sometimes specified are where the current has its maximum value and the feed point (input terminals). These two points are sometimes at the same place, as in a center-fed dipole, but they are not always the same. And in principle, *any* point may be specified. The value then obtained for the radiation resistance of the antenna depends on what point is specified; this value is the radiation resistance *referred to that point.*

The above words "maximum current" refer to the rms current in that part of the antenna where the current is maximum. It does *not* mean the *peak* value of the current located where the current is greatest. The reader will recall that, in accordance with equation (1–3), by definition the *amplitude* I_0 of a current sine wave is actually the peak value of current during its cycle. Furthermore, the reader is cautioned that, in some texts, formulas for radiation resistance are written as a function of current "amplitude" I_0, instead of rms current. Thus, use of the wrong combination of formula and current level will cause the radiation resistance to be incorrectly calculated.

The radiation resistance of some types of antennas can be calculated, and yet not for others. Sometimes radiation resistance can be obtained by measurement (see section 9.10, chapter 9). Typical values of the input radiation resistance of actual antennas range from a fraction of an ohm to several hundred ohms. The very low values are undesirable, because they imply large antenna currents (i.e., $P = I^2R$). Therefore, there exists the possibility of considerable ohmic loss of power, that is, dissipation of power as heat rather than as radiation. An excessively high value of radiation resistance is also undesirable, because this requires that a very high voltage (i.e., $P = E^2/R$) be applied to the antenna.

Antennas always have ohmic resistance, although sometimes it may be so small as to be negligible. The ohmic resistance is usually distributed over the antenna; and since the antenna current varies, the resulting loss may be quite complicated to calculate. In general, however, the actual loss can be considered to be equivalent to the loss in a fictitious lumped resistance placed in series with the radiation resistance. If this equivalent ohmic loss resistance is denoted by R_0, the full power (dissipated plus radiated) is $I^2(R_0 + R_r)$, whereas the radiated power is I^2R_r. Hence the antenna radiation efficiency k of (3–23) is given by

$$k_r = \frac{R_r}{R_0 + R_r} \qquad (3\text{–}29)$$

It must be acknowledged, however, that this definition of the efficiency is not really very useful even though it may occasionally be convenient. The fact is that both R_0 and R_r are fictitious quantities, derived from measurements of current and power; R_r is given in these terms by (3–28), and R_0 is correspondingly equal to P_0/I^2. Making these substitutions into (3–29) gives the more basic definition of the efficiency:

$$k_r = \frac{P_r}{P_0 + P_r} \qquad (3\text{–}30)$$

where P_r is the power radiated, and P_0 is the power dissipated.

3.8. Input Impedance

Rf current usually reaches to the antenna through a transmission line. The antenna input is at the point where the transmission line is connected to the antenna. At this location the antenna presents a load impedance to the transmission line, for example, Z_L of Fig. 2–2. This impedance is the input impedance of the antenna, and an impedance mismatch occurs unless the input impedance equals the characteristic impedance of the line Z_0. A mismatch leads to loss of power transfer and creates a standing wave on the line. Aside from the loss of power transfer, standing waves are the source of increased voltage along the transmission line. Consequently, because input impedance of the antenna in relation to Z_0 controls the standing wave ratio, it is a very important parameter. Measurement of the antenna input impedance is discussed in sec. 9.11.

In addition to its importance in determining whether or not there will be a standing wave on the transmission line, the input impedance determines how large a voltage must be applied at the antenna input terminals to obtain the desired current flow and hence the desired amount of radiated power. The impedance is in fact equal to the ratio of the input voltage E_i to the input current I_i, by definition:

$$Z_i = \frac{E_i}{I_i} \tag{3–31}$$

This impedance is in general complex. If the antenna input is at a current maximum, and if there is no reactive component to the input impedance, Z_i will be equal to the sum of the radiation resistance and the loss resistance; that is:

$$Z_i = R_i = R_r + R_0 \tag{3–32}$$

The input impedance will be nonreactive for this feed point if the antenna is resonant (as in the case of a wire approximately an integral number of half wavelengths long, discussed in secs. 4.2–4.4) or if the antenna is *terminated* by a resistance of proper value at its far end so that there is no standing wave of current on it (as described in sec. 4.4). In other cases, however, the input impedance may consist effectively of the radiation and loss resistances in series with a very high reactance.

If this reactance has a large value, the antenna input voltage must be very large to produce an appreciable input current. If in addition the radiation resistance is very small, the input current must be very large to produce appreciable radiated power. Obviously this combination of circumstances, which occurs with the "short dipole" antennas that must be used at very low frequencies, results in a very difficult "feed" impedance-matching problem. Methods of solving it are described in sec. 4.1 and 4.11.

The concepts of radiation resistance and feed point or input impedance have been discussed here in terms of antennas that have currents flowing in linear conductors as the basis of the radiation. As will be discussed in secs. 4.7, 4.8, and 4.10, other types of antennas exist with radiating properties difficult to analyze in these terms. They are, for example, fed by waveguides rather than by transmission lines. The equivalent of an input impedance can be defined at the point of connection of the waveguide to the antenna, just as waveguides have a characteristic wave impedance analogous to the characteristic impedance of a transmission line. It is difficult to define a "radiation resistance" for such antennas.

Even for some types of antennas consisting of current-carrying conductors this is difficult, and it may even be difficult to define an input impedance. This is true, for example, of an array of dipoles, when each dipole is fed separately; sometimes each dipole, or groups of dipoles, will be connected to separate transmitting amplifiers and receiving amplifiers. The input impedance of each dipole or group may then be defined, but the concept becomes meaningless for the antenna as a whole, as does also the radiation resistance. Both these terms have meaning primarily for simple linear-current radiating elements; but they comprise a very large class of antennas.

3.9. Bandwidth

All antennas are limited in the range of frequency over which they will operate satisfactorily. This frequency range, whatever it may be, is called the *bandwidth* of the antenna. If an antenna were capable of operating satisfactorily from a minimum frequency of 195 MHz to a maximum frequency of 205 MHz, its bandwidth would be 10 MHz. It would also be said to have a 5 percent bandwidth (the actual bandwidth divided by the center frequency of the band, times 100). This would be considered a "moderate" bandwidth. Some antennas are required to operate only at a fixed frequency with a signal that is narrow in its bandwidth; consequently there is no bandwidth problem in designing such an antenna. But in other applications much greater bandwidths may be required; in such cases special techniques are needed. Such techniques are known and will be described in secs. 7–1 and 7–2. In fact, some recent developments in broad-band antennas permit bandwidths so great that they are described by giving the numerical ratio of the highest to the lowest operating frequency, rather than as a percentage of the center frequency. In these terms, bandwidths of 20 to 1 are readily achieved with these antennas, and ratios as great as 100 to 1 are possible.

The bandwidth of an antenna is not as precise a concept as some of the other parameters that have been described, because many factors are involved in what is meant by "operating satisfactorily." The principal ones are input impedance, radiation efficiency, gain, beamwidth, beam direction, polarization, and sidelobe level.

These may not all be involved in every case, because one or another of them may be so much more critical than the others, in a particular case, that it alone determines the bandwidth. The two basic factors involved, between which a distinct separation may be made, are the antenna pattern and the input impedance. Accordingly, the terms *pattern bandwidth* and *impedance bandwidth* are sometimes used to emphasize this distinction. The beamwidth, gain, sidelobe level, beam direction, and polarization are parameters associated with the pattern bandwidth, whereas input impedance, radiation resistance, and efficiency are associated with the impedance bandwidth.

The definition of the bandwidth of an antenna is less precise than the definitions of other parameters for still another reason: there is no established criterion of "satisfactory" operation. In some applications, for example, an impedance variation of a factor of 2 over the operating frequency band may be acceptable; in others only a 10 percent variation may be tolerated. Similar statements apply to variations of beamwidth, gain, and so forth. When an antenna bandwidth figure is given, therefore, it should always be accompanied by a statement of "satisfactory operation" on which it is based, unless these criteria are fairly well established for the particular application involved.

Two categories of bandwidth requirement exist, and sometimes they allow different approaches. In some cases (category 1) the antenna is required to handle frequencies over a wide band simultaneously. This is called instantaneous bandwidth. An example is an antenna that must function properly when passing short pulses (wide bandwidths). There are also cases (category 2) in which the range of frequencies is covered over a period of time, but at any one time the bandwidth requirement is only a fraction of the long-term requirement. This is sometimes called tunable bandwidth. An example of this is a communication antenna that may operate with its carrier frequency anywhere within a band of 15 MHz, for instance, in the region of 300 MHz, a bandwidth requirement of 5 percent. But when it is operating at a particular time, its transmitted signal may cover a bandwidth of, for example, 50 kHz—a bandwidth of less than 0.02 percent. It is possible, in such a situation, for an operator to readjust the antenna impedance, if necessary, when the frequency of operation is changed.

These examples illustrate fundamental differences between instantaneous and tunable bandwidths. The first category presents the most difficult problem of course, because the antenna must meet the requirement without the possibility of any adjustments being made in going from one frequency to another. However, even when the bandwidth requirement is of the second type, it may be desirable to meet it without requiring adjustments to be made; the decision is primarily an economic one.

3.10. Polarization

The radiation of an antenna may be linearly, elliptically, or circularly polarized, as defined in sec. 1.1.4 (also see Appendix B). Polarization in one part of the total pattern may be different from polarization in another. For example, the polarization may be different in the minor lobes and in the main lobe, or may even vary in different parts of the main lobe.

The simplest antennas radiate (and receive) linearly polarized waves. They are usually oriented so that the polarization (direction of the electric vector) is either horizontal or vertical. Sometimes the choice is dictated by necessity, at other times by preference based on technical advantages, and sometimes one polarization is as good and as easily achieved as the other.

For example, at the very low frequencies it is practically impossible to radiate a horizontally polarized wave successfully (because it will be virtually canceled by the radiation from the image of the antenna in the earth); also, vertically polarized waves propagate much more successfully at these frequencies (e.g., below 1,000 kHz). Therefore vertical polarization is practically required at these frequencies.

At the frequencies of television broadcasting (between 54 and 698 MHz), horizontal polarization has been adopted as standard. This choice was made to maximize signal-to-noise ratios; it was found that the majority of man-made noise signals are predominantly vertically polarized. (Interestingly, in Great Britain the opposite choice was made, because from the pure wave-propagation point of view, vertical polarization provides maximum signal strength.)

At the microwave frequencies (above 1 GHz) there is little basis for a choice of horizontal or vertical polarization, although in specific applications there may be some possible advantage in one or the other. Of course in communication circuits it is essential that the transmitting and receiving antennas be polarization matched.

Circular polarization has advantages in some VHF, UHF, and microwave applications. For example, in transmission of VHF and low-UHF signals through the ionosphere, rotation of the polarization vector occurs, the amount of rotation being generally unpredictable. Therefore if a linear polarization is transmitted it is advantageous to have a circularly polarized receiving antenna (which can receive either polarization), or vice versa. Maximum power transfer is realized when both antennas are either left- or right-circularly polarized. (This applies, for example, to transmission and reception between the earth and a space vehicle.) Circular polarization has also been found to be of advantage in some microwave radar applications to minimize the "clutter" echoes received from raindrops, in relation to the echoes from larger targets such as aircraft.

It is apparent that the polarization properties of an antenna are an important part of its technical description—a parameter of its performance. Sometimes it may be desirable to provide a "polarization pattern" of the antenna, that is, a description of the polarization radiated as a function of angles within a spherical coordinate system, although such a complete picture of the polarization is not ordinarily required.

3.11. Interdependencies of Gain, Beamwidths, and Aperture Dimensions

Aperture area controls directivity and gain, linear dimensions control beamwidths and area, and thus directivity and gain depend on beamwidths. These interdependencies of directivity and gain, beamwidths, linear dimensions, and area on one another are important to the antenna design process, and are outlined below.

Equation (3–25) relates effective receive area A_e to gain G and wavelength λ. Because of reciprocity, it is applicable to both effective transmit and receive areas. The general relationship from antenna theory (Silver 1949, sec. 6.4) for directivity D is related to maximum effective area A_{em} and wavelength λ as follows:

$$D = (4\pi A_{em})/\lambda^2 \tag{3–33}$$

Since gain $G = kD$ from (3–23), we can express G in terms of an effective area A_e and λ as

$$G = (4\pi A_e)/\lambda^2 \tag{3–34}$$

where $k = A_e/A_{em}$.

The definitions of A_{em} and A_e are defined by (3–33) and (3–34). Physical aperture A_p is another frequently used aperture term, but it is less clearly defined. Obviously, A_p is a measure of the physical size of an antenna and it is an area over which radiation is transmitted or received. Physical area for a horn or reflector antenna can be readily visualized. Presumably A_p for a stub antenna is its cross-sectional area, but what about one attached to an automobile which affects its radiation pattern? Another definition sometimes used is aperture efficiency ε_{ap}, where

$$\varepsilon_{ap} = A_e/A_p \tag{3–35}$$

Depending on how A_p is defined, ε_{ap} can exceed unity. For a uniformly continuously illuminated aperture, that is, one for which the amplitude and phase are both constant over the physical area, $A_{em} = A_p$. This can be shown to be true from results of integrating the total radiation pattern for a uniformly illuminated aperture and calculating D from (3–33), as done by Silver (1949, p. 183). Thus, for a lossless, uniformly continuously-illuminated aperture $\varepsilon_{ap} = A_e/A_p = 1$ and

$$D = (4\pi A_p)/\lambda^2 \quad \text{(lossless, uniform illumination)} \tag{3–36}$$

The actual gain of an antenna is of course less than D of (3–36), because of losses that may occur from large and extraneous sidelobes, impedance mismatches, and dissipative (I^2R) losses.

Theoretically, the half-power beamwidth θ_{HP} for a uniformly illuminated line source is

$$\theta_{HP} = 50.8\ \lambda/d \quad (\theta_{HP} \text{ in degs., } \lambda/d \text{ dimensionless})$$

or (3–37)

$$\theta_{HP} = 0.887\ \lambda/d \quad (\theta_{HP} \text{ in rads., } \lambda/d \text{ dimensionless})$$

For the equations of (3–37), λ and d are in the same units. The equations of (3–37) can be derived from the pattern for a uniformly illuminated aperture, which is discussed in sec. 6.10.

Now consider a rectangular aperture. Its gain can be determined with (3–36) by expressing physical aperture A_p in terms of principal plane beamwidths, θ_{HP} and ϕ_{HP}, using (3–37). Accordingly, let d_θ and d_ϕ denote the linear dimensions that control the beamwidths in θ and ϕ directions, respectively. Then, theoretically, the gain G for a lossless, uniformly continuously-illuminated aperture is

$$G = 4\pi(d_\theta d_\phi)/\lambda^2 = 4\pi[(50.8\lambda)^2/(\theta_{HP}\cdot\phi_{HP})]/\ \lambda^2 = 32{,}429/(\theta_{HP}\cdot\phi_{HP}) \tag{3–38}$$

with G dimensionless and θ_{HP} and ϕ_{HP} in degrees.

Stutzman (1998) investigated equations for a number of theoretical patterns, including those for this case of a rectangular aperture. He notes that, ordinarily, patterns of real antennas do not have perfectly deep nulls. Also, because of the effects of installation environments, they do not have sidelobes that decrease uniformly at wide-angles, as do theoretical patterns. Further, the gain of an antenna is also reduced by lossy materials (I^2R losses), and the radiated power may be reduced by impedance mismatches. Stutzman suggests, without detailed measurement data being available, that a reasonable approximation, as a general rule, for an antenna having a beam normal to the aperture, is

$$G = 26{,}000/(\theta_{HP}\phi_{HP}) \qquad (G \text{ dimensionless}, \theta_{HP} \text{ and } \phi_{HP} \text{ in degs.}) \tag{3–39}$$

The approximate, "typical" gain of (3–39) is nearly 1.0 dB less than that of (3–38), which is for a lossless, uniformly illuminated rectangular aperture. Furthermore, the use of (3–39) is recommended only if the known antenna efficiency ("k" in $G = kD$) is nearly 1. The point being that directivity and thus gain are reduced by spurious radiation not readily detected and thus not ordinarily accounted for when determining directivity. For example, if only the usual principal-plane measurements are made, there may be unsuspected out-of-plane spurious radiation.

References

Friis, H. T., "A Note on a Simple Transmission Formula," *Proceedings of the IRE*, vol. 34, May, 1946, pp. 254–56.

Hollis, J. S., T. J. Lyon, and L. Clayton, *Microwave Antenna Measurements*, Scientific-Atlanta, Inc., 1970. This publication may be available through MI Technologies, Inc. (www. mi-technologies.com).

Jurgenson, R., and R. G. Brown, *Geometry*, Houghton Mifflin Co., 2000.

IEEE Standard 100-1992, *The New IEEE Standard Dictionary of Electrical and Electronic Terms*, 1993.

Silver, S., *Microwave Antenna Theory and Design*, McGraw-Hill, 1949.

Stutzman, W. L., "Estimating Directivity and Gain of Antennas", *IEEE Antennas and Propagation Magazine*, August, 1998, pp. 7–11.

Terman, F. E., *Radio Engineers' Handbook*, McGraw-Hill, 1943, p. 785.

Problems and Exercises

1. Indicate, by placing a letter T or F in each of the boxes, whether you think that the following statements are true (T) or false (F):

   (a) The largest antennas are those used to obtain high gain at high frequencies.

(b) A steel tower can be used to support an antenna, or sometimes it can itself be the antenna.

(c) The place at which the feed line connects to an antenna is called its input terminals or input port.

(d) Guy wires of antenna towers should be interrupted by insulators spaced a half-wavelength apart.

(e) Solid copper is always the preferred form of conductor for an antenna.

(f) A radome is a dome-shaped radar antenna.

2. A directional antenna has a maximum electrical dimension of 50 meters, and its operating frequency is 100 MHz (10^8 Hz). A field strength measurement is made at a distance of 1 km from this antenna, in the main beam. (a) Is this a near-field or a far-field measurement? (b) What is the approximate distance at which the near field ends and the far field begins?

3. The solid angle subtended by the sun as viewed from the earth is $\Omega = 6 \times 10^{-5}$ steradian. A microwave antenna, designed to be used for studying the microwave radiation from the sun, has a very narrow beam whose "equivalent" solid angle,in the sense of the denominators of equations (3–19) and (3–21), is approximately equal to that subtended by the sun. Assume that this antenna has no minor lobes. What is its approximate *directivity* D? Express this gain as both a power ratio and a decibel value.

4. An antenna radiates a total power of 100 watts. In the direction of maximum radiation, the field strength at a distance of 10 km (10^4 meters) was measured and found to be $E = 12$ millivolts (0.012 volt) per meter. (a) What is the directivity D of this antenna, assuming free-space propagation to the measuring point? (b) If its efficiency factor is $k_R = 0.92$, what is its gain G? (c) If the wavelength is $\lambda = 3$ meters, what is the effective area A_e in square meters?

5. If the operating wavelength of an antenna, whose gain $G = 30{,}000$, is $\lambda = 0.1$ meter, (a) what is its effective area, A_e, and (b) If the *actual* cross-sectional area of the antenna is the same as its effective area, and if the outline of this area is circular, what is the antenna diameter? (Recall from elementary geometry that the area of a circle of diameter d is $\pi(d/2)^2$.)

6. Derive the two forms of the Friis Transmission Equation given in equation (3–27). In doing so, start with equation (3–11) and the definition of gain. (These two forms of the Friis equation are in fact of greater practical value than equations that include power density.)

7. A dipole slightly shorter than a half wavelength, fed at the center, has an input impedance that is purely resistive and of value 75 ohms. The conductor has some ohmic resistance, and the resulting ohmic loss of power is equivalent to what would result if the dipole were a perfect conductor but had a "lumped" resistance of value $R_0 = 8$ ohms connected in series with it at the feed point. (a) What is the radiation resistance, R_r, of the dipole? (b) What is the radiation efficiency factor, k_r? (c) The *directivity* of a dipole approximately a half-wavelength long is $D = 1.64$. What is the *gain*, G, of this particular dipole?

8. The two VHF television bands are 54 to 88 MHz (low band) and 174 to 216 MHz (high band). (a) What are the percentage bandwidths of each of these two bands? (b) If a single receiving antenna is designed to perform satisfactorily at all frequencies between the bottom end of the low band and the top end of the high band, what is its bandwidth, expressed in the conventional way?

9. Assume N isotropes are placed along a line, and are energized equally in amplitude and phase by the same power source. By using equations (1–9) and (3–11), what is the theoretical gain perpendicular to the line of isotropes?

10. List *three* quantities pertaining to the electric field that should be plotted, as functions of the direction angles θ, ϕ, to present all possible information about the antenna pattern in the far field. (*Note*: Do not include the magnetic intensity or the power density, as these are both derivable from a knowledge of the electric field.)

CHAPTER 4

Basic Radiators and Feed Methods

The preceding chapters have been largely groundwork, covering principles, concepts, and terminology, as well as some basic antenna theory. It is now possible to discuss specific antennas.

Initially the basic forms of radiating structures will be discussed. They are sometimes used by themselves as simple antennas; they may be very effective in some applications. They are also used in combination with each other and with other components to form more complicated antennas having special properties such as high directivity, large bandwidth, omnidirectionality, steerable beams, low noise, and so on. These more complicated antennas are described in chapters 5 through 8. The properties of the basic radiators will be discussed in terms of their behavior in free space, except for specific types that require the presence of the earth for their operation, as will be indicated in the discussion. It will also be assumed, except where specifically otherwise stated, that current-carrying portions of the antennas are perfect conductors. The conductors of actual antennas are usually very good so that this assumption is reasonably well approximated in practice. When some conductor losses do occur, the principal effect is to reduce the efficiency, as defined by equation (3–30), chapter 3. Ordinarily the pattern (and hence the directivity and beamwidth) are not seriously affected, although appreciable conductor resistance would affect these parameters also.

4.1. Short Dipoles

Perhaps the simplest and most important radiating structure, from the viewpoint of antenna theory, is the electrically short dipole with uniform current along its length. "Electrically short" means "short compared to a half wavelength."

Throughout this book, the term *short dipole* is understood to mean simply a dipole that is much shorter than a half wavelength, but not necessarily one with a uniform current. The term is generally applied to any dipole that is no longer than about a tenth of a wavelength (0.1λ). Isolated short dipoles do not ordinarily have uniform current throughout their length, but approximate uniformity of the current may be achieved by capacitive end loading, as will be described later in this section.

A short dipole that does have a uniform current will be called an *elemental dipole*. Such a dipole will usually be considerably shorter than the tenth-wavelength maximum specified for a short dipole. The term *infinitesimal dipole* may be used to imply extreme shortness, as required in certain mathematical analyses. Other terms sometimes used for an elemental dipole are *elementary dipole, elementary doublet, and Hertzian dipole*. Part of the importance of this type of dipole is that many more complicated antennas can be analyzed by considering them to be assemblages of many elemental dipoles. For example, a long-wire antenna may be regarded as composed of many elemental dipoles connected end-to-end. Although the current is considered constant (at any instant of time) along the length of each elemental dipole, the currents in different dipoles may be different, both in magnitude and phase; therefore, a nonuniform current in the long wire can be approximated by this representation.

If a center-fed short dipole is initially in a neutral condition and then a current starts to flow in one direction, one half of the dipole will acquire an excess of charge and the other a deficit (since a current is a flow of electrical charge). There will then be a voltage between the two halves of the dipole. If the current then reverses its direction, this charge unbalance will be first neutralized and then reversed. Therefore an oscillating current will result in an oscillating voltage as well (or vice versa). If the current oscillation is sinusoidal, the voltage oscillation will also be sinusoidal and approximately 90 degrees lagging the current in phase angle; that is, the short dipole is capacitive in nature, from the viewpoint of its current-voltage relationship.

Since such a dipole can be regarded as one in which electric charge oscillates, it is an oscillating *electric* dipole. It is distinguished from an oscillating *magnetic* dipole, which is equivalent to a bar magnet whose magnetic strength and polarity oscillate. An example of a magnetic dipole is discussed in sec. 4.5.1.

The current, though uniform throughout the length of the elemental dipole at any instant, is assumed to vary sinusoidally in time, according to (4–1) that follows

$$I(t) = I_0 \sin(2\pi f t + \alpha) \tag{4–1}$$

where $I(t)$ is the current at any time t, I_0 is the amplitude of the current (the rf peak value), f is the frequency in Hertz, t is the time in seconds, and α is the phase angle (which simply means that when $t = 0$, $I(t) = I_0 \sin \alpha$).

4.1.1. Dipole Radiation

It is a well-known fact of elementary electrical theory that current in a wire is accompanied by a magnetic field surrounding the wire, and also that a voltage existing between two conductors, or different parts of a conductor, is associated with an electric field in the intervening and adjoining space. A dipole antenna, therefore, will be surrounded by an electric field and a magnetic field. The nature of these fields at an instant of time *in the vicinity of the dipole* is indicated in Fig. 4–1.

The current and voltage of an rf dipole change direction (polarity) at a rate determined by the frequency f and undergo a sinusoidal variation of their magnitudes as shown (for the current) by (4–1). At a given instant, however, they have a particular direction, and the field lines have a corresponding direction, as shown in Fig. 4–1. When the current direction reverses, the direction of the magnetic field lines reverses also; and when the voltage polarity reverses, the electric field reverses direction.

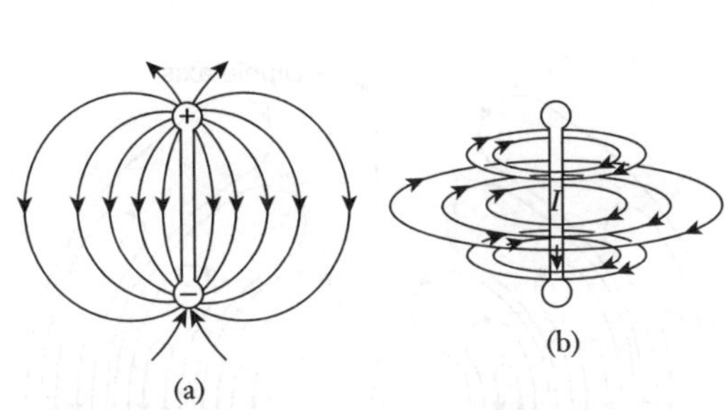

FIGURE 4–1.

Configuration of electric and magnetic fields (approximate) in the immediate vicinity of an elemental-dipole radiator. (a) Electric field lines. (b) Magnetic field lines.

The field lines are shown only in the immediate vicinity of the dipole, and only a few lines are shown. In principle, however, they fill the entire space around the dipole and would extend to an infinite distance from it if the dipole were located in empty space and if the current had been flowing in it for an infinite time. But the fields do not exist at an infinite distance as soon as the current starts flowing. They travel outward from the dipole at the finite speed $c = 3 \times 10^8$ meters per second (in empty space and at practically the same speed in air).

Therefore, by the time the field lines corresponding to a given polarity of the dipole have reached a distance from the dipole equal to $\frac{1}{2}(c/f)$, which is a half wavelength as defined by equation (1–1) of chapter 1, the dipole polarity has reversed, and the new field lines being set up in the region immediately adjoining the dipole have directions opposite to those at the distance $\frac{1}{2}(c/f) = \lambda/2$. As the oscillation of current and voltage in the dipole continues, the outward-traveling field lines will evidently have opposite directions at half-wavelength intervals along the direction of travel. This oscillating outward-traveling field is an *electromagnetic wave*, which has been *radiated* by the dipole. The approximate configuration of the *electric-field component* of this wave, in a region extending several half wavelengths from the dipole, is shown in Fig. 4–2a, and the *magnetic-field component* is shown in Fig. 4–2b.

It is noteworthy that some of the electric field lines, rather than terminating on charges in the conductors, form closed loops in space—something that cannot occur in the *electrostatic* case (where the field is due to a steady or d-c voltage). This field configuration, resulting in *radiation*, is an *electrodynamic* phenomenon; it happens only with varying currents and voltages, and with moving fields. At much greater distances than those shown in Fig. 4–2, however, the "closed ends" of the loops virtually disappear, leaving only field lines that are transverse to the direction of propagation of the waves, as in Fig. 1–1, chapter 1.

Not all the fields in the vicinity of the dipole represent radiation. When the dipole polarity reverses, some of these field components "collapse" upon the conductor, causing induced voltage and current associated with the inductance and capacitance of the dipole conductor. These are the field components that decrease rapidly with distance from the dipole, as discussed in sec. 3.2.5. One component, the *static* field, decreases as the inverse cube ($1/r^3$) of the distance r. A second component, the time varying *reactive* field, decreases as the inverse square ($1/r^2$) of the distance. These two components comprise the

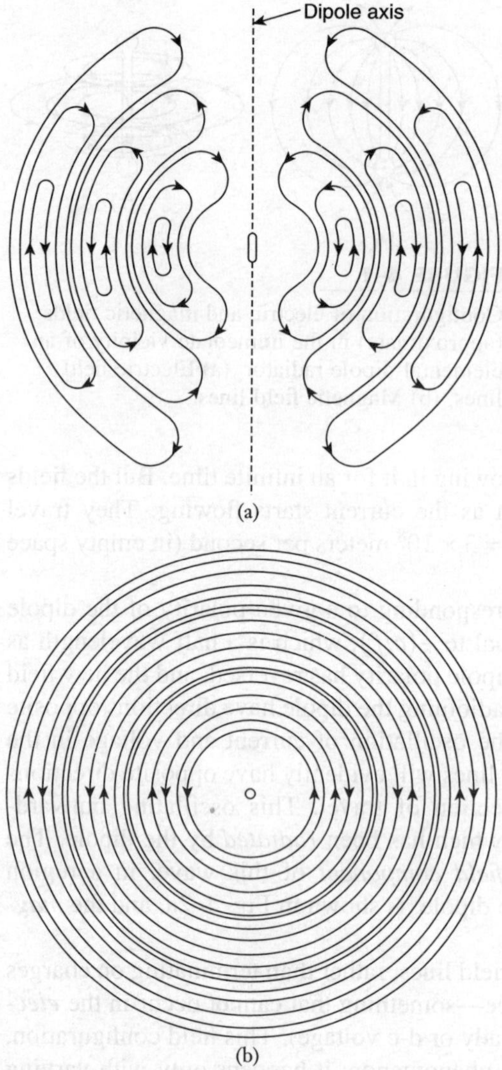

FIGURE 4–2.

Configuration of electric and magnetic field lines in radiation field of an elemental-dipole radiator. (a) Electric field. (b) Magnetic field. Electric field lines are shown in a plane containing the dipole axis, and magnetic field lines are shown in the plane through the center of the dipole perpendicular to its axis. (Dipole is perpendicular to plane of paper in Figure 4–2b.)

near field of the dipole. The third component, which decreases as the inverse first power of the distance ($1/r$), is the *radiation* field. Because of their more rapid decrease with distance, the static and reactive fields become very much smaller than the radiation field at great distances from the dipole; in fact, at a distance of a few wavelengths, the radiation field is so very much the strongest component that the near-field components are virtually negligible. Close to the dipole, however, the near-field components are much stronger than the radiation components.

The existence of a radiation field was unnoticed in the earliest experiments with electricity, because of the dominating reactive fields at short distances. Its existence was first demonstrated about 1887 by the classical experiments of the German physicist Heinrich Hertz, though it had been predicted theoretically about 25 years earlier by the English mathematical physicist James Clerk Maxwell (see Appendix A).

Electric and magnetic fields represent energy. The static and reactive fields represent stored energy that is returned to the conductor, just as the fields associated with coils and condensers of an electric circuit return energy to the circuit when the current or voltage maintaining the field is removed. The radiated fields, on the other hand, represent electromagnetic energy flowing outward into space. From the viewpoint of the dipole conductor, radiated energy is "lost" in the same sense that electrical energy is lost when it is converted into heat energy in a resistance. As mentioned in sec. 3.7, this energy loss is ascribed to a hypothetical "radiation resistance," which is a helpful concept for theoretical considerations involving the antenna input impedance, efficiency, and radiated power.

In the radiation field there is a continual exchange of energy between the electric and magnetic field components. As part of his theory, Maxwell postulated that an electric field acting in empty space causes a "displacement current" just as it causes an electron current in a conductor. He further hypothesized that this displacement current has the same ability to set up a magnetic field as does an electron current. Many experiments confirm this theory, which is now unquestioned. A varying electric field therefore causes a varying displacement current, which in turn results in a varying magnetic field. The magnetic field, in its turn, creates a varying electric field in accordance with Faraday's law. The cycle is thus complete; each field component sustains the other, and in regions remote from conductors or charges (empty space), one cannot exist without the other, in the fixed ratio given by equation (1–10), chapter 1.

That electric and magnetic fields represent energy may be demonstrated by placing a charged object in an electromagnetic field. The field will exert a force upon such an object and cause it to move if there are no restraining forces. This effect occurs, for example, when radio waves encounter the earth's ionosphere, in which there are free electrons. These electrons are accelerated by the field, which means that *kinetic energy* is imparted to them. The energy is supplied by the electromagnetic field. Similarly, an electromagnetic field impinging on a receiving antenna transfers energy (power) to it, which may be amplified by the receiver and eventually converted into sound variations in a loudspeaker, light variations on a television screen, or some other form of intelligence.

4.1.2. Pattern of an Elemental Dipole

If an elemental dipole (length $< 0.1\lambda$) is placed at the origin of a spherical-coordinate system (Fig. 3–1) with its axis (direction of its length) parallel to the $\theta = 0$ direction (the z-axis of the corresponding cartesian-coordinate system), the radiated field may be considered for any point in space whose position is given by the coordinates r, θ, ϕ; and the electric field intensity will then be designated $E(r, \theta, \phi)$. The geometry of this situation is shown in Fig. 4–3.

Analysis based on Maxwell's equations shows that the radiation field (far field) of this radiator is given by

$$E(r,\theta,\phi) = \frac{60\pi Il \sin\theta}{\lambda r} \tag{4–2}$$

where l is the length of the elemental dipole and I is the dipole current, in amperes. If l, λ, and r are in meters, and I is in rms amperes, E is obtained from this formula in rms volts per meter.

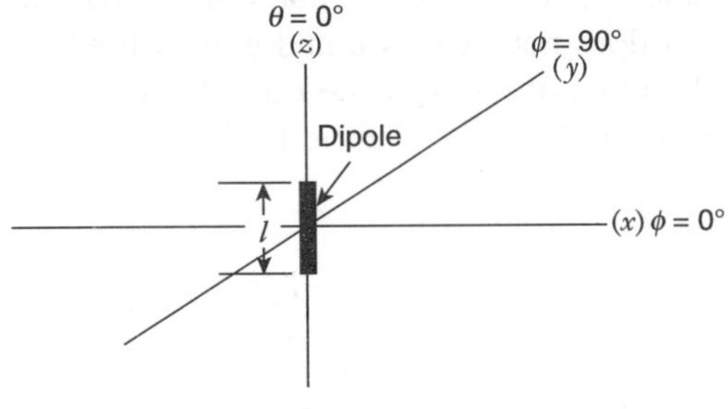

FIGURE 4–3.

Relationship of elemental dipole radiator to spherical coordinate system.

The fact that the angle ϕ does not appear in this expression means that for

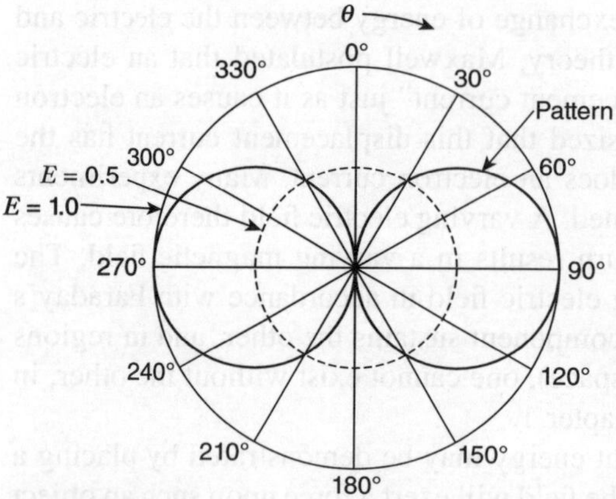

FIGURE 4–4.

Relative electric-intensity pattern of elemental (or short) dipole in a plane perpendicular to the dipole axis. ($E = |\sin\theta|$). (*Note:* The range of the angle θ in this diagram is 0–360°, to indicate that the pattern is shown in a whole plane. Strictly, however, since the spherical colatitude coordinate θ has a maximum value of 180°, the angles on the left side of the diagram should go from 0 to 180° like those on the right side.)

fixed values of r and θ, E does not vary as ϕ varies, that is, E is *independent* of ϕ. Stated otherwise, the pattern of E in any plane parallel to the xy-plane (i.e., a plane in which ϕ varies but θ does not) is a perfect circle. It also means that the pattern of E in all planes containing the z-axis (θ = 0-axis) will be exactly alike; for example, the pattern in the xz-plane will be the same as the pattern in the yz-plane. Finally, it means that all significant information concerning the three-dimensional pattern is contained in just *one* of these plane patterns in which θ is the angle variable. The relative pattern in such a plane, as given by (4–2), is shown in Fig. 4–4.

Figure 4–4 shows only the variation of the rms value of E (or the amplitude, depending on whether I in (4–2) is taken to be the rms value or the amplitude of the current), as functions of r and θ. The polarization is also of interest. It is linear, and in the $\theta = 90°$ plane (the plane through the dipole center perpendicular to the dipole axis) the polarization is parallel to the dipole axis. At any general field point the polarization is by definition the direction of the electric field lines. These lines, in the radiation field, are always perpendicular to a line from the dipole center to the field point, and they lie in a plane containing this line and the dipole axis.

The magnitude of E, given by (4–2), and its direction in space (polarization) are two properties of a radiation field that must be specified for a description of the field. A third quantity also to be specified is the relative phase of E as a function of θ and ϕ for a fixed value of r. For the elemental dipole field the phase is constant for a fixed value of r; that is, it does not vary as θ and ϕ are varied. The absolute phase of E may be expressed as a function of the distance r and the phase of the current I. Relative to the phase of I, the phase angle of the electric field E at distance r is

$$\gamma = \frac{\pi}{2} - \frac{2\pi r}{\lambda} = \frac{\pi}{2}\left(1 - \frac{4r}{\lambda}\right) \text{ radians} \tag{4–3}$$

Note that $-2\pi/\lambda$ is the delay of phase, in radians, created by the separation distance r. Equation (4–3), as well as (4–2), applies only in the far field, which means at values of r are of the order of λ or greater.

The relative-power-density pattern may be obtained from (4–2) by making use of the relation $p = E^2/377$ from (1–9). (It is useful here to note that the number 377 actually represents the quantity 120π.) The result is

$$p(r,\theta,\phi) = \frac{30\pi I^2 l^2 \sin^2\theta}{\lambda^2 r^2} \tag{4–4}$$

This formula gives p in watts per square meter when I is in rms amperes and all lengths are in meters.

4.1.3. Radiation Resistance

The total power radiated P_{total} by an elemental dipole is found by integrating $p(r, \theta, \phi)$ over the surface of an imaginary sphere at a fixed value of r. Then, in accordance with equation (3–15), chapter 3

$$\begin{aligned} P_{total} &= \int_0^{2\pi}\int_0^{\pi}[p(r,\theta,\phi)]\,r^2\sin\theta\,d\theta\,d\phi = \frac{30\pi I^2 l^2}{\lambda^2}\int_0^{2\pi}\int_0^{\pi}\left[\frac{\sin^2\theta}{r^2}\right]r^2\sin\theta\,d\theta\,d\phi \\ &= \frac{60\pi^2 I^2 l^2}{\lambda^2}\int_0^{\pi}\sin^3\theta\,d\theta = \frac{790 I^2 l^2}{\lambda^2}\text{ watts} \end{aligned} \tag{4–5}$$

The radiation resistance may now be calculated, from (3–28), by dividing P_{total} by I^2. The result is

$$R_r = 790\frac{l^2}{\lambda^2}\text{ ohms} \tag{4–6}$$

For example, if $l/\lambda = 0.1$, $R_r = 7.9$ ohms. (It will be recalled that this value of l/λ was stipulated at the beginning of this section to be approximately the maximum permissible length for an antenna to qualify as an elemental dipole.) The dipole current required for one kilowatt of power with this value of radiation resistance is 11.3 amp (a rather large current). This result indicates a major disadvantage of short dipoles, namely, the very large currents required for radiation of appreciable power. Therefore, radiators with larger values of radiation resistance are preferred when they can be used; but this is not always possible, and short dipoles are very useful radiators under these circumstances.

4.1.4. Directivity

The directivity of an elemental dipole can be computed by using foregoing results and the fundamental definition of directivity, equation (3–16), that follows:

$$D = U_{max}/U_{av} = p(r,\theta,\phi)_{max}/p(r,\theta,\phi)_{av}$$

providing $p(r, \theta, \phi)_{max}$ and $p(r, \theta, \phi)_{av}$ are evaluated at the same distance r. The numerator of (3–16), the equation above, is available from (4–4) with $\theta = 90°$, so that $\sin^2\theta = 1$ (the maximum value). The denominator is $P_{total}/4\pi r^2$, where $4\pi r^2$ is the area of a sphere of radius r and P_{total} is given by (4–5). Then, complete expression for the directivity (with 790 written as $80\pi^2$) is

$$D = \left(\frac{30\pi I^2 l^2}{\lambda^2 r^2}\right)\left(\frac{4\pi r^2 \lambda^2}{80\pi^2 I^2 l^2}\right) = 1.5 \tag{4–7}$$

Thus the directive is 1.5 regardless of the exact length l in relation to the wavelength λ, as long as the radiator qualifies as an elemental dipole. In fact, this result applies to any *short* dipole.

4.1.5. Beamwidth

The pattern of Fig. 4–4 (the two circles formed by heavy lines) is created by a "slice" through the three-dimensional pattern. However, the total pattern in space is shaped like a doughnut (with a pin-sized hole). The two lobes of Fig. 4–4 are really cross sections of the same lobe, and the angular width of this doughnut-shaped lobe will now be discussed.

The half-power beamwidth may be determined either by measuring the angular width of the pattern, as plotted in Fig. 4–4, between the points of electric intensity equal to $0.707E_{max}$, or from analysis of (4–4). The only angle-dependent term in this expression is $\sin^2\theta$, and it determines the pattern and the beamwidth. The quantity $\sin^2\theta$ has its maximum value of unity at $\theta = 90°$. Therefore, the half-power beamwidth is determined by finding the values of θ where $\sin^2\theta$ equals $\frac{1}{2}$. The values are $\theta = 45°$ and $\theta = 135°$ and thus the half-power beamwidth is $135° - 45° = 90°$.

4.1.6. Input Impedance

The input impedance of a short dipole, when it is fed at a small gap near its center, consists of the radiation resistance in series with a large value of capacitive reactance (equivalent to a small series capacitance). There is also, in series, an equivalent loss resistance R_0, included previously in (3–26), that may be large enough to be significant in relation to R_r. An equivalent circuit of the dipole, as it looks from the viewpoint of the transmission line, is shown in Fig. 4–5. Of course there is not actually a "series condenser" in the dipole; this circuit merely represents the impedance in a lumped-circuit equivalent form. Because the value of the equivalent series capacitance is very small, it represents a high value of capacitive reactance, which must be "tuned out" by including an inductive reactance of equal value in the feed circuit. Then the voltage supplied by the transmission line need not be extremely high. The current must be high, however, in order to radiate appreciable power, as indicated previously by (3–25). (In effect this equation shows that the radiated power is $P = I^2R_r$; so if R_r is small, I must be large to make P large.)

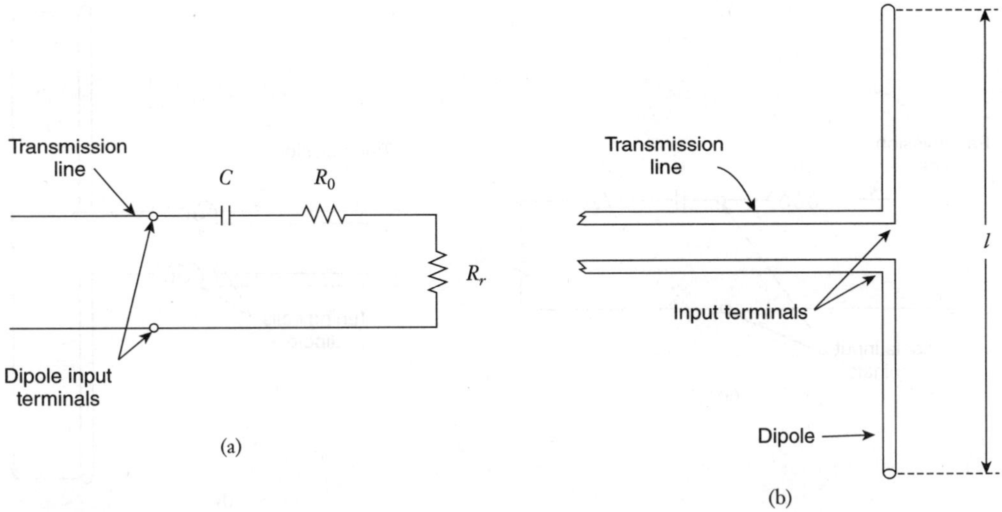

FIGURE 4–5.

Equivalent and actual circuits of center-fed short dipole. (a) Equivalent circuit. (b) Center-fed dipole and feed line.

This high current, flowing through the inductive and capacitive reactances, produces very high voltages across the feed-circuit inductor and across the antenna input terminals, even though the transmitter itself does not have to supply a high rf voltage (because the inductive and capacitive reactances cancel, leaving only R_r and R_0 as the effective transmitter load). If the input resistance R_i (= $R_0 + R_r$) is very small, a more complicated arrangement than that shown in Fig. 4–6 may be required to provide an impedance transformation in addition to reactance cancellation. Therefore feeding a short dipole antenna is somewhat difficult. In particular, the inductance in the feed circuit, when high power is being radiated, must be very large both to withstand the high voltage and to carry the heavy current without excessive loss. These are expensive requirements.

4.1.7. Short Dipole with Nonuniform Current Distribution

An isolated elemental dipole cannot actually be achieved as a physical reality; it is more of a concept, like the isotrope, than a practical radiator. Some types of dipole radiators do exist that approximate the properties of the elemental dipole. If an actual short dipole is fed in the manner shown in Fig. 4–5b, current will flow in the dipole conductor, and radiation will occur. The current in the conductor, however, will not be uniform as assumed for an elemental dipole, and therefore equations (4–2) to (4–6) will not apply to its radiation without modification. The necessary modification turns out to be very simple.

Because the short dipole conductor is "open" at both ends, that is, not connected to anything, the current at these points must be zero. (Physical theory exists to support this statement, although here it will simply be assumed to be intuitively obvious that a current

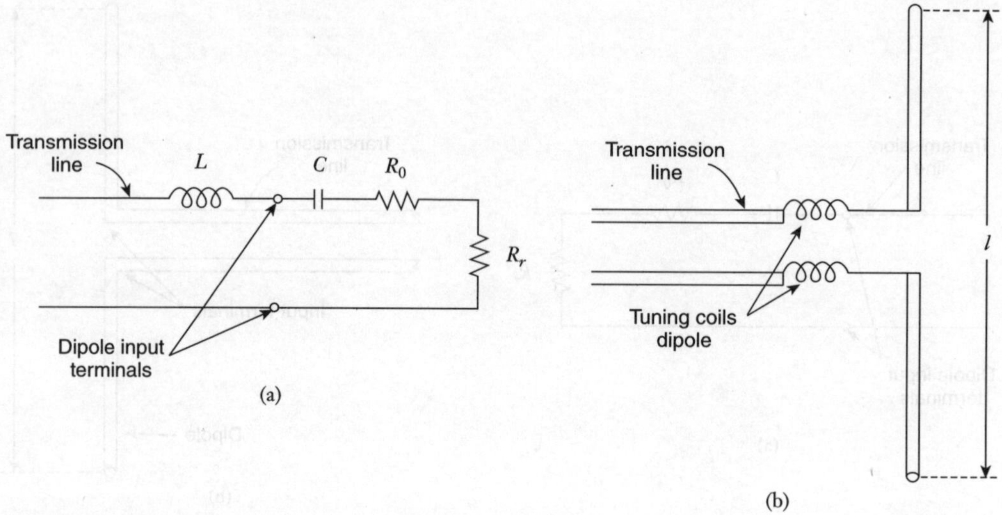

FIGURE 4–6.

Method of tuning out dipole capacitive input reactance with series inductance (L). (a) Equivalent circuit. (b) Dipole with input tuning coils. Reactance cancellation results when $2\pi fL = 1/2\pi fC$.

cannot exist where it has "no place to go.") At the same time, current can exist elsewhere in the dipole. This statement would seem to violate the physical principle of continuity for electric current, which implies that a current must have the same value everywhere along a continuous conductor. It will be recalled that this is not true in a transmission line on which a standing wave exists (sec. 2.1). The current in the dipole is a standing wave. It may be thought of as two equal and opposite currents (the reverse current is due to reflection from the open end) that, at the ends of the dipole, have exactly opposite phases and thus cancel, resulting in zero current. The cancellation is incomplete (because of the changing phase relationship) at points a short distance from the end and becomes progressively less complete going from the ends to the center. The principle of continuity is satisfied for the currents traveling in each direction, separately.

When the dipole is very short compared with a wavelength, as assumed, the current will vary approximately *linearly* along the dipole from end to center. This means that a graph representing the current as ordinate I, and distance from the end to the center of the dipole as abscissa x, is a pair of sloping straight lines forming a triangle, as shown in Fig. 4–7, with zero value at the left end (end of the dipole, $x = -l/2$), maximum value, I_{max}, at the center, $x = 0$, and zero value again at the right end ($x = +l/2$, l being the total length of the dipole). It can be shown that the short dipole with linear current distribution is like an elemental dipole with an "effective length" equal to half its actual length, and a uniform current equal to the current at the center of the actual dipole. Equations (4–2) to (4–6) may be used to describe the behavior of the actual short dipole if l in these equations is replaced by ($l/2$). With this modification, the entire discussion of the elemental dipole, including the feedpoint impedance considerations, applies to the actual short dipole. The directivity and the beamwidth—in fact, the total pattern—are the same for the open-ended short dipole and for the elemental dipole.

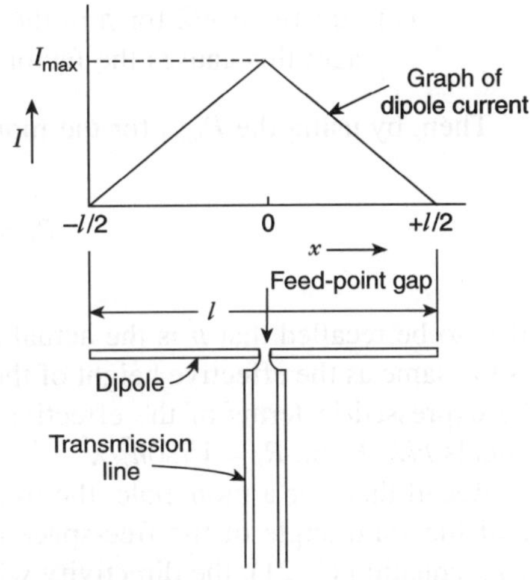

FIGURE 4–7.

Current distribution in a short open-ended center-fed dipole. (Gap at center is assumed to be of negligible length.)

4.1.8. Short Vertical Antenna with Ground Image

At very low frequencies, below 500 kHz, for example, the earth in most localities is a nearly perfect reflector of radio waves. Since a wavelength at these frequencies is physically quite long (600 m or about 2,000 ft. at 500 kHz, for example, and 30 km or about 19 miles at 10 kHz!) it is difficult to get a horizontal antenna high enough above the earth to produce appreciable low-angle radiation (based on the principles illustrated in Figs. 1–14 and 1–15). Moreover, antenna lengths that are an appreciable fraction of a wavelength are quite long, and expensive.

If a vertical antenna is erected with its base at the ground, it will be imaged in the earth in accordance with the principle of images (see sec. 1.2). The phase of the equivalent current in the image conductor is such that the antenna-plus-image may be considered a single antenna in free space. Since the height of the vertical antenna-plus-image, $2h$, will usually be a small fraction of a wavelength, the radiation is like that of a short dipole in free space. This combination of a half dipole, of height h, and its image in a reflecting surface is known as a *monopole*.

The pattern, however, is actually only half the free-space pattern, since the earth "cuts off" the other half. For a given current at the base of the antenna, the total radiated power is only half as great as it would be for the antenna-plus-image in (actual) free space with the same maximum current, as is found by substituting $\pi/2$ for π in the θ-integration of (4–5). Therefore, the radiated power and radiation resistance are only half as great as the values calculated on the free-space antenna-plus-image basis. Then, for a fixed current I, because of a smaller radiation resistance, both the input power and the radiated power are reduced.

As already discussed in connection with Fig. 4–7, the effective length of a short dipole being one-half its overall length may be used. Thus, although the length of the antenna-plus-image is $2h$, the effective monopole length is half as much, that is, h.

The total radiated power P_{total} of a short monopole is determined as follows:

(1) replace the length l of the elemental dipole of (4–5) with h, the effective length of the short monopole (i.e., the half-dipole plus image in ground plane), and

(2) substitute $\pi/2$ for π in the θ-integration of (4–5), because the earth's blockage; this causes the factor 790 to be replaced by 395.

Then, by using the P_{total} for the monopole, its radiation resistance becomes

$$R_r = \frac{P_{total}}{I^2} = \frac{395h^2}{\lambda^2} \tag{4–8}$$

It is to be recalled that h is the actual height of the half-dipole of the monopole, which is the same as the effective height of the half-dipole plus its image. Alternatively, R_r may be expressed in terms of the effective height (i.e., length) of the half-dipole h_e, which equals $h/2$. Then, $R_r = 1580h_e^2/\lambda^2$.

Recall that, for a monopole, the total power radiated is effectively concentrated into half the solid angle of the free-space case. Then, by the reasoning given in chapter 3, e.g., equation (3–21), the directivity will be twice that of a free-space short dipole. Thus for the monopole, $D = 3$, as compared to $D = 1.5$ given in (4–7) for the elemental dipole. The pattern in the horizontal plane is uniform (circular), that is, equal signal strength is radiated in all horizontal directions. The radiation at the peak of the beam is vertically polarized. The half-power vertical beamwidth is half that of the free-space short dipole (i.e., 45 degrees) since the earth eliminates half of the pattern. However, calculations of field strength at a distance in the actual earth environment cannot be made on the basis of these "semi-free-space" results because the propagation of the vertically polarized waves depends on the semi-guiding effect of the earth's surface, and at very great distances the ionosphere plays a part, as discussed in sec. 1.4.

A vertical radiator of this type may take the form of a steel tower with its base insulated from earth; then it is fed by connecting the source (transmitter) between the tower base and the ground, with an inductance in the feed line to compensate for the capacitive reactance of the antenna. The ground is a source of appreciable loss unless care is taken to minimize the resistance of the ground connection. In high-power transmitting installations an elaborate network of buried wires is used to make a good connection.

4.1.9. Top-Loaded Antenna

As has been indicated in the discussion of input impedance, in this section, the low radiation resistance of a short dipole together with the high capacitive reactance component of the input impedance create a difficult feed problem. As (4–8) above shows, the radiation resistance can be increased by increasing the effective height. This can be done either by increasing the actual height, or by changing the current distribution in the antenna so as to increase the effective height. As has been explained in the discussion of a short dipole with nonuniform current distribution, with a linearly decreasing current that has zero value at the end of the radiator the effective height is only half the actual height. If the current can somehow be made uniform, the effective height becomes equal to the actual height, and the radiation resistance is increased by a factor of 4 (because the effective height is squared in the radiation-resistance formula, i.e., the numerical constant 395 in (4–8) becomes 1580 if h is interpreted as the effective height).

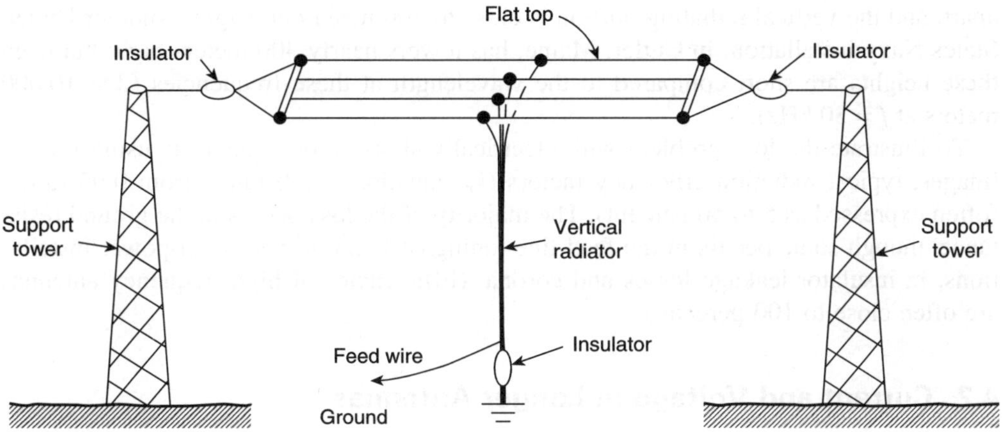

FIGURE 4–8.
A top-loaded short-monopole antenna, semischematic.

Current uniformity can be either totally or partially accomplished by "top loading"* the antenna. This procedure consists of running wires approximately horizontally from the upper end of the dipole. These wires do not radiate, but their capacitance to ground results in larger current at the upper end of the vertical conductor. If this "flat top" of horizontal wires is sufficiently extensive, and the vertical section is of "short dipole" length, the vertical current distribution may be made practically uniform (as assumed in analysis of elemental dipoles) so that the effective height is equal to the actual height. When the top loading does not produce approximately uniform current in the vertical section, the result is an effective height less than the actual height but greater than the effective height with no top loading.

The top loading also has the effect of reducing the magnitude of the capacitive-reactance component of the input impedance. This means that much less inductance is needed in series with the feed line, and also that for a given radiated power the voltage across this inductance and at the antenna base will be greatly reduced. This effect is perhaps the greatest benefit of top loading in high-power installations, since voltage breakdown and corona losses on the antenna are serious problems.

Top-loaded short vertical radiators at very low frequencies take many physical forms. A typical one is illustrated in Fig. 4–8. The flat top, as shown, is strung between two vertical towers, and the vertical radiating portion is supported at the center of the flat-top span. The flat top is insulated from the towers, and the antenna is fed at the bottom of the down lead through an inductance; the other side of the feed line is grounded through a network of buried conductors.

A dramatic form of this type of antenna is the United States Navy's Jim Creek VLF installation (in the state of Washington), which operates in the 10 to 30 kHz frequency region. This flat top is a conductor supported between two mountains about 2 kilometers

* The equivalent procedure for a dipole would be called *end loading.* The term *top loading* is used simply because the end of the monopole is at the top. On a dipole, both ends would be "loaded," symmetrically.

apart, and the vertical radiating portion is close to 300 meters in height. Another United States Navy installation, in Cutler, Maine, has towers nearly 300 meters high; but even these heights are short compared to the wavelength at these frequencies ($\lambda = 10{,}000$ meters at $f = 30$ kHz).

To illustrate the loss problem with electrically short vertical antennas using ground images, typical radiation efficiency factors (k_r, equation 3–30) range from 0.05 to 0.5 (often expressed as 5 to 50 percent). The majority of the loss occurs in the ground resistance, though some occurs in the feed-line tuning coil and, in very high-power installations, in insulator leakage losses and corona. (Efficiencies of high-frequency antennas are often close to 100 percent.)

4.2. Current and Voltage in Longer Antennas

Electrically short antennas have been discussed in some detail because they are of both theoretical and practical importance. At higher frequencies, beginning in the MHz region and especially in the HF region and above, longer electrical lengths become feasible, and their use results in certain advantages. In particular, the difficulties encountered in feeding short dipoles are eliminated, and higher directivities may be obtained. The input impedance of longer antennas may be made nonreactive, and the radiation resistance is usually much higher than that of a short dipole.

The variation of current and voltage along the length of longer antenna wires is more complicated than for short or elemental dipoles. For an elemental dipole it was assumed that the current is uniform (constant) along the conductor at any instant of time, although varying in time according to (4–1). For a short dipole without capacitive end loading, the current varies in a *linear* (straightline) fashion, as shown in Fig. 4–7. The voltage, though not shown in Fig. 4–7, is of opposite polarity on either side of the feed-point gap and has virtually constant amplitude along the conductor length.

The patterns of variation of the current and voltage along the conductor are called the *current* and *voltage distributions* of the antenna. These distributions are important in understanding the radiation properties of various antenna lengths and feed arrangements.

The current and voltage distributions on open-ended long antenna wires are basically similar to the standing waves of current and voltage on an open-ended two-wire transmission line. This standing-wave pattern is shown in Fig. 4–9a. (The voltage distribution is the same as shown in Fig. 2–5, chapter 2, for $Z_L \to \infty$.) The voltage maxima occur at the end of the line, and at other points an integral number of half wavelengths from the end. The voltage has zero values (nulls) at points an odd number of quarter wavelengths from the end. The current has maxima at the voltage minima, and the current minima are at the voltage maxima.

These patterns are plotted with both positive and negative "amplitudes" (I_0 and V_0) to emphasize the phase reversals. The same phase information is conveyed by the *phase distribution* patterns of Fig. 4–9b, which show that the phases of the voltage and current are constant in the intervals between the nulls and that a sudden change of 180 degrees occurs at the nulls. It is also shown that the current and voltage are everywhere 90 degrees out of phase with each other. (A 270-degree phase difference is equivalent to 90 degrees.)

If now the wires in the end quarter-wavelength section of the open-ended two-wire line are bent outwards at right angles to their original directions in the plane of the line, as shown in Fig. 4–10a, the result is a half-wave center-fed dipole. Figure 4–10b shows the current and voltage distribution on the dipole. Essentially it is the same pattern that existed on these wires before they were bent to form the dipole, with zero current at the ends and maximum current at the center. The voltage is maximum at the ends and zero at the center. These features are the same as those of the short open-ended dipole, whose current distribution is shown in Fig. 4–7. The difference is that the variation is no longer linear; it is sinusoidal. If the current and voltage are expressed as functions of the distance x measured along the wire from one of the open ends of the antenna, the *phasor** amplitudes are given by the equations:

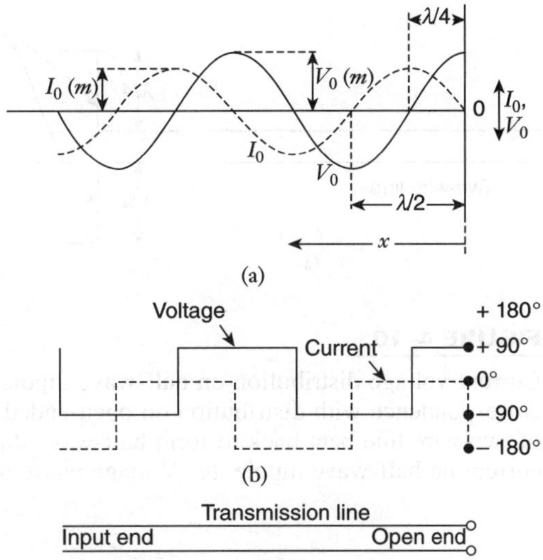

FIGURE 4–9.

Voltage and current standing wave patterns on an open-ended uniform transmission line, assuming no line losses. (a) Amplitude. (b) Phase angle.

$$I_0(x) = jI_{0(m)} \sin\left(\frac{2\pi x}{\lambda}\right) \tag{4–9}$$

$$V_0(x) = V_{0(m)} \cos\left(\frac{2\pi x}{\lambda}\right) \tag{4–10}$$

where $I_{0(m)}$ and $V_{0(m)}$ are the maximum amplitudes. These equations do not show the *time* variation, or instantaneous values; they are obtained by multiplying the amplitudes by the factor $\sin(2\pi ft + \alpha)$, as in (4–1).

The space–time relationships of current and voltage on a half-wave dipole are somewhat difficult to visualize at first. As an aid in this effort, Fig. 4–11 shows the *instantaneous* patterns of current and voltage on the dipole at several instants during a single rf cycle. In these diagrams, the rf period T is the time for completion of a single cycle;

* In these expressions, the j factor indicates that the current is 90 degrees out of phase with the voltage, and the positive and negative sign changes resulting from the sine and cosine functions of x indicate the 180-degree phase changes that occur at the standing-wave nulls. $I_{0(m)}$ is the value of $I_0(x)$ that occurs at $x = \lambda/4$, and $V_{0(m)}$ is the value of $V_0(x)$ that occurs at $x = 0$ and $x = \lambda/2$.

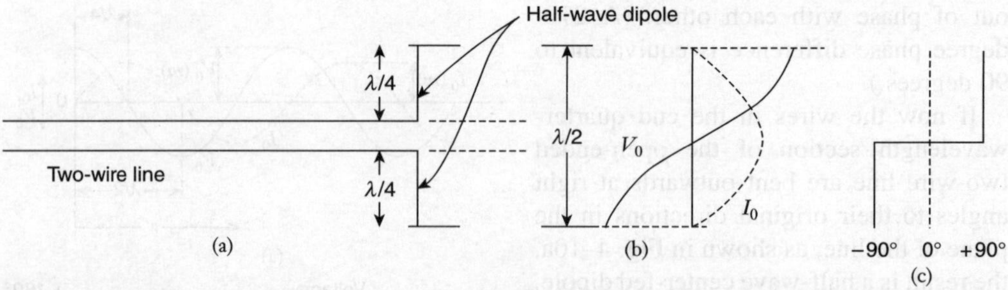

FIGURE 4–10.

Current-voltage distribution on half-wave dipole. Comparison with Figure 4–9 indicates correspondence with distribution on open-ended transmission line. (a) End-quarter-wave section of two-wire line bent back to form half-wave dipole. (b) Amplitude distribution of voltage and current on half-wave dipole. (c) Voltage phase distribution (solid) and current phase (dashed).

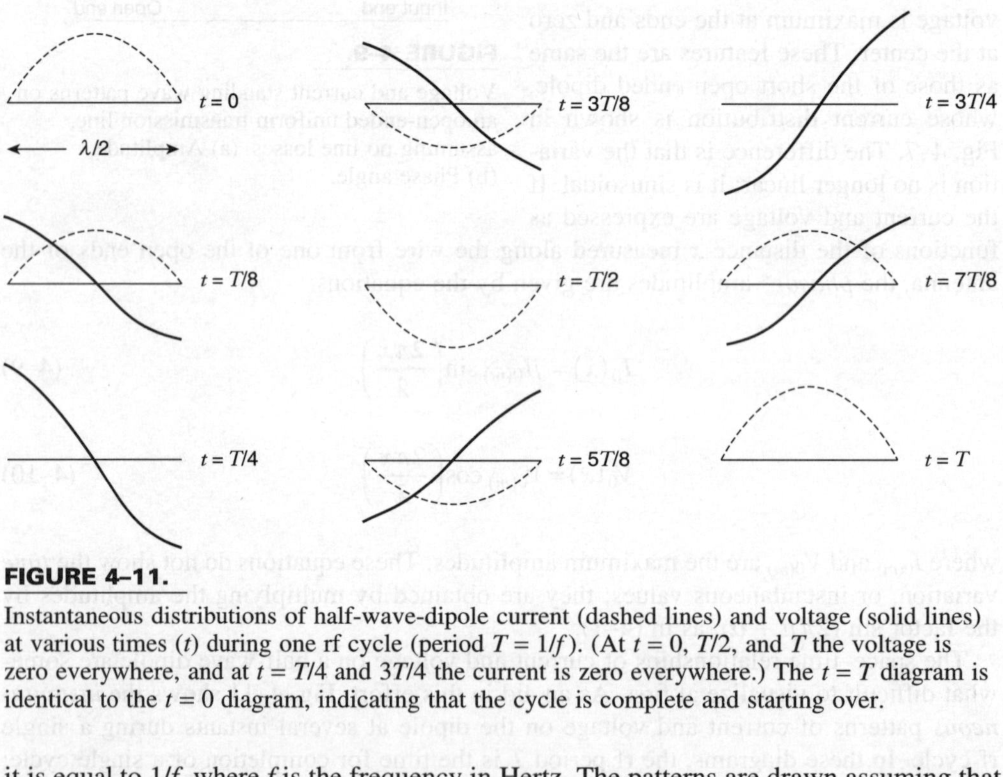

FIGURE 4–11.

Instantaneous distributions of half-wave-dipole current (dashed lines) and voltage (solid lines) at various times (t) during one rf cycle (period $T = 1/f$). (At $t = 0$, $T/2$, and T the voltage is zero everywhere, and at $t = T/4$ and $3T/4$ the current is zero everywhere.) The $t = T$ diagram is identical to the $t = 0$ diagram, indicating that the cycle is complete and starting over.

it is equal to $1/f$, where f is the frequency in Hertz. The patterns are drawn assuming that at zero time ($t = 0$) the current is at its instantaneous maximum value, corresponding to $\alpha = \pi/2$ in (4–1).

Linear antennas longer than a half wavelength are also used. They may or may not be fed at their centers. On each side of the feed point, the current and voltage distributions are determined by (4–9) and (4–10) above. For correct operation of such an antenna, with a balanced two-wire line, the lengths of wire on either side of the feed point must be the same or must differ by an integral number of half wavelengths. Linear antennas of this type, on which standing waves of current and voltage exist owing to reflections from the end of an open-ended wire, are called *resonant* antennas.

At the gap in the antenna wire across which the feed line is connected, the antenna voltage distribution undergoes a 180-degree phase reversal, but the current phase is the same on either side of the gap. Therefore, if the feed point is at a current maximum (voltage minimum), the distributions over the entire antenna length will be the same as they would be in an unbroken wire of the same length (case 1). This situation exists when the wire lengths on each side of the feed point are odd integral multiples of a quarter wavelength. But if the feed point is at a voltage maximum, which will be the case if the wire lengths on each side are integral multiples of a half wavelength, the antenna phase pattern is not the same as it would be on an unbroken wire (case 2). The voltage-current-phase patterns for these two cases are shown in Fig. 4–12, for a total antenna length of one wavelength. Antennas of the first type, having the unbroken-wire type of distribution (obtained by feeding either at one end or at a current maximum), are properly termed *long-wire resonant antennas*; those of the second type, in which the feed point is a voltage maximum, are actually *two-element collinear arrays*. (If the total antenna length is one wavelength, as in Fig. 4–12b, each element of this collinear array is a half-wave dipole, and for longer total lengths each element may itself be a long-wire antenna.) Because arrays are discussed in chapter 5, only the true long-wire types will be discussed in this chapter, although some types of collinear and other long-wire arrays are sometimes loosely referred to as long-wire antennas.

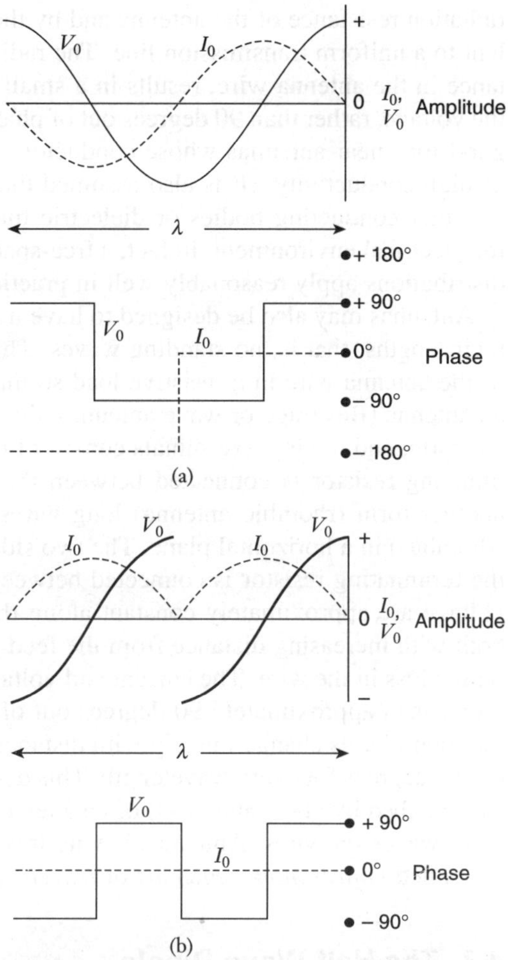

FIGURE 4–12.

Voltage-current distributions on a full-wave antenna fed (a) at end or current maximum in 4(a) and (b) at center (voltage maximum) in 4(b).

Actually these sinusoidal distributions of current and voltage are approximations rather than exact descriptions. They are slightly modified, on an actual antenna, by the radiation resistance of the antenna and by the fact that the antenna wires are not equivalent to a uniform transmission line. The radiation resistance, as well as any actual resistance in the antenna wire, results in a small component of current that is in phase with the voltage, rather than 90 degrees out of phase. But the sinusoidal approximation is quite good for linear antennas whose conductors are very thin compared to their length, and of high conductivity. (It is also assumed that the antenna wire is not close to any large irregular conducting bodies or dielectric material that would disturb the uniformity of the electrical environment. In fact, a free-space environment is assumed, but the assumed distributions apply reasonably well in practical situations.)

Antennas may also be designed to have uniform current and voltage amplitudes along their lengths, that is, no standing waves. This result is achieved by terminating the end of the antenna wire in a resistive load so that no reflection occurs. In one form of such an antenna (Beverage or wave antenna), the wire runs approximately horizontally above the earth, and the input terminals consist of one end of the wire and the ground. The terminating resistor is connected between the other end of the wire and the ground. In another form (rhombic antenna) long wires form an array in the shape of a diamond (rhombus) in a horizontal plane. The two sides of the diamond are fed at one vertex, and the terminating resistor is connected between them at the other vertex. The current and voltage are approximately constant along the wires, but there is a gradual decrease of both with increasing distance from the feed point, owing to the radiation losses and the ohmic loss in the wire. The current and voltage are in phase with each other everywhere, rather than approximately 90 degrees out of phase as with standing-wave distributions, but their phases change linearly with distance along the wire in the amount of 2π radians or 360 degrees for every wavelength. This description is characteristic of *traveling waves*, as described by (1–2) and (1–3) of chapter 1 for waves in space, and by (2–3) of chapter 2 for waves on wires. Antennas having traveling-wave current and voltage distribution are called *nonresonant antennas* or *traveling wave antennas*.

4.3. The Half-Wave Dipole

The radiation patterns of linear antennas that do not qualify as "short dipoles" may be found by considering them to be composed of a number of elemental dipoles placed end to end. For example, a dipole a half wavelength long might be approximated by five tenth-wavelength elemental dipoles end to end. The current in each elemental dipole would (by definition) be constant and equal to the average current in the corresponding section of the half-wave dipole, as indicated in Fig. 4–13. The current distribution is a half cycle of a sinusoid with the maximum at the dipole center, as in Fig. 4–10. The current has a constant phase angle everywhere on a half-wave dipole so that all the elemental dipoles are assumed to be in phase.

The radiated field intensity at a distant point (field point) due to each elemental dipole was given previously by (4–2), and its phase angle was given by (4–3), with the distance r taken to be the distance to the field point from the center of the elemental dipole; that is, r will have a slightly different value in computing the field-point contribution of each elemental dipole. These slight distance differences will not significantly affect the relative

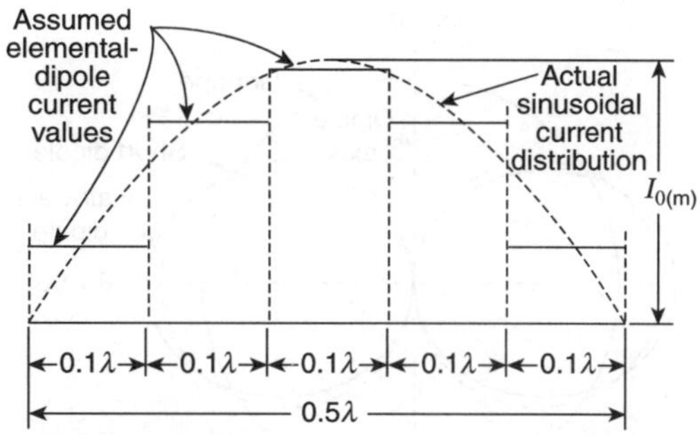

FIGURE 4–13.

Approximation of actual half-wave dipole by five tenth-wave-length elemental dipoles, with currents equal to average current in corresponding segment of half-wave dipole.

intensities of the individual elemental dipole fields, but they will affect the relative *phases* significantly. The total field at a distant point is the phasor sum of the contributions of the individual elemental dipoles, in accordance with the principle of interference in sec. 1.2.

This method of analysis, as described thus far, is obviously an approximation and a rather crude one, when the half-wave dipole is dissected into only five elemental dipoles. The accuracy of the approximation may be increased by dissecting it into more elemental dipoles of shorter individual lengths. But the labor of calculation is also thereby increased, if the phasor summation process is employed as described.

The approximation may be made exact, however, and the tedious summation process avoided, by applying the methods of calculus. The half-wave dipole is then considered to be composed of an infinite number of infinitesimal dipoles, and the phasor summation of their fields at a distant point is expressed as an integral. The resulting expression for the magnitude of the electric field of the half-wave dipole, at a distance r in the direction θ, ϕ, obtained by solving the integral expression, is

$$E(r,\theta,\phi) = \frac{60I}{r}\left[\frac{\cos\left(\frac{\pi}{2}\cos\theta\right)}{\sin\theta}\right] \tag{4–11}$$

where E is in rms volts per meter if r is in meters and I is the rms current in amperes at the center of the dipole. This pattern is seen to be a slightly more complicated mathematical expression than that of the short or elemental dipole of (4–2), but the patterns are only slightly different. They are compared in Fig. 4–14. The half-wave dipole has a slightly narrower beamwidth—78 degrees compared to 90 degrees for the short dipole. Consequently its directivity is slightly greater—1.64 compared to 1.5 for the short dipole. The power-density ratio is 1.64/1.5 = 1.093, and the field-strength ratio 1.047.

The slightly greater directivity of the half-wave dipole is thus almost insignificant. Its advantage lies primarily in its increased radiation resistance and reduced or nonexistent feed-point reactance. The radiation resistance for an exactly half-wavelength dipole is found, by the method illustrated in the case of the elemental dipole, to be 73.1 ohms, referred to the maximum current point (dipole center). Therefore this is also the resistive component of the input impedance when the dipole is fed at the center. There is also a small reactive component of 42.5 ohms, inductive. This small inductive reactance may

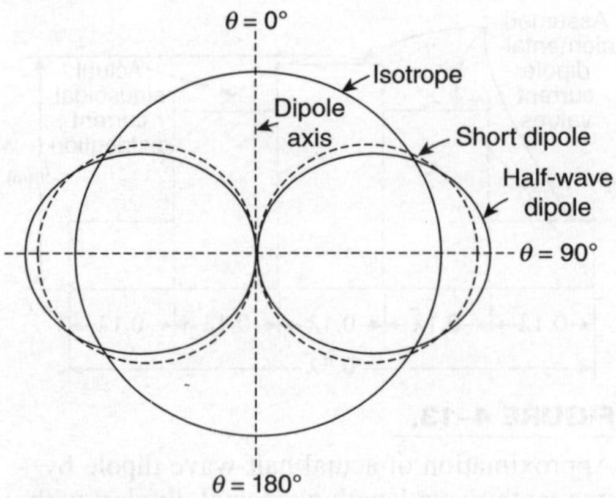

FIGURE 4–14.
Half-wave-dipole, short-dipole, and isotrope patterns compared for equal power radiated (electric-intensity patterns), in plane containing dipole axes.

be eliminated by shortening the dipole to about 95 percent of a half-wavelength (i.e., about 0.475λ). The radiation resistance (and input impedance) is then about 65 ohms (Kraus and Marhefka 2002, p. 182). The pattern (beamwidth and gain) is not significantly affected by this slight shortening.

These properties make the half-wave dipole especially attractive as a radiator for many purposes, at frequencies for which its length is not excessively large or minutely small. The results given for the radiation resistance and input impedance are free-space values for a conductor very thin compared to the length, with no ohmic resistance. Consequently they become somewhat modified for conductors of appreciable diameter or when the dipole is close enough to the ground or other conductors to result in "coupling." Usually ohmic loss is small enough to be disregarded. Dipoles of larger diameter, and of special shapes and configurations, are discussed in sec. 7.1.

When a vertical quarter-wavelength radiator is erected with its base at or just above the ground, it is imaged in the earth so that its radiation may be analyzed as if it were a half-wave dipole in free space, subject to the same modifications as discussed for the short vertical dipole imaged in the ground. When the quarter-wave vertical antenna (monopole) is fed at its base with the other side of the feed line connected to ground, its radiation resistance and input impedance are just half the values for the half-wave dipole in free space, and the directivity is twice as great. The radiation is vertically polarized at the peak of the beam. Vertical radiators of other lengths may be similarly analyzed, that is, by use of the image principle. Vertical-tower radiators of heights up to about 5/8 wavelength are much used for broadcasting and other applications in the medium-frequency range of about 500 to 3,000 kHz. (Even higher vertical antennas may be used if they are "sectionalized" so that they become, in effect, collinear-array antennas, described in sec. 5.2). A monopole too short to be a quarter-wavelength high, yet too long to be classed as a "short monopole," may be capacitively top loaded (in the same general manner as described for short vertical monopoles) to result in virtually quarter-wave performance.

4.4. Long-Wire Antennas

Antennas consisting of a single straight wire, either unbroken or with a feed-point gap at a current maximum when the antenna has standing-wave current distribution, are classed as long-wire antennas if their length is substantially greater than a half wavelength. Such antennas are not properly called dipoles. On the other hand, the half-wave antenna is commonly called a half-wave dipole, even though a true electric dipole is equivalent to two equal and opposite polarity point charges separated by a definite distance. The elemental dipole and the short dipole are, in essence, equivalent to oscillating electric dipoles, but longer antennas are not. However, usage sanctions the term for the half-wave dipole.

The radiation patterns of long-wire antennas may be determined by the method described for the half-wave dipole by considering them to be composed of end-to-end infinitesimal dipoles. The current amplitude and phase in each infinitesimal dipole are taken to be the values indicated by the current distributions calculated from (4–9), and as shown for a one-wavelength wire in Fig. 4–12 for a resonant antenna. For a nonresonant antenna a constant current amplitude along the wire is assumed, with a linear phase change corresponding to a traveling wave of current (2π radians or 360 degrees per wavelength). These current-distribution assumptions are valid for a thin wire of perfect conductivity, ignoring the effect on current distribution of the radiation losses. Therefore, the results are approximate, but useful in that they indicate the general nature of the radiation patterns.

4.4.1. Patterns of Resonant Antennas

As shown in Fig. 4–14, the pattern of a short or half-wave dipole consists of a single doughnut-shaped lobe of radiation (appearing as two oppositely directed lobes in a "slice" or plane pattern containing the dipole axis). Long-wire radiators have more than one three-dimensional lobe, taking the form of cones of radiation. The axes of the cones coincide with the axis of the wire, and the sides of the cones are inclined at various angles with respect to the wire. As for the short dipole, the patterns are uniform (circles) in the plane perpendicular to the axis of the wire.

There will be one cone-shaped lobe for each half wavelength of wire length, for both the standing-wave and traveling-wave antennas. The lobes are symmetrically disposed with respect to the plane that bisects the wire. Therefore, if there is an odd number of half wave-lengths, one lobe will be perpendicular to the wire, like the short-dipole lobe except that it is thinner (narrower beamwidth), more like a pancake than a doughnut when the wire is many wavelengths long. When the wire length is an even number of half-wavelengths, there is no perpendicular lobe.

For the standing-wave or resonant antenna, the amplitude of the electric field strength (pattern) is given by

$$E(r,\theta,\phi) = \frac{60I}{r}\left\|\left[\frac{\cos\left(\dfrac{n\pi}{2}\cos\theta\right)}{\sin\theta}\right]\right\| \tag{4–12a}$$

where n is the number of *half wavelengths* in the wire length, assumed to be an odd number, and as usual E is in rms volts per meter if r is in meters, and I is the rms current

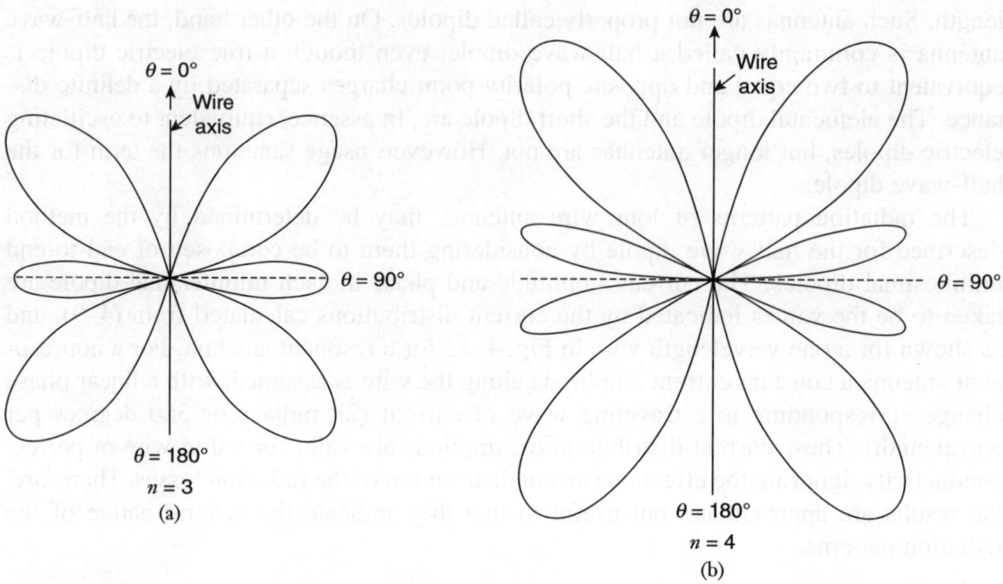

FIGURE 4–15.

Patterns of resonant long-wire antennas.

at a current maximum, in amperes. For a wire an even number of half-wavelengths long, the equation becomes

$$E(r,\theta,\phi)=\frac{60I}{r}\left[\frac{\sin\left(\frac{n\pi}{2}\cos\theta\right)}{\sin\theta}\right] \qquad (4\text{–}12b)$$

The nature of these patterns is shown in Fig. 4–15 for an odd and an even number of half-wavelengths.

In these formulas, it is assumed as usual that the antenna is located at the origin of a spherical coordinate system with the axis of the wire along the $\theta = 0°$ axis (z-axis, Fig. 3–1) and that I is the rms current at a current-maximum point of the sinusoidal standing wave. The patterns shown are for long wires of modest length ($n = 3$ and $n = 4$). As the number of half wavelengths is made larger, the number of lobes increases proportionately and the lobes of maximum radiation lie closer to the wire. Because of the factor "sin θ" in the denominator of (4–11) and (4–12), an *envelope* of the lobe pattern is, in three dimensions, a circular cylinder parallel to the axis of the wire. In a plane containing the wire axis, the edges of the envelope are straight lines parallel to the wire. The effect is shown in Fig. 4–16 for a many-lobed pattern.

These patterns, and equations (4–11) and (4–12), are for antennas an integral number (n) of half wavelengths long. The *total* length, however, should be shortened by about 5 percent of *one* half wavelength to eliminate a reactive component of input impedance. This will not affect the pattern appreciably.

4.4.2. Radiation Resistance and Directivity

The radiation resistance of a long-wire resonant antenna n half wavelengths long, in free space, is given approximately by

$$R_r = 73 + 69\log_{10} n \tag{4–13}$$

for values of n greater than 2 (Brainerd et al. 1942). The equation is also approximately correct for $n = 1$.

The angle of maximum radiation, that is, the angle that the strongest lobe makes with the wire axis (this is also the lobe closest to the axis, as Figs. 4–15 and 4–16 show), is given approximately by (4–14) below. This formula is quite accurate for small values of n and gives a result close enough for most purposes, even for large values of n.

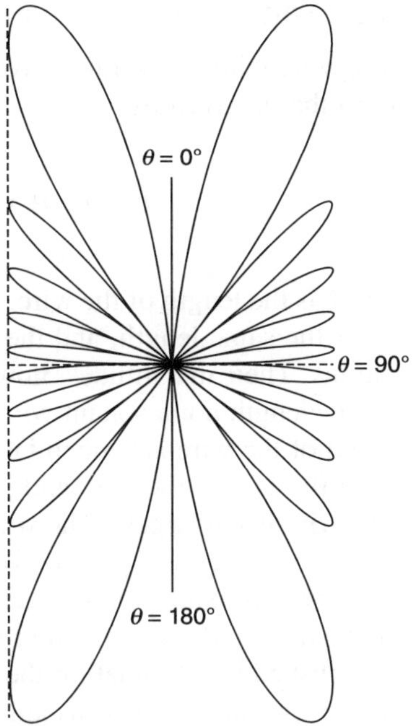

FIGURE 4–16.

Pattern of five-wavelength resonant antenna (n = 10).

$$\cos\theta_{max} = \frac{n-1}{n} \tag{4–14}$$

The maximum directivity may be attained through knowledge of the maximum field strength E_{max}, the radiated (transmitted) power P_t, and other previously developed relationships. By substituting $\cos\theta_{max}$ into (4–12a) or (4–12b), according to whether n is odd or even, the value $60I/(r\sin\theta_{max})$ for the maximum field strength E_{max} is obtained.* The power P_t is I^2R_r from equation (3–28). Furthermore, the maximum and average power densities p_{max} and p_{av} are $(E_{max})^2/377$ and $P_t/4\pi r^2$, respectively. Then, the maximum directivity D_{max} becomes

$$D_{max} = \frac{U_{max}}{U_{av}} = \frac{p_{max}}{p_{av}} = \frac{120}{R_r \sin^2\theta_{max}} \tag{4–15}$$

It is interesting to note that this formula gives the correct result for a half-wave dipole, D_{max} = 1.64, when R_r is taken as 73 ohms and θ_{max} = 90°; also, (4–13) and (4–14) are correct for n = 1.

* When (4–14) is substituted into (4–12a) and (4–12b), their numerators become, respectively, $60I|\cos\{(n-1)\pi/2\}|$ and $60I|\sin\{(n-1)\pi/2\}|$. For n odd, $|\cos\{(n-1)\pi/2\}| = 1$, and for n even, $|\sin\{(n-1)\pi/2\}| = 1$. The denominators become $r\sin\theta_{max}$.

4.4.3. Patterns of Nonresonant Antennas

A long wire with a traveling-wave current of uniform amplitude I has an electric-intensity pattern that is given by

$$E(r,\theta,\phi)=\left[\left[\frac{60I\sin\theta}{r(1-\cos\theta)}\right]\sin\left[\frac{\pi L}{\lambda}(1-\cos\theta)\right]\right] \quad (4\text{–}16)$$

where L is the length of the wire. This pattern has the same number of lobes as a resonant wire of the same length, and the maxima and minima occur at approximately the same positions. Their magnitudes, however, are quite different, as shown by the pattern of a 3/2-wavelength nonresonant wire in Fig. 4–17. As seen there, the lobes directed toward one end of the wire are much larger than those at the other end of the pattern. The lobe nearest the axis of the wire and pointed in the direction of the traveling wave of current on the wire is the largest. The smallest lobe is the one at the other end of the pattern, the magnitudes increasing progressively toward the large-lobe end.

This type of pattern has an advantage when it is desired to radiate or receive in predominantly one direction, rather than two. Suppression of the pattern in one direction is accomplished by eliminating the reflected current at the end of the wire by means of a resistive termination. This usually takes the form of a resistor connected from the end of the wire to ground. Such termination can be successful, however, only if the height of the antenna above ground is a very small fraction of a wavelength (otherwise the connection would have reactance as well as resistance and would not be a reflection-free termination). The correct value of the resistor, being connected between the end of the wire and ground, is half the value that matches the impedance of a transmission line consisting of the antenna wire and its earth image. If the antenna height is h and the wire diameter is d, the resistance is from equation (2–62), chapter 2:

$$R=138\log_{10}\left(\frac{4h}{d}\right)\text{ ohms} \quad (4\text{–}17)$$

However, this formula should be used only as a rough guide. The usual practice is to adjust the resistance until no standing wave exists on the antenna wire.

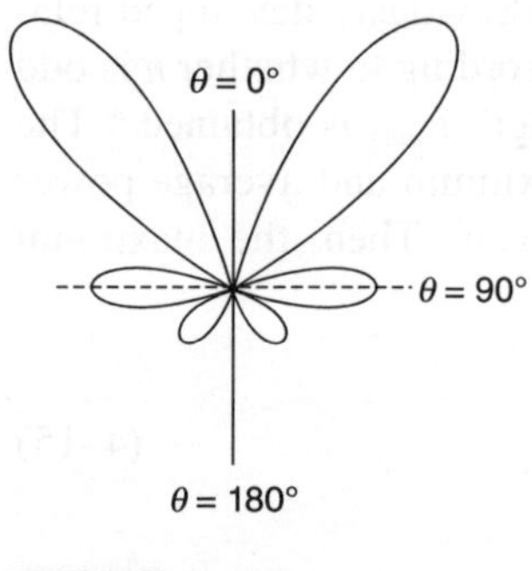

FIGURE 4–17.
Pattern of three-half-wavelength nonresonant long-wire antenna ($L = 1.5\lambda$). (Compare with resonant wire of same length, $n = 3$ pattern of Figure 4–15.)

4.4.4. Polarization

The radiation from a long-wire antenna is linearly polarized, but the polarization (electric field) direction is not the same in all parts of the pattern. (This is true even of short and half-wave dipoles, but for them the variation is not as great because there is only one lobe perpendicular to the wire; in the perpendicular plane the polarization is simply parallel to the wire.) The polarization in one of the oblique lobes of a long-wire antenna, or in fact in any particular part of the pattern, may be determined by the following procedure (assuming free-space propagation):

(i) Draw a line from the center of the antenna in the direction of interest.
(ii) Form the plane that contains both the antenna wire and this direction line.
(iii) At any point on this direction line the polarization (electric field) vector is perpendicular to the direction line and lies in the plane thus formed.

(This procedure is in fact applicable to the radiation from any straight-wire radiator, including short dipoles and half-wave dipoles.)

4.4.5. Effect of the Ground and Other Factors

The foregoing discussion of long-wire antennas has assumed perfect thin-wire conductors and a free-space environment. Ground reflection affects the vertical-plane pattern in the manner discussed in sec. 1.4.3 and illustrated for a special case by Fig. 1–15. The presence of the ground also affects the radiation resistance and the input impedance because of mutual coupling between the antenna and its image. Resistance of the wire itself is usually small, but in a very long wire the total resistance may be appreciable. In addition to its direct effect on the input impedance, this resistance also changes the form of the current distribution on the wire, in both the resonant and nonresonant antennas, and so affects the radiation pattern. Therefore the behavior calculated for the free-space perfect-conductor antenna serves primarily as a general guide to what will be observed with practical antennas. When correction for ground effects is made, the theoretical patterns agree quite well with those that actually occur.

4.4.6. Uses of Long-Wire Antennas

Both resonant and nonresonant long-wire antennas are used for transmitting and receiving in the MF and HF range, from perhaps 500 kHz to 30 MHz. They provide a simple and effective method of obtaining a directional pattern and gain. As will be described in Ch. 5, these properties can be further enhanced when long-wire antennas are used as elements in an array.

The single terminated wire used as a nonresonant antenna will not be effective for horizontal polarization, as already discussed, because of its small-fraction-of-a-wavelength height. As the discussion of polarization indicates, however, a lobe that makes a small angle with the axis of a horizontal wire in a vertical plane will radiate or receive waves whose electric field vector has an appreciable vertical component. Such an antenna is sometimes used as a rather highly unidirectional receiving antenna for vertically polarized waves. In this use, the long-wire nonresonant antenna is known as a *Beverage* or "wave" antenna (Beverage, Rice, and Kellog 1923).

The functioning of a Beverage antenna is now described. For a wave with propagation direction slanted between horizontal and vertical, there will be both a vertically- and a horizontally-polarized (V- and H-POL) component. Since the earth is an imperfect conductor, the H-POL component is not totally diminished. Thus, the incoming H-polarized fields, from the ground, induce voltages along the antenna that add in phase at the receiving end. Waves propagating along the wire from the opposite direction are, ideally, absorbed by the terminating resistor. Therefore, the Beverage antenna provides a highly directive pattern in the horizontal plane for vertical polarization. Beverage antennas are not ordinarily used for transmitting, because the power absorbed in the terminating resistor results in poor radiation efficiency.

4.5. Loop Antennas

Another basic form of radiator is the loop, which in its fundamental form is a single-turn coil of wire. A current can be made to flow in the loop by breaking it at some point and connecting the terminals of a transmission line (or other source) at the gap in the loop, as indicated in Fig. 4–18.

4.5.1. The Small Loop

The radius of the small loop, a, is assumed to be very small compared to the wavelength λ, so that the current in all parts of the loop will be of the same amplitude and phase at any instant. An analysis of the radiation from such a loop may be made by considering it to be made up of many elemental dipoles connected together. Since dipoles are straight rather than curved, the figure thus formed will be a polygon rather than a circle. However, the approximation to a circle can be made as good as desired by taking the elemental dipoles to be sufficiently short or, ideally, infinitesimal. The fields of the individual dipoles are then superposed in the manner described for analyzing the half-wave dipole, sec. 4.3. Here not all the electric vectors of the separate field components are parallel. Although this complicates the mathematics, the principle is the same. The superposition of nonparallel fields was discussed in sec. 1.2.

From such an analysis it is found that the field pattern of a loop has exactly the same shape as that of a single elemental dipole oriented with its axis coincident with the loop axis (i.e., with its axis perpendicular to the plane of the loop) (Fig. 4–4). However, the vector directions of the electric (E) and magnetic (H) components of this field are interchanged, relative to the E and H directions of the elemental-dipole field. The *polarization* is linear but perpendicular to that of the corresponding electric dipole. Therefore a loop with its axis horizontal radiates maximum field intensity in the plane of the loop, the pattern being doughnut-shaped; but with axis horizontal the polarization is vertical, rather than horizontal. If the plane of the loop is horizontal, the radiation pattern in the horizontal plane is uniform (a circle), like that of a vertical dipole, but the polarization is

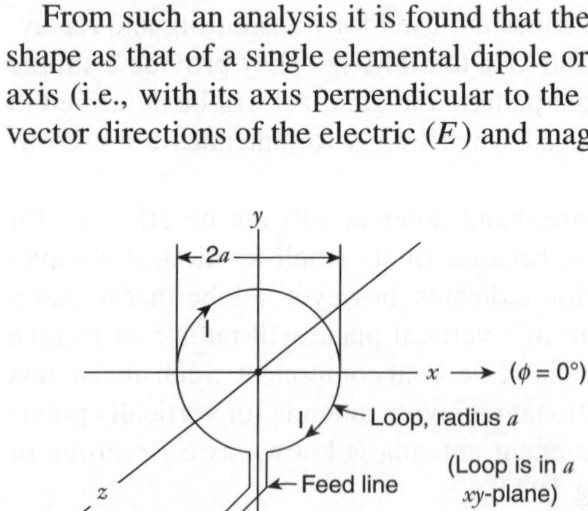

FIGURE 4–18.

Basic form of loop antenna.

horizontal. The small loop is an oscillating *magnetic dipole*, which is equivalent to a bar magnet whose magnetic strength and polarity oscillate. Because the pattern has the same shape as the elemental electric dipole, the directivity is the same ($D = 1.5$) and so is the half-power beamwidth ($BW_{3dB} = 90°$).

Now consider Fig. 4–18 and assume an observer is on the z-axis, which extends outward from the page, and where angle $\theta = 0°$. Recall that the current I is assumed constant and of the same phase everywhere on the loop. Then, the radiation reaching the observer from any two diametrically opposite located elemental dipoles are equal in magnitude and opposite in phase, and thus cancel. In other words, at $\theta = 0°$ the pattern has zero amplitude, as indicated in Fig. 4–4 for the dipole. Now notice that as θ is increased by being removed from the z-axis, the path length difference (and thus the phase difference) increases between the radiation from diametrically opposite elemental dipoles. Therefore, the pattern's amplitude increases with increases in θ. Furthermore, because of the symmetry of the loop about the z-axis, it is clear that the amplitude is constant and independent of θ. Therefore, analogous to the pattern of a short dipole, the E-field pattern of a loop antenna is donut shaped.

The polarization can also be determined from considering Fig. 4–18. Let an observer be anywhere on the x-y plane and far removed from the loop. Then, recalling that the polarization from each elemental dipole within the loop is aligned with the direction of its current, one can discern that the vectorial sum of the radiation at each angle θ is perpendicular to the z-axis. But, because of loop symmetry, the electric field lines are necessarily concentric about the z-axis. Thus, if the z-axis is vertical, the polarization is horizontal.

The relationship between the loop current and the radiated power is quite different for a loop, since the radiation resistance of the elemental dipole depends on the ratio of its length to the wavelength, and the geometry of a loop is not comparable. The formula for the radiation resistance of a small loop is

$$R_r \cong \frac{31{,}200 A^2}{\lambda^4} \text{ohms} \tag{4–18a}$$

where A is the area of the loop and λ is the wavelength. Since A can be expressed in terms of circumference C as $C^2/4\pi$, (4–18a) can also be expressed as

$$R_r \cong 197\left(\frac{C}{\lambda}\right)^4 \tag{4–18b}$$

In these formulas, A, C, and λ must be expressed in the same units of length.

The elemental-dipole pattern (with E and H directions interchanged) and these radiation-resistance formulas apply only to loops that are small compared to a wavelength. This criterion is considered to be met if the loop diameter is less than 0.1 wavelength. For this maximum size of loop, the radiation resistance is about 2 ohms. A very large current, therefore, is needed for radiation of appreciable power, as was also found to be true of short dipoles (sec. 4.1).

It turns out that the results found for a circular loop apply equally well for a loop of any shape as long as its dimensions are sufficiently small compared to a wavelength; the radiation resistance depends only upon its area, following (4–18a). The loop may be square, triangular, or even irregular in shape.

At very low frequencies it is common to make a loop with more than one turn of wire. If the number of turns is N, the resulting radiation resistance is found by multiplying the one-turn value of (4–18a) or (4–18b) by N^2. It is necessary that the total length of wire be small compared to the wavelength if the small-loop behavior is to apply, but if the frequency is very low (wavelength very long) this requirement is not difficult to meet. Because of the large wavelength, however, the radiation resistance may still be a very small value in spite of the number of turns, and the loop may have a significant ohmic resistance also. Therefore the radiation efficiency will be poor.

When such loops are used for receiving, the terminals of the loop may be connected to a very high-impedance receiver input circuit, so that the quantity of primary interest is the voltage induced in the loop rather than the power delivered. When the loop has its plane in the direction of a properly polarized incoming signal, if the incident-wave field intensity is E volts per meter, the induced voltage will be

$$V = \frac{2\pi NAE}{\lambda} \text{ volts} \tag{4–19}$$

where N is the number of turns of the loop and A is its area.

Small loops are often used for receiving as direction finders when the received signals are vertically polarized. The direction of the received signal is determined by orienting the loop with its axis toward the signal direction. The "null" (minimum value) of the pattern is in this direction and is very sharp (corresponding to the pattern in the direction of the axis of a dipole, Fig. 4–2). Thus, when the orientation of the loop is adjusted for minimum signal, the direction of the signal is accurately indicated. There is a twofold ambiguity in the direction, however, because a null exists in the pattern on both sides of the loop. This ambiguity may be resolved in various ways. A common way is to combine (in the receiver input circuit) the loop output with the output of a small vertical dipole, with a 90 degree phase difference (produced by the circuit arrangement). If the loop and dipole signal amplitudes are equal, the resulting combined pattern has only one null and is therefore unambiguous. However, loop direction finding is successful only when the loop can be located in an environment free from nearby large reflecting objects that may result in signals arriving at the loop position from more than one direction. This destroys the null effect, or at the least it destroys the sharpness of the null.

4.5.2. Other Loop Antennas

This section describes some other types of loops. Smith (2007) discusses these and other configurations, and includes an extensive annotated list of references.

Loops are fed by coaxial cables or two-wire lines. An interesting coax-fed loop configuration has some features common with the short vertical monopoles on automobiles.

In both cases, the outer conductor of the coaxial cable is attached to the base plate. Also in both cases, the center conductor passes through a hole in the conducting base plate, from which an image is formed. In the monopole arrangement, an extension of the center conductor serves as the half-dipole above the base plate. However, for the loop, the extension is bent into a half circle, whereby its image in the base plate forms the other half of the loop.

For light-weight receiver applications, a low-loss magnetic ceramic (ferrite) is commonly used as the core within a multiturn loop to improve efficiency. A reflecting backplane (parallel with the plane of the loop) can be used for providing a unidirectional pattern and increased directivity. Resonant loops (discussed below) are also used as the elements of phased arrays to increase directivity: an example being coaxially positioned loops to function as the reflector, driven element, and directors of a Yagi-Uda array (Fig. 5–11).

Small-loop analysis is applicable to loop wire-lengths of roughly 0.1λ or less, so that the current distribution around the loop is approximately uniform. Larger loops are also used, especially at the higher frequencies. Ordinarily the patterns of larger loops have multiple lobes, and the current distributions on these loops affect the patterns considerably.

The Alford loop, shown in Fig. 4–19, is an example of a larger loop. It is more efficient than, and has a pattern similar to, that of a small loop. It consists of a square one-turn loop with quarter-wavelength sides, and it is fed with opposite phases at opposite corners. The other two corners are capacitively connected. The out-of-phase feed is achieved by transposing one branch of the feed line as shown. The capacitors are commonly open-end sections of transmission line; with the reactance given in chapter 2 by (2–24). The radiation resistance of the Alford loop is about 80 ohms. Its radiation pattern is similar (though not identical) to that of a small loop, but it is much more efficient.

As the circumference C of a loop increases and approaches a wavelength, the peak of the beam moves toward the loop axis. Near this resonant length, the far field pattern is nearly the same as two parallel dipoles separated by approximately the loop diameter. The input impedance varies significantly with C, having large peaks in both the resistance and reactance for circumferences near odd multiples of $\lambda/2$. Near the resonant loop length of λ, the input resistance is about 100 ohms and the reactance component is relatively small. Thus, the input impedance for a loop with a one λ circumference can be readily matched to a transmission line.

The pattern of the resonant $C = \lambda$ loop can be made unidirectional and the directivity increased an axial direction by placing the loop over a planar reflector. With spacings between the reflector and

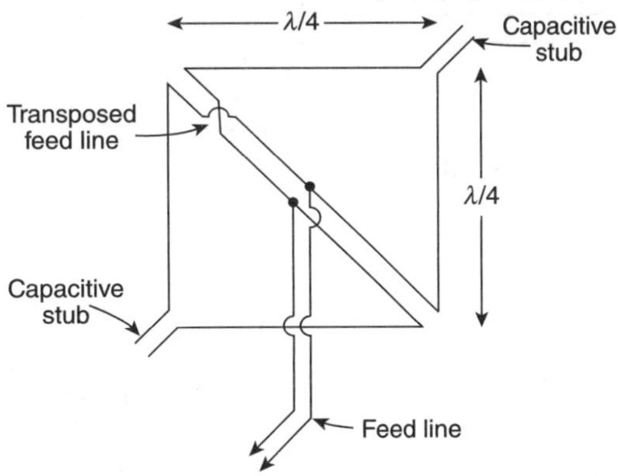

FIGURE 4–19.
The Alford loop antenna.

loop in the range of 0.05λ to 0.2λ, measurements have given directivities of approximately 10, and input impedances that can be readily matched (resistance $R \leq 135\ \Omega$). The reflector used was square reflector and had different side dimensions between 0.6λ and 1.9λ.

As already noted, when the loop circumference is increased to value near one wavelength, the maximum of the far field pattern is along the loop axis. Resonant loops of this type are used as the elements of a Yagi-Uda array to form a unidirectional beam along the axes of the loops and of the array. Details for choosing the dimensions of the loops and their spacings for a Yagi-Uda array are given by Balanis (2005, p. 599).

4.6. Helical Antennas

Another basic form of radiator is the helix, which is a wire (conductor) wound in the shape of a screw thread and used as an antenna in conjunction with a flat metal plate called a *ground plane*. Helixes are mostly used at relatively high frequencies so that their dimensions are appreciable compared to the wavelength. Theory and practice in the art of helical antennas has been developed largely by John Kraus and his associates at the Ohio State University (Kraus and Marhefka 2002, pp. 222–42).

As shown in Fig. 4–20, the helix is fed at one end, usually being connected to the center conductor of a coaxial transmission line whose outer conductor is connected to the ground plane. The basic geometry of the helix is described in terms of its diameter D and its turn spacing S. For an N-turn helix the total length of the antenna is equal to

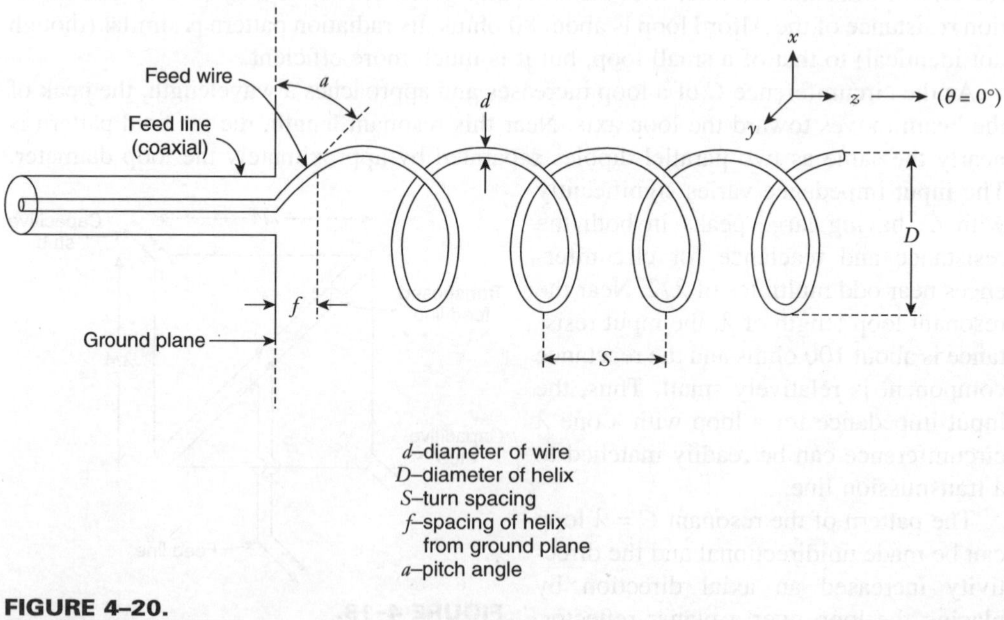

FIGURE 4–20.
Helical antenna.

NS, and the circumference $C = \pi D$. The length of the wire per turn of the helix is $L = \sqrt{S^2 + C^2} = \sqrt{S^2 + \pi D^2}$. The pitch angle α, an important parameter of the helix, is the angle that a line tangent to the helix wire makes with the plane perpendicular to the axis of the helix; and it can be found from this relation: $\sin\alpha = S/L$ or $\tan\alpha = S/\pi D = S/C$. The properties of helical antennas are described in terms of these geometric parameters. Many different radiation characteristics may be obtained by varying their magnitudes in relation to the wavelength λ.

The feed wire (Fig. 4–20), which connects the terminus of the co-axial center conductor to the beginning of the actual helix, lies in a plane through the helix axis and is inclined with respect to the ground plane at approximately the pitch angle of the helix. Variation of its geometry affects the input impedance of the antenna.

When the dimensions of the helix are very small compared with the wavelength, the maximum radiation is in the plane perpendicular to the helix axis, and the radiation pattern is a combination of the equivalent radiation from a short dipole positioned on the helix axis and a small loop also coaxial with the helix. This type of helix is known as a normal mode helical antenna (NMHA), and it is widely used in wireless handsets. To reduce cost of manufacture, NMHAs have been fabricated by printing a conducting path into a groove in a small, cylindrical plastic post or mast (see Fig. 36–2, Vardaxoglou and James 2007).

For a NMHA, the patterns of the two equivalent radiators are of course the same, but the linearly polarized components are at right angles, and the phase angles at a given point in space are 90 degrees apart. Therefore, as explained in sec. 1.1.3, the resultant field is elliptically polarized or circularly polarized, depending on the field-strength ratio of the two components. This ratio depends on the pitch angle α. When α is very small, the loop type of radiation predominates; when it becomes very large, the helix becomes essentially a short dipole. In these two limiting cases the radiated polarization is linear, in one having loop polarization, and in the other, dipole polarization. For intermediate values of α the polarization is elliptical, and at a particular value of α it will be circular. Wheeler (1947) showed that this result is obtained when $S = \pi^2 D^2/2\lambda$, which corresponds to a value of α given by

$$\tan\alpha = \frac{\pi D}{2\lambda} \qquad (4\text{–}20)$$

The analysis of the helix leading to these conclusions may be made by considering it to be equivalent to a number of small loops having the same diameter as the turns of the helix, with their planes parallel and their axes in line with the helix axis and spaced the same as the helix turn spacing. Then these loops are considered to be connected by short dipoles parallel to the helix axis and of length equal to the helix turn spacing. The radiation field of the helix is equivalent to that obtained by superposition of the fields of these elemental radiators.

When the diameter and spacing (D and S) are appreciable fractions of a wavelength, an entirely different radiation pattern is obtained. The maximum intensity is radiated in the direction of the helix axis, in the form of a directional beam with minor lobes at oblique angles. The radiation in the main lobe is circularly polarized. It is this feature of the helix, in this mode of radiation (the *axial* mode), that probably accounts for most of the practical applications of this type of antenna.

A typical helical antenna operating in this mode has a circumference C of approximately one wavelength and spacing S approximately a quarter wavelength. The antenna will operate quite well over a range of frequency so that these dimensions are noncritical. The ground plane (which may be either a solid sheet or a wire grid or mesh) should be at least $\frac{3}{4}$ of a wavelength in diameter. The pitch angle may range from about 12 to 18 degrees; approximately 14 degrees is optimum. The gain and beamwidth depend on the helix length (equal to NS, Fig. 4–20, where N is the number of turns). The feed-point impedance is resistive and of the order of 150 ohms at the frequency for which $C = \lambda$. At higher and lower frequencies the resistive component varies, and a reactive component appears. Detailed design information are available (Kraus and Marhefka 2002, ch. 8).

In terms of a three-dimensional spherical coordinate system (Fig. 3–1) with the $\theta = 0°$ axis coincident with the helix axis, the beam (pattern) has axial symmetry, that is, it is the same in any plane containing the axis (does not depend on the longitude angle ϕ). The 3-dB beamwidth, obtained imperically, is given approximately by the formula

$$\theta_{3\,\mathrm{db}} = \frac{52}{C}\sqrt{\frac{\lambda^3}{NS}}\ \text{degrees} \tag{4–21}$$

The formula assumes that the pitch angle is between 12 and 15 degrees, that N is equal to or greater than 3, that NS (the helix length) is not greater than 10 wavelengths, and that C is between 0.75λ and 1.33λ.

The directivity, subject to the same assumptions, is given by

$$D_{max} = \frac{12NSC^2}{\lambda^3} \tag{4–22}$$

In some applications it is necessary to pay attention to whether the helix is wound with a right-hand or a left-hand pitch (analogous to right-hand and left-hand screw threads). This determines whether the wave will be right- or left-hand circularly polarized. (A receiving antenna designed to receive right-hand circular polarization cannot receive left-hand circular, and vice versa.)

Helical antennas have found considerable application in space telemetry applications at the ground end of the telemetry link with ballistic missiles, satellites, and space probes, at HF and VHF. The circular polarization is useful in this application because of the polarization rotation of waves produced by the ionosphere (Faraday effect, sec. 1.4.6).

4.7. Horn Radiators

The radiators thus far discussed are based on the concept of fields set up by alternating currents in wires (in the generalized sense of the term "wire," which includes tubing, pipes, and bars). The most basic of them is the elemental dipole, since in principle all other current-carrying conductors can be regarded (mathematically and conceptually) as an assemblage of elemental dipoles, and the radiation field is then deduced by applying the principle of linear superposition to the fields of the individual dipoles.

Another class of radiators is based on the existence over a surface of a specific electromagnetic field configuration. The intensity, phase, and polarization of the field over this surface, or *aperture*, are analogous to the current amplitude, phase, and direction in antennas represented by an assemblage of dipoles. The description of the variation of these field quantities over the aperture is called the *aperture distribution*. When this distribution is known, it is possible in principle to calculate the radiation pattern, just as it is possible for a wire or arrangement of wires in which the current distribution is known. As for radiation due to currents, the analysis of radiation due to the field distribution of an aperture is based on Maxwell's equations.

An example of an aperture over which the field distribution is known is the cross section of a waveguide, in which a particular known mode is propagating, as described in sec. 2.5. It is a well-known experimental fact that if such a guide is "sawed off" in a plane perpendicular to the axis of the guide, leaving an open end, radiation will occur from this open mouth. The resulting field pattern can be calculated from the known configuration of the field for the particular waveguide mode. This is the simplest case of a *waveguide horn radiator*.

It should not be surprising that radiation occurs under these circumstances because the fields inside a waveguide are propagating in essentially the same way that fields propagate in free space; the only difference is that they are constrained from spreading spherically by the walls of the guide. When this propagating field reaches the guide mouth it continues to propagate in the same general direction except that, in accordance with Huygen's principle, it also spreads laterally, and the wavefront eventually becomes spherical, although there is a "near field" region in the vicinity of the mouth of the guide in which the wavefront is more complicated. It can be thought of as a transition region in which the changeover from guided propagation to free-space propagation takes place. This changeover involves a change of phase velocity and a change in the characteristic wave impedance, from those of the guide to the free-space values, $c = 3 \times 10^8$ meters per second and $Z_c = 377$ ohms.

Because the waveguide impedance is ordinarily different from this free-space value, the radiating open end does not usually present a matched-impedance load to the guide, resulting in an undesirable standing wave. This can be eliminated by some form of transformer matching device, such as those described in sec. 2.5. A better method, however, is to flare the walls of the guide. If this is done properly, it results not only in a matched impedance but also in a more concentrated radiation pattern, that is, narrower beamwidth and higher directivity. This flared structure is what is ordinarily meant by the term *horn radiator*.

Various possible flaring arrangements, resulting in different types of horns, are shown in Fig. 4–21. As shown, a rectangular guide may be flared on the narrow walls, the wide walls, or both. A *sectoral horn* is flared in only one dimension. If the flare is in the direction of the electric vector, as when the broad walls are flared with the TE_{10} mode in

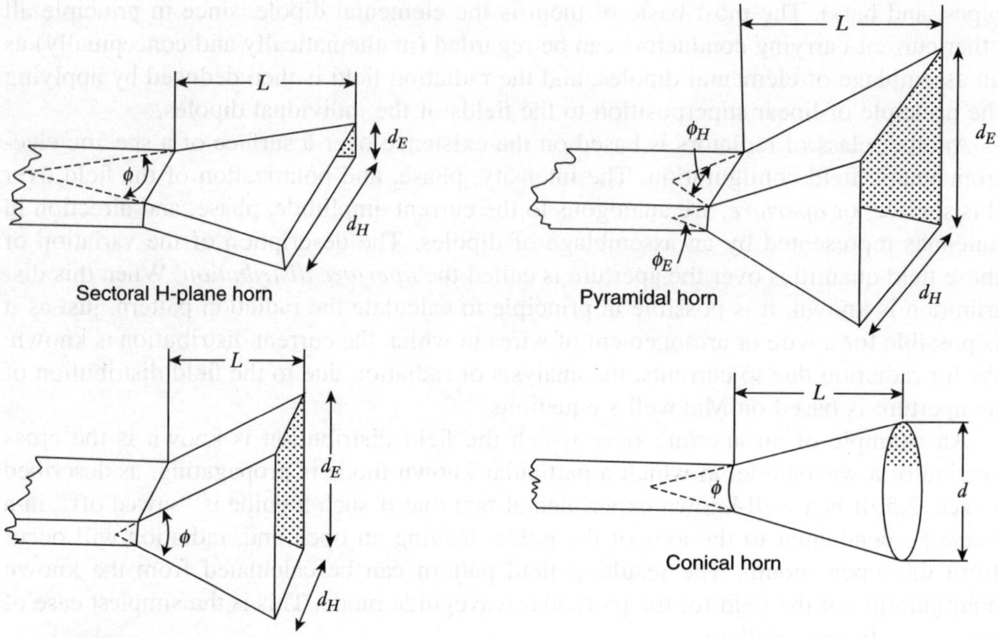

FIGURE 4–21.
Waveguide horn types.

rectangular guide, the result is an E-plane sectoral horn; when the narrow walls are flared, the radiator is an H-plane sectoral horn. Flaring both walls results in a *pyramidal horn.* A *conical horn* is formed by uniform flaring of the walls of a circular waveguide.

If the flare angle ϕ is too great, the wavefront at the mouth of the horn will be curved rather than plane. This means that the phase distribution over the aperture will be non-uniform, resulting in decreased directivity and increased beamwidth. On the other hand, too small a flare angle results in a small aperture area for a given length L of the horn. The directivity is proportional to the aperture size for a given aperture distribution. Thus, there is an optimum flare angle that provides the maximum gain for a given horn length, and therefore the optimum flare angle is intermediate between slight and abrupt. In other words, an *optimum horn* or *optimum-gain horn* is one that compromises in aperture phase error to maximize its gain for a given length L, and therefore its flare angle is intermediate between slight and abrupt.

Graphs of radiation patterns are available for a variety of horn types and dimensions (Balanis, ch. 13, 2005; Love 1993). These graphs, known as universal patterns, were generated by aperture theory and have been validated, generally, by measurements. The "universal" patterns provide details of the major lobe shapes for large as well as small horns, with aperture widths as small as 1.5 or 2λ. Even so, designs for center-fed reflectors and lenses often require feed-horn patterns with dimensions even smaller than 1.5λ. (Section 6.3.3 provides guidance on design for horn aperture widths less than 2λ).

It is apparent that the flare angle must be made smaller as the length is increased to maintain a given maximum phase variation across the aperture. Therefore there is a practical limit to the gain that can be obtained with a horn radiator; very high gain requires an excessive horn length. For moderate gains, however, horn radiators are very useful. They are of course especially appropriate when the feed line is a waveguide. Their bandwidth is then essentially the bandwidth of the guide—2:1 typically, for the TE_{10} mode in rectangular guide and a sectoral or pyramidal horn.

The published literature on optimum-gain horns includes somewhat different results for beamwidths versus horn dimensions, depending on how the horn dimensions are specified and the details of analysis. Kraus and Marhefka (2002, p. 339) provide simple equations for the beamwidths of optimum horns, that were obtained from analyses of measured beamwidths versus horn flare angle, for various horn lengths. Those equations for the 3 dB beamwidths of "optimally" tapered horns follow:

$$\theta_E = \frac{56}{d_E} \text{ degrees} \tag{4–23a}$$

and

$$\theta_H = \frac{67}{d_H} \text{ degrees} \tag{4–23b}$$

where E and H refer to the horn's E and H plane patterns. The symbols d_E and d_H are the aperture dimensions (widths), expressed in wavelengths along the E and H planes.

Use of (4–23a) and (4–23b) does not require detailed horn dimensions, yet they provide good "first" beamwidth estimates for an "optimumly" tapered horn. As already mentioned, the universal patterns are considered accurate when detailed horn dimensions are available. It is to be noted that optimum gain horns are often called standard gain horns, because of their wide laboratory usage. When detailed horn dimensions are available and more accurate calculated beamwidths are desired, the reader is referred to Bird and Love (2007, pp. 14–17). These authors also include an equation for the gain of an optimum-gain antenna, which follows

$$G = \frac{6.5 d_E d_H}{\lambda^2} = \frac{6.5A}{\lambda^2} \tag{4–24}$$

where $A = d_E d_H$ is the area of the horn-mouth opening (aperture). From (3–39) of chapter 3, a recommended formula for estimating gain is

$$G = \frac{26{,}000}{\theta_E \theta_H} \tag{4–25}$$

By using (4–23a) and (4–23b) with (4–24), one finds a difference of only 0.3 dB in gain from that provided by (4–25).

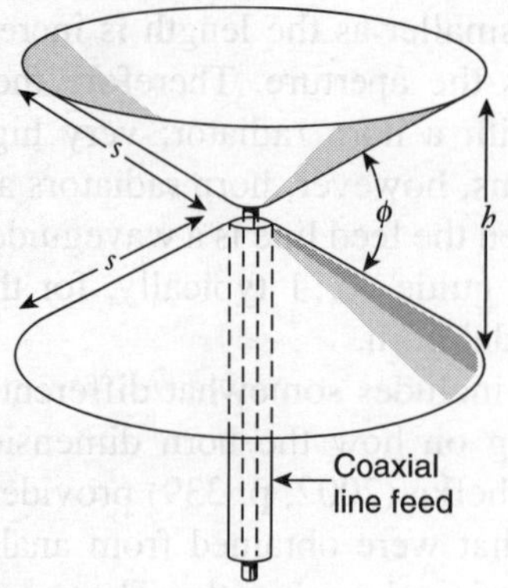

FIGURE 4–22.

Biconical horn.

Incidentally an unflared open-mouthed waveguide provides a slightly greater directivity than (4–24) indicates, because of its more nearly constant phase distribution. For such a radiator the factor 6.5 in (4–24) becomes approximately 10. For a typical rectangular guide A is approximately equal to $\lambda^2/4$; hence G is about 2.5 Thus this simple radiator has a somewhat greater gain than 1.64, the gain of a half-wave dipole.

Many special forms of horns are used. There are too many to describe in detail, but their basic principle is the same as those of the commoner types that have been discussed. One special horn that deserves a brief discussion, however, is the biconical horn, pictured in Fig. 4–22 . It consists of two conical metal surfaces with their axes collinear (in line with each other) and their vertexes opposed. As with sectoral horns, there is an optimum flare angle that depends on the mode of excitation employed (Terman 1943). With the coaxial-line feed shown, the polarization will be vertical, and the optimum-flare criterion is $h = \sqrt{2s\lambda}$. Since $\sin(\phi/2) = h/2s$, the optimum flare angle ϕ is the one that satisfies the relation

$$\sin\left(\frac{\phi}{2}\right) = \sqrt{\lambda/2s} \tag{4–26}$$

Horizontal polarization may be excited in this horn by means of a small loop antenna with its plane perpendicular to the cone axes and lying between the vertexes, and the loop axis collinear with the cone axes. The optimum flare angle is then given by

$$\sin\left(\frac{\phi}{2}\right) = \sqrt{3\lambda/4s} \tag{4–27}$$

The radiation pattern is omnidirectional in the horizontal plane with the cone axes vertical, the vertical beamwidth and directivity depending on the dimension h. For optimum flare angles the directivity is given by

$$D = m\left(\frac{2h}{\lambda}\right) \tag{4–28}$$

where for vertical polarization (assuming vertical cone axes) the factor $m \simeq 0.8$, and for horizontal polarization $m \simeq 0.6$. The vertical beamwidths may be estimated using (4–23a) for vertical polarization and (4–23b) for horizontal polarization, with d_E and d_H replaced by h.

The omnidirectional horizontal pattern is the attractive feature of the biconical horn, in the VHF and UHF bands, especially with horizontal polarization. Few antennas provide a truly omnidirectional horizontal-plane pattern and horizontal polarization.

4.8. Slot Radiators

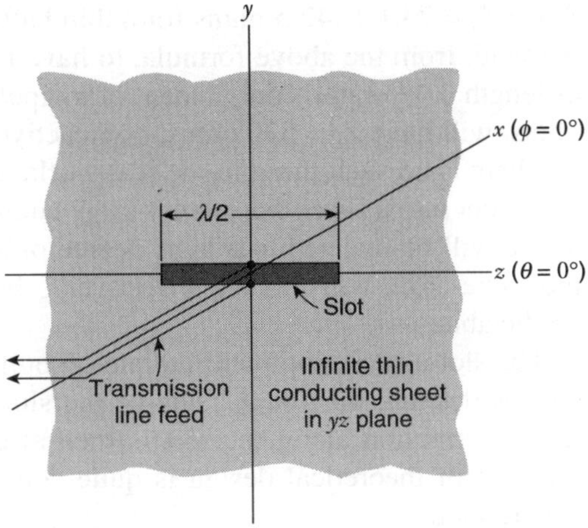

FIGURE 4–23.

Radiating slot in an infinite plane conducting sheet.

If a narrow slot-like opening is cut in a large flat sheet of metal, and properly connected to a source of rf power, it will radiate in a manner that bears a certain resemblance to the radiation by a dipole of the same dimensions as the slot. In fact, if the conducting sheet is a plane of infinite extent, the radiation pattern will have exactly the same shape as that of the corresponding dipole except that the electric and magnetic vectors are interchanged. (The same relationship exists, incidentally, between the patterns of a short dipole and a small loop.) Also, the impedance properties of the slot are somewhat different. These complementary properties of a slot in an infinite plane conductor, and a thin flat dipole of exactly the same dimensions as the slot, are predicted by an important result of electromagnetic theory known as *Babinet's principle*. It also relates the impedance properties of the two kinds of radiators.

Figure 4–23 shows such a slot and a two-wire transmission-line feed connected to it. For the half-wavelength-long slot shown, the radiation pattern will have the same angle dependence as that of a half-wave dipole, as given by (4–11) and plotted in Fig. 4–14. Note that only the term in square brackets of (4–11) applies; i.e., the *relative* patterns are the same. Also, since the E and H vectors are interchanged, the polarization is opposite to that of the corresponding (complementary) dipole. It is this fact that allows the three-dimensional "doughnut" pattern to exist unaffected by the presence of the conducting plane, and on both sides of it, except for the infinitesimally thin slice eliminated by the metal sheet. That is, the required electric field intensity can exist in the space at the surface of the conducting plane because the electric field lines are perpendicular to the plane. (It is a well-known principle of electromagnetic theory that they could not so exist if they were parallel to the surface.)

Thus beamwidth and directivity are the same as for the half-wave dipole; $\theta_{3dB} = 78°$ and $D = 1.64$. The input impedance Z_s for the connection shown in Fig. 4–23 is related to the input impedance of a center-fed half-wave dipole, Z_d, by the formula

$$Z_s = \frac{(120\pi)^2}{4Z_d} = \frac{35,530}{Z_d} \tag{4–29}$$

Since $Z_d = 73.1 + j42.5$ ohms for a thin half-wave dipole, a thin (narrow) half-wave slot is found, from the above formula, to have impedance $Z_s = 363 - j211$ ohms. A thin slot of length 0.475λ, the complement of a dipole having nonreactive input impedance of 67 ohms, will have $Z_s = 530$ ohms, nonreactive.

There is no such thing in the real world as an infinite plane conducting sheet, but if a slot is cut into a sheet that is very large compared to the slot, then the behavior predicted above will be realized to a high degree of approximation. Slots cut into sheets of even moderate size will radiate effectively, but their exact behavior is not as readily predictable.

The slot as described will radiate on both sides of the sheet. If radiation on one side only is desired, the "back" side of the slot may be enclosed by a box, or cavity. The field distribution along the slot is then affected by the dimensions of the cavity. The problem of theoretical design is quite complicated, and design is often determined by experiment.

A unidirectionally radiating slot may also be obtained by cutting it in a proper position and orientation in the wall of a waveguide. Figure 4–24 shows the appearance of several slots in a TE_{10}-mode rectangular waveguide that will radiate, and two that will not radiate. A waveguide slot, if it is to radiate, must be positioned so that it interrupts currents that would otherwise flow across its length in the inner walls of the guide. This is equivalent to saying that there must be a component of magnetic field (H) parallel to the slot at the

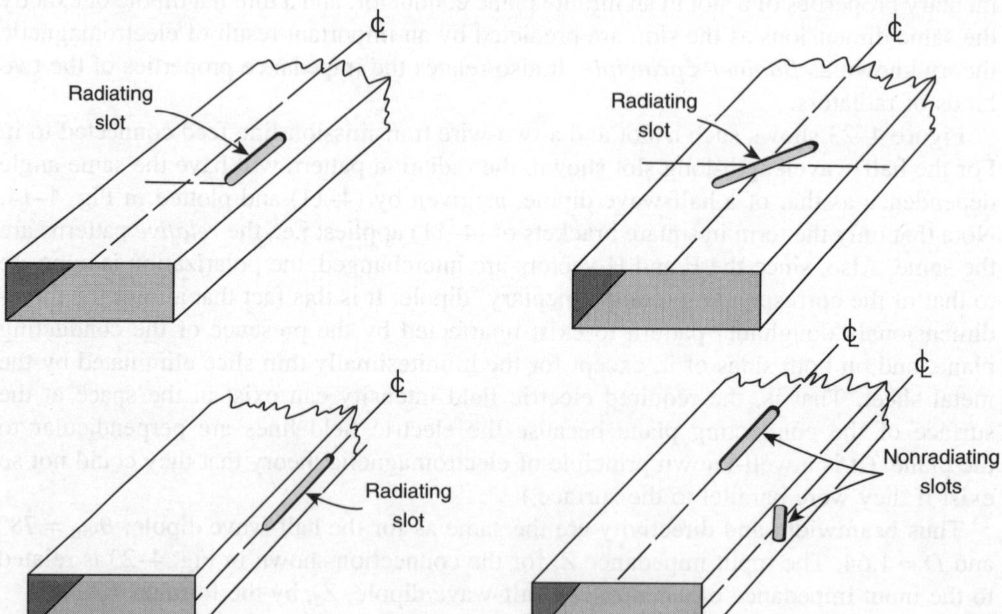

FIGURE 4–24.

Radiating and nonradiating waveguide slots in rectangular guide, TE_{10} mode.

inner surface of the guide. The field configurations in waveguide for various modes are given in advanced engineering textbooks and handbooks. The examples of radiating slots shown in Fig. 4–24 by no means exhaust the possibilities. To be most effective the waveguide slot should be resonant, which it will be if the length is approximately half a wavelength. However, the exact length for resonance depends on the position of the slot in the guide.

A waveguide slot does not radiate the total power flowing in the guide; it "extracts" or "couples out" some fraction of it. The remaining power continues on down the guide to whatever additional load there may be further on. Or if it encounters a "short circuit" (end cap), it is reflected. By impedance matching devices it may then be possible to couple all the power to the slot. Waveguide slots, however, are seldom used singly; usually an "array" of them is cut along the length of the guide, as will be described in sec. 5.9.

Slot radiators need not be complements of half-wave dipoles. Many other radiating shapes are possible, but all may be analyzed in terms of their complementary radiators. For example, an annular-ring slot in an infinite plane sheet will have a radiation pattern exactly like that of a loop of the same size, with *E*-fields and *H*-fields interchanged. Slot radiators are practically restricted to the higher frequencies by the requirement of a conducting sheet considerably larger than the slot. They are very useful when a radiator must be devised that will not project from a surface, for example, in an airplane wing or fuselage. (Here the opening may be covered by a protective cover of low-loss dielectric material.)

4.9. Patch or Microstrip Antennas

The geometry of a microstrip is well adapted to construction by printed-circuit techniques, in which the strip conductor and adjoining ground planes can be deposited on low-loss substrate material by mass-production methods. An unbalanced microstrip geometry is illustrated in chapter 2, Fig. 2–9 (lower right). The balanced form has the strip enclosed both below and above by a metallic ground plane. This transmission-line technology can be combined with ordinary printed-circuit techniques to permit construction of monolithic phased-array modules containing not only the transmission line components, but also phase shifters, couplers, control circuitry, radiating elements, and solid-state transmitting and receiving amplifiers. This fabrication technique greatly reduces the cost as well as the bulk of large phased arrays. Moreover, the "sheet" construction need not be completely planar; it can be made to conform to the surface of a vehicle such as the fuselage of an airplane. An array thus constructed in nonplanar form is known as a conformal array.

A patch or microstrip antenna is commonly a metal rectangular or circular metal surface (the patch) on a dielectric ground plane, such as a printed circuit board. The patch or microstrip antenna is useful as a single element antenna and as the element-type within multielement arrays. Their features include lightweight and ruggedness with low profile, and bandwidths typically less than a few percent. Patch antennas can be made that radiate either a linear or a circular polarization, and the use of two operating frequencies is

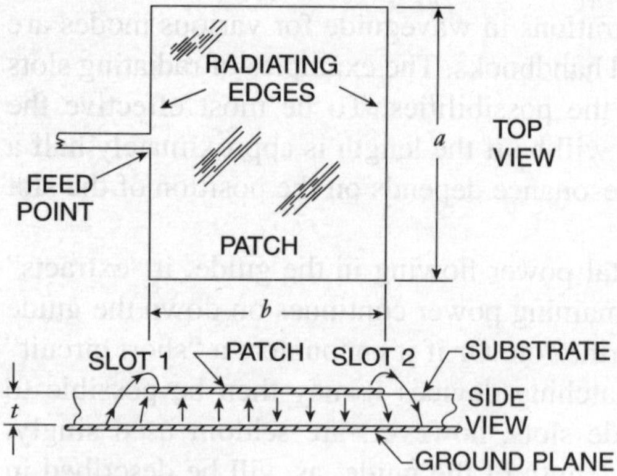

FIGURE 4–25.

Microstrip antenna, a thin conducting patch on a dielectric substrate above a conducting ground plane (from Carver and Mink 1981; © 1981, IEEE).

possible. Because of their ruggedness and lightweight, patches are especially useful for airborne or space applications (Howell 1975; Munson 1974). Practical patch antennas have been made for a wide range of wavelengths, covering at least from UHF into the millimeter wavelengths.

The top and side views of a rectangular patch or microstrip antenna are illustrated in Fig. 4–25. The patch is energized by a microstrip transmission line at the patch's left side, where the dipole launches radiation. Instead, the patch can be energized by a coaxial line in a configuration called a pin fed patch. Then, the outer coaxial conductor is connected to the ground plane of the printed circuit board and the center conductor is routed through a hole in the printed circuit board and connected to the patch. Sometimes proximity coupling is used, where the connection is electromagnetic instead of direct.

Figure 4–25 depicts a patch antenna, where a wave propagates in a dielectric substrate within parallel plates between the patch and the ground plane. The parallel plate medium is a resonant structure. With a relative dielectric constant ε_r, the between-plates wavelength is $\lambda/\sqrt{\varepsilon_r}$. The length, electrically, from the left to the right patch sides is approximately one-half λ, and thus the physical length is $\approx \lambda/2\sqrt{\varepsilon_r}$. This produces a phase difference between the left and right edges (designated as slots 1 and 2 in Fig. 4–25) of approximately 180°, making the vertical components of the edge *E*-fields of opposite polarity. However, the edge horizontal components are in time phase. The terminology underscores the fact that the fringing of the electric fields at the patch edges is similar to the electric fields that emanate from narrow slits. Therefore, the pattern has maximum amplitude in the direction normal to the patch (i.e., upward) and it is horizontally polarized (pointed to the right).

Patch antenna design and development became an active field in the early 1970s. By January 1981, a special issue of the *IEEE Transactions on Antennas and Propagation* was published that contained a number of especially significant papers (see, e.g., Carver and Mink 1981; Mailloux, McIlvenna, and Kernweis 1981). At that time, the perceived needs included, for example, increases in impedance bandwidth beyond the then available few percent, improved techniques to allow multifrequency operation, and small microstrip phase shifters for use in electronic scanning patch arrays.

Robust developments continued in the patch antenna field, resulting in reliable fabrication techniques, dramatically increased bandwidths, and reduced sizes. Novel designs now include patches that are stacked, stacked patches that are probe fed, and multiple shorting posts on stacked patches. For example, the literature describes stacked-patch antennas having bandwidths up to octave widths (Targonski, Waterhouse, and Pozar

1998; Waterhouse 1999) and electrical sizes small enough for hand-held mobile communications at frequencies less than 2 GHz (Waterhouse, Targonski, and Kokotoff 1998).

4.10. Surface-Wave and Leaky-Wave Antennas

In the years during and since World War II some rather exotic forms of antennas have been devised, primarily in the category of VHF, UHF, and microwave antennas. Two such types of antennas that may be in the class of basic radiators are the surface-wave and leaky-wave antennas. Their theory and applications are too complex and too extensive for a full discussion here (see, e.g., Kraus and Marhefka 2002, pp. 734–41).

These antenna types are analyzed in terms of guided electromagnetic waves propagated along a surface or other guiding structure that does not fully confine them. Radiation may take place at discontinuities of the structure, or gradually along an aperture. Prominent examples of such antennas are the polyrod antenna, the cigar antenna, the zigzag, the holey plate, and the mushroom antenna. Some of these antennas find use in applications requiring a high-gain radiator with a low silhouette, as on a streamlined aircraft. They are primarily microwave or near-microwave devices, but they are by no means limited to the microwave region. In fact, the Yagi-Uda antenna, usually discussed as an *array* antenna (sec. 5.3), can also be regarded as a surface-wave antenna. This antenna is often used at frequencies as low as the 20 meter (14 MHz) amateur radio band.

4.11. Basic Feed Methods

The usual arrangement for feeding power to an antenna from a transmitter, or to a receiver from the antenna, is indicated in block-diagram form in Fig. 4–26. The transmission line can be any of the types discussed in secs. 2–4 and 2–5. The function of transformer A is to match the antenna feed-point impedance to the characteristic impedance of the line and also to make a transition, if necessary, from one form of line to another (e.g., from balanced to unbalanced, or from coaxial line to waveguide). Transformer B serves the same functions between the transmission line and the internal impedance of the transmitter or receiver. The two transformers insure not only that the transmitter will be correctly "loaded" by the antenna and that the antenna will be correctly loaded by the receiver, but also that there will be no standing waves on the transmission line. Elimination of standing waves is desirable, but not essential. If standing waves are to be permitted, one transformer can be omitted, and the other transformer adjusted for correct loading of the

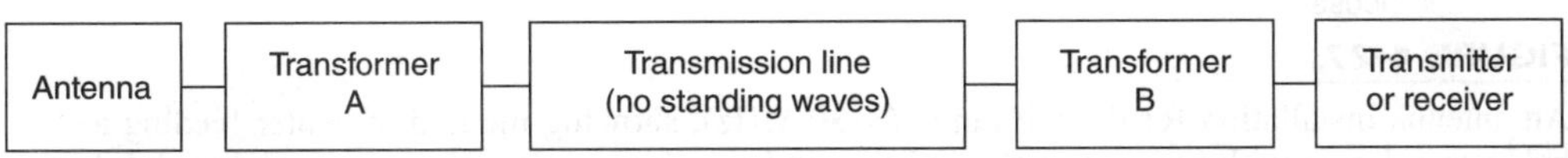

FIGURE 4–26.

Block diagram of basic antenna feeding arrangement.

transmitter (or, in reception, optimum transfer of received signal power from the antenna to the receiver).

Sometimes the transmission line can be eliminated altogether by making a direct connection from the antenna to the transmitter output terminals or the receiver input terminals. Here also only one transformer is required. This situation can exist at very low frequencies, where a "line" of even a few hundred feet in length may be in effect a direct connection. Any conductor of length less than about a hundredth of a wavelength may be so regarded, since no appreciable standing wave pattern can exist on a conductor so electrically short. The direct connection can also exist at higher frequencies when the antenna is "built into" a receiver or transceiver.

The transformers at low frequencies are inductor-and-capacitor devices. In addition to impedance step-up or step-down, they also can provide reactance cancellation; both effects may occur in the same circuit elements or they may be separated. At the higher frequencies the transformers may be composed of transmission-line or waveguide elements, as described in secs. 2–3 and 2–5.

At frequencies up to about 30 MHz, two-wire balanced transmission lines can be used, since at these frequencies radiation due to the line spacing being a significant fraction of a wavelength is not a serious problem. Line impedances range from slightly less than 100 ohms to perhaps 800 ohms. The lower impedances are achieved with close-spaced wires embedded in low-loss polyethylene plastic. The higher impedances result with air-insulated wires or tubing. The wire lines have spacing bars of porcelain or other insulating material at intervals of a few feet or more, depending on the spacing and the wire stiffness.

When the higher-impedance lines are used to feed an ordinary half-wave dipole at its center, or a long-wire antenna at a current maximum, a transformer must be used if the impedances are to be matched. One possible type of transformer is shown in Fig. 4–27.

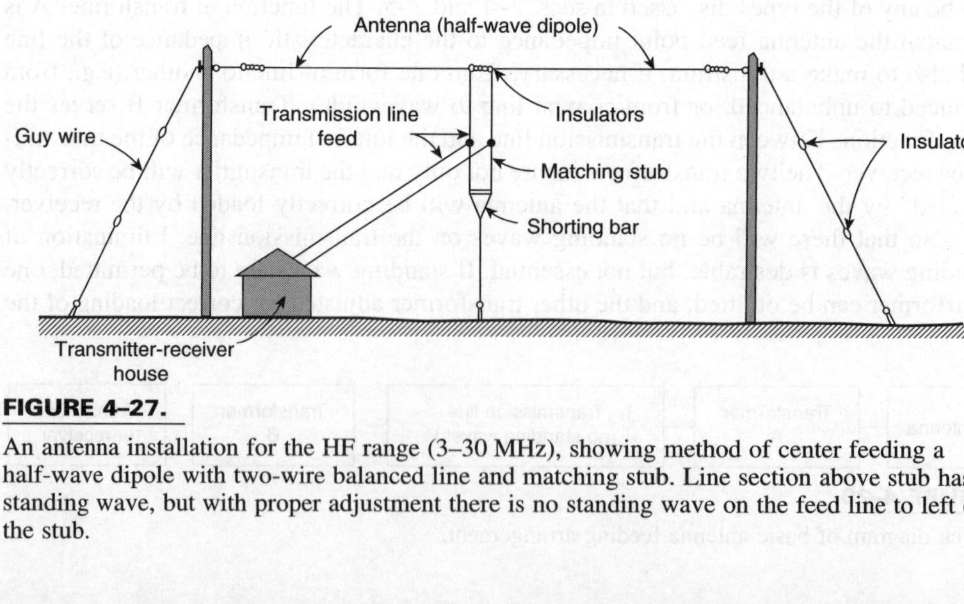

FIGURE 4–27.

An antenna installation for the HF range (3–30 MHz), showing method of center feeding a half-wave dipole with two-wire balanced line and matching stub. Line section above stub has standing wave, but with proper adjustment there is no standing wave on the feed line to left of the stub.

It is the shorted-stub arrangement whose principle is explained in chapter 2. (See Fig. 2–6.) An alternative method, which can be used when the antenna feed-point impedance is purely resistive, is the quarter-wave transmission-line transformer, whose transformation ratio is given by equation (2–22). (These methods are of course not limited to dipole and long-wire antennas; they are of general applicability.)

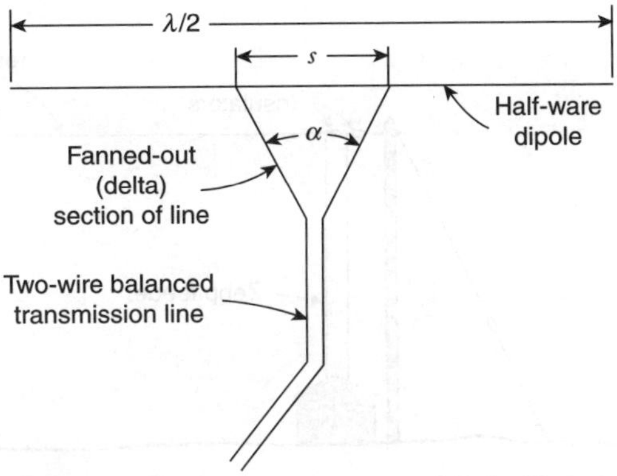

FIGURE 4–28.
Delta-match feed method applied to a half-wave dipole.

Another method, which can be used for feeding a wire antenna at a current maximum, is the "delta match," illustrated in Fig. 4–28. In this method there is no gap in the antenna at the feed point; the line spacing is gradually increased until it spans a section of the antenna of length denoted as s in Fig. 4–28. The effective impedance presented to the transmission line increases as s is increased. This spacing is adjusted until an impedance match results, as indicated by absence of standing waves on the line. Methods of measuring the voltage standing-wave ratio (VSWR), and of thereby determining the antenna input impedance, are described in chapter 9.

Another method of obtaining an impedance match to a dipole with a two-wire line of moderate impedance is to use a folded dipole, as described in sec. 7.1. In its simplest form the folded dipole has an input impedance that approximately matches a 300-ohm line.

Although it is not absolutely essential to operate the transmission line without standing waves, it may be important to do so in high-power applications to minimize line losses due to the high currents at the current maxima and to avoid excessive voltages at the voltage maxima. Radiation losses are also greater when there are standing waves, and the loading adjustment is more critical. A line operating with an appreciable standing wave is called a *resonant* line; one with little or no standing wave is called *nonresonant*.

A half-wave dipole or a long-wire antenna can be fed at one end (maximum-voltage point) with a two-wire resonant line. The antenna is connected to one side of the line, and the other side is simply left open, as indicated in Fig. 4–29. A line used in this way is called a "Zepp" feeder. An advantage of this arrangement is that the antenna can be operated at any integral multiple of the frequency for which the antenna length is a half wavelength. The antenna pattern will be different for each such frequency, in accordance with (4–12a) and (4–12b). The value of n in these equations is of course 1 for half-wavelength operation, 2 for full-wave operation, and so on. The frequency for which $n = 1$ is called the *fundamental* frequency of the antenna, and those for successively higher values of n are called *harmonic* frequencies. (For example, the frequency for $n = 3$ is called the third-harmonic frequency.)

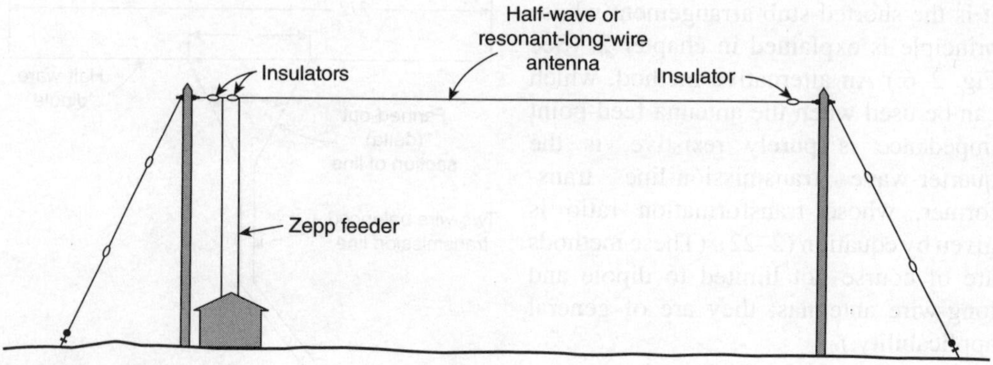

FIGURE 4–29.

Method of feeding a half-wave or resonant-long-wire antenna at one end by means of a two-wire line with standing waves (Zepp feeder).

The pure Zepp feeder arrangement, shown in Fig. 4–29, omits transformer A in Fig. 4–26. The line is operated with a standing wave. When the antenna is operated at more than one of the possible frequencies (values of *n*) transformer B must in general be adjusted differently for the different frequencies. In the HF band, where such antennas are most commonly used, this transformer typically consists of a variable inductance-capacitance circuit (*ARRL Antenna Book* 2007). This reference and its earlier editions contain much practical information on antennas and feed systems of the type described in this chapter and on some of those described in chapter 5.

A matching circuit (i.e., transformer A) can also be incorporated at the antenna end of this type of feeder, to eliminate standing waves on the line. The stub arrangement of Fig. 4–27 (and Fig. 2–6, chapter 2) is used for this purpose. When a half-wave vertical dipole is fed in this way, the resulting arrangement is called a "J" antenna. This matching will in general be effective at only one frequency.

As the Zepp feeder indicates, "balanced" two-wire lines may be used to feed an unbalanced antenna, though at the sacrifice of perfect balance of the line currents. (Therefore such lines will radiate somewhat more than would a perfectly balanced line.) In general, however, balanced two-wire lines are preferred when the antenna is fed at a point of symmetry—where the structure is electrically balanced with respect to the ground on both sides of a center feed point. But when one side of the feed point is the ground, or a metallic ground plane, the favored transmission line for feeding the antenna is coaxial line. Examples of such antennas are monopoles, antennas whose axes are perpendicular to a ground plane in which they are imaged. All the feed methods described for two-wire lines are applicable in these cases, except that the center conductor of the coaxial line connects in the manner indicated for one of the conductors of a two-wire line, and the coaxial outer conductor connects to the base of the antenna (ground).

Transmission-line feed is appropriate to such radiators as dipoles, long wires, loops, and helixes, whose radiation is based on currents flowing in wires. Waveguide feed is more appropriate for horns and waveguide-slot antennas. However, these "rules" have exceptions; it may at times be convenient to use a coaxial line to feed a horn—for example, when the frequency is low enough so that a waveguide would be very large and expensive, but yet high enough to make a horn radiator feasible. (This might be the case at a frequency in the region of 500 MHz.) Then a line-to-waveguide transition (described in sec. 2.5) is used, as indicated in Fig. 4–30.

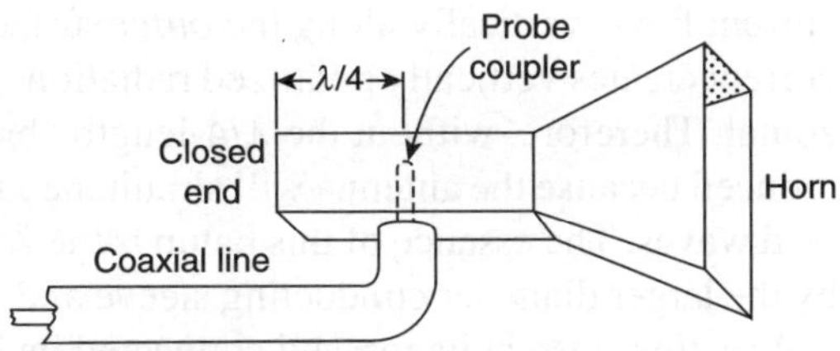

FIGURE 4–30.

Arrangement for feeding a horn radiator with a coaxial transmission line.

Coaxial lines are also often used when the ultimate load is balanced because of their nonradiating properties and the protection that the outer conductor affords against weather and physical damage, and because they have lower losses and higher voltage breakdown rating for the same conductor spacing. A wide variety of methods for accomplishing the connection of an unbalanced (coaxial) line to a balanced (two parallel-conductor) load are possible. The device used to make an unbalanced-to-balance connection is called a *balun*, an abbreviation of the words *bal*ance and *un*balance. Examples of baluns are shown in Fig. 4–31.

At low frequencies inductor-and-capacitor arrangements are used, as suggested by Fig. 4–31(a). At frequencies above about 100 MHz, transmission-line transformers are customary. Typically, as now briefly addressed, the basic configurations include either a $\lambda/4$- or and a $\lambda/2$-length transmission line.

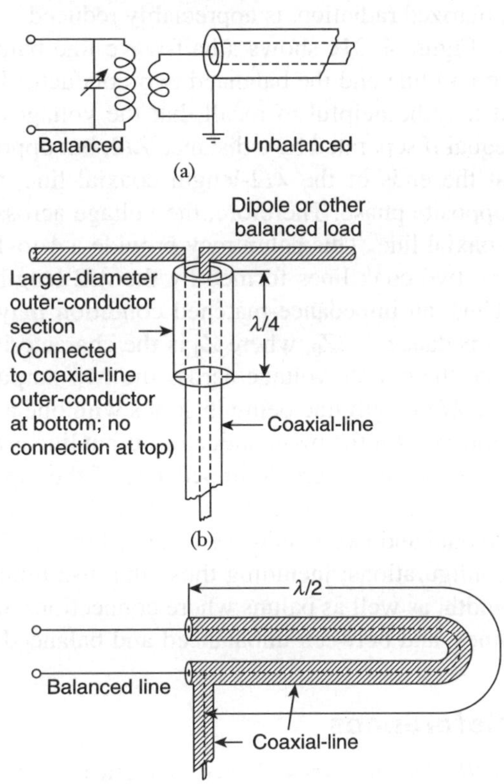

FIGURE 4–31.

Examples of balanced-to-unbalanced line coupling devices (baluns). (a) Coupled coils. (b) "Bazooka" balun. (c) Half-wave-line balun.

Figure 4–31(b) shows "Bazooka" balun that improves the coupling between a coaxial (coax) line and a dipole (or the balanced two-conductor load). Note that, in feeding a dipole in Fig. 4–31(b), the inner and outer coax conductors are connected to the right- and left-hand arms of the dipole. Ordinarily, current within a coax at high frequency travels along the outer surface of the inner conductor and the inner surface of the outer conductor. However, because of radiation from the dipole elements and from the coax-dipole junction discontinuity, and without the bazooka balun present, additional current flows vertically along the *outer* surface of the outer coax conductor. This vertical current creates vertically polarized radiation, yet the radiation of the dipole, per se, is horizontal. Therefore, without the $\lambda/4$-length "bazooka" sleeve, the effective antenna gain is reduced because the antenna will simultaneously radiate horizontally and vertically polarized waves. The essence of this balun is the $\lambda/4$ length conducting coaxial section, formed by the larger diameter conducting sleeve and the outer conductor of the coax line, with the $\lambda/4$ section open at its top and connected its bottom to the outer conductor of the coaxial line. In other words, looking from the top and downwards, the impedance of the $\lambda/4$ coax (formed by the sleeve and the outer conductor of the coax line) appears as an open circuit. Thus, the vertically moving outer coaxial-line surface current, and hence the vertically polarized radiation, is appreciably reduced.

Figure 4–31c shows a half-wave-line balun for coupling between the bottom coaxial (coax) line and the balanced two-conductor line. To recognize how this balun functions, it may be helpful to recall that the voltages between points on a transmission line are equal if separated by a distance $\lambda/2$, but opposite in phase. Then, one will recognize that, at the ends of the $\lambda/2$-length coaxial line, the voltages are of equal amplitude but of opposite phase. Therefore, the voltage across the balanced line is twice that at the input coaxial line. This balun may provide a 4-to-1 impedance transformation. First, note that the two coax lines formed by the $\lambda/2$ length line are in parallel across the input coax. Thus, an impedance-matched condition may exist if the $\lambda/2$ length coax characteristic impedance is $2Z_0$, where Z_0 is the characteristic impedance of the input coax line. Note that the double voltage across the two output conductors is consistent with the ends of the $\lambda/2$ length line being in series with one another. Thus, an impedance matched condition exists if the two-conductor output line is terminated with an impedance of $4Z_0$, where Z_0 is the characteristic impedance of the input coaxial line.

Figures 4–31(b) and (c) show only simple baluns that provide connections between coaxial and two-conductor balanced lines. Munk (2002) discusses numerous other balun configurations; including those that use multiple transmission lines for increased bandwidth, as well as baluns where connections are made between coax and balanced printed lines, and between unbalanced and balanced printed lines.

References

ARRL Antenna Book, 21st ed., American Radio Relay League, 2007.

Balanis, C. A., *Antenna Theory: Analysis and Design*, 3rd Edition, John Wiley & Sons, 2005.

Beverage, H. H., C. W. Rice, and E. W. Kellog, "The Wave Antenna: A New Type of Highly Directive Antenna," *Transactions of the AIEE*, vol. 42, 1923, p. 215.

Bird, T. S., and A. W. Love, "Horn Antennas," ch. 14 in *Antenna Engineering Handbook*, 4th ed., J. L. Volakis (ed.), McGraw-Hill, 2007.

Brainerd, J. G., ed., *Ultra-High-Frequency Techniques*, Van Nostrand, New York, 1942, p. 415. (The formula is there given as $R_r = 72.5 + 30\log_e n$.).

Carver, K. R., and J. W. Mink, "Microstrip Antenna Technology," *IEEE Transactions on Antennas and Propagation*, January 1981, pp. 2–24.

Howell, J. Q., "Microstrip Antennas," *IEEE Transactions on Antennas and Propagation*, January 1975, pp. 90–93.

Kraus, J. D., and R. J. Marhefka, *Antennas*, 3rd ed., McGraw-Hill, 2002.

Love, A. W., "Horn Antennas," ch. 15 in R. C. Johnson, *Antenna Engineering Handbook*, McGraw-Hill, 1993, pp. 15-6 through 15-9 and 15-35.

Munk, B. A., "Baluns, etc.," ch. 23 of Kraus and Marhefka, *Antennas,* 3rd ed., McGraw-Hill, 2002.

Mailloux, R. J., J. F. McIlvenna, and N. P. Kernweis, "Microstrip Array Technology," *IEEE Transactions on Antennas and Propagation*, January 1981, pp. 25–37.

Munson, R. E., "Conformal Microstrip Antennas and Microstrip Phased Arrays," *IEEE Transactions on Antennas and Propagation*, January 1974, pp. 74–78.

Smith, G. S., "Loop Antennas," ch. 5 in *Antenna Engineering Handbook*, 4th ed., J. L. Volakis (ed.), McGraw-Hill, 2007.

Targonski, S. D., R. B. Waterhouse, and D. M. Pozar, " Design of Wide-band Aperture Stacked Patch Microstrip Antennas," *IEEE Transactions on Antennas and Propagation*, September 1998, pp. 1245–51.

Terman, F. E., *Radio Engineers' Handbook*, McGraw-Hill, 1943, p. 836.

Vardaxoglou, Y. C., and J. R. James, "Mobile Handset Antennas," ch. 36 in *Antenna Engineering Handbook*, 4th ed., J. L. Volakis (ed.), McGraw-Hill, 2007.

Waterhouse, R. B., "Design of Probe-Fed Stacked Patches," *IEEE Transactions on Antennas and Propagation*, December 1999, pp. 1780–1784.

Waterhouse, R. B., S. D. Targonski, and D. M. Kokotoff, "Design and Performance of Small Printed Antennas," *IEEE Transactions on Antennas and Propagation*, November 1998, pp. 1629–33.

Wheeler, H. A., "A Helical Antenna for Circular Polarization," *Proceedings of the IRE*, vol. 35, December 1947, pp. 1484–88.

Problems and Exercises

1. At a distance of $r = 1$ meter from a particular short-dipole antenna, the reactive component of the total electric field is equal in strength to the *radiation* component. At a distance $r = 10$ meters in the same direction, which of these two components is stronger? How much stronger is it? That is, what is the ratio of their strengths?

2. A thin, perfectly conducting wire is fed as a short dipole at its center; its total end-to-end length is 0.04 wavelength. The wire has no capacitive end loading so that its *effective* length (in terms of an equivalent elemental dipole) is less than its actual length. The rf current at the feed point (center) is 10 amp, rms. (a) What is the radiation resistance? (b) How much total power is radiated?

3. The dipole described in Problem 2 is connected to another transmitter of the same frequency (and wavelength), but of higher power output, so that the feed-point current is now 25 amp. (a) At a point half way between the center and one end of the dipole, what is the current? (b) What is it at a point at either end,

which is at a distance from the center equally 90 percent of the distance from the center to the end? (c) What is the current at the end of the dipole?

4. A half-wave dipole in free space is center-fed with a current of 10 amp (rms). At a distance of 1,000 meters from the dipole, which is in the far field, and in a direction that is 60 degrees from the dipole axis, what is the field strength in volts per meter?

5. A medium-frequency (MF) radio station (for which a long-wire horizontal antenna is practical) is required to communicate with only four other stations. These stations are in four different directions; one is due north, one due south, one east, and one west. It is desired to utilize a single horizontal long-wire resonant antenna that will have four major lobes, one directed at each of the four other stations. (The major lobes are those nearest the wire axis.) (a) How many half wavelengths long should this antenna be? (b) What are the two possible directions of the antenna wire? *Suggestions*: Assume that equation (4–14) is valid for the value of n involved. Draw a diagram showing the relative positions and directions of the stations, and consider possible orientations of the antenna wire. Determine from this the required value of θ_{max} in equation (4–14). Then, using equation (4–14), solve for n. The value obtained for n will not be an exact integer; the correct value is the integer nearest to the value found.)

6. A helical antenna with a ground plane (as in Fig. 4–20) has a turn diameter and spacing that are appreciable fractions of a wavelength, so that it radiates in the axial mode. The circumference of a turn, C, is equal to the wavelength, λ, and the turn spacing S is equal to 0.25λ. The number of turns is $N = 16$. (a) What is the 3-dB beamwidth of this antenna? (b) What is its directivity?

7. A rectangular waveguide pyramidal horn has aperture dimensions, d_E and d_H of Fig. 4–21, of one wavelength. (a) Determine approximate E- and H-plane half power beamwidths. (b) What is the approximate directivity?

8. A slot in an infinite plane sheet of metal is in the form of an annular ring so that it is the complement of a small loop antenna. (The central portion of the sheet, inside the annulus, is supported by low-loss insulating material.) (a) Is the maximum radiation of this annular slot in the direction perpendicular to the plane of the sheet, or is it parallel to it? (b) What is the polarization of the field near the metal sheet at a point distant from the slot?

9. A thin vertical monopole antenna is 95 percent of a quarter wavelength in height above a ground plane of infinite extent and perfect conductivity. It is fed at a gap at its base by a coaxial line. No transformer is used at the feed point, yet there are no apparent standing waves on this line. What is the approximate characteristic impedance of the line?

10. Several means of delivering power to an antenna from a transmitter are listed below, and identified by capital letters:

    (A) Coaxial line.

    (B) Balanced two-wire line followed by an impedance transformer to provide nonresonant operation (no standing waves).

(C) Waveguide.

(D) Direct connection.

(E) Resonant two-wire line.

After each of the antenna types below, write in one of the above capital letters to indicate which form of line or connection you consider most appropriate. (Use each letter once and only once.)

(i) Automobile radio antenna for broadcast-band reception □ (535–1,605 kHz)

(ii) Helical antenna with ground plane □

(iii) Long-wire antenna fed at one end □

(iv) Horn radiator □

(v) Half-wave dipole having 20-meter length, fed at gap in center □

CHAPTER 5

Arrays

This chapter discusses array antennas that are designed so that the major lobe (the main beam) is pointed in one fixed direction or more. Commonly, array antennas are also designed to electronically, and thus almost instantly, change beam pointing direction. Such a beam pointing antenna is called a *phased array, electronic scanning array,* or *electronically steered array* (ESA). The general principles of arrays are discussed in the present chapter, and chapter 8, titled Electronically Steered Arrays, focuses on concepts and techniques more directly applicable to electronic beam steering.

The term *array*, as applied to antennas, means an assembly of radiating elements in an electrical and geometric arrangement of such a nature that the radiation from the elements "adds up" to give a maximum field intensity in a particular direction or directions and cancels or very nearly cancels in others. Obviously this principle can be used for the design of a directional antenna with increased gain.

The long-wire antennas discussed in sec. 4.4 may in a sense be regarded as arrays, since they are analyzable as an assembly of elemental dipoles in a geometric configuration that provides directionality and gain. (The resonant long-wire antennas also might be regarded as an array of half-wave dipoles.) The term array, however, is usually reserved for arrangements in which the individual radiators are separate rather than part of a continuous radiator.

5.1. Basic Array Theory

All the elements of an array (the individual radiators) are usually alike, or at least very similar. Perhaps the commonest array elements are the half-wave dipole, the half-wave microstrip patch, the half-wave slot, and the open ended waveguide, but practically all the basic radiators discussed in chapter 4 are employed as elements of arrays.

The radiation pattern of an array (in free space) depends on four factors: (1) the relative positions of the individual radiators with respect to each other; (2) the relative phases of the currents or fields in them; (3) the relative magnitudes of the individual-radiator currents or fields; and (4) the patterns of the individual radiators. The basic theory of arrays is developed in terms of the first three factors, on the assumption that the individual radiators are *isotropic point sources.* An isotropic point source is one that radiates with uniform intensity in all directions and has no physical size, and here it is assumed that it does not block or otherwise affect the radiation of the other elements of the array. An array radiation pattern can be calculated on the basis of these assumptions, and then a correction to it can be made to take into account the fact that the individual radiators in practical cases do affect each other and do not radiate isotropically.

5.1.1. The Two-Isotropic-Element Array

The simplest array is one that consists of just two isotropic point-source radiators. It will be discussed in some detail because it illustrates most of the principles of arrays of any number of individual radiators. The two-element array will be further specialized by assuming that the individual radiators are of "equal strength." If they are thought of as radiating a field intensity proportional to a current that flows in them (in some unspecified fashion), the currents in the two are assumed to be equal. (An isotropic point-source radiator is a fiction, and the idea of a current is introduced solely to illustrate the meaning of "equal strength.") The only remaining variables are the spacing of the two radiators and their phases.

The meaning of the term *phase* as applied to the radiating elements of an array is also most easily illustrated by considering that their radiation is related to currents that flow in them. Suppose that at some distant point the fields of the two radiating elements are examined and are found to be in phase with each other. If then the phase of the current in Radiator 2 is changed by an amount α radians whereas the phase of the current in Radiator 1 is not changed, it will be observed that the two fields at the distant point are now out-of-phase by the amount α radians. A phase can also be ascribed to radiators of the aperture type; the phase may be taken as that of the field at some reference point in the aperture.

The phase of a radiating element in an array is always discussed in relation to the phases of the other elements. In other words, if the phases of the two radiators in a two-element array are changed by the same amount, the array radiation pattern is unaffected; but changing the phase of one without changing the other will affect the pattern because it affects the way that the individual fields of the two radiators add up at a specified distant point.

The significant geometry of a two-element isotropic-point-source array is shown in Fig. 5–1. The two sources are positioned a distance d apart on the y-axis of an xy coordinate system, each distant $d/2$ from the origin. The point P is a distant point at which it is desired to calculate the field strength that results from the radiation of the array. The coordinates of P denoted r and ϕ are two coordinates of the spherical-coordinate system shown in Fig. 3–1, chapter 3. The third spherical coordinate, θ, is not shown because only a plane in which θ is constant is being considered here, namely, the xy-plane in which $\theta = \pi/2$ radians (90°).

In the parlance of electromagnetic theory (and antenna theory which is really an application of electromagnetic theory), P is the *field point,* that is, the point at which the field is to be calculated. Since the position of P will be specified only in general terms, it can represent any point in space; hence, an expression for the field strength at P applies

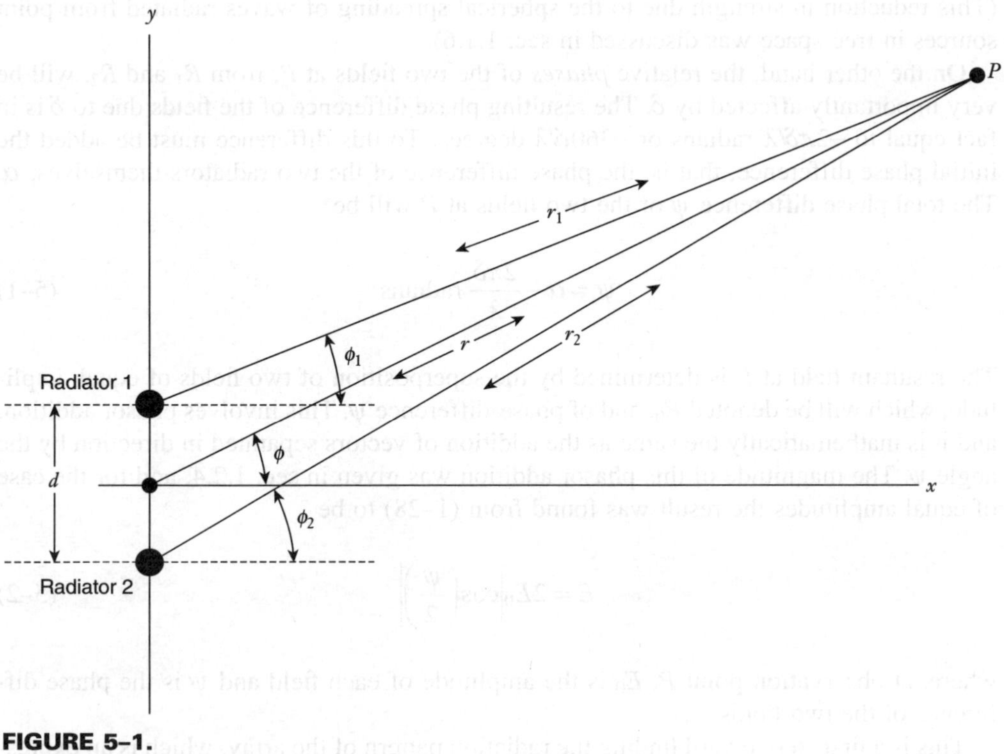

FIGURE 5–1.
Array of two isotropic point sources.

to all points and thus *defines the radiation pattern of the array.* Calculation of the field due to the array at an arbitrary point P is basic to the understanding of array theory. This calculation is here made for the two-element isotropic-point-source array, with the two sources of equal strength (intensity).

As shown, the distance from Radiator 1 at point R_1 to P is r_1, and from Radiator 2 at point R_2 to P the distance is r_2 (R_1 and R_2 are shown in Fig. 5–2). The two sources are assumed to lie on the y-axis of a cartesian coordinate system, and P is assumed to be in the xy-plane. Therefore, in terms of the corresponding spherical coordinate system (Fig. 3–1), the direction of P from R_1 is ϕ_1, and from R_2 it is ϕ_2.

The distances r_1 and r_2 are assumed to be very large compared to the distance d, the separation of the two radiators. If the difference of these two distances to the field point is $\delta = r_2 - r_1$, the maximum possible value that δ can have, whatever the location of P, is equal to d, the radiator separation. (This equality will occur when P lies on the y-axis; i.e., when $\phi_1 = \phi_2 = 90°$ or $270°$.) This means, since both r_1 and r_2 are very much larger than d, that δ will always be very much smaller than either r_1 or r_2. The very important conclusion that may then be drawn is that if the two radiators are of equal strength, the *amplitudes* of their separate fields at P will be *very nearly* the same; that is, both will be reduced in strength, because of the distance traveled, by virtually the same amount.

(This reduction in strength due to the spherical spreading of waves radiated from point sources in free space was discussed in sec. 1.1.6).

On the other hand, the relative *phases* of the two fields at P, from R_1 and R_2, will be very importantly affected by δ. The resulting phase difference of the fields due to δ is in fact equal to $-2\pi\delta/\lambda$ radians or $-360\delta/\lambda$ degrees. To this difference must be added the initial phase difference, that is, the phase difference of the two radiators themselves, α. The total phase difference ψ of the two fields at P will be*

$$\psi = \alpha - \frac{2\pi\delta}{\lambda} \text{ radians} \tag{5–1}$$

The resultant field at P is determined by the superposition of two fields of equal amplitude, which will be denoted E_0, and of phase-difference ψ. This involves phasor addition, and it is mathematically the same as the addition of vectors separated in direction by the angle ψ. The magnitude of this phasor addition was given in sec. 1.2.4, and for the case of equal amplitudes the result was found from (1–28) to be

$$E = 2E_0\left|\cos\left(\frac{\psi}{2}\right)\right| \tag{5–2}$$

where, at observation point P, E_0 is the amplitude of each field and ψ is the phase difference of the two fields.

This is a first step toward finding the radiation pattern of the array, which is an expression of E as a function of ϕ, the angle of the direction of P from the center of the array. To obtain such an expression, it is evidently necessary to express ψ in terms of ϕ. Equation (5–1), an expression for ψ in terms of δ and α, is already available. Since α is a (presumably) known quantity (the phase difference of the array elements), the only variable here is δ, which can be expressed in terms of ϕ. To see how this can be done, it is helpful to consider an enlarged diagram, Fig. 5–2, showing the region in the immediate vicinity of the array. As this diagram shows, because P is so distant in relation to the element separation d, the lines labeled r_1, r_2, and r can be considered almost parallel to each other, so that also $\phi_1 = \phi_2 = \phi$ to a very close approximation. If a construction line R_1Q is drawn as shown dashed, so that it is perpendicular to the line R_2P (also designated r_2), the distances R_1P and QP can be considered equal. Therefore, the distance R_2Q is the difference, δ, between R_1P and R_2P (i.e., between r_1 and r_2). The angle R_2R_1Q is equal to ϕ, since R_1R_2 is perpendicular to the x-axis and R_1Q is perpendicular to R_2P. The triangle R_1QR_2 is a right triangle, with base δ, hypotenuse d, and angle ϕ opposite the base. Therefore,

$$\sin\phi = \frac{\delta}{d} \tag{5–3}$$

* In (5–1) ψ and α denote phases of Radiator 2 field and current with respect to those of Radiator 1, that is, the Radiator 1 phase is the reference phase.

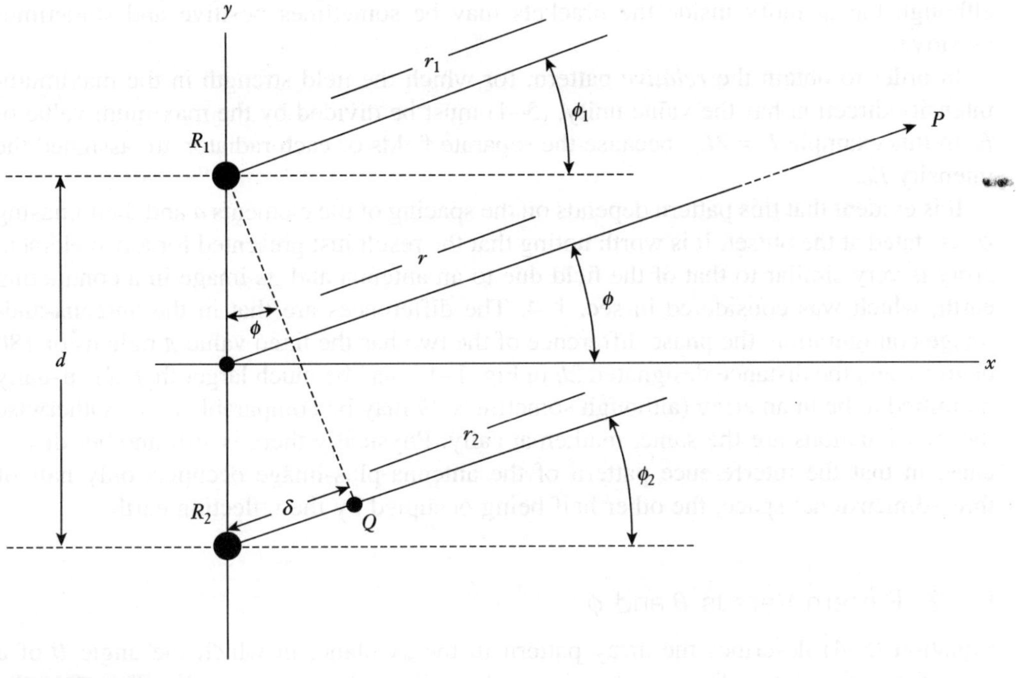

FIGURE 5–2.

Enlarged portion of two-element-array geometry.

or

$$\delta = d \sin \phi$$

Substituting this result into (5–1), and then substituting the resultant expression for ψ into (5–2), gives the following equation for the magnitude of the field at P:

$$E(\phi) = 2E_0 \left| \cos\left[\frac{\alpha}{2} - \frac{\pi d \sin \phi}{\lambda}\right] \right| \tag{5–4}$$

This is the desired expression for the magnitude of the field at P as a function of the angle ϕ that the direction of P makes with the line perpendicular to the line of the array. This equation gives the shape of the pattern in the xy-plane (which may also be called the $\theta = \pi/2$ plane). Recall from (5–1) that ψ is expressed in radians. Thus, for calculations using degrees, π in (5–1) and (5–4) is replaced by 180°, because π radians = 180°. The absolute-value brackets are used to indicate that the field intensity being calculated is proportional to the amplitude or to the rms value and is therefore a positive number, although the quantity inside the brackets may be sometimes positive and sometimes negative.

In order to obtain the *relative* pattern, for which the field strength in the maximum-intensity direction has the value unity, (5–4) must be divided by the maximum value of E. In this example $E = 2E_0$, because the separate fields of each radiator are assigned the intensity E_0.

It is evident that this pattern depends on the spacing of the elements d and their phasing α, as stated at the outset. It is worth noting that the result just presented for a two element array is very similar to that of the field due to an antenna and its image in a conducting earth, which was considered in sec. 1–4. The differences are that in the antenna-and-image configuration, the phase difference of the two has the fixed value π radians or 180 degrees, and the distance designated $2h$ in Fig. 1–14 may be much larger than d is usually permitted to be in an array (although sometimes $2h$ may be comparable to d). Otherwise the two situations are the same, mathematically. Physically there is still another difference, in that the interference pattern of the antenna-plus-image occupies only half of three-dimensional space, the other half being occupied by the reflecting earth.

5.1.2. Pattern Versus θ and ϕ

Equation (5–4) describes the array pattern in the xy-plane, in which the angle θ of a three-dimensional coordinate system is constant ($\theta = \pi/2$ radians, or 90°). Therefore the pattern *in this plane* is not a function of θ, and θ does not appear in the equation.

The complete pattern is actually a "figure of revolution," obtained by rotating the xy-plane pattern about the y-axis (line of the array). In other words, all patterns in planes through the y-axis are identical. For example, the pattern in the yz-plane is identical in shape and size to the pattern in the xy-plane. In this plane, however, the pattern equation is expressed as a function of the angle θ instead of the angle ϕ; in other planes, both angles are involved. Equation (5–4a) gives the pattern of amplitude versus θ and ϕ

$$E(\theta, \phi) = 2E_0 \left| \cos\left[\frac{\alpha}{2} - \frac{\pi d \cdot \sin\theta \cdot \sin\phi}{\lambda}\right]\right| \tag{5–4a}$$

The quantity $\sin\phi$ in (5–4) is merely replaced by the product $\sin\theta \cdot \sin\phi$. In the xy-plane, when $\theta = 90°$, $\sin\theta = 1$; hence (5–4a) becomes (5–4) in this plane, as it should.

5.1.3. Parallel-Dipole Two-Element Array

The pattern defined by (5–4) can be plotted as a function of the angle ϕ for various values of the parameters d and α. Although the various resulting patterns pertain basically to an array of isotropic elements, they also represent the patterns of an array of two dipoles in the plane perpendicular to their axes, if the dipoles are parallel to each other and perpendicular to the line joining their centers (line of the array). In terms of Fig. 5–1 the dipoles have their centers at the positions of the isotropic point sources on the y-axis, but their axes are parallel to the z-axis. In the xy-plane each dipole considered individually will have an omnidirectional pattern, that is, uniform radiation in all directions *in that plane*. Consequently the dipole-array pattern will be represented by (5–4) in the xy-plane only. These two-element dipole-array patterns for a number of values of d and α within the ranges of greatest practical interest are shown in Fig. 5–3, as originally published by G. H. Brown (1937). They may be thought of as the horizontal-plane patterns of a pair of vertical dipoles or monopoles separated by a distance d and with currents having phase difference α.

As shown in Fig. 5–3, the effect of the spacing and phasing of the dipoles is rather remarkable, and the variations in the patterns are extreme. The light-line circles represent the E-field pattern that would be obtained from a single dipole located at the midpoint of the array (with the array dipoles removed) radiating the same total power as the array. The heavy-line plots are the electric-intensity radiation patterns. A great deal can be learned about arrays in sgeneral by studying these two-element patterns.

It should be noted that when the two elements are in phase ($\alpha = 0°$), the radiation has a maximum in the direction perpendicular to the line joining the elements. That is, because the distances from the elements to the field point (P, Fig. 5–1) are equal in that direction ($\phi = 0°$), the phase difference due to path difference is zero also; hence the total phase difference of the superimposed fields is $\psi = 0°$. Consequently, the fields add directly, and the maximum possible resultant field is obtained. When $\alpha = 0°$ and a pattern maximum is in the direction perpendicular to the array line, the antenna is called a *broadside* array.

It should also be noted that for certain conditions the resultant field in some directions is zero—when the sum of the radiator phase difference (α) and the phase difference due to path difference ($2\pi\delta/\lambda$) is an odd integral multiple of π radians. The fields of the individual radiators are in this case of equal amplitude and opposite phase, so they cancel. This occurs, for example, when $\alpha = 0°$ and $d = \lambda/2$, in the $\phi = 90°$ and $270°$ directions, since in these directions the field phase-difference due to path difference is 180 degrees, whereas the phase difference due to radiator phase difference is zero. The same result occurs when the 180-degree net phase difference is due to a combination of path difference and radiator phase difference. These directions of zero intensity in a pattern are called *nulls*.

Finally, it is to be noted that certain combinations of d and α result in maximum radiation in the direction of the line joining the array elements. The array is then said to be operating as an *endfire* array. The radiation of an endfire array may be either bidirectional (radiation lobes in both directions along the line of the array) or unidirectional (a lobe in one direction and a null in the opposite direction). Examples of unidirectional endfire arrays are the case of $d = \lambda/8$ with $\alpha = 135°$, and the case of $d = \lambda/4$ with $\alpha = 90°$. When d is greater than $\lambda/2$, the array will have lobes in more than two directions, and may even be simultaneously broadside and endfire.

Although the two-element array is the simplest of all arrays, the variety of patterns obtainable makes it useful in many applications. In radio broadcasting in the MF band, for example, two vertical towers with appropriate spacing and phasing can be used to produce a horizontal-plane pattern (possibly one depicted in Fig. 5–3) to favor certain

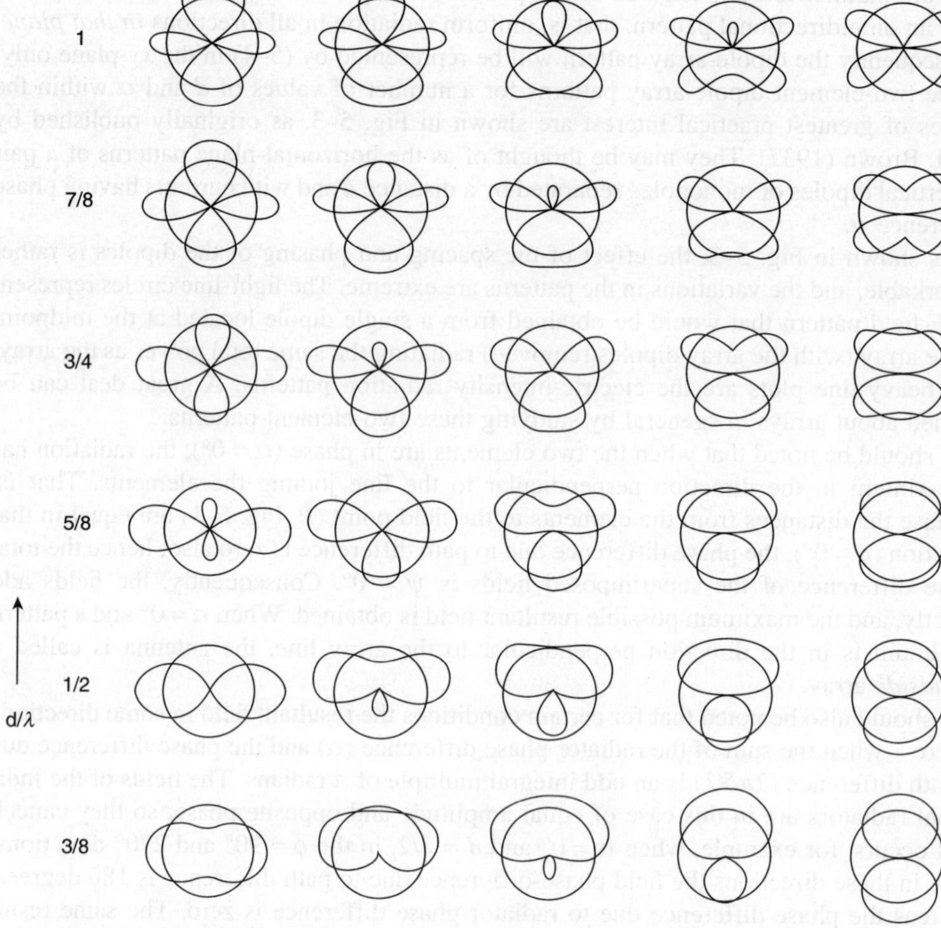

FIGURE 5–3.
Horizontal-plane patterns of two vertical dipoles (or monopoles). (*Proceedings IRE, 25,* 78–145, January 1937.)

directions, or to minimize radiation in certain directions, as may be required by the Federal Communications Commission to avoid interfering with the coverage area of another station on the same frequency.

Equations (5–2), (5–4), and (5–4a) and most equations in chapter 5 are based on assumptions that the radiating elements and input networks are lossless, and that each element radiates a fixed amount of power independent of element spacing or relative phasing. Thus, these assumptions include the input and radiated powers being equal and that there is no mutual coupling between elements. These oversimplifications are commonly used, so that the most basic of array concepts can be more easily addressed. In fact, although the coupling effects may sometimes be negligible, mutual coupling in principle causes changes in an element's radiation resistance and its input impedance, and it may also cause a change in an element's radiation pattern. Consequently, with a change in either element spacing or phasing, a fixed element current does not imply that there is a fixed radiated power from an element or conversely.

As already mentioned, in Fig. 5–3 the resulting field strength from the two elements is compared with the field strength from only one of the elements, and with the inputs for the two cases (two elements versus one element) always having the same radiated power (losses assumed zero) for each pattern. However, with constant power radiated, because of mutual-coupling effects on dipole radiation resistance and input impedance, the dipole currents may be different for the different spacings and phasings. Kraus and Marhefka (2002, pp. 529–52) include clear explanations on how to calculate the Fig. 5–3 patterns as well as patterns for other constant power, two-dipole arrays. Additionally, on page 535, Kraus and Marhefka note that Brown (1937) considered it important to provide analyses based on constant antenna input power, because "most transmitters are essentially constant power devices which can be coupled to a wide range of antenna impedance." The subject of mutual impedance is further addressed in secs. 5.1.4 through 5.1.7 of this chapter, and in chapter 8 in connection with electronically steered arrays.

5.1.4. Mutual Coupling

As indicated in the last two paragraphs, effects of a radiating element's input (driving-point) impedance and radiation resistance caused by mutual coupling between array elements need to be taken into account when calculating array performance. Therefore, the feed system of an array cannot be designed based on the input impedance of an isolated dipole, nor can the radiated power be calculated based on the radiation resistance of an isolated-dipole. In other words, *mutual impedances* should be included in the calculations of input impedance and radiation resistance. Furthermore, although usually of a lesser effect, the actual patterns of an element may be significantly *affected by the mutual coupling.* An element pattern, when operating within an array environment, is known as a scan element pattern (SEP). An SEP, previously known as an active element pattern, is found experimentally by connecting a receiver to only one element of the array, with all the other elements connected to terminating impedances of the value that would be effective if the array were operated normally. The pattern measurement of this element is accomplished in the usual fashion (see chapter 9). The currents induced in the single receiving element (as well as in the terminated elements) will be the same as in actual array operation, including mutual-coupling effects. The pattern measured under these conditions is in general different from the pattern of an isolated element. Although much of this discussion has been in terms of dipole elements, mutual coupling occurs with all types of array elements.

In the practical design of arrays, the effects of mutual coupling are often evaluated experimentally, because theoretical calculations are usually very difficult, although the theory is helpful in understanding the general nature of the effect. The electromagnetic analysis of element coupling involves complex mathematics and detailed use of Maxwell's equations. Such analysis will of course depend on the shape and size of the elements and on their electrical properties, element spacing, locations of the elements within the array aperture, wavelength, polarization, and the amplitudes and phases of the element input currents. The total of the electric and magnetic fields near an element includes the fields generated by its currents and the coupling from reactive near-fields from the other elements and possibly from nearby objects. For antennas with dimensions of many wavelengths, the fields of an element may also include significant radiating near-field components from other elements. Computer codes are used to compute the effects of mutual coupling among the elements of an array (Hansen 2007, pp. 20–24).

5.1.5. Input and Mutual Impedances, and Radiation Resistance

Because of mutual coupling among elements, the amplitude and phase of the input current of a specific array element cannot be adjusted independently of other elements. In other words, the driving-point (i.e., input) impedance of an individual element might differ considerably from its self-impedance, because of its mutual coupling with other array elements. In a multielement array, terminal voltages and element currents behave, conceptually, like a conventional mesh circuit network. Thus, the sum of the voltages around a current loop equals zero, as follows:

$$\begin{aligned} V_1 &= I_1Z_{11} + I_2Z_{12} + \ldots + I_nZ_{1n} \\ V_2 &= I_1Z_{12} + I_2Z_{22} + \ldots + I_nZ_{2n} \\ &\vdots \\ V_n &= I_1Z_{1n} + I_2Z_{2n} + \ldots + I_nZn_{nn} \end{aligned} \tag{5–5}$$

where

V_1, V_2, *etc.* = voltages applied to elements 1, 2, etc.
I_1, I_2, *etc.* = currents flowing in elements 1, 2, etc.
Z_{11}, Z_{22}, *etc.* = self-impedances of elements 1, 2, etc.
Z_{12}, Z_{2n}, *etc.* = mutual impedances between elements denoted by the subscripts

The driving-point (input) impedance offered to the voltage applied to the kth element is the phasor ratio (in general complex) V_k/I_k, obtained by dividing the right-hand side of the above equation by I_k. Thus for $k = 1$, the input (i.e., driving-point) impedance follows:

$$Z_{1input} = \frac{V_1}{I_1} = Z_{11} + \frac{I_2}{I_1} Z_{12} + \frac{I_3}{I_1} Z_{13} + \ldots \tag{5–6}$$

From above, it is seen that the input or driving-point impedance of a particular element is not only a function of its own self-impedance, but also a function of the relative currents flowing to the other elements and possibly in nearby objects. Thus, it is important in an array to design the feed system to match the input impedances instead of simply the self-impedances.

Radiation resistance is the resistance R_r that, inserted at the point where a current I is flowing, dissipates the same energy that radiates from the antenna. Thus R_r equals radiated power divided by I^2 (sec. 4.1.6). In an array composed of several radiating elements, the total radiation resistance of an element may be expressed in terms of the radiation resistance of the individual element and its mutual impedances. Specifically, the effective radiation resistance encountered by a voltage V_1 applied to element 1 of an antenna array is the resistance component of the driving-point (input) impedance Z_{1input} offered to V_1, as calculated by (5.6). The power radiated by element 1 delivered by the voltage V_1 is the square of the current multiplied by this effective radiation resistance. Likewise, the total power delivered to an element is the square of the current at the input multiplied by the resistive component of Z_{1input}. This resistive component consists of the radiation resistance R_r, plus whatever additional resistance is needed to account for the dissipated (heat) losses that may arise from the presence of earth, and from the conductors and dielectrics within the antenna. The radiation resistance to the voltages applied to other elements in the array and the power delivered by these other voltages is determined in the same way. The total radiated power is then the sum of the powers supplied by the various applied voltages. Likewise, total power input to the elements is the sum of the powers delivered to all elements.

5.1.6. Principle of Pattern Multiplication

Equation (5–4) describes the pattern in one plane of either a two-element array of isotropic radiators or a two-element dipole array if the dipoles have their axes perpendicular to the line of the array and parallel to each other. Equation (5–4a) describes the pattern versus θ and ϕ for the array of isotropic elements, but it does not describe pattern versus θ and ϕ for the dipole array. In planes other than the one perpendicular to the dipole axes, the pattern is affected by the nonisotropic patterns of the individual dipoles. The question to be answered is, what is the complete far-field pattern of any array?

The answer is provided by the *principle of pattern multiplication*, which is described below by use of (5–7). If an array consists of elements whose electric field patterns are all alike, and described by an expression that will be denoted $E_e(\theta, \phi)$, and if the array pattern for isotropic point source elements has a pattern that will be denoted by $E_a(\theta, \phi)$, then the pattern of the array of actual elements, $E_A(\theta, \phi)$, is given by the formula

$$E_A(\theta, \phi) = k_n \cdot E_e(\theta, \phi) \cdot E_a(\theta, \phi) \tag{5–7}$$

That is, the pattern of the array of actual elements is obtained by multiplying together the pattern of a single element and the pattern of the array as calculated for isotropic point-source elements. The function $E_A(\theta, \phi)$ is sometimes referred to as the *antenna pattern factor*, which is the product of the *element factor* $E_e(\theta, \phi)$ and the *array factor* $E_a(\theta, \phi)$. Squaring both sides of this equation converts it into a relationship of power-density patterns, in which the squares of the electric-intensity factors may be replaced by corresponding power-density pattern factors, $P_A(\theta, \phi)$, $P_e(\theta, \phi)$, and $P_a(\theta, \phi)$, in accordance with equation (1–9), chapter 1.

The factor k_n is included in this equation as an arbitrary numerical constant to be adjusted to whatever value is required to make $E_A(\theta, \phi)$ a true *relative* pattern. That is, it is desired that $E_A = 1$ for the particular values of θ and ϕ in the direction of maximum field intensity, in accordance with the definition of a relative pattern. If both E_e and E_a are relative patterns, it may happen that E_A will automatically be a relative pattern also, that is, with $k_n = 1$. This will happen only when a maximum direction of E_e coincides with a maximum direction of E_a, which it will not necessarily always do, although it often does. The factor k_n is called a *normalizing* constant.

As an example of the application of (5–7), the pattern versus θ and ϕ will be determined of a two-element array of dipole radiators, spaced a distance d apart on the y-axis, with phasing α. For the case of isotropic radiators instead of dipoles, the pattern is given by (5–4a). The pattern of a half-wave dipole with its axis parallel to the z-axis is given by equation (4–11), sec. 4–3. (This is the complete dipole pattern, even though it involves only the angle θ rather than both θ and ϕ, because the pattern for this particular dipole orientation is independent of the angle ϕ. That is, the pattern in any plane corresponding to a particular value of ϕ is exactly like the pattern in a plane corresponding to any other value of ϕ.) The complete pattern follows in (5–8). It is a function of θ and ϕ, of a two-element dipole array with this orientation of the dipole axes and is attained by multiplying the patterns of (4–11), sec. 4–3 and (5–4a) together:

$$E_A(\theta, \phi) = k_n \left| \cos\left(\frac{\alpha}{2} - \frac{\pi d \cdot \sin\theta \cdot \sin\phi}{\lambda}\right) \cdot \left[\frac{\cos\left(\frac{\pi}{2}\cos\theta\right)}{\sin\theta}\right] \right| \tag{5–8}$$

In using the principle of pattern multiplication, certain rules apply:

1. The pattern to be used for the array elements is the pattern that a single element would have in the array environment, i.e., the "active pattern"—not the pattern in isolation other elements or objects.
2. The pattern of the array factor to be used is the one calculated for isotropic point-source elements spaced and phased the same as the actual elements. The phasing cannot be calculated on the basis of a transmission-line feed system designed for the input impedances of the elements operating as isolated

elements. Their actual input impedances will be affected by mutual coupling with other elements.

3. All the array elements must be alike; they must have similar patterns and polarizations, similarly oriented. For example, if the elements are dipoles, they must have their axes parallel to one another. If the elements are horns, they must be of the same form and size, and all "aimed" in the same direction.

The principle of pattern multiplication and the calculation of array patterns in general have been discussed from the *relative*-pattern point of view. To attain the *absolute* value of the E-field pattern, one must return to the definitions of directivity D and gain G. As discussed in sec. 3.3.4, the directivity of an antenna, D, can in principle be calculated if the relative pattern is known, although the actual process may be very difficult. Additionally, D can be measured, as discussed in chapter 9. If both D and the total radiated power, P_t, are known, the absolute pattern may be calculated. To do this, one multiplies the relative E-field pattern by $\sqrt{30P_tD/R}$ from equation (1–45), chapter 1, where R is the distance from the antenna to a far-field point.

5.1.7. Effects of Element Directivity and Mutual Coupling

An interesting conclusion may be drawn from the principle of pattern multiplication concerning the use of directive elements in arrays. The conclusion is that *if* the pattern of the array factor itself, that is, (5–7) has a much narrower beamwidth than the element-pattern beamwidth, the overall pattern beamwidth and gain are determined primarily by the array factor. Element beamwidth and gain then have little effect for a given array configuration (fixed number of elements). However, the use of directive elements may permit achieving a desired antenna beamwidth and gain with fewer elements spaced farther apart than would be permissible with isotropic or wide-beamwidth elements, resulting in economy of elements and a simpler feed system, but not in a reduction of overall antenna size.

Experience shows that an active element pattern (i.e., SEP) may be narrower than the pattern of the same element when isolated from surrounding objects (see, e.g., Mailloux 1994, p. 324). Then, for large arrays having many elements, the dominating array factor tends to mitigate the element pattern narrowing effect of mutual coupling. However, the array factor does limit the angle over which an array beam can be electronically scanned without appreciable pattern degradation.

The previous discussions on mutual coupling are mostly about the inadequacy of using element impedance, radiation resistance, and radiation patterns applicable to an isolated array element environment. Consequently, one might logically ask why, in the remaining parts of chapter 5, is there so much emphasis on the use of (a) array element characteristics that are in isolation of other elements and (b) array factors that, by definition, assume no mutual coupling? Firstly, these subjects are basic to the principles of arrays and to understanding array performance. In addition, although likely different in an array environment, knowledge of such gross features as self-impedance, polarization, general element pattern shape, and resonant frequency are useful, generally, toward a preliminary design. As discussed later throughout much of chapter 5, the amplitudes and phases of element excitation currents are critical to the control of the overall array patterns. These quantities are needed when calculating array factors, yet they do not include, explicitly, effects of mutual coupling. Furthermore, these are the currents needed, when effects of mutual impedance are included, to determine the required element input voltages and radiated power. One must also recognize that element beam shapes change, because of being within an array environment. However, because of the dominating effect of the array factor on overall array patterns (sec. 5.1.6), useful pattern shape approximations are often possible without the use of measured in-array "active" element patterns.

5.2. Multielement Uniform Linear Arrays

When more than two elements are used in an array, the principle of calculating the pattern (from which in turn the beamwidth and directivity can be computed) is the same as for a two-element array except that the fields of all the elements must be superposed at the field point. The simplest type of multielement array is one in which all the radiators are in a line, with equal spacing between adjacent pairs, as shown in Fig. 5–4. The method

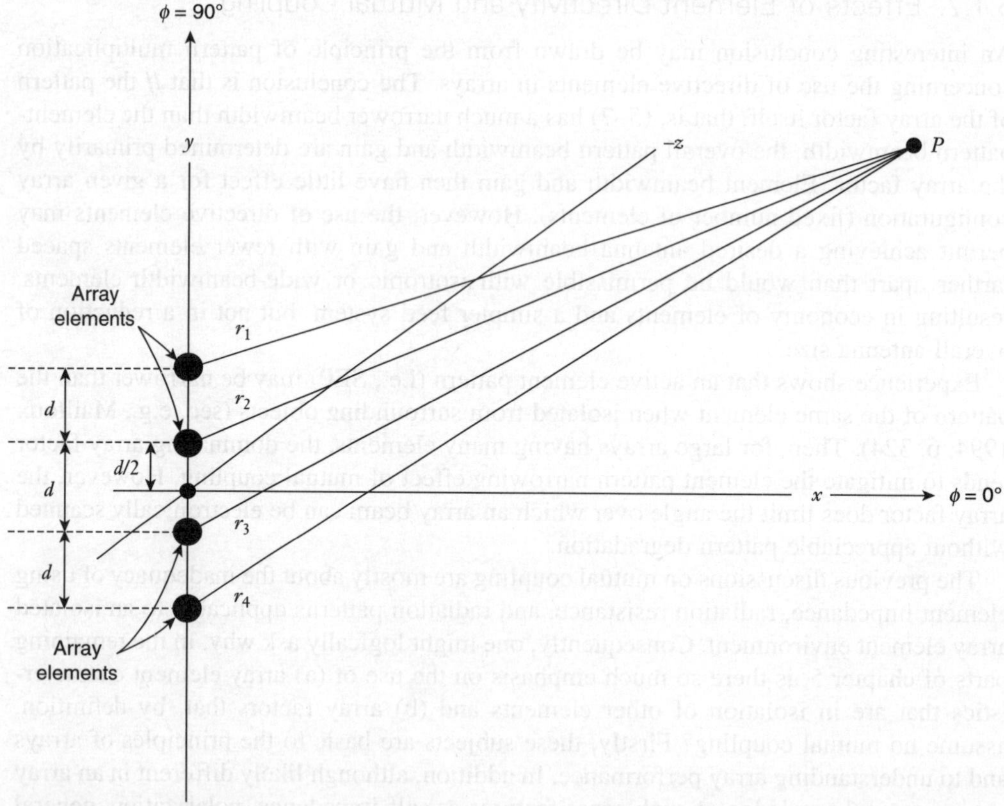

FIGURE 5–4.
Linear array of four radiating elements.

of analysis is suggested by showing a field-point P joined by ray lines to each element. Such an array is called a *linear* array. When all the elements are radiating with equal intensity, and the phase difference between adjacent elements is constant, the array is called *uniform*. This section deals with the properties of *uniform linear arrays*.

5.2.1. Radiation Pattern

If the array contains N isotropic point-source elements, with equal spacing d and phase difference α between adjacent elements, the pattern in a plane containing the line of the array can be shown to be

$$E_{rel} = \left| \frac{\sin\left[N\left(\frac{\pi d \sin\phi}{\lambda} - \frac{\alpha}{2}\right)\right]}{N \sin\left[\frac{\pi d \sin\phi}{\lambda} - \frac{\alpha}{2}\right]} \right| \tag{5–9}$$

where ϕ, as in (5–4), is the angle between the direction of the field point and a perpendicular to the line of the array. For $N = 2$ this expression can be shown to be equivalent to (5–4) (despite the seeming dissimilarity). As in the two-element case, the pattern versus θ and ϕ is obtained simply by replacing $\sin\phi$ by the product $\sin\phi \cdot \sin\theta$. The factor N in the denominator is a normalizing factor, as discussed for (5–7); that is, in this case $k_n = 1/N$.

The pattern has its maximum values at angles ϕ such that the quantity $(\pi d \sin\phi)/\lambda - \alpha/2 = 0$; that is, when $(\pi d \sin\phi)/\lambda = \alpha/2$. The pattern will have additional maxima at angles for which this quantity is equal to an integral multiple of π radians. At the maxima, (5–9) is equivalent to

$$E_{rel} = \lim_{x\to 0}\left|\left(\frac{\sin Nx}{N\sin x}\right)\right| \quad or \quad \lim_{x\to m\pi}\left|\left(\frac{\sin Nx}{N\sin x}\right)\right| \tag{5–10}$$

where m is any integer. For either limit, this expression is an "indeterminate form" (zero divided by zero), but application of a method of differential calculus shows that the limit is unity. The pattern has secondary maxima, or minor lobes, when the numerator of (5–9) attains values expressed by $\sin[(2m + 1)(\pi/2)]$, where again m is any integer (i.e., $m = 1, 2, 3, \ldots$).

The variety of possible patterns for an array with a given number of elements, obtained with different values of d and α, is very great, but many of the possibilities are primarily curiosities, of no practical value. Two basic types of pattern are of special interest.

5.2.2. Broadside Linear Arrays

When $\alpha = 0°$, all the elements are "in phase," and pattern maxima occur at $\phi = 0°$ and $\phi = 180°$, that is, in the directions perpendicular to the line of the array, which is then

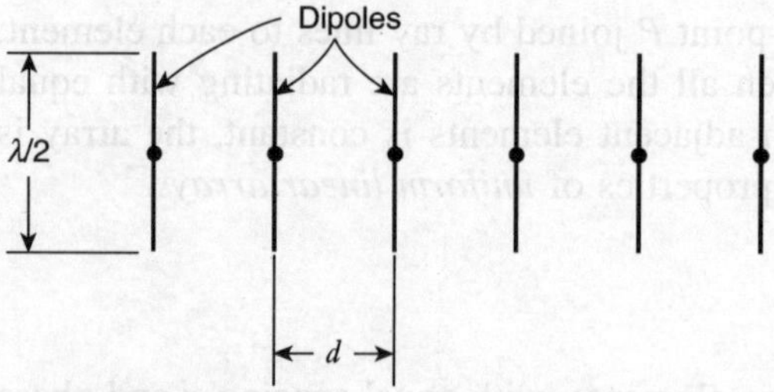

FIGURE 5–5.
Linear horizontal array of six vertical dipoles.

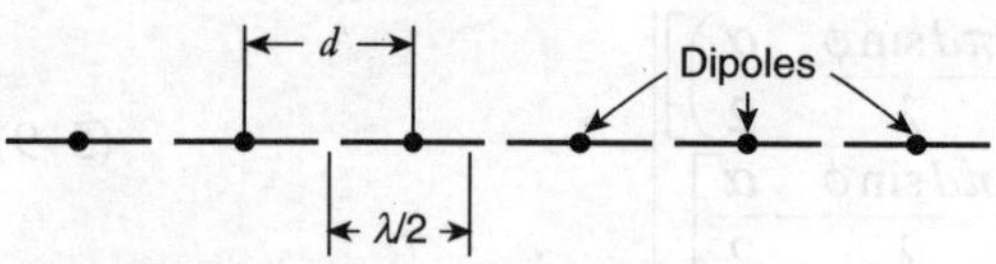

FIGURE 5–6.
Collinear broadside array.

called a *broadside* array. The pattern will be maximum in these directions regardless of the element spacing, d. These will be the only primary maxima if d is less than λ. If $d = \lambda$, additional maxima occur at $\phi = 90°$ and $270°$; as d is increased still further, additional maxima occur as cones of radiation about the axis of the array. They are known as *grating lobes* (so called because they are analogous to the lobes observed in the optical study of a diffraction or reflection grating). Ordinarily, therefore, the spacing of elements in a broadside array is kept less than a wavelength.

However, it has been shown that, subject to this restriction, there is an advantage in spacing the elements of an array by somewhat more than half a wavelength. For a two-element array the optimum spacing is about 0.7λ, for four elements it is about 0.8λ, and for a large number of elements the optimum is about 0.95λ (Tai 1964). The directivity increases gradually as the spacing is increased until the optimum is reached, then drops rather sharply with further increase. It is to be emphasized, however, that the advantage of the wider spacings is in the directivity obtainable with a *given number of elements*. In terms of the ratio of the directivity to the *total length of the array*, there is no advantage in the wider spacing.

The foregoing observations are based on a uniform linear broadside array of point-source isotropic radiators. They apply also to a similar array of dipoles with their centers on the array line and their axes perpendicular to the array line and parallel to each other, as in Fig. 5–5, with respect to the pattern in the plane perpendicular to the dipole axes, that is, the xy-plane in Fig. 5–4. If the array line is horizontal, the dipole axes are vertical, and the radiation is vertically polarized. (It is also possible to make the array line vertical and have the dipole axes horizontal, and the radiation will then be horizontally polarized.) The spacing effects for an array of isotropes also apply to the dipoles in this case because their individual patterns are omnidirectional in the plane perpendicular to their axes.

The dipoles can also be arranged with their axes parallel to the line of the array, which is then called a *collinear* broadside array. This arrangement, pictured in Fig. 5–6, allows a center-to-center dipole spacing somewhat greater than is permissible with parallel dipoles, because the patterns of the individual dipoles have nulls in the $\phi = 90°$ and $\phi = 270°$ directions (i.e., in line with their axes and the line of the array). Therefore the wide-angle grating lobes of radiation that appear with greater spacings are suppressed, for element spacings somewhat greater than a wavelength, in accordance with the principle of pattern multiplication.

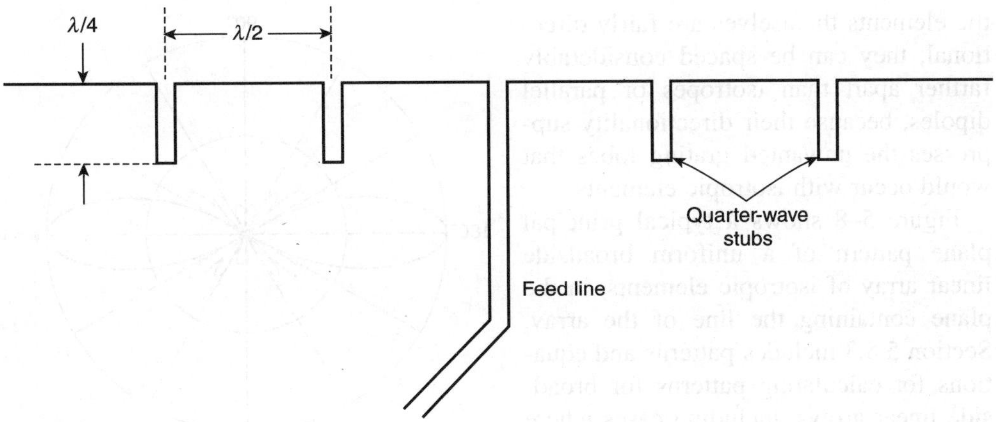

FIGURE 5–7.

A six-half-wave Franklin antenna (six-element collinear dipole array).

The in-phase currents in the individual dipoles, required for a broadside pattern, may be obtained by properly connecting a branched transmission line to the feed point of each dipole. In other words, if the total line length from the transmitter to each dipole is the same, as in Fig. 2–8a, chapter 2, the dipoles will be fed in phase. (Care must be taken to see that the same side of the line is connected to the same side of each dipole; reversing this connection reverses the phase.)

In an alternative feed arrangement, shown in Fig. 5–7, the feed line is connected between the ends of one pair of dipoles, which causes them to be in-phase. (This is a high-impedance feed point, since the ends of the dipoles are voltage-maximum points.) Then quarter-wave stubs are connected between the ends of the additional adjacent pairs of dipoles, providing simultaneously a feed connection and proper phasing. The $\lambda/4$ stubs provide open circuit impedances, and their $\lambda/2$ round-trip lengths cause a phase reversal at each of their input terminals. This arrangement is known as a *Franklin antenna*. (Recall that if the dipoles are directly connected end to end, *without* the quarter-wave stub, the current in alternate half-wave sections will be out of phase; the antenna will be of the long-wire type, and the pattern will be entirely different.)

The collinear array can also be fed by transmission lines connected between the ends of pairs of adjacent dipoles. This has an advantage over center-feeding each dipole individually, in that only one transmission-line branch is required for each pair of dipoles. Also, the relatively high feed-point impedance is usually more easily matched to a two-wire line. The dipole spacing is then restricted to one-half wavelength (as is also true for the Franklin antenna), but this is a fairly satisfactory spacing.

Broadside arrays may also be formed from other types of elements, such as horns, slots, microstrip patches, helixes, and polyrods. If the individual elements are themselves directional, their maximum radiation should be in the broadside direction. If they are unidirectional radiators, such as sectoral or pyramidal horns, waveguide slots, microstrip patches, axial-mode helixes, and polyrods, a unidirectional broadside array results. When the elements themselves are fairly directional, they can be spaced considerably farther apart than isotropes or parallel dipoles, because their directionality suppresses the unwanted grating lobes that would occur with isotropic elements.

Figure 5–8 shows a typical principal plane pattern of a uniform broadside linear array of isotropic elements, in the plane containing the line of the array. Section 5.5.3 includes patterns and equations for calculating patterns for broadside linear arrays, including cases where array elements are not identical.

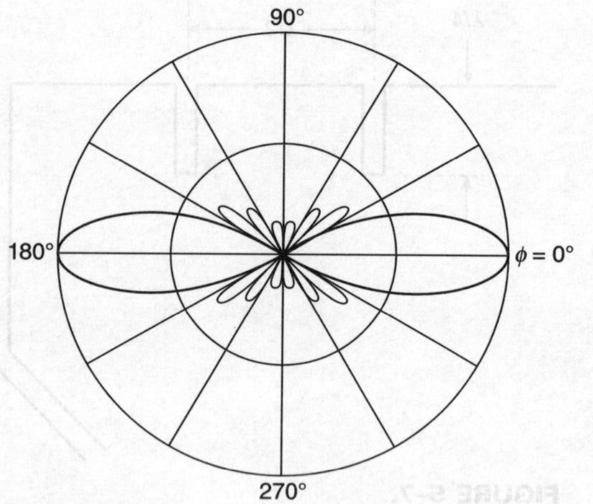

FIGURE 5–8.

Approximate pattern of an eight-element uniform broadside linear array of point-source isotropic elements.

5.2.3. Endfire Arrays

If in (5–9) the phase-difference α between adjacent elements is equal to $2\pi d/\lambda$ radians, the condition for a maximum of radiation is satisfied when $\phi = 90°$, and *for this value only*, provided that d is less than $\lambda/2$. The maximum field intensity is radiated in a direction along the line of the array, "off the end" rather than broadside; hence the name *endfire array*. The maximum is toward only one of the ends of the array, rather than in both the endfire directions. In terms of Fig. 5–4, if the progressive phase change is a retardation going in the direction of the positive y-axis by the amount α per element, the beam will be in the $\phi = 90°$ direction. If the sign of α is changed, or its amount is increased by 180 degrees without changing the element spacing, the beam will be in the direction $\phi = 270°$.

Although the condition stated above for the value of α results in an endfire array, it does not result in an endfire pattern with the maximum possible directivity and narrowest possible beam. It has been shown by Hansen and Woodyard (1938) that an endfire beam with somewhat greater gain results if the phase change per element satisfies the following condition:

$$\alpha = \left(\frac{2\pi d}{\lambda} + \frac{\pi}{N}\right) \tag{5–11}$$

where N is the number of elements in the array. This relationship is referred to in the antenna literature as the *Hansen-Woodyard condition*. (This condition does not necessarily result in a unidirectional pattern, however, as does the basic endfire condition.)

The correct phase of current or field to each radiating element of an endfire array requires a feed system in which the current or field must travel through a longer path in the transmission line or waveguide to each successive element along the array, the increased length of line or guide per element being equal to $\alpha\lambda/2\pi$, where α is the

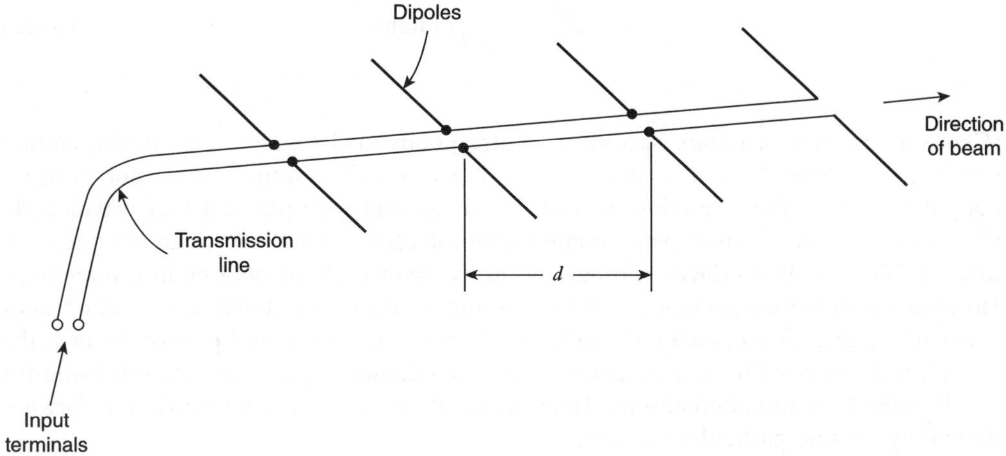

FIGURE 5–9.

One form of feed arrangement suitable for an endfire array.

required phase change per element expressed in radians and λ is the wavelength. If a waveguide line is used, λ in this formula is the guide wavelength, λ_g given as (2–68) in chapter 2. Figure 5–9 illustrates this principle for a four-element endfire dipole array. Incidentally the basic endfire analysis assumes isotropic radiators, but it applies also to other radiators that have radiation along the line of the array.

The feed system must also be a matched-impedance system, that is, one with hardly any standing wave on it, in order to produce the required phasing of the elements in accordance with this formula. There must be an impedance match at each branch point of the line, in accordance with principles described in chapter 2; see, for example, Fig. 2–7. The impedance relations must also be adjusted so that equal currents are fed to all the dipoles in order for equation (5–9) to apply. A typical endfire array pattern is shown in Fig. 5–10, for isotropic point-source radiators, in a plane containing the array line. The beam has axial symmetry; for example, if the beam axis is horizontal, the horizontal and vertical beamwidths are the same.

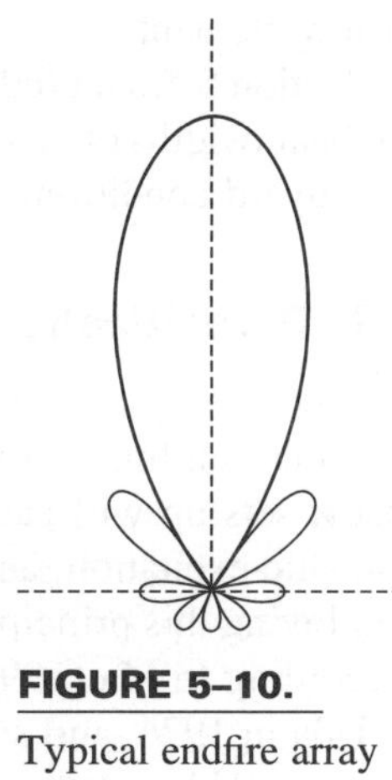

FIGURE 5–10.

Typical endfire array pattern in a plane containing the line of the array.

Some of the patterns shown in Fig. 5–3 are those of two-element endfire arrays. A few of them have not only a maximum in one endfire direction (the "front" direction) but also a complete null, or zero field intensity, in the opposite (back) direction. The cases $d = \lambda/8$ with $\alpha = 135°$ and $d = \lambda/4$ with $\alpha = 90°$ are examples. These particular patterns are advantageous in applications where a high *front-to-back ratio* is desired. The condition for a null in one endfire direction is

$$\alpha = \pi\left(1 \pm \frac{2d}{\lambda}\right) \text{ radians} \tag{5–12}$$

(Choosing the plus or minus sign merely corresponds to changing the particular endfire direction in which the null occurs.) Satisfying this null condition does not insure a maximum in the other direction. In fact, if d is an odd multiple of a half wavelength, (5–12) corresponds to an in-phase condition of the elements ($\alpha = 0°$ or an integral multiple of 360°). This produces a broadside array, with nulls in both endfire directions. However, with some spacings, of which examples are given above, a maximum does occur in the direction opposite the null, producing a *unidirectional* pattern. In fact, the two-element array with $d = \lambda/8$ and $\alpha = 135°$ simultaneously satisfies the condition for a null in the back direction and the Hansen-Woodyard condition for maximum forward directivity for that particular spacing.

Incidentally, the null condition of (5–12), applies not only to the two-element array but also to any uniform linear endfire array with an even number of elements, since the elements cancel in pairs in the null direction. It may also be noted that the null is never absolute because of unavoidable imperfections in the spacing and phasing of the elements, and many-element arrays are more susceptible to such imperfections than those of few elements.

Section 5.5.6 includes further discussion on endfire arrays and Fig. 5–18 that compares the beamwidths of an ordinary endfire array and an endfire array that satisfies the Hansen-Woodyard condition.

5.3. Parasitically Excited Endfire Arrays

It is not necessary to feed each element of an endfire array by direct connection to a transmission line. If only one dipole of such an array is directly fed, or driven, the field that it sets up will cause currents to flow in adjoining elements. This process is called parasitic excitation, and the elements thus excited are *parasitic elements*. Endfire arrays employing this principle are known as Yagi-Uda antennas (often called simply "Yagis"). According to Ma (1993, pp. 3–13), this type of array was first described in Japanese by S. Uda in 1926, and subsequently in English by H. Yagi in 1928. As noted in sec. 4.10, the Yagi-Uda antenna can also be regarded as a *surface-wave* antenna.

Parasitic excitation cannot be employed in broadside arrays. To produce the in-phase currents required for a broadside pattern, a full-wavelength element spacing would be required. There would then be two endfire lobes of radiation as well as the two broadside lobes, and this type of pattern is not a true broadside pattern. Therefore broadside arrays are always driven rather than parasitic. (There are some antennas that might be considered exceptions to this statement. In them parasitically excited elements produce a broadside beam, but the exciting source is not itself part of the array.)

The phases of the currents in parasitic dipole elements are determined by their spacing from the adjacent element, and also by their lengths. A parasitic dipole electrically exactly a half wavelength or slightly longer will be inductive, and the phase of its current will

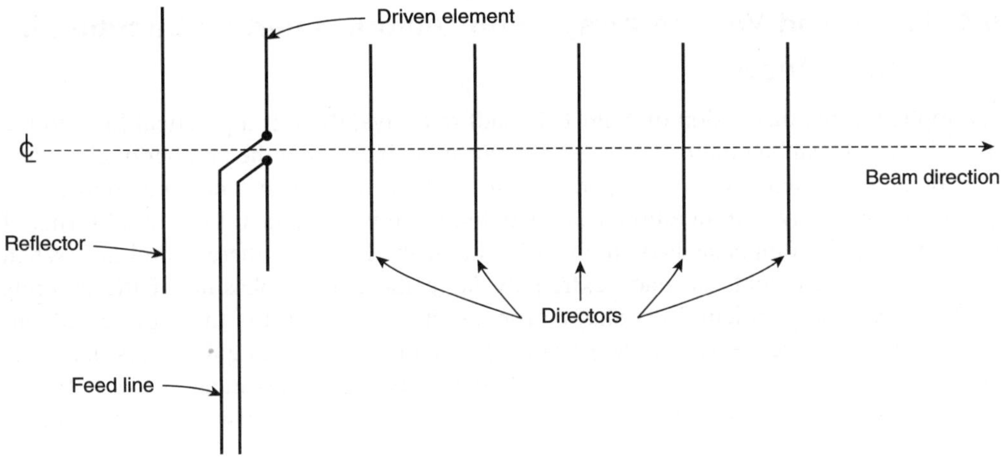

FIGURE 5–11.

A Yagi-Uda parasitic endfire array with one reflector and five directors.

lag the induced emf. A dipole shorter electrically than a half wavelength will be capacitive, and the current in it will lead the induced emf. Comparatively close spacing of elements is used in parasitic arrays to obtain good excitation, and the induction fields of the elements play a major role, so that an exact analysis is very complicated. It is known, however, that properly spaced dipole elements that are electrically slightly shorter than a half wavelength act as *directors*, reinforcing the field of the driven element in the direction away from the driven element. Thus a line of directors may be used, and each one will excite the next one. On the other hand, an element that is electrically one-half-wavelength long or slightly longer will act as a *reflector*, if correctly spaced, reinforcing the field of the driven element in a direction toward the driven element from the reflector. Therefore if a reflector element is placed adjacent to a driven element, another element placed beyond the reflector will not be appreciably excited, as very little field exists beyond the first reflector. For these reasons a Yagi-Uda endfire array usually consists of one driven element, one reflector on one side of it, and a number of directors on the other side of it.

A typical Yagi-Uda configuration is shown in Fig. 5–11. Antennas of this type offer the advantages of a unidirectional beam of moderate directivity with light weight, simplicity of feed-system design, and low cost. The design becomes critical, however, if high directivity is attempted through the use of many elements. Up to five or six may be used without difficulty, and arrays of thirty or forty elements are possible. The input impedance of a Yagi-Uda array tends to be low, and the bandwidth is limited to around 2%, typically. Directivity of around 10 dB is readily achieved with a moderate number of elements (five or six). Higher gains may be achieved by making a broadside array of which the elements are Yagi-Uda arrays.

5.4. Planar and Volume Arrays with Uniform Aperture Distribution

5.4.1. Planar Arrays

As implied in the discussion of Yagi-Uda endfire arrays, there is a practical limit to the directivity that can be obtained from a linear array by increasing the number of elements. The limit is reached sooner in a parasitic array than in a driven one, and sooner in a driven endfire array than in a broadside one, but there is a practical limit in all forms of linear arrays. The emphasis is on the word "practical"; in theory there is no limit. When the number of elements is made extremely large the correct phasing of the currents becomes extremely critical. Very slight errors of phasing will nullify the expected advantage of additional elements, and the practical problem of maintaining the necessary exact phasing is virtually impossible to solve. A linear array that results in about a 0.1° beamwidth represents approximately a practical limit. (Such an array would have about a thousand elements.)

The directivity of an array can be increased, however, by combining broadside linear arrays to form a broadside planar array. A broadside linear array of isotropic elements has a pattern that may have a narrow beamwidth in a plane containing the line of the array, but it radiates uniformly in all directions of a plane perpendicular to the line of the array. Thus a many-element linear broadside array has a pattern that was earlier described as like a "pancake" (as compared with the relatively fat "doughnut" pattern of a dipole). But when broadside linear arrays are arranged in parallel rows with correct phasing to form a broadside planar array, the pattern becomes two separate lobes, each having a maximum in one of the two opposite directions perpendicular to the plane of the array. The two lobes are identical (mirror images of each other) and are characterized in general by two beamwidths measured in planes perpendicular to each other through the beam axis. (The two planes are usually chosen parallel to and perpendicular to the line of the basic linear arrays of which the plane array is formed.)

If the number of linear arrays thus "stacked" in rows is equal to the number of elements in one of the linear arrays, and the spacing of the rows is equal to the spacing of elements in each linear array, the total plane array is a square. In fact, if the plane of the array is vertical, it is impossible to say whether it consists of horizontal linear arrays stacked vertically in rows, or vertical linear arrays arranged horizontally in columns; the array is in fact a matrix of rows and columns. It is often convenient for purposes of analysis however, to consider the planar array as a plane assembly of parallel linear arrays. When the array is rectangular rather than square the linear arrays are usually considered to run parallel to the longer dimension.

A common array element is the dipole, and the dipole axes are ordinarily parallel to one side of the array. In a vertical planar array, the dipoles are placed vertically if vertical polarization is desired and horizontally to obtain horizontal polarization. Then linear arrays considered in one direction are collinear arrays, and in the other direction they are parallel-dipole arrays. Figure 5–12 illustrates a vertical planar dipole array that is two (vertical) dipoles high and four dipoles wide (a "two-by-four"). Such arrays are sometimes called *curtains*.

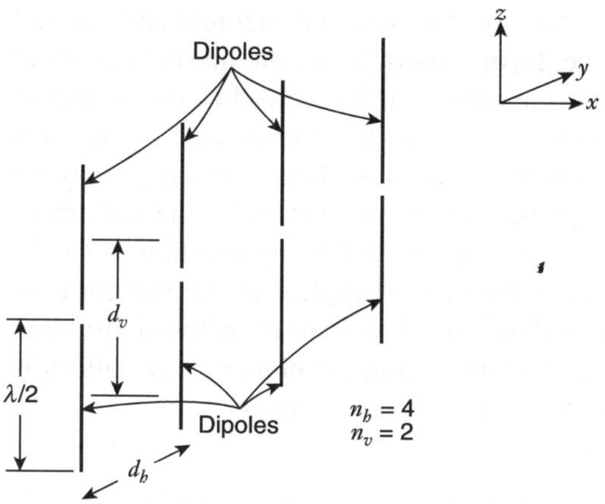

FIGURE 5–12.

A two-by-four, dipole broadside planar array in *y-z* plane. (Beam is in the *x* direction.)

5.4.2. Pattern Versus θ and φ

The theory of planar arrays is best approached assuming isotropic point-source radiators. Consider Fig. 5–13 that consists of equal amplitude, in-phase ($\alpha = 0°$) isotropes with element spacings d_h and d_v in the horizontal (*y*-axis) and vertical (*z*-axis) directions. The equation of the horizontal-plane broadside pattern for a horizontal row of elements is given by (5–9), with $\alpha = 0°$. This linear array pattern, when expressed in terms of θ and φ is, in accordance with (5–4a), attained by replacing $\sin\phi$ with $\sin\phi\sin\theta$. Thus, the pattern for a horizontal broadside linear array, parallel to the *y*-axis, is

$$E_h(\theta,\phi) = \frac{\sin\left[N_h\left(\dfrac{\pi d_h \sin\phi\sin\theta}{\lambda}\right)\right]}{N_h \sin\left[\dfrac{\pi d_h \sin\phi\sin\theta}{\lambda}\right]} \tag{5–13}$$

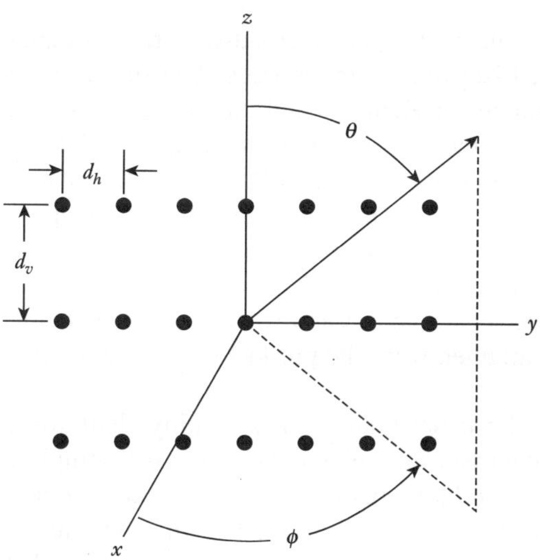

FIGURE 5–13.

A three-by-seven broadside planar array of equal-amplitude, equal-phase isotropes in *y-z* plane. (Beam is in the *x* direction.)

A vertical column of elements in the planar array is a line array along the *z*-axis of Fig. 5–12. Obviously the pattern of such an array will have the same shape (for a given number of elements *N*) as a horizontal linear array, but rotated in the coordinate system to agree with its vertical axis. This results in a different mathematical expression for the pattern, which is

$$E_v(\theta,\phi) = \frac{\sin\left[N_v\left(\dfrac{\pi d_v \cos\theta}{\lambda}\right)\right]}{N_v \sin\left[\dfrac{\pi d_v \cos\theta}{\lambda}\right]} \tag{5–14}$$

Note that the angle φ does not enter into (5–14), even though it describes the complete pattern. This is because of the orientation of the vertical array with respect to the coordinate system.)

Equations (5–13) and (5–14) express separately the patterns of horizontal and vertical linear arrays into which the plane array may be decomposed. Thus, the question is, what is the pattern of the complete array? Note that the array can be viewed as consisting of vertical line arrays that are equally spaced along the y-axis (the horizontal), where each vertical array is a triplet, containing three isotropic elements. Thus, the array may be viewed as a horizontal linear array of the triplets, and (5–14) expresses the pattern of each triplet. Therefore, the planar array pattern may be attained by application of (5–7), the principle of pattern multiplication. This principle can be applied in the present case by considering the planar array to be a horizontal uniform linear array, whose individual *elements* are vertical arrays (the triplets). Therefore the complete planar array pattern is attained by simply multiplying E_h and E_v of (5–13) and (5–14); namely

$$E(\theta,\phi)=E_h(\theta,\phi)\times E_v(\theta,\phi)=\frac{\sin\left[N_h\left(\dfrac{\pi d_h\sin\theta\sin\phi}{\lambda}\right)\right]\sin\left[N_v\left(\dfrac{\pi d_v\cos\theta}{\lambda}\right)\right]}{N_hN_v\sin\left[\dfrac{\pi d_h\sin\theta\sin\phi}{\lambda}\right]\sin\left[\dfrac{\pi d_v\cos\theta}{\lambda}\right]} \tag{5–15}$$

Equation (5–13) gives the pattern versus θ and ϕ of a planar broadside array of equal amplitude, equal phase, and uniformly spaced isotropic point sources. The subscripts h and v are used with N and d to denote the number of elements and their spacing in both the horizontal and vertical dimensions. Here the factor k_n of (5–7) is equal to $1/N_hN_v$. It is to be noted that use of the principle of multiplication for (5–15) is possible because of the uniformity of the array, that is, the array description in the x direction is independent of position along the y-axis; and conversely, the array description in the y direction is independent of position along the x-axis. This independence between the x and y directions causes the planar array mathematics to be separable in x and y. However, in general, complete patterns of planar arrays cannot be attained from the product of principal plane patterns (see sec. 5.7.3).

There is a further step required, because the usual planar array employs half-wave dipoles or elements of another type, rather than isotropic elements. Then, the complete pattern is obtained by multiplying (5–15) by the relative pattern of the element. If dipole elements are used and are placed with their axes vertical (i.e., lying along the z-axis), their patterns are given by equation (4–11) (only the part in the square brackets is needed for the relative pattern). If instead, dipole elements are horizontal (parallel to the y-axis), the relative pattern (corresponding to (4–11) for a vertical half-wave dipole) is

$$E(\theta,\phi)=\frac{\cos\left(\dfrac{\pi}{2}\sin\theta\sin\phi\right)}{\sqrt{1-\sin^2\theta\sin^2\phi}} \tag{5–16}$$

(This additional multiplication will not be performed explicitly here because the principle has already been adequately illustrated.)

5.4.3. Volume Arrays and Plane Reflectors

Just as a planar array was formed by stacking linear arrays in parallel rows, a *volume array* can be formed by combining planar arrays. As noted, a single broadside planar array has a bidirectional pattern. If two such arrays are placed parallel to each other a distance *d* apart and phased so that the corresponding array of the two isotropic elements would be a *unidirectional* endfire array in accordance with (5–12), the resulting complete pattern will be unidirectional. Ordinarily, two planes of elements will suffice. The complete pattern is then obtained by further application of the principle of pattern multiplication.

Still another method of obtaining a unidirectional beam is to place a plane reflecting surface parallel to a single planar array, with a suitable spacing between the array and the reflector. The resulting pattern may be calculated by considering the actual array in combination with its image in the reflector, according to the image principle described in sec. 1.2. The spacing between the planar array and its image will be twice the spacing of the array and the reflector, and the phases will be opposite, that is, 180 degrees apart. Thus the array plus its image are in effect a volume array, two elements deep.

The reflector method has advantages over the actual volume-array method, in that since there are actually only half as many dipoles the feed system is less complicated. Also the reflector effectively prevents back radiation except for a small amount due to diffraction around the edges of the reflector, provided that the reflector is either a solid sheet of metal or a fine-mesh screen. However, a fairly coarse mesh or even a parallel-wire grating (wires parallel to the antenna polarization) gives satisfactory results, with much-reduced weight and wind resistance, if the spacing between reflector wires in the direction perpendicular to the polarization is a small fraction of a wavelength. The reflecting surface should extend some distance beyond the edge elements of the array—usually a distance comparable to the spacing between elements.

The dipole-to-reflector spacing, within certain limits, is not critical. The useful range of spacings is from about 1/16 to 1/4 wavelength. Close spacing gives somewhat greater gain with an array of few elements, but at the expense of low dipole-feed-point impedance and reduced bandwidth. With large arrays the gain does not depend appreciably on the spacing, within the permitted range. Too large a spacing, however (greater than half a wavelength), will "split" the pattern and result in more than one beam. A good compromise among the competing factors—directivity, ohmic losses, and bandwidth—is a spacing of about 1/8 wavelength. (Ohmic losses increase with the closer spacings because of lowered radiation resistance and higher currents.)

The two-element-deep volume array, consisting of two large-area vertical planar arrays, may be preferable at the lower frequencies because a reflector of sufficient size would be much more expensive and would have excessive wind resistance. Such antennas, known as "double curtain" arrays, can be used in the frequency range from about 3 to 30 MHz or higher. Above 30 MHz the use of a reflector instead of a true volume array becomes increasingly advantageous. A compromise method is the use of parasitic dipoles as the reflecting device. Planar arrays with plane reflectors, sometimes called "mattress" or "bedspring" antennas, are much used in the VHF and UHF bands. As radar antennas

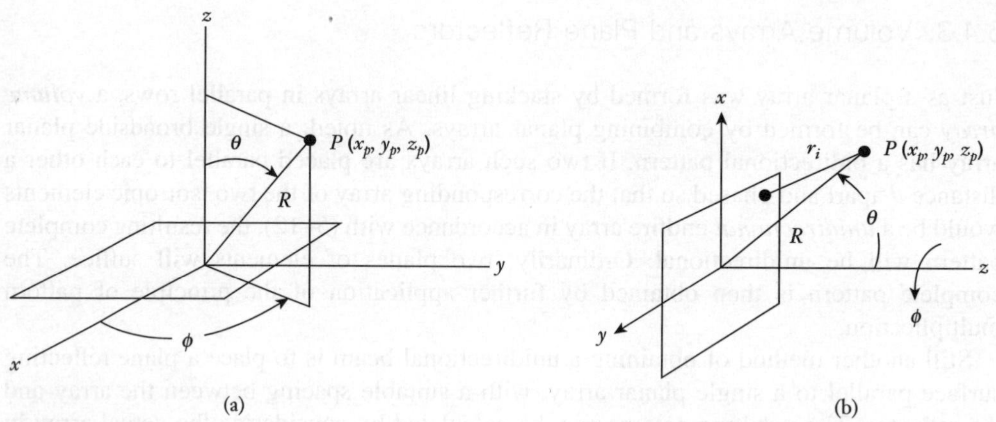

FIGURE 5–14.

Spherical coordinates with array elements in *x-y* plane. (5–14a) shows point *P* at distance *R* from origin; (5–14b) shows point *P* and distance *R*, and distance r_1 from a position x_i, y_i on the *x-y* plane.

they are often mounted on a rotating platform so that the beam "scans" the horizon, typically at rotation speeds of 1 to 30 rpm, depending on the antenna size. Such reflecting screens are commonly as large as 30 feet or more with hundreds of elements, and much larger ones can be used on occasion for special purposes.

5.5. Linear Array Pattern Calculations

Section 5.5 includes general equations for calculating the patterns of array factors, including cases where array elements are not excited with equal currents. Patterns for broadside and endfire arrays are determined, comparisons are made between the patterns for linear arrays and continuous linear aperture antennas, and the dependence of grating lobes on element spacing is discussed.

5.5.1. General Equations for Array Patterns

An array factor is the radiation pattern of an array antenna when each of its array elements is considered to radiate isotropically (IEEE 1993, p. 55). Now assume isotropic array elements of arbitrary amplitude and phase are located on the *x-y* plane of Fig. 5–14. Then, the array factor $F(\theta, \phi)$ is the complex sum (phase and amplitude) of the electric fields in the far zone from each element as follows:

$$F(\theta,\phi) = A_0 \exp(-jk\delta_0) + A_1 \exp(-jk\delta_1) + \cdots + A_{(N-1)} \exp(-jk\delta_{(N-1)})$$
$$= \sum_{i=0}^{N-1} A_i \exp\left(-j\frac{2\pi}{\lambda}\delta_i\right) \qquad (5\text{–}17)$$

where

$A_i = a_i \exp(j\alpha_i)$, where a_i is the amplitude and α_i is the phase of the radiated E-field of the ith element

$k = 2\pi/\lambda$

$\delta_i = r_i - R$

r_i = distance from i^{th} element to an observation point in the far zone

R = distance from the reference point on the array to the observation point in the far zone

N = total number of isotropic elements

An array factor is a complex function of angle. Therefore, a graph of the amplitude of an array factor $F(\theta, \phi)$ is obtained by plotting $|F(\theta, \phi)|$. To obtain a normalized amplitude pattern of an array factor, one must of course divide $|F(\theta, \phi)|$ by the peak amplitude of $|F(\theta, \phi)|$.

Note that δ_i is the distance between the ith element and an observation point that exceeds the distance between the origin ($x = y = z = 0$), the array reference point, and the observation point, said point being in the far zone. Thus, when including the effects of path length differences, the relative far-zone phase contribution of the ith element ψ_i follows:

$$\psi_i = \alpha_i - \left(\frac{2\pi}{\lambda}\right)\delta_i \tag{5–18}$$

Then, the array factor of (5–17) may be expressed as

$$F(\theta, \phi) = \sum_{i=0}^{N-1} a_i \exp j\psi_i = \sum_{i=0}^{N-1} a_i \exp\left[j\left(\alpha_i - \left(\frac{2\pi}{\lambda}\right)\delta_i\right)\right] \tag{5–19}$$

From Appendix H, for observations in the far zone, δ_i may be expressed as

$$\delta_i = -\sin\theta(x_i \cos\phi + y_i \sin\phi) \tag{5–20}$$

where

x_i, y_i is the ith element position within the x-y plane

and

θ, ϕ are the angles from the origin to the observation point

Recall that $F(\theta, \phi)$, as defined, is the pattern calculated under the assumption that each array element radiates isotropically. Then, the far-field pattern $E(\theta, \phi)$ of an array having identical elements can be calculated by using the principle of multiplication. In reality, however, element patterns of physically identical elements are never the same when the elements are actually placed in an array. However, in principle, if each element pattern is described by the function $f(\theta, \phi)$, the far-field pattern $E(\theta, \phi)$ is

$$E(\theta,\phi) = f(\theta,\phi)\cdot F(\theta,\phi) \tag{5–21}$$

It is to be noted the $F(\theta, \phi)$ and $E(\theta, \phi)$ are generally complex, and therefore their amplitude patterns are created by plotting magnitudes only, that is, $|F(\theta, \phi)|$ and $|E(\theta, \phi)|$.

In summary, (5–17) and (5–19) are equal and are general expressions for the array factor if each array element is an isotrope; and (5–21) is the far-zone E-field array pattern if the pattern of each element can be expressed as $f(\theta, \phi)$. A note of caution: effects of mutual coupling between elements may cause the "in-place" element patterns (called scan element pattern, SEP) to differ from their "free space" patterns. Because of this, even for an array of physically identical elements, the actual array pattern may not equal $F(\theta, \phi)$ times the "free-space" element pattern $f(\theta, \phi)$, as indicated by (5–21). Conventionally, however, (5–21) is used as a "best" estimate until more detailed information is available.

5.5.2. Linear Array Patterns

In this section, the radiation pattern in the x-y plane is investigated for a linear array of elements located along the y-axis. With these constraints, from Fig. 5–14a it can be seen that $\theta = 90°$ and each $x_i = 0$, and from (5–20) one attains $\delta_i = -y_i \sin\phi$. Thus, the array factor of (5–19) becomes

$$F(90°,\phi) = \sum_{i=0}^{N-1} a_i \exp\left[j\left(\alpha_i + \left(\frac{2\pi}{\lambda}\right) y_i \sin\phi\right)\right] \tag{5–22}$$

In (5–22) the element amplitudes, phases, and separation distances are arbitrary. Equation (5–9), previously introduced in sec. 5.2 is also for arrays along the y-axis, but it is applicable only to arrays for which the element amplitudes, phase differences, and physical separations are all equal.

Equation (5–22) can be further simplified if, between adjacent elements, the separation distance d and the phase difference α are constant, as is common in practice. Furthermore, frequently the input current amplitude and phase of an array are symmetrical about the array center. Then, $F(90°,\phi)$ with its phase reference at the array center can be expressed as follows:

$$F(90°,\phi) = \sum_{n=-(N-1)/2}^{(N-1)/2} a_n \exp\left[jn\left(\alpha + \left(\frac{2\pi}{\lambda}\right) d \sin\phi\right)\right] \tag{5–23}$$

where

a_n = amplitude of the element located on the y-axis at $y_n = n \cdot d$
α = phase difference between adjacent elements

d = separation distance between elements along the y-axis
N = total number of isotropic elements

As previously mentioned, (5–9) in sec. 5.2 pertains only to arrays having n equal amplitude isotropic elements, with equal amplitude, equal spacing d, and equal phase difference α between adjacent elements. For this special case, (5–23) can be further simplified and becomes (5–9), except for the fact in (5–23) the total number of elements is designated as N, not n.

5.5.3. Broadside Linear Array Patterns

A broadside array is one in which the main beam direction is normal to the line of the array. Then, for a linear array located along the y-axis of Fig. 5–14a, ϕ is either 0° or 180°. Then, with equal phase excitation (i.e., $\alpha = 0$), the pattern from (5–23) has equal-amplitude maxima at 0° and 180°. Consequently, each maximum equals the sum of the element amplitude terms a_n, and the broadside pattern of an array of isotropic radiators is bidirectional. Broadside arrays are made unidirectional through use a reflecting back plane or elements with unidirectional element patterns. In further discussions on broadside arrays in this book, it is assumed that means have been taken to assure unidirectional performance.

Figure 5–15 shows patterns for two arrays with the same array factor, each array having element excitations with equal amplitudes ($a_n = 1$) and equal phases ($\alpha = 0$). In each case, the element spacing d is $\lambda/2$ and the number of elements N is 10. Each array pattern is normalized so that its peak is unity (0 dB) and graphed versus ϕ over ±90°. For one array the elements are isotropic radiators, and for the other the pattern $f(\theta, \phi)$ of each element pattern is $|\cos\phi|$ for ϕ between ±90°. The $|\cos\phi|$ dependence approximates the pattern of a simple element. The array factors are obtained by calculating the absolute value of (5–23), and (5–21) is used to apply pattern multiplication for obtaining the effects of the $|\cos\phi|$ element patterns. By comparing the two patterns of Figure 5–15, it may be seen that the $|\cos\phi|$ element patterns do not reduce the magnitude of the major side lobes, but the minor lobes are reduced at angles near 90° from the main beam. Thus, although the major side-lobe to main-lobe ratio is the same for the two arrays, the array with the $\cos\phi$ elements has a slightly higher directivity (greater beam concentration). It is also to be noted that (a) side lobes are large (approximately −13 dB) when all elements are excited with equal amplitude and (b) wide-angle element patterns can affect a reduction in the wide-angle sidelobe levels.

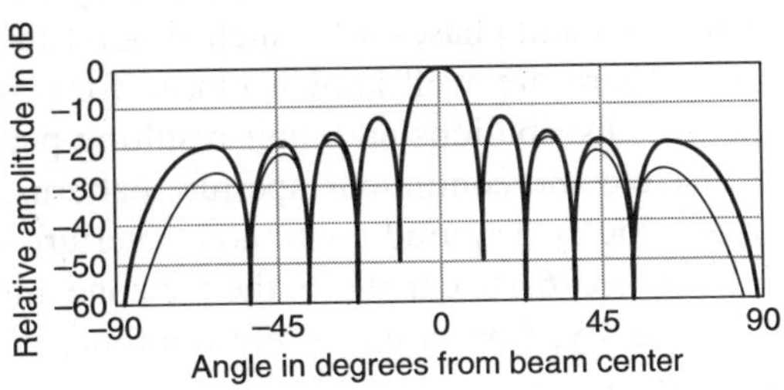

FIGURE 5–15.

Radiation patterns of two ten-element broadside arrays, with element excitations of equal amplitudes and phases. Heavier pattern for isotropic element patterns; thinner pattern for $\cos\phi$ amplitude element patterns.

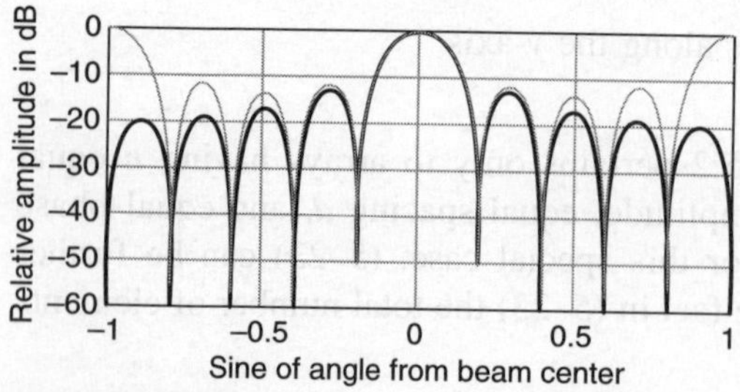

FIGURE 5–16.

Radiation pattern of a ten-element linear array of isotropic radiators spaced $\lambda/2$ apart (heaviest curve), and a five-element linear of isotropic radiators spaced λ apart (thinner curve).

5.5.4. Grating Lobes

As mentioned for broadside arrays in sec. 5.2.2, periodically occurring major lobes exist when the spacing between uniformly spaced elements is λ or greater. These periodically occurring lobes are called grating lobes. As a cautionary note, if a beam is focused to point in a direction other than broadside, a grating lobe may occur at smaller element spacings. For arrays designed for changing the beam-pointing direction (chapter 8), element spacing is ordinarily limited to $\lambda/2$ or somewhat less, to avoid grating lobes.

Figure 5–16 includes two patterns, one for a ten-element linear array of isotropic radiators spaced $\lambda/2$ apart (heaviest curve) and the other for a five-element linear array of isotropic radiators spaced λ apart (thinner curve). The curves are graphed as a function of $\sin\phi$, Notice that, graphed in this manner, the grating lobes at $\sin\phi = \pm 1$ (i.e., $\phi = \pm 90°$) are the same magnitude and shape as the major lobe at $\phi = 0$ (i.e., $\sin\phi = 0$).

5.5.5. Comparisons: Broadside Array and Continuous Aperture Antenna

Reflector and lens antennas are discussed in chapter 6. Unlike the discrete excitation of array apertures at each element location, the illumination of reflector and lens apertures is continuous. In the limit of very close spacing between elements, array apertures become continuous. A comparison of the patterns from discrete and continuous apertures is included here, because knowledge of the patterns from continuous apertures provides useful insights about patterns from arrays. As will be shown, the patterns of the two aperture types are similar if: (1) the array element spacing is $\lambda/2$ or less and (2) the array amplitudes and phases are matched point-to-point with the continuous aperture distributions. There are well-known closed-form mathematical relations between continuous aperture distributions and their resulting patterns. Therefore, because of the similarities of discrete and continuous aperture patterns, much is known about array patterns based on previously acquired continuous aperture patterns.

From sec. 6.10, chapter 6, the far-zone amplitude pattern in a principal plane, normalized to unity, from a uniformly illuminated (constant amplitude and phase) continuous aperture is

$$E(u) = |\sin u/u| \tag{5–24}$$

where

$$u = (\pi L/\lambda)\sin\phi$$

and ϕ denotes the angle measured from normal to the aperture of width L. In comparison, from (5–7), for a broadside linear array of isotropes having equal amplitude and phase with spacing d, the normalized amplitude pattern is

$$\left|\frac{\sin\left[N\left(\dfrac{\pi d \sin\phi}{\lambda}\right)\right]}{N\sin\left[\left(\dfrac{\pi d \sin\phi}{\lambda}\right)\right]}\right| \qquad (5\text{–}25)$$

where N is number of elements. With the approximation n times d used as the array aperture width L, the numerator of (5–25) becomes $\sin u$ as in (5–24). Of course, the array width is actually $N - 1$, but the difference between N and $N - 1$ diminishes for large values of N. Therefore, for a continuous aperture and an array with a large number of elements, each of the same width, the zeros of $E(u)$ and $E(\phi)$ occur at practically the same angle ϕ.

There are also other close similarities between the broadside patterns for closely spaced arrays and continuous aperture antennas. For example, because $\sin x \approx x$, if x is small and in radians, the numerator of (5–25) becomes approximately u at near-broadside where ϕ is small. Figure 5–17 includes patterns of a uniformly excited broadside array with spacing d of $\lambda/2$ and of a continuous aperture, each of the same length. The patterns are virtually equal at angles near the direction of the main beam. As also apparent from Fig. 5–17, the peaks in the minor lobes differ increasingly as the angle ϕ becomes closer to ±90°. For aperture widths of about 5λ and larger, the side-lobe peaks at wide angles (ϕ near ±90°) may differ by several decibels. Even so, at these wide angles the field strength, and thus the energy, in either pattern is small compared to the energy in the major lobes. Therefore, since the two major lobe patterns are almost identical, the directivity of the two antennas of Fig. 5–17 are virtually the same.

For most practical purposes, the approximate equality of broadside antenna patterns, whether from closely spaced ($\lambda/2$ or less) elements or continuous apertures, is retained provided the array amplitudes and phases are matched point-to-point with the continuous aperture distributions. This near-equality of patterns exists provided also that the apertures are of equal length and exceed 5λ.

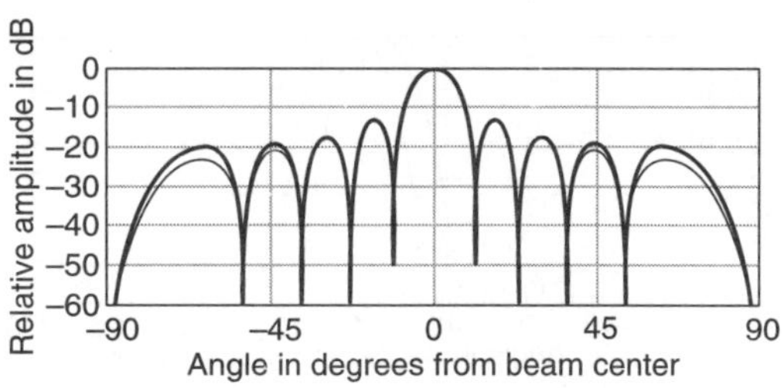

FIGURE 5–17.

Radiation pattern of a ten-element linear array of isotropic radiators spaced $\lambda/2$ apart (heaviest curve), and a continuous linear aperture of 5λ width (thinner curve).

5.5.6. Endfire Array Patterns

Endfire arrays are discussed in sec. 5.2.3. The present section includes pattern calculations of endfire arrays having elements aligned along the y-axis (Fig. 5–14). Endfire array patterns may have two principal lobes, in opposing directions along the array axis. On the other hand, there will be only one major lobe (unidirectional pattern) if the array element spacing d is less than $\lambda/2$. An endfire array can provide higher directivity for a given number of elements than a broadside array. However, endfire arrays require larger dimensions in the along-beam direction. For an ordinary (conventional) endfire array, the phase difference between elements is opposite to the phase delay due to element spacing, thereby causing the radiation of all elements to add constructively at the center of the beam. Thus $\alpha = -2\pi d/\lambda$ for an ordinary endfire array, where α is the phase difference between elements.

The directivity is said to be extraordinary if it satisfies the Hansen and Woodyard (H-W) condition, and then its directivity is larger than that of the ordinary endfire array. For an H-W array, there are N equal amplitude isotropic elements and the phase α between elements is

$$\alpha = \left(\frac{2\pi d}{\lambda} + \frac{\pi}{N}\right) \tag{5–26}$$

The patterns of ordinary and extraordinary endfire arrays are now compared.

Assume the elements are equally spaced isotropic elements of equal amplitude and located on the y-axis of Fig. 5–14a. Now consider the pattern of an endfire linear array in the x-y plane, for which $\theta = 90°$. Then, with $N = 10$, each amplitude $a_n = 1$, and the element spacing d of $\lambda/4$, (5–23) becomes

$$F(90°, \phi) = \sum_{n=-4.5}^{4.5} \exp\left[jn\left(\alpha + \left(\frac{\pi}{2}\right)\sin\phi\right)\right] \tag{5–27}$$

Now assume that the beams of the ordinary endfire array and of the one satisfying the Hansen and Woodyard condition are pointed in direction $\phi = 90°$. The phase α between elements for an ordinary endfire array equals the phase delay due to propagation between elements; thus, $\alpha = -\pi/2$ because $d = \lambda/4$. From (5–26), for the extraordinary (H-W) condition, with $d = \lambda/4$ and $n = 10$ elements, $\alpha = -0.6\pi$.

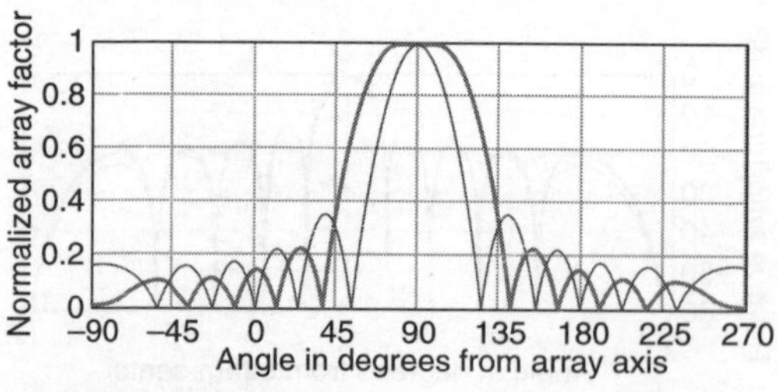

FIGURE 5–18.

Normalized patterns for ten-element endfire arrays with $d = \lambda/4$ element spacing: ordinary endfire (bold line) and endfire satisfying Hansen-Woodyard condition (fine line).

The *normalized* patterns for the two unidirectional endfire arrays having 10 elements and $\lambda/4$ element spacing, using (5–27), are included in Fig. 5–18. Notice that the Hansen-Woodyard array has a substantially narrower beamwidth, and larger side lobes. On the other hand, the shape of the major lobe of the ordinary endfire array is flatter at its peak.

From (5–27), the values of the array factors along the y-axis are

$$F(90°, 90°) = \left| \sum_{n=-4.5}^{4.5} \exp\left[jn\left(-\frac{\pi}{2} + \frac{\pi}{2} \right) \right] \right| = 10 \quad \text{ordinary endfire array} \qquad (5\text{–}28)$$

and

$$F(90°, 90°) = \left| \sum_{n=-4.5}^{4.5} \exp\left[jn\left(-0.6\pi + \frac{\pi}{2} \right) \right] \right| = 6.392 \quad \text{extraordinary endire array} \quad (5\text{–}29)$$

Recall that electric field strength is proportional to array factor F. Although (5–29) is smaller than (5–28), the directivity of the Hansen-Woodyard array is larger. This is because the Hansen-Woodyard pattern (and thus energy) is more closely confined to the y-axis. Additionally, F(90°, 90°) is largest in (5–28), because the radiation from all elements adds in-phase but not so for (5–29). Kraus and Marhefka (2002, pp. 115) report the directivities obtained by integrating the patterns, including the minor lobes, for the two ten-isotrope arrays. They give the approximate directivities for the ordinary and Hansen-Woodyard arrays to be approximately 11 and 19, respectively. For these directivities, the Hansen-Woodyard directivity is the largest by the factor 1.73.

A focused broadside array of ten isotropes has in theory a directivity of 10. Thus, from the directivities given above and the same number of elements, lossless endfire arrays can provide greater gain, as well as larger directivity, than a broadside array.

5.6. Array Tapering for Side-Lobe Reduction

5.6.1. Introduction

A principal advantage of a directional antenna is the gain that it provides in the desired direction, but sometimes it is equally important to minimize radiation toward or reception from an undesired direction. The matter is especially serious in congested areas where interference from other systems is a problem or for radar when signals from objects located in minor-lobe directions may obscure weak target signals of interest.

The minor lobes immediately adjacent to the main lobe are side lobes. Since these are usually the largest of the minor lobes, and hence of greatest importance, the words "side lobes" are often used when the more inclusive term "minor lobes" would be more appropriate. (*Note:* confusion is occasionally also caused by the fact that a "low side-lobe level" means a high main-beam to largest minor lobe ratio. That is, the smaller the side lobes are, the larger will be the number, whether expressed as a power-density ratio or as a decibel value to describe their level relative to the main lobe.)

A technique called "tapering" is used to reduce side lobes, and it refers to providing a variation in the element excitations (e.g., element currents) in a linear array. Namely, minor lobes are reduced if the center elements of the array radiate more strongly than the end elements, the strengths being gradually tapered from center to end according to some prescription.

When array elements are excited with equal amplitude and phase to maximize antenna gain, the ratio of main-beam power density to the first-side-lobe power density is approximately 20, or 13 dB. A side-lobe level −13 dB below the major lobe peak is often unacceptably high. It is common to design high-gain narrow-beam antennas for side-lobe levels down at least 30 dB, especially for radar use. A −30 dB level is considered good, and −40 dB excellent. A level of 50 dB below the main lobe is very difficult to achieve, but even somewhat better side-lobe levels have been obtained. Planar arrays are typically tapered by different amounts in the horizontal and vertical dimensions, because side-lobe requirements versus principal plane differ depending on an antenna's application.

5.6.2. Amplitude Tapering of Broadside Arrays: General

This section compares the patterns for five-element arrays having uniform, binomial, optimum, and edge distributions; and its content follows Kraus (1988, pp. 159–62). Broadside arrays having uniform distributions (all element amplitudes and phases equal) ordinarily provide maximum directivity, but their minor lobes are relatively large. A five-element uniform amplitude distribution provides a 23° half-power beamwidth and peak side lobes of −12.4 dB relative to the peak of the main beam. The binomial distribution, although generally impractical, has no side lobes and its directivity and beamwidth are relatively large. Moreover, the theoretical absence of side lobes is not likely to be achieved in practice, because of unavoidable imperfections in the antenna geometry, phasing, and feed system. A five-element binomial distribution provides a 3 dB beamwidth of 31°. The relative amplitudes for the binomial distribution are in accordance with Pascal's triangle, as shown in Table 5-1 for N elements.

The distribution having the narrowest 3 dB beamwidth and the strongest side lobes is the so-called edge distribution. It contains only the two outer-edge elements, and no elements in between. Thus the five-element, $\lambda/2$ spacing edge distribution array is identical to a two-element array having 2λ spacing. Such an array has many side lobes, and each has the same amplitude as the center lobe. The 3-dB half-power beamwidth for this array is 15°.

The names Tschebyscheff, Tchebyscheff, Tchebyschev, Chebyshev, and Chebishev appear in the technical literature. All of these names refer to the one person who developed the well-known polynomials, for whom they are named. Chebyshev is used here, following the IEEE standard (IEEE 1993).

TABLE 5-1 Relative Amplitudes of Binomial Distributions for Three- to Eight-Element Arrays

N	Relative amplitudes
3	1 2 1
4	1 3 3 1
5	1 4 6 4 1
6	1 5 10 10 5 1
7	1 6 15 20 15 6 1
8	1 7 21 35 35 21 7 1

The Dolph-Chebyschev (D-C) distribution is considered the optimum aperture distribution, but its use for more than about eight elements is impractical. In theory, the Dolph-Chebyschev distribution optimizes the relationship between beamwidth and side-lobe level. Specifically, if the maximum side-lobe level is specified, the beamwidth between the first nulls is minimum. A five-element Dolph-Chebyschev distribution designed for –20 dB side lobes has a 3 dB beamwidth of 27°.

Figure 5–19 includes the patterns for the distributions discussed above. By considering this figure, certain general conclusions can be made, namely: (a) low side lobes can be obtained if the amplitude tapers down to small values out at the aperture edges, and (b) an abrupt change in amplitude versus aperture position creates large side lobes. In addition to the Dolph-Chebyschev amplitude distributions for beam shaping and side-lobe reduction, there is a wide variety of distributions that can be used; and these depend on methods available for implementation, desired beamwidth, and side-lobe levels. As will be discussed later in sec. 5.6, a method devised by T. T. Taylor probably achieves the best balance among all three factors: side lobes, beamwidth, and directivity.

5.6.3. Dolph-Chebyshev Synthesis

Array design by Dolph-Chebyshev synthesis produces the narrowest beamwidth subject to a given peak side-lobe level. In theory, all side lobes of a D-C array are of the same level. Dolph-Chebyshev synthesis is a mathematical procedure that equates the currents in an array to a Chebyshev polynomial. The required element current distributions as a function of number (three up to eight) of elements that provide calculated side lobes (in 10 dB steps) as low as –40 dB are available (see, e.g., Ma 1993). A sample of tabulated values appears below, as an indication of the general nature of D-C distributions. This table is for an eight-element linear array designed for a –30 dB side-lobe level. The array elements are numbered 1 through 8 progressively from one end of the array to the other, numbers 4 and 5 being the two center elements.

Element Numbers	Relative Currents
1 and 8	0.26
2 and 7	0.52
3 and 6	0.81
4 and 5	1.00

The current distribution is symmetrical about the center of the array; hence the elements can be grouped in pairs as shown. The current values are normalized to the value unity at the center of the antenna. As the table shows, for this –30 dB side-lobe level, the end-element currents are only 26 percent of the center-element current. The 3 dB beamwidth of this array is 16.4 degrees, and the gain, for half-wavelength element spacing, is 8.3 (9.2 dB).

Unfortunately, antennas having a large number of elements and designed for low side lobes using D-C aperture distributions are impracticable. For example, since the side-lobe levels are constant (independent of direction), directivity and thus gain decrease with

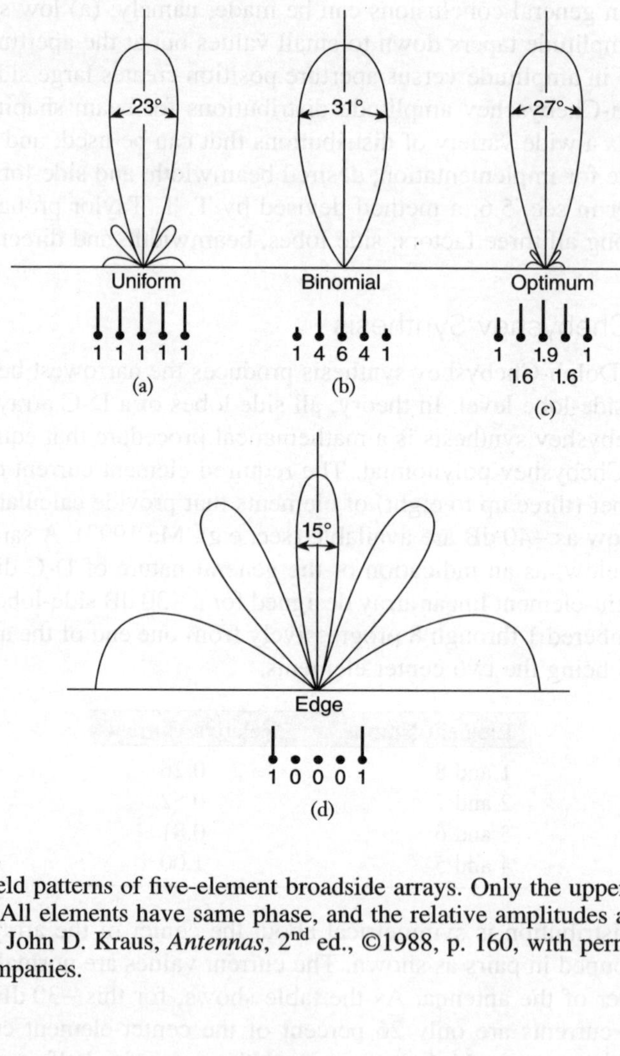

FIGURE 5–19.

Normalized far-field patterns of five-element broadside arrays. Only the upper half of each pattern is shown. All elements have same phase, and the relative amplitudes are included below each figure. From John D. Kraus, *Antennas*, 2nd ed., ©1988, p. 160, with permission of The McGraw-Hill Companies.

increase in array size. This is because, as the principal beamwidth is reduced, a larger fraction of the radiated power is within the side lobes. Also, for increasingly larger arrays, the required array element excitation becomes nonmonotonic, requiring high peak currents at the end elements that causes large I^2R losses. This feature reduces available gain. Another problem with low side-lobe D-C designs is that the element currents must be controlled to an impracticably high accuracy, which contributes to them being unrealizable. Therefore, aside from the application to arrays with a small number of elements, D-C patterns are important for identifying the narrowest beamwidth theoretically available for a given peak side-lobe level. A simplified method is described in the next section for calculating theoretical, yet unattainable, D-C patterns for arrays having a large number of elements.

5.6.4. Simplified Calculations for Dolph-Chebyshev Patterns

Van der Mass (1954) discovered a relatively easy way to obtain the theoretical D-C patterns for arrays with a large number of elements. This was done by replacing the array with a continuous line source formed by letting the number of array elements approach infinity. Then, line-source D-C patterns can be obtained without the tedious calculations of D-C synthesis, and the beamwidths are almost as narrow as had the calculations been with discrete elements.

The "optimum" line-source patterns of Van der Mass, like other D-C patterns, has side lobes of constant amplitude (Mailloux 1994, pp. 127–28), and are therefore physically unrealizable. These far-field E-field patterns are expressed as

$$E(u) = \cos\sqrt{u^2 - (\pi A)^2} \tag{5–30}$$

where $u = (\pi L/\lambda)\sin\theta$

$A = (1/\pi)\operatorname{arccos}h(R)$
R = ratio of electric field strength of the peak side lobes to main beam, and

where $\operatorname{arcos}h$ is the inverse hyperbolic cosine, λ is wavelength, and θ is the observation angle measured from the normal to the aperture.

The 3 dB beamwidth for a D-C pattern expressed in radians is

$$BW_{HPCheb} = (\lambda/L)\beta_0$$

Where (5–31)

$$\beta_0 = (2/\pi)\left[(\operatorname{arccos}h(R))^2 - \left(\operatorname{arccos}h(0.70R\right)^2\right]^{0.5}$$

As an example of the optimum yet unrealizable 3 dB beamwidth for a D-C pattern in accordance with equation (5–31), we now calculate β_0 for R = 100 (i.e., 40 dB) side lobes. Then

$$\beta_0 = (2/\pi)\left[(5.298)^2 - (4.952)^2\right]^{0.5} = 1.20$$

Therefore, the "optimum" 3 dB beamwidth for constant 40 dB peak side lobes, although unrealizable, expressed in radians, is

$$BW_{HPCheb} = 1.20(\lambda/L) \tag{5–32}$$

The broadside beamwidths for continuous line apertures are discussed in sec. 6.10. The narrowest broadside continuous line-source beamwidth is one that has an aperture distribution of constant amplitude and equal phase (uniform distribution). The 3 dB beamwidth for this basic aperture, expressed in degrees is

$$BW_{HPu} = 50.8(\lambda/L) \tag{5–33}$$

with λ/L dimensionless. When expressed in radians, (5–33) becomes

$$BW_{HPu} = 0.887(\lambda/L) \tag{5–34}$$

Therefore (5–31) and (5–34) can be used to provide a comparison between the most efficient distribution (which gives −13 dB peak side lobes) and the D-C pattern (which gives the narrowest major lobe for a specified constant side-lobe level). However, as already stated, D-C patterns are not always practical or realizable.

Figure 5–20 is included to compare the patterns for a uniform aperture distribution and a D-C distribution with 26 dB side lobes. Each aperture is 2 m wide and the frequency is 3 GHz. Although the beamwidth for the uniform aperture is slightly narrower than provided by the D-C distribution, the much larger side lobes created by the uniform distribution are apparent.

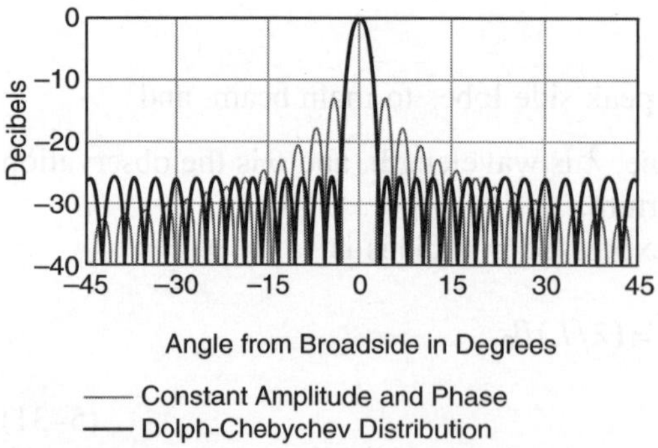

FIGURE 5–20.

Two patterns, one for a uniform amplitude distribution and the other for a Dolph-Chebychev distribution with 26 dB side lobes. Each aperture is 2m wide and the frequency is 3 GHz.

5.6.5. The Taylor Distribution

The Taylor aperture distribution is often used where narrow broadside beams and low side lobes are needed. Taylor (1955) analyzed the deficiencies of Dolph-Chebyshev arrays and formulated a combined radiation pattern and aperture distribution that provides narrow beamwidths, and yet has good efficiency for large arrays. His analysis began with the line-source D-C patterns given by Fig. 5–15 above. In so doing Taylor developed a method for avoiding the D-C directivity (and gain) loss problem caused by no decay in the side lobes. This was accomplished by approximating, arbitrarily closely, the D-C pattern with a physically realizing pattern. He retained an approximate constant side-lobe pattern close to the main beam, but let the wide-angle side lobes decay in amplitude like the side lobes from a uniform continuous line source.

Taylor's method is basically designed to apply to continuous aperture distributions rather than to an array of discrete elements, but it can be applied to linear arrays of a large enough number of elements (about twenty or more). This is the case where the Dolph-Chebyshev distribution results in poor directivity. Taylor's method gives improved directivity for a given peak minor-lobe level, because it allows the far-out side lobes to diminish in amplitude.

A parameter $\bar{n}$, called *nbar*, defines the number of nondecaying side lobes on each side of the main lobe. Thus as $\bar{n}$ becomes large, the Taylor pattern (and aperture distribution) approaches the Dolph-Chebyshev pattern (and distribution). Then, ordinarily, one uses the largest $\bar{n}$ that still provides a monotonically declining amplitude distribution out to each end of the aperture. In doing so, the beamwidths obtained are almost as narrow as with the D-C pattern—and the resulting aperture efficiency is excellent.

The Taylor aperture distribution provides a beamwidth wider than that of a D-C pattern by an approximate factor σ. From Mailloux (1994 p. 129), the 3 dB beamwidth for a Taylor distributed aperture can be expressed as

$$BW_{HPTaylor} = \sigma(BW_{HPCheb}) = \sigma(\lambda/L)\beta_0$$

where (5–35)

$$\sigma = \bar{n}\left[A^2 + (\bar{n} - 1/2)^2\right]^{-0.5}$$

with

$\bar{n}$ = number of equal-amplitude side lobes on either side of the main beam
L = total length of aperture
$A = (1/\pi)\text{arccos}\,h(R)$
R = design side lobe voltage ratio

Now to compare the beamwidths of the unrealizable D-C pattern of (5–30) and a realizable Taylor pattern, consider an array with $\bar{n} = 4$ and 40 dB peak side lobes. Then, from the definitions given above

$$A = (1/\pi)\text{arccos}\,h(100) = 1.686 \tag{5–36}$$

and

$$\sigma = 4\left[(1.686)^2 + (4 - 0.5)^2\right]^{-0.5} = 1.03 \tag{5–37}$$

Thus for $\bar{n} = 4$ and 40 dB peak side lobes, the 3-dB width of the main beam of the Taylor pattern is only 3 percent wider than a D-C pattern having 40 dB side lobes.

Recall from (5–32) that the beamwidth for a D-C pattern with 40 dB side lobes is 1.20 (λ/L).

As already mentioned, in addition to the Taylor 3-dB beamwidth being broader than that of the Chebyshev pattern, in principle the $\bar{n} = 4$ Taylor pattern contains four equal-amplitude side lobes on either side of the major lobe. Also, in principle, the remaining side lobes have widths and amplitudes like those from a continuous uniform aperture distribution.

Figure 5–20 is useful for roughly illustrating the formation of a Taylor pattern by a merger of two patterns: one from a uniform aperture distribution and the other from the D-C distribution with 26 dB side lobes. Each aperture is 2m wide and operates at 3 GHz. Ideally, the Taylor side lobes predominate in close to the major lobe and out to angles where the side lobes of the uniform amplitude pattern are the smallest. Then, the uniform amplitude pattern dominates a Taylor pattern. From Fig. 5–20, a reasonable guess is that a resulting Taylor pattern might have four or five side lobes ($\bar{n} = 8$ or 10) at the –26 dB level on either side of the major lobe. However, care is required in a Taylor design when selecting the nbar and side-lobe levels, because calculated Taylor patterns are seldom as precise as theory predicts. In addition, the choice of $\bar{n}$ is not arbitrary, because increasing it retains more of the side lobes at the design side-lobe level and this makes the calculated Taylor closer to a D-C pattern. In other words, increasing $\bar{n}$ eventually leads to aperture illuminations that do not decrease monotonically down to the aperture edges (Mailloux 1994, p. 133). Thus, the act of increasing $\bar{n}$ too much can destroy the usefulness of the aperture distribution.

In summary, the Taylor distribution is widely used, because it is a realistic way of providing the narrowest beamwidth from a broadside array, given a specific peak side-lobe level and an aperture width. Neither the theory nor design for Taylor distributions is simple. However, the necessary equations for calculating aperture distributions and patterns are available (see, e.g., Mailloux 1994, pp. 128–29; Balanis 2005, pp. 408–10). Additionally, tables are available that give required array element amplitudes, for a variety of $\bar{n}$ values, for Taylor arrays having side-lobe levels for 20 to 40 dB, inclusive, in 5 dB steps (*Reference Data for Radio Engineers* 1979, pp. 27–29 through 27–31).

5.6.6. Other Low-Side-Lobe Array Distributions

A tapering effect is also achieved by "thinning," or space-tapering, that is, by removing some of the elements. Suppose that initially an array has elements that are uniformly spaced, and fed with equal amplitudes. Then, if some elements are removed, with more elements removed near the edges than near the center of the array, the average density of elements will exhibit a taper from center to edge. This taper will have a side-lobe-suppressing effect, somewhat like that of an amplitude taper in an unthinned (filled) array. The pattern of element removal may be random, rather than regular, to avoid the creation of the grating lobes that occur when the spacing of array elements is large. Clearly, the gain is less than that of the filled array of the same size and taper. The primary application of the thinned space-tapered technique is with arrays that have many elements.

As discussed previously, the patterns of arrays and continuous apertures are similar if (1) the array element spacing is $\lambda/2$ or less and (2) the array amplitudes and phases are matched point-to-point with the continuous aperture distributions. Consequently, from previously developed knowledge about continuous apertures there are simple amplitude distributions that are known to provide low side-lobe levels. For example, a cosine-shaped amplitude distribution with its peak at the aperture center will provide a reasonably efficient, low side-lobe pattern. Digital filter algorithms (Harris 1978) also provide useful aperture amplitude distributions, the Hamming function being an example. Bodnar (2007; pp. 55–16 through 55–19) provides graphs that show beamwidth versus side-lobe level and aperture efficiency versus side-lobe level, for the better-known uniform aperture distributions. These graphs are useful for estimating performance available from array antennas.

5.7. Planar Arrays: Patterns, Directivity, and Gain

The subject of broadside planar array patterns is introduced in sec. 5.4. There it is assumed the array elements were located in the *y-z* plane, and the pattern equations considered are only for the simplest case of elements having equal amplitude and equal phase. Sections 5.7.1 through 5.7.5 that follow discuss general equations for calculating patterns of planar arrays, as well as simpler special cases. Finally, sec. 5.7.6 addresses the beamwidths and gain of practical planar arrays.

5.7.1. Introduction

A planar array pattern can be calculated by summing the vector contributions of each array element at every direction and at a distance where far zone approximations are valid. Then, for an array located in the *x-y* plane, the array factor is

$$F(\theta, \phi) = \sum_i a_i(x, y) \exp j\psi_i \tag{5–38}$$

where

θ, ϕ = angles to a far-zone point from the aperture origin

a_i = amplitude of element i

$\psi_i = \alpha_i(x, y) - \dfrac{2\pi}{\lambda}\delta_i(x, y)$, the phase contribution of element i at the observation point

α_i = phase of element i

$\delta_i = -\sin\theta(x_i \cos\phi + y_i \sin\phi)$, which is the difference in distances to an observation point in the far zone (see Appendix H), from (a) a point x_i, y_i on the aperture and from (b) the aperture origin

The reader will recognize that (5–38) is a summation that includes each a_i, α_i, and δ_i over all *x* and *y* values. Consequently, the calculation of $F(\theta, \phi)$ is, in general, complicated because δ_i (contained in ψ_i) is a function of both θ and ϕ. Furthermore, for calculations

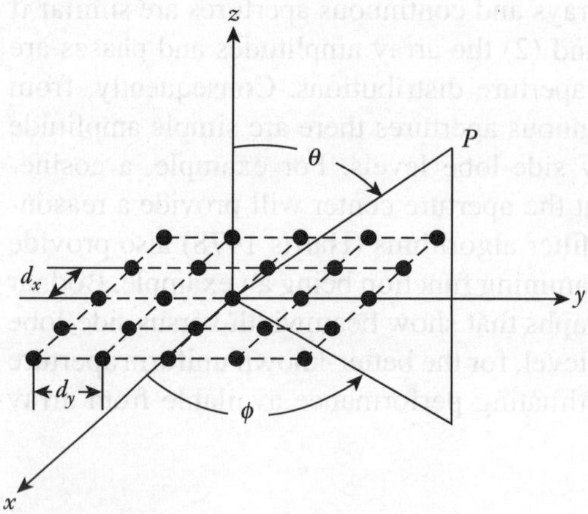

FIGURE 5–21.

A Planar array in the x-y plane. Element spacings are d_x and d_y, respectively, along the x and y axes.

of patterns in the radiating near field, the δ_i above must be replaced by equation (H-4), Appendix H.

5.7.2. Principal Plane Patterns: Equal Element Spacings

Pattern calculations versus θ and ϕ are made in this section using Fig. 5–21, which provides a systematic method for describing the x and y coordinates of a planar array. Since the element spacings d_x and d_y are constants, the x and y coordinates can be expressed as $x_m = md_x$ and $y_m = nd_y$. Similarly, one attains

$$\psi_{mn} = \alpha_{mn} - \frac{2\pi}{\lambda}\delta_{mn} \tag{5–39}$$

and

$$\delta_{mn} = -\sin\theta\left(md_x\cos\phi + nd_y\sin\phi\right) \tag{5–40}$$

Then, by letting $A_{mn} = a_{mn}\exp j\alpha_{mn}$, where a_{mn} is an element amplitude and α_{mn} is its phase, a general expression for the planar array factor is as follows:

$$F(\theta,\phi) = \sum_m\sum_n A_{mn}\exp\left[j(ms_x + ns_y)\right] \tag{5–41}$$

with

$$s_x = \frac{2\pi}{\lambda}d_x\sin\theta\cos\phi \tag{5–42}$$

and

$$s_y = \frac{2\pi}{\lambda}d_y\sin\theta\sin\phi \tag{5–43}$$

where

d_x and d_y are the element spacings along the x and y axes
m is an integer such that md_x denotes a coordinate of an array element on x-axis
n is an integer such that nd_y denotes a coordinate of an array element on y-axis

5.7.3. Separable Aperture Distributions

Planar arrays that have a large number of elements are usually constructed so that $A_{mn} = A_m A_n = a_m \exp(jm\alpha_x) \times a_n \exp(jn\alpha_y)$. Here a_m and a_n are element amplitudes, where a_m is a function of x only and a_n a function of y only. In addition, α_x and α_y are fixed phase differences between adjacent elements in the x and y dimensions, respectively. Expressing A_{mn} in this manner makes it mathematically separable between the x and y coordinates. Methods by which the element excitations are made separable are as follows:

(a) by stacking above one another identical x-axis line arrays (each with element excitation A_m), and exciting the separate x-axis arrays in accordance with A_n, or
(b) by placing alongside one another identical y-axis line arrays (each with element excitation A_n), and exciting the separate y-axis arrays in accordance with A_m

Then, with A_{mn} expressed as the product of A_m (a function of x only), and A_n (a function of y only), equation (5–41) can be expressed as

$$F(\theta,\phi) = \sum_m a_m \exp jm(\alpha_x + s_x) \times \sum_n a_n \exp jn(\alpha_y + s_y) \tag{5–44}$$

Thus, for separable array distributions, we see from (5–44) that a planar array factor is the product of two terms. On careful examination, it may be seen that the first and second terms are the array factors for line arrays along the x and y axes, respectively. In other words,

$$F(\theta,\phi) = F_x(\theta,\phi) \times F_y(\theta,\phi) \tag{5–45}$$

Thus, $F_x(\theta, \phi)$ and $F_x(\theta, \phi)$ are array factors for line sources along the x and y axes, as follow

$$F_x(\theta,\phi) = \sum_m a_m \exp jm(\alpha_x + s_x) = \sum_m a_m \exp\left[jm\left(\alpha_x + \frac{2\pi}{\lambda} d_x \sin\theta\cos\phi\right)\right] \tag{5–46}$$

$$F_y(\theta,\phi) = \sum_n a_n \exp jn(\alpha_y + s_y) = \sum_n a_n \exp\left[jn\left(\alpha_y + \frac{2\pi}{\lambda} d_y \sin\theta\sin\phi\right)\right] \tag{5–47}$$

The mathematics of complete patterns are complex, partly because s_x and s_y are both functions of θ and ϕ. Thus, the complexity of array factors exists, even for arrays having element excitations that are separable in the x and y dimensions.

For principal plane patterns, the equations for patterns with separable distributions are considerably less complex, especially if the phase excitations of all elements are equal. By setting $\phi = 0°$ and $90°$ in (5–46) and (5–47), and with $\alpha_x = \alpha_y = 0$, (5–45) for the principal plane patterns becomes

$$F(\theta, \phi = 0°) = \sum_m a_m \exp\left[jm\left(\frac{2\pi}{\lambda} d_x \sin\theta\right)\right] \times \sum_n a_n \quad \textbf{(x-z plane)} \tag{5–48}$$

$$F(\theta, \phi = 90°) = \sum_n a_n \exp\left[jn\left(\frac{2\pi}{\lambda} d_y \sin\theta\right)\right] \times \sum_m a_m \quad \textbf{(y-z plane)} \tag{5–49}$$

In (4–46) and (4–47), notice the following:

(1) $\sum_m a_m \exp\left[jm\left(\frac{2\pi}{\lambda} d_x \sin\theta\right)\right]$ is a principal plane pattern for a linear array located along the x dimension

(2) $\sum_n a_n \exp\left[jn\left(\frac{2\pi}{\lambda} d_y \sin\theta\right)\right]$ is a principal plane pattern for a linear array located along the y dimension

(3) $\sum_m a_m$ and $\sum_n a_n$ are simply constant multiplicative factors.

Items (1) through (3) above relate to the principal plane patterns for an array with separable amplitude distribution and ones for which each element has the same phase. From these items it may be seen that the equations for the principal plane patterns are much simpler than those of the three-dimensionl patterns. In fact, each principal plane pattern is the same as that of a linear array.

5.7.4. Patterns Versus θ and ϕ: Equal Amplitude, Separable Arrays

Still simpler equations are possible if the arrays have elements of equal amplitude, and the phases along the x- and y-dimensions are separable. The simplest case is, of course, where both the element amplitudes and the element phases are equal. By using (5–46) and letting the amplitude of each array element a_m be unity, the linear array factor $F_x(\theta, \phi)$ along the x-axis becomes

$$F_x(\theta, \phi) = \sum_m \exp jm(\alpha_s + s_x) = \sum_m \exp jm\psi_x \tag{5–50}$$

where $\psi_x = \alpha_s + s_x$.

Equation (5–50) is a geometric progression. Its sum is complex (amplitude and phase) and can be expressed in closed form. This sum, for a total of M identical elements along the x axis, with the phase reference taken at the center of the line array, and with the amplitude normalized for a maximum of unity, is derived by Kraus (1988, pp. 138–40), and is as follows

$$F_x(\theta, \phi) = \frac{\sin(M\psi_x/2)}{M \sin(\psi_x/2)} \tag{5–51}$$

Then, because F_x and F_y are both geometric progressions of the same general form, and with N being the total number of elements along the y axis,

$$F_y(\theta, \phi) = \frac{\sin(N\psi_y/2)}{N\sin(\psi_y/2)} \tag{5–52}$$

Then, according to (5–45), and with all element amplitudes a_m and a_n being unity, $F(\theta, \phi)$ for a planar array with separable phase distributions can be expressed as follows:

$$F(\theta, \phi) = F_x \times F_y = \frac{\sin(M\psi_x/2)}{M\sin(\psi_x/2)} \times \frac{\sin(N\psi_y/2)}{N\sin(\psi_y/2)} \tag{5–53}$$

where

$$\psi_x = \alpha_x + s_x = \alpha_x + \left(\frac{2\pi}{\lambda} d_x \sin\alpha \cos\phi\right) \tag{5–54}$$

and

$$\psi_y = \alpha_x + s_y = \alpha_x + \left(\frac{2\pi}{\lambda} d_y \sin\theta \sin\phi\right) \tag{5–55}$$

The simplest equation occurs for the case where the phases as well as the amplitudes are equal, which results if each α_m and α_n in equations (5–54) and (5–55) is zero. This simplest condition is the one addressed by (5–13), sec. 5.4.2, but it applies to the case of equal element amplitudes and phases when the array elements are located in the y-z plane. Instead, the various equations in secs. 5.7.1 through 5.7.4 are applicable when the array elements are in the x-y plane.

As seen above, the equations for far-field planar array patterns are not mathematically simple, even for simpler ones like (5–53) above. The creation of patterns is discussed further in chapter 6, where example patterns for continuous aperture antennas are included. Papers on calculations of patterns versus θ and ϕ that use Matlab software include Bregains, Ares, and Moreno (2004) and Sevgi and Uluişik (2005). SM 5.0 included in the accompanying website gives equations for, and examples of, 3-D plots of patterns versus θ and ϕ using Mathcad software.

5.7.5. Summary of Planar Array Patterns

This section summarizes equations for patterns of planar arrays that are given in secs. 5.7.1 through 5.7.4, where the planar arrays are located in the x-y plane. Previously, in sec. 5.4, the broadside patterns of planar arrays were discussed, where the array elements are located in the y-z plane, and the only patterns considered are those with elements having equal amplitudes and equal phases.

Equation (5–38) is a general equation for the *E*-field radiation pattern for a planar array, where the element amplitudes, phases, and spacing are completely arbitrary. This equation is written for the radiating far-field; but, as indicated in the text, it can be readily changed for applicability to the radiating near-field patterns.

Equation (5–41) is a general equation for patterns versus θ and ϕ, but it requires there be equal spacing between elements along the x dimension and along the y dimension. However, the spacings along the x direction need not be equal to the spacing along the y direction. The amplitudes and phases of the elements may be arbitrary. Although the equation is complex, it has wide applicability because, for practical reasons, multielement arrays are usually constructed with equal spacing between elements.

In addition to having equal spacing between elements, multielement arrays are often constructed so that the element amplitudes and phases are mathematically separable. This means that the variations in amplitude and phase along the x dimension are independent of the variations in amplitude and phase along the y dimension. Equation (5–44) describes the pattern when the element excitations are separable, but otherwise the amplitudes and phases of the elements are arbitrary. The requirement of (5–41) for equal spacings along the x and y dimensions is also applicable to (5–44).

From (5–44) it can be seen that, for separable aperture distributions, the equation for three-dimensional patterns reduces to the product of two line sources. Equations (5–46) and (5–47) are the array factors for these line sources, one that has amplitude and phase variations along the x dimension, and the other has amplitude and phase variations along the y dimension.

For principal plane patterns, the equations for apertures with separable distributions are considerably less complex, especially if the phase excitations of all elements are equal. As may be seen, (5–48) and (5–49) for these principal plane patterns for planar arrays are of the same form as principal plane patterns for linear arrays.

Equation (5–53) describes the pattern if an array has elements of equal amplitude, and if the phases along the x- and y-dimensions are separable. The equation is simplified even further if both the element amplitudes and the element phases are equal. Previously, in sec. 5.4.2, equation (5–13) was introduced for the simplest case when the amplitudes and phases of all elements are equal. For (5–13), the array elements are located in the y-z plane, instead of in the x-y plane for which the equations of secs. 5.7.1 through 5.7.4 apply.

As previously discussed, the array factor $F(\theta, \phi)$ is the array pattern calculated under the assumption that each array element radiates isotropically. In reality, element patterns are never isotopic, but they may be described by a function $f(\theta, \phi)$. If all element patterns were identical in an actual array antenna, the far-field pattern $E(\theta, \phi)$, because of the principle of multiplication (sec. 5.1.6), would be

$$E(\theta,\phi) = f(\theta,\phi)\cdot F(\theta,\phi) \tag{5–56}$$

Mutual coupling between elements may limit the validity of (5–56) (see secs. 5.1.4 through 5.1.7, and 5.9). Often, however, when (5–56) is normalized to have a maximum of unity, it provides a practical estimate for actual array patterns. $F(\theta, \phi)$ and $E(\theta, \phi)$ are generally complex, and therefore their E-field amplitude patterns are created by plotting their absolute magnitudes.

5.7.6. Beamwidth and Gain of Broadside Arrays

In principle, beamwidths and directivity can be calculated when a complete, relative pattern is available, as was illustrated for the short dipole in sec. 4.1. However, whether such a pattern is available as an equation or is compiled from measured data, the required calculations for directivity are not simple. Therefore, and because of interdependencies of directivity on principal-plane beamwidths, approximation formulas for beamwidth and directivity are useful. Such formulas are available for broadside arrays, which are the most common type of arrays in narrow-beam high-directivity applications.

The simplest example is a uniform broadside linear array of N isotropic elements spaced a half-wavelength apart. For values of N larger than 3, the beamwidth is approximately $102/N$ degrees. (For $N = 3$, the beamwidth is 36 degrees, and for $N = 2$ it is 60 degrees.) The directivity of such an array is equal to N. Since isotropic elements do not exist, these results are somewhat academic. However, the beamwidth formula can also be applied to an array of parallel dipoles in the plane perpendicular to the dipole axes. (This is the type of linear array pictured in Fig. 5–5.) Furthermore, the beamwidth and gain results for the array of isotropes are directly applicable to an array of many collinear dipoles (as illustrated by Figs. 5–6 and 5–7), since for a long-enough array the array pattern alone will primarily determine the beamwidth and directivity. The dipole pattern will have little effect near the beam center.

When the element spacing of a linear array is approximately a half-wavelength, the beamwidth formula becomes

$$BW = \frac{51\lambda}{Nd} \text{ degrees} \tag{5–57}$$

(which for $d = \lambda/2$ is $102/N$ as given above). The variation of the directivity with element spacing for a given number of elements is not expressible by a simple formula. Curves showing this variation have been published by Tai (1964) for both uniform and nonuniform linear arrays. As mentioned for broadside arrays in sec. 5.2.2, the gain for a given number of elements increases as the spacing is increased up to a maximum which occurs at slightly less than one wavelength spacing (about 0.95 λ) for a large array (many elements). For $N = 3$ the maximum directivity occurs at about $d = 0.8\ \lambda$.

The beamwidth formula, equation (5–57), can also be applied to the horizontal and vertical beamwidths of a vertical planar array by considering it to be a linear array in each direction, of N_h elements with spacing d_h horizontally, and N_v elements with spacing d_v vertically. Although this formula is for an array without a reflecting screen it also applies with a reflector if N is large.

Broadside arrays are often made unidirectional by placing a reflecting screen behind the array, or by using two curtains of arrays with endfire phasing between the curtains.

When such arrays are large (many wavelengths) the beamwidths and directivity are given by formulas of the following type:

$$BW = k_1\left(\frac{\lambda}{Nd}\right) \tag{5–58}$$

$$D = k_2\left(\frac{4\pi A}{\lambda^2}\right) \tag{5–59}$$

where k_1 and k_2 are of the order of one or slightly less, if the beamwidth is expressed in radians and if all array elements are similar and radiating in phase with equal intensity. If the beamwidth is expressed in degrees, k_1 is in the vicinity of 60—somewhat less for a uniform array and somewhat more for tapered arrays. For a tapered array the constant k_2 in (5–59) is less than one. Commonly, k_2 is known as the aperture efficiency.

Equation (5–59) with $k_2 = 1$ represents the maximum directivity that can be obtained with an ordinary unidirectional planar array of area A. As mentioned, $k_2 = 1$ applies to a broadside uniformly excited planar unidirectional array (all elements in phase and radiating with equal intensity). Similarly, the directivity $D = N$ for a broadside half-wave-spaced uniform linear array of N elements (no reflector) is ordinarily the maximum obtainable value of directivity for an array of that length. Thus, for array length L and element spacing $\lambda/2$, the maximum directivity is $D = (2L/\lambda) + 1$.

However, it is possible, in an array of closely spaced elements, to achieve directivities greater than the above mentioned uniform-array maximum values by properly phasing the elements. An array in which this is accomplished is a supergain or superdirective array. This possibility, however, is not as attractive as it seems at first. The superdirective array is characterized by relatively large phase changes within a relatively small distance. The mutual coupling between elements cause much larger currents fields than in a normal array. The currents increase enormously if any substantial amount of superdirectivity is attempted, to the extent that ohmic losses quickly overcome any increase in directivity, so that gain is not increased.

Except for very small arrays, super directive illuminations (Hansen 1964, pp. 82–91) have proven impractical, because of the high I^2R losses resulting from these very large currents. Also, the bandwidth of arrays having superdirective illumination becomes extremely small as the superdirectivity is increased. Therefore, the supergain effect is not practical except in very limited degree in special situations. Moderate superdirectivity is achieved, however, in endfire arrays phased according to the Hansen-Woodyard condition, but even moderate superdirectivity is impractical in broadside arrays.

Even so, as now discussed, the endfire array is being used successfully to obtain a higher gain for a given *frontal* area than available from a broadside planar aperture. An endfire array may provide higher directivity and gain for a given number of elements than a broadside array. However, endfire arrays require larger dimensions in the along-beam direction. The UHF array on the United States Navy E-2C aircraft uses the endfire principle to advantage (Long, 2004). It has a horizontal array of horizontally polarized

Yagi antennas, which permits a small vertical dimension. The horizontal array provides a relatively narrow azimuth beam. Of especial importance is that its desired broad elevation beam is obtained with a much smaller aperture height than would be required of a broadside planar antenna. The result is an antenna with small vertical dimension having low aerodynamic drag. Additionally, the antenna gain is about four times the gain that is available from a continuous aperture of the same frontal area.

The physical aperture A_p is a measure of the physical size of an antenna area over which radiation is transmitted or received. For a uniformly illuminated aperture, that is, one for which the amplitude and phase are both constant over the physical area and one that is lossless, the gain G is as follows:

$$G = (4\pi A_p)/\lambda^2 \tag{5–60}$$

Equation (5–60) was shown by Silver (1949, p. 183) to be true by integrating the total radiation pattern for a uniformly illuminated aperture and calculating D. The actual gain of a real antenna is of course less, depending on losses that can occur because of discrepancies in the antenna pattern, impedance mismatches, and dissipative (I^2R) losses.

In sec. 3.3.4, chapter 3, directivity is defined as $D = 4\pi/\Omega$, where Ω is the imaginary solid angle that contains all radiated power if it were distributed uniformly and totally within said solid angle. Thus, directivity and consequently gain are in approximate inverse proportion to the products of 3 dB principal-plane beamwidths. Theoretically, the half-power beamwidth θ_{HP} for a uniformly illuminated line source of length L

$$\theta_{HP} = 50.8\lambda/L \tag{5–61}$$

when θ_{HP} is expressed in degrees, and λ and L are in the same units. Equation (5–59) can be obtained from the table in sec. 6.10–2, chapter 6.

Now consider a rectangular aperture. Its gain can be determined with (5–61) by expressing physical aperture A_p in terms of principal plane beamwidths, θ_{HP} and ϕ_{HP}, by using equation (5–60). Then, the approximate gain G for a lossless, uniformly illuminated aperture is

$$G \approx 32{,}400/(\theta_{HP}\phi_{HP}) \quad (G \text{ dimensionless}, \theta_{HP} \text{ and } \phi_{HP} \text{ in degs.}) \tag{5–62}$$

Stutzman (1998) investigated equations for a number of theoretical patterns, including those for this case of a rectangular aperture. He notes that actual patterns due to antenna fabrication do not ordinarily have perfectly deep nulls; and because of the effects of installation environments, they do not have side lobes that decrease uniformly at wide angles, as do theoretical patterns. Obviously, the gain of an actual antenna is also reduced by lossy materials (I^2R losses). Additionally, the radiated power may be reduced by impedance mismatches. As a general rule if detailed measurement data are unavailable, Stutzman suggests that a reasonable approximation for gain, for a beam normal to the aperture, is

$$G = 26{,}000/(\theta_{HP}\phi_{HP}) \quad (G \text{ dimensionless, } \phi_{HP} \text{ and } \phi_{HP} \text{ in degress.}) \tag{5–63}$$

The approximate, "typical" gain of (5–63) is nearly 1.0 dB less than gain of (5–62) determined by using theoretical beamwidths and for a lossless, uniformly illuminated rectangular aperture. It is to be underscored that use of (5–63) is recommended only if the antenna efficiency ("k" in $G = kD$) is known to be approximately 1. The point being that directivity and thus gain are reduced by spurious radiation not readily detected and thus not ordinarily accounted for when determining directivity. For example, if only the usual principal-plane measurements are made, there may be unsuspected out-of-plane spurious radiation.

Equation (5–63) is applicable to arrays as well as continuous aperture antennas (chapter 6). Stutzman (1998, pp. 7–11) cautions the reader regarding the use of the following equation for directivity of arrays that appears often in antenna literature, namely:

$$D = D_e D_i, \tag{5–64}$$

where

D_e = directivity of each element in the array
D_i = directivity of the array with isotropic elements

This formula is for large arrays without grating lobes. Even when the transmission efficiency ("k" in $G = kD$) is large, Stutzman recommends the use of (5–63) instead of (5–64). This he notes is because the accuracy of (5–64) can vary greatly with the details of array geometry. For example, small changes in array element position can increase spurious radiation above what is indicated by a theoretical calculation for directivity (even though there may be no perceptible change in principal-plane beamwidths), thereby contributing to a loss in gain.

5.8. Some Other Array Types

5.8.1. Long-Wire Arrays

The directional properties of single long-wire antennas, described in sec. 4.4, can be augmented by combining two or more of them into an array. The simplest such array is the V antenna, consisting of two long-wire antennas each with one of its ends at the apex of the V. If the angle between the two sides of the V is equal to twice the angle that the cone of maximum radiation of each wire makes with the axis of that wire, the two cones will "add up" in the direction of the line bisecting the angle of the V, and there produce a maximum lobe of radiation. If the wires of the V are resonant, there will be an equal lobe in the opposite (back) direction; that is, a resonant V is bidirectional. A V of two nonresonant wires will have a single unidirectional beam. Figure 5–22 shows schematically a resonant V antenna and a typical pattern oriented to correspond to the schematic of the antenna. The gain is approximately twice the gain of one leg of the V by itself.

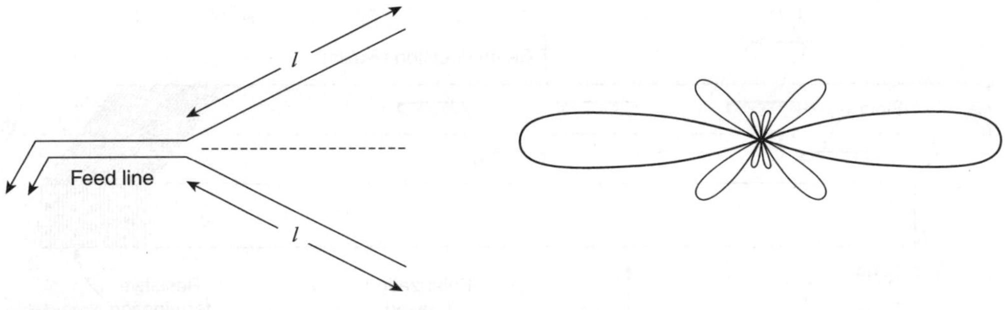

FIGURE 5–22.

Resonant V antenna and typical pattern.

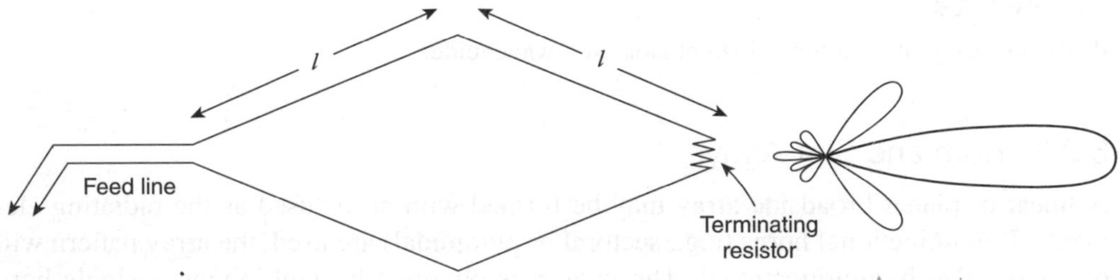

FIGURE 5–23.

Rhombic antenna and typical pattern.

The principle of the V antenna may be extended by connecting two Vs together at their open ends to form a diamond, or *rhombic* antenna. This antenna is fed at one end, as if it were a V antenna; a terminating resistor is usually connected across the far ends to make the antenna nonresonant and hence unidirectional. The resistor used must be noninductive at the frequency of the antenna. A value of about 800 ohms is usually required for proper termination. A schematic diagram of a rhombic and a typical pattern are shown in Fig. 5–23.

The rhombic is usually used in preference to the V if a nonresonant antenna with unidirectional pattern is wanted, since the V is much more difficult to terminate. (A ground connection is needed, as described in sec. 4.4). However, a rhombic may also be operated unterminated; the pattern will then be bidirectional.

Both V and rombic antennas can be "stacked" vertically or side by side, forming an array of Vs or an array of rhombics, to achieve additional directivity. Long-wire arrays are used chiefly in the MF and HF bands, from about 3 to 30 MHz; they are seldom used above 100 MHz.

If the angle between the legs of a V is made less than twice the single-wire lobe angle, the maximum of the resulting single lobe will still be in the plane that bisects the V, but it will be tilted upward out of the plane of the V itself. This result may be desired to receive waves reflected downward from the ionosphere or to transmit upward at a slight angle for optimum ionosphere reflection. The same principle can also be applied to the rhombic.

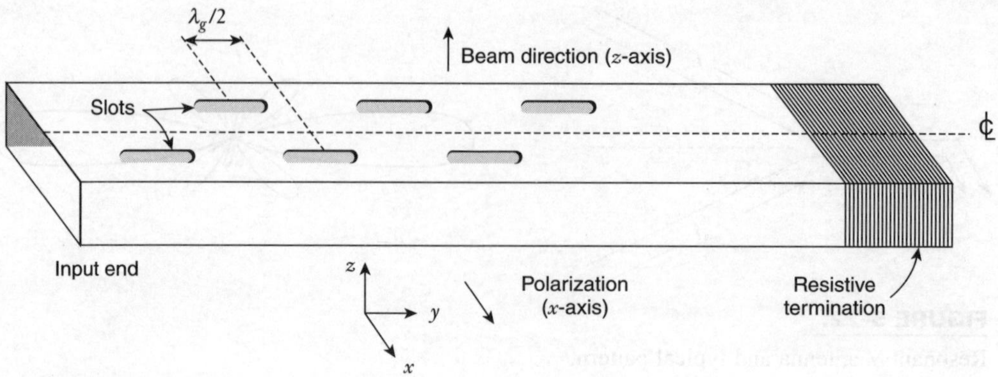

FIGURE 5–24.
Broadside array of longitudinal shunt slots in a waveguide.

5.8.2. Horn and Slot Arrays

A linear or planar broadside array may be formed with horns used as the radiating elements. If unidirectional horns (e.g., sectoral or pyramidal) are used, the array pattern will of course also be unidirectional. The pattern is obtained by multiplying a single-horn pattern by the pattern of the equivalent array of isotropic point sources. Horn arrays are not in very common use, but they do have some applications.

Waveguide slot arrays, on the other hand, are much used at microwave frequencies. They consist of a set of slots cut along the face of a waveguide. A typical form of slot array is shown in Fig. 5–24. The longitudinal shunt slots are cut in the broad face of a rectangular waveguide operating in the TE_{10} mode. They are parallel to the longitudinal center line of the guide and displaced laterally from it. The slots are spaced a half (guide) wavelength apart along the length of the guide, and they alternate on opposite sides of the center line; this results in in-phase operation, and hence a broadside pattern. The polarization is perpendicular to the axes of the slots.

The lateral displacement of the slot from the guide center line determines its degree of coupling to the wave in the guide, and hence the percentage of the power flowing down the guide that will be extracted and radiated. Therefore, variation of this displacement provides a convenient means of controlling the array taper, or amplitude distribution.

The last slot in the array cannot extract all the remaining power. The residue in the guide is ordinarily absorbed in a resistive termination, to prevent reflection and standing waves that would upset the intended amplitude distribution and phasing.

Many other forms of slot arrays are possible and useful. The array of longitudinal shunt slots is perhaps the most common.

5.8.3. Patch or Microstrip Arrays

Microstrip, also commonly known as patch, antennas are described in sec. 4.9. The patch antenna is made by reliable fabrication techniques, has acceptable bandwidths, and is lightweight and small. For these reasons, patch arrays are widely considered for airborne and spacecraft applications. In addition, design and construction techniques exist that exhibit low mutual coupling between array elements, thereby suppressing the likelihood of blind angles, that is, blindness (Yang, Mosallaei, and Rahmat-Samii 2007).

5.8.4. Phased Arrays for Scanning

Thus far this chapter has discussed antenna arrays that are designed for the major lobe or beam being pointed in one direction or more. If all the elements of a linear array or a plane array are in phase, the beam will be directed broadside. On the other hand, if the phases of the elements of a linear array progressively change by an amount per element that is equal, in radians, to $2\pi d/\lambda$, where d is the element spacing and λ is the wavelength, the beam direction will be parallel to the line joining the elements (endfire). Furthermore, by progressive phase changes, beams may be directed at intermediate angles. Advantage of this fact is taken in the so-called *phased arrays,* or electronically steered arrays, to produce a beam that may be directed at various angles by changing the progressive phase shift along the array. Concepts and techniques of array antennas that are designed to electronically change beam-pointing direction are discussed in chapter 8, Electronically Steered Arrays.

5.9. General Remarks on Mutual Coupling

Most basic discussions on array pattern analysis assume that all elements radiate isotropically, or at least the radiation pattern of each element is identical in shape. These assumptions amount to assuming that the mutual coupling between elements is negligible. For some element configurations, this assumption may provide a useful estimate for an overall normalized array pattern. However, generally, by neglecting mutual coupling, the calculated array element input currents and radiated power will be incorrect, and the validity of the estimated pattern shape may be in question (secs. 5.1.4–5.1.7).

A few comments follow about the environment within which elements are located. In an array with many elements, those elements near the center are within similar electric and magnetic environments, with the outermost (edge) elements being subjected to asymmetrical mutual coupling. However, for purposes of side-lobe control, amplitudes are tapered to smaller values toward the edge elements. This tapering tends to minimize some of the effects of asymmetrical. Furthermore, often dummy edge elements are included, to provide a greater uniformity in the mutual coupling environment for the energized elements that are thusly removed from the aperture edges.

Ideally, an antenna should provide a good impedance match between the transmitter and free space. If there are impedance mismatches, a loss of input and radiated power occurs. Thus a mismatch, even at one element, changes the array aperture illumination and may cause an appreciable pattern change from that which would occur based on the element's assumed radiated power. A mismatch causes standing waves, which produce undesirable, higher voltage levels than a matched condition. Furthermore, internal reflections may cause the generation of spurious lobes in the overall array radiation pattern.

In fact, there are conditions, sometimes observed, where a matched condition exists at the broadside beam direction, but at some other angle most of the power is reflected and thus a scan "blindness" results. In spite of the difficulty of dealing with mutual coupling, especially with electronically steered arrays (chapter 8), well-functioning fixed-beam as well as electronically steered arrays have been developed and operating for a number of decades (Hansen 2007; Oliner and Knittel 1972).

References

Balanis, C. A., *Antenna Theory*, Wiley-Interscience, 2005.

Bodnar, D. G., "Materials and Design Data," ch. 55 in *Antenna Engineering Handbook*, 4th edi, J. L. Volakis (ed.), McGraw-Hill, 2007.

Bregains, J. C., F. Ares, and E. Moreno, "Visualizing the 3D Polar Power Patterns and Excitations of Planar Arrays with MATLAB," *IEEE Antennas and Propagation Magazine*, April 2004, pp. 108–112.

Brown, G. H., "Directional Antennas," *Proceedings IRE*, vol. 25, January 1937, pp. 78–145.

Dolph, C. L., "A Current Distribution for Broadside Arrays Which Optimizes the Relationship between Beamwidth and Side-Lobe Level," *Proceedings IRE*, vol. 34, June 1946, 335–48.

Hansen, R. C., *Microwave Scanning Antennas*, vol. 1, Academic Press, 1964.

Hansen, R. C., "Phased Arrays," ch. 20 in *Antenna Engineering Handbook*, 4th ed., J. L. Volakis (ed.), McGraw-Hill, 2007.

Hansen, W. W., and J. R. Woodyard, "A New Principle in Directional Antenna Design," *Proceedings IRE*, vol. 26, March 1938, 333–35.

Harris, F. J., "On the Use of Windows for Harmonic Analysis with the Discrete Fourier Transform," *Proceedings of the IEEE*, January 1978, pp. 51–83.

IEEE Standard Dictionary of Electrical and Electronics Terms, 5th ed., Institute of Electrical and Electronics Engineers, 1993.

Kraus, J. D., *Antennas*, 2nd ed., McGraw-Hill, 1988.

Kraus, J. D., and R. J. Marhefka, *Antennas,* 3rd ed., McGraw-Hill, 2002.

Long, M. W., *Airborne Early Warning System Concepts*, SciTech Publishers, 2004, pp. 235–36 and 405–08.

Ma, M. T., "Arrays of Discrete Elements," ch. 3 in *Antenna Engineering Handbook,* R. C. Johnson, 3rd ed., McGraw-Hill, 1993, p. 3–23.

Mailloux, R. J., *Phased Array Antenna Handbook*, Artech House, 1994.

Oliner, A. A., and G. H. Knittel, *Phased Array Antennas*, Artech House, 1972.

Reference Data for Radio Engineers, 6th ed., Howard W. Sams & Co, Inc., 1979.

Sevgi, L., and Çağatay Uluişik, "A MATLAB-Based Visualization Package for Planar Arrays of Isotropic Radiators," *IEEE Antennas and Propagation Magazine*, vol. 47, February 2005, pp. 156–63.

Silver, S., *Microwave Antenna Theory and Design*, McGraw-Hill, 1949.

Stutzman, W. L., "Estimating Directivity and Gain of Antennas," *IEEE Antennas and Propagation Magazine*, August 1998, pp. 7–11.

Tai, C. T., "The Optimum Directivity of Uniformly Spaced Broadside Arrays of Dipoles," *IEEE Transactions on Antennas and Propagation*, July 1964, pp. 447–54.

Taylor, T. T., "Design of Line-Source Antennas for Narrow Beamwidth and Low Side Lobes," *IRE Trans on Antennas and Propagation*, January 1955, pp. 16–28.

Van der Mass, C. J., "A Simplified Calculation for Dolph–Tchebycheff Arrays," *J. Appl. Phys.*, vol. 25, no. 1, pp. 121–124, January 1954.

Yang, F., H. Mosallaei, and Y. Rahmat-Samii, "Low Profile Antenna Performance Enhancement Utilizing Engineered Electromagnetic Materials," ch. 34 in J. L. Volakis, *Antenna Engineering Handbook*, 4th ed., 2007, p. 34–12.

Problems and Exercises

1. Two dipoles have their centers positioned at R_1 and R_2 in Fig. 5–1 (and Fig. 5–2), with their axes parallel to the z-axis (perpendicular to the plane of the paper). Their separation is $d = \lambda/6$. (a) What must be their phase difference, α, in order for the field intensity to be zero in the direction $\phi = 270°$ (direction of the negative y-axis)? (b)If E_0 in equation (5–4) has the value $\frac{1}{2}$ volt per meter, calculate $E(\phi)$, for these values of d and α, and plot the resulting pattern using polar coordinates. The shape of the resulting pattern should resemble those of comparable phasing and spacing in Fig. 5–3. (Note that the maximum value of this pattern is less than one; it needs a normalizing factor to make it a proper relative pattern.)

2. (a) A central transmitting station communicates only with three other fixed stations, which are all at about the same distance but in directions that are 120 degrees apart. The frequency is in the LF region, and two vertical towers are to be used as a two-element monopole array for the central station. To provide equal signal strength at all three of the other stations, and as strong a signal as possible with a given amount of transmitter power, what spacing and phasing of the monopole elements (towers) would you employ? (Base your answer on inspection of Fig. 5–3). (b) What would your answer be if there were four other stations, instead of three, in directions 90 degrees apart (e.g., one to the north, one east, one south, and one west)?

3. A uniform linear array consists of four *short* dipoles, spaced a distance $d = \lambda/2$ apart, as in Fig. 5–4. The phase difference between elements is $\alpha = 0°$, so that it is a broadside array. The short-dipole axes are parallel to the z-axis of the coordinate system, so that their individual *relative* patterns are, from equation (4–2) of chapter 4, $E_{rel} = \sin\theta$. (This is the complete pattern even though only one angle is involved.) Write the equation for the complete pattern (versus θ and ϕ) of this dipole array. Three steps are necessary: (a) Modify equation (5–9), following the instruction given in the text, to convert it to a pattern for an array

of isotropic elements. (b) Substitute into this expression the appropriate values for n, d, and α. (c) Apply the principle of pattern multiplication to obtain the pattern versus θ and ϕ of the dipole array.

4. A uniform broadside array of twelve point-source isotropic elements has an element spacing of 0.65 wavelength ($d = 0.65\lambda$). (a) What is the approximate beamwidth? (b) If the spacing is $d = 0.5\lambda$ (instead of 0.65λ), what will the beamwidth be? (c) What is the directivity for $d = 0.5\lambda$? Will the directivity for $d = 0.65\lambda$ be less than or greater than this value?

5. A five-element driven endfire dipole array has element spacing $d = \lambda/8$. (a) What should the *phasing* (α) of the elements be to obtain maximum directivity of the beam? Express the result in both radians and degrees. (b) Using the value of α found in part (a), calculate $E(\phi)$ from equation (5–9) for $\phi = 90°$ and $\phi = 270°$ (the two "endfire" directions). What is the front-to-back ratio of this antenna, expressed as a ratio of electric field strengths? Express it also as a decibel value. *Note*: In part (b), you will find that the initial calculation indicates a "negative" electrical intensity for $\phi = 270°$, but recall that absolute-value brackets are used in equation (5–9) to indicate that the calculated field is regarded as always positive.)

6. Check the box that you think precedes the correct answer to the following multiple-choice problems:

   (a) A Yagi-Uda antenna has a beam that is

   ☐ unidirectional ☐ omnidirectional

   ☐ bidirectional ☐ multilobed (many equal-strength lobes)

   (b) If the total number of dipole elements in a Yagi-Uda antenna is five, the usual number of these that will be *parasitic directors* is

   ☐ one ☐ three

   ☐ two ☐ four

   (c) The principal advantage of a Yagi-Uda antenna over a fully driven endfire array with the same number of elements is

   ☐ higher gain ☐ simpler feed system

   ☐ easier adjustment of element length and spacing ☐ better polarization characteristics

7. It is desired to obtain a directivity of 1,000 with a large uniform planar dipole array backed by a reflecting screen. The wavelength is $\lambda = 0.5$ meter ($f = 600$ MHz). (a) What must be the *area* of this array? If the array is square, what is the length of each side? (b) If the dipoles of the array have their centers spaced a half wavelength apart in both vertical and horizontal dimensions, with dipoles located at each corner of the square, how many dipoles does the array contain? (Disregard the fact that the edge dimension is not exactly an integral multiple of a half wavelength; it is very nearly so.)

8. Multiple choice (check one box in each part):

(a) *Tapering* the currents in a dipole array is done for the following reason:

- ☐ To avoid corona in the end elements
- ☐ To reduce the minor-lobe level
- ☐ To minimize ohmic losses
- ☐ To increase the directivity

(b) The absolute minimum side-lobe level is achieved in array design by using:

- ☐ The Dolph-Chebyschev distribution
- ☐ A Taylor distribution
- ☐ A binomial distribution
- ☐ A truncated Gaussian distribution

(c) The Taylor distribution is superior to the Dolph-Chebyschev when:

- ☐ It is applied to a uniform linear array
- ☐ It is applied to a linear array of many elements
- ☐ Minimum beamwidth is desired for a given side-lobe level
- ☐ It is desired to have all minor lobes of equal magnitude

9. A V antenna has resonant-long-wire legs that are each 5 wavelengths long (10 half wavelengths). What must be the angle at the apex of the V for the beam to have maximum directivity and to lie exactly on the bisector of the V? For solution, see equation (4–14), chapter 4.

10. Calculate the patterns shown in Fig. 5–20 for two, 2-m line apertures that operate at 3 GHz. One aperture has constant amplitude and phase and the other has a Dolph-Chebychev distribution that gives 26 dB side lobes.

CHAPTER 6

Reflectors and Lenses

It has been shown in sec. 5.1 that an *array* antenna can be used to achieve a directional radiation pattern in which the radiated power is concentrated in a beam. This chapter treats an entirely different method of achieving essentially the same result, by the use of reflectors and lenses. Antennas using these devices achieve a directional effect most readily explained in terms of optical principles described in sec. 1.2—the principles of reflection and refraction.

The branch of optical science that deals with these phenomena in terms of rays and wave fronts, rather than in terms of electromagnetic-wave theory, is called *geometric optics*. The principles of geometric optics can be applied (as mentioned in sec. 1.2) only when the dimensions of the optical surface are large compared with the wavelength. This means, for example, that a reflector 3 meters in diameter would not behave in accordance with a geometric-optics analysis at a frequency of 1 MHz, for which the wavelength is 300 meters. It would do so very well, however, at 10,000 MHz, for which the wavelength is 3 cm. Generally speaking, therefore, antennas based on geometric-optics principles are very-high-frequency devices. They are used mainly above 30 MHz, and arguably above about 1 GHz they are more common than arrays.

Even when the dimensions of the antenna are large compared to the wavelength, the principles of geometric optics cannot be applied to all aspects of its behavior. For example, diffraction will occur at the edges of a lens or reflector and at small irregularities in the structure if such exist. Diffraction is not explainable by geometric optics. A qualitative description may be given verbally or graphically in terms of Huygens' principle, as was done in sec. 1.2, but an exact description requires the mathematical expressions of electromagnetic theory.

The diffraction effects are of secondary importance, however, and are ignored here, in the aperture field formulation of lens and reflector antennas, although they cannot be ignored when an exact far-field analysis is desired. Diffraction must be considered, for example, in analysis of the minor-lobe formation, and the main-beam pattern shape and width. The method of geometric optics (ray-wave front analysis) is basically an approximate rather than an exact method. But it is so nearly exact for many purposes, and is so much simpler than the exact mathematics, that it is usually employed wherever possible. Also, it conveys a useful intuitive conception of some aspects of antenna behavior.

6.1. Focusing and Collimation

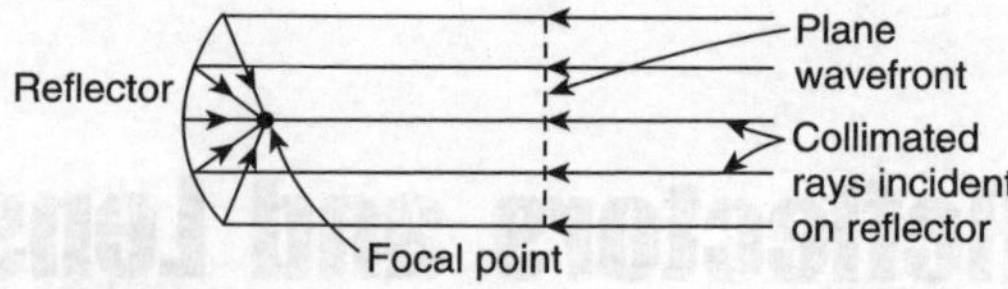

FIGURE 6–1

Focusing by a curved reflector.

An important geometric-optics concept, *focusing*, is familiar in connection with optical devices such as cameras, projectors, search-lights (and automobile headlights), telescopes, and the like. Antennas utilizing radio-wave reflectors* and lenses focus rays in a similar way. *Collimation* is a special case of focusing.

6.1.1. Focusing by a Parabolic Reflector

If a beam of parallel rays is incident on a suitably curved reflector, the rays will be brought to focus at a point, as shown in Fig. 6–1. Similarly, if a point source of radiation is placed at this focal point, the rays from it will be reflected in such a way that they emerge as a parallel beam. That is, the directions of all ray lines in Fig. 6–1 are reversed. This is in effect a simplified statement of the principle of reciprocity discussed in sec. 1.3.

Rays that are parallel are said to be *collimated.* In a sense, they are focused "at infinity." It can be shown that this collimation occurs if the shape of the reflector is parabolic. The automobile headlight is a familiar example of this type of reflector. The giant searchlight, once used for finding enemy bomber aircraft at night (before radar became available) and still used for some purposes, is another example.

The geometry of a parabola can be expressed in terms of the coordinate system of Fig. 6–2. The basic coordinates are cartesian (rectangular). The horizontal axis, labeled z, lies along the axis of the parabola, which is a line of symmetry. (That is, if the lower half of the parabola were folded over this axis it would lie exactly on the upper half.) The point at which this axis intersects the parabolic curve is called the *vertex*. The second coordinate axis, labeled x, passes through this point also. At a certain distance f from the vertex, on the parabolic axis, is a point labeled *focus*. The equation of the parabolic curve, in terms of these coordinates and the parameter f is

$$x^2 = 4fz \tag{6–1}$$

The focal point, or focus, at distance f from the vertex, is the point at which incoming collimated rays will converge (as indicated in Fig. 6–1) or from which the diverging rays of a point source will be collimated.

The bilateral symmetry of the curve is inherent in the x^2 term of the equation; that is, if a given value of z is chosen and the positive value of x is found that satisfies the equation, it will also be satisfied by minus the same value of x. The curve defined by (6–1) extends to infinity in the $+z$-direction (and consequently also in the $+x$ and $-x$ directions).

* The word "reflector" in this chapter implies a nonplanar reflector—either one that is curved or a system of plane reflectors set at different angles with respect to a reference plane. A simple plane reflector, such as might be used in conjunction with an array, does not provide a focusing action.

Practical parabolic reflectors, of course, are of finite depth; they terminate, or are "cut off," at some finite value of z, denoted z_{ap} in Fig. 6–2, graphed in decibels.

The open mouth of the parabola is known as the *aperture*. The aperture dimension is labeled D_a in Fig. 6–2.* It is apparent that if z_{ap} is smaller than f, the focus will lie outside the aperture instead of inside as shown in the diagram. The ratio of the focal length to the aperture size f/D (commonly referred to as the "f over D ratio") is an important characteristic of a parabolic reflector. It is determined by the depth of the reflector, z_{ap}, in relation to the focal length f.

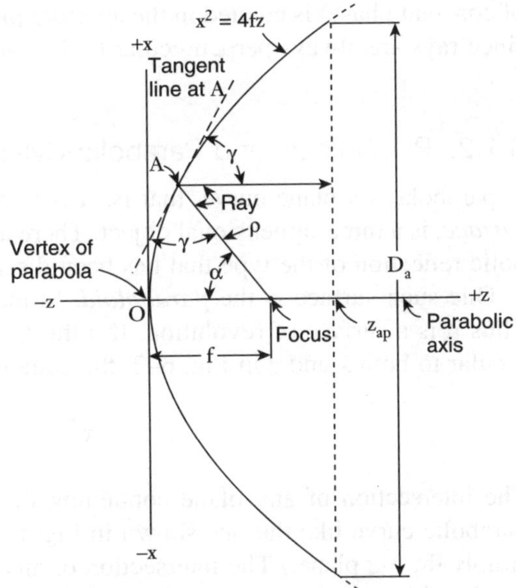

FIGURE 6–2

Geometry of parabolic reflection.

A parabola whose depth is exactly equal to the focal length ($z_{ap} = f$) will have a value of D equal to $4f$, and therefore for this parabola $f/D = f/4f = \frac{1}{4}$, or 0.25. For reasons that will appear later, it is generally inadvisable to make a parabolic reflector deeper than the focal length (although in special cases it may be done), and ordinarily the f/D value will range from about 0.25 to 0.5.

The focusing action of the parabolic reflector can be understood by considering a ray that leaves the focal point at an angle α with respect to the parabolic axis, as shown in Fig. 6–2. At the point A where this ray encounters the parabolic curve, a tangent to the curve is drawn, as shown by a dashed line. By the laws of reflection (sec. 1.2), the ray will be reflected in such a direction that the incident and reflected rays make equal angles (γ) with the tangent line. This causes the reflected-ray direction to be parallel to the parabolic axis, regardless of the particular value of α that may be considered. In other words, *all* rays emanating from the focal point will be reflected parallel to the parabolic axis. By the principle of reciprocity, incoming parallel rays will be reflected so that they converge to focus at the focal point of the parabola.

This result can also be shown in another way by considering the total distance that a ray travels in going from the source (focal point) to the reflection point (A), and thence to the aperture plane (the dashed vertical line of length D). By simple geometric analysis it can be shown that the length of this path is equal to $f + z_{ap}$, for all values of the angle α. (This result is obvious for the special case of $\alpha = 0$). This means that the *phases* of all waves thus arriving at the aperture plane are the same. Thus a *wavefront* (a surface

* Since the symbol D is also used to denote the *directivity* of an antenna, the aperture linear dimension will be designated D_a in applications where it might be confused with directivity symbol. But often it is called simply D because this symbol has traditionally been used, especially in referring to the f/D ratio.

of constant phase) is created in the aperture plane. Hence the rays are parallel to the axis, since rays are always perpendicular to a wavefront (Sec. 1–1).

6.1.2. Paraboloids and Parabolic Cylinders

A parabola is a plane curve, that is, it is two dimensional. A reflector, being a curved *surface*, is a three-dimensional object. There are two types of surfaces that produce parabolic reflection of the type that has been discussed.

One such surface is the *paraboloid*, formed by rotating the parabola about its axis. Thus it is a surface of revolution. If a third cartesian coordinate, y, has its axis perpendicular to both x and z in Fig. 6–2, the equation of the paraboloid is

$$x^2 + y^2 = 4fz \tag{6–2}$$

The intersection of any plane containing the z-axis with the paraboloidal surface is a parabolic curve like the one shown in Fig. 6–2. (The intersecting plane in this figure is simply the x-z plane.) The intersection of any plane perpendicular to the z-axis with the paraboloidal surface is a circle. Thus the open mouth of a paraboloidal reflector, the aperture, is circular (as in a conventional automobile headlight) if the reflector has the same depth in all planes containing the parabolic axis, that is, the z axis.

It is possible, however, to "cut away" portions of a paraboloidal reflector in such a way that it does not appear circular when viewed from a point on the parabolic axis. Such *cut paraboloids* have certain advantages in some applications, as will be discussed in sec. 6.3.

The second type of surface is the *parabolic cylinder*, formed by translating the parabola of Fig. 6–2 in the direction of the y-axis, that is, by "moving it sideways." The intersections of all planes parallel to the x-z plane with the parabolic cylinder are parabolas like the one shown in Fig. 6–2. The intersections of all planes parallel to the y-z plane with the parabolic cylinder are straight lines. If the cylindrical surface has a finite dimension in the y-direction, the reflector as viewed from a distant point on the z-axis will appear rectangular, that is, it has a rectangular aperture. The parabolic cylinder has a *focal line*, rather than a focal point, and a *vertex line*. The approximate appearances of the full paraboloid, a cut paraboloid, and a parabolic cylinder are shown in Fig. 6–3.

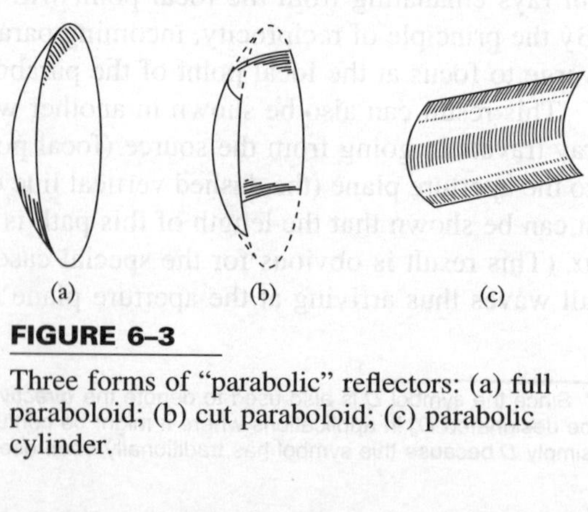

FIGURE 6–3

Three forms of "parabolic" reflectors: (a) full paraboloid; (b) cut paraboloid; (c) parabolic cylinder.

6.1.3. Space Attenuation for Point and Line Sources

The strength of the illumination on an aperture depends on whether the reflector or lens feed functions as a point or line source of radiation. The strength of the radiation versus distance is described by a term called space attenuation. Thus, knowledge of space attenuation is an important aspect of the design of reflector and lens antennas. As may be seen in Fig. 1–2, chapter 1, rays emanating from a point source diverge spherically. Thus, the wave energy from a point source is constant within a tube of solid angle. Therefore, the power density varies in proportion to $1/r^2$, where r is the distance from the source. On the other hand, as will now be discussed, the power density varies in proportion to $1/r$ for radiation from a line source.

Consider a line source that radiates radially with equal intensity perpendicular in every direction from its axis. Now imagine a concentrically placed cylinder that intercepts the radiated power. The cylinder's surface area will vary in direct proportion to r, and hence the power density at the cylinder would vary in direct proportion to $1/r$. Therefore, as a consequence of energy conservation, the power density from a line source varies with distant r as $1/r$; yet it varies as $1/r^2$ from a point source.

In Fig. 6–1, both focused (collimated) and unfocused rays are shown near the reflector. The collimated (focused) rays are parallel, and thus the power density for focused rays is independent of distance r near the parabola's aperture (open mouth). Refer now to Fig. 6–2 to develop equations for the field strength (illumination) over the apertures of paraboloids (parabolas of revolution) and parabolic cylinders. Radiated rays diverge along the distance ρ from the focal point to the reflector, but they are focused after reflection. Consequently, for a paraboloid illuminated by a point source, the power density varies as $1/\rho^2$, where ρ is the distance between the focal point and the reflector. Similarly, for a parabolic cylinder illuminated by a line source, the power density varies as $1/\rho$ between the focal line and the reflector.

In Fig. 6–2, note that $z_{ap} - f$ is the distance that the aperture point z_{ap} is to the right of the focal point. Recall that, for a focused antenna, all ray path lengths between the focus and aperture are equal. Then, to determine ρ versus angle α by using Fig. 6–2, one observes:

$$(\text{focus-to-point A}) + (\text{point A-to-aperture}) = (\rho) + (\rho\cos\alpha + z_{ap} - f) \qquad (6\text{–}3)$$

In addition, note that along the parabolic axis:

$$(\text{focus-to-point A}) + (\text{point A-to-aperture}) = (f) + (f + z_{ap} - f) \qquad (6\text{–}4)$$

By equating (6–3) and (6–4), it can be seen that $2f = \rho + \rho\cos\alpha$. Then, by using the trigonometric identity $(1 + \cos\alpha)/2 = \cos^2(\alpha/2)$, one finds

$$\frac{f}{\rho} = \frac{1+\cos\alpha}{2} = \cos^2\left(\frac{\alpha}{2}\right) \qquad (6\text{–}5)$$

We now use the fact that, for a point source, power density varies as $1/\rho^2$. Then, from (6–5), for a paraboloid with an isotropic radiator at its focus, power density p_α on the aperture versus angle α is

$$\frac{p_\alpha}{p_0} = \left(\frac{1+\cos\alpha}{2}\right)^2 = \cos^4\left(\frac{\alpha}{2}\right) \tag{6–6}$$

In (6–6), p_0 is power density at the aperture center, where angle α is zero. Similarly, for a parabolic cylinder, power density p_α on the aperture versus angle α is

$$\frac{p_\alpha}{p_0} = \left(\frac{1+\cos\alpha}{2}\right) = \cos^2\left(\frac{\alpha}{2}\right) \tag{6–7}$$

In (6–7), p_0 is the power density at the center of the parabolic cylinder, where angle α is zero.

To obtain electric field strength E versus angle α, the fact is used that E varies as the square root of power density. Then, from (6–6) and (6–7), the variation of E versus α along the aperture of a paraboloid and a parabolic cylinder can be expressed, respectively, as

$$\frac{E_\alpha}{E_0} = \frac{1+\cos\alpha}{2} = \cos^2\left(\frac{\alpha}{2}\right) \quad \text{(for paraboloid)} \tag{6–8}$$

and

$$\frac{E_\alpha}{E_0} = \sqrt{\frac{1+\cos\alpha}{2}} = \cos\left(\frac{\alpha}{2}\right) \quad \text{(for parabolic cylinder)} \tag{6–9}$$

Equations (6–8) and (6–9) describe the variations in the aperture amplitude E_α versus angle α caused by divergence of rays. Thus, (6–8) describes the amplitude on the aperture of a paraboloid if the feed radiates isotropically, and (6–9) describes the amplitude distribution if a line source radiates uniformly at all angles about its axis.

Another useful expression is the attenuation, expressed in decibels, between focus or focal line and the aperture, caused by the divergence of rays. From (6–8), this attenuation in decibels for a paraboloid is

$$20\log(E_\alpha/E_0) = 40\log\cos(\alpha/2) \quad \text{(for paraboloid)} \tag{6–10}$$

Similarly, from (6–9), this attenuation in decibels for a parabolic cylinder is

$$20\log(E_\alpha/E_0) = 40\log\cos(\alpha/2) \quad \text{(for parabolic cylinder)} \tag{6–11}$$

The equations in the present section describe the effects of space attenuation. These equations provide a necessary step toward accurately determining the aperture strength versus position along an aperture, and therefore often they are essential for calculating the side-lobe levels and beamwidths available from reflector and lens antennas. Sometimes, however, as discussed in sec. 6.4, approximations are made for antenna designs that use only the relative field strengths between the aperture center and its edges.

6.2. Beamwidth and Directivity

It has been shown in sec. 6.1 that if a source of radiation is placed at the focus of a parabolic reflector, a beam of parallel (collimated) rays will be produced. Since the rays do not diverge and the wavefront is plane, it might be deduced that the resultant beamwidth is zero (because a nonzero beamwidth implies that the wavefront is spherical and that the rays are diverging within a cone).

This reasoning is not correct, and it is an aspect of lens and reflector analysis to which geometric optics gives incorrect answers. As discussed in sec. 3.2.5, within the radiating near-field or Fresnel region (see also Fig. G–1 of Appendix G), the wavefront gradually changes with increased distance from being plane to becoming spherically-shaped on reaching the radiating far-field or Fraunhofer region. Thus, the radiating near-field region extends from the plane-wavefront region to essentially the spherical-wavefront region, and the radiating far-field extends outward to all greater distances. Although the boundary between radiating near-field and radiating far-field regions is not sharply defined, for approximate purposes it is usually considered to be at a distance from the antenna equal to $2D^2/\lambda$, where D is the largest aperture dimension and λ is the wavelength. (The same units of length are to be used for both D and λ in making this computation.) This criterion, as has been indicated, applies to electrically large arrays as well as to reflectors, and it also applies to lenses and to any other highly directive antenna.

6.2.1. Shape of Aperture

Figures 6–1 and 6–2 illustrate typical shapes of parabolic reflectors in cross section as viewed from the side, that is, from a direction perpendicular to the optical axis. When they are viewed along the axis—from "in front"—the area projected onto the aperture plane is the *aperture area*, or simply the aperture, which is the area containing the collimated radiation. The shape of this aperture area is an important characteristic of an antenna. As has been mentioned in sec. 6.1, if a paraboloidal reflector is a figure of revolution the resulting aperture is circular. However, the full circular aperture may not be desired in some cases, and portions of the reflector can be cut away so that a noncircular aperture results, as indicated in Fig. 6–3. Commonly used apertures of antennas are elliptical, square, and rectangular as well as circular, and occasionally odd shaped. The shape of the aperture affects the solid-angular shape of the beam.

6.2.2. Primary and Secondary Patterns

The feed radiator, considered by itself, has a radiation pattern and a beamwidth that are different from the pattern and beamwidth of the antenna as a whole. The feed-radiator beamwidth must be comparable (but not usually exactly equal) to the angle subtended at the focus by the edges of the reflector in order for the entire surface to be illuminated. The feed radiator is also known as the primary radiator, and its pattern is called the *primary pattern*. The pattern of the entire antenna is called the *secondary pattern*. When the term *antenna pattern* is used, the secondary pattern is meant. The primary pattern may also be called the feed pattern.

6.2.3. Beamwidth

The secondary radiation pattern of a lens or reflector antenna is very similar to that of a unidirectional planar array backed by a plane reflector, of the same size and aperture shape. The beamwidth is given by a formula of the same type used in chapter 5:

$$BW = k_1 \frac{\lambda}{D_a} \tag{6–12}$$

where λ is the wavelength, D_a is the aperture width of the reflector or lens, and k_1 is a constant, depending on the units in which the beamwidth is to be expressed and on some other factors. If the beamwidth (BW) is desired in degrees, and if both λ and D_a are expressed in the same units of length, k_1 is of the order of 60 to 70. This means, for example, that if the aperture width D_a is equal to 10 wavelengths, the beamwidth will be about 6 or 7 degrees.

For a paraboloid of noncircular aperture, the value of D_a to be used in (6–12) is the aperture dimension in the plane in which the beamwidth is to be calculated. If the aperture has different dimensions in different directions, the beam will have different widths in these directions.

6.2.4. Directivity

The directivity (D) of a reflector antenna may be expressed in terms of the *area* (A) of its aperture. The formula is the same as that for a large planar array:

$$D = k_2\left(\frac{4\pi A}{\lambda^2}\right) \tag{6–13}$$

The constant k_2 will usually have a value between about 0.5 and 0.7, depending on the shape of the aperture and the characteristics of the source of the radiation used.

The general relationships discussed in chapter 5 between beamwidths, directivity, and gain are also applicable to continuous apertures. The factor k_2 used above that relates directivity with aperture area is commonly called aperture efficiency.

6.3. Reflector Illumination

A complete parabolic-reflector antenna has two basic components—the reflector and a source of primary radiation placed at or near the focal point. (When the antenna is used for receiving, this primary "radiator" receives the signal concentrated on it by the focusing action of the antenna.) The primary radiator is commonly called simply the *feed*.

Ideally, the feed should have a pattern of such nature that it radiates toward the reflector so as to "illuminate" the entire surface, with little or no energy radiated in other directions. Such an ideal pattern is of course unattainable, but some types of primary radiators are much better suited than others. Obviously an isotropic radiator would be a poor choice. A dipole is likewise not very well adapted to this task, although dipole feeds are sometimes used. More often, a dipole is used in conjunction with a small reflector to provide a better pattern, and sometimes a small dipole array may be used as a feed. The most common choice of a feed radiator for paraboloidal reflectors is the waveguide horn, which was described in sec. 4.7. The parabolic-cylinder reflector has special feed requirements that will be discussed separately.

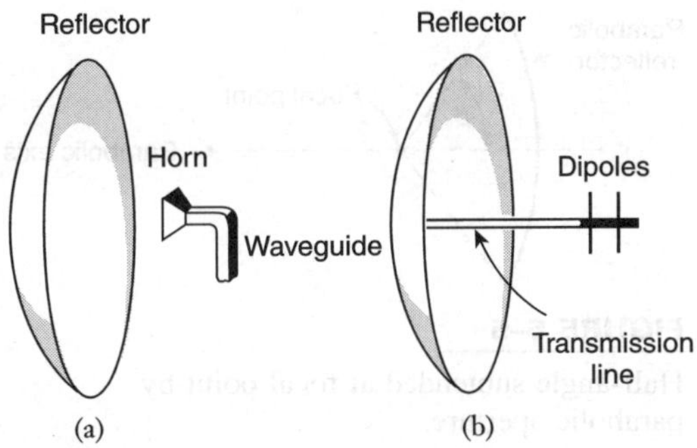

FIGURE 6–4

Paraboloidal-reflector antenna fed by (a) horn radiator and (b) double-dipole endfire array.

Practically all the basic radiator types described in chapter 4 may be adapted to feeding a reflector. When circular polarization is desired, the helix is often used. The conical horn can also be used for this purpose. Figure 6–4 shows the general appearance and arrangement of a paraboloidal-reflector antenna with two different types of feed. The horn feed is waveguide-fed. The double-dipole feed consists of two dipoles, spaced and phased to produce an endfire pattern that illuminates the paraboloidal reflector. Various other feed arrangements are possible. Representative feed types are described in Silver (1949, chs. 8, 9, and 10).

6.3.1. Primary Pattern Requirements

The problem of feed design for a reflector or lens is to obtain a primary pattern that is the best compromise between fully covering the surface of the reflector or lens and not "spilling over" the edge any more than necessary. When the nature of typical patterns is considered (e.g., chapter 3, Fig. 3–2), it is evident that both requirements cannot be satisfied simultaneously. In practice, some spillover is accepted. This spillover represents a loss of power from the main-beam. However, if the pattern of the feed radiator were narrowed appreciably in order to avoid spillover, the power density at the edges of the reflector or lens would be reduced greatly compared to that at the center. The effect would be very similar to that in an array with an excessive "taper" of the currents in the elements. As discussed in sec. 5.6, an excessive taper causes severe gain reduction and widening of the beam, although it also has the beneficial effect of reducing side-lobe amplitudes.

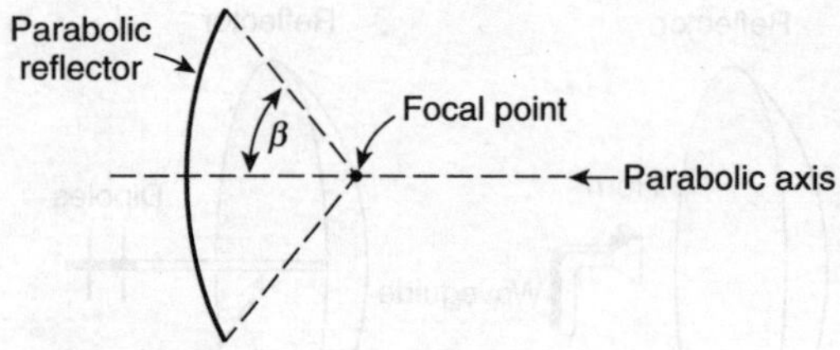

FIGURE 6–5

Half-angle subtended at focal point by parabolic aperture.

The radiation from the feed is called the *illumination* of the reflector. The variation of the intensity of the radiation over the aperture is called the *aperture distribution*. The *edge taper* is the ratio of the power density at the edge of the aperture to that at the center, or the decibel equivalent of this ratio. An excessive taper causes loss of gain and widening of the beam due to inefficient use of the available lens or reflector area; it results in a larger-than-necessary value of k_1 in (6–12) and a smaller-than-necessary value of k_2 in (6–13). Too little taper causes loss of gain due to excessive spillover and it also causes larger-than-necessary side lobes and back lobes. Exactly what amount of illumination taper will be employed in a given case depends on the relative importance, for the application at hand, of achieving maximum gain and reducing side lobes and back lobes to the minimum practical level.

The problem is somewhat complicated by the fact that a certain amount of illumination taper will occur even if the primary pattern has a uniform intensity within the solid angle subtended by the reflector. This inherent taper is due to the way in which the curvature of the reflector redistributes the power density in the aperture, compared to its original distribution in the primary radiation from the feed. The amount of taper thus produced may be calculated by geometric analysis. The inherent taper is greater with small *f/D* ratios than with large *f/D*.

For the paraboloidal reflector the inherent taper (space attenuation) may be expressed in terms of half the angle subtended by the reflector aperture edge at the feed, that is, at the focal point. This half angle is designated β in Fig. 6–5.

From (6–6) of sec. 6.1.3, the ratio of the power density at an angle α (Fig. 6–2) to that at the center, for a uniform-intensity primary pattern, is given by $\cos^4(\alpha/2)$. Since angle α equals β at the reflector edge (Fig. 6–5), the edge taper (space attenuation) expressed in decibels is, therefore,

$$\tau_1 = 40 \log \cos \frac{\beta}{2} = -40 \log \sec \frac{\beta}{2} \qquad (6\text{–}14)$$

The taper due to the primary pattern, in decibels, is approximately given by the formula:

$$\tau_2 = -12 \left(\frac{\beta}{BW} \right)^2 \qquad (6\text{–}15)$$

where *BW* is the half-power beamwidth (as defined in sec. 3.5) of the feed radiator. (The tapers are here expressed as power ratios less than one, or negative decibel values.)

The value of β for a given paraboloidal reflector may be expressed in terms of its *f/D* ratio. The formula is

$$\cot\beta = \frac{2f}{D} - \frac{1}{8(f/D)} \qquad (6\text{–}16)$$

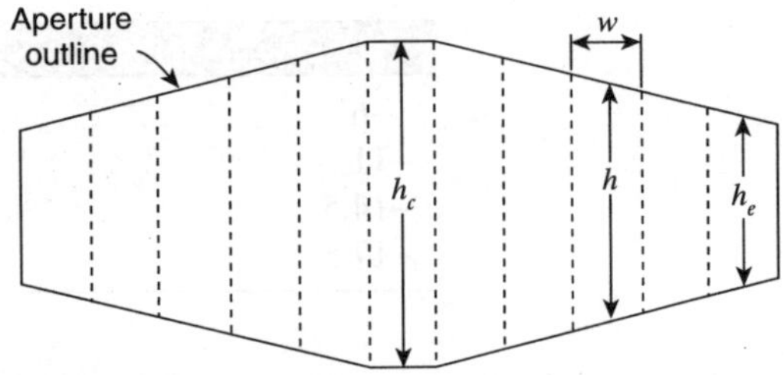

FIGURE 6–6
Equal-width vertical strips on a tapered aperture.

The following table of values of β was calculated by using (6–16). It gives the value 2β rather than simply β because 2β is the total angle subtended by the aperture (see Fig. 6–5) and is thus a rough indication of the feed beamwidth required.

f/D	2β
0.10	273°
0.25	180°
0.50	106°
1.00	56°

(This table indicates why the *f/D* ratio is seldom smaller than 0.25 or larger than 0.50, i.e., the required feed beamwidths become impractically large or small, respectively.)

A further tapering effect occurs if the aperture is not rectangular. Consider, for example, an approximately hexagonal aperture as illustrated in Fig. 6–6, with height h_c at the center and h_e at the edge. Consider vertical strips of this reflector, of width w and height h. If the illumination of the aperture is uniform, the total power radiated from a given strip is proportional to its area, hw. Therefore the ratio of the power radiated from the center strip to that from the edge strip is h_c/h_e. This is equivalent to a horizontal illumination taper (in the direction perpendicular to the strips) given in decibels by

$$\tau_3 = -10\log\frac{h_c}{h_e} \qquad (6\text{–}17)$$

The analysis is of course more complicated for an aperture having a curved outline, or for nonuniform illumination in the vertical direction, but the principles are the same. The total illumination taper, expressed as the ratio of the edge illumination to the center illumination in decibels, is the sum of the three component tapers, τ_1, τ_2, and τ_3.

6.3.2. Taper and Side Lobes for Elliptical Apertures

The total taper that should be used for a given case depends on the side-lobe level required. A published study (Adams and Kelleher 1950) for elliptical apertures (including circular apertures) gives the following indicative values for the sum of τ_1 and τ_2. (The factor τ_3 is implicitly included by the stipulation that the aperture is elliptical.)

$\tau_1 + \tau_2$, Decibels	Side-Lobe Level, Decibels
−6	−20
−11	−25
−14.5	−30
−17.5	−35

An example illustrates the use of these principles and results. Suppose that it is desired to design a circular-aperture paraboloidal-reflector antenna for a 30 dB side-lobe level. A horn is to be used as the feed radiator, and the *f/D* ratio is 0.4.

From (6–16) it is first calculated that the value of β is given by

$$\cot\beta = 0.8 - \frac{1}{3.2} = 0.4875$$
$$\therefore \beta = 64°$$

Hence the primary radiator must illuminate a reflector that subtends an angle of 128 degrees.

The taper due to reflector curvature is calculated from (6–14):

$$\tau_1 = 40\log_{10}\cos(32°) = 40\log_{10} 0.848$$
$$= -2.9\,\text{dB}$$

The table above indicates that for −30 dB side lobes a total taper of −14.5 dB is required. The feed pattern must therefore provide a taper of −14.5 + 2.9 = −11.6 dB. This is the required value of τ_2 in (6–15).

The next step is to determine the required primary-pattern beamwidth, *BW*. That is, (6–15) must be solved for the value of *BW* corresponding to the given value of τ_2, which is −11.6, and $\beta = 64°$. The result is

$$BW = 64\sqrt{12/11.6} = 65°$$

This means that a feed horn with a 65-degree half-power beamwidth is required. Equations (4–23a) and (4–23b) in chapter 4 provide for the design of a horn of a given beamwidth. It is thus found that an optimum-flare pyramidal horn must have an *E*-plane mouth dimension (d_E) of 0.86λ, and an *H*-plane dimension (d_H) of 1.03λ, where λ is the wavelength.

6.3.3. Optimum Illumination Taper

The preceding discussion of pattern requirements and taper of the total illumination in relation to side-lobe level, beamwidth, and gain is for the special case of elliptical-aperture paraboloidal reflectors. As has already been shown, this taper is affected by both the primary (feed) radiation pattern and by the geometry of the surface of the reflector, and also by the shape of the aperture outline. The formulas given are based on experimental investigation rather than theoretical analysis.

Aperture tapers for arrays were discussed in chapter 5, where the similarities in the effects of tapers on arrays and continuous apertures were briefly discussed. In addition, Tables 6–1 and 6–2 in sec. 6.10 include a number of different continuous aperture distributions, and the beamwidths and relative gains that result therefrom.

In sec. 5.6.5 the Taylor distribution is said to be widely used in the design of efficient and low side-lobe-level arrays, providing there are 20 or more elements (Taylor 1955). Although widely used in the design of arrays having a large number of elements, the Taylor distribution is basically a design for continuous apertures, and thus it provides an efficient aperture design for continuous distributions. In other words, the Taylor distribution is generally considered to be an optimum aperture distribution that is applicable both to arrays and continuous aperture antennas.

6.3.4. Line-Source Feeds

The foregoing example of a required primary-radiator beamwidth calculation applies specifically to the feed for a paraboloidal reflector, but the principles apply to other types of antennas characterized by an illuminated surface, such as parabolic-cylinder reflectors and lenses. The paraboloidal reflector requires a feed that approximates a point source, which is located at or near the focal point. As mentioned, the paraboloid is geometrically a figure of revolution. But the parabolic-cylinder reflector, and also lenses whose surfaces are cylindrical, are characterized by a *focal line*. The feed must therefore be a *line source*, rather than a point source.

The simplest example of a line source is the linear array described in sec. 5.2. (At microwave frequencies a commonly used line source is a waveguide-slot array.) When the linear array is used with a cylindrical reflector, the length of the array is made approximately equal to the cylindrical length dimension of the reflector. The line of the array is positioned on the focal line.

The beamwidth and pattern in the plane containing the line feed and the parabolic axis are determined entirely by the array, according to the principles discussed in sec. 5.2. (A parabolic-cylinder reflector functions in this dimension as if it were a plane reflector.) In the perpendicular plane the pattern is determined by the aperture dimension, and the beamwidth is given by (6–12). Thus a cylindrical reflector is, with this type of feed, a hybrid antenna—a sort of cross between an array and an "optical" antenna.

The total illumination taper in the cylindrical direction is that of the array (or other feed); but in the other direction there is space attenuation introduced because of path-length differences. The formula for this taper (space attenuation) with a parabolic-cylinder reflector is *not* the same factor that applies for the paraboloidal reflector. From (6–7) of sec. 6.1.3, the ratio of the power density at an angle α (Fig. 6–2) to that at the center, for a uniform-intensity primary pattern, is given by $\cos^2(\alpha/2)$. Since angle α equals β at the reflector edge (Fig. 6–5), the edge taper (space attenuation) expressed in decibels is, therefore,

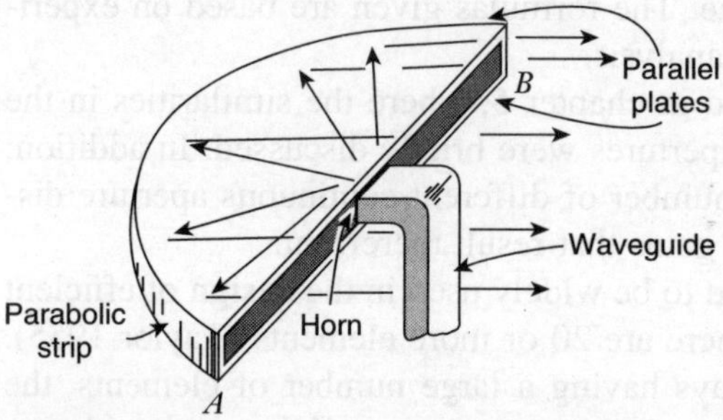

FIGURE 6–7
Pillbox antenna (line source of radiation).

$$\tau_1 = 20 \log \cos \frac{\beta}{2} \qquad (6\text{–}18)$$

To this must be added the feed-pattern taper and any other aperture-shape taper, as with a paraboloidal reflector, to obtain the total taper.

Arrays are not the only possible form of line-source feed. At microwave frequencies a "pillbox" feed may be used, a device sketched in Fig. 6–7. It consists of a parabolic strip of metal, bounded on both sides by flat metal plates. A feed horn placed at the focal point illuminates the parabolic strip so that collimated rays issue from the open mouth of the pillbox. Since the parabolic strip is very narrow compared to the parabolic aperture (*AB*), the radiation from the pillbox is distributed along a long narrow opening—in effect, along a line. Typically, the width of the strip, and hence the spacing between the parallel plates, is comparable to the lateral dimensions of waveguide at the frequency of operation, as indicated in Fig. 6–7. The waves propagating in the space between these plates are then essentially guided waves. They propagate in waveguide fashion rather than like free-space waves and are subject to many of the effects discussed in connection with waveguides (sec. 2.5). For example, the phase velocity of the waves is not that of free space; it varies with the frequency. For a given plate spacing, a low-frequency cutoff exists, below which waves will not propagate in a TM mode. However, the TE mode cutoff is always well below any frequency at which the parabolic reflector will function as a geometric-optics device. The pillbox may be operated in the TE mode, but the TM mode is more commonly employed. Because the electric field in this mode is parallel to the plates, metallic support pins perpendicular to this field may be used between the plates. This is not possible with the TE mode, and providing adequate plate stiffness may be a serious problem.

Special techniques may be employed to avoid the "blocking" that results due to the presence of the feed horn in the aperture. In one technique a "double pillbox" is used in which there are two parallel-plate spaces, coupled by an opening at the parabolic surface in such a way that the illuminating rays propagate in one parallel plate region but are reflected into the other. The pillbox aperture allows these reflected rays to escape, unobstructed by the horn feed. A cross section of this arrangement is sketched in Fig. 6–8. Another technique is the use of an "offset" parabolic section. This technique is described in this section in connection with paraboloidal reflectors (see Fig. 6–10), where it is also used to avoid aperture blocking by the feed radiator.

The pillbox, like other feed radiators, is sometimes used by itself as a complete antenna. It provides a radiation pattern that is relatively narrow in the plane of the parallel plates and broad in the perpendicular direction. It is in effect a parabolic-cylinder antenna of very short cylindrical length. When it is used as the line-source feed of another parabolic-cylinder reflector, the final pattern is the result of two parabolic reflections, one in each of the perpendicular (principal) planes of the pattern. It might seem that it would be simpler just to use a paraboloidal reflector in the first place. But the double-cylindrical-reflector arrangement is sometimes advantageous in that it allows the pattern to be controlled in each plane somewhat independently of the other plane.

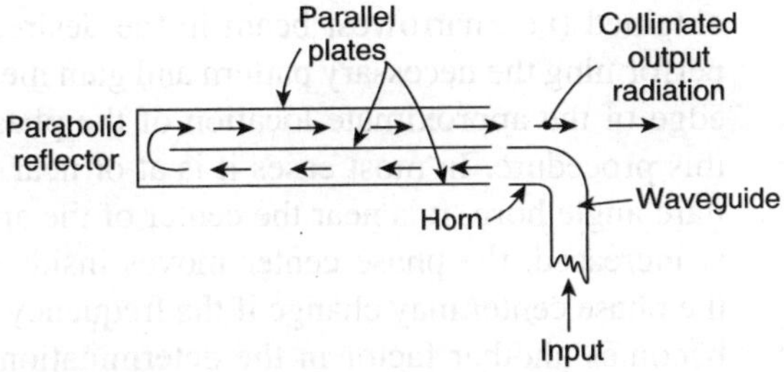

FIGURE 6–8
Cross section of double-pillbox arrangement.

6.3.5. Feed-Positioning Requirements

If a parabolic reflector is to be used to obtain a beam pattern that is maximized on the axis of the antenna, the feed must be located at the focal point, or for the parabolic-cylinder reflector or cylindrical lens, on the focal line. If the feed is moved a small amount laterally—that is, perpendicularly to the parabolic axis so as to keep it in the focal plane—the beam will still be formed but its direction will be changed. This effect may be used (as will be discussed in sec. 6.9) to cause the beam to change direction without moving the entire antenna. However, if the feed is moved too far laterally from the focus, the beam will deteriorate, and therefore the amount of beam motion that can be obtained in this way is limited.

If the feed is moved off the focal point or line in a direction *along* the axis, the radiation pattern will be broadened, since the rays will no longer be collimated (parallel). Therefore it is important to position the feed correctly at the focal point (or, when it is desired to direct the beam off axis, in the focal plane).

The focal point (or line) may be located by simple geometric measurement—that is, with a steel tape, or by the use of a surveyor's transit if the reflector is very large. The theoretical location is of course determined by the parameter f in (6–1) (or 6–2).

The question arises, exactly what point of the feed structure is to be positioned at the focus of the reflector? Consider, for example, a horn radiator. Should the mouth of the horn be at the focus, or should the point at which the flare starts, or some other point? There is a similar question if the feed consists of a dipole backed by a parasitic reflecting element or a small sheet reflector.

To answer this question it is necessary to introduce the concept of the *phase center* of a radiating source. This concept is based on the fact that in the far-field region of any radiator, the wavefront is spherical (even though, as has been discussed in this chapter, the aperture wavefront may be plane). In this spherical-wavefront region of the main beam (i.e., in the far field), if the ray lines are drawn perpendicular to the wavefront, they will constitute a set of diverging (nonparallel) rays. They will appear to be emanating from a point. In the language of geometry, this point is the *center of curvature* of the wavefronts. This point is also called the phase center of the antenna. It is the point from which the radiation appears to be originating.

The calculation of the phase-center location for a given feed radiator may be a complex problem; it is often simpler to adjust its position experimentally until the best pattern is obtained (i.e., narrowest beam in the desired direction, and greatest gain). Methods of performing the necessary pattern and gain measurements are discussed in Ch. 9. A knowledge of the approximate location of the phase center of the feed is of course helpful in this procedure. In most cases it is at or near the geometric center of the feed. For a low flare angle horn, it is near the center of the aperture plane (mouth). However, as the flare is increased, the phase center moves inside the horn. For some types of feed radiators the phase center may change if the frequency of operation is changed; thus this parameter becomes another factor in the determination of the bandwidth of the antenna. (Certain types of log-periodic radiators, discussed in sec. 7.2, are especially subject to this effect, so that their otherwise excellent bandwidth properties may be severely limited when they are used as feed radiators for reflectors and lenses. However, this is not true of all log-periodic types of radiators.)

In addition to the problem of knowing where to position the feed, there is the companion problem of insuring that it will remain at the correct position when subjected to various stresses that may occur due to wind, gravity, ice loading, and so forth. The obvious method of accomplishing this is to support the feed with a strong and rigid mechanical structure. Unfortunately, in the case of a reflector antenna, there is the conflicting requirement that the feed support must not block too many of the reflected rays; it must not be opaque if it is bulky, and if it is opaque it must not be bulky. A common method of support in large paraboloidal reflectors is a tripod or quadrupod attached to the reflector with its apex somewhat beyond the focal point, so that the feed may be nested under the apex. The support booms may be either hollow metal tubes or solid pieces of insulating material, such as fiberglass. When the reflector is small and of short focal length, the waveguide or transmission line may furnish adequate support. Reflectors with feeds supported by these methods are shown in Fig. 6–9.

The fact that the feed support (and the feed itself) blocks the aperture is a disadvantage of many reflector antennas. However, if a paraboloid or parabolic cylinder is cut so that the collimated rays do not "see" the feed radiator, the problem of feed blockage is thereby solved. Figure 6–10 shows how this is done. The parabolic section actually used is shown by the solid curve, while the full (symmetrical) parabolic section is shown dotted. This arrangement avoids blockage but somewhat complicates providing the desired primary pattern taper.

The feed-support is most severe for paraboloidal reflectors when the beam direction must be steerable in any direction, or over a large range of angles. This means that some method of moving the reflector (often called a "dish") must be provided, and the feed must be moved at the same time so as to keep it at the focal point; that is, the feed and the dish must be mechanically connected by a rigid structure. The arrangements of Fig. 6–9 meet this requirement. Feed support is simplified when the antenna need not be moved, that is, when the beam is always to point in a fixed direction. The feed support can then be attached to the antenna base (e.g., the ground) rather than to the dish, and light weight is not as important. This situation occurs, for example, with large reflector antennas used for tropospheric-scatter point-to-point communication at VHF or UHF.

When the feed is located in the aperture of the dish, so that it blocks some of the reflected radiation, the antenna pattern is adversely affected in two ways. The gain is

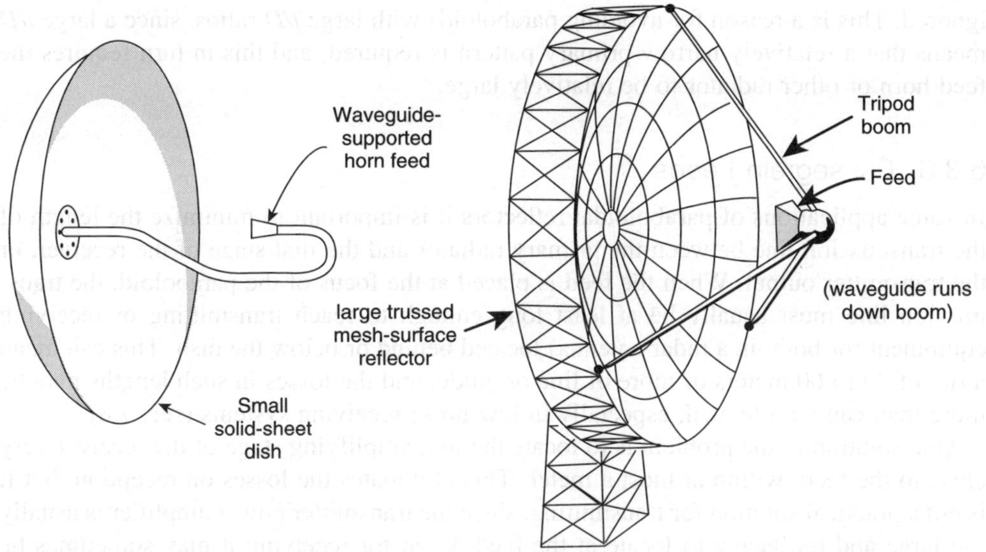

FIGURE 6–9

Two methods of reflector feed support.

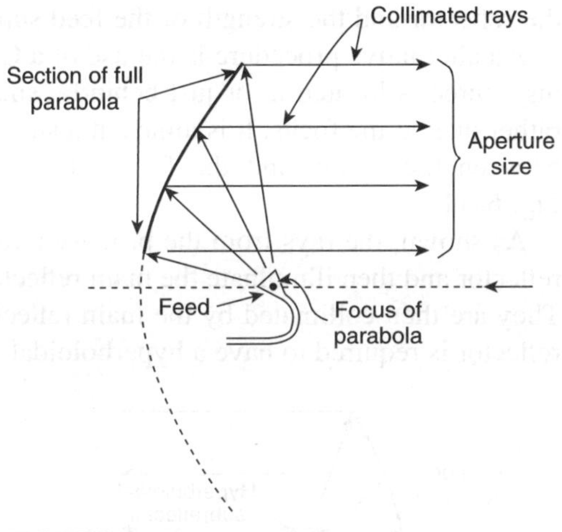

FIGURE 6–10

Offset or "cut" parabolic reflector, showing that collimated rays are not intercepted (blocked) by feed.

somewhat reduced, because some power is reflected into directions other than the forward direction. The side-lobe level is also increased. These are the principal reasons that blocking of the aperture by the feed is undesirable, and for employing a cut reflector, as in Fig. 6–10, if the feed is large, to minimize or eliminate blocking. Another undesirable effect occurs also when the feed is in the collimated beam. Some of the radiation blocked by the feed is reabsorbed—for example, if the feed is a horn, it enters the horn mouth and propagates back down the guide. This in effect creates a reflection mismatch, even though the horn radiating into empty space would properly match the guide. This effect can be compensated for by impedance-matching devices such as those described in sec. 2.3, but this method has the disadvantage of reducing the bandwidth of the antenna. The method of using an offset feed with a cut paraboloid is better; but if the feed is small compared to the total aperture of the antenna, the effects of aperture blocking will be small and can usually be ignored. This is a reason for avoiding paraboloids with large *f/D* ratios, since a large *f/D* means that a relatively narrow primary pattern is required, and this in turn requires the feed horn or other radiator to be relatively large.

6.3.6. Cassegrain Feeds

In some applications of paraboloidal reflectors it is important to minimize the length of the transmission line between the primary radiator and the first stage of the receiver, or the transmitter output. When the feed is placed at the focus of the paraboloid, the transmission line must usually be at least long enough to reach transmitting or receiving equipment (or both, in a radar antenna) located behind or below the dish. This can mean a run of 30 to 60 meters or more of line or guide, and the losses in such lengths may be more than can be tolerated, especially in low-noise receiving systems (sec. 7.8).

One solution to the problem is to locate the first amplifying stage of the receiver very close to the feed, within at most a meter. This eliminates the losses on reception, but it is not a practical solution for transmitting, since the transmitter power amplifier is usually too large and too heavy to locate at the feed. Even for receiving it may sometimes be impractical to locate a preamplifier at the focus because of the difficulty of performing servicing and adjustments. Requirements for cooling and weatherproofing may also be difficult to meet. Finally, some of the very low-noise microwave preamplifiers, such as the maser, may be too large and complicated for this location, depending on the size of the reflector and the strength of the feed support structure.

An alternative procedure is the use of a Cassegrain feed, in which the primary radiating source is located in or just behind a small opening at the vertex of the paraboloid, rather than at the focus. It is aimed at a small secondary reflector or *subreflector* located between the vertex and the focus. The arrangement is shown diagrammatically in Fig. 6–11.

As shown, the rays from the primary radiator are reflected from the Cassegrain subreflector and then illuminate the main reflector just *as if* they had originated at the focus. They are then collimated by the main reflector in the usual way. As indicated, the subreflector is required to have a hyperboloidal curvature to reflect the rays from the source in the correct manner, so as to produce a "virtual source" at the paraboloidal focus. Since the transmitter and receiver are now located out of the ray paths and at a location where mechanical support is not usually a problem, they may be as large and heavy as required. Also, they are relatively accessible for servicing and adjustment.

However, aperture blocking is now produced by the Cassegrain subreflector. This blocking may be tolerated in many

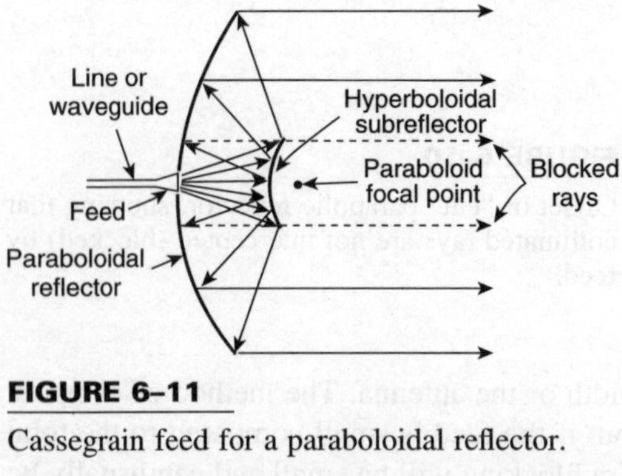

FIGURE 6–11
Cassegrain feed for a paraboloidal reflector.

large-antenna applications in order to gain the advantages of an accessible primary radiator, but it is a defect of the Cassegrain scheme that may be serious. One way of avoiding it is by using an offset reflector, as is sometimes done with focal-point feeds. Another method is a polarization-twisting scheme (Hannan, 1961), if the primary radiator is linearly polarized. The Cassegrain reflector is made in the form of a wire grating rather than a solid metal sheet. The grating wires are parallel to the primary polarization so that total reflection occurs, as required. On the surface of the main paraboloidal reflector there is a special polarization-rotating structure, such that the collimated rays have a polarization rotated 90 degrees with respect to the primary polarization. The Cassegrain grating reflector is transparent to this polarization and hence does not block the radiation. (This polarization-rotation technique can also be used with ordinary paraboloidal feed systems to eliminate mismatch effects resulting from reentry of the reflected waves into the primary radiator. When the polarization is rotated, this reentry will not occur if the feed radiator is insensitive to the reflected polarization, which it ordinarily will be.)

The Cassegrain system is directly copied from the reflector system used in large astronomical optical telescopes, so as to permit the eyepiece to be placed below the main reflector. Fittingly, Cassegrain antennas have often been used as "radio telescopes" for radio astronomy.

6.4. Radiation Patterns of Horn Antennas

6.4.1. Horn Patterns, in General

Waveguide horns are commonly used as feeds for reflectors and lenses. The radiation in front of a horn appears essentially as if radiated from a specific point, that is, the phase front at a fixed distance is almost spherical. Consequently, horns are excellent primary feeds for reflectors and lenses. A good approximation is that the phase center is in the plane of the aperture (the horn's mouth), but waveguide flaring outward toward the mouth may cause the phase center to be slightly behind the aperture plane (Muehldorf 1980).

Beamwidth, and thus gain, of a horn depends mainly on its aperture size relative to wavelength, but beamwidth and gain depend also on the amount of flaring (tapering) of the horn. For a given aperture size, the phase variation across a horn aperture is least, and the gain is maximum, for a long horn with small flare angles. However, for convenience in handling, a horn should be short. An optimum horn is one that compromises in aperture phase error to maximize its gain for its length, and therefore its flare angles are intermediate between slight and abrupt.

Without having specific feed design data available, 3 dB beamwidths for "optimally" flared horns may be used as first estimates. Those beamwidths, repeated from sec. 4.7, are:

$$\theta_E = \frac{56}{d_E} \text{ degrees} \tag{6–19}$$

and

$$\theta_H = \frac{67}{d_H} \text{ degrees} \tag{6–20}$$

where E and H refer to the horn's E and H plane patterns. The symbols d_E and d_H are the aperture dimensions (widths), expressed in wavelengths along the E and H planes.

Graphs of radiation patterns, developed from aperture analyses, known as universal patterns, are available for a variety of horn types and dimensions (Balanis 2005; Love 1993, pp. 15–6–15–9, 15–35). These "universal" patterns provide details of the major lobe shapes for aperture widths as small as 1.5 or 2λ. However, designs for center-fed reflectors and lenses often require feed-horn patterns with dimensions even smaller than 1.5λ. Section 6.4.3 provides guidance on feed design for aperture widths less than 2λ.

Sometimes identical E- and H-plane feed patterns are desired. However, for a conventional tapered waveguide horn, these patterns are unequal and the side lobes are higher in the E plane. This is because the E- and H-plane amplitude distributions of a waveguide are different, with no amplitude taper in the E-plane. Horns designed with corrugated inner walls near the horn's mouth (aperture) reduce differences in E- and H-plane patterns (Love 1993, pp. 15–43), but corrugated horns are heavier, larger, and more expensive than smooth-walled horns.

6.4.2. Shapes of Major Lobes

The design of a wide-angle feed pattern is often critical, because reflector and lens patterns are highly sensitive to the strength of the primary feed pattern at the reflector or lens aperture edges, where the amplitude versus angle of the horn pattern is steepest and thus hardest to control. Therefore, detailed knowledge of the primary feed pattern shape is desired, but sometimes only the horn beamwidth is known. Following (6–15), a good estimate of normalized pattern amplitude, within a main lobe, in terms of 3 dB beamwidth BW_3 is

$$20 \log E(\beta) = -12\left(\frac{\beta}{BW_3}\right)^2 \tag{6–21}$$

Thus, solving for E(β), one obtains

$$E(\beta) = 10^{-0.6\left(\frac{\beta}{BW_3}\right)^2} \tag{6–22}$$

Note that BW_3 is the feed beamwidth between half-power points, but β is measured from the beam center.

For primary feed patterns, antenna designers usually prefer working with the beamwidths between the −10 dB points, instead of the 3 dB beamwidths. Reasons include

(i) the −10 dB levels are nearer the reflector or lens edges, and the antenna side-lobe levels are highly sensitive to the edge illumination, and
(ii) near the −10 dB angles the primary feed (horn) pattern changes more rapidly with angle than at the −3 dB angle, causing overall antenna performance to be more sensitive to the −10 dB locations.

Now let BW_{10} be defined as the full −10 dB beamwidth and let $\beta_{0.1}$ be the angle between the feed's beam center and a −10 dB direction, that is, $BW_{10} = 2\beta_{0.1}$. Then, the relationship between BW_{10} and BW_3 is as follows:

$$20\log E(\beta_{0.1}) = -10 = -12\left(\frac{\beta_{0.1}}{BW_3}\right)^2 = -12\left(\frac{0.5 \cdot BW_{10}}{BW_3}\right)^2 \tag{6–23}$$

or

$$\frac{BW_{10}}{BW_3} = 2\sqrt{\frac{10}{12}} \approx 1.83 \tag{6–24}$$

Finally, the amplitude $E(\beta)$ at angle β, measured from the beam center, in terms of the full −10 dB beamwidth BW_{10} can be expressed as

$$20\log E(\beta) = -12\left(\frac{\beta}{BW_3}\right)^2 = -40\left(\frac{B}{BW_{10}}\right)^2 \tag{6–25}$$

or

$$E(\beta) = 10^{-2\left(\frac{\beta}{BW_{10}}\right)^2} \tag{6–26}$$

6.4.3. Measured Wide-Beamwidth Horn Patterns

As already mentioned, when only major lobe shapes are needed, published universal patterns may be adequately reliable for dimensions as small as 1.5 or 2λ. In reality, patterns from small horns can be affected significantly by radiation from aperture edges. Therefore, for horns having widths of less than 2λ, measured patterns should be used whenever possible.

Figure 6–12 shows −10 dB beamwidth data measured on waveguide horns with small width D to wavelength λ ratios (note that the abscissa is λ/D, not D/λ.). They were obtained from a large number of measurements made over several years at the Radiation Laboratory during *WW* II (Risser 1949, ch. 10, pp. 341–66). The flare angle of the *average* horn is about 20°, which ordinarily indicates small phase variations across the mouths of the horns. Thus, although specific information on phase is unavailable, Fig. 6–12 is useful for providing first approximations for pattern beamwidths for dimensions smaller than 2λ. For brevity, BW_{10} is used herein to denote −10 dB beamwidth (the angle in a principal plane between the two −10 dB directions). Without other measured pattern data available, Fig. 6–12 can serve as a useful starting point for estimating the shape of the major lobe with (6–26), at least for the amplitude at angles between the beam center and the −10 dB points.

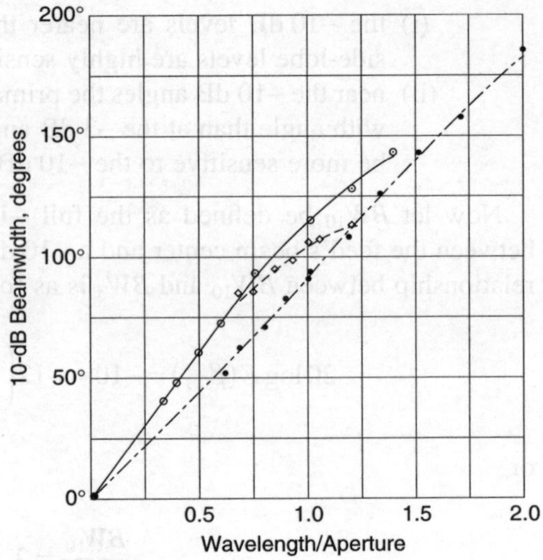

FIGURE 6–12

Measured −10 dB beamwidths of waveguide horns having small phase variations over the apertures. – – – *E*-plane of sectoral horns, —— *H*-plane of pyramidal horns with *E*-plane aperture $\geq\lambda$, ——— *H*-plane of sectoral horns. From Risser (1949, ch. 10, p. 364).

6.4.4. Summary

- Equations (6–19), (6–20), and (6–22) are useful for estimating horn beamwidth and major lobe shape, if the required in-plane horn width exceeds 2λ.
- When more detailed information and level of the larger side lobes are needed, horn dimensions can be obtained from published universal patterns, provided the required in-plane horn width exceeds 2λ.
- When patterns are needed that require feed dimensions smaller than 2λ, a possible step is to estimate aperture dimensions from the −10 dB beamwidth data of Fig. 6–12 and to estimate major lobe shape by using (6–26).
- Primary-feed patterns are critical to antenna design and ordinarily, after initial calculations are made, pattern measurements are necessary if the overall design goals are to be assured.
- In cases involving very low side lobes or patterns of unusual shapes, an overall antenna development may entail several iterative steps including measurement, modification, and analysis.

6.5. Pattern Calculation and Reflector Antenna Design

6.5.1. General Remarks

Calculations for radiation patterns of continuous aperture antennas are in many ways like those for arrays. Basic to the likeness of the two aperture types is a similarity of their main lobe patterns and of details of their patterns at angles out to nearly 90° from broadside (see sec. 5.5.5). Specifically, nearly identical patterns exist if three conditions are met, namely; (1) the aperture widths are at least 5λ in the plane of the patterns, (2) the separation of array elements is $\lambda/2$ or less, and (3) the amplitude and phase distribution on the continuous aperture are, at the coordinates of the array elements, the same as those of the array elements.

A major difference in pattern design between arrays and reflector antennas is, however, that reflectors are illuminated by a primary feed; thus, feed pattern shapes critically affect the secondary (overall) patterns of reflector antennas.

The table of 2β (the total angle a paraboloid subtends) versus f/D ratio, that follows equation (6–16), illustrates the range of feed pattern widths required to subtend the aperture dimension D of a paraboloid versus its f/D ratio. However, as can be seen from Fig. 6–10, smaller feed beamwidths are needed if a sectionalized (cut) parabolic cylinder or a "cut" paraboloid is used. Larger f/D ratios (requiring smaller beamwidths) are usually avoided because, for mechanical rigidity, short focal lengths are desired. On the other hand, short focal lengths require wide feed patterns that require electrically small feeds; and, as discussed in sec. 6.4.3, their patterns are generally less predictable than those of larger feeds.

There are two general types of primary feeds: (a) the point source and (b) a line source. A point source feed is used for illuminating a reflector having axial symmetry (e.g., a paraboloid). Because of this symmetry and for effective use of the cross-sectional area, the limits on compatible feed beamwidths relative to aperture widths constrain the ratio of maximum-to-minimum principal plane patterns to approximately two or three. Consequently, when point-like feeds are used, the range of possible azimuth-to-elevation beamwidth ratios is quite limited. On the other hand, line-source feeds are usually used where azimuth and elevation beamwidths differ greatly. For example, line-source feeds for antennas having beamwidth ratios as large as 20 : 1 are commonly used with surveillance radar.

As discussed for arrays in chapter 5, a pattern versus θ and ϕ is relatively easy to determine, if the aperture distributions are separable in the principal planes and the linear aperture patterns for the two aperture distributions are known. Then, the patterns may be determined from the product of the two linear aperture patterns. Otherwise, as with arrays, the complete pattern calculations require computational intensive, point-to-point numerical calculations. For apertures with nonseparable distributions, patterns for the principal planes are much simpler to calculate than the complete patterns. Then, also as with arrays, the principal plane patterns may be calculated by using an equivalent line aperture for each principal plane and integrating each line aperture distribution over the relevant line aperture.

An example follows in the next section for calculating the illumination along the positive x-axis (in the upper half) of a parabola. In addition, the far-zone pattern in the x-z plane is calculated, based on the calculated x-axis amplitude distribution. In this example, the feed for the parabola is a line source. Thus, the space attenuation between feed and reflector is caused by two-dimensional spreading of the radiation between feed and reflector. A line-source feed is commonly used to illuminate a parabolic cylinder. Then, the illumination is separable because the x-axis illumination of the parabola's aperture will be independent of the illumination of the parabolic cylinder along the length of the line-source feed (y-axis). Thus, as in the case of separable distributions for arrays, the normalized far-zone pattern in the x-z plane is controlled by the x-axis distribution and the pattern in the y-z plane is controlled by the distribution by the y-axis distribution. Additionally as described in chapter 5 for arrays having independent (mathematically separable) x- and y-axis distributions, the pattern versus θ and ϕ may be determined as the product of the two patterns created by the x- and y-axis distributions.

For a paraboloid or a sectional surface area thereof, the steps in calculating detailed patterns are different than for a parabolic cylinder. This is so because the axial symmetry of the reflector surface shape prohibits the illumination of the principal planes being independent of one another. Therefore, as in the case of arrays having nonseparable distributions, a detailed principal plane pattern calculation uses an equivalent line aperture distribution, and each line aperture distribution is integrated over the relevant line aperture. Principal plane patterns are of course much simpler to determine than complete patterns, which require point-to-point numerical calculations over the whole aperture.

6.5.2. Aperture Distribution and Pattern of a Half Parabolic Cylinder

This section describes results of pattern calculations for the top half of a parabolic cylinder that are included in SM 4.9 of the accompanying website. The calculations are made using Mathcad software, and they determine the amplitude distribution for a half parabolic cylinder and its far-zone pattern. The coordinates of Fig. 6–2 are used. In the x-z plane the reflector is a parabola with vertex at $x = z = 0$, with focus on the z-axis, and located only in x-z plane at $x \geq 0$. Additionally, the feed for the reflector is a broadside line source located in the y-z plane and extends from the parabola focus in the negative y direction (into paper). Thus, since the feed radiation versus distance ρ from the focal line diverges only in angle α, the power density and the amplitude of the feed radiation is directly proportion to $1/\rho$ and $1/\sqrt{\rho}$, respectively.

The problem is to determine the amplitude distribution, including the effects of space attenuation, alone the x-axis and the far-zone radiation pattern in the x-z plane. As an example, let the aperture dimension be 1 m in the x-z plane, focal length be 0.5 m, and operating wavelength be 0.1 m. In addition, let the reflector be illuminated with a horn feed located along the focal line that has a 45° half-power width in the x-z plane. The horn feed is set in its elevation angle so that its pattern is centered so that the strength of the feed horn pattern, after including effects of space attenuation, is equal at the top and bottom reflector edges. By trial and errors, it is found that equal edge amplitudes exist if the horn beam center at angle α that is 48° above the z-axis.

Figure 6–13 includes the relative feed amplitude pattern, the space attenuation and the resulting aperture distribution; each expressed in terms of the reflector x coordinate. From these results, the reader will notice that the aperture amplitude illumination is equal at both the top and bottom reflector edges. However, the amplitude is asymmetrical along the x coordinate, and the peak amplitude is not at the center of the parabola's x coordinates. As expected and may be seen in Fig. 6–13, because of path length differences, the space attenuation is asymmetrical along the x coordinate.

Figure 6–14 is a graph of the far-zone pattern, of the illuminated half parabolic cylinder, in the x-z plane. Note that the pattern lacks the deep nulls that are ordinarily seen in calculated far-zone patterns, and the first side lobes are almost indistinguishable from the outer edges of the major lobe. This loss in null-depth is caused by the asymmetry in an aperture amplitude distribution along the x dimension.

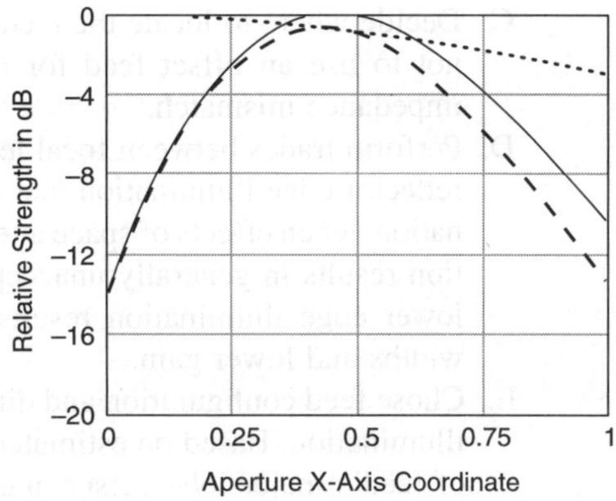

FIGURE 6–13

Relative feed pattern amplitude, space attenuation, and field strength in decibels versus aperture x-axis coordinate.

6.5.3. Steps for Reflector Antenna Design

Steps for developing a parabolic reflector antenna follow. Similar steps are appropriate for other reflector shapes and lenses.

A. Choose approximate overall reflector aperture size. As first approximations:
   - $BW = 70\lambda/D$ for overall aperture dimensions. BW is a desired half-power principal plane beamwidth in degrees, D is antenna dimension in plane of BW, and λ/D is dimensionless.
   - $G = 26{,}000/\theta_1\theta_2$ for gain, where θ_1 and θ_2 are principal plane beamwidths in degrees. Special beam shapes will result in smaller gain. For example, a cosecant-shaped pattern typically causes gain to be reduced by factor of 0.7 (1.5 dB).
   - Allow for increased antenna size needed for structural integrity.

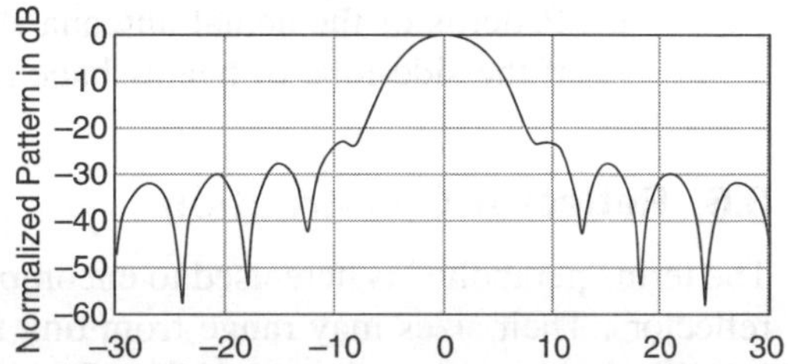

FIGURE 6–14

Normalized far-zone pattern in x-y plane.

B. Select a general reflector shape: e.g., a paraboloid or a parabolic cylinder
   - A simple pyramidal feed horn usually suffices for a paraboloid, if focal-length to aperture-dimension ratios are within acceptable bounds, for example, see table that follows equation (6–16). Consequently, for a paraboloidal reflector, the ratio of large-to-small principal-plane beamwidths is ordinarily limited to less than 2 : 1.
   - Parabolic cylinders require line source feeds, which permit large ratios of principal plane beamwidths and wide-angle scanning. Line source feeds are, however, more difficult to design and fabricate than horns.

C. Decide where to locate the feed with respect to the aperture, i.e., whether or not to use an offset feed for reducing aperture blockage and minimizing impedance mismatch.
D. Perform trades between focal length and feed pattern beamwidths to furnish reflector edge illumination that is at least 10 dB below reflector peak illumination, when effects of space attenuation are included. A larger edge illumination results in generally unacceptable reflector spillover and loss of gain. A lower edge illumination results in lower side lobes, slightly wider beamwidths and lower gain.
E. Chose feed configuration and dimensions based initially on the reflector edge illumination. Based on estimated feed beamwidths, calculate expected shape of feed's major lobe versus angle, by using either (6–22) or (6–26). It may be necessary to make feed measurements, especially if −30 dB or lower side lobes are required or if the estimated feed dimensions are less than 2λ.
F. Calculate illumination versus aperture coordinates based on expected shape of feed's major lobe and reflector geometry.
G. Calculate patterns in principal planes. Special requirements may also require pattern specifications in other planes.
H. Continue the iterative process of selecting focal length and feed configuration until acceptable secondary patterns are calculated. Before desired patterns are obtained, it may be necessary to revise the original estimate of overall reflector dimensions.
I. Patterns of the actual antenna should be measured for assurance, especially if the side-lobe or beam-shape requirements are stringent.

6.6. Reflector Construction

The term "parabolic" is here used to encompass both paraboloidal and parabolic-cylinder reflectors. Their sizes may range from tiny microwave dishes whose apertures are measured in centimeters and up to 100 m. Possibly the largest reflector antenna is located at the Arecibo Ionospheric Observatory at Arecibo, Puerto Rico, where it is used as a scientific instrument for probing the earth's ionosphere, principally at 435 MHz. It is not parabolic but spherical in shape, and uses a specially designed feed for correcting phase errors (spherical aberrations) caused by its shape. The diameter and depth are 305 m and 51 m, respectively; and its surface contains forty-thousand aluminum panels. The reflector was fashioned in a natural "bowl" in the earth and the reflector axis points vertically. The beam may be steered within a moderate angular range about the vertical axis by moving the feed, which is suspended by a system of towers and cables high above the reflector. The reflector itself is of course fixed in position.

The largest fully steerable radio-telescope antennas have diameters of 100 m, and there are two. One is in Effelsberg, Germany, which began operations in 1972. Afterwards, another fully steerable 100-m reflector was constructed at U.S. National Radio Astronomy Observatory at Green Bank, West Virginia (Imbriale and Jones, 2007). The third largest is the 76.2-m diameter radio telescope antenna at Jodrell Bank, in northwest

England. When completed in 1957, it contained the largest fully steerable reflector. There are several in the 45- to 60-m size range, and dishes of 20 and 25 meter diameter are fairly common. However these are still "huge" antennas, especially if they are steerable.

6.6.1. Fabrication Methods

The smaller dishes are generally made of aluminum. They are formed by spinning or stretching aluminum on a solid form, which may be made of wood by standard woodworking techniques, using a parabolic template to check the shape. The template is in the form of a parabolic curve conforming to equation (6–1) for the desired value of f, the focal length. It may be made of metal, plastic, or any stiff material. If a paraboloid is being formed, the template is arranged to rotate about the desired parabolic axis. For a parabolic cylinder, it is provided with a translational axis on which it can be moved along a line parallel to the desired focal line. This technique can be employed for fabricating dishes up to about 3 meters in diameter. Very small reflectors may be cast and then machined if a precise surface is required.

For larger dishes the parabolic reflector must usually be supported by structural stiffening members attached to its back surface. The usual fabrication procedure is to construct this backup structure first. Radial members that are parabolically curved to the correct shape are joined by circular members to form a paraboloid, or similar pieces are connected by straight pieces to form a parabolic cylinder. Additional interconnections may be made to provide the required strength and stiffness. Finally, the reflecting surface is laid over and attached to this structural support. Again, the parabolic shape may be checked for correctness by means of a template. Shims may be added or removed to make final corrections. The surface may be solid sheet metal, perforated sheets, or a metallic mesh, in the form of panels of convenient size. If each panel is large compared to the wavelength of operation, it is ordinarily not necessary to provide electrical bonding of adjacent panels at the adjoining edges, although it may be mechanically desirable to do so. The purpose of using perforated sheets or mesh material instead of solid sheets is to reduce the total weight of the dish and to make it have less wind resistance. The perforations or mesh openings must be small compared to the wavelength, preferably less than 1/16 wavelength in the direction perpendicular to the polarization of the radiation if the polarization is linear. In the other direction the opening size is noncritical.

These descriptions of fabrication techniques are not detailed, and do not cover all possible techniques and materials. The purpose here is solely to convey a general idea of the methods used. Furthermore, it is to be recognized that the criticalness of reflector surface details is dependent on possible special patterns requirements, such as very low side lobes and/or back radiation.

6.6.2. Reflector Surface Accuracy Requirements

The surface of a reflector must conform to the true parabolic curve described by equations (6–1) or (6–2) to within a fraction of a wavelength in order to provide the desired plane wavefront of the reflected radiation. But perfect accuracy is unattainable, and construction of a precise surface is very expensive. It is desirable, therefore, to know what degree of inaccuracy can be tolerated without serious sacrifice of performance. Theoreticians have studied the question of how much deviation from a true parabolic surface is permissible, assuming that the deviations are of a *random* nature—that is, that they are not of a regular nature. An intuitive understanding of the effect of surface irregularities can be obtained from Fig. 1–6 (chapter 1). As shown, the total reflection consists of a specular (desired) component and a scattered or diffuse (undesired) component.

The generally accepted rule-of-thumb figure is that the permissible deviation is 1/32 to 1/16 wavelength. Thus the irregularity of the reflector surface in effect determines the maximum frequency at which it can be used successfully; the higher the frequency of operation desired, the more precisely accurate the surface must be. Appendix I discusses relatively simple calculations on the effects of random phase errors on antenna patterns.

An analysis performed by Ruze (1966) gives detailed information on this matter. The random deviations of the surface from a true parabolic shape cause diffuse reflection that increases the side-lobe level and reduces the directive gain. Ruze has shown quantitatively how these effects are related to the root-mean-square (rms) deviation of the reflector from the exactly correct surface. He showed that a given rms deviation has a greater effect on side-lobe level in a small reflector than in a large one, and also that the effect depends on the *correlation interval* of the irregularities. Correlation interval is a statistical concept. If the individual "bumps" of the surface extend over a small area, the correlation interval is small. If they extend over a larger area, as would be true of a "wavy" rather than a "bumpy" surface, the correlation interval is larger. In terms of these concepts, Ruze showed that a given magnitude of rms deviation from the true surface causes a greater increase of side lobes and reduction of gain when the correlation interval is large than when it is small.

His paper contains curves giving the results for specific cases. As an illustration, a paraboloidal reflector of circular aperture, having a diameter of 25 wavelengths and typically tapered illumination, will have an additional side-lobe level of −20 dB when the rms deviation of the reflector is 1/32 wavelength if the correlation interval is one wavelength. But if the correlation level is only a quarter of the wavelength, the additional side-lobe level will be only about −35 dB. By "additional side-lobe level" it is meant that the relative power of the side lobes due to reflector inaccuracies will be added to the relative power of whatever side lobes would be present if the reflector were perfect. As an example of how this "addition" would be computed, suppose that the side-lobe level with a perfectly accurate reflector would be −20 dB, which corresponds to a power level of 1/100 or 0.01 of the main-beam level. Then an additional −20 dB side-lobe level would add another relative power level of 0.01, giving a total level of 0.02. Thus the combined effects give a net side-lobe level of −17 dB. On the other hand, an additional −35 dB side-lobe contribution corresponds to an additional 1/3000, or roughly 0.0003, so that the total in this case becomes 0.0103, which is negligibly different from −20 dB.

Another factor of great importance is the rigidity of the reflector—its resistance to deformation due to wind or gravitational forces (including additional loading that may be imposed by ice in the colder climates). Gravitational forces are usually important only in steerable reflectors that may point sometimes at the horizon and sometimes at the zenith or intermediate elevation angles. If the reflector shape is paraboloidal at one of these angles, the loading at other angles may be such that it will deform, that is, the edges of the dish may sag differentially. This effect is important only for large heavy reflectors. Deviations of this type will have a serious effect on the pattern, however, since they are of the "large correlation interval" type. A related effect is the possible variable effect of gravity on sag of the feed support structure, for different elevation angles of the antenna. The net effect of reflector deformation and feed-support deformation can be separated into two parts. One is a deterioration of the pattern—increase of side-lobe level and reduction of gain; the other is a shift in the direction of the maximum of the beam, which may cause angle-measurement errors in a radar or radio-astronomy system unless the shift is known and corrected in interpretation of data.

Distortion of the antenna by wind forces can also be serious, and resulting shifts of the beam direction cannot be corrected by a "calibration" as can be done for gravitational shifts. Wind forces, as previously mentioned, can be reduced by using perforated or mesh material for the reflector surface ("skin"). However, the most serious consideration in the reduction of wind force is usually that the antenna may be overturned in a high wind, or that the steering motors may be unable to overcome an opposing wind force. Most large steerable antennas, in fact, will not operate in very high winds, and are usually stowed (locked in a fixed position) when winds exceed 30 or 40 mph. Some types of moderate-sized steerable antennas, however, such as those of radars for air traffic control or for military and naval applications, are capable of operating in fairly high winds.

6.7. Corner-Reflector Antennas

Although the reflectors considered in this chapter are basically restricted to those having curved surfaces to produce a focusing or collimating action, thus eliminating plane reflectors from consideration, there is a type of reflector that represents an intermediate case, namely, the corner reflector. It is somewhat analogous to a parabolic cylinder in that it is a "surface of translation," requiring a line source of illumination. It is formed by the intersection of two plane reflectors, usually at right angles ("square corner"). It is most often fed by a dipole or a collinear dipole array. A cross section of a typical arrangement is shown in Fig. 6–15a, and a perspective view is given in Fig. 6–15b.

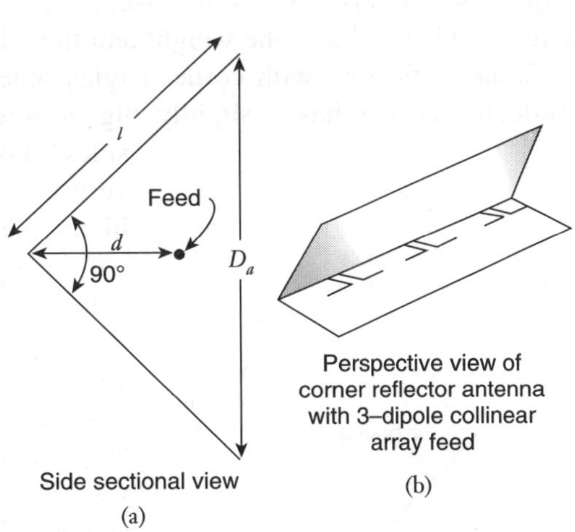

FIGURE 6–15
Corner-reflector antenna.

The aperture dimension, D_a, may be between one and two wave-lengths. The feed-to-vertex distance, d, is made equal to half the side length, l. Thus the design equations are

$$d = \frac{l}{2} \tag{6–27}$$

$$D_a = 1.414l = 2.828d \tag{6–28}$$

(The second equation is obtained from fact that the hypotenuse of a right triangle is the square root of the sum of the squares of the other two sides.) The distance d is generally made to be between 1/3 and 2/3 wavelength. A thorough discussion of corner-reflector antenna design is given by Kraus and Marhefka (2002).

These equations are valid only within the stated range of values of D_a. Within this range, increasing the size does not greatly affect the beamwidth and gain, but the radiation resistance and the bandwidth are increased. It is apparent from the fact that the maximum allowable value of D_a is about two wavelengths that the beamwidth in this dimension is fairly broad; it is about 40 degrees. In the other dimension, as with the parabolic cylinder the beamwidth is determined entirely by the feed radiator, which may be a linear array with a fairly narrow beam. If a beamwidth in the corner-aperture dimension of appreciably less than 40 degrees is desired, a parabolic-cylinder reflector should be used instead of the corner. (The same feed may be used, positioned on the focal line of the parabolic cylinder.) The directivity of a corner-reflector antenna is approximately 10 dB greater than that of a dipole or of a linear dipole array by itself.

The surfaces of a corner reflector are frequently, in fact usually, made of spaced wires or tubes parallel to the vertex, rather than solid sheet metal. The spacing is a small fraction of a wavelength, and for polarization parallel to the wires the reflection is practically as good as that from a solid reflector. If the feed is a dipole or dipoles parallel to the vertex, as is almost always the case, the polarization will be correct. The use of spaced wires or tubes reduces the weight and the wind resistance.

Corner reflectors with corner angles other than 90 degrees are sometimes used. A 60-degree corner has a slightly higher directivity than a 90-degree corner, but the sides must be longer to realize the increase. (The vertex-to-feed distance must also be greater.) It is likely that the greater directivity may be obtained with less total reflector surface by using a parabolic cylinder, or by stacking two 90-degree corners as shown in Fig. 6–16. This arrangement is in effect an array of corner reflectors. The two line sources must of course be fed in phase with each other. (Incidentally, parabolic cylinders may also be stacked in this way. The gain will be about the same as that of a single reflector of the same total aperture, but there may be some advantages in reduction of reflector depth.)

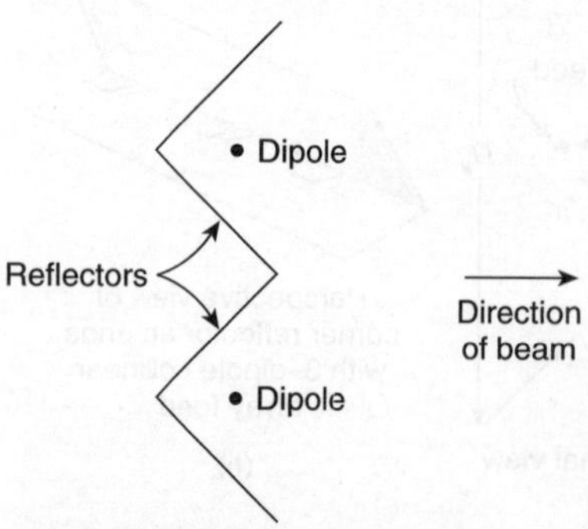

FIGURE 6–16

Stacked corner reflectors.

6.8. Lens Antennas

Lenses are used in approximately the same applications as are paraboloidal and parabolic-cylinder reflectors, though the frequency range of common use is somewhat higher, beginning at perhaps 1 GHz. Their greatest use is at 3 GHz and above. At the lower frequencies they become too bulky and heavy.

6.8.1. Optical Lenses

The collimating action of a simple optical lens is shown in Fig. 6–17. The behavior is shown for a source on the axis at the focal distance from the lens, resulting in collimated rays (plane wavefronts) on the other side of the lens. These collimated rays are parallel to the lens axis, an imaginary line through the optical center of the lens from the focal point.

The rays from the point source at the focus diverge uniformly in all directions. A cone of these rays is intercepted by the lens. The material of the lens has an index of refraction that is (in the usual case when the external medium is air or vacuum) greater than that of the surrounding medium. (Optical lenses are of course usually made of glass, although transparent plastics are sometimes used.) In accordance with the principle illustrated by Fig. 1–3, chapter 1, the lens bends the rays that impinge upon it at any angle other than perpendicularly to the surface. That is, all rays are bent except the one from the focus through the center of the lens. Unlike the flat surface shown in Fig. 1–3, the lens surfaces are curved, so that different parts of the lens produce different amounts of bending. The result is that the rays from the focal point, upon emerging from the opposite side of the lens, are parallel rather than divergent. For a simple thin optical lens, the surface curvature to produce this result is spherical; that is, the lens surface conforms to a portion of the surface of a sphere.

This collimating action does not occur if the source is placed closer to or farther from the lens than the focal point. Then the rays on the emergent (right-hand) side of the lens will (respectively) diverge or converge. Both these types of behavior are useful in optical applications of lenses, but in radio applications the collimating behavior depicted in Fig. 6–17 is practically always desired. The rays on the right-hand side of the lens, in Fig. 6–17, are in effect "focused at infinity," that is, parallel rays may be regarded as converging to a point at an infinite distance. This description is, however, the geometric-optics approximation of the actual behavior, as has been noted in sec. 6.2.

A lens, like a reflector, is a reciprocal device. A source at the focus, on (say) the left-hand side of the lens, produces parallel rays on the right-hand side. Conversely, incoming parallel rays on the right-hand side will converge to a point on the left-hand side, at the focus. These two cases correspond to the use of a lens antenna for transmitting and receiving, respectively. They also illustrate the general principle of reciprocity, discussed in sec. 1.3.

Many of the principles and practices discussed in connection with parabolic reflectors also apply to lenses used as antennas. In particular, this is true of the principles of illumination taper, aperture shape, and taper due to surface curvature in relation to side-lobe

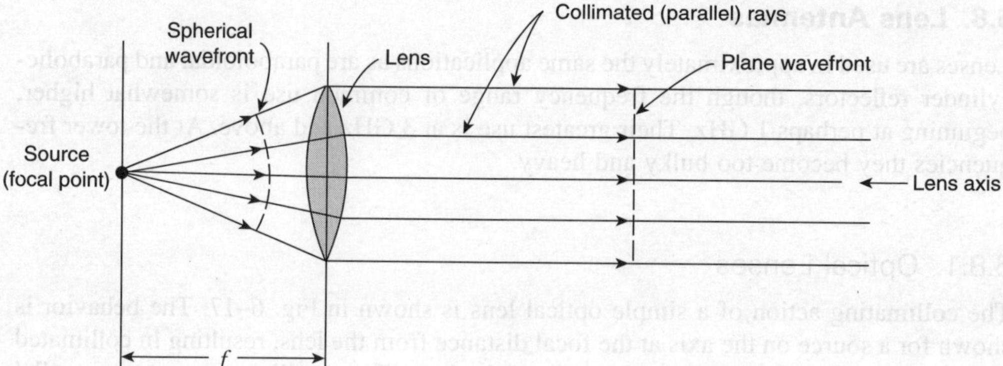

FIGURE 6–17.

Collimation of rays by a simple converging lens.

levels, and of the relations between aperture size, beamwidth, and gain. Feed radiator requirements are in general quite similar, except that aperture blocking effects do not occur, as already noted. As will be discussed in sec. 6.7 in more detail, a collimated beam may also be formed in a direction not parallel to the lens axis, by moving the source (feed) away from the focus in the focal plane—that is, perpendicularly to the lens axis—as was also indicated to be true for parabolic reflectors, for limited deviations from the optical axis.

6.8.2. Lens Surface Configurations

The foregoing discussion of the optical properties of lenses considers the ray behavior in a single plane. If the surfaces of the lens have the same shape in all axial planes—that is, if they are "surfaces of revolution"—the same ray behavior is observed in all planes through the lens axis, and rays from a point source will be collimated (as in Fig. 6–17). A lens of this type is known in antenna applications as a *rotational lens*. If, on the other hand, the lens surfaces are curved in one direction only and are straight in the perpendicular direction, the focusing or collimating action will take place in one plane only, so that a line source of radiation is required. This type of lens is a *cylindrical* lens. The two types are analogous in their behavior and feed requirements to the paraboloidal and parabolic-cylinder reflectors. Lenses may also have apertures that are circular, elliptical, rectangular, or other shapes.

The surfaces of simple optical lenses are spherical. Those of lenses used for radio applications generally have a more complicated curvature. One surface of a lens may be curved and the other plane, or both surfaces may be curved. Whereas the refracting material (e.g., glass) of optical lenses usually has an index of refraction (n) greater than one, the refracting region of a radio lens may have n either greater or less than one. Therefore the curved surfaces of convergent radio lenses may be either convex or concave. (A glass optical lens, to be convergent—that is, capable of collimating rays from a point or line

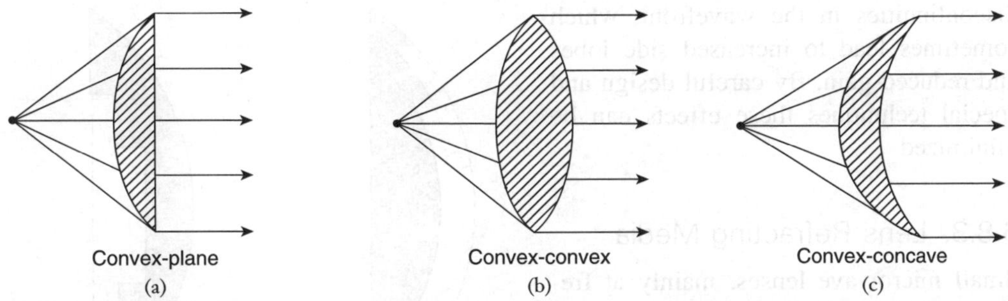

FIGURE 6–18.

Lens surface curvature combinations for $n > 1$.

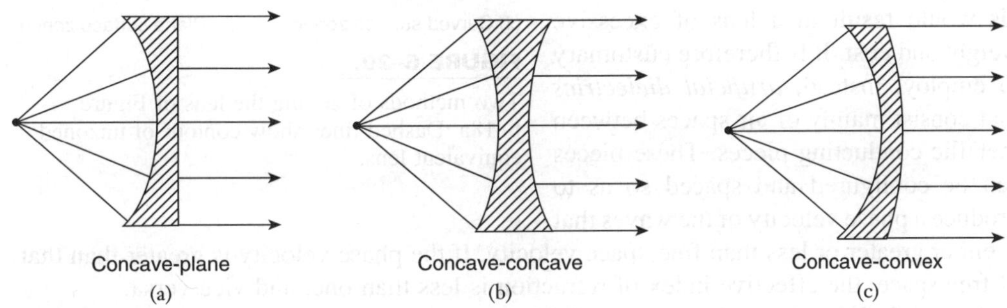

FIGURE 6–19.

Lens surface curvature combinations for $n < 1$.

source—must have at least one convex surface.) If the index of refraction is less than one ($n < 1$), one or both of the curved surfaces will be concave, whereas for $n > 1$ one or both will be convex. It is also possible to have one surface convex and one concave, provided that the convex surface has the greater curvature for $n > 1$ and vice versa for $n < 1$. The various possibilities are shown in Figs. 6–18 and 6–19. The curvatures are in all cases calculated to produce the right amount of total ray bending at the two surfaces so that the rays from a focal point or line will issue from the opposite lens surface all parallel, that is, collimated.

Lenses having simple curved and plane surfaces may be very thick, and therefore excessively bulky and heavy. Also, waves passing through the thickest portions of the lens may suffer considerable loss of power, since the lens structure or material may be dissipative. To offset these effects, lens surfaces can be *zoned*. That is, at definite distances from the center of the lens, the surface is "stepped" so that its total thickness is reduced. The depth of each step is such that the rays passing through the lens on each side of the step have path lengths that differ by a full wavelength; hence they are in-phase. The wavefront issuing from the lens is therefore the same as if zoning were not used. Figure 6–20 shows cross sections of zoned lenses corresponding to the unzoned types of Fig. 6–18a. Although zoning provides the benefits mentioned, it also introduces discontinuities in the wavefront, which sometimes lead to increased side lobes and reduced gain. By careful design and special techniques these effects can be minimized.

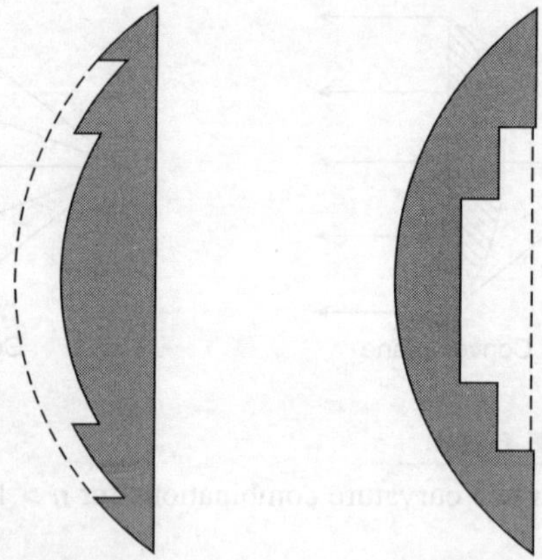

FIGURE 6–20.

Two methods of zoning the lens of Figure 6–18a. Dashed lines show contour of unzoned equivalent lens.

6.8.3. Lens Refracting Media

Small microwave lenses, mainly at frequencies above 10 GHz, can be made of solid dielectric materials having indexes of refraction greater than one ($n > 1$). For the larger lenses, however, these materials would result in a lens of excessive weight and cost. It is therefore customary to employ, instead, *artificial dielectrics* that consist mainly of air spaces between metallic conducting pieces. These pieces can be configured and spaced so as to produce a phase velocity of the waves that is either greater or less than free-space velocity. If the phase velocity is greater than that of free space, the effective index of refraction is less than one, and vice versa.

Artificial-dielectric media may be divided into three classes: (1) path-length media; (2) metallic-obstacle delay media; (3) metal-plate waveguide media. The first two types produce the effect of an index of refraction greater than one; the last type has a phase velocity greater than that of free space (just as ordinary waveguides do, as discussed in sec. 2.5), and hence an index of refraction less than one.

A path-length medium is created by forcing the waves to follow a path within the lens that is longer than a straight-line path. Thus, even though the actual velocity in the medium may be the same as in free space, the effect is that of a lower phase velocity. One way of accomplishing this, for example, is to force the waves to travel between parallel metal plates that are formed into a special tin-hat shaped "geodesic" lens (see sec. 6.8.8).

The metallic-obstacle delay medium consists of an array of small metallic objects, such as spheres or cubes, separated by a nonconducting low-dielectric-constant material (such as "polyfoam") that is used primarily to support the metallic objects. (This type of lens would function equally well with air between the metal pieces if they could somehow be supported by the air.) The size, shape, and spacing of the metal pieces determine the effective dielectric constant and refractive index.

The metal-plate waveguide refracting medium consists of thin metal plates parallel to one another in the direction of propagation through the lens. The velocity of propagation (phase velocity) through the space between the plates is determined by the plate spacing just as it is for ordinary waveguides. Such a parallel-plate region is like a waveguide with the dimension b of Fig. 2–11 (chapter 2) of very large value, and with the dimension

a close to the cutoff value (half of the free-space wavelength) so that the phase velocity will be high. The plates must operate in the fundamental TE mode (electric field parallel to the plates), and thus such a lens will function properly only for a proper polarization of the feed. However, it is also possible to have two sets of plates running in perpendicular directions so that a set of square waveguide channels is formed. This is known as "egg crate" construction, and it may be used with waves of any polarization.

6.8.4. Variable-Index-of-Refraction Lenses

The lenses considered thus far depend for their action on the curvature of their surfaces. The medium between these surfaces must have an index of refraction different from that of the surrounding medium, which is generally air with $n \approx 1$. Within the lens, however, the index has been assumed to be the same everywhere. It is entirely possible, however, to construct a lens in which the index of refraction varies within the lens. It would be possible in this way to construct a converging lens whose thickness was constant, that is, with plane surfaces. Alternatively, the variable-index construction may be used to make lenses with most unusual properties.

An example that has found important applications is the *Luneberg lens*, which is a sphere whose index of refraction (n) varies as a function of the radial distance from the center of the sphere according to the formula:

$$n(r) = \sqrt{2 - (r/R)^2} \tag{6–29}$$

where R is the radius of the sphere and r is the radial coordinate of any point within the sphere. It is apparent that $n = 1$ at the surface of the sphere ($r = R$) and has a maximum value of $\sqrt{2}$ at the center of the sphere ($r = 0$). Such a lens has an interesting and useful property; it will collimate the rays from a feed source placed anywhere on its surface. The collimated rays will emerge on the opposite side of the sphere from the feed point, traveling in the direction of the line from the feed point through the center of the sphere. Thus a beam can be caused to point in any direction by moving the feed to an appropriate point on the lens. The behavior of the rays in a Luneberg lens is shown in Fig. 6–21. A sphere having the required variation of refractive index can be made using either an artificial dielectric medium or concentric spherical shells of solid dielectric material of different indexes of refraction. The effective refractive index of a solid dielectric material can be reduced to a desired value for this purpose by manufacturing it in the form of a "foamed" solid containing air spaces.

There are also two-dimensional instead of spherical (three-dimensional) Luneberg lenses. Two-dimensional variable-index-of-refraction lenses focus in only one plane (Johnson 1993, p. 16–26). They have dielectric properties like a thin cylindrical slice cut through the center of a 3-D Luneberg lens. An early type consisted of nearly flat plates partially filled with dielectric material and it operated in the TE_{10} waveguide mode. In addition, there have been flat-plate lenses that operated in the TEM mode. One of these used concentrate rings of different dielectric constants and another used partially filled

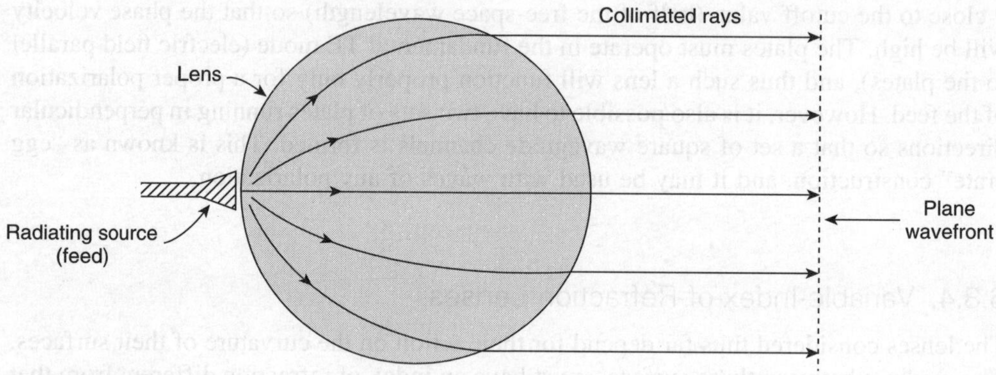

FIGURE 6–21.
Rays in a Luneberg lens.

dielectric plates that are tapered to zero thickness at the lens edges. Another 2-D type lens is the geodesic Luneberg lens, described in sec. 6.8.8.

6.8.5. Focusing with Dielectric and Metal Plate Lenses

A number of lens shapes for dielectric and metal-plate lenses are shown, respectively, in Figs. 6–18 and 6–19. The index of refraction for dielectric lenses (Fig. 6–18) is greater than unity, and less than unity for TE_{10}-mode waveguide lenses (Fig. 6–19). Only the simple lenses of Figs. 6–18(a) and 6–19(a) will be addressed here. They have one refracting surface, the other being normal to the rays. The other lens shapes of Figs. 6–18 and 6–19 have two refracting surfaces. Although more complex, the techniques for designing lenses with double refractive surfaces are also well established.

Discussions on lens focusing are limited in this book to determining lens shapes needed to equalize electrical path lengths. A proper lens design includes other specifications. For example, beamwidths and side lobes depend on the amplitude distribution across the aperture. However, control of the aperture amplitude requires an understanding of how refraction within a lens modifies the amplitude across the aperture. Also, to reduce weight and size, lenses are shaped by zoning as illustrated in Fig. 6–20. Lens designs also must address losses caused by air-lens reflections and absorption, and the effects of lens dimensions on the operating bandwidth. Kock (1946), Risser (1949, ch. 11), and Bodnar (2007) are recommended additional reading on the design of lenses.

6.8.6. Dielectric Lenses

Figure 6–22 shows ray paths through a plano-convex lens, which is symmetrical about the line FQ_2. Assume that a focused antenna consists of a primary feed at point F and the lens. Then the phase along the aperture of dimension D is constant, and the electrical lengths FPP_2 and FQQ_2 are equal. The phase delay for a path length l, expressed in radians is $(2\pi l)/\lambda$. Then, setting the electrical lengths FPP_2 and FQQ_2 equal gives

$$\frac{r}{\lambda_0}+\frac{PP_2}{\lambda_d}=\frac{L}{\lambda_0}+\frac{QQ_1}{\lambda_d}+\frac{Q_1Q_2}{\lambda_d} \quad (6\text{–}30)$$

Note from Fig. 6–22 that $PP_2 = Q_1Q_2$ and $r\cos\beta = (L + QQ_1)$. Therefore, from (6–30), the electrical lengths of paths FPP_2 and FQQ_2 are equal when

$$\frac{r}{\lambda_0}=\frac{L}{\lambda_0}+\frac{r\cos\beta-L}{\lambda_d} \quad (6\text{–}31)$$

where

λ_0 = wavelength in free space (air or vacuum)
λ_d = wavelength in the dielectric lens

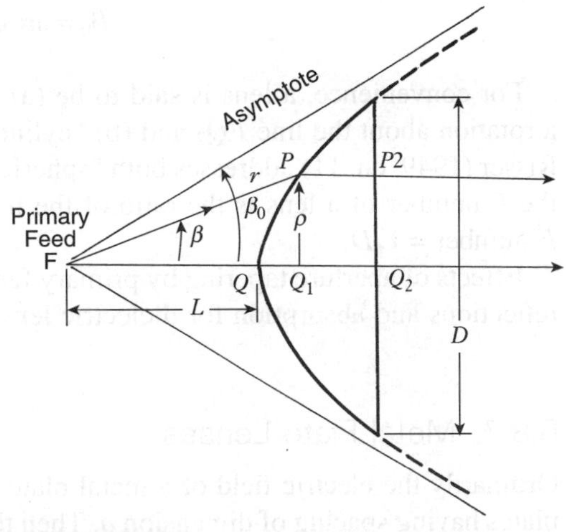

FIGURE 6–22.
Path lengths in a dielectric lens.

From equation (1–19), chapter 1, the index of refraction n of a lossless substance is expressed as

$$n=\frac{c}{v}=\frac{\sqrt{\mu\varepsilon}}{\sqrt{\mu_0\varepsilon_0}} \quad (6\text{–}32)$$

For most dielectric materials $\mu = \mu_0$, and thus for a lossless material usually

$$n=\sqrt{\varepsilon/\varepsilon_0} \quad (6\text{–}33)$$

where $\varepsilon/\varepsilon_0$ is the relative permittivity of the material having index of refraction n.

Now, from the general relationship $f\lambda = v$ and (6–32), for a material having index of refraction n, and with its wave velocity v_d and wavelength λ_d

$$n=\frac{c}{v_d}=\frac{f\lambda_0}{f\lambda_d}=\frac{\lambda_0}{\lambda_d} \quad (6\text{–}34)$$

Then, multiplying (6–31) by λ_0, and solving for r the following is obtained

$$r=\frac{(n-1)L}{n\cos\beta-1} \quad (6\text{–}35)$$

Equation (6–35) gives the shape of the lens, and it describes a hyperbola having asymptotes at an angle β_0 with respect to the axis of symmetry. With r very large, it can be seen from (6–35) that $n\cos\beta$ is then approximately one, and thus $\cos\beta_0 \cong (1/n)$ and

$$\beta_0 = \arccos(1/n). \tag{6–36}$$

For convenience, a lens is said to be (a) "spherical" if the surfaces are generated by a rotation about the line FQ_2 and (b) "cylindrical" if it has symmetry along a focal line. Risser (1949, ch. 11) addresses both "spherical" and "cylindrical" lenses. Parenthetically, the F number of a lens is the ratio of the focal distance L to the lens diameter D; thus, F number = L/D.

Effects of aperture tapering by primary feeds, and losses caused either by air-dielectric reflections and absorption for dielectric lenses are addressed by Risser (1949, ch. 11).

6.8.7. Metal Plate Lenses

Ordinarily the electric field of a metal plate lens is oriented parallel to the planes of the plates having spacing of dimension a. Then the plates are a guide for the waves providing that $a \geq \lambda_0/2$. If $a \leq \lambda_0$, the spacing is said to be below critical and the plates are then opaque. In accordance with equations (2–70) and (2–72), chapter 2, the wavelength of the waves propagating within air-filled plates is

$$\lambda_g = \frac{\lambda_0}{\sqrt{1-(\lambda_0/2a)^2}} \tag{6–37}$$

Thus, following (6–34),

$$n = \frac{\lambda_0}{\lambda_d} = \sqrt{1-(\lambda_0/2a)^2} \tag{6–38}$$

Figure 6–23 illustrates a cylindrical metal-plate lens illuminated by an E-plane line source feed. The plates are each identically shaped and spacing between plates is a constant value a. Therefore n is determined by (6–38) above.

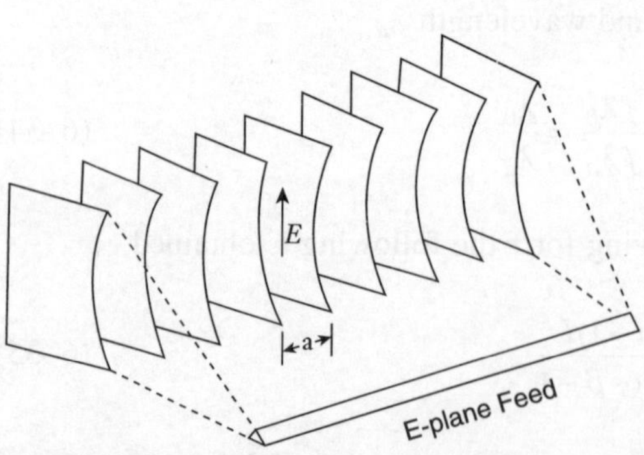

FIGURE 6–23.
Cylindrical metal waveguide lens with plate spacing a and illuminated by a vertically polarized line-source feed.

Figure 6–24 shows ray paths through a metal plate lens, which is symmetrical about the line FQ_1. Assume a focused antenna consists of a primary feed at point F and the lens. Then the phase along the aperture of dimension D is constant, and the electrical lengths FPP_1 and FQQ_1 are equal. Recall that electrical phase of a path of length l expressed in radians is $2\pi l/\lambda$ Thus, by equating the electrical lengths of paths FPP_1 and FQQ_1 and dividing by 2π, one finds

$$\frac{L}{\lambda_0} + \frac{QQ_1}{\lambda_g} = \frac{r}{\lambda_0} + \frac{PP_1}{\lambda_g}$$

or

$$\frac{L}{\lambda_0} = \frac{r}{\lambda_0} + \frac{PP_1 - QQ_1}{\lambda_g} = \frac{r}{\lambda_0} + \frac{L - r\cos\beta}{\lambda_g} \tag{6–39}$$

Finally, by substituting n for λ_0/λ_g in (6–39) and solving for r, one obtains

$$r = \frac{(1-n)L}{1 - n\cos\beta} \tag{6–40}$$

where

λ_0 = wavelength in free space (air or vacuum)
λ_g = wavelength between the metal plates

The reader will notice that (6–40) for the metal plate lens is equal to (6–35) for the dielectric lens. However, because $n < 1$, to make both the numerator and denominator of (6–40) positive, one had to first multiply both by –1. As noted previously with $n > 1$, (6–35) has the shape of a hyperbola. However, with $n < 1$, (6–40) has the shape of an ellipse.

Generally, a metal plate lens is more frequency sensitive than a dielectric lens, in that it focuses only for a relatively small bandwidth. Recall that (6–40) must be satisfied for the lens to be perfectly focused. However, for waveguide, n is frequency dependent. Thus, a metal plate lens can be perfectly focused only at one frequency. As with dielectric lenses (Fig. 6–20), metal plate lenses are zoned (stepped) to reduce weight and to increase bandwidth. Even so, depending on the desired side-lobe level, good metal-plate lens performance is limited to bandwidths of only a few percent (Kock 1946).

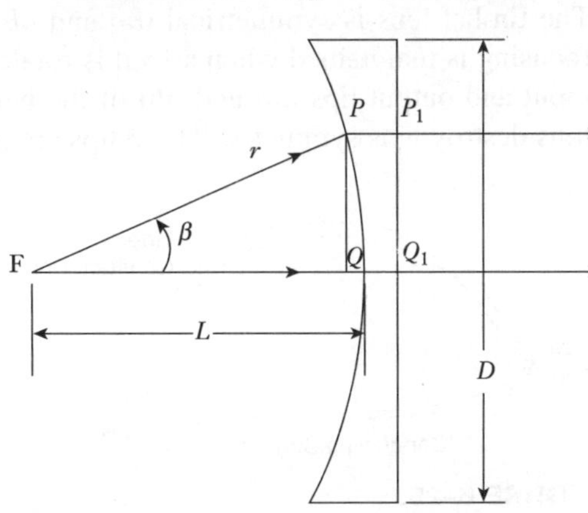

FIGURE 6–24.
Air and waveguide paths within a metal plate lens.

6.8.8. Geodesic Luneberg Lenses

Fermat's principle of least time is a fundamental law of optics. It may be expressed as follows: "When a ray passes from one point to another by any number of reflections or refractions, the path taken by the ray is the one for which the corresponding time of traversal is the least." Another relevant definition is that of a geodesic: which is the shortest line between two points, where the line is constrained to follow a surface. Thus, the shortest path that a person can travel between New York and London is a geodesic, because the shortest path is constrained to follow the earth's surface. Therefore, for a medium that provides a constant propagation velocity, a natural result of Fermat's principle is that the path of an electromagnetic wave is a geodesic. Consequently, focusing occurs by forcing electromagnetic waves in air to travel along curved surfaces.

To appreciate what a geodesic lens accomplishes, we first consider the length required of a sectorial H-plane horn (Fig. 4–21, chapter 4), if it has an aperture width d_H of 50λ at $\lambda = 0.1$ m. The far-zone equation $L = 2D^2/\lambda$ of Appendix F, that results in 22.5° phase error across an aperture, indicates a required horn length L of 500 m. Obviously, this length is impractical. However, as will now be discussed, a geodesic lens of 50λ i.e., 5 m diameter can provide a 5 m aperture with no phase error.

Geodesic lenses focus in one plane by having equal physical path lengths between a point and a line, as now described. Advantages over dielectric lenses include very wide bandwidth, and excellent impedance properties. Additionally, mechanical tolerances are not severe, and appropriate manufacturing techniques coupled with good shop practice can produce effective geodesic lenses at moderate cost.

A basic geodesic lens consists of two evenly spaced, rotational symmetric, conducting surfaces. Ordinarily, propagation within the surfaces is in the TEM mode for which wave velocity is that of free space. Thus, the focusing between a feed point and the aperture results because all path lengths are equal, and consequently such a lens is focused over a very wide bandwidth. Figure 6–25 shows an example lens with dashed lines indicating two of the equal path lengths between a point and a straight line. The paths of the rays as seen from a top view, when projected onto a planar surface, are the same as the paths within a thin cylindrical slice cut through the center of a three-dimensional Luneberg lens. Consequently, a geodesic lens focuses in only one plane.

Figure 6–26 shows cross sections of previously developed geodesic Luneberg lenses. Note the input and output lips designated *oa* and *ob* at the edges (rims) of the lenses. The tin-hat lens is symmetrical (*ao* and *ob* are identical) and has horizontal lips. Thus focusing is maintained when a feed is rotated along the rim through 360°. However, the input and output lips (*ao* and *ob*) of the helmet and clam-shell lenses are different and thus destroy lens symmetry. These lips are provided to allow beam scanning with multiple, rotating feeds over a limited angular sector.

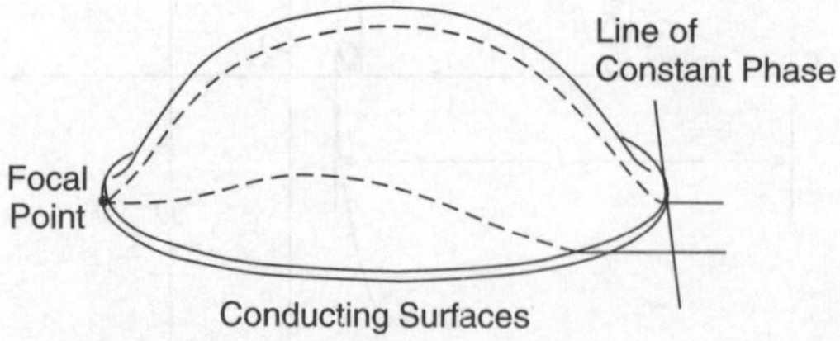

FIGURE 6–25.

Paths through a geodesic lens for two of the rays of a collimated beam (from Johnson 1962), courtesy of *The Microwave Journal*.

Figure 6–27 illustrates the use of a geodesic lens for exciting a line source reflector feed for a scanning antenna. The geodesic lens and nonfocusing flat-plate extensions transform a point source at the lens feed horn into a linear wave front along the reflector feed assembly. The linear wave front from the lens is directed diametrically opposite the lens feed point. Therefore, the angle of incidence at the

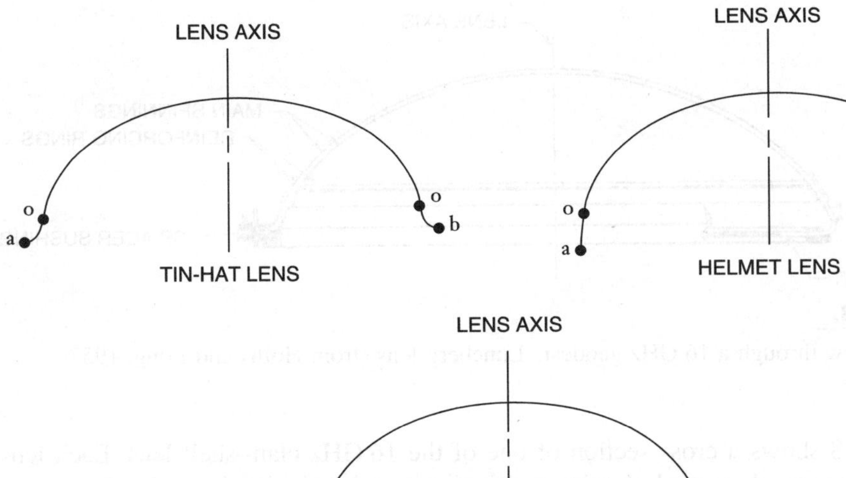

FIGURE 6–26.
Sectional views of mean surfaces for common types of geodesic lenses (from Johnson 1962), courtesy of *The Microwave Journal*.

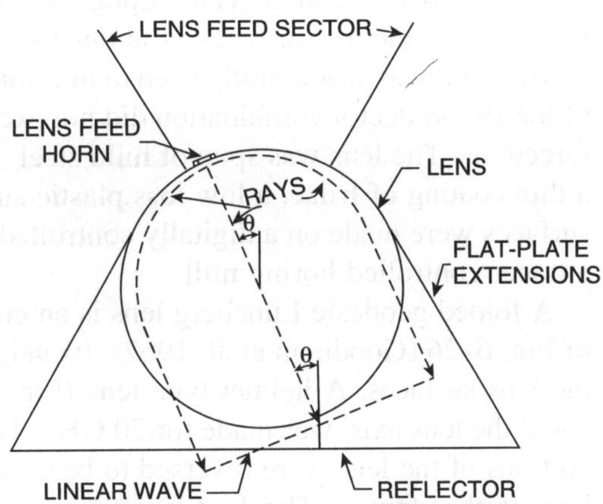

FIGURE 6–27.
Projected ray paths from geodesic lens to the linear aperture of reflector feed horn.

reflector feed assembly (and the scan angle of the radiated beam) is changed by moving the lens feed-horn along the periphery of the input lips.

Geodesic Luneberg lenses have been used with centimeter and millimeter wavelength, rapid mechanical-scan antennas. In a 16-GHz dual-beam radar application (Hollis and Long, 1957), two identical 127 cm clam-shell lenses were housed in an antenna that scanned a 40° azimuth sector alternately, each beam at a rate of 17 scans per second (see Fig. 7–27, sec. 7.7.2). Half-power azimuth beamwidths were 1.07°. The two beams were separated 1.85° in elevation and had 0.76° half-power beamwidths. Focusing in elevation was accomplished with one parabolic cylinder reflector, illuminated with two vertically offset line source feeds.

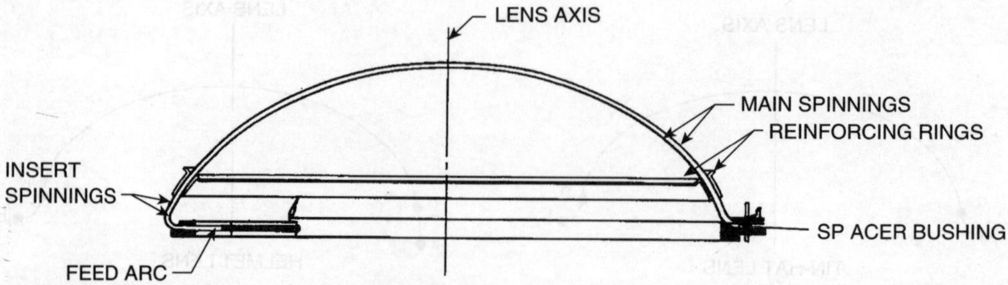

FIGURE 6–28.

A sectional view through a 16 GHz geodesic Luneberg lens (from Hollis and Long, 1957; © 1957, IEEE).

Figure 6–28 shows a cross section of one of the 16 GHz clam-shell lens. Each lens consists of two closely nested aluminum spinnings; each spinning is made of two sections: a main spinning, and an insert that replaces a section of the main spinning between the periphery and the reinforcing ring. This insert forms an internal feed arc that permits sectoral feed horns to rotate in a plane about the lens axis. The insert subtends 110° on the lens periphery, to permit the lens to focus for all feed positions over the 40° scan sector. The fabrication tolerance for the lens surfaces was set at $\frac{1}{32}$ inch. Although this tolerance was maintained over most of the lens surface areas, greater deviations did exist. Pattern measurements indicated a maximum side-lobe level of –25 dB.

A narrow-beam geodesic Luneberg lens was used in the AN/MPS-29 (XE-1), a 70-GHz radar (see sec. 7.7.2). The lens diameter is 350λ, that is, 60 inches (152 cm), that provides a 0.2° scanned beam (Long, Rivers, and Butterworth 1960). Spacing between the lens conducting surfaces is about 1.4λ. This dimension is oversized for the TEM mode, yet it was successfully used to minimize lens attenuation. Measured side-lobe level of the lens-reflector combination did not exceed –22 dB for any of the feed horns or scan directions. The lens was spun of mild steel, machined, copper-plated, and protected with a thin coating of Irilac, a low loss plastic surface coating. Templates for the conducting surfaces were made on a digitally controlled profiler, and the surfaces were machined on a tracer controlled boring mill.

A folded geodesic Luneberg lens is an entirely different configuration than the lenses of Fig. 6–26 (Goodman et al. 1967). Its height-to-diameter ratio is reduced by "folding" the lens surfaces. A helmet-type lens (Fig. 6–26) with one fold, located symmetrically about the lens axis, was made for 70 GHz. To affect the height reduction, the upper-dome sections of the lens were reversed to become bowls, with their troughs along the centerline of the domes. The lens aperture was approximately 23 inches (58 cm) and its maximum mean-surface height was 3.6 inches (9.4 cm). Measured side lobes of the folded lens were, surprisingly, smaller than for the unfolded lenses. The side lobes were "lost" in the receiver noise, which was at least 36 dB below the peak of the main lobe. The –3 dB beam width was 0.56°, the same as expected for an unfolded lens. However, the folding broadened the base of the main lobe at angles wider than the –10 dB angles. Thus, the folded geodesic lens provided reduced profile height and lowered side lobes, and these were achieved with negligible degradation of antenna gain or beamwidth. This lens was installed in an azimuth scanning, 70 GHz armored-vehicle mounted radar that provided adequate vision for night driving (Dyer and Goodman 1972).

Geodesic Luneberg lenses have been used in other types of scanners. For example, Allen (1956) designed a tin-hat lens that was sector-scanned with multiple waveguides in a configuration called organ-pipe feed; and Schaufelberger (1960) employed the ultra-wide-band millimeter wavelength feature of a geodesic Luneberg lens to provide the detection sensitivity needed for target detection by radiometry.

6.9. Beam Steering by Feed Offset

The Luneberg lens described above is an ideal device for producing a beam that changes direction when the feed alone is moved, without moving the entire antenna. As indicated, the beam direction will be along the line from the feed phase center through the center of the lens. The quality of the beam will be equally good for all feed positions on the lens surface; that is, the gain, beamwidth, and side-lobe level will remain constant for all beam positions.

Obviously, much less mechanical energy is required to move a small feed horn than to move an entire antenna. This requires, however, a flexing or rotating joint in the waveguide so that the feed horn can be moved while the transmitter remains stationary. An alternative is to place a number of horns at fixed points to provide fixed beams in desired directions, and then to switch from one to another in accordance with the requirements of the particular application.

A beam may be similarly steered with an ordinary lens or with a parabolic reflector, by moving the feed off the lens or reflector axis but keeping it in the focal plane. The off-axis collimation of a beam of rays using an offset feed with an ordinary lens is shown in Fig. 6–29a. The same effect with a parabolic reflector is shown in Fig. 6–29b. However, the angular deviation θ of the beam from the axial direction that can be obtained in this way is much more limited with ordinary lenses than with the Luneberg lens, and still more limited with a parabolic reflector. As the steering angle is increased, the beam shape deteriorates, resulting in increased beamwidth, decreased directivity, and increased side-lobe level. At large values of offset of the feed, the beam deterioration becomes excessive; in fact, the pattern can hardly be referred to as a beam, and it is not usable as such.

The permissible scan angle (or steering angle) by the feed-offset method is roughly proportional to the on-axis beamwidth and is generally of the order of a few beamwidths. The maximum scan angle is greater with large than with small *f*/*D* ratios. It may also be increased with lenses by the use of special surface curvatures, and with reflectors by combining special curvature with special feed design.

6.10. Pattern Calculations for Continuous Apertures

The aperture of an antenna is an area through which the radiation passes, and it is a plane surface near the antenna and perpendicular to the direction that the maximum radiation passes. Pattern calculations for continuous apertures are commonly made with equations

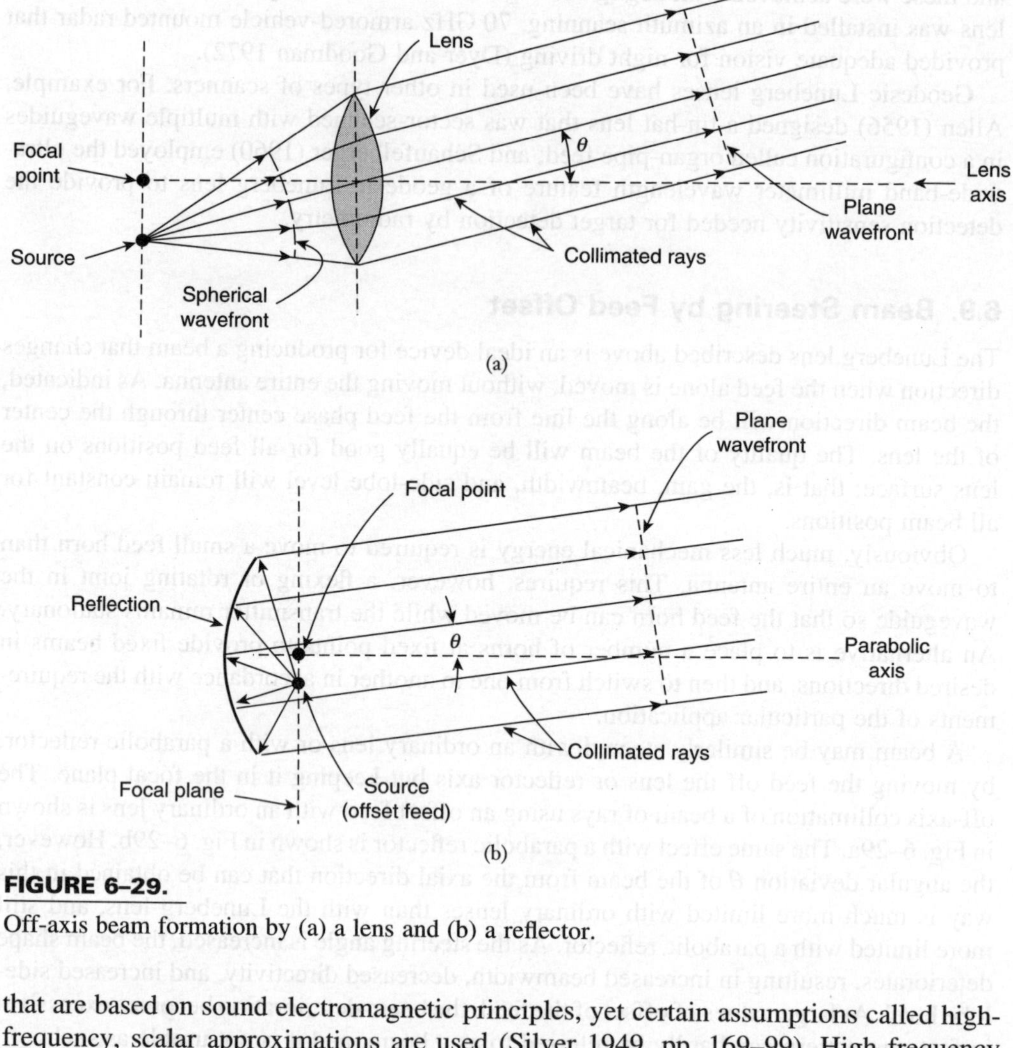

FIGURE 6–29.
Off-axis beam formation by (a) a lens and (b) a reflector.

that are based on sound electromagnetic principles, yet certain assumptions called high-frequency, scalar approximations are used (Silver 1949, pp. 169–99). High frequency refers to the aperture being large enough that the effects of radiation from aperture edges are negligible; and scalar refers to the field over the aperture being almost completely linearly polarized, with only a small fraction of the energy being cross-polarized.

6.10.1. Historical Note on Aperture Analyses

In his classic antenna book, Silver (1949) describes microwave antenna theory and hardware developments made during World War II at the MIT Radiation Laboratory. There he references (Silver 1949, pp. 182–95) research reports on the application of mathematical techniques for calculating aperture antenna patterns. By 1946, antenna specialists knew that far-zone radiation patterns could be calculated, in principle, using the Fourier integral of aperture distributions. At that time, however, user-friendly computer means for doing aperture calculations and pattern plotting were not available.

Beginning in the 1950s, antenna developments within the Engineering Experiment Station, Georgia Institute of Technology (now Georgia Tech Research Institute), benefited from the use of an analog Fourier integral computer. Searcy Hollis built the computer and designed it specifically for antenna analyses (Hollis, 1956). A paper by Clayton and Hollis (1960) describes the development of this Fourier integral computer, its use in calculating and plotting antenna patterns, and how linear aperture distributions can be used to determine patterns versus θ and ϕ. The paper also describes a version of the Fourier integral computer manufactured and sold by Scientific Atlanta, Inc. That computer used a phototube reader that inputted data from graphs of aperture amplitude and phase distributions, and computed patterns were printed on a paper recorder.

Later, calculated patterns versus θ and ϕ became more easily attainable through use of general-purpose digital computers. Often the pattern calculations incorporated previously developed mathematical equations, for approximating the patterns of continuous line sources. Nowadays, generally available personal computers (PCs) can readily provide detailed pattern calculations using point-to-point amplitude and phase data over an entire aperture. Consequently, today there is an extensive body of knowledge on using PCs for antenna aperture analyses (Diaz and Milligan 1996).

6.10.2. Continuous Line Source

As with planar arrays, radiation pattern calculations for line sources are basic to the understanding of pattern calculations for continuous planar apertures. Figure 6–30 describes the coordinate system used for the material that follows. Based on equations

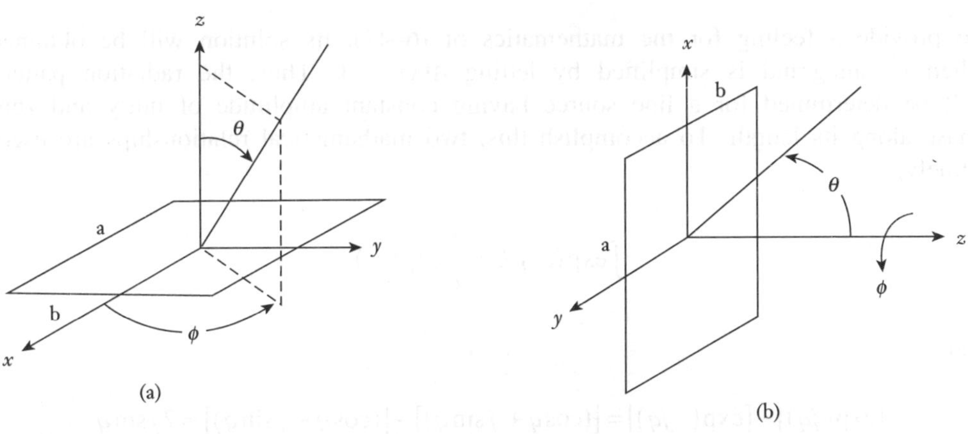

FIGURE 6–30.

Coordinates for a rectangular aperture located in the x-y plane.

given in Johnson (1993, p. 2–15), the normalized radiation pattern in the *x-z* plane of a continuous line source on the *x*-axis may be expressed as

$$E(\theta)=\frac{1}{L}\int_{-L/2}^{L/2}A(x)\exp\left[j\left(\frac{2\pi x\sin\theta}{\lambda}\right)\right]dx \qquad (6\text{–}41)$$

where $E(\theta)$ = electric far-field pattern versus observation angle θ, normalized for peak amplitude of unity

θ = observation angle measured from normal to aperture
L = overall length of aperture
x = position along the aperture: $-L/2 \geq x \leq L/2$
$A(x) = a(x)e^{j\alpha(x)}$
$a(x)$ = aperture amplitude versus position x
$\alpha(x)$ = aperture phase versus position x

The analogy between equations for linear arrays and linear continuous apertures may be apparent. Equation (6–41) is a summation of amplitude and phase contributions, at each observation angle θ from aperture currents of infinitesimal length dx. For mathematical convenience, solutions for are usually expressed in terms of the variable u, where $u=\frac{\pi L}{\lambda}\sin\theta$.

The factor $1/L$ normalizes (6–41), so that the maximum of $E(\theta)$ is unity. Thus, an *unnormalized* pattern $g(\theta)$ in the *x-z* plane for a continuous line source along the *x*-axis is

$$g(\theta)=\int_{-L/2}^{L/2}A(x)\exp\left[j\left(\frac{2\pi x\sin\theta}{\lambda}\right)\right]dx \qquad (6\text{–}42)$$

To provide a feeling for the mathematics of (6–42), its solution will be obtained when its integrand is simplified by letting $A(x) = 1$. Thus, the radiation pattern will be determined for a line source having constant amplitude of unity and zero phase along its length. To accomplish this, two mathematical relationships are used; namely,

$$\int\exp(cz)\,dz=\frac{1}{c}\exp(cz)$$

and

$$[\exp(jq)]-[\exp(-jq)]=[(\cos q+j\sin q)]-[(\cos q-j\sin q)]=2j\sin q$$

Then with $A(x) = 1$, (6–42) becomes

$$\int_{-L/2}^{L/2} A(x)\exp\left[j\left(\frac{2\pi x\sin\theta}{\lambda}\right)\right]dx = \frac{1}{j\left(\frac{2\pi}{\lambda}\right)\sin\theta}\left[\exp\left(\frac{2\pi}{\lambda}\right)\frac{L}{2}\sin\theta - \exp\left(-\frac{2\pi}{\lambda}\right)\frac{L}{2}\sin\theta\right]$$

$$= \frac{1}{j\left(\frac{2\pi}{\lambda}\right)\sin\theta}\left[2j\sin\left[\left(\frac{2\pi}{\lambda}\right)\frac{L}{2}\sin\theta\right]\right] = L\frac{\sin\left[\left(\frac{\pi L}{\lambda}\right)\sin\theta\right]}{\left(\frac{\pi L}{\lambda}\right)\sin\theta} = L\frac{\sin u}{u} \qquad (6\text{–}43)$$

where $u = \frac{\pi L}{\lambda}\sin\theta$. Now, since $\sin u/u$ equals unity when u is zero, the normalized amplitude pattern for a uniformly illuminated line source is

$$E(u) = \frac{\sin u}{u} \quad \text{(for constant amplitude and phase)} \qquad (6\text{–}44)$$

Another line amplitude distribution frequently used is cosine amplitude and constant phase. In this case, the amplitude is made unity at the aperture center and zero at its edges. Then $A(x) = a(x) = \cos(\pi x/L)$ for $-L/2 \le x \le L/2$. From Silver (1949, p. 187) and other references, the pattern obtained using this cosine distribution with (6–41) is

$$E(u) = \frac{\cos u}{1-\left(\frac{2u}{\pi}\right)^2} \quad \text{(for cosine amplitude distribution)} \qquad (6\text{–}45)$$

where $u = \frac{\pi L}{\lambda}\sin\theta$.

Graphs of $E(\theta)$ from (6–44) and (6–45), expressed in decibels, for the uniform and cosine amplitude distributions are included in Fig. 6–31. There the first side lobes for the uniform distribution are only 13.2 dB less than the peak of the major lobe. On the other hand, the peak side lobes for the cosine distribution are smaller, being 23 dB below the major lobe.

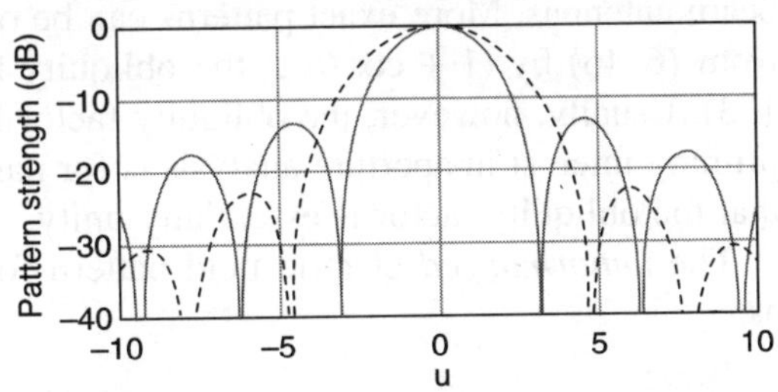

FIGURE 6–31.

Normalized pattern amplitudes expressed in decibels versus $u = \pi(L/\lambda)\sin\theta$. — Constant aperture amplitude distribution; . . . . . Cosine aperture amplitude distribution.

Mathematical solutions for the radiation patterns of a variety of continuous linear aperture distributions are tabulated in various books (see, e.g., Silver 1949, p. 187). Table 6-1 includes the half-power beamwidths and maximum side-lobe levels for several aperture amplitude distributions for which the phase is assumed constant over the aperture. In Table 6-1, aperture dimensions are normalized so

TABLE 6-1 Beamwidth, Maximum Side Lobes, and Relative Gain Versus Linear Aperture Amplitude Distribution (from Silver 1949, p. 187)

Type of Distribution $-1 \geq x \leq 1$	Half-Power Beamwidth (degrees)	Intensity 1st side lobe (dB below max)	Relative Gain
$a(x) = 1$	$50.8\ \lambda/L$	13.2	1.00
$a(x) = 1 - 0.2x^2$	$52.7\ \lambda/L$	15.8	0.99
$a(x) = 1 - 0.5x^2$	$55.6\ \lambda/L$	17.1	0.97
$a(x) = 1 - x^2$	$65.9\ \lambda/L$	20.6	0.83
$a(x) = \cos(\pi x/2)$	$68.8\ \lambda/L$	23.0	0.81
$a(x) = \cos^2(\pi x/2)$	$83.2\ \lambda/L$	32.0	0.67
$a(x) = 1 - \lvert x \rvert$	$73.4\ \lambda/L$	26.4	0.75

that coordinate x is between -1 and $+1$. Notice that the first side lobes are appreciably reduced by the tapering of amplitudes to small values at the aperture edges. The relative gain in Table 6-1 is commonly called aperture efficiency. It is the gain relative to the gain available if the aperture were illuminated with constant amplitude and constant phase.

In the previous discussions, the phase over the aperture is assumed constant. A major effect of aperture phase errors is to reduce the gain and broaden the major lobe. In addition, phase errors reduce the depth of pattern minima between the lobes and raise the side lobes. Very large phase errors over the aperture can cause the main lobe to be split into parts and cause large side lobes. For a detailed discussion on phase errors along a continuous aperture, the reader is referred to Johnson (1993, pp. 2-21–2-27).

6.10.3. Aperture Analysis: General

A discussion follows on the calculation of patterns for a planar aperture located in the x-y plane of Fig. 6–30. Let the excitation on the aperture be $A(x, y) = a(x, y) \exp[j\alpha(x, y)]$, where $a(x, y)$ describes the amplitude and $\exp[j\alpha(x, y)]$ the phase. The beam points in the positive z direction. Equation (6–46) below is the usual starting point for narrow beam antennas. More exact patterns can be obtained simply by multiplying the patterns from (6–46) by $(1 + \cos\theta)/2$, the obliquity factor (see Appendix G or Silver 1949, p. 173). Usually, however, the obliquity factor is assumed to be unity. This is because the primary interest in aperture analysis is for narrow beam antennas and small θ values, so that the obliquity factor is essentially unity.

The *unnormalized* electric field pattern for a rectangular aperture can be expressed as

$$g(\theta, \phi) = \int_{-a/2}^{a/2} \int_{-b/2}^{b/2} A(x, y) e^{j\frac{2\pi}{\lambda}\sin\theta(x\cos\phi + y\sin\phi)}\, dx dy \qquad (6\text{–}46)$$

and it expresses the relative electric field strength at a fixed distance from the aperture origin versus the angles θ and ϕ. Here a is the aperture length along the x-axis, and b is the length along the y-axis. Note that the aperture distribution $A(x, y)$ is a function of two variables, and thus it describes the amplitude and phase at the aperture's x and y coordinates. With reflector and lens antennas, often the dependencies of $A(x, y)$ on x and y are interdependent so that it is difficult or impossible to describe $A(x, y)$ with a simple equation. Then, it may be necessary to solve (6–46) by point-to-point integrations over the aperture.

The simplest $g(\theta, \phi)$ calculation is one for a line source along either the x- or the y-axis. Then from (6–46), for an x-axis continuous distribution

$$g(\theta,\phi)=\int_{-a/2}^{a/2}A(x)e^{j\frac{2\pi}{\lambda}x\sin\theta\cos\phi}dx \tag{6–47a}$$

because all y values are zero. Notice that the integrand in (6–47a) is the same as in (6–42), except that the product $\sin\theta\cos\phi$ replaces $\sin\theta$. Consequently, solutions of (6–47a) are the same as solutions for (6–42), except that their solutions in terms of the variable u, where $u = (\pi L/\lambda)\cdot\sin\theta$, are replaced by

$$U_x=(\pi a/\lambda)\cdot\sin\theta\cos\phi \tag{6–47b}$$

Likewise, for a y-axis continuous distribution, for which all x coordinates are zero

$$g(\theta,\phi)=\int_{-b/2}^{b/2}A(y)e^{j\frac{2\pi}{\lambda}y\sin\theta\sin\phi}dy \tag{6–48a}$$

Then, similar to solutions for (6–47a), solutions of (6–48a) are the same as solutions for (6–42), except that the solutions in terms of the variable u, where $u = (\pi L/\lambda)\cdot\sin\theta$, are replaced by

$$U_y=(\pi b/\lambda)\cdot\sin\theta\sin\phi \tag{6–48b}$$

6.10.4. Apertures Having Separable *x* and *y* Distributions

If he aperture distribution $A(x, y)$ at the x coordinates is independent of the y coordinates and visa versa, it can be expressed as

$$A(x,y)=A1(x)\cdot A2(y)=a1(x)\exp[j\alpha1(x)]\cdot a2(y)\exp[j\alpha2(y)] \tag{6–49}$$

Equation (6–49) is said to be mathematically separable or factorable. Separable equations are applicable to the case of a line source feed that illuminates a parabolic cylinder or a cylindrical lens. For example, suppose the line source and the focal line of the cylinder coincide along the y-axis. Then the excitation along the line source defines the term $A2(y)$. Now suppose the radiation pattern about the y-axis is shaped by a flared line source feed horn. Then the shaped radiation pattern and the space attenuation determine the excitation $A1(x)$. Thus, $A(x, y)$ is separable and (6–46) can be simplified to become

$$g(\theta,\phi)=\int_{-a/2}^{a/2} A1(x)e^{j\frac{2\pi}{\lambda}x\sin\theta\cos\phi}\,dx\cdot\int_{-b/2}^{b/2} A2(y)e^{j\frac{2\pi}{\lambda}y\sin\theta\sin\phi}\,dy \qquad (6\text{–}50)$$

Equation (6–50) is simplified further if patterns only in the *x-z* and *y-z* planes are considered. Then, the two principal plane patterns are dependent on aperture distributions along the *x*- and *y*-axes, as follows:

$$g(\theta,0^\circ)=\left[\int_{-b/2}^{b/2} A2(y)dy\right]\cdot\int_{-a/2}^{a/2} A1(x)e^{j\frac{2\pi}{\lambda}x\sin\theta}\,dx\,(X\text{-}Z\text{ plane}) \qquad (6\text{–}51a)$$

$$g(\theta,90^\circ)=\left[\int_{-a/2}^{a/2} A1(x)dx\right]\cdot\int_{-b/2}^{b/2} A2(y)e^{j\frac{2\pi}{\lambda}y\sin\theta}\,dy\quad(y\text{-}z\text{ plane}) \qquad (6\text{–}51b)$$

Notice that the bracketed terms of (6–51a) and (6–51b) are constants. Also, notice that the integrals outside the bracketed terms are similar in form to (6–42). Thus, except for a multiplicity factor, (6–51a) and (6–51b) for planar apertures are describable by radiation patterns of line sources. Therefore, knowledge of linear aperture patterns is often beneficial to an understanding of the patterns of continuous planar apertures.

The simplest planar aperture distribution has unity amplitude and zero phase, and its pattern versus θ and ϕ can be determined with relative ease. For this case,

$$A(x,y)=1\cdot\exp 0\times 1\cdot\exp 0=1.$$

Then, since $A(x, y)$ is separable, $g(\theta, \phi)$ is the product of two integrals and each is the pattern of a line source of constant amplitude and phase. Thus, from (6–47b), (6–48b), and (6–50), the radiation pattern for a distribution of constant amplitude and phase becomes

$$g(\theta,\phi)=A\left[\frac{\sin U_x}{U_x}\right]\cdot\left[\frac{\sin U_y}{U_y}\right]=A\left[\frac{\sin\left(\frac{\pi a}{\lambda}\sin\theta\cos\phi\right)}{\frac{\pi a}{\lambda}\sin\theta\cos\phi}\right]\cdot\left[\frac{\sin\left(\frac{\pi b}{\lambda}\sin\theta\sin\phi\right)}{\frac{\pi b}{\lambda}\sin\theta\sin\phi}\right] \qquad (6\text{–}52)$$

where A is the aperture area (a times b).

Figure 6–32 is a plot of $20\log|g(\theta, \phi)|$ versus θ and ϕ) of (6–52), normalized to zero dB. From this figure it can be seen that the patterns in the principal planes (*x-z* and *y-z*) are similar, and they are identical if the aperture dimensions a and b are equal. From (6–44), it is known that each principal plane pattern, when normalized to unity, has the form $\sin u/u$. Here u is $(\pi w/\lambda)\sin\theta$ with w being the aperture width within the plane of the pattern. As previously noted; the function $\sin u/u$ is at its maximum of unity at u = 0 and its first side lobes are relatively large, being only 13.2 dB below the peak of the major lobe.

6.10.5. Equivalent Linear Apertures in Principal Planes

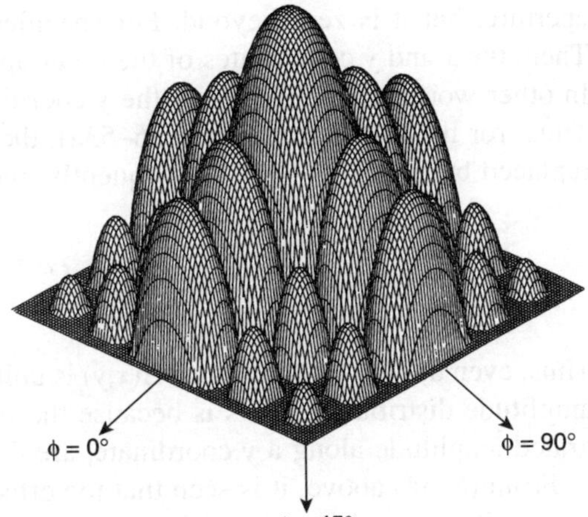

FIGURE 6–32.

Radiation pattern for a uniformly illuminated square aperture, graphed in decibels. Courtesy of J. W. Cofer, Georgia Tech Research Institute, calculations made circa 1969.

Equations (6–51a) and (6–51b) give principal plane patterns for a planar aperture, expressed as functions of separable linear aperture distributions. In theory, principal plane patterns for nonseparable aperture distributions also may be expressed in a closed, integratable mathematical form. However, in practice, principal plane patterns often are determined by numerical integration of measured or estimated aperture distributions. The concept of equivalent linear aperture distributions, now discussed, is applicable to antennas having nonseparable aperture distributions. It can provide insight into how a principal plane pattern is affected by changes in the amplitude and phase distribution of a planar aperture.

The pattern $g(\theta, \phi = 0°)$ in the *x-z* principal plane for an equivalent line source along the *x*-axis can be obtained by rearranging the terms in (6–46) as follows:

$$g(\theta, \phi = 0°) = \int_{-a/2}^{a/2} \left[\int_{-b/2}^{b/2} A(x, y)\,dy \right] \cdot e^{j\frac{2\pi}{\lambda} x \sin\theta}\,dx \tag{6–53a}$$

Similarly, the pattern $g(\theta, \phi = 90°)$ in the *y-z* principal plane for an equivalent line source along the *Y*-axis, can be obtained by rearranging the terms in (6–46) as follows:

$$g(\theta, \phi = 90°) = \int_{-b/2}^{b/2} \left[\int_{-a/2}^{a/2} A(x, y)\,dx \right] \cdot e^{j\frac{2\pi}{\lambda} y \sin\theta}\,dy \tag{6–53b}$$

Now compare (6–53a) with (6–42) for the *x-z* plane pattern of an *x*-axis linear aperture. Note that the bracketed integral of (6–53a) functions for (6–42) as the equivalent linear aperture distribution along the *x*-axis. However, this bracketed integral (the equivalent linear aperture distribution) is a function of *x* and *y*. Thus, to evaluate the bracketed integral at each *x* coordinate, $A(x, y)$ is integrated over all *y* coordinates between $-b/2$ and $b/2$. Likewise, the pattern in the $\phi = 90°$ plane is attained from (6–53b). The principles of evaluating (6–53a) and (6–53b) are beneficial in envisioning the effects of aperture tapers, as is discussed below.

A simple mathematical example is now given, which is that of determining the equivalent linear aperture distribution and the pattern for a uniformly illuminated circular aperture. Then, the aperture amplitude may be expressed as $A(x, y) = 1$ over the circular aperture, but it is zero beyond. For specificity, let the radius of the aperture be unity. Then, the x and y coordinates of the outer aperture edges are interrelated by $x^2 + y^2 = 1$. In other words, at each x-value, the y coordinate at the aperture edge is $y_e = (1 - x^2)^{1/2}$. Thus, for the bracketed term of (6–53a), the limits of integration $b/2$ and $-b/2$ may be replaced by $y_e/2$ and $-y_e/2$. Consequently, the bracketed term of (6–53a) then becomes

$$\int_{-b/2}^{b/2} A(x, y)\,dy = \int_{-y_e/2}^{y_e/2} 1 \cdot dy = y_e = \left(1 - x^2\right)^{1/2} \tag{6–54}$$

Thus, even though the amplitude $A(x,y)$ is unity when not zero, it is in fact a nonseparable amplitude distribution. This is because the limits of integration, and therefore the integrated amplitude along a y coordinate, are dependent on its x-value.

From (6–54) above, it is seen that the effective illumination along the x-axis is mathematically tapered toward each aperture edge. In other words, the bracketed term of (6–53a), that is, equivalent linear aperture distribution, is $(1 - x^2)^{1/2}$. Thus, (6–53a) becomes

$$g(\theta) = \int_{-a/2}^{a/2} \left(1 - x^2\right)^{1/2} e^{j\frac{2\pi}{\lambda} x \sin\theta}\, dx \tag{6–55}$$

Consistent with the original assumption, $g(\theta)$ of (6–55) is the equation for a principal plane pattern of a uniformly illuminated circular aperture. The beamwidth and maximum side-lobe level for this aperture distribution are included in Table 6-2 (distribution: $f(r) = 1$) of the next section. Parenthetically, by using variable instead of fixed integration limits when determining an equivalent linear aperture distribution, the above example shows that $g(\theta)$ can be determined using (6–53a) or (6–53b) for planar apertures that are not rectangular.

The determination of equivalent line-source apertures for nonseparable distributions is usually more difficult than in the above example. However, the concept of equivalent linear apertures helps to show how aperture amplitude shaping of planar apertures affects side lobes and beamwidths, similar to how amplitude tapering affects the pattern of a linear aperture. Relationships between the physical shaping of a planar aperture and the tapering of an effective linear aperture are discussed also in connection with Fig. 6–6.

TABLE 6-2 Beamwidth, Maximum Side lobes, and Relative Gain Versus Circular Aperture Distribution (from Silver 1949, p. 194)

Type of Distribution $0 \le r \le 1$	Half-Power Beamwidth (degrees)	Intensity 1st Side Lobe (dB below max)	Relative Gain
$f(r) = 1$	$58.9\ \lambda/D$	17.6	1.00
$f(r) = (1 - r^2)$	$72.7\ \lambda/D$	24.6	0.75
$f(r) = (1 - r^2)^2$	$84.3\ \lambda/D$	30.6	0.56

6.10.6. Circular Apertures

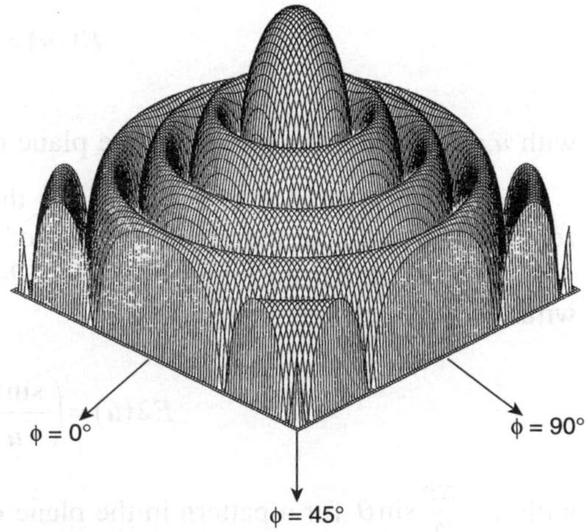

FIGURE 6–33.
Radiation pattern for a uniformly illuminated circular aperture, graphed in decibels. Courtesy of J. W. Cofer, Georgia Tech Research Institute, calculations made circa 1969.

Beamwidth, maximum side lobes, and relative gain for three circular apertures are given in Table 6-2. Each aperture distribution is a function of radius r, where r is normalized to unity. Equations of the patterns for these distributions have been solved in closed analytical form (Johnson, p. 2–21). Figure 6–33 shows the amplitude of the radiation pattern, expressed in decibels, of a circular aperture that is illuminated with constant amplitude and phase. There are major differences between this pattern and the pattern for a uniformly illuminated square aperture of Fig. 6–32. The first side lobes for the circular aperture are −17.6 dB with respect to the major lobe peak and the −3 dB beamwidth is $58.9\lambda/D$ degrees. On the other hand, for a square aperture, the comparable numbers along the principal planes are −13.2 dB and $50.8\lambda/L$ degrees. Thus, the effect of the circular shape, relative to the square shape, is to decrease (taper) the aperture amplitude toward the outer edges.

6.10.7. Patterns Versus θ and ϕ: A Summary

As already discussed, a pattern versus θ and ϕ is relatively easy to determine, if the aperture distributions are separable and the linear aperture patterns for both the x- and y-axis distributions are known. Then, as illustrated in the remainder of this section, patterns are determined as the product of two line-source patterns, in accordance with (6–50). Otherwise, calculations of patterns versus θ and ϕ require computational intensive, point-to-point numerical calculations in accordance with (6–46). For apertures with nonseparable distributions, patterns for the principal planes are much simpler to calculate than patterns versus θ and ϕ. These principal plane patterns are calculated by obtaining an equivalent line aperture for each principal plane and then integrating each line aperture distribution over the relevant line aperture following (6–53a) and (6–53b).

The remainder of section 6.10–7 focuses on patterns for separable distributions. Previously, (6–52) was derived to show how the simplest of patterns versus θ and ϕ is obtained. Its aperture distribution is separable, because the amplitude and phase are constant. Another separable planar aperture distribution is now discussed, that includes constant amplitude $a1(x)$ along the x-axis and a cosine-squared amplitude distribution $a2(y)$ along the y-axis.

The radiation patterns for the two distributions, $A1(x)$ and $A2(y)$, are now used to obtain the pattern versus θ and ϕ. The normalized pattern for a uniform line-source distribution, from (6–44), is

$$E1(u) = \left(\frac{\sin u}{u}\right) \tag{6–56}$$

with $u = \frac{\pi a}{\lambda} \sin\theta$ for a pattern in the plane of the line source.

The cosine-squared distribution along the *y*-axis is unity at the aperture center and zero at each end, and the phase is assumed to be zero. Then, $A2(y) = \cos^2(\pi y/b)$, with $-b/2 \geq y \leq b/2$; and from Johnson (1993, p. 2–16), the normalized pattern for a line-source with a cosine-squared distribution is

$$E2(u) = \left(\frac{\sin u}{u}\right)\left(\frac{\pi^2}{\pi^2 - u^2}\right) \tag{6–57}$$

with $u = \frac{\pi b}{\lambda} \sin\theta$ for a pattern in the plane of the line source.

To obtain the pattern $E(\theta, \phi)$ for a planar aperture having line source distributions in accordance with (6–56) and (6–57),

$-u$ in $E1(u)$ of (6–56) is replaced by U_x to obtain $E1(U_x)$,

and

$-u$ in $E2(u)$ of (6–57) is replaced by U_y to obtain $E2(U_y)$.

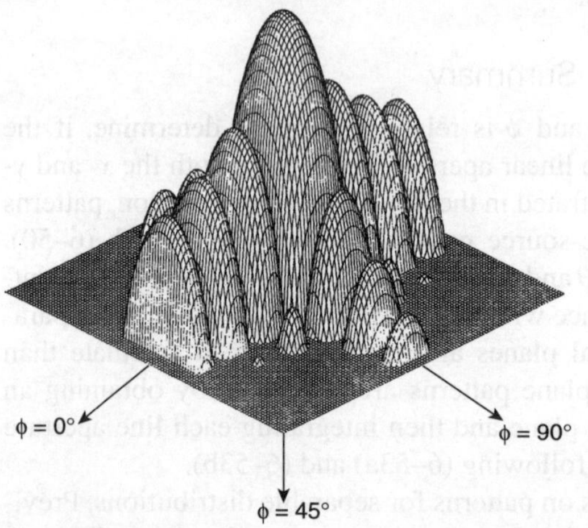

FIGURE 6–34.
Radiation pattern graphed in decibels, with uniform amplitude along one axis and cosine-squared tapered amplitude along the other axis. Courtesy J. W. Cofer of Georgia Tech Research Institute, calculations made circa 1969.

Then, the pattern $E(\theta, \phi)$ is

$$E(\theta,\phi) = E(U_x, U_y) = E1(U_x) \cdot E2(U_y) \tag{6–58}$$

where $U_x = (\pi a/\lambda) \cdot \sin\theta\cos\phi$ and $U_y = (\pi b/\lambda) \cdot \sin\theta\sin\phi$.

Figure 6–34 includes a pattern graphed in decibels for an aperture having a uniform distribution along the *x*-axis and cosine-squared distribution along the *y*-axis. Notice that the side lobes of the $\phi = 45°$ pattern are much smaller than along either the $\phi = 0°$ or $\phi = 90°$ pattern cuts, and this also was the case for the pattern of Fig. 6–32. Generally, however, the side-lobe levels in a $\phi = 45°$ pattern depends on the relative *a* and *b* widths of the aperture, in addition to the detailed shapes of the aperture distributions. Consequently, the side lobes for $\phi = 45°$ patterns are not always smaller than those of both the $\phi = 0°$ or $\phi = 90°$ patterns. However, for some operational scenarios, the effect of a side-lobe reduction in a plane, without loss of gain, sometimes may be obtained by rotating the aperture 45° about its z-axis.

6.11. Comparison of Directive Antenna Types

Two somewhat different ways of achieving directional antenna patterns have been described—the method of *arrays* in chapter 5, and the method of *ray collimation* by reflectors and lenses in the present chapter. Each of the two methods has advantages and disadvantages; in some applications one is preferred, in other applications the other is better. Arrays have been more commonly used at lower frequencies, and now they are being used more or less commonly at frequencies up to 10 GHz. Although arrays are not commonly used above about 30 GHz, they may be used up to at least 100 GHz (Emrick and Volakis 2007). Reflectors and lenses are most common above 3 GHz, although parabolic reflectors are fairly common down to at least 100 MHz. Lenses are basically microwave devices, not ordinarily used below about 3 GHz.

In the frequency region from about 300 to 3,000 MHz, and exclusive of the need for rapid electronic beam positioning or shaping, the choice between an array and a paraboloidal reflector may sometimes be difficult. Reflectors are favored when the desired beamwidth is less than a few degrees, and arrays are favored when high aperture efficiency is desired. Additionally, reflectors are usually indicated if broadband operation or low noise temperature (see secs. 7.1 and 7.8) are required.

Electronic scanning arrays are, generally, expensive but they may be the only solution for applications requiring rapid beam pointing, adaptive beam shaping, or a combination of rapid beam pointing, beam shaping, and signal processing (see chapter 8). However, a combination of electronically controlled primary feed and a reflector or a lens may be more cost-effective and lighter. For beam scanning only in an angular sector at speeds up to at less 20 scans per second, mechanically moving feeds in combination with reflectors or lenses have been successful (see sec. 7.7.2).

The principal advantage of lenses over reflectors is that the feed and feed-support structures do not block the aperture, since the rays are transmitted through the lens rather than returned toward the feed. Lenses can also be designed to operate satisfactorily with the feed farther off the optical axis, and hence are useful in applications requiring a beam that can be moved angularly with respect to the axis (although, as has been mentioned in sec. 6.3.5, this is possible in a moderate degree with reflectors). A further advantage is that permissible mechanical tolerances are somewhat greater for lenses than for reflectors. On the other hand, lenses are usually bulkier, heavier, more complicated to design and construct, and more expensive for the same gain and beamwidth than are reflectors. These factors become somewhat less significant at the very short wavelengths, above 10 GHz, and it is in this region that lenses are most commonly used.

References

Adams, R. J., and K. S. Kelleher, "Pattern Calculation for Antennas of Elliptical Aperture," *Proceedings IRE*, vol. 38, September 1950, pp. 1052 ff. See also K. S. Kelleher, "Reflector Antennas," ch. 12 in *Antenna Engineering Handbook*, H. Jasik (ed.), McGraw-Hill, 1961.

Allen, C. C., "Geodesic Lens With Organ Pipe Feed," *Record of the Georgia Tech-SCEL Symposium on Scanning Antennas*," Georgia Institute of Technology, 18–19 December 1956, pp. 297–314.

Balanis, C. A., *Antenna Theory: Analysis and Design*, 3rd ed., John Wiley & Sons, 2005, ch. 13.

Bodnar, D. G., "Lens Antennas," ch. 18 in *Antenna Engineering Handbook*, 4th ed., J. L. Volakis (ed.), McGraw-Hill, 2007.

Clayton, L., Jr., and J. S. Hollis, "Calculation of Microwave Antenna Radiation Systems By the Fourier Integral Method," *Microwave Journal*, Sept. 1960, pp. 59–66.

Diaz, L., and T. Milligan, *Antenna Engineering Using Physical Optics*, Artech House, 1996.

Dyer, F. B., and R. M. Goodman, Jr., "Vehicle Mounted Millimeter Wave Radar," *18th Tri-Service Radar Symposium Record*, University of Michigan, 1972. Reprinted in S. L. Johnston, *Millimeter Wave Radar*, Artech House, pp. 485–506, ch. 19.

Emrick, R., and J. L. Volakis, "Millimeter-Wave and Terahertz Antennas," ch. 23 in *Antenna Engineering Handbook*, 4th ed., J. L. Volakis (ed.), McGraw-Hill, 2007.

Goodman, R. M., Jr., R. C. Johnson, H. A. Ecker, and W. K. Rivers, Jr., "A Folded Geodesic Luneberg Lens Antenna," presented at the 17th Annual Symposium on USAF Antenna Research and Development at the University of Illinois, November 1967.

Hannan, P. W., "Microwave Antennas Derived from the Cassegrain Telescope," *IRE Transactions on Antennas and Propagation*, March 1961, 140–53.

Hollis, J. S., "A Fourier Integral Computer for Calculation of Antenna Radiation Patterns," MSEE Thesis, Georgia Institute of Technology, 1956.

Hollis, J. S., and M. W. Long, "Luneberg Lens Scanning System," *IRE Transactions on Antennas and Propagation*, vol. AP-5, January 1957, pp. 21–25.

Imbriale, W. A., and D. L. Jones, "Radio-Telescope Antennas," ch. 49 in *Antenna Engineering Handbook*, 4th ed., J. L. Volakis (ed.), McGraw-Hill, 2007.

Johnson, R. C., "The Geodesic Luneberg Lens," *Microwave Journal*, vol. 5, August 1962, pp. 76–85.

Johnson, R. C., *Antenna Engineering Handbook*, 3rd ed., McGraw-Hill, 1993.

Johnson, R. C., and R. M. Goodman, Jr., "Geodesic Lenses for Radar Antennas," *Record of IEEE EASCON '68*, Washington, DC, 1968, pp. 64–69.

Kock, W. E., "Metal Plate Antennas," *Proceedings of the IRE*, November 1946, pp. 828–36.

Long, M. W., W. K. Rivers, Jr., and J. C. Butterworth, "Combat Surveillance Radar AN/MPS-29 (XE-1)," *Record of the Sixth Annual Radar Symposium*, University of Michigan, 1960. Reprinted in S. L. Johnston, *Millimeter Wave Radar*, Artech House, pp. 461–78, 1980.

Love, A. W., "Horn Antennas," ch. 15 in R. C. Johnson, *Antenna Engineering Handbook*, 3rd ed., McGraw-Hill, 1993.

Kraus, J. D., and R. J. Marhefka, *Antennas,* 3rd ed., McGraw-Hill, 2002, pp. 352–64.

Muehldorf, E. I., "The phase center of horn antennas," *IEEE Transactions on Antennas and Propagation*, vol. AP-18, November 1980, pp. 753–60.

Risser, J. R., "Waveguide and Horn Feeds," ch. 10, in S. Silver, *Microwave Antenna Theory and Design*, McGraw-Hill, 1949.

Risser, J. R., "Dielectric and Metal Plate Lenses," ch. 11 in S. Silver, *Microwave Antenna Theory and Design*, McGraw-Hill, 1949.

Ruze, J., "Antenna Tolerance Theory: A Review," *Proceedings of the IEEE*, April 1966, 633–40.

Schaufelberger, A. H., "An Airborne High Speed Scanning Antenna for a Millimeter Radiometer," *Symposium Record on the USAF Antenna Research and Development Program, Vol. II*, University of Illinois, Monticello, Illinois, 3–7 October 1960.

Silver, S., *Microwave Antenna Theory and Design*, McGraw-Hill, 1949.

Taylor, T. T., "Design of Line-Source Antennas for Narrow Beamwidth and Low Side Lobes," *IRE Transactions on Antennas and Propagation*, January 1955, pp. 16–28.

Problems and Exercises

1. A circular-aperture paraboloidal reflector has a focal length of 10 feet. The depth of the reflector (z_{ap} in Fig. 6–2) is 6.4 feet. (a) What is the aperture diameter, D_a? (b) What is the f/D ratio? (*Hint*: Use equation (6–1), noting that when $z = z_{ap}$, $x = D/2$.)

2. A paraboloidal reflector of circular aperture has a diameter D_a = 30 feet. The frequency of operation is 450 MHz. (a) If the constant k_1 of equation (6–12) is 70 degrees for this antenna, what is the beamwidth? (b) If k_2 in equation (6–13) is 0.6, what is the directivity, D? Express this result as both a power ratio and in decibels. (*Note*: All length and area quantities in equations (6–12) and (6–13) must be expressed in a consistent system of units.)

3. A paraboloidal reflector has an aperture dimension D_a = 40 feet, in a particular plane. The focal length is 12 feet. (a) What is the angle (2β) subtended by the reflector as viewed from the focus, in this plane? (b) If a primary horn feed of beamwidth 100 degrees in this plane is placed at the focus of this reflector, approximately what will be the illumination edge taper (τ_2)? (c) Approximately what will be the side-lobe level, in decibels?

4. A rectangular-aperture parabolic-cylinder reflector is to be operated with a uniform collinear-dipole array as the feed radiator. The cylindrical axis and the array are aligned horizontally. It is desired to obtain a horizontal beamwidth of 2 degrees and a vertical beamwidth of 20 degrees. (*Note*: The horizontal beamwidth is determined by the array, whereas the vertical beamwidth is determined by the parabolic aperture.) The wavelength of operation is λ = 0.25 meter (f = 1200 MHz). The array spacing d of equation (5–57) is 0.7λ, and the constant k_1 of equation (6–3) is 60 degrees. It is deemed advisable to extend the horizontal

dimension of the reflector a distance of one wavelength beyond the centers of the end elements of the array. What must be the dimensions of reflector aperture? *Hints*: The horizontal beamwidth will be the same as that of a uniform linear array of isotropic elements; the element pattern in this case has virtually no effect, and the reflector does not affect the horizontal beamwidth. The length of an array of n elements, between the centers of the end elements, is $(n - 1)d$. In solving equation (5–57) to find the required value of n, the initial solution will not be an exact integer; but of course n must be an integer. Therefore, take for n the nearest integer to the nonintegral value found from equation (5–57).

5. A 90-degree corner-reflector antenna operating at a wavelength of one meter ($f = 300$ MHz) has a dipole feed positioned one-half wavelength from the vertex of the corner. Approximately what should the side length (l) and the aperture dimension (D_a) be? Express the result in meters, and also in feet and inches.
6. State whether you would use an array, a paraboidal reflector, or a lens to meet the following antenna requirements: (a) A beamwidth of 50 degrees in both principal planes, at a frequency of 50 MHz. (b) A beamwidth of approximately one degree in both principal planes, at a frequency of 30 GHz, with considerable capability of angular beam motion by off-axis feed positioning, and freedom from aperture-blocking effects. (c) A beamwidth of approximately one degree in a fixed direction in both principal planes, at a frequency of 5 GHz, with the lightest possible weight, lowest cost, and good bandwidth properties.
7. List three advantages of a paraboloidal-reflector antenna over a lens antenna, for the same aperture size.
8. List three advantages of a lens antenna over a reflector antenna, for the same aperture size.
9. A rectangular aperture in the yz coordinate plane has a y-dimension $D_y = 10\lambda$. The field in the aperture is of uniform intensity and phase. At what positive and negative values of the azimuth angle ϕ, in the xy-plane, will the first nulls of the pattern occur?
10. Show that for the aperture of Problem 9 ($D_y = 10\lambda$), the relative value of $E(\phi)$ is approximately 0.707 when ϕ has the value $25.4\lambda/D_y$ degrees. This result confirms the fact that k_1 in equation (6–12) has the value 50.8 (twice 25.4) for this particular case, since the $E(\phi) = 0.707$ point on the beam pattern corresponds to the half-power-density points, which define the beamwidth.

CHAPTER 7

Antennas with Special Properties

Chapter 7 discusses properties of antennas and antenna analysis techniques not addressed in other chapters. Antennas are used in many different applications, and consequently there are numerous special properties needed to satisfy their requirements. The range of topics addressed in this chapter is wide, and includes techniques for providing wide bandwidths, multiple polarizations, low receiver noise, and extremely low side lobes. A specific application may, of course, employ more than one of these techniques. There is also a section solely on antennas for direction finding and another on antennas that accomplish beam scanning mechanically. The concept of synthetic-aperture antennas, although perhaps more of a signal processing than an antenna topic, is also discussed here, because it is a uniquely effective way of attaining very narrow antenna beamwidths through use of a relatively small antenna on a moving platform. Finally, the chapter closes with a section on seemingly unrelated subjects, namely, geometrical theory of diffraction (GTD), method of moments (MoM), and fractals. These topics are, however, connected by the subject of radiation from sharp edges (curvatures small compared to a wavelength), which currently cannot be analyzed by exact theoretical methods.

GTD and MoM analyses are computer programmed for solutions to complex antenna configurations. GTD uses ray-optics representation of electromagnetic propagation, and it also incorporates diffraction theory and surface waves for surfaces large compared to a wavelength. MoM, on the other hand, is applicable primarily to wire antennas (e.g., dipoles and longer wire radiators), but it has also been used for patch antennas. MoM programs compute currents, from which radiation can be calculated. In contrast, fractals are computer-generated random shapes proven useful as novel antenna configurations, and for which MoM programs are used to analyze the radiation from their sharp edges.

7.1. Broad-Band Antennas

As discussed in sec. 3.9, the bandwidth of an antenna can be defined in various ways, depending on the requirements. It is customary to speak of the *impedance bandwidth*, *gain bandwidth*, *polarization bandwidth*, and the *pattern bandwidth* separately when a precise description of antenna bandwidth is required.

Bandwidths are sometimes specified in terms of percentage of the center frequency and sometimes as the ratio of the maximum to the minimum frequency. Which method of specification is used depends on the magnitude of the bandwidth. If the ratio of maximum to minimum frequency is less than 2 : 1, the percentage figure is often given (a 1.1 : 1 ratio, for example, corresponds to roughly 10% bandwidth). The higher bandwidth ratios are generally given as ratios. Bandwidths of 10 : 1 and higher are achievable with special types of antennas. On the other hand, a 10 percent bandwidth or even less may represent a great engineering achievement in some applications—for example, in a large array antenna. Since broad bandwidth is often a necessary property of an antenna, much research and development have gone into improving the techniques of designing antennas for broad-band operation, and much progress has been made.

7.1.1. Basic Broad-Band Principles

Conventional antennas are essentially resonant structures. They have properties that go through maximum and minimum values at particular frequencies. These properties are the input impedance and the various pattern properties that have been mentioned. A center-fed linear wire is an example. At the frequency at which its length is (approximately) a half wavelength, the reactive component of the input impedance is minimum (or zero), and the radiation is maximum in the direction perpendicular to the dipole, as was discussed in sec. 4.3. As the frequency is increased indefinitely, the impedance and the radiation in the perpendicular direction go through successive maxima and minima, although the two properties do not go through these in step with each other. This fact indicates why, in this case, the impedance bandwidth and the pattern bandwidth have to be considered separately.

It is well known that if a resonant circuit is "loaded" by connecting or coupling a dissipative element (e.g., a resistor) to it, the sharpness of the resonance, and also the amplitude of variation of impedance and other properties, will be reduced. This is another way of saying that the bandwidth will be increased. This fact provides one approach to broadening the impedance bandwidth of antennas, at the sacrifice of efficiency. This method is used in the terminated rhombic and V antennas (sec. 5.8.1), and it is the basis of the well-known excellent bandwidth properties of these antennas. Resistive loading can also be used with short-monopole VLF antennas to broaden the bandwidth when wide-band modulation of the transmitted signal makes increased bandwidth necessary. Without such loading these antennas may be very narrow-band because of the large reactive component of the input impedance; when this reactance is tuned out by means of a large inductance, a "high Q" resonant circuit may result. (High Q implies narrow bandwidth.) However, a resistive loading is unnecessary when ground losses and other conductor losses reduce the Q sufficiently.

At higher frequencies, where antennas are usually full length, conductor losses may be very low compared to their radiated power. Consequently, simple antennas may be found to have inadequate bandwidth. But at these frequencies, deliberate loading with resistance is seldom practiced. In the first place, the extremely narrow bandwidth sometimes encountered at VLF is not usually found at higher frequencies, because there is a better ratio of radiation resistance to reactance. In effect, the *radiative* loading lowers the Q. Moreover, other methods of improving bandwidth have been discovered. These methods may be separated into two classes—those that apply to basic radiators, and those that apply to complex antennas, such as arrays, reflector-feed combinations, and lens antennas (in which the refracting element as well as the feed may be frequency-sensitive). This separation is not absolute, but it is of some value.

The methods that apply to basic radiators, such as dipoles, are mostly *geometric* in nature. That is, the employment of certain shapes, and certain size ratios, have been found to be beneficial. A dramatic extension of this class of methods has been made in the development of the spiral and log-periodic antennas, or frequency-independent antennas as they are also called.

Other methods apply to complex antennas. In some cases it is possible to combine elements whose variations of impedance (or other properties) are *complementary* in such a way that they tend to offset each other, as the frequency is varied. The bandwidth of an array is, naturally, improved by employing broad-band radiators as the elements. It is important to note, however, that the element bandwidth *in the array environment* may be less than it would be when isolated, because of mutual coupling effects.

Another important factor in broad-band array design is the transmission-line or wave-guide feed system that distributes the rf power of the transmitter, to provide the required amplitude and phase to each array element. Certain possible arrangements are much less frequency-sensitive than others. The two basic methods are shown in Fig. 2–8, chapter 2. For broadside arrays, the method of Fig. 2–8a is much better than that of Fig. 2–8b, because it preserves the same total length of line from the common input point to each element of the array; therefore all elements will be in-phase regardless of the frequency. But with the arrangement of Fig. 2–8b, the elements will be in-phase only at frequencies for which the interconnecting line length, d, is an integral multiple of a wavelength. The arrangement with all input-to-element path lengths equal is called a *corporate structure* feed system.

It is often necessary to provide impedance-matching transformers at an antenna's input terminals or at the elements of an array. Baluns (sec. 4.11) may also be required. The bandwidth of the transformers and baluns is an important factor in determining the overall impedance bandwidth. It is desirable to employ a transformer and balun whose reactance variations with frequency are in such a direction that they tend to cancel the reactance variation of the antenna or the array element. For example, a dipole fed at the center has inductive reactance at frequencies above the resonant frequency, and capacitive reactance at lower frequencies. A possible method of adjusting the dipole input impedance is to make it shorter than the resonant length, so that it is capacitive; then a short-circuited section of transmission line (shorted stub) is connected across the antenna input terminals, and its length is adjusted until it has an inductive reactance just sufficient to counteract the capacitive reactance of the dipole. For example, the required stub length is obtainable by rearranging equation (2–36), chapter 2. The resulting input resistance will have different values for different amounts of shortening of the dipole from the resonant length. The reactances of the stub and of the dipole will tend to cancel as the frequency is varied up or down. The cancellation will be imperfect, but there will be less net reactance change with frequency than there would be for a resonant dipole without the stub. This is a relatively simple illustration of a principle. More elaborate and effective methods may be used in practice.

These observations serve mainly to convey some of the general ideas and a few particulars of the art of making complex antennas broad-band. The remainder of this section is devoted to a discussion of the design of individual radiators of broad bandwidth.

7.1.2. Broad-Band Dipoles

Since dipoles are the most useful of radiators over a large part of the radio spectrum, considerable study has been devoted to designing them for broad bandwidth. The principal factor determining the bandwidth of a dipole has been found to be its thickness relative to its length. A "fat" dipole has much broader bandwidth than a thin one.

This principle can of course be more readily exploited at the moderately high frequencies where the dipole length is not too great—generally at frequencies above about 100 MHz, occasionally at somewhat lower frequencies. Dipoles are commonly employed as radiators up to about 1 GHz, occasionally up to a few gigaHertz. Therefore the practical region of application of the principles to be discussed is about 30 MHz to 3 GHz.

The discussion of dipole properties in sec. 4.3 is based on the assumption that the length-to-diameter ratio is very large, that is, that the dipole is thin. Fat dipoles do not have the same input impedance and current distribution as thin dipoles. Their radiation patterns are similar, although not identical. The important property of the thick dipole is that its impedance variation with frequency is much less than for a thin dipole.

It is common practice, therefore, in the frequency region mentioned, to make dipoles using large-diameter tubing or pipe rather than thin wire. This results in a cylindrical dipole, as illustrated in Fig. 7–1a. A length-to-diameter ratio as low as 10 is not uncommon. The shape is sometimes modified as shown in Fig. 7–1b and 7–1c.

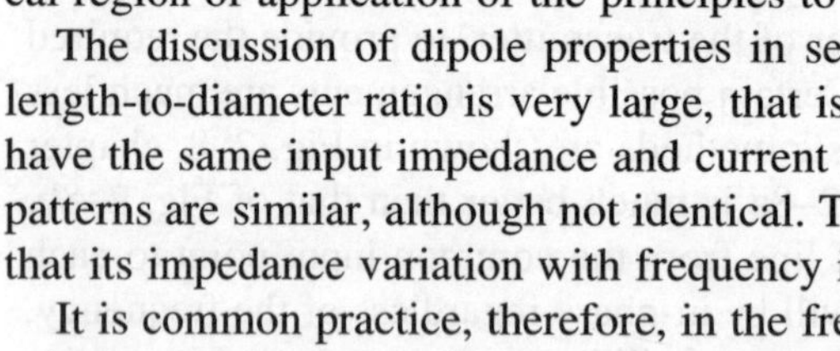

FIGURE 7–1.

Several forms of fat dipoles. (a) Cylindrical dipole. (b) Cylindrical with conical ends at gap. (c) Prolate spheroidal antenna.

The variation of the input impedance of the simple cylindrical dipole for three different values of the length-to-diameter ratio (L/D) is shown in Figs. 7–2 and 7–3. These curves are based on calculations of Kennedy and King (1953). Because of effects at the point of connection of the transmission line, these values may not be observed exactly in practice, but they serve as a guide to the approximate values and the nature of the variation. It is apparent from these curves that the variations of resistance and reactance are much less for fat dipoles ($L/D = 17$ and $L/D = 122$) than for thin dipoles ($L/D = 11{,}000$). The frequency f_0 is the value at which the dipole is a half wavelength—that is, $L = \lambda/2$ when $f = f_0$. The resulting values of the voltage standing-wave ratio (VSWR) on a transmission line for the various values of f/f_0 could be calculated by taking the values of R and X given by these curves to determine the quantities R_L/Z_0 and X_L/Z_0 for use in equation (2–45), chapter 2, from which the line voltage variation may be plotted. Alternatively, the Smith Chart, described in sec. 9.12, could be used to determine the VSWR directly from the values of R_L/Z_0 and X_L/Z_0.

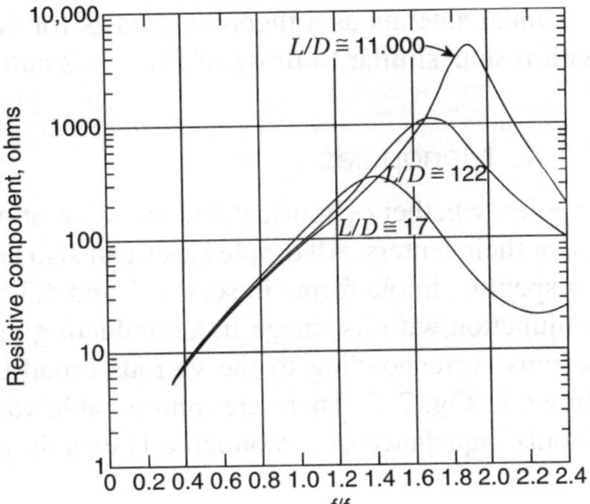

FIGURE 7–2.

Resistive component of input impedance of a center-fed cylindrical dipole as a function of frequency, for three values of length-diameter (L/D) ratio. Plotted from values calculated by Kennedy and King (1953).

7.1.3. Biconical Antennas

A radiator generally regarded as a form of dipole is the biconical antenna, shown in Fig. 7–4. This type of antenna is usually analyzed in terms of the cone half-angle θ together with the parameters s and h. As seen by comparison of Fig. 7–4 with Fig. 4–22 of chapter 4, it is virtually identical to the biconical horn. Whether it is regarded as a dipole or a horn is partly a matter of preference in some cases. Conventionally it may be considered a dipole if θ is less than 45 degrees and a horn if θ is greater than 45 degrees. The mode of excitation also affects this distinction. The biconical antenna can be regarded as a dipole only if it is excited to produce polarization parallel to the conical axes (TEM mode). In either case, however, the antenna has broad-band properties. The broad-band qualities of horns have already been mentioned. As a dipole, the biconical antenna has a bandwidth roughly equivalent to that of a cylindrical dipole whose diameter is somewhat less than the maximum cone diameter. Biconical antennas have been extensively analyzed by Schelkunoff (1943). He has also used the

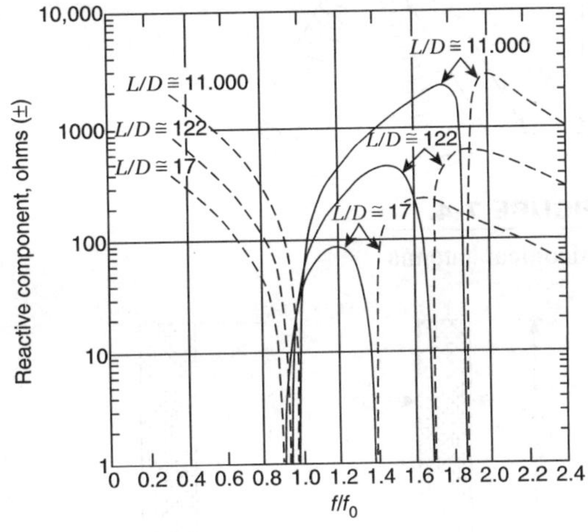

FIGURE 7–3.

Reactive component of input impedance of a center-fed cylindrical dipole as a function of frequency, for three values of length-diameter (L/D) ratio. Dashed-line portions of curves represent negative (capacitive) reactance, and solid-line portions represent positive (inductive) reactance. Plotted from values calculated by Kennedy and King (1953).

biconical antenna as a theoretical basis for deducing properties of cylindrical antennas, with results similar to those of Figs. 7–2 and 7–3.

7.1.4. Monopoles

Dipoles, whether cylindrical, biconical, or of other shape, are symmetrical radiators when fed at their centers. All dipole types can also be used as monopoles, which were discussed for specific dipole forms in secs. 4.1 and 4.3. A monopole is half of a dipole operated in conjunction with its image in a conducting ground plane perpendicular to it. Monopole designs corresponding to the various broad-band dipoles that have been discussed are shown in Fig. 7–5. There are innumerable variants of the shapes shown. The feed-point (input) impedance of a monopole is exactly half the value of the corresponding dipole, if the ground plane is a perfect conductor and of infinite extent, and the pattern corresponds exactly to half the pattern of the dipole. Since for a given input power the radiation is concentrated into half the solid angle occupied by the dipole pattern, the directive gain of the monopole is twice that of the dipole in free space. (See discussion of directivity in sec. 3.3 and of vertical radiators in secs. 4.1 and 4.3.) In practice, of course, the ground plane will not be a perfect conductor of infinite extent, but the properties of the monopole will approximate those just described if the ground plane is a good conductor extending to a distance several times as great as the height of the monopole.

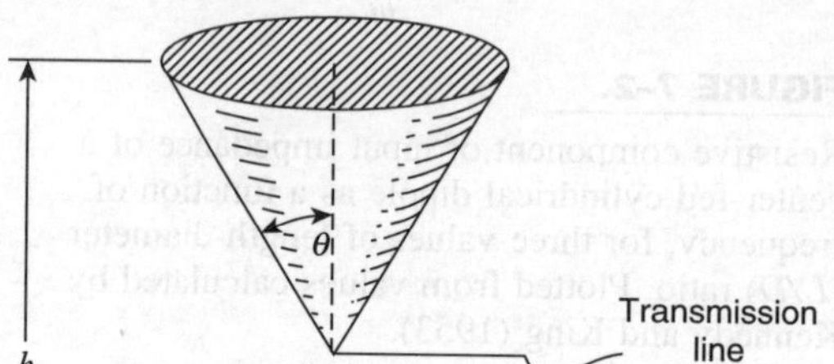

FIGURE 7–4.
Biconical antenna.

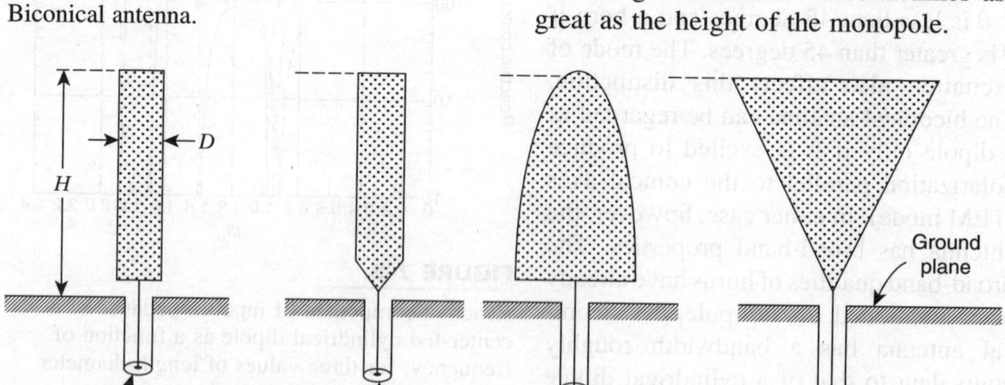

FIGURE 7–5.
Monopole antennas corresponding to the dipoles of Figures 7–1 and 7–4.

Monopoles are especially useful as vehicle antennas where the ground plane is the "skin" of the vehicle (ship, boat, automobile, tank, aircraft, spacecraft). On aircraft the monopole may for aerodynamic reasons take the shape of a streamlined "blade" rather than the circular-cross-section shapes commonly used in other applications. Another advantage of the monopole is that it is conveniently fed by a coaxial line. (The advantages of coaxial lines are discussed in sec. 2.4.) A monopole has the same bandwidth properties as the corresponding dipole.

7.1.5. Folded Dipoles

A very important variation of the simple dipole is the folded half-wave dipole, depicted in Fig. 7–6. A principal advantage of the folded dipole is its higher input impedance that can be more readily matched to the characteristic impedance of a two-wire line given by equation (2–62) of chapter 2. The folded construction results in a step-up of the approximately 70-ohm simple-dipole input impedance by a factor of 4. Hence the input impedance of a basic folded dipole is about 300 ohms (actually slightly less). Folded dipoles are often used as elements of television receiving antennas and as the feed element for Yagi-Uda arrays.

This statement applies only to a folded dipole by itself. When it is an element of an array, or is used with a reflector, its input impedance may no longer have this value, and an impedance-matching device may then be required. Even so, the matching to a two-wire line is easier to accomplish than it would be with a simple dipole.

The folded dipole also has somewhat better intrinsic bandwidth properties than a simple dipole of the same size conductors. The folded construction tends to produce the reactance-canceling action of a short stub line in parallel with the simple-dipole reactance, at frequencies off resonance. The great difference between the impedance behavior of the folded dipole and the ordinary dipole may be seen by considering a very short folded dipole (short compared to a half wavelength) in comparison with a very short ordinary dipole; the short folded dipole will have a very low inductive impedance whereas the short ordinary dipole will have a very high capacitive input impedance. For longer-than-half-wave dipoles the opposite comparison of reactances applies; the folded dipole is capacitive, and the simple dipole is inductive. The folded dipole has bandwidth properties equivalent to those of a fat dipole of diameter somewhat less than the spacing of the folded-dipole conductors.

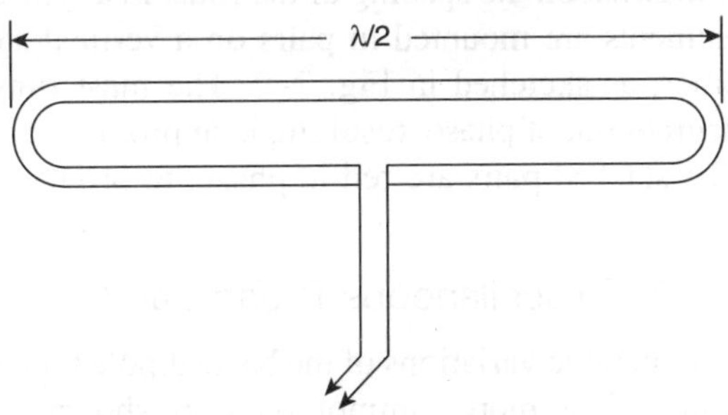

FIGURE 7–6.
Folded dipole.

Additional step-up of the simple-dipole impedance may be obtained by adding more "folded" conductors. A three-wire folded dipole is shown in Fig. 7–7. Its input impedance is approximately nine times the normal 70-ohm impedance, or about 630 ohms. Still more conductors can be added to obtain

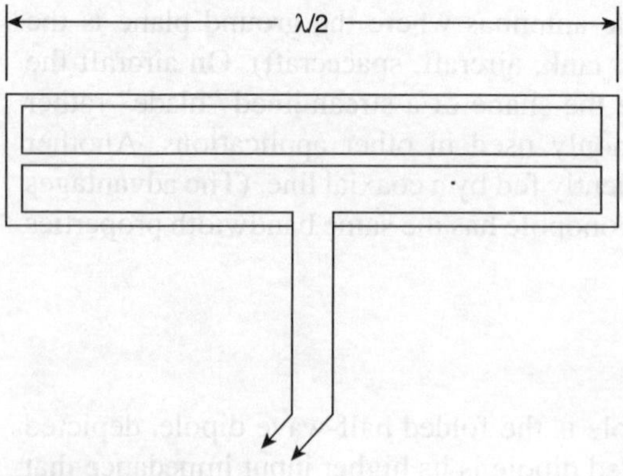

FIGURE 7–7.
Three-wire folded dipole.

even higher impedance, though an input impedance higher than about 600 ohms is seldom desired. The step-up ratio may also be altered by making the folded conductors of different size from the basic conductor. Many other variations of the folded-dipole principle have been devised.

7.1.6. Superturnstile Antenna

A form of broad-band dipole much used as the element of a TV transmitting array, known as the superturnstile, is shown in Fig. 7–8. This element is partly a dipole and partly a slotted-sheet antenna. The slot is vertical and the dipole horizontal; hence the polarization is horizontal. It is fed by a balanced line at the center of the slot. The input impedance is about 75 ohms. This radiator has a 30 to 35 percent impedance bandwidth for a VSWR not exceeding 1.1 : 1. Its broad-band properties stem partly from the large dipole width and partly from the fact that the dipole and the slot have "complementary" impedance variation characteristics that tend to offset each other as the frequency is varied.

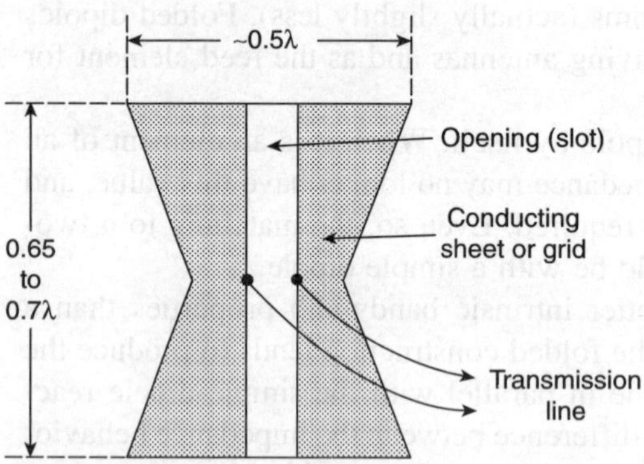

FIGURE 7–8.
Element of a superturnstile antenna.

To reduce wind resistance, the solid sheets are replaced by horizontal conducting rods, as depicted in Fig. 7–9. The dimensions given in Fig. 7–8 are approximate for the center frequency, and they will depend somewhat on the spacing of the rods. In a typical VHF TV transmitting array, the antenna elements are mounted in pairs on a vertical steel mast, the pairs stacked one above the other, as sketched in Fig. 7–9. The mast runs "through" the slot. Each pair is fed 90 degrees out of phase, resulting in approximately circular coverage in the horizontal plane. The stacked pairs are fed in phase, to produce array gain horizontally (in elevation).

7.1.7. Miscellaneous Broad-Band Dipoles and Other Radiators

Innumerable variations of the basic dipole types, previously described, have been devised. Some of the more common ones are shown in Fig. 7–10.

Broad-band dipoles have been discussed extensively because of their importance in many applications, and also because many of the principles discussed apply to other radiator types as well. It is not possible here to discuss the broad-banding of every type of radiator, but some general observations can be made.

Horns and axial-mode helixes are basically broad-band radiators, since their operation does not depend on any critically resonant element or elements. They do of course have maximum and minimum frequencies. For the rectangular horn these are usually the frequency limits of the rectangular waveguide, which is a 2 : 1 range. (See sec. 2.5.) Slot radiators have bandwidth properties similar to those of dipoles. The various nonresonant antennas described in sec. 4.4 have excellent bandwidths, but the resonant long-wire types do not.

In all this discussion, and in what follows, the bandwidth is considered for operation of the antenna without any adjustments when the frequency is changed. It is of course possible to operate an essentially narrow-band antenna over a considerable frequency range if some provision is made for adjustment of critical lengths, or for adjusting an impedance-matching transformer. In some applications this type of operation is possible, and is employed. Possibly the most common example is the adjustable "rabbit ears" indoor antenna sometimes used with television receivers, the dipole length being adjustable by means of a telescoping construction.

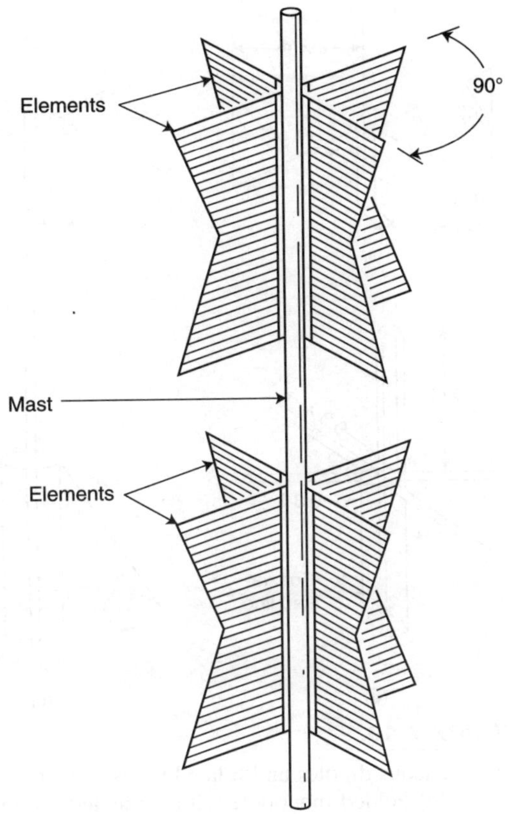

FIGURE 7–9.

Two vertically stacked "bays" of a superturnstile TV transmitting antenna.

7.2. Frequency-Independent Antennas

A very sophisticated and effective approach to achieving broadband antenna design has evolved from the initial work of a number of researchers at the University of Illinois (Rumsey 1957, 1966; DuHamel and Isbell 1957). The class of antennas that has resulted are called frequency-independent or log-periodic antennas. (The term log-periodic is perhaps too restrictive since it refers to only one aspect of their behavior.) These antennas achieve bandwidths of 10 : 1 with ease, and much larger values are possible with careful design. Their broad-band behavior includes both impedance and pattern characteristics. They are a class rather than a type of antenna, because there are many different types. They have a wide variety of physical appearances, some of them quite bizarre in

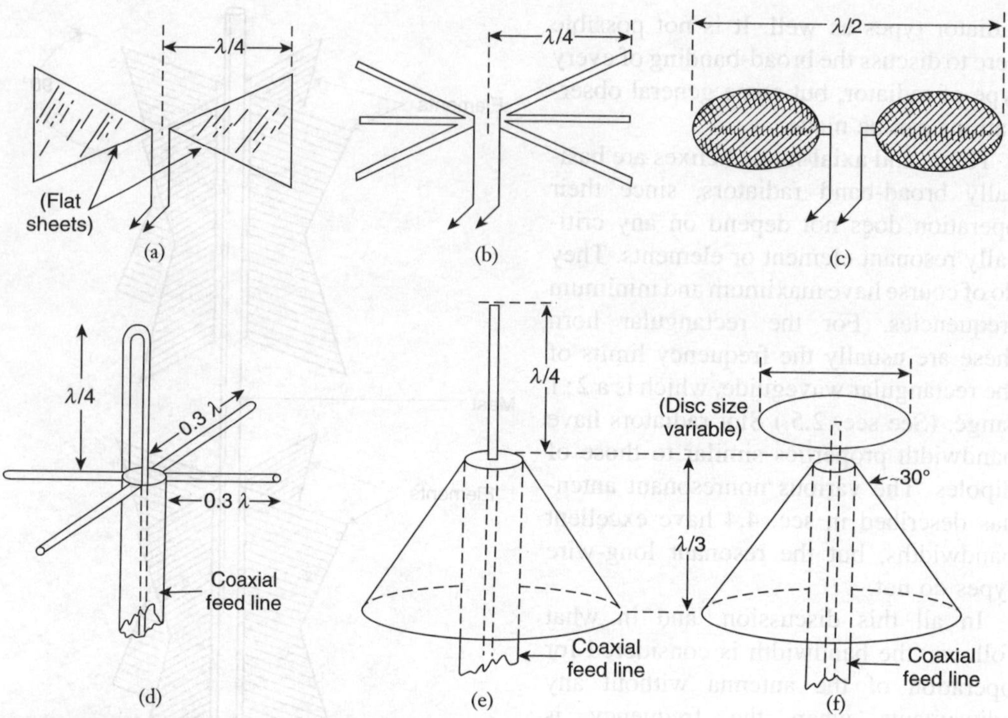

FIGURE 7–10.

Miscellaneous dipoles and related types. (a) Triangular dipole. (b) Fan dipole. (c) Ellipsoidal dipole. (d) Folded monopole with simulated ground plane. (e) Conical skirt monopole. (f) Discone antenna.

comparison with more conventional antennas. They may have unidirectional or bidirectional patterns of low to moderate directive gain. Higher directive gain may be obtained by using them as elements of an array or as feeds for parabolic reflectors and lenses, in which use, however, a design must be chosen that maintains a constant or nearly constant phase center. (Many log-periodic types do not.) Log-periodic array design presents special problems not encountered in ordinary arrays. Excellent discussions of the subject have been published by Deschamps and DuHamel (1961), Jordan, Deschamps, Dyson, and Mayes (1964), and Rumsey (1966).

7.2.1. The Log-Periodic Principle

All the frequency-independent antennas have a special kind of repetitiveness in their physical structure, which results in a repetitive behavior of the electrical characteristics. That is, the design involves a basic geometric pattern that is repeated, but with a changing size of the pattern. The pattern size changes with each repetition by a constant scale factor so that the structure "grows" (or shrinks, depending on the direction considered). These principles are illustrated by the log-periodic "dipole array" of Fig. 7–11, which is

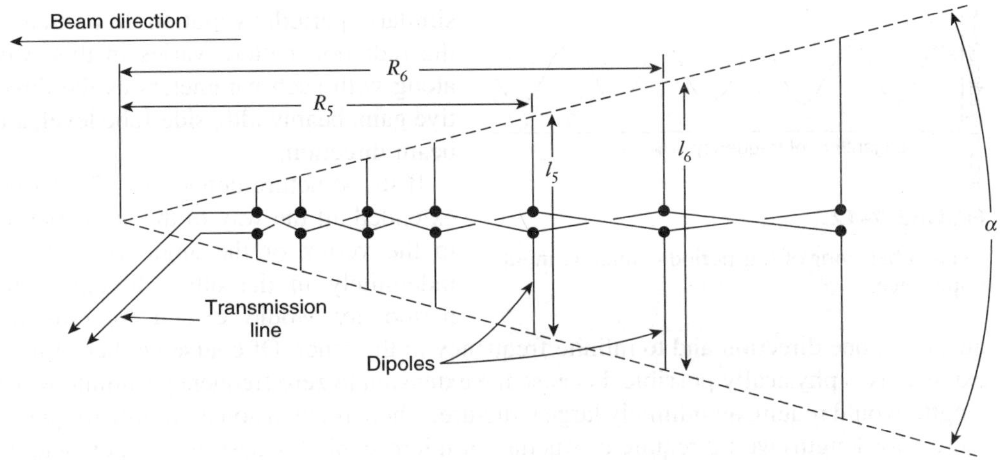

FIGURE 7–11.
Log-periodic dipole array.

perhaps the nearest that a log-periodic design can come to resembling a conventional antenna. (There is a marked similarity to the end-fire dipole array described in sec. 5.2.)

This particular form of dipole array was devised by Isbell (1960). It consists of a number of dipoles of different length and spacing, fed by a two-wire line that is transposed between each adjacent pair of dipoles. The array is fed at the small end of the structure, and the maximum radiation is toward this end. The lengths of the dipoles and their spacing are graduated in such a way that certain dimensions of adjacent elements bear a constant ratio to each other; these are the quantities designated R and l in Fig. 7–11. That is, if this *design ratio* is designated by τ (a number less than one), then

$$\frac{R_2}{R_1} = \frac{R_3}{R_2} = \frac{R_4}{R_3} = \frac{1}{\tau} = \frac{l_2}{l_1} = \frac{l_3}{l_2} = \frac{l_4}{l_3} \tag{7–1}$$

It is apparent that these conditions cause the ends of the dipoles to lie along straight lines that meet at an angle designated α. It is a characteristic of the frequency-independent antennas that certain aspects of their structures can be specified in terms of an angle or angles.

The result of these structural conditions is that if a plot is made of the input impedance as a function of frequency, the variation will be found to be repetitive. If the plot is made against the *logarithm* of the frequency, rather than the frequency itself, this variation will be *periodic*—that is, the impedance will go through cycles of variation in such a way that each cycle is exactly like the preceding one. A typical plot is shown in Fig. 7–12. It is this behavior that gives rise to the name "log periodic"; the impedance is a logarithmically periodic function of the frequency. (It is not implied, however, that the variation is necessarily sinusoidal.) Moreover, all the electrical properties of the antenna undergo a

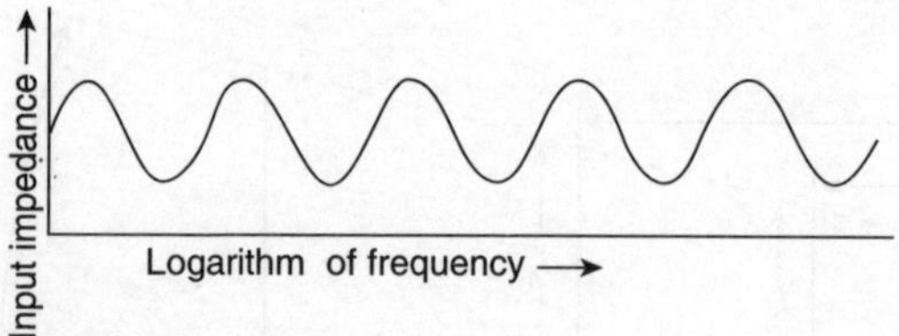

FIGURE 7–12.

Typical behavior of log-periodic antenna input impedance.

similarly periodic variation. In particular, the radiation pattern varies in this way, along with such parameters as the directive gain, beamwidth, side-lobe level, and beam direction.

If the structure defined by (7–1) were extended all the way to the apex, that is, to the vertex of the angle α, and also indefinitely in the other direction, this periodicity would extend to zero frequency in one direction and to infinite frequency in the other. Of course neither of these extensions is physically possible, because the extension to zero frequency (infinite wavelength) would require an infinitely large structure, whereas extension to infinite frequency (zero wavelength) would require a structure of microscopic fineness at the apex; and the transmission line feeding would have to be of infinitesimal conductor size and spacing—an obvious impossibility. Therefore, the structure must be *terminated* at some point in each direction, and these points determine high and low cutoff frequencies, beyond which the log-periodic property does not extend.

This periodicity does not by itself insure that the antenna will be broad-band. But if the impedance and pattern variation over one cycle of the periodic variation can be made sufficiently small, so that some bandwidth criterion is satisfied, the same criterion will be satisfied over all periods. The requirement, therefore, is to find structural patterns that do provide the necessary behavior over one log-periodic cycle. The possible bandwidth is then limited only by the number of cyclic structures employed in the antenna. Fortunately, many such structural patterns have been found.

The magnitude of the log-frequency periods is determined by the design ratio, τ, and is in general of magnitude log $(1/\tau)$.* That is, if two successive maxima of the impedance or pattern variation occur at frequencies f_1 and f_2, it will be found that they are related by the formula

$$\log f_2 - \log f_1 = \log \frac{f_2}{f_1} = \log \frac{1}{\tau} \tag{7–2}$$

from which it follows that $f_2/f_1 = 1/\tau$, or $f_1 = \tau f_2$. Therefore, if the log-periodic antenna has certain measured properties (e.g., impedance, gain) at any particular frequency f, it follows that it will have exactly the same properties at frequencies τf, $\tau^2 f$, $\tau^3 f$, and so on, and also at $f/\tau, f/\tau^2, f/\tau^3, \ldots$, provided that these frequencies are all within the cutoff limits.

The word "exactly" in the foregoing statement applies only if the structural scaling by the design ratio τ is exact and is applied to every detail of the structure. For example, in the antenna of Fig. 7–11 not only the dimensions R and l must be scaled but also the sizes of the conductors. If, for example, the dipoles are made of tubing, the tubing must

* In certain cases the impedance (but not the pattern) may vary with a period half as large (that is, with period $\frac{1}{2}$ log $(1/\tau)$). But these cases do not violate Eq. 7–2, since a variation with periodicity $\frac{1}{2}$ log $(1/\tau)$ is *also* periodic with period log $(1/\tau)$.

be of properly increasing thickness as the distance from the apex of the structure increases. The width of the gaps at the dipole centers must also increase. However, these relatively minor factors can be ignored without serious effect if the overall bandwidth (ratio of maximum to minimum cutoff frequencies) does not exceed about 10:1.

When a log-periodic antenna is fed at a particular frequency, it is found that the radiation occurs from a certain portion of the structure, and that other portions do not radiate. This "active" region of the antenna of Fig. 7–11 is the region in which one or more of the dipoles is nearly half a wavelength. The cutoff frequencies are those at which the shortest and longest dipoles are approximately half a wavelength. Thus the active region of the antenna is near the apex for the highest frequencies radiated, near the large end for the lowest frequencies, and at intermediate positions for frequencies in between. This behavior may also be expressed by saying that the *phase center* of the antenna progresses from the large end to the small end as the frequency goes from minimum to maximum of the band-width range.

Log-periodic antennas may be either unidirectional or bidirectional in their pattern characteristics. The bidirectional types are characterized by two active regions that move apart as the frequency is decreased; in these types the phase center remains fixed and coincides with the feed point.

For the antenna of Fig. 7–11 typical values of the design ratio and apex angle are $\tau = 0.8$ and $\alpha = 30°$. For any given value of α, there is a minimum permissible value of τ (which is always a number between 0 and 1). Larger values of α and smaller values of τ go together and result in more compact design for a given bandwidth. On the other hand, smaller values of α and larger values of τ result in improved performance—smaller variation of impedance and pattern, and higher gain, at the cost of a larger structure. The reason for this effect may be intuitively understood by realizing that for small α and large τ, at any given frequency, there are more dipoles of nearly half-wavelength; hence the active or radiating region of the antenna encompasses more dipoles than for large α and smaller τ. As is always true, the gain increases with the number of radiating elements and with the size of the radiating region. Also, the impedance and pattern variations are smaller because of the smoother transition in the configuration of the radiating region when it encompasses several dipole elements.

7.2.2. Practical Log-Periodic Designs

As mentioned, numerous structural forms have been found to be suitable for log-periodic antennas. Three representative ones are shown in Fig. 7–13.

First we refer to the wire-trapezoidal-tooth antenna of Fig. 7–13b, which is frequently used as a moderately directive steerable (rotatable) HF communication antenna. It has two arms or branches originating at the apex of the antenna. Each branch has a characteristic angle α that plays the same role in the antenna design as the angle α in the log-periodic dipole array (Fig. 7–11). The other angle, γ, affects the directional characteristics. When γ is 180 degrees, which it is for the trapezoidal-tooth structure shown in Fig. 7–13a, the radiation is bidirectional and perpendicular to the plane of the antenna. When γ is an acute angle, the radiation is unidirectional and toward the apex of the structure. The dipole array, Fig. 7–11, at first glance does not seem to conform to these observations.

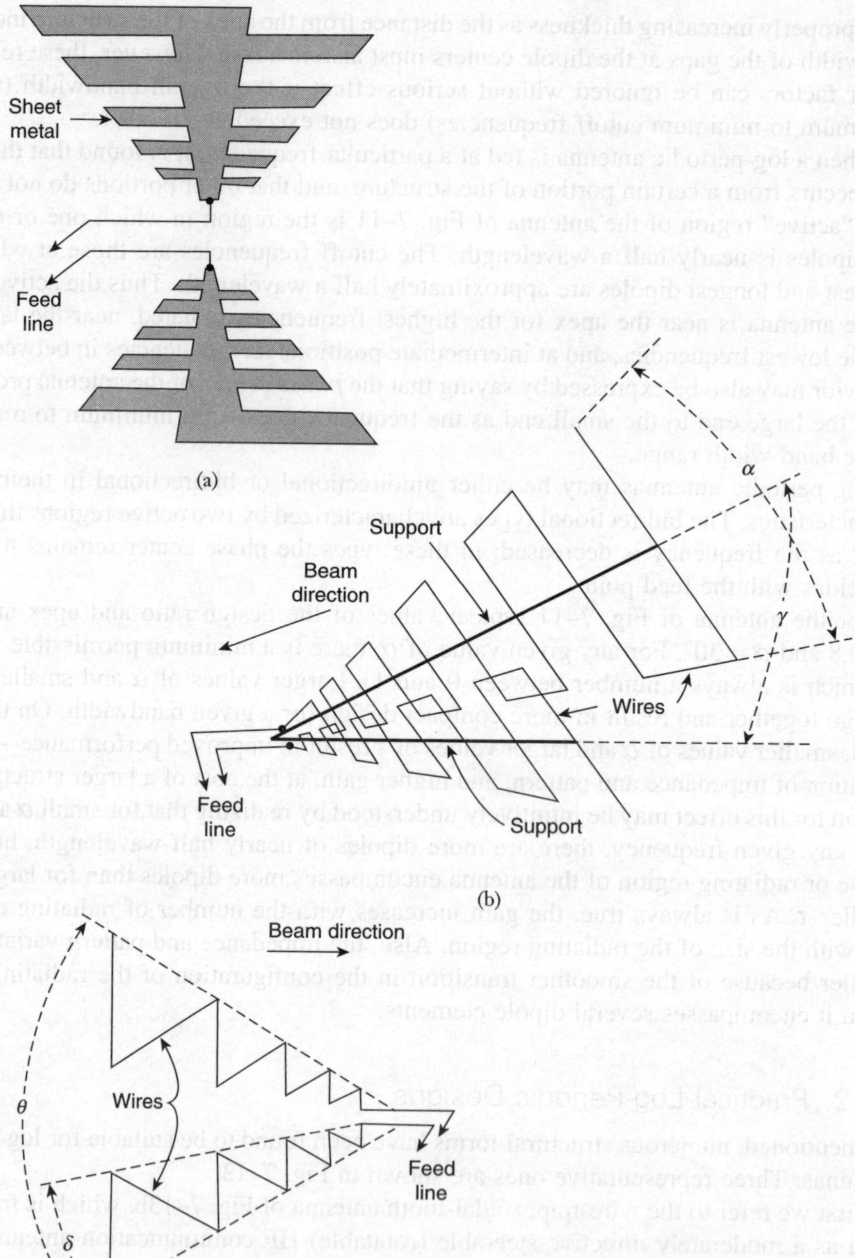

FIGURE 7–13.

Some practical log-periodic antenna designs. (a) Trapezoidal tooth structure. (b) Wire trapezoidal tooth antenna. (c) Wire triangular tooth antenna.

It can be shown, however, that actually it is a specialization of the trapezoidal-tooth structure (Fig. 7–13a), in which the width of the teeth is reduced to nearly zero, and the angle γ has been reduced from 180 degrees to zero. That is, the two branches have been folded over until they are in the same plane, but not in electrical contact. The wire triangular tooth antenna (Fig. 7–13c) is another plane structure that results in a unidirectional pattern.

A variation of the Isbell log-periodic dipole array, developed by Mayes and Carrel (see Mayes, 1982) at the University of Illinois, employs resonant-V dipole elements instead of conventional straight dipoles, with the acute angle of the V toward the small end of the array (in the direction of the beam). The dipole elements of this array operating as half-wave radiators provide a moderate bandwidth. Slightly beyond the upper limit of this basic band, the elements again become active in a 3/2-wavelength mode, and at still higher frequencies they operate in a 5/2-wavelength mode. The V configuration provides good directivity at the higher frequencies, and the multiple-mode operation provides a large operating bandwidth (as much as 20 : 1) in a relatively compact antenna. This design has been in wide use as a TV receiving antenna for covering the entire spectrum from the lowest TV VHF channel (54 MHz) to the previous highest TV UHF channel (890 MHz), although the current highest U.S.-allocated TV UHF frequency is 698 MHz (see sec. 1.1.2). Other modifications of the Isbell array employ folded-dipole and folded-monopole elements (the latter being operated against a ground screen or the actual ground).

7.2.3. Equiangular Log-Periodic Antennas

It has been noted that certain features of the structure of a log-periodic antenna may be specified in terms of an angle or angles (Dyson 1959, 1965). When the structure can be *entirely* specified in terms of angles, it is found that the impedance variation is very small over the log-periodic frequency cycle. Hence it is highly desirable to use structures that meet this criterion. An example of such a structure, the conical spiral antenna shown in Fig. 7–14, is characterized by the half angle of the cone and by the angle that the

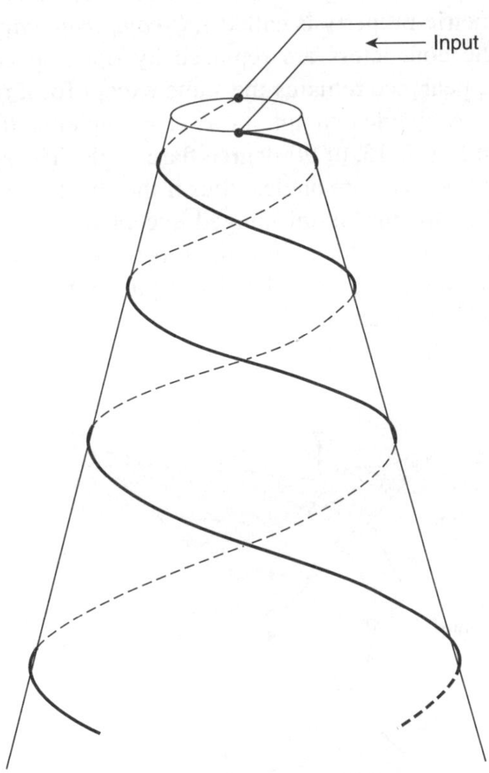

FIGURE 7–14.

Sketch indicating general nature of a conical logarithmic-spiral antenna. (A practical antenna would have a smaller pitch angle—i.e., more turns per unit length of cone.)

spiral makes with a circumference, or its complement that the spiral makes with a radial line from the apex. There are two interleaved spiral conductors lying on a conical (non-conducting) surface. Each spiral is connected at the apex to one side of the feed line. The radiation is unidirectional, going in the direction toward which the apex of the cone points. The peak of the beam is polarized elliptically, becoming virtually circularly polarized as the number of turns per unit length is increased.

7.2.4. Self-Complementary Antennas

As mentioned in sec. 4–8, a certain relationship exists between the patterns and impedances of *complementary* antennas (e.g., a "flat" dipole in free space and a slot of the same size and shape in an infinite conducting plane). Booker (1946) showed that if an antenna consisting of both conducting-sheet elements and openings between them (e.g., slots) can be so configured that the conductors and the open spaces are of identical shape and size, its input impedance is independent of frequency. An antenna having this geometric property is called *self-complementary.* The test of self-complementarity is that if the conductors are replaced by open spaces and the open spaces by conductors, the appearance remains the same except for a rotation through an angle.

A simple example of a self-complementary structure is a pair of triangular sheets, as in Fig. 7–15, of 90-degree flare angle. The spaces between them will of course also have 90-degree flare angles; thus if the sheets are replaced by spaces and the spaces by sheets, the structure is unchanged except for a rotation through 90 degrees. The self-complementarity holds only if the sheets extend to infinity; therefore, this arrangement does not constitute a practical self-complementary antenna. It is shown here solely to explain the self-complementarity principle.

If the log-periodic principle is combined with the self-complementary principle, the structure need not extend to infinity since it is only necessary for self-complementarity to exist in the active regions of the structure. A sheet-logarithmic-spiral structure, shown in Fig. 7–16, which is also an equiangular structure, can be made self-complementary. It provides bidirectional circularly polarized radiation in directions perpendicular to the plane of the sheet, with excellent impedance characteristics; that is, the impedance is virtually constant over the frequency range between the log-periodic cutoff points. Other self-complementary designs have also been devised. The impedance of a two-terminal self-complementary antenna, according to Booker's principle, is 60π

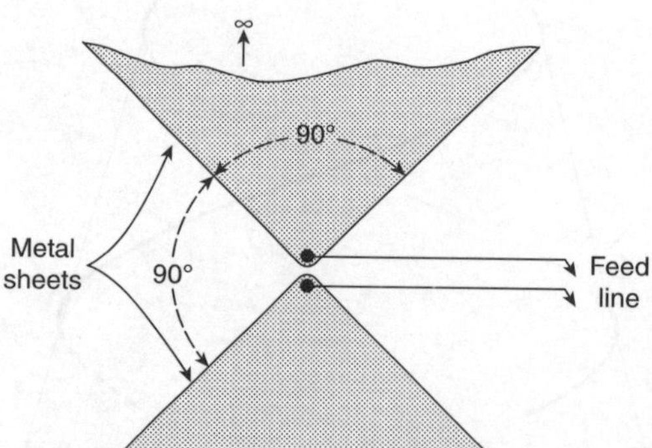

FIGURE 7–15.
Triangular sheet self-complementary structure.

(about 189) ohms. (It is also possible to have structures of more than two terminals, i.e., with more than twofold angular symmetry, and such structures have other values of impedance.)

This discussion of frequency-independent antennas has presented the elementary principles and some of the highlights of current designs. Such antennas are practical in the frequency region of perhaps 10 MHz to 10 GHz. The theory and practice are in relative infancy, although great strides have been made.

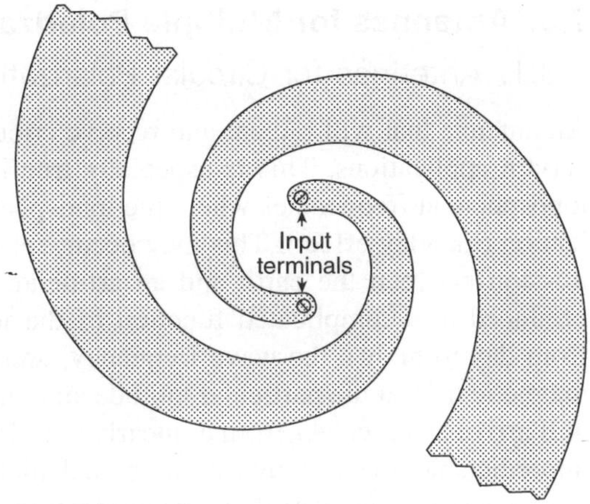

FIGURE 7–16.

Central portion of a logarithmic-spiral self-complementary antenna. Shaded portions are sheet metal. Note that rotation of the figure through 90° carries the shaded portions into the clear areas and vice versa and rotation through 180° leaves the figure unchanged.

7.2.5. Spiral Antennas

Spiral antennas consist of conducting wires or tapes arranged in spiral shapes, on either a conical or planar surface (Filipovic and Cencich 2007). Spiral antennas are inherently circularly polarized (CP) and have relatively constant input impedance and radiation patterns over a wide range of frequencies. Without modification, planar spiral antennas are bidirectional with opposite circularity in the two directions perpendicular to the planar surface. Planar spiral antennas are made unidirectional by placing either absorbing materials or a reflecting surface on one side of the planar surface. The reflecting plate is spaced at $\lambda/4$ distance, and then the wave to be rejected is polarization reversed and adds constructively to wave of the other direction, causing unidirectional performance. The conductors of conical spiral antennas are wound along a cone and their patterns are unidirectional, with the beam maximum directed toward the apex of the cone.

The conducting spirals are called arms. Customarily, the shapes of the spiral arms have been either Archimedean or equiangular. The Archimedean spiral has a constant arm width and constant separation between arms throughout the spiraling aperture. The equiangular spiral has progressively increased arm width and separation between the arms until they open to the outside aperture dimension. Although the antenna of Fig. 7–16 is a self-complementary spiral, the spiral shape is equiangular.

Spiral antennas may be made in a number of different geometries not only for improved electrical performance, but also for better packaging, arraying, and mounting. A square shape may allow closer spacing for array elements, and wiggly or zig-zag shapes permit longer conductor lengths and thereby enhance low-frequency performance. Spiral antennas can be flush mounted, made on antenna reflectors, or placed on aircraft and other vehicle surfaces.

7.3. Antennas for Multiple Polarizations

7.3.1. Antennas for Circular Polarization

An antenna that will radiate and receive circularly polarized waves may be required for certain applications. This is especially true in uses involving transmission through the ionosphere at frequencies where the ionosphere may produce rotation of the wave polarization (Faraday effect). This may occur, for example, in communication or radar transmission between the earth and an artificial satellite, or other spacecraft. The rotation produced is a complicated function of the ionospheric electron density (which varies from day to night), the wave frequency, and the orientation and strength of the earth's magnetic field at the particular latitude and longitude involved. Thus the polarization that will arrive at a receiver from a linearly polarized transmitting antenna may be practically unpredictable, even though it can be calculated if the electron density and earth's field are known. If it happens that the polarization is rotated just enough to put it at 90 degrees with respect to a linearly polarized receiving antenna, no signal will be received. This is the extreme case; for other angles of rotation, the signal strength (power) will be reduced to a fraction equal to the square of the cosine of the angle between the wave polarization and the receiving antenna polarization. These effects occur in the frequency range of, roughly, 10 to 1,000 MHz, although ordinarily not above about 500 MHz in daytime and perhaps 100 MHz or less at night.

If either the transmitting or the receiving antenna is circularly polarized (i.e., transmits or receives circularly polarized waves), signal reception is possible regardless of polarization rotation by the ionosphere. Circular polarization is also desirable in certain radar and communications applications at higher frequencies.

A number of methods exist for producing circularly polarized radiation or reception by an antenna. Some of them have already been mentioned in connection with the description of specific antenna types, for example, the helix (sec. 4.6) and the spirals (either conical or planar).

An important method of achieving circular polarization is the use of two dipoles arranged to form a cross, that is, with their centers at the same point and their axes at right angles to each other. If a transmission line connects directly to the center of one of them, and if the two dipole-center feed points are joined by a quarter-wave line section, there will be a 90-degree phase delay between the currents in the two dipoles in accordance with equation (2–23), chapter 2, provided that the length of each dipole is adjusted to make its input impedance nonreactive. The pair of dipoles will thus radiate two linearly polarized waves at right angles to each other with 90-degree phase difference. As stated in sec. 1.1, this combination produces an elliptically polarized wave, or if the two linear-polarization amplitudes are equal it results in a circularly polarized wave. The two amplitudes will be equal in the two directions perpendicular to the dipole axes. Thus in these directions the radiation will be circularly polarized and also will have maximum power density. In the plane of the two dipoles, the radiation will be linearly polarized and of somewhat reduced power density. In this plane the radiation will be almost (but not quite) uniform in all directions, that is, throughout 360 degrees. In all other directions

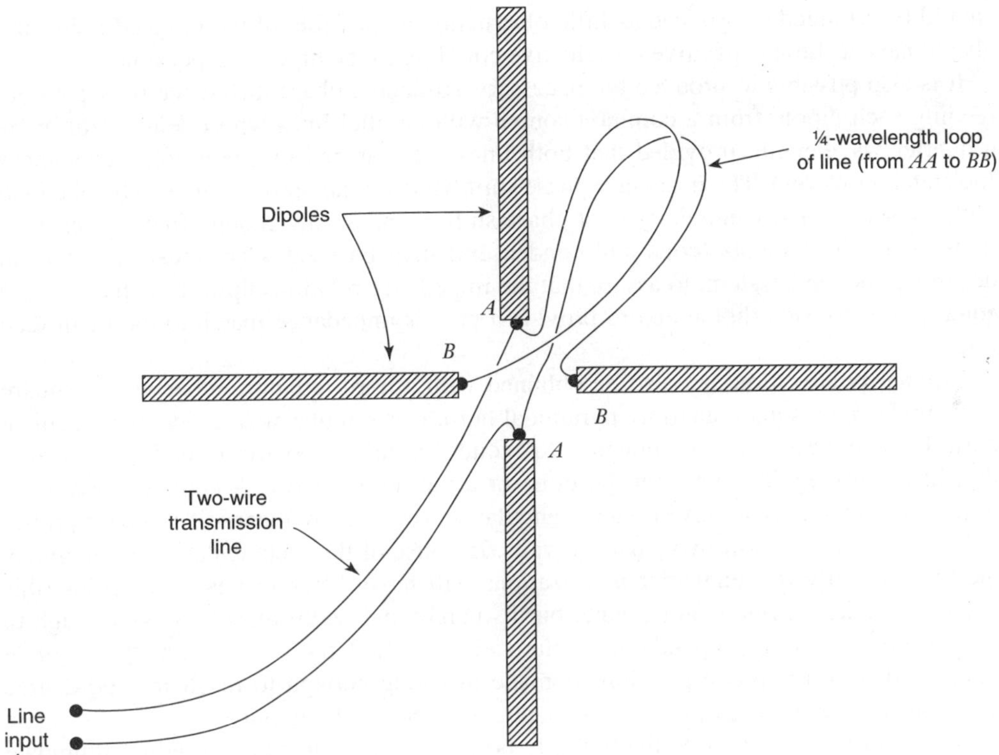

FIGURE 7–17.

Arrangement of crossed dipoles for radiation of circular polarization (turnstile antenna).

the radiation will have varying degree of ellipticity, going from circular on the perpendicular axis to linear polarization in the plane of the dipoles.

This arrangement of dipoles and the feed system is shown in Fig. 7–17. It is an especially important arrangement for two reasons. First, it is a basic method of producing circular polarization. The pattern in this polarization is bidirectional but can readily be made unidirectional by placing a reflector behind the dipoles, or combining several pairs in an endfire array (with the cross-dipole planes perpendicular to the line of the array). Second, it is useful when approximately uniform radiation is desired in a horizontal plane with horizontal polarization.

This configuration is known as a *turnstile* antenna. To provide increased gain in the horizontal plane and to reduce or eliminate the circularly polarized upward and downward radiation, several turnstiles can be stacked vertically and fed in broadside-array fashion. This arrangement is much used for television and FM broadcasting, using broad-band dipoles. When a particular form of slotted-sheet dipole is used, the arrangement is known as the superturnstile antenna, as was mentioned in the discussion of broad-band dipoles (see Fig. 7–9). The quarter-wave phase-delay line section, if this phasing method is used, should be arranged to produce as little obstruction as possible of the radiated fields and also to have as little capacitive or inductive coupling to the dipoles as possible.

It is also possible to produce the necessary 90-degree phase difference by separately feeding each dipole from a common source with parallel lines whose lengths differ by a quarter wavelength, provided that both lines are matched by the dipole impedances (no standing waves). The necessary phase shift between the dipoles can also be obtained with a coaxial- or waveguide-type of phase shifter, and at low enough frequencies even lumped-circuit elements (coils and condensers) may be used. Care must be taken, in designing the feed system, to assure that the impedance relationships are such as to feed equal power to each dipole and to provide a proper impedance match to the main feed line.

Circular polarization can also be obtained with a horn radiator, either with a square waveguide and a square-aperture pyramidal horn, or a circular waveguide and a conical horn. In either case, the requirement is to excite a circularly polarized mode of propagation in the waveguide. This can be done in a variety of ways. A common way is to introduce both polarizations into a rectangular waveguide, by means of in-phase probes (Fig. 2–15, chapter 2) in two adjacent walls. Because of the rectangularity of the guide, the two mutually perpendicular polarizations will have different phase velocities (this assumes the waveguide is not square, but its height and width must be large enough to permit propagation of perpendicular polarizations). The length of the rectangular guide (measured from the probe position) is made just long enough to result in a 90-degree phase difference between the two polarizations at the guide output.

A horn or other radiator with circularly polarized radiation can be used to illuminate a paraboloidal reflector to produce a high-gain circularly polarized beam. Pyramidal horns that are not square can be used to illuminate noncircular apertures, but special methods must be used to compensate for the differences in phase velocities of the two polarizations in the horn flare (since the flares are different for the different polarizations). Lenses can also be used with such horns if the refracting medium is capable of passing both polarizations with the same phase velocities.

A linearly polarized wave can be directly converted to circular polarization by means of special transmission or reflection devices. An example of such a transmission medium is a set of straight parallel vanes or plates with their planes parallel to the direction of propagation and their direction inclined at 45 degrees to the linear polarization, so that the wave in the regions between the plates can be considered to have two mutually perpendicular components, one parallel to the plates and one perpendicular to them. The latter component will travel through the region at free-space velocity, but the former will have a phase velocity that is determined by the plate spacing, according to the principle of the metal-plate waveguide lens (except that the boundary surfaces of the parallel-plate region are flat, or plane, instead of curved). If the thickness of this "lens" is properly chosen, the two component waves can be caused to have a 90-degree phase difference and the wave that emerges will be circularly polarized. This device is known as a *quarter wave plate*, since it produces a quarter-wavelength effective path difference for the two polarizations. A reflecting device that accomplishes the same result can be constructed by using a similar set of vanes of half the depth, backed by a plane reflector.

Circularly polarized high-gain arrays can be constructed by using crossed dipoles as the radiating elements, fed as previously described, or by using helixes, pairs of slots, or circularly polarized horns. Cross-polarized Yagi-Uda arrays, fed 90 degrees out of phase, may also be used. Similarly, pairs of unidirectional log-periodic antennas can be used, such as the wire-trapezoidal-tooth antenna of Fig. 7–13b, with a "staggered" arrangement of the teeth so that the two polarizations are radiated with 90-degree phase difference at all frequencies within the bandwidth range.

Many other forms of circularly polarized antennas are possible. The types that have been described serve to indicate the general principles.

As mentioned in sec. 1.1, circular polarization is characterized as "right-hand" or "left-hand" according to whether the electric vector is rotating clockwise or counterclockwise, respectively, as viewed *from the source*. Which of these senses of circular polarization will be radiated by a given antenna depends on whether the phases of the orthogonal dipoles or fields *lead* or *lag* each other by 90 degrees. Moreover, if a given circularly polarized antenna is connected to receive a given sense of circular polarization, it will reject signals of the opposite sense. Therefore, to be able to receive signals of both senses, an antenna should be connected to two receivers with different phasings, one appropriate for one sense and one for the other. The above-mentioned four-port hybrid ring coupler is especially convenient for this purpose; the desired result is accomplished by connecting the antenna elements to two of the ports and the two receivers to the other two ports.

A radar that transmits circularly polarized waves will receive from symmetrically reflecting targets, like a sphere or a flat plate, echo signals that require the receiving connection to the antenna to be phased in the sense opposite to the transmitting connection. For many types of complex targets, however, the reflected waves will contain both circular-polarization senses. This fact can be used to allow receiving echo signals from a desired unsymmetrical target (e.g., an airplane) while rejecting those from areas of rainfall, since the raindrops reflect in the symmetrical manner.

7.3.2. Polarizers and Dual-Mode Transducers

Polarizers change polarization from one to another, and dual-mode transducers permit transmitting or receiving more than one polarization. The output waveguide of a polarizer or a dual-mode transducer is usually round or square.

Figure 7–18 shows a polarizer in square waveguide, with wave propagation from left to right. To understand its operation, one can think of a vertically polarized wave being resolved into two equal magnitude, equal phase waves oriented at ±45° to vertical. Now assume the following:

- waveguide dimensions are small enough so that only one waveguide mode (the dominant mode) is propagated
- a thin dielectric slab, as depicted in Fig. 7–18, is aligned at +45° to vertical
- the length of the slab is long enough that the phase delay of the +45° polarized wave is 90° greater than that of the –45° wave

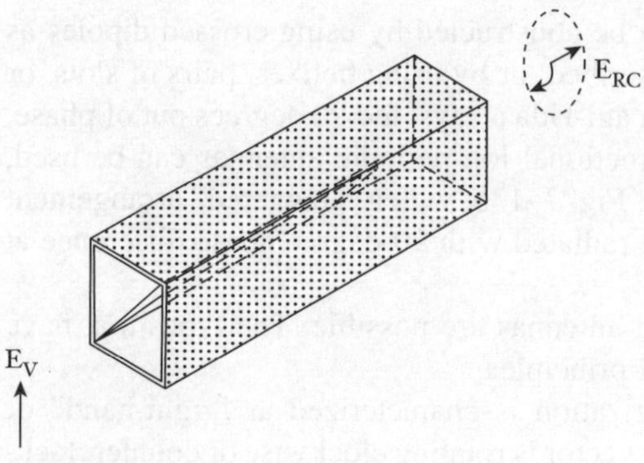

FIGURE 7–18.

Circular polarizer with thin dielectric slab oriented at 45° to vertical.

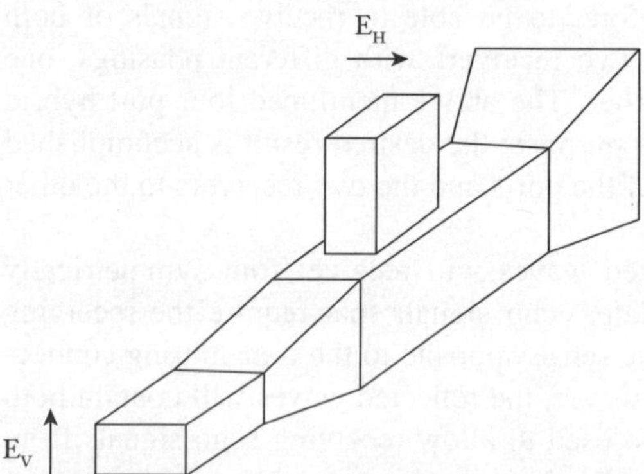

FIGURE 7–19.

Dual-mode transducer in square waveguide feeding a horizontally and vertically polarized horn.

Then, looking from left to right (the direction of propagation), the resultant electric field is rotating clockwise. Thus, the dielectric slab converts the vertically polarized (V-POL) wave to a right circularly (RC) polarized wave. Similarly, a like slab oriented at –45° would generate a left-circularly (LC) polarized wave.

For the polarizer of Fig. 7–18, a change from right to left circular polarization can occur by changing the input polarization from vertical to horizon. Thus, the +45° slab polarizer of Fig. 1–18 in combination with a V-POL input can be used to transmit or receive one circular polarization (CP), and alternatively the other CP is available with an H-POL input. If instead, the slab causes 180° relative phase delay, the V-POL input is transformed to H-POL output. The operating principle of a polarizer in circular waveguide is similar to that of the square waveguide example of Fig. 7–18. For either the square or circular waveguide case, tapering or notching both ends of the dielectric slab reduces wave reflections.

A polarization transducer permits the adding of waves of different polarizations to create a wave of another polarization. Most transducers function reciprocally, so that they can separate waves into specific polarizations. Figure 7–19 shows a dual-mode (i.e., dual-polarization) transducer that can provide separately a horizontally or a vertically polarized wave into a square waveguide. Note that separate rectangular waveguides couple V- and H-polarized waves independently to the square waveguide. Although not shown, internal impedance matching is required if there are abrupt changes in waveguide dimensions. Levine and Sichak (1954) provide input to a square waveguide with separately polarized waves by using dipoles fed by coaxial cables, and Johnson (1967) inputs a square waveguide with rectangular waveguides. Typically, the length of transition (taper) between waveguide sizes is short, and often abrupt for compactness. Bandwidths are ordinarily 5 to 10 percent for VSWR of 1.2 or less, and isolation between V- and H-polarization inputs are at least 40 dB.

Figure 7–20 shows photographs of two commercially available transducers with rectangular waveguide inputs, one having a square and the other a circular waveguide output. Note the abrupt changes in waveguide size that permit compact designs.

7.3.3. Corrugated Horn Feeds

FIGURE 7–20.

Transducers having square and circular waveguide outputs. (Courtesy of Microwave Development Laboratory, Inc.)

It is sometimes desired that dual-polarization reflector antennas and their feeds have equal azimuth and elevation beamwidths. From sec. 6.4 it may be seen that, for a square horn, the side lobes are larger and the pattern is narrower in the E plane than in the H-plane. Particularly for small horns, the lack of amplitude taper in the E plane may cause even greater diffraction from the E-plane waveguide walls. Some of these problems can be minimized through use of corrugated horns. However, they are heavier, larger, and more expensive than smooth-walled horns. Universal patterns for corrugated horns are given by Love (1984, pp. 15–19).

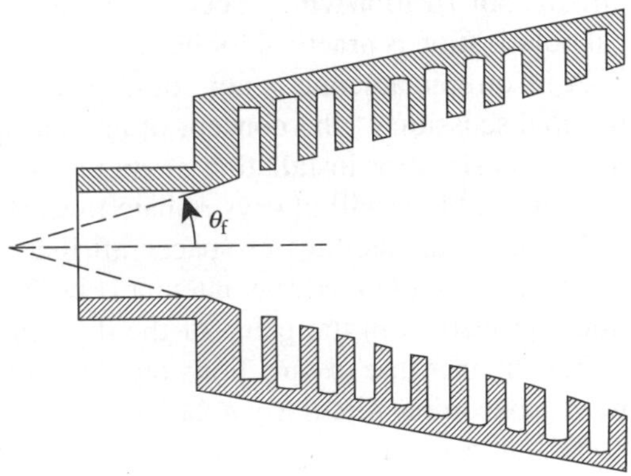

FIGURE 7–21.

A cone-shape tapered corrugated horn with circular aperture. After Thomas (1978), © 1978 IEEE.

Figure 7–21 illustrates a commonly used corrugated horn, which is tapered outward from a circular waveguide and thus has a circular aperture. It has axially symmetric beams, low side lobes, and low cross-polarization. The concept of corrugations is as follows: where the horn taper begins, the slot depth is roughly $\lambda/2$ (giving an approximate short circuit like a shorted $\lambda/2$ length transmission line), to keep the wave bound as though next to a conducting wall. In addition, as the mouth of the horn is approached, the slot depth is tapered so that near the throat the slot depths are roughly $\lambda/4$. The $\lambda/4$ slots approximate the open circuit effect of a $\lambda/4$ line) to detach the wave from the walls and thereby reduce E-plane diffraction from the walls. The performance of sectoral and pyramidal horns can also benefit from having corrugations, which cause the E-plane beamwidth to be broadened and the side lobes to be greatly suppressed (Love 1984, pp. 15–43).

7.4. Omnidirectional Antennas

Much of the emphasis in antenna theory and practice is on increased directivity, which improves the system performance in any point-to-point radio application. Narrow beamwidth allows discriminating (on reception) against interfering signals from directions other than that of the desired signal, and on transmission it minimizes interference with receiving stations in other than the desired direction. The resulting increased antenna gain improves the signal strength in the desired direction.

Nevertheless in some applications a narrow beam is undesirable. In entertainment broadcasting and in certain forms of communication an omnidirectional horizontal pattern is required. In unstabilized spacecraft applications, isotropicity may be desired. Omnidirectional refers to a constant pattern in one plane whereas isotropic refers to a constant pattern over a sphere.

Omnidirectionality is fairly simple to obtain. For example, a vertical dipole or monopole has an omnidirectional pattern in the horizontal plane, with vertical polarization. If horizontal polarization is required, the turnstile antenna that has been described will give a fairly uniform omnidirectional pattern; these can be arrayed vertically to give a narrow vertical beamwidth and corresponding gain, as is commonly done for TV and FM broadcasting. At still higher frequencies the biconical horn can be used for either vertical, horizontal, or even circular polarization with proper excitation. At the lowest frequencies, of course, only vertical polarization is practical for horizontal-plane applications above a conducting earth.

An isotropic antenna is not possible to achieve, even theoretically, as was mentioned in the discussion of the concept of an isotropic radiator, in sec. 3.3. Such an antenna is usually desired for installation on an unstabilized spacecraft, so that even though it may spin or tumble it will always radiate toward the earth.

On artificial satellites or spacecraft that are not large in comparison with the wavelength, the simple turnstile antenna (Fig. 7–17) works quite well. Its nearly omnidirectional properties in the plane of the dipoles have already been mentioned in sec. 7.3.1, as has the fact that in directions other than in this plane it radiates elliptically polarized waves, becoming circularly polarized on the axis perpendicular to the antenna plane. The polarization is anything but uniform over the entire pattern, but if the antenna on the earth end of the circuit can receive circular polarization of both senses, there will always be some signal of proper polarization for reception. This antenna has been used successfully on artificial earth satellites of diameters up to about one meter at frequencies up to about 150 MHz (wavelength 2 meters). Each dipole is mounted so that each half projects radially from the surface of the satellite, that is, the body of the satellite occupies the space between the two halves of the dipoles. This fact does not seriously modify the turnstile performance as long as the satellite is not too large and if its surface is fairly "clean"—uncluttered by sizable projections.

At very much higher frequencies isotropicity is more difficult, because of the larger size of the satellite in relation to the antenna size. One practical solution is to do away with the need for omnidirectional radiation by stabilizing the satellite or spacecraft. (On some spacecraft this has been done so that a directional antenna, aimed at the earth, can be used.) Otherwise, it is necessary to place individual radiators at a number of points around the surface of the vehicle so that at least one of them will be on the side toward the earth at all times. At sufficiently high frequencies these radiators may take the form of slots in the metal skin of the vehicle.

7.5. Electrically Small Antennas

In some circumstances it is impossible to accommodate an antenna of sufficient size to have appreciable gain and high efficiency, owing to limitations of space or cost.

This situation occurs most often at low frequencies, where an antenna of wavelength dimensions is extremely large. Then it becomes important to consider antennas that are physically and electrically small. The emphasis of the discussion is on their electrical smallness, since mere physical smallness does not by itself make an antenna unusual. An electrically small antenna is one that is small compared to the wavelength.

Some basic forms of electrically small antennas have already been discussed in secs. 4.1 and 4.5—the short dipole and the small loop. Their inefficiency was noted, particularly in connection with the use of vertical grounded antennas for transmitting at LF and VLF. These are actually monopoles or half dipoles operated in conjunction with their ground-reflection images. They may sometimes be one hundred or more meters high, yet they are electrically small because the wavelength may be several kilometers. Their inefficiency is due to a combination of factors. The radiation resistance is very low, so that a high current is required. At the same time the input impedance includes a high capacitive reactance. If the required high current is to be obtained with a reasonable generator (transmitter) rf voltage, this capacitive reactance must be tuned out with a large series inductance (coil). The coil, in turn, has some resistance, in which appreciable loss can occur due to the heavy current. The heavy current also flows into the ground so that further losses will occur unless the ground conduction is excellent.

There are various means of reducing these losses. Capacitive top loading is used to increase the radiation resistance, thus lowering the current required for a given radiated power. Extensive systems of buried wires are used to increase the effective ground conductivity. Loading coils (tuning inductors) are made of large conductors to reduce resistance. These measures are necessary when the electrically short, grounded antenna is used for transmitting. Consequently, at higher frequencies where efficient antennas may be of reasonable size, electrically small antennas are not generally used in transmitting applications.

There are times, at the low and medium frequencies especially, where electrically small antennas may be necessary for receiving. Moreover, it is fortuitous that in receiving applications at these frequencies the antenna efficiency may be unimportant, so that the electrically small antenna may function very effectively. This may seem to be a contradiction of the "reciprocity" that has been ascribed to antennas in their transmitting and receiving behavior, but it really is not. The reciprocity principle is correct and does hold for electrically small antennas as long as only the radiated and received *signal* is considered. In reception, however, the important consideration is the *signal-to-noise ratio*.

The electrically small antenna of low efficiency may be effective when the alternative is a larger antenna of about the same *directivity*, and when the predominant noise is external, that is, enters the receiver via the antenna. These circumstances occur primarily at frequencies below about 10 MHz. The predominant noise is atmospheric static, and high-directivity antennas are usually out of the question, especially below 2 or 3 MHz. Thus the alternative antennas may be a tall tower, possibly top-loaded, or a very much shorter vertical monopole. The patterns, and hence the directivities, will be practically the same in either case. The difference being considered between antennas is efficiency (the factor k defined in sec. 3.3.5) and thus gain, and it can be shown that, within wide limits, this will not affect the signal-to-noise ratio under the stated conditions.

Very common examples of electrically small antennas are those used for reception in the broadcast band—535 to 1,605 kHz (approximately 200 to 600 meters wavelength). As is well known, a short random length of wire serves very well as an antenna for local reception, and at night even distant reception is possible. Automobile radios typically use a short vertical monopole, about one meter in length, or about 0.01 wavelength or less. Small "table radios" and also some larger sets often have built-in small-loop antennas that are resonated by means of a parallel variable condenser; the combination then serves as the tuned input circuit of the receiver rf amplifier. The ultimate in smallness is the tiny "ferrite rod" antenna used in transistor pocket portable radios. This antenna is actually a small-diameter elongated coil wound on a rod of ferrite material up to perhaps 10 cm in length, connected in parallel with the rf amplifier tuning capacitor; it thus serves as a combination antenna and tuned circuit as does the somewhat larger loop antenna of the table radio. The ferrite core increases the rf flux in the coil. It also allows the necessary inductance to be obtained with relatively few turns of wire so that the resistance is kept low; hence the coil Q is high. Consequently both the induced voltage and the selectivity of the circuit are greater than with an air-wound coil of the same size.

Electrically small loop antennas are also very commonly used for receiving at MF, LF, and VLF, again because efficiency is not important. Also, since the wave polarization is always vertical at the low frequencies (below 2 MHz), advantage may be taken of the nulls that occur in the directions perpendicular to the plane of the loop, to eliminate interfering signals from a particular direction, if the loop is made rotatable.

Sometimes an electrically small antenna may be desirable for transmitting at frequencies where a quarter-wavelength vertical antenna would be possible but fairly expensive and perhaps inconveniently large. A "short monopole" antenna will, in this case, have just as good *directivity*, but the radiation resistance will be very low so that the efficiency may be poor. A method of improving the efficiency, which has been incorporated in a number of commercial designs, is the use of a resonant top-loading structure. In effect, the antenna consists of a short vertical section that radiates (with vertical polarization) and a horizontal section that is nonradiating (because of cancellation due to ground reflection) but is of sufficient length, inductance, and capacitance to make the entire structure resonant. That is, the input impedance is nonreactive and the radiation resistance is much higher than it would be for a monopole without top loading. A metallic ground plane is also employed. Therefore such antennas may be reasonably efficient even though electrically small.

7.6. Direction-Finding Antennas

The term *direction finding* has a special and a general sense. In its special sense it refers to the process of determining the direction of arrival of a signal from a distant source purely by means of receiving equipment connected to a directional antenna system. In the more general sense it may include systems that transmit as well as receive (e.g., radars). The term is used here in the general sense. The subject is very large, but all that will be attempted here is a brief sketch of the antenna types and techniques, since the basic operation of the antennas has already been covered in chapters 4, 5, and 6.

7.6.1. Low-Frequency Null Systems

The term *passive* is applied to systems or devices that function only when acted upon by an external signal, as opposed to *active* systems that generate their own signals. Direction finders at low frequencies (LF and VLF) are generally passive. They are used as aids to navigation and for locating the sources of unidentified signals, for various purposes. They almost always utilize a null indication, that is, the direction of minimum signal (ideally, zero) is determined, rather than maximum.

Multiturn small-loop antennas are customarily used. Since the wave polarization at LF and VLF is always vertical, the plane of the loop is vertical, and provision is made for rotating it about a vertical axis. An electrically small loop pattern in a horizontal plane is like that of the short horizontal dipole (Fig. 4–4, chapter 4), with nulls in the directions perpendicular to the plane of the loop. Therefore there is a 180-degree ambiguity of the measured direction. This ambiguity may be resolved by employing in conjunction with the loop a short vertical monopole located nearby (a negligible distance away in terms of the wavelength). The null direction is first found with the monopole disconnected. Then its output is connected to the receiver so that it adds to the loop voltage, but with a 90-degree phase delay introduced by inductive reactance. The effective pattern of the loop-monopole combination is an asymmetrical cardioid rather than the symmetrical pattern of the loop alone, and by rotating the loop for maximum signal with the monopole connected it can be decided which of the two null directions, observed with it disconnected, is the true direction of the incoming signal. This type of direction finding is subject to errors from many causes, and numerous techniques have been devised for minimizing them.

At somewhat higher frequencies, the ionosphere can produce appreciable horizontally polarized downcoming signal components that tend to "fill in" the pattern nulls of a loop and destroy the direction-finding accuracy. The Adcock antenna can overcome this effect. It consists of two vertical dipoles or monopoles spaced a quarter wave or less apart and connected to the receiver input with opposite polarity so that nulls occur in the directions perpendicular to the plane of the dipoles (as in the patterns of the right-hand column of the top row of Fig. 5–3, chapter 5). The pattern is essentially the same as that of a loop, but the antenna is insensitive to horizontal polarization. The null ambiguity can be resolved by the use of an additional (third) dipole or monopole, just as for the loop.

A goniometer is an electrical combining device used with multiple fixed antennas, having a stator connected to the fixed antennas and a rotor connected to a receiver or transmitter, allowing the pattern of the fixed antenna system to be rotated as the rotator is rotated. By using two fixed vertical loops at right angles to each other (crossed loops) in conjunction with a goniometer, mechanical rotation of the rotor may be made equivalent electrically to rotating a loop antenna (Terman 1943, p. 879). Thus, this combination of loop antennas with a goniometer permits the use of large fixed loops and also permits locating them at a distance from the receiver, with transmission-line connections. Crossed Adcock antennas can also be used with a goniometer.

7.6.2. Beam-Maximum Systems

At VHF and above it is more practical to employ an antenna with a very narrow directional beam, and to determine the signal direction by rotating the antenna until a signal maximum is observed. This is the technique used for ordinary radar direction finding. Radar antennas are usually rotatable, or the beam may be pointed in some manner. Beamwidths as small as one degree or even less can be used, although at the VHF radar frequencies beamwidths of 10 to 20 degrees are more common. The antennas may be arrays, parabolic reflectors, or lenses. In special cases other antenna forms may be used, such as surface-wave antennas. They may be mechanically steerable in both elevation angle and azimuth angle. Beam steering by varying the phasing of an array is commonly used for direction finding.

7.6.3. Lobing Antennas

When a narrow beam is "scanned" through the direction of an incoming signal, the location of the maximum direction can be determined to within some fraction of the beamwidth. By employing optimum techniques this fraction can be made fairly small. It is about one-tenth of the beamwidth for a radar system employing simple visual observation of the signals on a cathode-ray-tube indicator. Even with optimum processing, however, the accuracy is limited by the fact that the "nose" of a beam is blunt, rather than sharp.

A method of measurement that circumvents this difficulty has been devised for use when extreme accuracy is required, as in weapon-pointing radars—the method of lobe comparison, or lobing. In this method, the beam is shifted, without moving the antenna as a whole, by equal fractions of a beamwidth in both directions from the nominal beam direction. This beam shifting can be done either in rapid time sequence (sequential lobing) or by generating two beams at the same time (simultaneous lobing). The patterns of the two beams then overlap, as shown in Fig. 7–22. The theory of operation can be described by considering signals arriving first from point A, and then from point B.

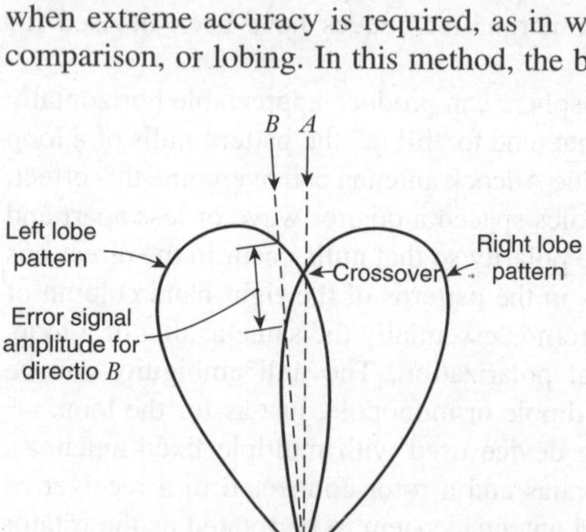

FIGURE 7–22.
Patterns of a lobe-comparison antenna.

The antenna output in the simultaneous-lobing case is connected to two receivers, one of which receives the difference of the signals from the two lobes, whereas the other receives the sum. If the signal is coming from A, there will be no difference signal, since the amplitudes of the two lobes are equal. If the signal is coming from *B* (an "off-axis" direction), there will be a difference, or error, signal, as shown by the fact that the dashed line crosses the two lobe patterns at different levels. The sense (direction) of the error is found by comparison of the phases of the sum and difference signals in special receiver circuits that convert the error signal into a d-c voltage; the polarity of this voltage will reverse as the signal direction changes from right-of-center to left-of-center. The sum signal is also used, in radar systems, for signal detection and range measurement. In the sequential-lobing scheme a single receiver is used, and the received signals from the two beams are switched so that their amplitudes can be compared.

It is apparent that the "difference pattern" of the two lobes (the difference of the pattern amplitudes plotted as a function of angle) will be very sharp, rather than blunt like the nose of a lobe. Because of this fact the accuracy possible by lobing is much greater than by simply observing the maximum direction of a beam.

The two displaced beams can be generated in a number of ways. With an array antenna, changing the phasing of the elements will produce the desired result. With a paraboloidal reflector or lens antenna, the beam may be shifted in the desired manner by moving the feed slightly off the optical axis, as shown in Fig. 6–3b, chapter 6. In a sequential lobing system this shift may be made by mechanically moving the feed off-axis first in one direction, then in the opposite direction, at a rapid rate. In either a sequential or a simultaneous lobing system, two feeds may be used, each displaced a small amount from the optical axis, in opposite directions. In the simultaneous lobing system both feeds are connected to the receiver through a hybrid junction (coupler) (sec. 2.6) so that a difference (error) signal is received. For sequential lobing, the receiver is switched between the lobes.

Thus far, lobing only in one plane has been discussed. It may be desired, however, to measure the incoming signal direction in two mutually perpendicular planes, for example, vertically and horizontally. This can be accomplished by generating four lobes—left, right, up, and down with respect to the nominal beam axis. With a paraboloidal reflector or a rotational lens this requires four fixed feeds. A typical arrangement of four horns is shown in Fig. 7–23. Their waveguide outputs are combined by means of hybrid junctions in such a way that one receiver is fed the difference between the signals of the upper and lower pairs, and another the difference between the left and right pairs. A third receiver is fed the sum of all four horns.

The sequential-lobing equivalent of the four-lobe simultaneous system is accomplished by moving a feed (of a reflector or lens) in a circle around the zero axis. The beam direction then sweeps out a cone about this axis. This method is called *conical scanning*. It is most feasible

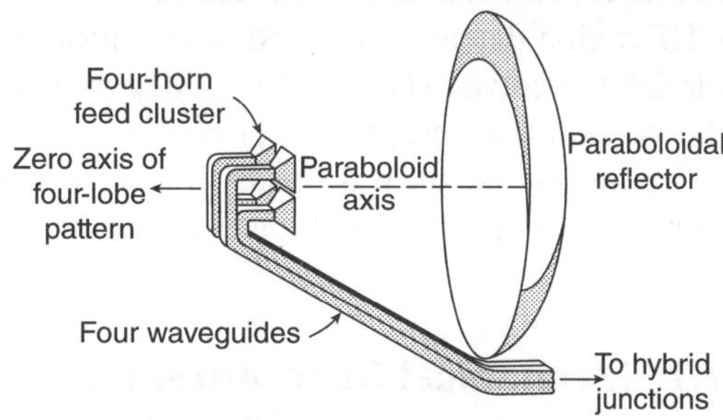

FIGURE 7–23.

Four-horn simultaneous-lobing (monopulse) feed for paraboloidal reflector.

with small microwave antennas, where the required mechanical motion is not very great.

The simultaneous-lobe-comparison method, when used in a pulse radar system, is known as *monopulse* lobing, since the signal amplitudes can be compared on a single-pulse basis; the sequential-lobing system requires at least two successive pulses for its operation. The method that has been described is also called *amplitude monopulse*, since it is based on comparing the signal amplitudes in two angularly displaced lobes of a single antenna. Another method, *phase monopulse*, uses two or four antennas placed side by side, with their beams pointing in the same direction but with their phase centers separated. If a signal arrives from an off-axis direction it will be received with *equal amplitude* in each beam but with *a phase difference*, which may be used to generate an error signal. When this phase method is used with nonpulsed systems it is referred to as phase-comparison lobing or as an *interferometer* system. It is capable of greater accuracy with a given antenna size because the sharpness of the error response is determined by the separation of the antennas rather than by their individual beamwidths. The amplitude-comparison lobing system, on the other hand, is more compact and more readily steerable as a unit, for the same antenna gain and beamwidth.

In the phase-comparison or interferometer system, the interference pattern between the two beams becomes multilobed as the separation of the antennas is increased. The principle is identical to that of the interference between an antenna and its image in a reflecting surface, as discussed in sec. 1.4 (see also Figs. 1–14 and 1–15). Therefore ambiguity can exist if the individual beamwidths are appreciably greater than the lobe widths, but the ambiguity can usually be resolved by one of a number of methods. This technique is used in VHF satellite tracking systems. Interferometers are also commonly used in radio astronomy applications.

Aircraft landing systems use a technique similar to the amplitude lobing principle, where antenna patterns are transmitted from fixed ground stations and received by aircraft receivers. For lateral guidance, ILS (Instrument Low-Approach System) radiates, from the far end of a runway, two identical beams in the high-VHF region that are separated in azimuth, but modulated at different frequencies. When the signal strengths of the differently modulated VHF signals are equal, the aircraft is on lateral course. For vertical guidance, ILS radiates, from the near end of a runway, two identical beams in the low UHF region that are separated in elevation, but modulated at different frequencies. When the UHF received signals of the differently moduated signals are equal, the aircraft is on the vertical (i.e., proper glide) course.

Lobing is also used for passive direction finding at high frequencies, where it is superior to the loop or Adcock antenna methods.

7.7. Mechanical Scan Antennas

7.7.1. Introduction

In some applications, especially radar, it is necessary to "scan" a directional beam through some angular sector—for example, around the horizon (360°) or through the vertical angle sector from the horizon to the zenith (90°). Sometimes a more limited sector can be scanned in repetitive fashion, an extreme example being the conical scan lobing system, which was described in sec. 7.6. Scanning in the horizontal plane is known as azimuth scanning; vertical-plane scanning is called elevation scanning. The two motions may sometimes be combined when it is desired to scan a large solid angle with a narrow beam; typically, the azimuth scan is performed at a relatively slow rate and the vertical scan is a rapid saw-tooth motion, with at least one vertical sawtooth scan occurring during the time it takes for the azimuth scan to progress one beamwidth. (This insures that there will be no gaps in the scan coverage.)

Relatively slow azimuth scanning is commonly accomplished by simply rotating the entire antenna about a vertical axis at a constant rate. Typical speeds for radar antennas are 1 to 30 rpm, depending on the antenna size. Limited sectors can be scanned with the antenna as a whole remaining stationary, either by moving the feed of a reflector or lens, or by varying the phasing of an array. These beam steering methods permit higher scanning speeds. In fact, for many applications inertial-less scanning by electronic phasing of an array is the preferred method for rapid beam scanning and/or tracking. Consequently, chapter 8 is devoted entirely to the concepts of electronically scanned antennas (ESA).

7.7.2. Rapid Mechanical Scan Antennas

High-speed repetitive scanning of limited sectors is sometimes accomplished at microwave frequencies through the use of devices in which a reciprocating or sawtooth beam motion is produced by purely rotational mechanical motion of a feed or mirror. These devices often involve combinations of specially curved reflectors and parallel-plate regions; typical examples are the Foster, Lewis, and Robinson scanners. The organ-pipe scanner is another mechanism that includes a rotating waveguide horn that consecutively energizes waveguides that have outputs arranged in a line, thereby transforming a continuous rotating motion into a reciprocating motion. The above-mentioned scanners are described by Kelleher (1993).

Several different types of high-speed, mechanical scanning antennas were developed at the Engineering Experiment Station (EES), Georgia Institute of Technology (now Georgia Tech Research Institute). These antennas scanned, typically, 20 times per second over an azimuth sector, and the active sector itself could be rotated in azimuth. Design frequencies included 9, 16, 24, and 70 GHz. Two general configurations were used: (1) multiple rotating, back-to-back reflectors and (2) multiple rotating horns feeding one or two geodesic Luneberg lens that illuminated one reflector. Some of the back-to-back scanners were used to transmit or receive either horizontal, vertical, or left or right circular polarization, and simultaneously receive two polarizations: horizontal and vertical, or left and right circular.

Back-to-back reflector antennas were developed at EES during the late 1940s, 1950s, and 1960s for radar tracking of projectiles down to the point of impact. Examples include naval ship gun shells, bombs, and air-dropped mines. Attributes of the fast scan rate include improved tracking of high-speed targets and elimination of the radar display

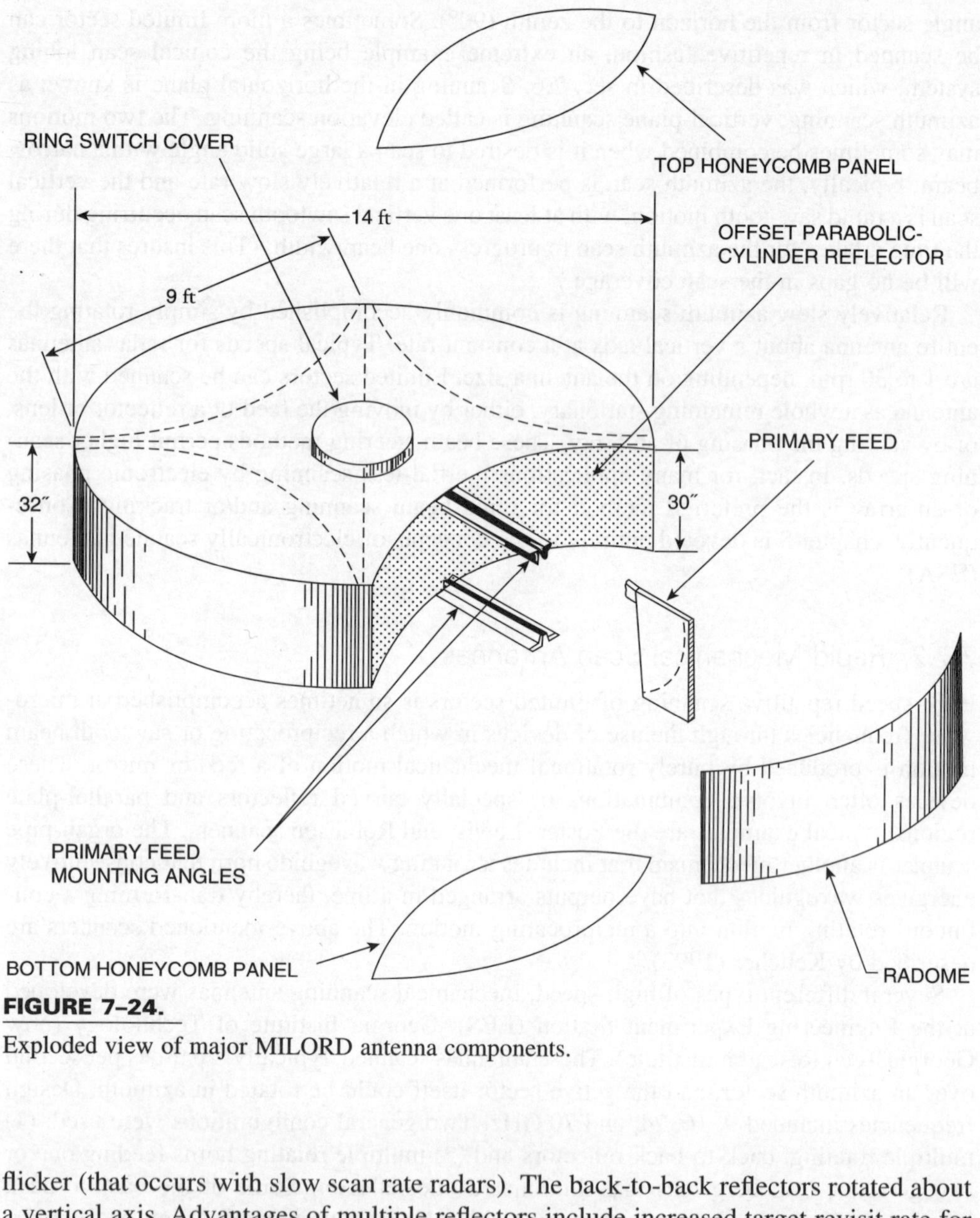

FIGURE 7–24.
Exploded view of major MILORD antenna components.

flicker (that occurs with slow scan rate radars). The back-to-back reflectors rotated about a vertical axis. Advantages of multiple reflectors include increased target revisit rate for a given antenna spindle rotation rate, and increased beam-time on target for a given target revisit rate. An azimuth sector of about 110 or 80 degrees was viewed by a radar, depending whether the scanner had three or four reflectors.

Figure 7–24 shows the principal components of the MILORD antenna (Holliman and Hollis, 1956). MILORD is an acronym formed from the words Mine Impact LOcating Radar Device.

Key features of the MILORD antenna follow:

Frequency = 9.375 GHz
Gain ≈ 39 dB
Horizontal polarization
Azimuth beamwidth = 0.7°
Elevation beamwidth = 3.5°
Weight = 5600 pounds (2540 kg)
Rotation rate = 240 RPM
Linear velocity at rim = 120 mi/h (193 km/h)
Beam scans at 16/s over 85° azimuth sector
Waveguide switch activates one reflector feed at a time over a 85° azimuth sector
For reduced aerodynamic drag, the honeycomb panels and the radomes enclose the antenna to form a cylinder.

Figure 7–25 shows an exaggerated cross section through a feed and a reflector. Each feed is of the hog-horn type, which consists of a parabolic reflecting barrier between closely spaced aluminum plates and an H-plane sectoral horn at the focal point. The linear aperture of each feed is 61 cm. The offset angle of the feed is 2°, giving a reduction in power reflected back into a feed. VSWR at the feeds was approximately 1.05 over a 2 percent band.

A key component for a rapid sector-scan antenna is the high-speed waveguide switch. The first sector scanners used a turnstile type switch. A turnstile switch is, in essence, a rotary joint having multiple outputs, with all but one being short-circuited at a given time (Long 1951). Later, the scanners used a ring switch design having a wider bandwidth, and higher peak power performance (Johnson, Holliman, and Hollis 1960). A ring switch contains one input junction and multiple output junctions. The basic junction geometry consists of a cavity that couples energy to two rectangular waveguides, one is split longitudinally in the E-plane and the other is an output junction. The junction has a simple geometrical configuration, requires no additional matching devices, and has a useful bandwidth that exceeds 25 percent.

Figure 7–26 shows four dual polarized back-to back paraboloidal antennas that rotate about a spindle at 150 RPM. The paraboloids are separately activated over a 70° sector, and the sector is positionable over 226°. The 3 dB azimuth and elevation beamwidths are each 1.5°; and the beams scan a 70° sector at 10, 5, or 2.5 scans per second. Separate waveguides supply horizontal and vertical polarizations, and orthogonal circular polarizations are obtained by appropriate addition and subtraction of the H- and V-polarized waves. The relative phase shift through the separate ring switches for the H and V polarization paths was necessarily small, to provide isolation greater than 30 dB between the two circular polarizations.

Figure 7–27 is a photograph of a rapid-scan, geodesic Luneberg lens antenna mounted on a test stand (Hollis and Long 1957). The antenna, developed for use with a mortar locating radar, produces two beams from separate geodesic lenses that scan sequentially across a 40° azimuth sector. A parabolic cylinder reflector focuses the beams in elevation. Parallel extensions connect the lenses with the reflector focal line, and they are folded

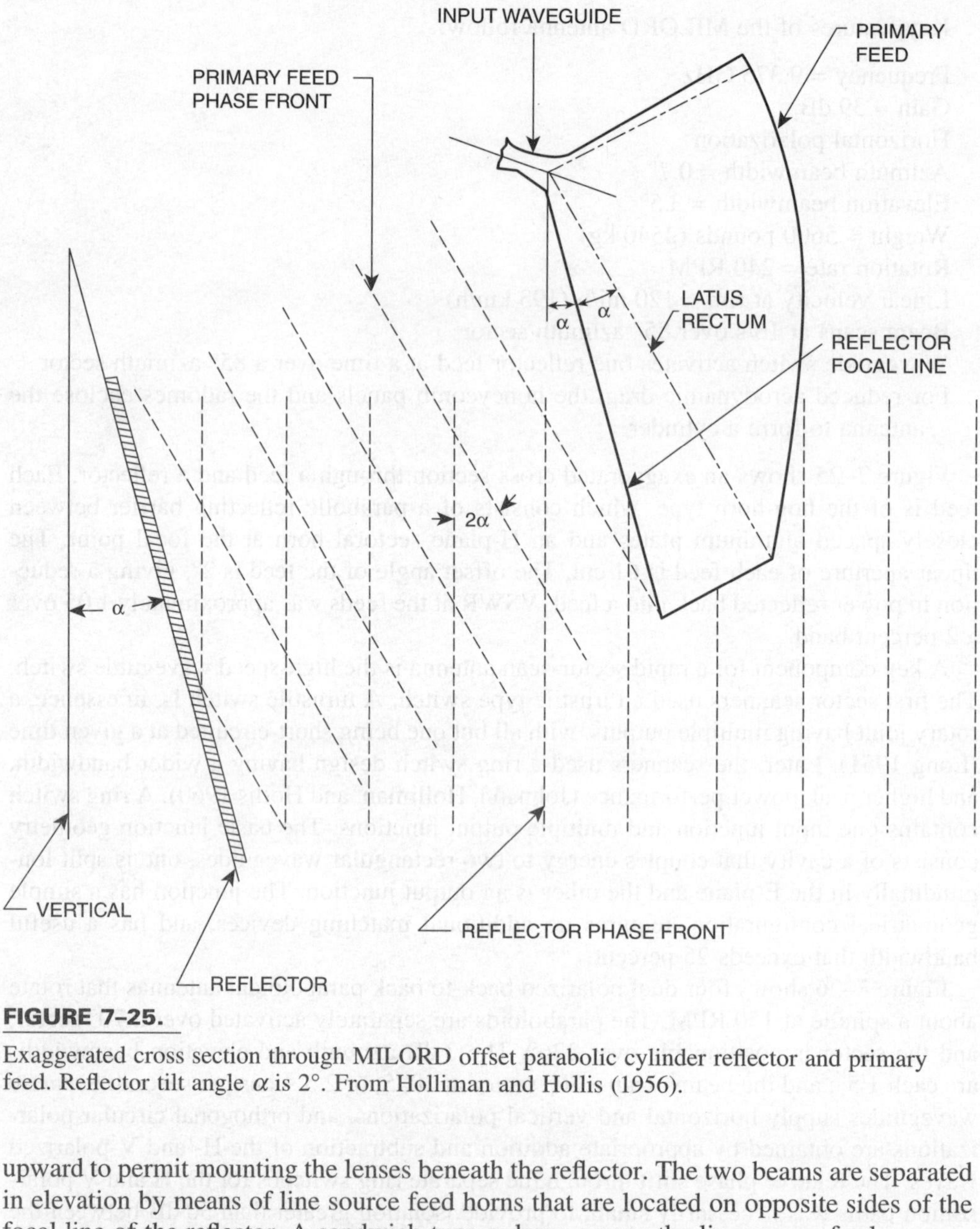

FIGURE 7–25.

Exaggerated cross section through MILORD offset parabolic cylinder reflector and primary feed. Reflector tilt angle α is 2°. From Holliman and Hollis (1956).

upward to permit mounting the lenses beneath the reflector. The two beams are separated in elevation by means of line source feed horns that are located on opposite sides of the focal line of the reflector. A sandwich-type radome covers the line source feeds.

The scanning mechanism is located in the cavity formed between the two lenses. Four sectoral lens feed horns are spaced at intervals of 90° on two feed wheels, one for the upper- and the other for the lower-elevation beam. The wheels are mounted coaxially and the lens feed horns of one wheel are spaced 45° in azimuth from those of the other. The feed-switching mechanism includes a four-way switch at the center of each feed wheel, and a two-way chopper switch that rotates at four times the speed of the feed wheels. When the feed wheels rotate, the upper and lower beams alternately scan the 40° azimuth sector, each at a rate of seventeen scans per second.

Figure 7–28 illustrates the geodesic lens-scanning antenna for the Combat Surveillance Radar AN/ MPS-29 (XE-1), which operates at 70 GHz (Long, Rivers, and Butterworth 1960). Key operating parameters are gain 54.7 dB (includes 2.8 dB loss); 0.2° and 0.3° azimuthal and elevation beamwidths, respectively; twenty scans per second over a 30° scan sector; vertical polarization. Details of the lens, which is of a helmet type configuration, are given in sec. 6.8.8. A ring switch, which serves as a commutator for the lens feeds, consists of a stationary input section and a rotary output section that has eleven sectoral horns that energize the geodesic lens. The feed horns, seen protruding below the rotating ring, are activated sequentially as each passes through the scan sector of the input lips. The lens feed horns, shown protruding below the rotating ring, are activated as each passes through the scan sector of the input lips.

FIGURE 7–26.

A dual-polarization rapid-scanner having four back-to-back paraboloids, shown within the machine shop of Engineering Experiment Station at Georgia Tech, circa 1963.

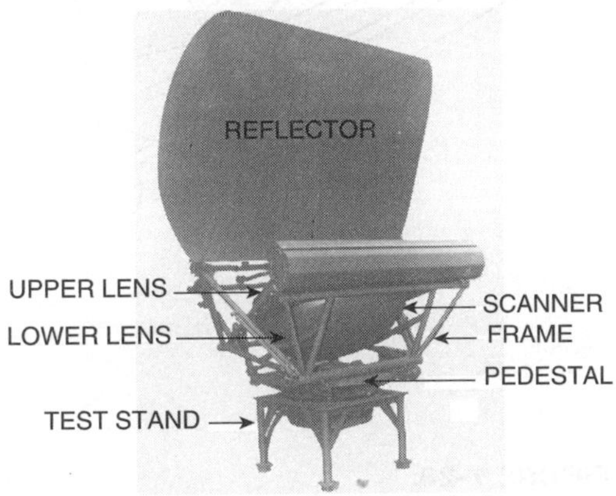

FIGURE 7–27.

A rapid-scan, geodesic Luneberg lens-scanning antenna mounted on a test stand (from Hollis and Long 1957; © 1957, IEEE).

The path of the microwave energy through the ring switch is shown in Fig. 7–28. For 70 GHz, where waveguide losses are appreciable, the E-dimension of the ring switch waveguide and junction is 1.375λ, corresponding to the conducting surface spacing of the lens. This height was selected to minimize lens losses, and was a compromise between ohmic losses and losses from mode conversion (of the propagating waves) caused by bending in the E-plane. The other switch cross-sectional dimension is the H-plane width of RG-98/U waveguide, which is 0.875λ. A hydraulic brake system allows, on operator command, the beam scan to be stopped and positioned in 2 seconds to within less than 0.5 milliradian, anywhere in the 30° scan sector.

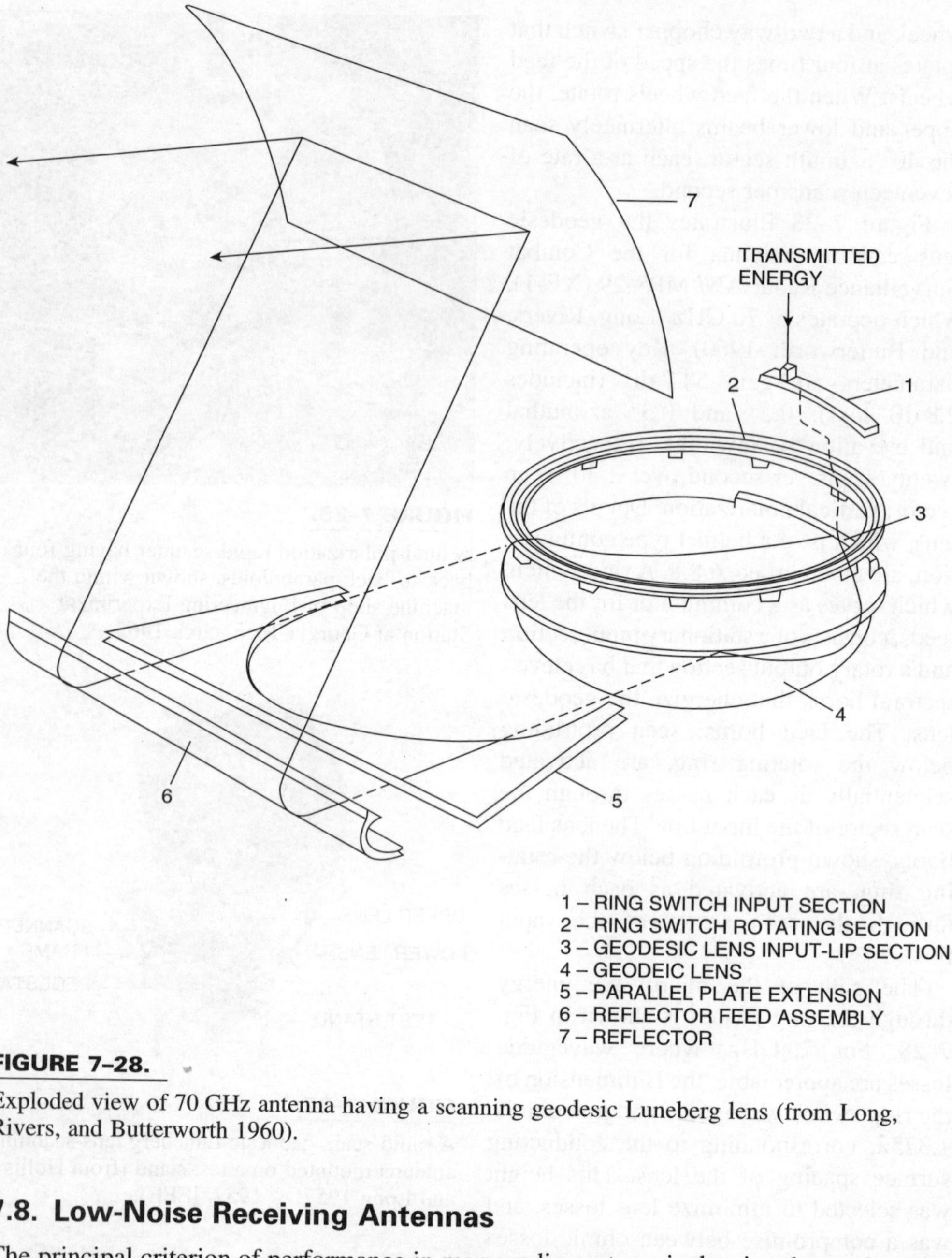

FIGURE 7–28.

Exploded view of 70 GHz antenna having a scanning geodesic Luneberg lens (from Long, Rivers, and Butterworth 1960).

7.8. Low-Noise Receiving Antennas

The principal criterion of performance in many radio systems is the signal-to-noise ratio in the receiver. Noise is always present at some level, and the signal level must usually be greater than the noise level for successful reception, although by special averaging or integrating techniques some types of signals may be detected or read even though their amplitudes are below the noise level. In all cases there is a minimum useful signal level that is expressed in terms of its ratio to the noise level. Consequently, it is important to keep the noise level as low as possible.

Noise in radio systems is of various types and origins in different parts of the spectrum. In the frequency region below about 10 MHz the principal noise is usually "static," which is generated in the atmosphere by lightning discharges and propagates for great distances by ionospheric reflection. It enters the receiver via the antenna along with the desired signal, and little or nothing can be done to minimize it. (A high-gain antenna will help by increasing the received signal while the received noise remains virtually unchanged. But at the very lowest frequencies, directive antennas are not feasible.)

In some situations, especially in the HF through UHF regions, man-made noise from electrical machinery, appliances, power lines, and automotive ignition is the prime offender. Much of this noise tends to be vertically polarized and to be stronger closer to the ground. For the first of these reasons, horizontal polarization may be advantageous, and is therefore used for FM and TV broadcasting. It is also beneficial, in these frequency regions, to employ an elevated antenna connected to the receiver via a balanced or coaxial transmission line, so that all reception takes place well above the ground.

From about 30 to 300 MHz, in the absence of man-made noise, cosmic noise predominates. This noise originates in the galactic system and is heard in audio-output receivers as a "hiss" when the receiver gain is sufficiently high; on a radar A-scope it is called "grass," and on an analog TV screen it is sometimes referred to as "snow." These terms describe its approximate appearance. It is not seen or heard when a strong signal is received because the receiver gain is then reduced (usually automatically). Cosmic noise is, like static, unavoidable; it is received via the antenna along with the signal. (A high-gain antenna is beneficial, however, because it increases the signal strength without increasing the noise. This is true because the signal comes from a single direction whereas the cosmic noise comes from virtually all directions of the sky.)

The cosmic noise decreases with increasing frequency, so that above about 1 GHz it is of negligible importance. Some noise is radiated by the earth's own atmosphere, and by the ground. The atmospheric noise does not become significant until the frequency is about 3 GHz or higher, and is not severe below about 10 GHz. The ground noise, on the other hand, is relatively constant at all frequencies. The result of all these effects is that there is a region of minimum noise between about 1 and 10 GHz, with cosmic noise and static predominating at lower frequencies and atmospheric noise predominating at higher frequencies. (See also sec. 9.13.2).

The foregoing discussion refers solely to noise that enters the receiver via the antenna. Additional noise is generated within the receiver itself. Techniques exist, however, for reducing this internal noise to such a level that the system performance is largely determined by the external noise, even in the low-external-noise frequency region. (Masers, parametric amplifiers, and tunnel diodes and low-noise transistors are the basis of especially low noise amplifiers.) When the predominant noise is the noise that enters from external sources, via the antenna, it is desirable to consider antenna designs that reduce the reception of noise relative to the received signal reception.

In the frequency region UHF and above where the noise from the ground radiation is a significant portion of the total noise, certain aspects of the antenna design do affect the system noise level. As has been mentioned in chapters 3, 5, and 6, directional antennas always have some side lobes and back lobes, through which some reception of ground noise can occur even when the main-beam is pointed upward. Therefore, the objective in designing a low-noise antenna is primarily to reduce the level of these lobes as much as possible. It is especially important to do this when the antenna will be used for such applications as space communication, radar, or telemetry with a low-noise receiver in the frequency range somewhat below 1 GHz to somewhat above 10 GHz.

The design techniques that minimize side and back lobes have been discussed in sec. 5.6 and 6.3. There is, however, one further factor to be considered; namely, the ohmic losses between the waves in space and the input terminals of the first amplifier of the receiver. Because noise will be generated by any loss that exists in this part of the system the length of transmission line or waveguide must be kept to a minimum. For this reason, arrays are not ordinarily used as low-noise antennas, even though their side-lobe and back-lobe characteristics can be controlled more readily than those of reflectors. The losses in a typical array feed system (especially if the array is large) may generate more thermal noise than would be avoided by total elimination of the side and back lobes. (Thermal noise generation is discussed in sec. 9.13.)

The effect of these array losses can be circumvented by placing a low-noise receiver-preamplifier *at each element* of the array, ahead of the feed-system losses. The signal phase must be preserved in the preamplifier, so that the signals from the various elements can be combined in correct phase relationship in the usual way, to form a beam in the desired direction. By definition (IEEE 1993), an active antenna array is an array which all or some of the elements are equipped with their own transmitter or receiver or both. Usually there is not a complete transmitter or receiver located at an element. Instead, located at the elements must of course be at least those components necessary for minimizing losses and for providing the proper array element phases. Generally, the active array antenna technique is very expensive, and it is therefore used only in special applications such as in electronically beam-steered arrays for radar (chapter 8).

Lenses can be designed for low side lobes, and also they offer the possibility of locating the receiver near the feed. For very high gain applications, however, lenses become unwieldy in the low-noise frequency region below 10 GHz. Therefore, except for electronic beam scanning radar, the greatest emphasis in low-noise antenna design is on the use of paraboloidal reflectors.

It is well known that a highly tapered aperture illumination will reduce the side-lobe level, and somewhat greater tapering is usual in low-noise designs than when maximum gain is the paramount consideration. At least equally important for reflector antennas is the minimization of illumination spillover, because spillover causes back lobes directed toward the ground. For the same reason it is important to minimize leakage through the openings of a mesh reflector surface; that is, the openings must be very small compared to the wavelength.

The Cassegrain feed system (sec. 6.3) is frequently employed to minimize the transmission line length, to reduce or eliminate noise due to transmission-line loss. The Cassegrain system is also less likely to result in back lobes due to spillover. The spillover

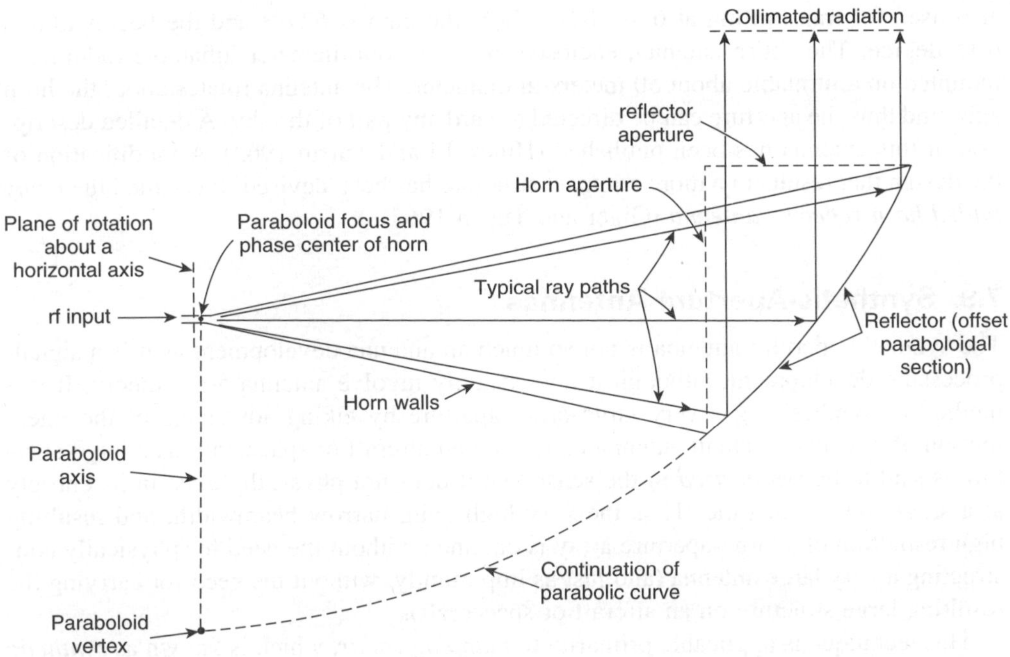

FIGURE 7–29.
Sectional view of a conical-horn-reflector antenna. Metallic enclosure (heavy line) is complete except for opening at reflector aperture.

that occurs at the subreflector causes side lobes that look at the sky rather than at the ground; hence they result in little or no additional ground-noise. When a conventional focal-point feed is used, if low noise is important it is desirable to locate a receiver preamplifier at the apex of the feed support. Care should be taken, when this is done, to minimize aperture blockage, which also causes higher side-lobe levels. Parenthetically, offset-fed reflectors are commonly used to reduce feed blockage and side-lobe levels for home-use direct-broadcast satellite TV reception.

An antenna design that is perhaps ultimate in low-noise performance is a very large, conical-horn-reflector antenna used by the Telstar satellite-communication ground terminal at Andover, Maine. Figure 7–29 is a diagram of this type of antenna. Its design dramatically reduces spillover and reflector leakage, and also permits the receiver and transmitter to be located close to the feed point, at the apex of the horn. The axis of the horn is horizontal, but the mouth of the antenna can be pointed upward. This is possible because a section of a paraboloidal reflector is inserted in front of the mouth of the horn, so that the wavefront is redirected at a 90-degree angle from the horn axis. The apex of the horn is at the focus of the paraboloid. The paraboloidal aperture is circular, 20.7 meters in diameter. The antenna is used for reception at a frequency of 4.08 GHz and provides high gain and a narrow beam in combination with extremely low noise. The gain is approximately 58 dB, and the beamwidth is about 0.23 degree. The antenna is also used for transmitting at 6.39 GHz, where the gain is 62 dB and the beamwidth is 0.15 degree. The entire antenna, enclosed in a 210-foot-diameter inflatable radome, is mounted on a turntable about 50 meters in diameter. The antenna rotates about the horn axis, and thus the aperture can be directed toward any part of the sky. A detailed description of this antenna has been published (Hines, Li and Turrin 1963). A modification of the design that results in a more compact structure has been devised. It is called the *triply folded horn reflector antenna* (Giger and Turrin 1965).

7.9. Synthetic-Aperture Antennas

The synthetic-aperture antenna is not so much an antenna development as it is a signal-processing development, although it does heavily involve antenna array theory. It is a method of synthesizing a very large array aperture by taking advantage of the linear motion of a relatively small antenna carried by an aircraft or spacecraft. The large aperture is said to be *synthesized* in the sense that it does not physically exist in its entirety at a single instant of time. Thus the very high gain, narrow beamwidth, and resulting high resolution of a large-aperture array is obtained without the need for physically constructing a very large antenna (and just as importantly, without the need for carrying the resulting large structure on an aircraft or spacecraft).

This technique is applicable primarily to *mapping radar*, which is known as *synthetic aperture radar,* or SAR (Cutrona 1990). The radar equipment and its actual side-looking antenna are carried by the aircraft or spacecraft (e.g., an earth-orbiting satellite), which travels a straight course at constant altitude. (An earth orbit sufficiently approximates a straight course during the array-synthesis processing time.) The region that can be mapped by this method is a swath parallel to the vehicle's course; the minimum and maximum distances of this swath from the vehicle are determined by the downward angles of the lower and upper boundaries of the vertical-plane beam pattern, subject to additional constraints imposed by the horizon, and by the radar sensitivity and resolution considerations.

The synthetic aperture can be regarded as a linear array, of which the actual antenna is a single element. The linear motion of the vehicle positions this single element for successively radiated radar pulses, at successively displaced positions. Now consider n such positions and let the n successive radar echoes received at these positions be stored in some manner that both amplitudes and phases are preserved. Then by suitable phasor addition of these stored (time-delayed) signals, a resulting signal can be obtained that is *as if* it had been received by a linear array of n elements. The effective angular resolution of this synthetic aperture is the same as that of an n-element linear array.

It is evident that the storage and processing of the successively received echo signals is the key to the feasibility of this scheme. All of the beam-forming considerations applicable to "real" arrays are applied in this processing, such as tapering of the effective element amplitudes (processing weights) to result in a desired side-lobe level. The first SARs used special optical processing methods, because of the extremely large amount of processing required. However, by 1984 digital signal processing (DSP) was fast enough that it was used on the space shuttle-imaging-radar-B (SIR-B).

There are three SAR modes of operation: stripmap, spotlight, and scan. In stripmap SAR, the beam remains at a constant squint angle, which is usually perpendicular to the flight. Spotlight is used to obtain an improved angular resolution of a known location of a target of interest. As the platform moves, the beam-pointing direction is changed so as to keep pointing at the target. Lastly, the scan mode is seldom used; but by means of beam direction changes, it does permit observing a straight path that is not parallel to the flight path. Even though there are different SAR modes of operation, the technique employs *side-looking* from an elevated platform, and the resultant improvement in angular resolution is one-dimensional, in the direction parallel to the vehicular motion.

The required resolution in the orthogonal (range) direction is obtainable because the radar employs pulses. By means of *pulse compression*, a relatively long-duration transmitted pulse can be transformed into a very short received pulse, and the range-dimension resolution is determined by this received pulse length. Pulse compression is accomplished by transmitting a very wide-band coded pulse, which is decoded and compressed by an appropriate receiver filter. The pulse at the filter output is much shorter in duration than the transmitted pulse, and the received signal sensitivity is dependent only on the transmitted pulse energy; and the range resolution obtained depends only on the compressed pulse length.

This combination of angle resolution by means of the synthetic aperture technique and range resolution by pulse compression allows very high-resolution mapping of the surface of the earth and other planets, monitoring of the positions of ships at sea, and study of changes in the configuration of the earth or sea surface over time (Elachi 1987).

An interesting aspect of the SAR technique from the antenna-theory viewpoint is that the best performance is obtained by processing the data so that, in effect, the antenna beam is *focused* on the earth surface at the point of reflection of the radar pulse. Ordinary arrays, as well as reflectors and lenses, usually produce a collimated beam, in which the rays are parallel; in effect they are "focused at infinity." This is the appropriate strategy for transmission distances that are in the far-field region of the antenna. The simplest types of SAR also produce a collimated beam. But by suitable data processing the SAR beam can in effect be focused so that the rays converge to a point at the earth's surface (and this can be done at all ranges, since the data are separately processed for different target distances). The advantage of this type of processing is that it permits a much larger synthetic aperture to be formed than would be possible if a parallel-ray beam were used.

For this synthetic-aperture procedure, the ordinary concept of a beamwidth is not applicable. The relevant consideration in mapping is the azimuthal resolution, which is expressed as a distance rather than an angle. For ordinary radar, and for far-field targets, the resolution is of the order of $\theta_b R$, where θ_b is the azimuthal beamwidth in radians and R is the target range. But, for sufficiently large synthetic apertures, targets are not necessarily in the far-field. It is shown by Cutrona (1990, pp. 21.4–21.7) that for the *focused* case, and for a sufficiently large synthetic aperture *D along the flight path*, the azimuthal resolution is equal to *D/2,* independent of the range and also independent of the frequency (or wavelength) of the radar. Cutrona also shows that for the unfocused synthetic aperture, the resolution is $\sqrt{\lambda R}/2$ where λ is the wavelength.

7.10. Antennas with Extremely Low Side Lobes

In many applications, a low-antenna-pattern side-lobe level is of great importance. This is especially true for radar antennas if the radar can be expected to operate in an environment that results in a significant level of "clutter" echoes; that is, a profusion of echoes from such reflecting objects as sea waves, rain, or irregular terrain. It is also true for radars for military use, which may be subject to interference from enemy jamming transmitters located in side-lobe directions of the radar antenna pattern. Low side lobes are also important for satellite-relay communications where it may be desired to utilize the same frequency for two or more antenna beams that are simultaneously transmitting or receiving different messages to or from separate locations on the earth surface. Obviously these transmissions will mutually interfere if the side-lobe levels are too high. These are major reasons for desiring low side lobes. There are lesser reasons as well, such as the general desirability of noninterference with other services and considerations of low-noise antenna design.

The basic principles of achieving low side-lobe radiation or reception have been described for array antennas in chapter 5 and for reflectors and lenses in chapter 6. As described there, side lobes are reduced by appropriate tapering of the array-element power distribution or of the lens or reflector aperture illumination intensity and by constructing reflectors and lenses with accurate surfaces. The lowest side-lobe levels attainable are generally with array antennas, for which the element power distribution is more accurately and flexibly controllable than is the illumination taper for a reflector or lens. For arrays as well as reflectors and lenses, a −20 dB side-lobe level is sometimes adequate, −30 dB is considered good, and −40 dB is excellent. A level of −50 dB is very difficult to achieve, but side-lobe levels of −50 dB and better have been achieved with both array and reflector antennas.

The pioneering antenna design that proved the feasibility of obtaining ultralow side lobes, as described by Schrank, was the AWACS radar antenna—an airborne system operating at S-band (vicinity of 3 GHz) designed by the Westinghouse Corporation for the E-3A airplane. This slotted waveguide array, of size about 7.6 meters wide by 1.5 meter high, has over four thousand radiating slot elements. The antenna is housed in a so-called rotodome mounted above the aircraft fuselage; this is an aerodynamically shaped radome, of dimensions that allow horizontal-plane rotation of the antenna for azimuth scanning. Vertical steering of the beam is accomplished by means of high-precision ferrite phase shifters.

The key to the AWACS antenna achievement has been primarily

(1) the sophisticated computer calculations of the exact phases and amplitudes of the required element excitations, taking into account mutual coupling effects, and

(2) the preservation of extremely close mechanical tolerances in the construction of the array. An excellent review of this subject has been published by Schrank (1983).

Other array antennas have subsequently been designed and built with side-lobe levels comparable to those of the AWACS, including at least one with dipole radiators rather than waveguide slots, thus demonstrating that the technology is not confined to slot arrays.

Although it is generally considered that better control of side-lobe levels can be achieved with array antennas than with reflectors, side-lobe levels in the 40 to 50 dB range have been reported for reflector antennas. These results are accomplished using computer-aided design and precision construction. In addition to his review of low-side-lobe array technology, Schrank also published a review article on low-side-lobe reflector antennas (Schrank, 1985).

The decibel side-lobe level is conventionally expressed as the ratio applicable to the *highest* side-lobe level. In some contexts, the *average* side-lobe level may be of greater importance than the level of the highest side lobe. The average side-lobe level is usually expressed in terms of its ratio to the *isotropic* level, denoted in decibels by the notation dBi. For high-gain (narrow-beam) antennas, this ratio is approximately equal to the fraction of the total power radiated (in transmitting-antenna terms) in the side lobes. Thus, –20 dBi means that approximately one percent of the total power radiated is side-lobe radiation. Since the main-beam power gain is also referred to the isotropic level, this means that if the main beam gain is 35 dBi, for example, and the average side-lobe level is –5 dBi, then the average side-lobe level is 40 dB below the main beam radiation. (Note that in the dBi notation, positive numbers refer to levels above isotropic and negative numbers refer to dB below isotropic level.)

In addition to airborne radar applications, low side-lobe design is especially important for reflector or lens antennas used on satellites for earth communication when frequency reuse is an objective. A paper by Burdine and Wilkinson (1980) discusses this matter and describes techniques for minimizing the side lobes of reflectors and lenses. (Many of the principles discussed in that paper are also described in chapter 6 of this book.).

As discussed in secs. 7.8 and 9.13.2, as major objective in designing a low noise antenna is to reduce the side lobes and back lobes as much as possible. The well-known horn-parabola, a successful technique for reducing wide-angle and rear lobes, is discussed in sec. 7.8. Interestingly, a conical horn-parabola design provided one of the lowest noise temperatures ever achieved (see sec. 9.13.2). In addition, this low-noise satellite-communication ground terminal type of antenna has been also commonly used for commercial microwave ground links, where the extremely low, wide-angle side lobes allow high back-to-back isolation between antennas. Even so, strictly speaking, the horn-parabola antenna is not an extremely low side-lobe type, because, according to Schrank (1985), the near-in side lobes are not very low (about –20 dB).

An important aspect of the low side-lobe problem is measurement. Great care must be taken to ensure that the side-lobe level measured on an antenna range is the true far-field side-lobe level. As discussed in chapter 3, sec. 3.2.5, the conventional criterion for an acceptable far-field measurement distance is $2D^2/\lambda$, where D is the largest aperture dimension and λ is the wavelength. However, it has been pointed out by Hacker and Schrank (1982) and Hansen (1984) that this criterion is inadequate for some types of measurement, in particular for the measurement of very low side-lobe levels. The paper by Hansen (1984) shows that for a Taylor-type pattern having a 50 dB first side-lobe level, accurate measurement of this level to within 0.5 dB requires separation of the measured and measuring antennas by at least $12D^2/\lambda$. (However, according to Hacker and Schrank (1982), measurement at lesser distance initially affects the measurement accuracy for only the side-lobes nearest to the main-beam.)

7.11. Geometrical Theory of Diffraction, Method of Moments, and Fractals

In the last several decades, new electromagnetic analysis techniques have evolved in an effort to meet growing antenna design requirements. Many of these stem from mathematical approximation methods made possible by readily available, powerful computer capabilities. Use of the fast Fourier transform (FFT) was, of course, a major step toward increasing computational speeds needed for pattern calculations. Plane-wave-spectrum (PWS) scattering is another example of a mathematical technique made practical by application of the FFT computer algorithm (Booker and Clemmow 1950; Wu and Rudduck 1974; Ryan 1981). Although the subject of advanced mathematical techniques is beyond the scope of this book, this section addresses the Method of Moments (MoM), geometrical theory of diffraction (GTD), and fractals. These are modern, advanced theoretical models that, through the use of computer programs, are contributing to the development of entirely new antenna types.

Each of these models (MOM, GTD, fractals) is connected with diffraction (radiation) from sharp edges (curvatures small compared to a wavelength), which currently cannot be analyzed by exact theoretical analyses (Balanis 2005, p. 721). Even so, the amount of use of these models for providing practical antennas solutions is, seemingly, ever increasing. This increased use has resulted because the necessary complex mathematical equations are expressed in computer algorithms. Although solutions for some problems involve heavy computational loads, new problem solutions are possible (with various degrees of approximation) because of rapid increases in computer speeds and memories. A brief summary follows.

7.11.1. Geometric Theory of Diffraction

In this book, much of the discussion on pattern calculations of aperture antennas involves integrating the effects of amplitude and phase over the aperture (sec. 6.10), sometimes referred to as the Kirchhoff method. Aperture calculations of this type are accurate for calculation in the forward direction, which includes the main-beam and much of the side-lobe region. It does not, however, properly account for "edge effects," and for that reason it does not correctly predict the pattern of an antenna in the lateral and backward directions where edge effects predominate.

Another method of calculation called the geometric theory of diffraction (GTD) has been developed that is useful when surfaces are large compared to a wavelength. With GTD, the propagation of electromagnetic waves can be analyzed through use of ray optics, like the reflection of rays from a large surface is calculated by use of the Fresnel equations (Appendix D). Although GTD uses the ray-optics representation of electromagnetic propagation, it also incorporates diffraction theory and surface waves to account for the effects of edge and surface discontinuities and surface-wave propagation. Surface waves were briefly introduced in sec. 1.4.2.

Effects of each of the different electromagnetic phenomena used in GTD analyses are discussed in the literature and are computed as coefficients (Hansen 1981). Then, each of the coefficients, after being computed appropriately with algorithms, is used as a step in the computational process for a specific antenna analysis. Depending on the geometry, in GTD analyses there may be higher order effects like multiple reflections and diffractions. These occur in a complex environment, like an antenna on an automobile, near ship structure, or near aircraft wings and engine nacelles. Burnside and Marhefka (1988) published an extensive, one-hundred page treatment of GTD theory. Burnside, Rudduck, and Marhefka (1980) published a summary of GTD computer codes developed at the Ohio State University, and Marhefka (2000) is an example of more recently developed GTD code. Examples of successful uses of GTD in calculating patterns of antennas mounted on modeled aircraft and investigating the effects of the aircraft on the patterns are addressed by Oortman and Ryan (2007).

An extensive set of antenna pattern calculations versus beam pointing direction for a large, low-side-lobe beam-steered L-band (approximately 1.3 GHz) array, that includes effects of aircraft interactions, is given by Allen (1992; 2004). The objective of the study was to determine the optimum antenna location, when antenna performance and flight dynamics are included. The required computations were very time intensive when made with a major computer system at Lockheed Martin. Even so, the GTD method of locating and moving an array on an aircraft was determined to be more cost-effective than a program of measurements using a full-scale antenna and airframe or using a scale model of antenna and aircraft.

7.11.2. Method of Moments

GTD applies to predicting antenna radiation from large aperture antennas, which are usually very high frequency devices (VHF and above); and it can also be applied to large planar arrays whose element excitations over the array surface can be considered equivalent to a field distribution over an aperture. The method of moments (MoM), on the other hand, is applicable primarily to *wire* antennas (e.g., dipoles and longer wire radiators), but it has also been used for patch antennas (Harrington 1968). A class of user-oriented digital computer programs called NEC (Numerical Electromagnetics Code) implements MoM. For wire antennas see Djordjevic, Bazdar, Vitosevic, Sarkar, and Harrington (1990), and for surface patches see Rao, Wilton, and Glisson (1982). MoM programs compute currents, from which radiation patterns can be calculated. Feed-point impedance, radiation efficiency, and gain can also be calculated. Most of the early work was done on large-scale and/or microcomputers, but there are now programs available that can be used with personal computers (Campbell 1984; Djordjevic et al. 1990; Miller and Burke 1983).

7.11.3. Fractals and Fractal Antennas

A fractal is a design, shape, or figure that is generated by a methodology that repeatedly uses an identical shape but of same and different sizes. A fractal antenna is constructed to approximate fractal geometry. The mathematics of fractals is well suited for computer computations because of their repetitive nature. Fractals can be used to generate profoundly intricate and complex shapes, and they can be deterministic or random. Random fractals contain a degree of randomness that permits the simulation of natural phenomena, like trees or mountains, in great detail. A comprehensive review of fractal antennas with an extensive list of references is included in Werner, Petko, and Spence (2007).

The fineness of detail of an object described with fractal geometry can be controlled mathematically. For example, when a picture of a bush is generated, one only needs to have a resolution small enough to be discernible to the eye. Similarly, in the case of constructing an antenna, intricacies that are much, much smaller than the smallest applicable wavelength need not be included. The procedure of dropping unnecessary details of a fractral-generated configuration permits desired fractal antenna structures to be manufacturable. Fractal antennas may be constructed through use of wire elements, and these of course have multiple edges. As a consequence, user-oriented MoM computer programs are used to analyze the edge diffraction effects of fractal wire antennas.

The use of a wire in short, more or less zig-zag, sections provides a greater overall wire length in a smaller space than if the wire were straight. This fact, when generalized, is known as the "space-filling" feature of fractal geometry. Figure 7–30 compares an ordinary circular loop antenna with a fractal "Koch" loop antenna. Both loops have the same outer radius, but it is obvious that the total wire length of the Koch loop is considerably greater. In fact, the perimeter lengths of the circular and the Koch loops are 0.26λ and 0.68λ and their calculated input impedances are 1.17 ohm and 26.7 ohms, respectively. Thus, although each loop has the same outer radius, it is much easier to couple power to the fractal loop. It is important to recognize that the impedance of the fractal antenna is increased because its effective length in increased, and consequently fractals provide a means of miniaturizing.

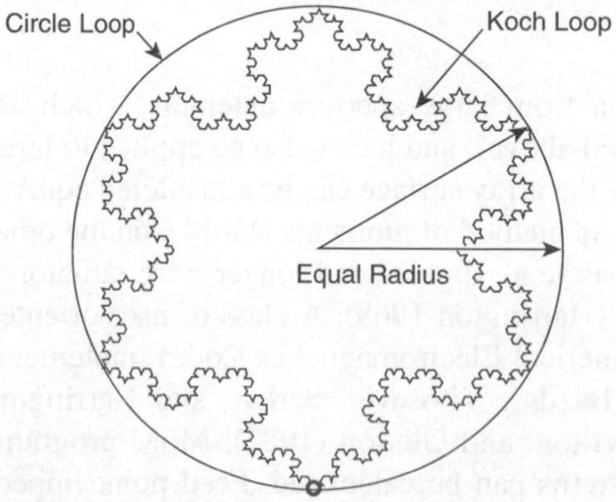

FIGURE 7–30.

Two wire loop antennas having the same outer radius: a Koch fractal loop and a conventional circular loop (from Gianvitttorio and Rahmat-Samii, 2002; © 2002, IEEE).

Fractal dipoles and patches are also possible. Gianvitttorio and Rahmat-Samii (2002) compare the performance of a conventional dipole with the fractal dipole models of Fig. 7–31. In each case, the overall dipole lengths are equal. The wire elements are contained within a plane for the Koch and quasi-fractal tree dipole, but not so for the three-dimensional quasi-fractal tree dipole. These fractal "trees" are similar to a real tree in that the top of every branch splits into more branches.

As with the Koch loop, the fractal dipoles possess features of miniaturization. In other words, for increases in the iterations (beginning with straight wires) shown in Fig. 7–31, the resonant frequencies are reduced. However, beyond the second iteration, the benefits of frequency reduction appear small, especially for the Koch and fractal tree dipoles. The resonant frequency for the conventional dipole (iteration 0) is given as 1.90 GHz, and it is about 1.15 GHz for the second iteration of the three-dimensional fractal tree dipole (see Fig. 14 of Gianvitttorio and Rahmat-Samii, 2002).

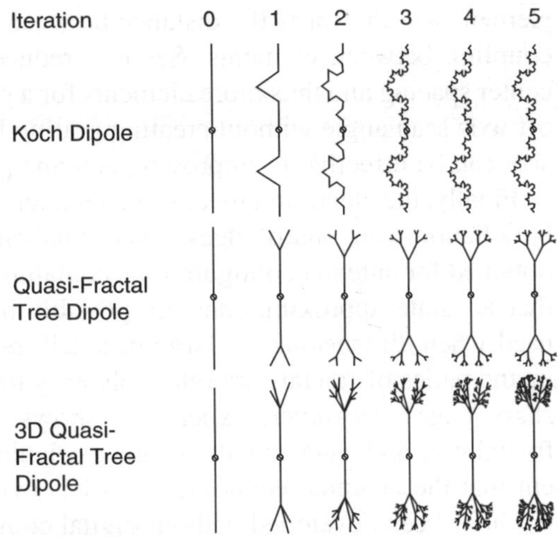

FIGURE 7–31.

Three types of fractal dipole antennas with different iterations: Koch, fractal tree, and three-dimensional fractal tree. In each case, iteration 0 is the ordinary linear dipole (from Gianvitttorio and Rahmat-Samii, 2002; © 2002, IEEE).

Patch antennas are described in sec. 4.9. A fractal patch can be made by increasing the electrical length along the sides of a patch, by using fractal-shaped (serrated) sides, instead of straight ones. The characteristics of a 30 mm by 19.46 mm rectangular patch and a 30 mm by 12 mm "torn-square" fractal patch, shown in Fig. 7–32, are compared by Gianvitttorio and Rahmat-Samii (2002). Reportedly, fractal patches offer the space-filling properties of fractal loops and dipoles. Namely, when compared with a conventional patch of the same resonant frequency, the dimensions are smaller and the radiation patterns are approximately the same. Both of the patches described above were resonant at 5.2 GHz, but the bandwidth of the rectangular patch was 1.8 percent and that of the fractal patch was only 0.4 percent. For some applications, reduced size can be a worthwhile trade for reduced bandwidth.

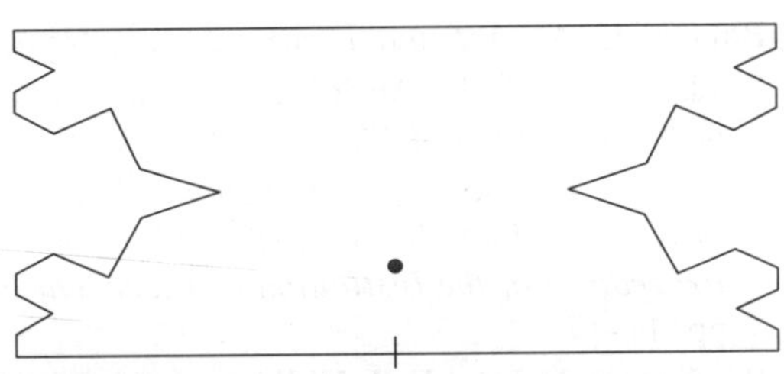

FIGURE 7–32.

A fractal patch antenna, where the edges along the resonant dimension are a "torn-square" fractal shape. The dot is a feed point (from Gianvitttorio and Rahmat-Samii, 2002; © 2002, IEEE).

Gianvitttorio and Rahmat-Samii (2002) also discuss the effects of reduced element size on arrays. They compared array pattern measurements with calculations using MoM, and reported similar results. Even though the size reduction of the elements is small in terms of miniaturizing, patch-size reduction can significantly improve array performance in two ways. First, with fixed center-to-center spacing of the elements, the reduced element size increases the distance between element edges, and this reduces the mutual coupling between elements. Second, reduced element size permits smaller center-to-center spacing and thus more elements for a given array width, thereby permitting a wider off-axis scan angle without creating grating lobes. Either type of use of reduced element size can be effective in improving antenna patterns for off-normal beam directions.

Finally, the electromagnetics phenomena common to GTD, MoM, and fractal antennas is radiation from sharp edges. Exact mathematical electromagnetic solutions cannot be obtained for antenna configurations containing sharp edges, but it has been demonstrated that accurate approximations are possible by using GTD and MoM. GTD or MoM is used when dimensions are large or small, respectively, compared to a wavelength. The mathematics of fractals are relatively easy to computer-generate, but fractal shapes have sharp edges. However, experience shows that the electromagnetic characteristics of fractal wire and patch antennas can be calculated with MoM techniques. Thus, it is apparent that the antenna technology that has evolved from GTD, MoM, and fractals could not have been developed without digital computers, because reduction to practice would have been a mathematically impracticable procedure.

References

Allen, W. P., "Aircraft Interference Effects on AEW Antenna Patterns," pp. 326–44 of M. W. Long, *Airborne Early Warning System Concepts*, Artech House, 1992 and SciTech, 2004.

Balanis, C. A., *Antenna Theory*, 3rd ed., John Wiley & Sons, 2005.

Booker, H. G., "Slot Aerials and Their Relation to Complementary Wire Aerials," *Journal of the Institution of Electrical Engineers* (London), 93, pt. IIIA, no. 4, 1946.

Booker, H. G., and P. C. Clemmow, "The Concept of an Angular Spectrum of Plane Waves, and Its Relation to That of a Polar Diagram and Amplitude Distribution," *Proeedings of the Institution of Electrical Engineers*, vol. 97, pt. III, January 1950, pp. 11–17.

Burdine, B. H., and E. J. Wilkinson, "A Low-Sidelobe Earth-Station Antenna for the 4/6 GHz B and," *Microwave Journal*, vol. 23, no. II, November 1980, pp. 53–68.

Burnside, W. D., and R. J. Marhefka, "Antennas on Aircraft, Ships, or Any Large Complex Environment," Ch. 20 in *Antenna Handbook—Theory, Applications, and Design*, Lo, Y. T. and S. W. Lee, eds., Van Nostrand, Reinhold Co., 1988.

Burnside, W. D., R. C. Rudduck, and R. J. Marhefka, "Summary of GTD Codes Developed at the Ohio State University," *IEEE Transactions on Electromagnetic Compatibility*," EMC-22, November 1980, pp. 238–243.

Campbell, D. V., "Personal Computer Applications of MININEC", *IEEE Antennas and Propagation Society Newsletter*, February 1984.

Cutrona, L. J., "Synthetic Aperture Radar," ch. 21 in *Radar Handbook*, M. I. Skolnik (ed.), McGraw-Hill, New York, 1990.

Deschamps, G. A., and R. H. DuHamel, ch. 18 in *Antenna Engineering Handbook*, H. Jasik (ed.), McGraw-Hill, New York, 1961.

Djordjevic, A. R., M. B. Bazdar, G. M. Vitosevic, T. K. Sarkar, and R. F. Harrington, *Analysis of Wire Antennas and Scatterers: Software and User's Manual*, Artech House, 1990.

DuHamel, R. H., and D. E. Isbell, "Broadband Logarithmically Periodic Antenna Structures," *IRE National Convention Record*, 1957, Part I, pp. 119–28.

Dyson, J. D., "The Unidirectional Equiangular Spiral Antenna," *IRE Transactions on Antennas and Propagation,* AP-7, October 1959, pp. 329–34.

Dyson, J. D., "The Characteristics and Design of the Conical Log-Spiral Antenna," *IEEE Transactions on Antennas and Propagation,* AP-13, July 1965, pp. 488–99.

Elachi, C., *Spaceborne Radar Remote Sensing: Applications and Techniques*, IEEE Press, 1987, pp. 11–50.

Filipovic, D. S., and T. Cencich, "Frequency Independent Antennas," ch. 13 in *Antenna Engineering Handbook*, 4th ed., J. L. Volakis (ed.), McGraw-Hill, 2007.

Gianvitttorio, J. P., and Y. Rahmat-Samii, "Fractal Antennas: A Novel Antenna Miniturization Technique, and Applications," *IEEE Antennas and Propagation Magazine*, Feb. 2002, pp. 20–35.

Giger, A. J., and R. H. Turrin, "The Triply-Folded Horn Reflector: A Compact Ground Station Antenna for Satellite Communication," *Bell System Technical Journal*, Sept. 1965, pp. 1229–53.

Hacker, P. S., and H. E. Schrank, "Range Distance Requirements for Measuring Low and Ultralow Sidelobe Antenna Patterns," *IEEE Transactions on Antennas and Propagation*, AP-30, September 1982, pp. 956–66.

Hansen, R. C., *Geometric Theory of Diffraction*, IEEE Press, Institute of Electrical and Electronics Engineers, 1981.

Hansen, R. C., "Measured Distance Effects on Low Sidelobe Patterns," *IEEE Transactions on Antennas and Propagation*, AP-32, no. 6, 1984, pp. 591–94.

Harrington, R. F., *Field Computation by Moment Methods*, The Macmillan Company, 1968.

Hines, J. N., T. Li, and R. H. Turrin, "The Electrical Characteristics of the Conical-Horn Reflector Antenna," *Bell System Technical Journal.*, July 1963, pp. 1187–1211.

Hollis, J. S., and M. W. Long, "Luneberg Lens Scanning System," *IRE Transactions on Antennas and Propagation*, vol. AP-5, January 1957, pp. 21–25.

Holliman, A. L., and J. S. Hollis, "An X-Band Wide-Angle Scanner," *Record of the Georgia Tech-SCEL Symposium on Scanning Antennas*, Georgia Institute of Technology, December 18–19, 1956, pp. 75–85.

IEEE Standard 100-1992, *The New IEEE Standard Dictionary of Electrical and Electronic Terms*, 1993.

Isbell, D. E., "Log Periodic Dipole Arrays," *IRE Transactions on Antennas and Propagation*, AP-8, May 1960, 260–67.

Johnson, R. C., "Dual-Mode Coupler," *IEEE Transactions on Microwave Theory and Techniques*, November 1967, pp. 651–52.

Johnson, R. C., A. L. Holliman, and J. S. Hollis, "A Waveguide Switch Employing the Offset Ring-Switch Junction," *IRE Transactions on Microwave Theory and Techniques*, September, 1960, pp. 532–37.

Jordan, E. C., G. A. Deschamps, J. D. Dyson, and P. E. Mayes, "Developments in Broadband Antennas," *IEEE Spectrum*, 1, no. 4, April 1964, pp. 58–71.

Kelleher, K. S., "Electromechanical Scanning Antennas," ch. 18, pp. 18-2 to 18-23, in Johnson, R. C., *Antenna Engineering Handbook*, 3rd ed., McGraw-Hill, 1993.

Kennedy, P. A., and R. W. P. King, Cruft Laboratory, Harvard University, *Technical Report* 155, April 1, 1953, "Experimental and Theoretical Impedances and Admittances of Center-Driven Antennas" (work done under an Office of Naval Research contract). Also reported in *The Theory of Linear Antennas*, by R. W. P. King, Harvard University Press, Cambridge, Mass., 1956.

LeVine, D. J., and W. Sichak, "Dual-Mode Horn Feed for Microwave Duplexing," *Electronics*, September 1954, pp. 162–64.

Long, M. W., "A High-Speed K-Band Switch," *Proceedings of the IRE*, December 1951, pp. 1566–67.

Long, M. W., W. K. Rivers, Jr., and J. C. Butterworth, "Combat Surveillance Radar AN/MPS-29 (XE-1)," *Record of the Sixth Annual Radar Symposium*, University of Michigan, 1960. Reprinted in S. L. Johnston, *Millimeter Wave Radar*, Artech House, pp. 461–78, 1980.

Love, A. W., "Horn Antennas," ch. 15 in R. C. Johnson and H. Jasik, *Antenna Engineering Handbook*, McGraw-Hill, 1984.

Mayes, P. E., "Frequency-Independent Antennas," *IEEE Antennas and Propagation Society Newsletter*, August 1982.

Marhefka, R. J., "Numerical Electromagnetic Code—Basic Scattering Code , NEC–BSC (version 4.2)", *ElectroScience Laboratory Technical Report*, The Ohio State University, October 2000.

Miller, E. K., and G. J. Burke, "Personal Computer Applications in Electromagnetics," *IEEE Antennas and Propagation Society Newsletter*, August 1983.

Oortman, G. J., and C. E. Ryan, Jr., "Aircraft Antennas," ch. 40, pp. 40-25 to 40-28, in *Antenna Engineering Handbook*, 4th ed., J. L. Volakis (ed.), McGraw-Hill, 2007.

Rao, S. M., D. R. Wilton, and A. W. Glisson, "Electromagnetic Scattering by a Surface of Arbitrary Shape," *IEEE Transactions on Antennas and Propagation,* May 1982, pp. 1396–1423.

Rumsey, V. H., "Frequency Independent Antennas," *IRE National Convention Record*, 1957, Part I, pp. 114–18.

Rumsey, V. H., *Frequency Independent Antennas*, Academic Press, 1966.

Ryan, C. E., "PWS Scattering Computation," *IEEE Antennas and Propagation Society Newsletter*, June 1981.

Schelkunoff, S. A., *Electromagnetic Waves*, Van Nostrand, Princeton, NJ, 1943. Also, Schelkunoff and Friis, *Antennas: Theory and Practice*, Wiley, New York, 1952; and Schelkunoff, *Advanced Antenna Theory*, Wiley, New York, 1952.

Schrank, H. E., "Low Sidelobe Phased Array Antennas," *IEEE Antennas and Propagation Society Newsletter*, April 1983.

Schrank, H. E., "Low Sidelobe Reflector Antennas," *IEEE Antennas and Propagation Society Newsletter*, April 1985.

Terman, F. E., *Radio Engineers' Handbook*, McGraw-Hill, 1943.

Thomas, B. M., "Design of Corrugated Conical Horns," *IEEE Transactions on Antennas and Propagation*, vol. AP-26, March 1978, pp. 367–72.

Werner, D. H., J. S. Petko, and T. G. Spence, "Fractal Antennas," ch. 33, pp. 33-1 through 33-28 in *Antenna Engineering Handbook*, 4th ed., J. L. Volakis (ed.), McGraw-Hill, 2007.

Wu, D. C. F., and R. C. Rudduck, "Plane Wave Spectrum-Surface Integration Technique for Radome Analysis," *IEEE Transactions on Antennas and Propagation*, May 1974, pp. 497–500.

Problems and Exercises

1. (a) A center-fed cylindrical dipole has a length-to-diameter ratio (L/D) of approximately 122. It is $\frac{1}{2}$ wavelength long ($L = \lambda/2$) at a frequency $f_0 = 500$ MHz. At approximately what two frequencies between 500 and 1,000 MHz will the reactive component of its input impedance be approximately +100 ohms (neglecting effects due to the feed-point connection)? (b) Another dipole of the same length has an L/D ratio of approximately 17. At about what two frequencies in the same range will the resistive component of its input impedance be 100 ohms? (Use Figs. 7–2 and 7–3.)

2. (a) A cylindrical dipole, at a particular frequency, has an input impedance $Z = 75 + j30$ ohms. What are the values of input resistance and reactance of a vertical monopole whose height (H of Fig. 7–5) above the ground plane is exactly half the length of the dipole, and whose diameter is the same as the dipole? Assume that the monopole ground plane is of infinite extent and perfectly conducting. (b) If the dipole has a free-space directivity (D) of 1.5 relative to an isotropic radiator, what is the directivity of the monopole?

3. A log-periodic antenna has a design ratio $\tau = 0.8$. At a frequency of 60 MHz, its input impedance is purely resistive and 82 ohms in value. The upper and lower cutoff frequencies are 300 MHz and 30 MHz. Assuming an ideal log-periodic behavior between the cutoff frequencies, at what frequencies (in addition to 60 MHz) will the input impedance be exactly 82 ohms and purely resistive? (Disregard fractions of a MHz.)

4. In each part, check the one of the four choices that you think is correct:

   (a) An equiangular log-periodic antenna is desirable because:

   (i) It is simpler to construct ☐

   (ii) It has noncritical length dimensions ☐

   (iii) It has very small impedance variation over its range of operation ☐

   (iv) Its phase center does not vary with frequency ☐

   (b) A self-complementary antenna is desirable because:

   (i) Its phase center does not vary with frequency ☐

   (ii) Its impedance does not vary with frequency ☐

(iii) It is light in weight □

(iv) The pattern does not have sidelobes □

(c) Some types of log-periodic antennas used as feeds for paraboloidal reflectors are deficient for broad-band operation because:

(i) The beamwidth cannot be made narrow enough for proper illumination taper □

(ii) The phase center varies with frequency □

(iii) The beam direction varies with frequency □

(iv) The beam cannot be made wide enough for proper illumination □

5. Name three basic types of antennas that can provide circularly polarized radiation.
6. Name one type of antenna that will provide each of the following types of radiation (or reception) characteristics: (a) Omnidirectionality (a theoretically perfect circular pattern) in the horizontal plane, with vertical polarization. (b) Same pattern as in (a) but with horizontal polarization. (c) An approximately uniform pattern in the horizontal plane with horizontal polarization in that plane, and that uses multiple dipoles.
7. State two conditions under which an *electrically small* antenna may be used for reception with results virtually as good as would be obtained with a much larger antenna.
8. With various types of direction-finding antennas, the direction of a received signal is determined by finding the null direction rather than the direction of maximum signal. In a single brief sentence, state why the null is used rather than the maximum.
9. An antenna has a one-degree beamwidth in the vertical plane and a three-degree beamwidth horizontally. The beam is scanned in both elevation and azimuth. The elevation scan is a sawtooth motion, and each sawtooth scan takes 0.1 seconds. The azimuth scan is a much slower motion with constant angular speed. What must this azimuth angular speed be in order for the azimuth scan to progress one azimuth beamwidth during the time of one vertical scan? Express the result in terms of revolutions per minute.
10. Name two antenna design factors to which special attention must be paid to achieve low-noise operation in the frequency range of 1 to 10 GHz. (One of these factors relates to external noise, and one to internal noise.)

CHAPTER 8

Electronically Steered Arrays

This chapter discusses electronically steered arrays (ESAs), also commonly called phased arrays. These antennas have beams that can be electronically steered in pointing direction or beam shape, without mechanical motion, and accomplished in microseconds. Although the operation of all arrays depends on the proper phasing of the individual array elements, the terms ESA and *phased array* have by usage come to mean an array in which the beam is *steered* in direction and shape by varying the phasing of the elements. Present-day ESA (or phased array) technology includes adaptive beam forming (ABF), which merges rapid beam pointing and shaping with digital signal processing separately. With ABF arrays, the phasing and time delaying of the signals from individual elements are jointly adaptively adjusted and then summed to rapidly beam point, beam shape, and Doppler filter desired received signals. In this way, the received signal output, from the summed individual array signals, may be optimized, simultaneously, for both the strength of the desired signal relative to thermal noise and relative to interference from undesired signals.

The advancements in ESA (i.e., phase array) technology has resulted from intensive and continuing research and development in the following areas:

(i) Improvement of the devices and circuitry used for producing the required phase shifts and power division among the array elements;

(ii) Use of microprocessors or special-purpose computers to determine the optimum phasing and power division to carry out a particular beam-steering command;

(iii) Better understanding of factors affecting side-lobe levels, mutual coupling effects on array-element patterns (and methods of minimizing the deleterious effects of such coupling), and effects of phase errors on side lobes and main-beam gain;

(iv) Development of *adaptive* receiving arrays that are capable of automatically adjusting their overall patterns to optimize signal-to-interference ratio by placing pattern nulls in the directions of interfering signals;

(v) Development of solid-state amplifiers suitable for use at transmit-receive array elements, making the use of amplifiers distributed among the array elements more economically feasible and the arrays more efficient; and

(vi) Development of fabrication techniques such as the microstrip technology, which further contributes to the economic feasibility of large arrays, especially when combined with solid-state technology. It also makes possible *conformal* arrays—i.e., arrays that can conform to the surface contour of a vehicle or to other nonplanar shape requirements.

8.1. Phased Array Principles

With all the elements of a linear array or a planar array in phase, the beam is directed broadside, that is, perpendicular to the line or plane of the elements. On the other hand, if the phases of the elements of a linear array progressively change by an amount per element that is equal, in radians, to $2\pi d/\lambda$, where d is the element spacing and λ is the wavelength, the beam direction will be parallel to the line joining the elements (endfire). These facts suggest that a progressive phase change per element along the array intermediate between the broadside and endfire values might result in a beam directed at some intermediate angle, as is the case.

An electronically steered array (ESA), or simply a phased array, is an antenna that uses variable phase, frequency, or time delay at the array elements to scan the beam to a designated angle in space.

Advantages of electronic steering include

- rapid beam pointing
- inertialess beam movement
- fast beam shaping by aperture control

Disadvantages

- high cost
- high complexity
- long, expensive design cycle

Because of its relative simplicity, frequency-scan arrays were the first widely used electronically agile arrays for radar. However, because of the potential advantages of electronic steering with phase shifters, momentum increased during the 1950s for the development of practical, rapid phase changers that operate over a wide range of microwave frequencies. Motivation for rapid, inertialess scan, narrow beam arrays continued for years, but various technological limitations and costs continued as prohibiting factors. Even today, although costs are greatly reduced, complexity and cost are still limitations for the production of large (hundreds or more elements) phased arrays. Of course, phased arrays for wireless, which generally require fewer array elements, are now widely used. A major new thrust for array development began with the invention of adaptive digital signal processing concepts for "smart" antennas, which require array elements to be rapidly and independently controlled from instructions generated by digital computations. Today, phased array research, development, and production are presently major technological activities.

8.1.1. Time Delay and Phase Shift Requirements

Figure 8–1 illustrates a linear array with the main-beam electronically steered to a scan angle θ_L, measured from broadside. The beam can be steered from one angle to another by changing the relative time delay between elements. Note that, for a focused beam, the wave phases from the elements on arriving perpendicular to the wavefront are equal. This is true if, for each element, the overall time delay from element input to wavefront is equal, and this can be done by adding a time delayer at the input of each element. Then focusing is accomplished because, for each element, the delay time of the time delayer plus the propagation time from element is equal. To illustrate, the path length difference between the bottom and top elements to the wavefront is $L \sin \theta_L$. Thus, the propagation time for the radiation from the bottom element to wavefront exceeds that from the top element by $L \sin \theta_L / c$, where c is 3×10^8 m/s. Therefore, to retain focus at all frequencies and at scan angle θ_L, a time delay increase of $L \sin \theta_L / c$ is needed for the

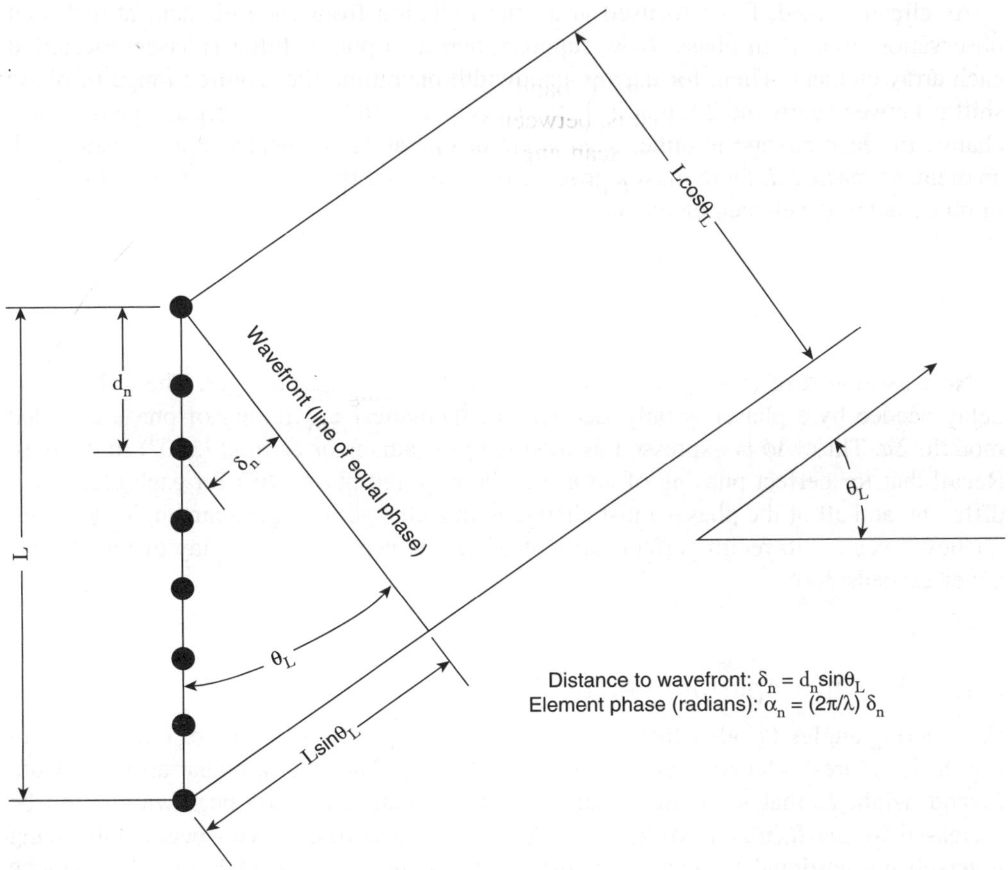

FIGURE 8–1.

Effective aperture (line of equal phase, $L\cos\theta_L$) versus scan angle θ_L.

top element relative to the bottom element. Appropriate, decreasingly less time delay is required for the lower elements for scan angle of θ_L. Clearly, for the beam to be scanned in the $-\theta_L$ direction, the larger time delays will be needed for the lower elements.

Consider now the following example, with $\theta_L = 30°$ and $L/\lambda = 20$. Then focusing will occur if a time delay is added to the top element that corresponds to the time it takes for a wave in free space to traverse a distance of 10λ. This delay can in principle be obtained by adding a transmission line. However, for each scan angle a different length of transmission line would be required—and the lengths would be different for each array element. Now imagine an array with several hundred (or perhaps thousands of) elements; and the capability to change to a different length of transmission line at each element and each scan angle. Although time delayers permit an array to be focused over a wide bandwidth, time delayers are bulky, heavy, and expensive. Therefore, time delayers are used only when very broad-band performance is required. Instead, phase shifters (often called phasers) are commonly used to provide agile beam-pointing capabilities.

As already noted, for a focused array the radiation from each element at a distant observation point is in-phase. Now suppose there is a phase shifter (phaser) located at each array element. Then, for narrow bandwidth operation, the required range of phase shift is between zero and 2π, that is, between zero and 360°. However, each phaser must change for each change in either scan angle or operating frequency. For focusing with an element spacing d, there must a progressive decrease, from top to bottom in Fig. 8–1, in phase delay α between elements as follows:

$$\alpha = \left(\frac{2\pi d}{\lambda}\right)\sin\theta_L \tag{8–1}$$

Now assume α of (8–1) equals $\Delta\phi + 2\pi I$, with I being any integer. Then, the phase delay needed by a phaser is only $\Delta\phi$. This mathematical unwinding of phase is called modulo 2π. Thus, $\Delta\phi$ is expressed as mod (2π) in radians or as mod (360°) in degrees. Recall that for perfect phasing of an array, the required phase shift for each element is different, and all of the phases must change with a change in either scan angle θ_L or frequency. Even so, to retain perfect array phasing, the needed phase delay of the phasers never exceeds 360°.

8.1.2. Effective Aperture Versus Scan Angle

For steering angles θ_L other than zero, the effective aperture (the line of equal phase in Fig. 8–1) is foreshortened in accordance with $L\cos\theta_L$. Then, for a planar array of width L_x and height L_y that scans in azimuth AZ and elevation EL, the beamwidths will be increased by the factors $1/\cos\theta_{AZ}$ and $1/\cos\theta_{EL}$, in accordance with beamwidth being inversely proportional to aperture width. Perhaps more detrimental, the gain will be reduced by the product $\cos\theta_{AZ}\cdot\cos\theta_{EL}$. The practical effect of gain loss due to aperture foreshortening generally limits the use of off-normal scan angles to 60° and less.

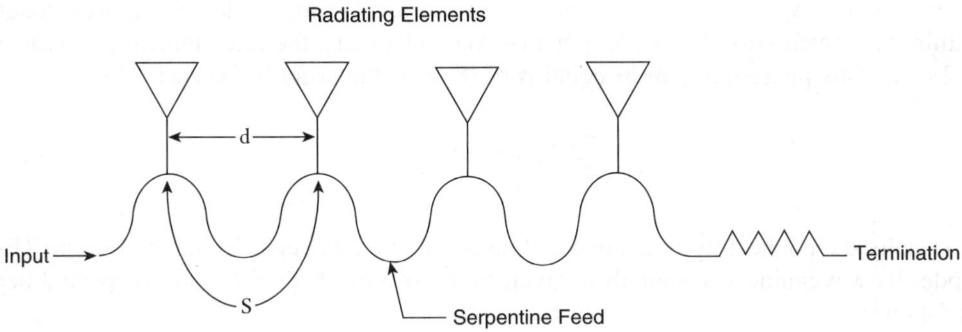

FIGURE 8–2.

Frequency scan linear array.

8.1.3. Frequency-Scan Antennas

In earlier times, ESA arrays that functioned by frequency scan were widely employed for radar. This was because, for radar applications where transmit frequency can be controlled, frequency-scan is a low-cost method for inertialess antenna beam scan (Ajioka 1993). Frequency scan antennas offer simplicity, low cost, and high reliability. Consequently, frequency scan has been widely used for inertialess beam scanning. There are, however, limitations because frequency beam-scan prevents other uses of frequency change, such as for pulse compression or pulse-to-pulse frequency agility. Another disadvantage is caused by the wide frequency spectrum needed, and the likelihood of interference with other electronic systems. In addition, the transmitting and receiving equipment required to accommodate changing frequency adds complexity and expense.

With frequency scan, the desired change in array phasing is caused by changing frequency. This changes the wavelength, so that if the phase change per element depends on the phase delay in a transmission line or waveguide, the phase will vary as the frequency varies. For a linear array, a basic series feed system is shown in Fig. 8–2, where the length of line s is greater than the element-to-element spacing d. This effect is accomplished by "folding" or "snaking" the waveguide or line between elements to increase its length. The resulting feed is called a serpentine or snake feed. This type of feed results in an increased phase change between adjacent elements for a given frequency change.

Following (8–1), the angle of the beam with respect to the broadside direction can be expressed in terms of the progressive phase change per element α and the frequency. Then, for the beam focused in direction θ_L and spacing d between elements, the required phase difference in radians between elements is

$$\alpha = \left(\frac{2\pi d}{\lambda}\right)\sin\theta_L + 2\pi I \tag{8–2}$$

where λ is free space wavelength and I is an integer. Letting λ_s denote the wavelength within the transmission line of length s between elements, the interelement phase delay is $2\pi s/\lambda_s$. This phase delay must equal α of (8–2) if the array is focused. Thus,

$$\left(\frac{2\pi d}{\lambda}\right)\sin\theta_L + 2\pi I = \frac{2\pi s}{\lambda_s} \tag{8–3}$$

Usually the connecting transmission line is air-filled waveguide operated in the TE_{01} mode. Its waveguide wavelength is given by (2–69) of chapter 2, and is repeated here as follows:

$$\lambda_g = \frac{c}{\sqrt{f^2 - f_c^2}} \tag{8–4}$$

In (8–4), c is the free space velocity of propagation and f_c is the waveguide cutoff frequency. If waveguide is used for the transmission line, $\lambda_s = \lambda_g$. Then from (8–3), if θ_L is zero

$$I = \frac{s}{\lambda_{g0}} \tag{8–5}$$

Here λ_{g0} is the wavelength within each connecting line of length s at the frequency f_0 for which the beam is pointed in the broadside direction, that is, $\theta_L = 0$. In other words, I is the integer number of wavelengths along the transmission line at the wavelength λ_{g0}.

Using (8–3), (8–4), and (8–5), it can be shown that

$$\sin\theta_L = \frac{I\lambda}{d}\left[1 - \left(\frac{f^2 - f_c^2}{f_0^2 - f_c^2}\right)^{1/2}\right] = \frac{cI}{fd}\left[1 - \left(\frac{f^2 - f_c^2}{f_0^2 - f_c^2}\right)^{1/2}\right] \tag{8–6}$$

In (8–6), only values of f within the interval for which $|\sin\theta_L| \le 1$ are permitted.

8.1.4. Array Bandwidth

Usually, modern phased arrays use phase shifters for rapid angle scanning and hopping, but time delayers (sec. 8.2.4) are needed when wide-band performance is required. This section discusses the principles that control the bandwidth of arrays that employ phase shifters and time delayers.

Two categories of bandwidth are discussed in chapter 3. Category 1 in which an antenna is required to handle frequencies over a wide band simultaneously; and category 2 in which the range of frequencies is covered over a period of time, but at any one time the bandwidth needed is only a small fraction of the long-term requirement. The simultaneous case is called instantaneous bandwidth. It is the one needed to pass the signal's spectrum, and therefore the shape of a short pulse. Category 2, called tunable bandwidth, is one where there is enough time available for setting antenna parameters prior to a frequency change. Instantaneous bandwidth (category 1) presents the more difficult problem, because the antenna must function properly, without adjustments, at any frequency within the band.

As already discussed, arrays having broad instantaneous bandwidth must use time delayers. Time delayers are heavy and expensive. For these reasons, most scanning arrays use phase shifters for scanning, and consequently they have only limited instantaneous bandwidths. Array elements and phase shifters (phasers) can limit overall bandwidth. However, array elements usually can perform over bandwidths of 10% without major changes in impedance or beamwidth. Recall that elements of a focused array require equal time delay to a point in space, and phase delay for a given time delay is directly proportional to frequency. Therefore, bandwidth is limited by phase shifters, because their phase delay is nearly independent of frequency.

The beam direction of an array that is steered by phase shifters will automatically shift as the frequency is changed. This beam shifting limits the array bandwidth. Most modern arrays can, however, be "tuned" (by resetting the phase shifters) over a bandwidth of five to perhaps ten percent. Frank (1972) gives an estimated first guess at bandwidth, without tuning, as

$$\text{bandwidth } (\%) = 3\,\text{dB beamwidth (degrees)} \tag{8–7}$$

In other words, a phased array will have roughly a one percent instantaneous bandwidth if it has a broadside −3 dB beamwidth of one degree. The actual bandwidth will depend on the feed architecture, transmitted waveform, and scan angle. According to Frank, (8–7) above will provide a bandwidth estimate that is rarely off by a factor of more than two.

Determining a more accurate estimate requires a thorough examination of how the array will be used. For example, the bandwidth decreases with increases in scan angle. In addition, signals that are modulated, for example, pulsed signals, have a widened spectrum, and this must be allowed in estimating needed bandwidth. In other words, because of the different frequencies within a modulated signal, an array beam is spread in angle. This spreading reduces the effective gain.

For a scanned beam to remain perfectly focused when frequency is changed, the element phases must be changed. Without resetting, phase shifters are essentially constant phase devices, with changes of only a few degrees over their operating bandwidths. For (8–8), (8–9), and (8–10) that follow, it is assumed that the transmission lines to the array elements are identical and phases of the phase shifters are independent of frequency.

From (8–1), the beam is steered to a direction θ_L with a phase of

$$\phi = \frac{2\pi x}{\lambda_1}\sin\theta_L = \frac{2\pi x}{c} f_1 \sin\theta_L \tag{8–8}$$

at an element located a distance x from the array center. With the same phase setting, a frequency f_2 steers the beam to a new position $\theta_L + \Delta\theta_L$. Then,

$$\phi = \frac{2\pi x}{c} f_1 \sin\theta_L = \frac{2\pi x}{c} f_2 \sin(\theta_L + \Delta\theta_L) \tag{8–9}$$

It can be shown that, for small changes in Δf, where $\Delta f = f_2 - f_1$, the change in direction of the beam $\Delta\theta_L$ is small, and then (8–9) can be approximated as

$$\Delta\theta_L = \frac{\Delta f}{f} \tan\theta_L \tag{8–10}$$

The relationship (8–10) indicates that the amount of beam squint $\Delta\theta_L$ increases in proportion to the product of fractional change in frequency and tangent of scan angle. However, (8–10) is of limited usefulness, because it is valid only for small changes in frequency.

To make practical estimates of beam shift, one must resort to approximations using (8–9). Furthermore, the loss in signal strength for a given beam squint will necessarily depend on beamwidth, and hence on aperture size. Frank gives graphs of loss in gain as a function of beamwidth, scan angle, and spectral width. Equation (8–7), a commonly used estimate for bandwidth, gives a gain loss of approximately 0.8 dB (due to the beam shift) for an unmodulated signal with the beam scanned 60° from broadside. For a signal with a broad spectrum, such as a short pulse, effective bandwidth may be less than indicated by (8–7). This is because an array must be focused at all frequencies contained within the spectral bandwidth of the signal being either transmitted or received.

Interestingly, antenna performance with short pulses can also be analyzed in terms of the time required for a received pulsed wave to reach all of the array elements (Frank, 1972). This time is called the array fill time, which is $(L \sin\theta_L)/c$. Thus, fill time is the time it takes for a wave traveling at speed c to traverse the distance $L \sin\theta_L$. The role of a time delayer is, of course, to add delay that equals the fill time that will, in principle, result in focusing that is independent of frequency.

8.1.5. Phased Array Patterns

Assume a planar array is located in the x-y plane (see, e.g., Fig. 5–14). Then, in accordance with sec. 5.5.1, far-zone patterns can be calculated by summing the excitation of the elements over their x and y values as follows:

$$g(\theta,\phi) = \sum\sum a(x,y)\exp[j\Psi(x,y)] \tag{8–11}$$

where

$a(x, y)$ = the amplitude excitation of each element
$\Psi(x, y) = \alpha - (2\pi/\lambda)\delta$

with

α = phase excitation of each element and
δ = pathlength difference of each element (radiator) to the observation point relative to pathlength from the array center, with the observation point in the far zone (see Appendix H),
$\delta = -\sin\theta\,(x\cos\phi + y\sin\phi)$

Usually, the elements of rectangular arrays are energized so that their amplitudes and phases along the x-axis aperture coordinates are independent of the y-axis coordinates, and conversely. In that case, the element amplitudes and phases can be expressed as products of terms that depend only on one coordinate, either x or y, as follow:

$$a(x, y) = a(x)a(y)$$

$$\alpha(x, y) = \alpha(x)\alpha(y)$$

Then, the integrand of (8–11) is separable as two products, one that is a function of the x coordinates and the other a function of the y coordinates. In addition, electronically steered arrays are usually designed so the separations between elements are evenly spaced, but not necessarily the same along the x and y axes. Then, the x and y coordinates can be expressed as $x_m = md_x$ and $y_n = nd_y$, where d_x and d_y are the element spacings in the x and y directions. Similarly, $a(x)$, $a(y)$, $\alpha(x)$, and $\alpha(y)$ can be expressed as a_m, a_n, α_m, and α_n, respectively. Then (8–11) can be written as the following product of two summations

$$\begin{aligned} g(\theta, \phi) = &\sum a_m \exp[j(\alpha_m + (2\pi/\lambda)md_x \sin\theta\cos\phi)] \\ &\cdot\sum a_n \exp[j(\alpha_n + (2\pi/\lambda)nd_y \sin\theta\cos\phi)] \end{aligned} \quad (8\text{–}12)$$

where far-zone amplitude patterns are calculated by summing the excitation of the elements over all m and n (x and y) values. The reader will recognize that each of the two product terms of (8–12) is an array factor for a linear array, and thus each can be considered separately as if describing the radiation from a linear array.

Effects of beam steering are now considered, recognizing that scanning may be accomplished separately in each plane. An array beam is focused if the phases of the fields from its elements are equal at a great distance. In other words, a focused antenna provides a field of equal phase along a line normal to the beam-pointing direction, as in Fig. 8–1. Consider now the pattern in the x-z plane for a line source along the axis. Then, since there are no elements along the y axis a_n and α_n are zero. In addition, since the pattern in the x-z plane is being considered, $\phi = 0$ and $\cos\phi = 1$. Therefore, from (8–12), the pattern in the x-z plane for a line source along the x-axis versus observation angle θ is

$$g(\theta) = \sum_{m=0}^{M-1} a_m \exp\left[j\left(\alpha_m + \frac{2\pi}{\lambda} md_x \sin\theta \right) \right] \quad (8\text{–}13)$$

where M is the number of elements and there are equally spaced elements located at coordinates md_x.

The pattern amplitude $|g(\theta)|$ is maximized when in (8–13) the term $\left(\alpha_m + \frac{2\pi}{\lambda} md_x \sin\theta\right) = 0$. Thus, for the beam to be steered for its peak amplitude in direction $\theta = \theta_L$, each element phase α_m must be as follows:

$$\alpha_m = -\frac{2\pi}{\lambda} md_x \sin\theta_L \tag{8–14}$$

Then, when the phases are set in accordance with (8–14) to maximize the pattern in direction θ_L, the pattern is as follows:

$$g(\theta) = \sum_{m=0}^{M-1} a_m \exp\left[j\frac{2\pi}{\lambda} md_x(\sin\theta - \sin\theta_L)\right] \tag{8–15}$$

The reader should recall that θ_L in (8–15) is the pointing direction of the major lobe and θ is the observation angle in an arbitrary direction.

8.1.6. Grating Lobes

A grating lobe is any lobe other than the major lobe that occurs when the radiation from all elements add in-phase. Grating lobes for a nonscanning broadside array were discussed in sec. 5.5.4, where it is seen that additional major lobes will occur when the element spacing is greater than λ. Grating lobes can occur for a beam pointed off of broadside if the element spacing is less than λ. This occurs because the term $g(\theta)$ of (8–15) can have maximum values if

$$\frac{2\pi}{\lambda} md_x(\sin\theta - \sin\theta_L) = \pm 2\pi I \tag{8–16}$$

where I is an integer. When (8–16) is satisfied, the maxima of $g(\theta)$ are grating lobes. As a consequence of (8–16), element spacing must be less than λ for an array that is scanned. In particular, to prohibit grating lobes when the major lobe is pointed in directions other than broadside, the maximum acceptable element spacing d_{max} is

$$d_{max} = \frac{\lambda}{1 + \sin|\Delta\theta|} \tag{8–17}$$

where $\Delta\theta$ is the largest angle θ_L to be scanned away from broadside. Parenthetically, the derivation is not oblivious and to derive it the reader is referred to Ajioka (1993, pp. 19–6 and 19–7).

From (8–17), for $\Delta\theta$ equaling 90°, d_{max} is $\lambda/2$. Because of loss in effective aperture due to pointing off of broadside, ESA designs typically limit the scan to a maximum of 60° off-broadside. Then, $\sin\Delta\theta = 0.866$ and $d_{max} = 0.54\ \lambda$. Consequently, the element spacings for ESAs are usually about $\lambda/2$, or slightly less, to avoid the risk of creating part or all of a full grating lobe.

Thus far it has been assumed that the array elements are arranged in a square grid with separation in height and width of d_{max} between elements. Now consider a lattice configuration of equilateral triangles, with each triangle leg having length d_{max}. Such a configuration, when considering only the avoidance of grating lobes, will allow (depending on maximum scan angle off-broadside) a 10 to 15 percent reduction in the overall number of required elements (Sharp 1961). However, the triangular configuration creates a somewhat more stringent requirement on the fineness of phase quantization for controlling side-lobe levels (Nelson 1969).

8.2. Beam-Steering Technology

8.2.1. Phase Shifters

An essential ingredient of a beam-steered phased-array is a device that can produce a variable and controllable phase shift. Phase shifters are sometimes call *phasers*. (They should not, however, be referred to as *phasors*, because that term denotes a mathematical complex variable characterized by an amplitude and a phase angle.) Three basic methods of producing phase shifts are: (i) variation of the velocity of propagation of waves in a segment or segments of the antenna feed system; (ii) variation of the lengths of segments of the feed path; and (iii) variation of the frequency, which results in a change in the phase at the output of a fixed-length transmission-line. The frequency-variation method (frequency scanning) already has been discussed (sec. 8.1.3).

Control of propagation-velocities or line lengths can be either analog (continuous) or digital (step-wise variable). Both methods are used. The digital method can approximate the continuous variation of phase to any desired degree of accuracy if a sufficient number of digital bits is used. The most popular electronic phase shifters employ either ferrites or diodes, but other technologies have matured in the last ten or so years (Romanofsky 2007). Phase shifter cost is a major factor in overall cost of electronically steered arrays (ESAs), because it must be multiplied by the number of phasers used. For some arrays, the number of phasers exceeds ten thousand; and an estimate (Romanofsky 2007, p. 21–2) includes total phaser cost that approach 40 percent of the overall cost of steerable receive arrays.

The principal method of controlling the propagation velocity in waveguides and transmission lines is through the use of ferrite material inserted into the space occupied by the propagating waves. Ferrite is a ceramic-like insulator material that possesses magnetic properties, and has high resistivity which permits wave propagation with low loss. The wave propagation velocity in ferrites can be varied by applying varying amounts of a constant magnetic field to the material (superimposed on the propagating electromagnetic fields). The strength of the constant field can be controlled by varying the magnitude of a magnetizing direct current.

Some ferrite phase shifters require a continuous magnetizing current, while others are of the "latching" type, in which a relatively short pulse establishes a magnetization level; this level is maintained until it is reset by another dc pulse. However, when the magnetization level is to be changed for either the continuous-current or the latching type of ferrite phase shifter, it is necessary first to set the magnetization momentarily at the saturation level and then to apply the current required to set the desired level. This avoids errors that would otherwise occur due to the hysteresis effect.

Ferrite phase shifters can be reciprocal or nonreciprocal. In the former case, the same amount and direction of phase shift occurs for either direction of propagation. In the latter case, the sign of the phase shift is reversed when the direction of propagation is reversed. When a nonreciprocal phase shifter is used for both transmission and reception with the same antenna (as is the case for many radar systems), the phase shifter must be switched rapidly between the transmitting and receiving modes of operation. Despite this requirement, nonreciprocal phase shifters are sometimes used in radar applications because of other desirable characteristics. Switching times of a few microseconds are achievable.

Ferrite phase shifters can be either analog or digital, and even when an intrinsically analog shifter is used, it may be digitally controlled. These phase shifters become increasingly inefficient and bulky as the frequency is decreased. They are not generally used below about 1 GHz, although they have been used at frequencies as low as 200 MHz. On the other hand, ferrite phase shifters are usable at frequencies of the order of 10 GHz or higher.

The primary electronic method employed for varying the *length* of a transmission line is *diode switching*. Diode phase shifters, unlike ferrite phase shifters, become increasingly efficient as the frequency decreases, although they also can be used up to 10 GHz. For purposes of basic understanding of its phase-shifting capability, the diode can be regarded as a switch, although in one type of phase-shifter it behaves as a variable capacitive susceptance. The simplest type of diode phase shifter is the *switched line* phase shifter, consisting of elements in which diode switches select either of two transmission line lengths. This is a digital device, as are most diode phase shifters. As an example of its action, if the two transmission-line segments through which the signal can be alternately switched differ in length by a quarter wavelength, the resulting phase shift will be 90 degrees (since a 360-degree phase change occurs for each wavelength of a propagation path). Other well-known types of diode phase shifters are the hybrid-coupled phase shifter and the periodically-loaded-line phase shifter (Tang and Burns, 1993).

A digital phase shifter is constructed by cascading several units, each of which can be switched between two fixed phase-shift values. The incremental phase shift of each successive unit is twice as large as that of the next-smaller unit, and the largest increment is 180 degrees. This permits all possible phase shifts to be achieved, in increments of the smallest unit, by switching the appropriate elements from one state to the other. For example, a 4-bit phase shifter has incremental phase-shift elements of 22.5, 45, 90, and 180 degrees (and zero), as shown in Fig. 8–3. This permits phase delays of 22.5, 45, 67.5, 90, 112.5, 135, 157.5, 180, 202.5, . . . , and so on. (For an n-bit phase shifter, the number of possible delays is 2^n, including zero phase shift which is equivalent to 360 degrees.) This description of digital phase shifting is applicable to digital ferrite phase shifters as well as to diode shifters.

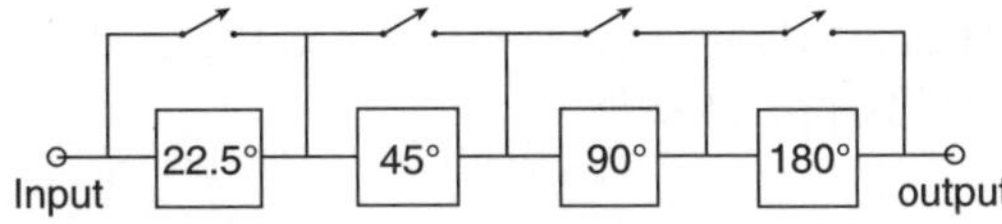

FIGURE 8–3.

Schematic of a 4-bit digital phase shifter.

The choice between ferrite and diode phase shifters is made on the basis of many factors, of which the principal ones other than cost include the frequency of operation, the rf power handling needs, the permissible insertion loss, permissible switching power, available space, and allowable weight. The relative importance of these factors varies for different applications, so it is difficult to make any general statements of preferences. Ferrite phase shifters are capable of handling higher power levels and of operating efficiently at higher frequencies (although both types are operable to at least X-band), and their insertion loss is usually lower. Diode phase shifters become increasingly efficient at lower frequencies, and are somewhat less critical in adjustment.

It is to be noted that, where phasers are used with either a receive module or a transmit-receive (T/R) module (see Fig. 8–7), phaser losses are less critical. This is because the phasers follow low-noise receive amplifiers and precede the transmit amplifiers. In addition, where T/R modules are used, the phaser power handling requirements are reduced because total transmit power is distributed between modules. Furthermore, other advantages of diode phasers over ferrite phasers include lower cost, smaller size and less weight. Therefore, diode phasers are used with receive or with T/R modules at higher frequencies than might otherwise be possible.

8.2.2. Effects of Phase Quantization

It is evident that a digital phase shifter cannot provide the *exact* phase shift theoretically required for the specified beam direction. However, it has been shown (Miller 1964) that for a linear array of many elements the effect of phase errors is not great if the *average* phase error over the array is algebraically near zero and if the errors are random from element to element (i.e., not periodic). This conclusion is very similar in its principles to the analysis of Ruze (sec. 6.6.2) concerning the effect on side-lobe levels of deviations of a reflector surface from a true parabolic shape. When these conditions are fulfilled (Cheston and Frank 1970, pp. 11–37), a 4-bit phase shifter will add less than an additional 1.4 percent of the total radiated power to the average side-lobe power level in a linear array of 100 elements, with a correspondingly negligible reduction of the main-beam gain (0.06 dB). There may also be a slight but insignificant shift of the main-beam direction. However, if the phase errors have any periodicity, from element to element, much more significant effects will occur, including the formation of *phase-quantization lobes*, which are analogous to grating lobes. There will also be some shift of the main-beam direction. At some angles the phase-quantization lobes can be significant. However, a method of reducing the peak phase-quantization lobes, attributed to Miller (1964), consists of inserting fixed randomized phase shifts in the feed paths to each array element. Quantization lobes can also arise due to *amplitude* quantization effects when subarrays are used. For details of these matters, see Cheston and Frank (1970, pp. 11–37).

8.2.3. Effects of Element Mutual Coupling

The design of large-scale electronically beam-steered arrays should include analyses on effects of mutual impedance between array elements and on possible radiation blind directions that can occur. In the early days of array development, unexpected "blind spots" were observed for some arrays at certain scan angles (see, e.g., Allen 1962; Cheston and Frank 1970; Hansen 1973, 2007; Stark 1974; Tang and Burns 1984, pp. 20–25/20–28; Mailloux 2005, ch. 6). It was eventually determined that mutual coupling between array elements was a major cause. As discussed in sec. 5.5.1, the overall array pattern is the product of an array factor (the pattern that would result if an equivalent array of isotropic elements were used) and the actual pattern of a single element of the array. However, as stated, the element pattern to be used is that of an element *in the array environment*. That is, the element pattern to be used is *not* the pattern that is measured for an isolated element.

Ideally, an antenna should provide a good impedance match between the transmitter and free space. If there are impedance mismatches, a loss of input and radiated power occurs. Thus a mismatch, even at one element, changes the array aperture illumination and may cause an appreciable pattern change from that which would occur based on the element's assumed radiated power. A mismatch causes standing waves which produces undesirable, higher voltage levels than does a matched condition. Furthermore, internal reflections may cause the generation of spurious lobes in the overall array radiation pattern. In fact, there are conditions, sometimes observed, where a matched condition exists at the broadside beam direction, but at some other angle most of the power is reflected and thus a scan "blindness" results. In spite of the difficulty of dealing with mutual coupling, especially with beam scanning arrays, fixed-beam and electronically steered arrays have been developed and satisfactorily operating for a number of decades (Oliner and Knittel, 1972; Hansen, 2007).

It will be recalled, from secs. 5.1.4 through 5.1.7, that mutual coupling between elements changes the input impedance, radiated power, and the pattern of an array element. Consequently, when phase changes are introduced to change the beam pointing direction or operating frequency, element input impedances and radiated power change, and, in general, the changes are different for each element. In addition, it has been found that the major effect of beam scanning is individual element impedance change (thus change in element current and element radiated power) and not element pattern change. Consequently, a major design issue is to address the input impedances of the elements. This means that mutual coupling analysis is needed to solve for the input voltages (V_1, V_2, *etc.*) of Eq. 5–5, sec. 5.1.5, that produce the required currents.

There have been numerous publications written on the design of arrays (see, e.g., Allen 1962; Cheston and Frank 1970; Hansen 1973, 2007; Stark 1974; Tang and Burns 1984; Mailloux 2005). Hansen (2007) is a recommended starting place before plans are set in place for a major new steered-array development. There he outlines important steps for avoiding major flaws in design, which include detailed preliminary design, simulation, computer analyses, and measurements.

8.2.4. Time Delayers

An array beam can be steered in any direction (subject to some constraints imposed by the element pattern and by the array geometry) by varying the element phases over a maximum range of zero to 360 degrees or 2π radians. In other words the maximum phase shift required per element is modulo 2π radians. However, if a wide band of frequencies is to be radiated or received, especially with large arrays (high gain, narrow beam), an additional requirement is imposed because the desired phase shift cannot then be preserved over the full frequency range. That is, the modulo 2π principle does not then apply. For very wide band operation, "true time delay" is required, which means that the *propagation times* for the paths from a common point in the feed system to any point on the radiated or received plane wavefront must be equal in the absolute sense, rather than in the modulo 2π phase sense.

This means that instead of a phase delay of up to 360 degrees maximum, the delay to some elements must have additional increments of full-wavelength path delays (at the nominal frequency), so that this propagation time criterion will be satisfied. Devices to accomplish this, though identical in nature to a phase shifter, must provide effective path lengths equal to or greater than a wavelength at the nominal frequency.

Because of the much longer lengths of line involved, the insertion loss of time delayers can be unacceptable in a passive array. This difficulty can be overcome, however, by the use of transmitting and receiving amplifiers at the array elements; then the time-delayer losses occur at low transmitter power levels so that the total power wasted is not large; and in the receiving mode, the additional noise due to the time-delayer loss occurs after sufficient amplification of the received signal so that the signal-to-noise ratio is not appreciably degraded. An array using this principle is defined as an "active array," and the concept was introduced in sec. 7.8 in connection with low-noise receiving antennas.

8.3. Phased Array Feed System Technology

The general principles of array feed systems are discussed in chapter 5 in terms of transmitting. In summary, the total power radiated must be divided among the array elements with some constant uniform phase gradient along any straight line through the array. The greatest array gain and narrowest beamwidth is achieved with uniform distribution of power among the elements, while an improved (reduced) side-lobe level results if the power fed to the elements is reduced (tapered) toward each end element.

In the present chapter an additional requirement has been stated for broad-band arrays; namely, the propagation *times* from the common feed source point (e.g., transmitter) to all points on the radiated wavefront must be equal. For a broadside array this can be achieved by either using equal-length paths from the source point to each element or by use of a *corporate* feed structure. The difficulty with the first scheme is power division among the elements; it is difficult to accomplish this for a many-element array by branching from a single transmission line or waveguide into many lines all at one division point. The corporate feed scheme, shown in chapter 2, Fig. 2–8(a), avoids this problem while still preserving equal line lengths by the branching method. At each branch, equal power division or any desired tapering can be obtained by suitable impedance relationships at the junctions. Alternatively, hybrid couplers can be used to minimize the coupling between element transmission lines, caused by impedance mismatches.

If a beam at some direction other than broadside is wanted, then the lengths of the lines to the various elements can be made unequal to provide the desired phase progression, or alternatively, phase shifters and/or time delayers can be inserted in the lines.

8.3.1. Feed Systems

ESA feed systems take many forms. Figure 8–4 shows multiple waveguide array elements (at left side) being fed by a corporate feed (at right side). Corporate feeds provide equal path lengths and equal power to their outputs. This particular corporate feed supplies four of the waveguide array elements of a multielement array that has apertures oriented for vertical polarization. Moving to the left and down from the corporate feed input, one can see a four-port hybrid junction, known as a hybrid tee. Its fourth port is a "stubby" load (termination) at the top of the tee. The magic tee divides input power equally between its two symmetrical ports, and each of these ports deliver power to two additional magic tees. The load dissipates power reflected (by impedance mismatches) from the symmetrical ports. There are, of course, many magic tees required for providing equal power and equal path lengths to each of the multiple waveguide array elements. In addition, there is a ferrite phase shifter in each waveguide path (between corporate feed and array element) to provide separate phase control for each array element. The phase shifter within the waveguide on the far left side is shown by means of a cutaway view.

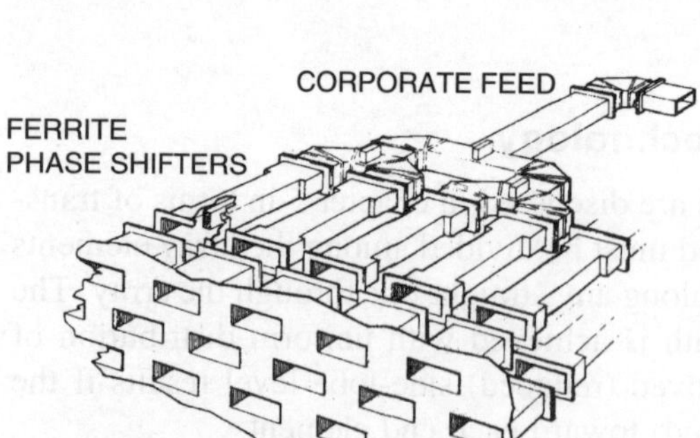

FIGURE 8–4.

Phased array network with magic tee dividers and ferrite phase shifters. From Stark 1974; © 1974, IEEE.

Figure 8–5 is a sketch of an eight-element corporate-fed linear array with eight phase shifters and two time delayers. The time delayers may be unnecessary, but they will increase the array bandwidth. Let us assume the elements are in a horizontal plane, so that the beam is steered in azimuth. More complex arrays can be formed by adding arrays like the one in Fig. 8–5. For beam steering in both azimuth and elevation, vertical array elements are required. These might be on arrays each like Fig. 8–5, with each array replacing an array element of Fig. 8–5. Then the antenna would be

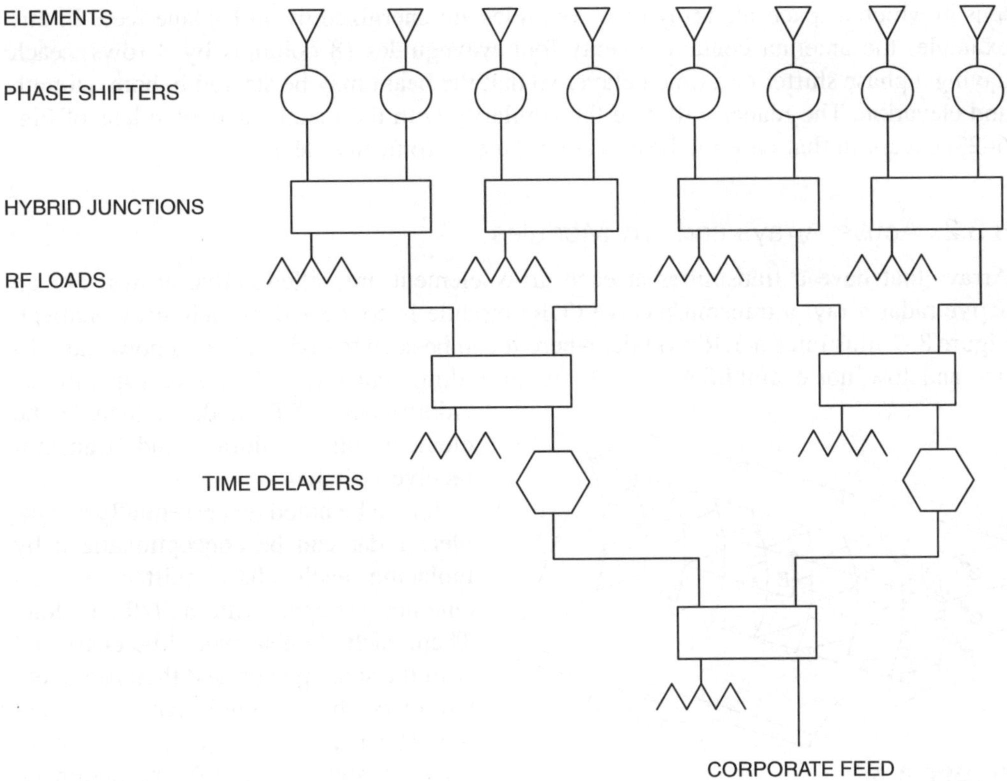

FIGURE 8–5.

Corporate feed for an eight-element array, consisting of eight phase shifters and two time delayers.

an 8 by 8 planar array having 64 elements. It should be apparent that large, multielement arrays may be devised by adding numerous sets of corporate fed arrays. When there are a large number of array elements, tapering for side-lobe reduction may be implemented by gradually reducing the number of elements toward the ends of the array.

Thus far the feed systems for arrays have been assumed to consist of transmission lines or waveguides. It is also possible to feed an array optically—that is, in the same manner that a reflector or lens would be fed (as illustrated in chapter 6, Figs. 6–1, 6–4, 6–10, and 6–14). An antenna having elements fed in this manner is called a space-fed array. The "array" in this case is an assemblage of delay lines and/or phase shifters with input and output ports (e.g., horns, dipoles, etc.) arranged as array elements. In this case, the "array" and not a reflector or lens, does the focusing.

Examples of this type of antenna include the Rotman lens (Rotman and Turner 1963) and the Bootlace lens (Volakis 2007, pp. 20–33). In the Rotman lens, the "array," that is, an assemblage of delay lines with input and output ports are located at the output of a 2-D wave-guiding medium (see, e.g., Fig. 6–8). Figure 8–6 is an example of a Bootlace lens in which a space-fed array of waveguides are energized by an E-plane feed. In this example, the antenna contains twenty-four waveguides (8 columns by 3 rows), each having a phase shifter or a time delayer so that the beam may be steered in both azimuth and elevation. The reader will note the similarity with the metal waveguide lens of Fig. 6–23, except in that case the beam cannot be electronically steered.

8.3.2. Active Arrays and T/R Modules

Arrays that have a transmitter at each array element are called active arrays. For an active radar array, a transmit/receive (T/R) module is connected to each array element. Figure 8–7 illustrates a T/R module, where it can be seen to contain both a power amplifier and low noise amplifier (LNA), for providing transmit and receive capabilities. Additionally, T/R modules include the element phase shifter and transmit/receive switches.

It is to be noted that essentially a complete radar can be conceptionalized by replacing each phase shifter at each antenna element with a T/R module. Then, each element would be energized with the same power, and therefore there would not be amplitude taper on transmit. This is commonly done to maximize transmit power. Side-lobe reduction on reception is customarily done by tapering on receive by control of the T/R receive gains or use of attenuation.

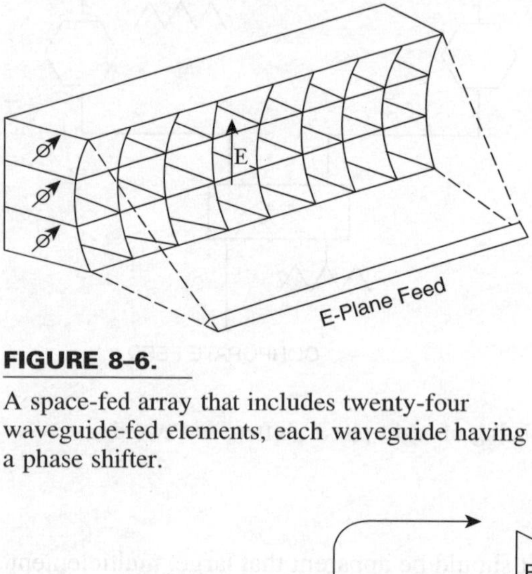

FIGURE 8–6.

A space-fed array that includes twenty-four waveguide-fed elements, each waveguide having a phase shifter.

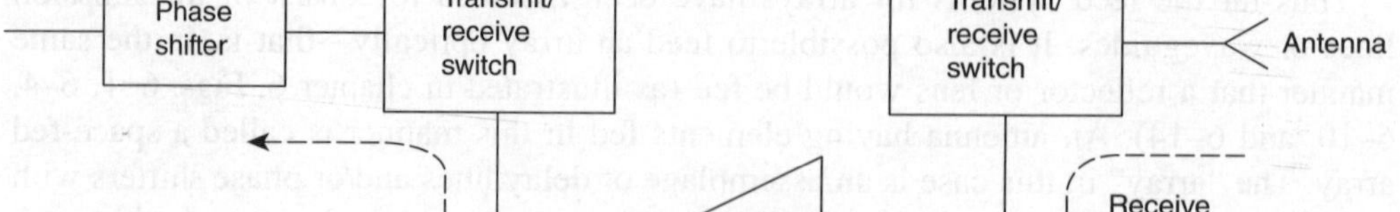

FIGURE 8–7.

Simplified diagram of a T/R module that serves as both transmitter and receiver at each element of an active array. From Merrill I. Skolnik, *Introduction to Radar Systems*, 3rd ed., © 2001, p. 600, with permission of The McGraw-Hill Companies.

An additional advantage of using multiple active (transmit or receive) components is reliability, because the loss of one or a few elements in a large array may not cause a system outage.

8.3.3. Alternative Configurations, Including Subarrays

As may be imagined, there are many possible array network configurations. Return now to Fig. 8–5, and assume each phase shifter is replaced by a T/R module. Each module has a phase shifter, a low-noise receive amplifier (LNA), and possibly a low-power transmit amplifier plus a transmit/receive switch. If the network were used for radar, an initial transmitter signal at the network input provides an excitation for each low-power transmit amplifiers via transmission through the hybrid junctions, and the low-transmit power of each element is summed upon radiation. Amplitude taper is often not used for transmitting, but it can be implemented by gain adjustments of the transmit amplifiers within the T/R modules.

On receive, the signals from the array elements are summed coherently (phase and amplitude) at each hybrid junction to provide a summed signal at the network output. It is to be noted that, for a lossless network of eight elements, the signal to noise ratio is substantially increased. For example, for an in-phase summation of eight equal amplitude signals, the voltage would be increased by a factor of 8, that is, power increased by the factor of 64. However, the summed noise power of eight equal-power independent noise sources is increased by eight. Thus, the signal-to-noise improvement for this assumed case is eight. For side-lobe reduction, gains of the LNA may be adjusted and some attenuation may be desired for refined adjustments.

Modern solid-state amplifiers have considerably reduced the cost of large phased arrays that use amplifiers located at the array elements, although this is still a fairly expensive type of antenna. The cost can be reduced, however, by dividing the array into subarrays, each of which contains several array elements, with only one amplifier per subarray. It will still be necessary (if wide-angle two-dimensional scanning is required) to provide a separate phase shifter for each element. However it then becomes possible to provide only one time delayer per subarray. Each subarray is then regarded as an element, and the steering of the actual individual elements is regarded as "steering" the subarray-element patterns (Cheston and Frank 1970, Fig. 31, pp. 11–45). The time-delayers then provide the array steering control.

8.3.4. Butler Matrix

Several *matrix* methods of feeding an array have been devised that result in the *simultaneous* generation of a number of beams at different directions from the array normal, in such a way that receivers connected to different ports of the feed matrix will each receive signals from only one of the beams, and a transmitter connected to one port will generate only the radiated beam corresponding to that port. Or, if the power from a single transmitter is divided equally and in-phase among the ports, all of the beams will be radiated simultaneously. The resulting total pattern will then be the far-field vector-phasor sum

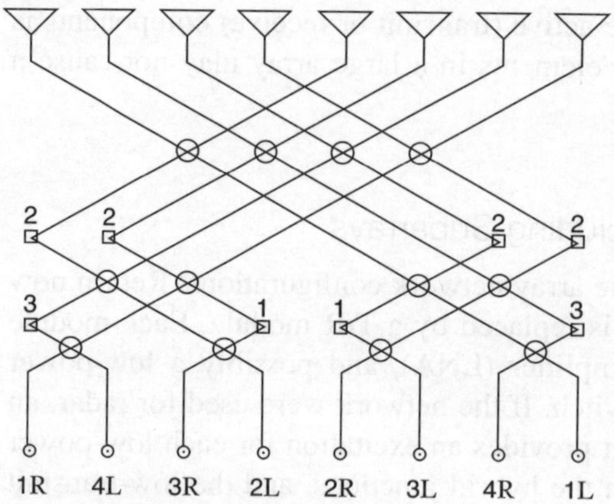

FIGURE 8–8(a).

The Butler matrix for an eight-element, eight-beam array (after Butler 1966).

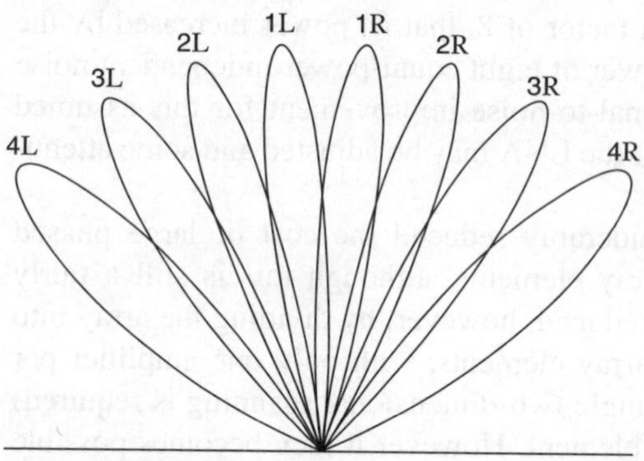

FIGURE 8–8(b).

Beam pattern of the eight-beam Butler matrix antenna (after Butler 1966).

of the individual beam patterns. Finally, if the transmitter power is divided unequally among the ports, or with some phase variation, the far-field superposition of the individual beams will be correspondingly modified. This allows generation of a "shaped beam" tailored to any desired spatial coverage requirement. Various modifications of this beam-shaping principle are also used (Shelton and Kelleher 1961).

An example of this matrix type of feed—possibly the one that is best known—is the Butler matrix (Butler and Lowe 1961). This and other matrix feeds, including the Blass matrix, have been discussed by Butler (Butler 1966). A schematic of the Butler matrix, applied to an eight-element, eight-beam array, is shown in Fig. 8–8(a). In its basic form, this matrix is applicable to any number of elements equal to an integral power of 2, that is, 2^n, and there will then be m beams and m ports, where m is an integer equal to or less than 2^n. The m beams are *orthogonal*, which means (in this context) that the peak of each beam corresponds to nulls of the other beams. The matrix contains fixed phase shifters and hybrid couplers, denoted respectively in Fig. 8–8(a) by circles and rectangles. For this particular matrix the couplers are 3 dB couplers (equal power in the two coupled arms), and their two output arms are phased 0 and 90 degrees, or 90 degrees and 0, depending on which arm is the input arm. The phase shift of each phase shifter is in units of 22.5 degrees, or $\pi/8$ radians; the integer in each of the phase shifter rectangles indicates the number of $\pi/8$ radian units that are shifted by that phase shifter. The output ports in Fig. 8–8(a) are labeled numerically and by letter—*L* for left, *R* for right—and the corresponding beams are similarly labeled in Fig. 8–8(b).

Numerous variations of this scheme, as described by Butler (1966), are possible, including methods that produce a tapered power distribution for side-lobe reduction, "true time delay" (wideband) matrices, and matrices that do the beam forming at the intermediate frequency of a receiving system.

8.3.5. Array Sum and Difference Patterns

The *radar monopulse* method of direction finding is described in sec. 7.6 of chapter 7. It uses sum and difference patterns of an antenna for greater accuracy in determining direction than possible if only the ordinary (sum) beam is used. This method was described there in terms of a reflector type antenna with a multihorn feed. The desired sum and difference patterns, in that case, are separately obtained at different receiver ports by combining the separate feed-horn outputs in a system of hybrid couplers.

The same result can be obtained in an array (including electronically beam-steered arrays) by feeding two symmetrical halves of the array separately and then combining the signals from the two halves in a hybrid coupler to produce the desired sum and difference signals. This permits monopulse operation in the plane perpendicular to the line dividing the two halves. If the array is divided into quadrants, simultaneous monopulse in both perpendicular planes (e.g., azimuth and elevation) can be obtained. However, many special considerations arise in the application of monopulse techniques to phased arrays for optimum generation of sum and difference patterns (Stark 1974, p. 1694).

8.3.6. Microstrip and Printed-Circuited Technology

The geometry of the *strip line* is well adapted to construction by printed-circuit techniques, in which the strip conductor and adjoining ground planes can be deposited on low-loss substrate material by mass-production methods. An unbalanced stripline geometry is illustrated in chapter 2, Fig. 2–9 (lower right), and a patch or microstrip antenna is shown in chapter 4, Fig. 4–25.

The balanced form has the strip enclosed both below and above by a metallic ground-plane. This transmission-line technology can be combined with ordinary printed-circuit techniques to permit construction of monolithic phased-array modules containing not only the transmission line components but also phase shifters, couplers, control circuitry, radiating elements, and solid-state transmitting and receiving amplifiers. This fabrication technique greatly reduces the cost as well as the bulk of large phased arrays. Moreover, the "sheet" construction need not be completely planar; it can be made to conform to the surface of a vehicle such as the fuselage of an airplane.

8.3.7. Conformal Arrays

An array thus constructed in nonplanar form is known as a conformal array. It is apparent that the phasing of the elements must be calculated to produce a beam by taking the nonplanar shape into account, but this can readily be done by a digital computer or, for beam-steered arrays, by a dedicated microprocessor. The radiating elements can be conventional dipoles mounted outside the ground plane, or suitably excited slots in the ground plane, or so-called patch elements that can be regarded as a special form of slot radiator (Mailloux 1982. For a general discussion of slot radiators see chapter 3, pp. 196–199). Incidentally, the problem of controlling the side-lobe level is more difficult in conformal arrays than in planar arrays because the element patterns in different parts of the conformal array are oriented differently.

8.4. Adaptive Array Antennas

Adaptive array antennas have been developed from the technology of rapid beam pointing and shaping, along with being jointly merged with digital signal processing. The term *adaptive array* refers to an array-type antenna that has the capability of adjusting (adapting) its pattern and the frequency filtering of the signals received from each array element in some prescribed way that depends on phases and amplitudes, as well as the time delay of signals received from external radiating sources. The full capabilities of adaptive array antennas stems from the technology advancements made for beam scanning and beam shaping of electronic steered arrays (ESAs), that is, phased arrays that were outlined as items (i) through (vi) at the introduction to this chapter.

8.4.1. Background System Developments

An excellent review of the early state of development of adaptive array antennas was published by Gabriel (1983), and the discussion in this section is based largely on that paper.

In the early 1980s, the most common example of an adaptive array is the so-called side-lobe canceller antenna, which adjusts its side-lobe pattern so that pattern nulls occur in the side lobes that are in the directions of the sources of jamming (jammers), thus in principle reducing the total received jamming signal to zero. In practice, of course, the nulls are not absolute, yet a high degree of cancellation of the jamming signals can be obtained, subject to certain restrictions. The restrictions are that there is a maximum number of separate jamming directions that can be nulled, and the nulling performance may be degraded for some angular distributions of the individual jammers. Also, the adjustment (adaptation) of the pattern is not instantaneous; a finite time is required, and this may place a limit on the radar scan rate.

The typical side-lobe canceller (SLC) consisted of a high-gain main antenna, which was any type (e.g., a reflector, a lens, or an array), and an auxiliary array consisting of several low-gain elements. These auxiliary elements are usually omnidirectional or nearly so in the horizontal plane, with polarization identical to that of the main antenna. The number of these auxiliary elements determines how many adaptive side lobe nulls can be positioned arbitrarily to cancel jamming signals. This type of antenna is sometimes referred to as a *coherent* side-lobe canceller (CSLC) to differentiate it from the noncoherent device called a side-lobe blanker (SLB). The SLB utilizes a single low-gain horizontally omnidirectional element, and when the signal received by this element is equal to or greater than the signal received by the high-gain main antenna, the receiver output is switched off, or "blanked." This prevents side lobe jamming signals from being received, but it does not permit detection of a desired main-antenna (higher gain) signal if it is weaker than a jamming signal received by the low-gain antenna.

In the side-lobe canceller, the signals received by the auxiliary elements are processed with the main-antenna signals in such a way that they create nulls of the main antenna pattern in the jammer directions. The theory of this processing involves the concept of the "degrees of freedom" available, which are equal to the number of low-gain elements in the auxiliary array. This number in turn determines (generally is equal to) the number of separate jamming-signal directions that can be nulled.

The mathematical algorithms of this signal processing and control tend to be very complicated because they are partly based on multivariate estimation theory. Implementation of some of these algorithms can be either analog or digital, but in modern systems digital technology is predominant. The adaptive process usually involves a "convergence time," and some of the simpler algorithms may converge relatively slowly, especially for certain angular distributions of the interfering signals. However, rapid convergence times are obtainable with the more sophisticated algorithms and techniques.

The side-lobe canceller, using a relatively few auxiliary array elements, is a "partial" adaptive array. A fully adaptive array is one in which the entire system is an array and all of the array elements contribute equally to the operation of the adaptive processor. This allows much greater flexibility and control of the total pattern (i.e., there are more degrees of freedom). However, the cost of the processor is much higher for arrays having a very large number of elements, such as those used in many radar systems.

The principle of a fully adaptive array was demonstrated with computer computations, however, in the above-referenced paper by Gabriel. In that 1983 paper, Gabriel's array had sixteen elements and was assumed to operate at S-band (approximately 3,000 MHz). Further assumptions included a separate receiver for each array element and each of the received signals, after conversion to an intermediate frequency (IF), was split into two baseband *I* and *Q* signals (see Fig. 8–11). As is customary, *I* and *Q* denote the in-phase and phase-quadrature components of an IF signal, and they preserve the phase information in the "zero frequency" (baseband) channels that is necessary for digital processing.

Figures 8–9(a) and 8–9(b) show results of Gabriel's computer analyses. In Fig. 8–9(a), the "quiescent" pattern of the array is shown—that is, the pattern in the absence of any jamming. Figure 8–9(b) then shows the adaptive patterns at successive time intervals in a continuous adaptive process. As shown, a null region exists at the angles of the three jamming transmitters, which are indicated by the three vertical arrows. Note that the average side-lobe levels of the adaptive patterns in the unjammed regions are somewhat higher than those of the quiescent pattern; this is the price paid for creation of the nulls in the jammer directions. It is

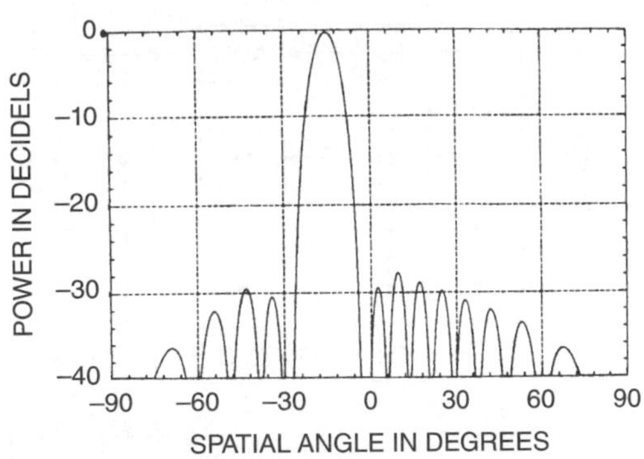

FIGURE 8–9(a).

Adaptive array pattern with no interfering (jamming) signal present (from Gabriel 1983; © 1983, IEEE).

possible to retain the quiescent side-lobe levels in the adaptive patterns, but this requires the application of additional computations in the adaptive algorithm (Frost 1972).

The technology of fully adaptive arrays is still in a state of intensive development, and this was also the case as pointed out by Gabriel (1983). Some of the other early classic papers include Gabriel (1976), Childers (1978), Gabriel (1980), Brennan and Reed (1973), Brennan, Reed, and Swerling (1974), and Monzingo and Miller (1980). As already indicated, development of adaptive or "smart" arrays continues to be an active field, having its origins in the suppression of side lobes of a main antenna by use of several smaller auxiliary antennas (Gabriel 1976). Today pattern optimization is done with real-time weighting of received signals in such a way that the array on reception can adapt to the interference environment. In principle it can also be done by weighting the transmit antenna pattern, but this generally is not done. An extensive list of up-to-date references is given by Gross (2007).

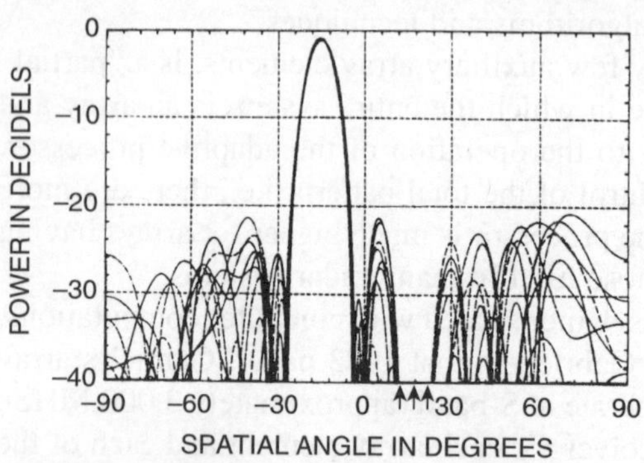

FIGURE 8–9(b).

Patterns of the adaptive array at successive time intervals after reception of a jamming signal (from Gabriel 1983; © 1983, IEEE).

8.4.2. Adaptive Beam-Forming Arrays

Figure 8–10 is a simplified example of an adaptive beam-forming (ABF) system. The phase and amplitude of signals from each individual array element are amplified and filtered by a low-noise receiver (Rx), converted to baseband, and digitized with analog-to-digital (ADC) converters. Next, the digital signals are processed by

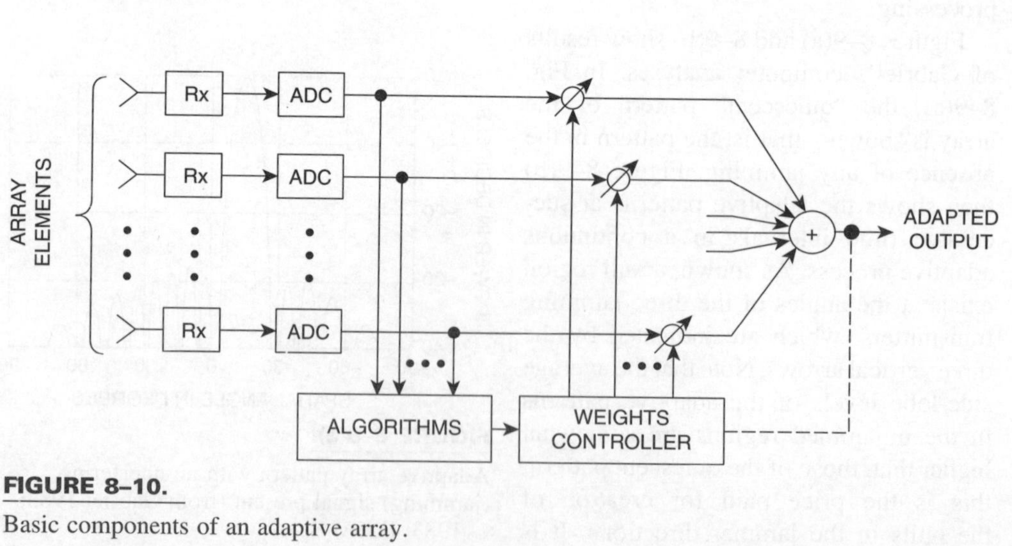

FIGURE 8–10.

Basic components of an adaptive array.

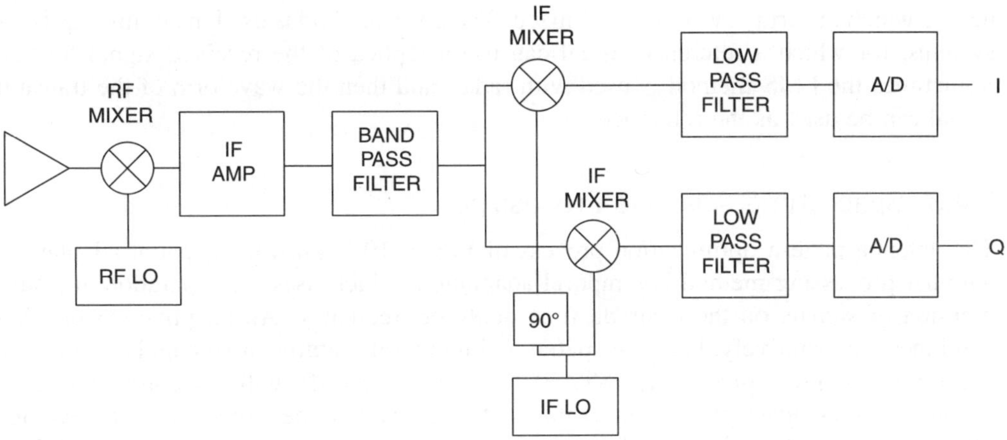

FIGURE 8–11.

Typical low-noise coherent (phase and amplitude) I and Q detection receiver.

computer algorithms for establishing phase and amplitude weights that modify the individual received signals. Then, the modified signals are summed for providing interference-suppressed outputs. The outputs can be from multiple signals that may have simultaneously arrived at the array elements. For some algorithms, a sample of the summed signals is fed back to the weight controller, as suggested by the dashed line in Fig. 8–10.

Figure 8–11 illustrates the principal features of a receiver that supplies, in digital format, the I and Q signals that contain phase and amplitude information, where amplitude "a" is

$$a = \sqrt{I^2 + Q^2}$$

and phase φ is

$$\varphi = arc\tan\left(\frac{Q}{I}\right)$$

The mathematics of pattern optimization uses complex matrix theory. There is currently much activity in the development in adaptive algorithms, in computational capabilities, and in improved array hardware (see, e.g., Balanis 2005). Presently used algorithms are generally based on the early work of (1) the Howells-Applebaum method (Applebaum 1976) and (2) a procedure due to Widrow and McCool (1976) that minimizes the least square mean (LMS) between the array output signal and a reference signal. The Howells-Applebaum method is commonly used with radar systems to affect signal-to-noise optimization, subject to an array pattern formed in the absence of interference. This requires sampling over a large number of range and Doppler cells to obtain data to which the array system is optimized. The LMS method is used in communications systems, for which a reference signal can use a replica of the received signal format. Sometimes the LMS method is used with radar, and then the waveform of the transmit signal can be used as the reference.

8.4.3. Space-Time Adaptive Processing

The antenna pattern optimization process of Fig. 8–10 is known as spatial adaptation. Another processing method is temporal adaptation, which uses the separation and suppression of signals on the basis on time delay or frequency. An adaptive system that combines, cooperatively, both the spatial and temporal features of signals is said to use space-time adaptive processing (STAP). The use of STAP, with its combined beam shaping and Doppler processing features, has proved to be especially effective for improving signal detection and clutter suppression for radar and mobile communications on moving platforms.

Figure 8–12 is an oversimplified schematic for a generalized steerable array and signal processor to provide both space and time adaptivity for the output voltage $v(t)$. There are N array elements and M time delays. The processing of time-delayed signals offers a

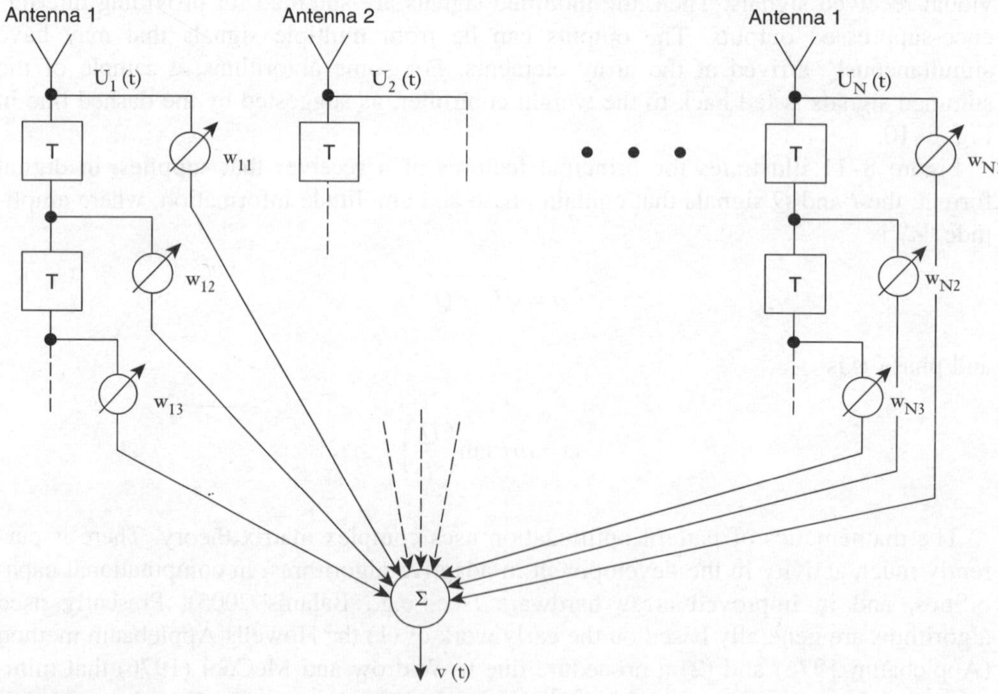

FIGURE 8–12.

Generalized Space-Time Processor having N element channels and M delay taps per channel, for cooperative space and time adaptive processing. From Barile, Fante, and Torres (1992); © 1992, IEEE).

variety of frequency filtering options. For example, the availability of complex (amplitude and phase) time-delayed signals permits fast Fourier transform (FFT) processing that provides, in essence, signals from multiple band-pass filters. Finally, it is to be noted that, in principle, the Fig. 8–12 configuration permits optimized frequency filtering and beam shaping to be accomplished independently, or cooperatively (i.e., optimized collectively).

As may be imagined, there are numerous design options. For example, the Fig. 8–12 configuration permits each antenna element to have a phase response that varies with frequency. A phase response can compensate for the fact that a given path length l gives a phase delay $(2\pi l)/\lambda = (2\pi l)f/c$ that depends on frequency. In other words, the tapped delay-line may perform as an equalizer, to make the array have approximately the same pattern over a range of frequencies. Wireless arrays using this phase feature are known as wideband arrays and they are said to employ space-time, spatio-temporal, or two-dimensional processors.

Thus, the wireless "two-dimensional" adaptive array provides the structure for suppressing interfering signals based on frequency differences and on spatial separations cooperatively. This configuration is said to be particularly valuable in heterogeneous communications environments where signals of different bandwidths and different carrier frequencies may be incident on the array (Liberti and Rappaport 1999, p. 102).

Features of a wideband wireless array are also of advantage for narrow band signals. Consider, for example, multipath signal components that may or may not be separated in angle or by significant time delays. The two-dimensional adaptive array can capture multipath components separated in either time or angle, and thereby combine features of both a spatial processor and a temporal equalizer (Liberti and Rappaport 1999, p. 102).

Computer throughput requirements and ultimate system performance can be altered considerably, depending on how the element signals are processed. Processing may be done on the signals from each array element, and then the separately processed element signals can be jointly optimized. For example, one might first frequency-filter the M time-delayed signals from each of the elements separately and then optimize the N frequency-filtered element signals by adaptive beam-shaping and pointing. Alternatively, the processing might first optimize beam shape and pointing direction for each of the M different time delayed signals of the N elements separately, and then frequency-filter the N signals that had previously been optimized by beam shaping and pointing.

Some readers may recognize that tapped delay-line filtering is commonly used in pulse Doppler radar for suppressing clutter and noise. This filtering when combined with the spatial adaptive features of Fig. 8–12 offers improved clutter and noise suppression capabilities that are especially beneficial for radars on moving platforms (Skolnik 2001, pp. 168–71).

Finally, fully adaptive arrays are costly and complex, but they offer many advantages including

- Simultaneous transmission of independent messages in different directions at the same frequency for increasing the capacity of band-limited cellular telephone networks

- Fast adaptive pattern nulling for minimizing interference
- Corrections from array component imperfections and mutual coupling between array elements
- Closely spaced multiple beams for increased network capacity
- Flexible time management in beam positioning and shaping the beams for increasing network capacity and minimizing interference
- Improved detection and interference suppression for radar and communications on moving platforms.

8.5. Examples of Electronically Steered Arrays

Enormous progress has been made in the technology of large electronically steered arrays, nevertheless, they are still very expensive, and they are used only in very special applications that justify the cost. The principal application is for military radars. The most complex and expensive antennas of this type utilize phase shifters for scanning simultaneously in two orthogonal directions, for example, in azimuth and elevation. These are sometimes referred to as *phase-phase steered scanning arrays*. Somewhat less expensive are arrays that use phase scanning (either of the "true" phase-shifter type or of the frequency-scan type which was described in sec. 8.1.3) in one direction (usually elevation), and mechanical motion of the entire antenna in the orthogonal direction (usually azimuth).

FIGURE 8–13.

The array antenna of the AN/TPS-59 radar operates at L-band, and combines mechanical rotation in azimuth with phase scanning in elevation. (Courtesy of Lockheed Martin.)

An example of this arrangement is the Marine Corps AN/TPS-32, an S-band radar that scans by mechanical rotation of the antenna in azimuth, with frequency scanning from the horizon to about 20 degrees in elevation (Brookner 1977). The pattern is a pencil beam of about 2 degrees azimuth beamwidth and 1 degree elevation beamwidth. The antenna gain is 41 dB, and the side-lobe level is −25 dB relative to the peak of the main beam. The azimuth rotation rate is 6 rpm, and during each 10-second azimuth scan the number of elevation scans is sufficient to provide azimuthal overlap of adjacent beams.

Figure 8–13 shows the Marine Corps AN/TPS-59 radar, operating at L-band, utilizes an array that combines mechanical rotation in azimuth with true phase scanning in elevation (Johnson and Jasik 1984, p. 32–12). The array is rectangular, 30 feet in height and 15 feet wide, with beamwidths of 1.6 and 3.2 degrees in elevation and azimuth, respectively. The elevation coverage is from 0 to 19 degrees, with azimuth scan rates of either 6 or 12 rpm (optionally). The power gain is 38.9 dB. Radiating elements are arranged in rows and columns, and each of the fifty-four rows is fed by solid-state transmitter amplifiers; the needed relatively large average power is made possible by the use of many low-power transmitter amplifiers. Advantages of this technology are that failure of one or even a few of the amplifiers does not totally disable the radar, and no portion of the system is subjected to extremely high power levels with attendant problems of heating and voltage breakdown. Receiver solid-state amplifiers and low-power-level phase shifters are similarly distributed. Both the TPS-32 and the TPS-59, incidentally, are transportable radars which can be set up for temporary operation at field sites.

The Navy AN/SPY-1 shipboard multifunction S-band radar, a part of the Aegis weapon system, has a phased-array antenna with true phase scanning in both azimuth and elevation (Bookner 1977; Scudder and Sheppard 1974). Four separate arrays are mounted on four faces of the ship superstructure so that each covers an azimuth quadrant. The vertical coverage of each array is sufficient so that the four arrays provide virtually hemispheric coverage for the radar. Each array is of approximately hexagonal shape, about 12 feet in width and 12 feet 7 inches in height. The vertical and horizontal beamwidths are of the order of 2 degrees.

The radiating elements are rectangular horns (chapter 4, sec. 4.7), grouped into subarrays as described in the preceding section of this chapter. The subarray arrangement is somewhat different for transmitting and receiving. There are 32 transmit subarrays, each containing 128 horn radiators. For receiving, the same horns are grouped into 64 subarrays of 64 horns each. However, on reception four more subarrays are added to the complete array, that is, these four subarrays are utilized for reception only. Thus there is a total of 4,096 horns in the transmitting array and 4,352 horns in the receiving array. The purpose of the additional four subarrays used on reception is to improve the symmetry of the array monopulse difference patterns, which are generated simultaneously with the normal "sum" pattern, as described in Sec 8.3.3. The additional reception subarrays also contribute to an improved side-lobe level on reception.

The phasing of the individual horns of the array is accomplished by ferrite (garnet) nonreciprocal digitally-controlled latching phase shifters. The phasing is done on an individual-element basis; the steering commands are based on the so-called row-column method. The subarrays are not involved in this aspect of the antenna operation.

This description applies to the first operational model of the antenna, which differs from the earlier experimental model described by Scudder and Sheppard (1974). As with most major systems, newer antenna designs have been developed since the first operational model.

Each transmit subarray is fed by a separate high-power amplifier, whose output power is then divided equally among the 32 subarray horns. On reception, the individual subarrays do not have corresponding rf amplifiers; but there is a low-noise rf amplifier mounted on the back of the array for each of the three monopulse channels (sum, azimuth difference, and elevation difference). This does not eliminate the signal-to-noise reduction caused by losses in the on-array transmission-line components and phase shifters,

FIGURE 8–14.

Photograph of the Cobra Dane (AN/FPS-108) phased array antenna at Shemya, Alaska. (Courtesy Raytheon Company.)

but it does avoid the loss that would otherwise occur in the transmission line from the array to the receiver components that are located in the deckhouse.

The transmit array is fed with uniform power distribution for maximum gain. The receive array, however, has a modified Taylor distribution for the sum monopulse beam, to reduce the side-lobe level. The difference monopulse beams utilize a Bayliss distribution, a special distribution for providing difference patterns with low side lobes (Hansen 2007, p. 20–19). The approximately hexagonal shape of the array also contributes to side-lobe reduction, for both transmitting and receiving, in accordance with the principle discussed for geometrically tapered apertures in sec. 6.3.1, Fig. 6–6. In fact, the general configuration of the AN/SPY-1 aperture is similar to that illustrated in Fig. 6–6 except that the height-to-width ratio of the AN/SPY-1 antenna is closer to unity. This antenna represents near-ultimate sophistication of phased-array design, exclusive of adaptive arrays.

An example of an extremely large array of the phase-phase scanning type, also representative of the most advanced phased-array technology, is the Air Force AN/FPS-108 "Cobra Dane" system which operates at L-band. The Cobra Dane is a one-of-a-kind, ground-based multifunction radar used for intercontinental ballistic missile (ICBM) detection and analysis. It is located at Shemya, Alaska. Figure 8–14 is a photograph of the antenna, which has a diameter of 95 feet (Johnson and Jasik 1984, pp. 32–14 to 34–17; Brookner 1977, p. 34). It consists of a total of 15,360 active and 19,408 passive elements in a "thinned" array. The passive elements, which are connected to dummy loads, are placed in the otherwise empty positions where active elements would be if the array were filled. Thinning can reduce the side-lobe levels in a manner similar to that achieved by *tapering* of element excitations. From Willey (1962), a thinned array of a given aperture size has a narrower beamwidth (and lower near-in side lobes) than would a filled array with the same number of active elements (but smaller aperture size).

This antenna has a subarray structure with "true time delay" phasing of the subarrays. This is required because of the large size of the antenna and the large bandwidth of the transmitted and received signals. There are 95 subarrays, each containing 160 elements. The phasing of the individual elements is accomplished by 3-bit digital diode phase shifters. In the transmit mode, each subarray is individually fed by a traveling-wave-tube power amplifier, and in the receive mode each subarray feeds a low-noise amplifier.

There are many array antennas employed in airborne and space applications. The U.S. Air Force E-3 Sentry airborne warning and control system (AWACS), which became available in the 1970s, is an example of an early operational airborne ESA radar that employs an electronically scanned array (ESA). It scans mechanically in azimuth and electronically in elevation to obtain height measurement and stabilize the beam to compensate for aircraft roll and pitch. Today there are several recently developed military radars that have active ESA antennas (AESAs), where transmit and receive (T/R) modules are placed directly at the array elements (Hendrix 2008). An advantage of these antennas over mechanical rotating antennas is the ability to point its beam essentially instantaneously in any direction within its field of view. This flexibility enables an operator to use the radar in almost unlimited combinations of surveillance and tracking. Additionally, having separate receivers at each AESA element permits adaptive nulling for the suppression of interference.

FIGURE 8–15.

Ultra side lobe array that scans electronically (and adaptively) in elevation and mechanically in azimuth. (Reprinted with permission of MIT Lincoln Laboratory, Lexington, Massachusetts.)

Figure 8–15 shows an ultralow side lobe UHF (approximately 440 MHz) radar array antenna that scans electronically (and adaptively) in elevation and mechanically rotates in azimuth. It was developed and tested by Westinghouse Electric Corporation (now Northrop Grumman) to be a central part of a Lincoln Laboratory experimental radar system for the U. S. Navy. The antenna consists of 14 horizontal line arrays, each with 24 elements having a 65-dB Chebyshev amplitude taper (Carlson, Goodman, Austin, Ganz, and Upton, 1990). Array aperture dimensions are 5 meters height by 10 meters width, with gain of 29 dB. Fabrication includes a dielectric stripline construction with equal path lengths to each element for improved bandwidth, and extreme accuracy was required to achieve its ultra-low azimuth sidelobe levels, reported to be more than 50 dB below the peak of the main beam.

As already noted, beam pointing in azimuth is accomplished mechanically, but in elevation the transmit and receive patterns are controlled electronically. On transmit, the fourteen rows of line arrays are separately energized and phased for pointing the transmit beam in elevation. On reception, signals from the fourteen rows are separately amplified, converted to digital format with phase and amplitude preserved, and adaptively processed with phase and amplitude weighting for maximizing signal to interference levels in the elevation dimension. Therefore, interference is suppressed in the azimuth dimension by the ultra-low azimuth sidelobe patterns of the fourteen rows of line arrays, and interference in the elevation dimension is suppressed by adaptively processing the signals received from the fourteen horizontal rows of line elements.

References

Ajioka, J. S., "Frequency-Scan Antennas," ch.19 in R. C. Johnson, *Antenna Engineering Handbook*, 3rd Edition, McGraw-Hill, 1993.

Allen, J. L., "Gain and Impedance Variation in Scanned Dipole Arrays," *IEEE Transactions on Antennas and Propagation*, vol. AP-10, September 1962, no. 5, 567–69.

Applebaum, S. J., "Adaptive Arrays," *IEEE Transactions on Antennas and Propagation*, Sept. 1976, pp. 585–98.

Archer, D., "Lens-Fed Multiple-Beam Arrays," *Microwave Journal*, vol. 18, no. 10, October 1975.

Balanis, C. A., *Antenna Theory, Analysis and Design*, 3rd ed., Wiley-Interscience, 2005, ch. 16.

Barile, E. C., R. L. Fante, and J. A. Torres, "Some Limitations on the Effectiveness of Airborne Adaptive Systems," *IEEE Transactions on Aerospace and Electronic Systems*, vol. 28, no. 4, October 1992, pp. 1015–32.

Brennan, L. E., and I. S. Reed, "Theory of Adaptive Radar," *IEEE Transactions on Aerospace and Electronic Systems*, AES-19, no. 2, March 1973, pp. 237–52.

Brennan, L. E., I. S. Reed, and P. Swerling, "Adaptive Arrays," *Microwave Journal*, vol. 17, no. 5, May 1974, pp. 43 ff.

Brookner, E., *Radar Technology*, Artech House, 1977.

Butler, J. L., "Digital, Matrix, and Intermediate Frequency Scanning," in *Microwave Scanning Antennas*, vol. III, R. C. Hansen, ed., Ch. 3, Academic Press, 1966.

Butler, J., and R. Lowe, "Beamforming Matrix Simplifies Design of Electronically Scanned Antennas," *Electronics Design*, April 1961, pp. 170–73.

Carlson, B. D., L. M. Goodman, J. Austin, M. W. Ganz,and L. O. Upton, " An Ultralow-Sidelobe Adaptive Array Antenna," *The Lincoln Laboratory Journal*, Vol. 3, No. 2, 1990, pp. 291–310.

Cheston, T. C., and J. Frank, "Array Antennas," ch. 11 in *Radar Handbook*, M. I. Skolnik (ed.), McGraw-Hill, 1970.

Childers, D. G., *Modern Spectrum Analysis*, IEEE Press, 1978.

Frank, J., "Bandwidth Criteria for Phased Array Antennas," in A. A Oliner and G. H. Knittel, *Phased Array Antennas*, Artech House, 1972, pp. 243–53.

Frost III, O.L., "An Algorithm for Linearly Constrained Adaptive Array Processing," *Proceedings of the IEEE*, vol. 60, no. 8, August 1972, pp. 926–35.

Gabriel, W. F., "Adaptive Arrays: An Introduction," *Proceedings of the IEEE*, Feb. 1976, pp. 239–72.

Gabriel, W. F., "Spectral Analysis and Adaptive Arrays Superresolution Techniques," *Proceedings of the IEEE*, vol. 68, June 1980, pp. 654–66.

Gabriel, W. F., "Adaptive Processing Antenna Systems," *IEEE Antennas and Propagation Newsletter*, October 1983.

Gross, F. B., "Smart/Antennas," ch. 25 in *Antenna Engineering Handbook*, 4th ed., J. L. Volakis (ed.), McGraw-Hill, 2007.

Hansen, R. C. (ed.), *Significant Phased Array Papers*, Artech House, 1973.

Hansen, R. C., "Phased Arrays," ch. 20 in *Antenna Engineering Handbook*, 4th ed., J. L. Volakis (ed.), McGraw-Hill, 2007.

Hendrix, R., "Aerospace System Improvements Enabled by Modern Phased Array Radar—2008," *Proceedings of the 2008 Radar Conference*, Rome, Italy, May 26–30, 2008, pp. 275–280.

Johnson, R. C., *Antenna Engineering Handbook*, 3rd ed., McGraw-Hill, 1993.

Johnson, R.C., and H. Jasik, *Antenna Engineering Handbook*, 2nd ed., McGraw-Hill, 1984.

Liberti, J. C., Jr., and T. S. Rappaport, *Smart Antennas for Wireless Communications*, Prentice Hall PTR, 1999, p. 102.

Mailloux, R. J., "Phased Array Theory and Technology," *Proceedings of the IEEE*, vol. 70, no. 3, March 1982, pp. 263–64.

Mailloux, R. J., *Phased Array Antenna Handbook*, Artech House, 2005.

Miller, C. J., "Minimizing the Effects of Phase Quantization Errors in an Electronically Scanned Array," *Proceedings of the 1964 Symposium*, Rome Air Development Center Document RADC-TDR-64–225, vol. 1, pp. 17–38.

Monzingo, R. A., and T. W. Miller, *Introduction to Adaptive Arrays*, John Wiley and Sons, 1980.

Nelson, E. A., "Quanization Sidelobes of a Phased Array with a Triangular Element Arrangement," *IEEE Transactions on Antennas and Propagation*, vol. 17 (May 1969), pp. 363–65.

Oliner, A. A., and G. H. Knittel, *Phased Array Antennas*, Artech House, 1972.

Romanofsky, R. R., "Array Phase Shifters: Theory and Technology," ch. 21 in J. L. Volakis, *Antenna Engineering Handbook*, 4th ed., McGraw-Hill, 2007.

Rotman, W., and R. F. Turner, "Wide-Angle Microwave Lens for Line-Source Applications," *IEEE Transactions on Antennas and Propagation, AP-11*, no. 11, November 1963, pp. 623–32.

Scudder, R. M., and W. H. Sheppard, "AN/SPY-1 Phased-Array Antenna," *Microwave Journal*, vol. 17, no. 5, May 1974.

Sharp, E. D., "A Triangular Arrangement of Planar-Array Elements that Reduces the Number Needed," *IEEE Transactions on Antennas and Propagation*, AP-9, March 1961, pp. 126–29.

Shelton, J. P., and K. S. Kelleher, "Multiple Beams from Linear Arrays," *IEEE Transactions on Antennas and Propagation*, March 1961, pp. 154–61.

Skolnik, M. I., *Introduction to Radar Systems*, 3rd ed., McGraw-Hill, 2001.

Stark, L., "Microwave Theory of Phased Array Antennas: A Review," *Proceedings of the IEEE*, December 1974, pp. 1661–1701.

Steyskal, H., "Digital Beamforming at Rome Laboratory," *Microwave Journal*, Feb. 1996, pp. 100–124.

Tang, R., and R. W. Burns, "Phased Arrays," pp. 20–31 to 20–48, in R. C. Johnson, *Antenna Engineering Handbook*, 3rd ed., McGraw-Hill, 1993.

Thomas, D. T., "Multiple Beam Synthesis of Low Sidelobe Patterns in Lens Fed Arrays," *IEEE Transactions on Antennas and Propagation, AP-26*, no. 6, November 1978, pp. 883–86.

Volakis, J. L., *Antenna Engineering Handbook*, 4th ed., McGraw-Hill, 2007.

Widrow, B., and J. M. McCool, "Comparison of Adaptive Algorithms Based On The Method Of Steepest Descent And Random Search," *IEEE Transactions on Antennas and Propagation*, Sept. 1976, pp. 615–37.

Willey, R. E., "Space Tapering of Linear and Planar Arrays," *IEEE Transactions on Antennas and Propagation*, July 1962, pp. 369–77.

Problems and Exercises

1. An array of 1 m width is to be designed for $\lambda = 0.1$ m and for a maximum scan angle 30° from broadside. If time delayers are used for scanning, what is the maximum time delay needed?
2. Assume that a planar ESA array has gain of 100 in broadside direction. When steered in azimuth 60° off broadside, what is the estimated gain in that off-broadside direction?
3. If instead of time delayers, assume that phase shifters are used in Problem 1. What phase delay in degrees expressed less than 360° (mod 360°) is required for an end element when the beam is scanned 30° from broadside direction? Express this phase delay relative to the phase at the opposite end of the array.
4. To avoid grating lobes from a line array having equal spacing between elements, what is the recommended maximum spacing between elements for the following: (a) a nonscanning broadside array, (b) an electronically steered array?
5. Assume an ESA designed for 2.0 GHz with the following features: 16 elements spaced 0.4λ along a horizontal line at 2 GHz. (a) What is the end-to-end length between the first and last elements? (b) If delay-only phasing is used, what is the maximum delay time required if steered in azimuth 60° from broadside?
6. Using the ESA of problem 5, prepare a graph of phase (relative to an end element) versus element number, with phase expressed less than 360° (mod 360°), for the beam steered 30° from broadside.
7. An ESA has a 3 dB beamwidth of 4.0 degrees in azimuth when steered in broadside direction. What is its estimated azimuthal beamwidth when steered in azimuth 60° from broadside?
8. Assume the ESA of problem 5 has the phases calculated in problem 6. In addition, assume the element amplitudes are equal. Show calculated normalized patterns for 2.0 and 2.1 GHz on one graph, for azimuth angles of –90° to 90° with amplitude graphed from 0 to –40 dB.
9. (a) How many phase-shift elements are needed with a 5-bit phase shifter? (b) What are the minimum and maximum phase shifts required?
10. A linear array is to be used as a scanning antenna by varying the frequency to change the phasing. The array element spacing is $d = \lambda_0/2 = c/2f_0$, in the notation of equation (8–6). The array is fed with a serpentine feed for which $I = 5$, using coaxial line for which $f_c = 0$. When the frequency of operation is $f = 0.98f_0$, by what amount will the angle of the beam be shifted from the broadside direction?

CHAPTER 9

Antenna Measurements

Every experienced antenna engineer knows that successful antenna design requires a knowledge of antenna theory, and except for the very simplest antennas, a certain amount of "cut and try" is necessary before an initial design will perform satisfactorily. An essential part of this cut-and-try process is measurement of the antenna's performance.

The majority of antenna measurements lie within two basic categories: impedance measurements and pattern measurements. The first category deals with one of the most important antenna parameters—the input impedance. The second category is a very broad and equally important one, with many subcategories, such as measurements of beamwidth, minor lobe level, gain, and polarization characteristics. Measurements of efficiency and noise may also be desired in some instances.

Not all these possible measurements need be made in every situation. It is seldom that the complete antenna pattern is measured, including side lobes and polarization characteristics in all directions. Often, at the higher frequencies, it can be assumed that antenna ohmic losses are negligible, and therefore the radiation efficiency need not be measured. The input impedance is practically always important, however. The beamwidth, gain, and side-lobe levels are also usually important, especially at the higher frequencies where directional antennas are often used. Detailed polarization measurements are important in special cases. For example, dual transmit and receive polarizations may permit doubling the number of available communications channels. Measurement of antenna bandwidth is not actually a separate measurement category; it consists of measuring impedance, pattern characteristics, and other critical parameters over a band of frequencies.

As discussed in sec. 7.8, the antenna may affect the noise level of a receiving system in special cases. Consequently, the technique of antenna noise measurements is especially important in the lower atmospheric noise region of about 1 to 10 GHz. Therefore, the basic technique of antenna noise measurement and the effect of antenna noise on overall receiving system noise are described in the present chapter.

9.1. Antenna Patterns, General

The *pattern* (transmission or reception) of an antenna is a description (in the transmitting case) of the field strength, and sometimes phase, at a fixed far-field distance from the

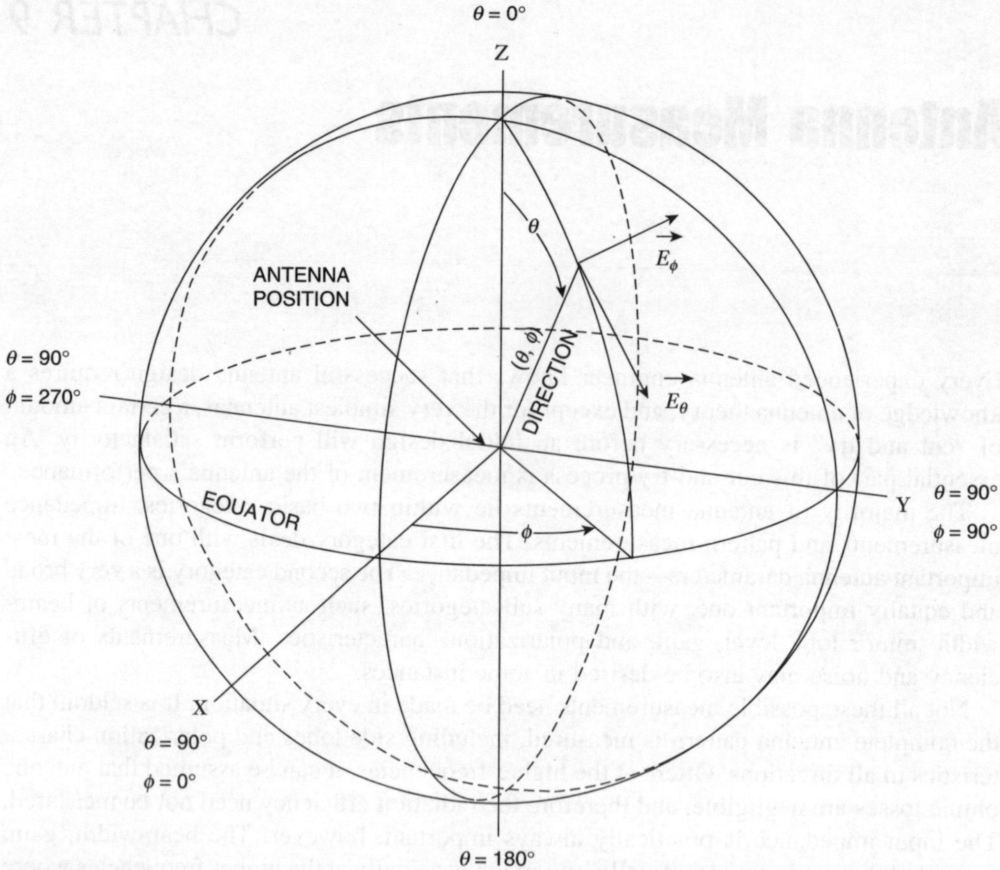

FIGURE 9–1.

Standard Spherical Coordinate System Used in Antenna Measurements. Source (IEEE 1979, p. 4); © 1979, IEEE.

antenna, as a function of direction. In accordance with Fig. 9–1, direction is conventionally expressed in terms of the two angles, θ and ϕ, of a spherical coordinate system whose origin is at the antenna. In the fullest sense the pattern also includes a description of the *polarization*, that is, the spatial direction of the electric field within a plane tangent to the far-field sphere.

The unqualified term "antenna pattern" implies that the pattern was that of the radiating far-field. In practice, this may be accomplished by placing the test antenna in a radiating field having essentially constant amplitude and phase. The traditional method of accomplishing this is to satisfy the $2D^2/\lambda$, 20λ, and $20D$ rules of thumb of sec. 3.2.5, where D is the maximum antenna dimension as viewed from the measurement point and λ the wavelength.

The $2D^2/\lambda$ criterion ordinarily dictates large distances and out-of-doors environments for large antennas (in terms of wavelength) at higher frequencies. Measurements satisfying this criterion, referred to as far-zone measurements, are discussed in sec. 9.2. In addition, well-developed measurement methods that permit the use of much shorter separation distances are described in later sections and include compact ranges (sec. 9.3), near-field ranges (sec. 9.4), and scale models (sec. 9.6).

A complete pattern measurement consists of measuring field strength and electric field direction (polarization) for many different values of the angles θ and ϕ for all values, in principle. In practice, the number of θ and ϕ directions in which measurements must be made depends on the complexity of the pattern and the need for detailed information in the particular application.

Since complete three-dimensional patterns are difficult to plot on a plain sheet of paper, and since the patterns in particular planes usually provide adequate information, patterns are usually measured and plotted in planes. Sometimes the pattern in only one plane conveys the information of AUT interest for a particular antenna. For example, in most earth-to-earth communication or broadcasting systems, the horizontal-plane pattern is the major consideration. Vertical-plane patterns in these cases usually have significance only to the extent that they affect the gain of the antenna in the horizontal plane (i.e., the less power that is radiated uselessly upward, the more there is available for radiation in the horizontal plane). Exceptions to this statement include earth-to-earth systems that involve propagation via an elevated reflection point or medium.

The vertical pattern is often of interest more directly, in applications involving an earth-based antenna and some elevated receiving point (or vice versa), as in radio astronomy, space communications, and in radar intended for air or space target detection and tracking. The patterns in these two planes—horizontal and vertical (azimuth and elevation)—suffice for practically all applications. The main-lobe pattern in other planes can usually be adequately estimated from these principal-plane patterns. However, if the detailed side-lobe patterns are of concern, as they may be in some radar applications and in other special cases, oblique-plane patterns will be of interest, for the side lobes in these planes cannot be inferred from the principal-plane patterns.

9.1.1. Radiating Near- and Far-Field Patterns

Figure 9–2 is a far-zone pattern of a paraboloidal reflector antenna, taken from a classic measurements paper (Cutler, King, and Kock 1947). There one can see the wide-angle lobe structure, which was attainable through careful measurement. Factors that affect, generally, the lobe structure for a reflector antenna include:

- limitations of feed pattern amplitude and phase
- effects of aperture blocking by the feed
- feed pattern spillover from the reflector edges and effects of edge diffraction
- reflector surface inaccuracies

As discussed in chapters 5 and 6, strengths of close-in minor lobes can be controlled by an antenna's aperture amplitude and phase distribution. The vestigial (or shoulder) lobe in Fig. 9–2 is a visible part of a first minor lobe (adjacent to major lobe) that remains after the first null is destroyed by aperture phase error. Typically, with reflector antennas,

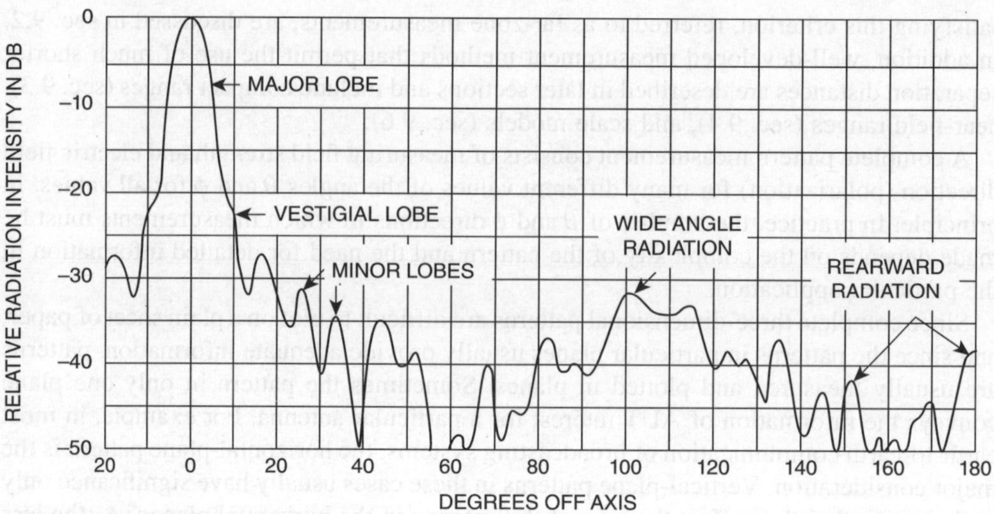

FIGURE 9–2.
Measured wide-angle far-zone amplitude (in dB) pattern of a reflectorantenna. From Cutler, King, and Kock (1947); © 1947, IEEE.

vestigial lobes occur because of a misaligned feed. Although patterns that include the major lobe and close-in minor lobes may be calculated, ordinarily it is impossible to precisely calculate the effects of wide-angle and rearward radiation caused by such factors as aperture blockage, spillover, and edge diffraction. Obviously, effects of random mechanical errors may be computed (accounted for) only in a statistical sense.

The radiating near- and far-field patterns of the close-in minor lobes, including the vestigial lobe, may be calculated following the discussions of Appendix G. In addition, the accompanying website includes example pattern calculations using Mathcad software. These calculations include the more easily defined effects of aperture amplitude and phase on the major lobe and close-in side lobes. However, measurements are required in order to determine effects of aperture blocking, feed pattern spillover, edge diffraction, and reflector surface inaccuracies. In other words, calculations cannot determine all of the factors that affect side lobes, and thus the final appraisal of antenna performance usually must be made based on measurements.

Although far zone patterns are nearly always needed, sometimes it is important to measure and understand field behavior in the radiating near-field. Results of calculations for the field distributions near an aperture are now discussed, where the phase and amplitude of the field are strongly influenced by distance to the observation point. As a consequence, Figs. 9–3 and 9–4 that follow show major effects of radiation from an aperture, per se; that is, effects of edge radiation, spillover, and random phase errors are neglected. Thus, the figures show only how reduced separation may affect amplitudes near the center of radiation patterns. The calculations were made by following the methodology used in the attached SM 4.4 and SM 4.5.

Figure 9–3 shows how the constant K, where the observation point is separated a distance $K(D^2/\lambda)$ from the aperture center, affects pattern shape. The reader will recall that, from the rule of thumb of sec. 3.2.5, the far-radiating field for electrically large antennas exists where K is two or greater. The effect of increased phase error, with reduced K (i.e., distance), on filling the first pattern null may be seen. This null-filling effect due to phase error is closely related to the creation of the vestigial lobe of Fig. 9–2.

Figure 9–4 shows an entirely different aspect of separation distance than does Fig. 9–3. It shows how the amplitude of the radiated field, near an aperture, varies as a function of position along the aperture. It depicts the near-field region where radiation approximates a nearly uniform plane wave, as conceptualized by Fig. G–1 of Appendix G. Existence of this approximation to a plane-wave field permits, for antennas within this radiating near-field, the measurement of far-field patterns within a compact range (see sec. 9.3).

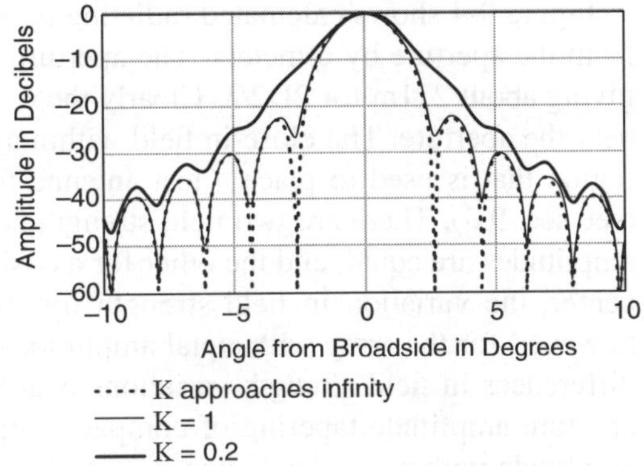

FIGURE 9–3.

Calculated radiation for three separation distances $K(2D^2/\lambda)$ versus angle from broadside.

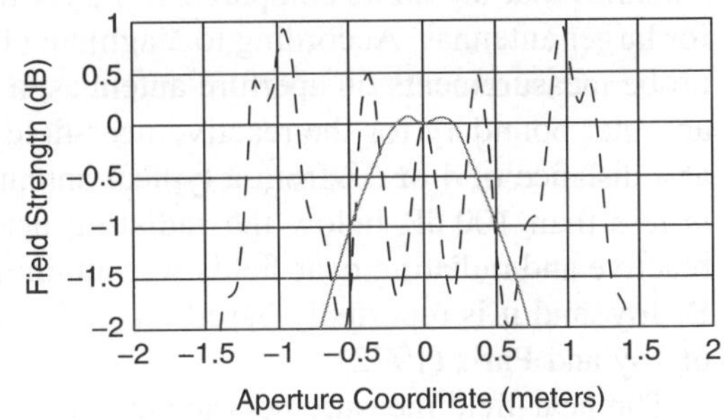

FIGURE 9–4.

Relative field strength in dB along the aperture and separated by 6 meters from the array. The irregular and smooth field strength variations are caused by the equal and cosine aperture amplitude distributions, respectively.

Figures 9–3 and 9–4 were made from calculations for a linear array of 66 isotropic elements, with element spacing of $\lambda/2$ and with $\lambda = 0.1$ m (3 GHz). The calculation for Fig. 9–3 assumed a cosine amplitude aperture distribution, and for Fig. 9–4 both a constant and a cosine amplitude distribution were assumed.

Figure 9–3 includes field distributions for three different separation distances. It can be seen that the pattern nulls are deepest if the observation distance approaches infinity. By reducing the distance to $2(D^2/\lambda)$, the usual rule of thumb for approximating far-field conditions, there is no apparent change in the amplitude peaks, but the nulls near the major lobe are less deep. For the $0.2(D^2/\lambda)$ distance, close-in nulls are no longer apparent, and the rapid amplitude change versus θ of the major lobe has been destroyed and the beamwidth is increased. Then, from this example, it is seen that although the $2(D^2/\lambda)$ distance permits retention of most of the pattern detail, some is lost. Thus, it should be apparent that if accurate measurements of deep nulls and very low side lobes are needed, observation distances greater than $2(D^2/\lambda)$ may be required.

Figure 9-4 shows calculated radiating near fields along a line parallel to and separated from the aperture by 6 meters. The aperture width and wavelength are 3.25m and 0.1m, giving about 211m for 2D2/λ. Clearly the 6-meter separation is electromagnetically very near the aperture. The close-in field within a compact range, called the quiet zone, is the region that is used to place a test antenna for measuring its radiating far-field patterns (see sec. 9.3). There are two field strength curves in Fig. 9-4; one for which the element amplitudes are equal, and the other for a cosine amplitude distribution. Near the aperture center, the variation in field strength for the cosine tapered aperture is small. There, however, for the array with equal amplitude elements, the variation is about 2 dB. These differences in field strength variations near the aperture center underscore the fact that aperture amplitude tapering of compact range antennas will improve the uniformity of amplitude within the quiet zone.

It is appropriate to mention that the above-mentioned compact range quiet zone, although being close to its radiating source, is at a distance great enough so that the magnitude of the reactive near-field is negligible. In sec. 3.2.5, it is stated that $\lambda/2\pi$ is the generally accepted boundary between the reactive and the radiating near-fields for antennas that are short compared to λ, yet there is not a commonly accepted guideline for larger antennas. According to Yaghjian (1986, p. 33), from experience with near-field probe measurements on aperture antennas, a distance of "λ or so" appears reasonable as an outer boundary for the reactive near-field. More specifically, according to E. B. Joy, at a distance of 4 or 5λ from a typical antenna under test (AUT), the reactive near-field is less than 100 dB below the radiating near-field. This guide to relative strengths of reactive and radiating near-fields was attained through personal communications with E. B. Joy, and it is reportedly based on studies by him that follow equations (10) and (11) of Joy and Paris (1972).

The near-field measurement technique (sec. 9.4) is entirely different from a compact range measurement. It uses a sampling probe to measure the near-field radiation on a planar, cylindrical, or spherical surface enclosing the antenna-under-test (AUT), and the results are used to accurately determine far-field patterns of the AUT. To accomplish this, detailed computer calculations are made based on carefully measured point-to-point amplitude and phase measurements over the near-field measurement surface. The measurements are made near the aperture, but ordinarily at a great enough distance so that the reactive near-field is negligible, typically four to five wavelengths from the AUT. Preferably, the measurements are made with a small sampling probe, to minimize probe-aperture multiple reflections. In addition, the computer calculations commonly include corrections to compensate for the probe pattern, gain, and polarization.

9.1.2. Pattern Statistics: Near- and Far-Field Statistical Gain

Accurate and detailed antenna patterns of the type acquired under controlled measurement conditions are not always required. An example case is where interference from an antenna is to be predicted. Recall from sec. 9.1.1 that the shapes of major lobes and the side lobes depend on observation distance, when it is less than approximately $2D^2/\lambda$. In other words, the details of patterns are range dependent within the radiating near-field region. Yet, interference levels are generally strongest between closely located systems, for which separation distance and observation angles are often unknown. In addition, the impracticability of using detailed patterns to predict susceptibility to interference is compounded because of minor-lobe structure changes with frequency and site configuration.

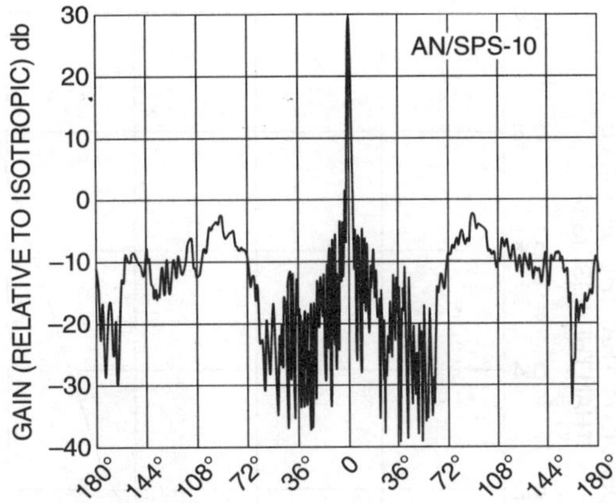

FIGURE 9–5.

360 degree pattern through azimuth plane of AN/SPS-10 antenna. From Cain and Byers (1968); © 1968, IEEE.

It is now known, from measurements, that the statistics of patterns within either the radiating-near- or far-field regions can be useful for predicting radio-frequency interference. This occurs because the statistical distributions of antenna patterns taken over wide angles are nearly invariant to observation distance, whether within either the near- or far-fields. In other words, for a given antenna, the probability of its gain at any angle exceeding a given value is dominated principally by the radiation patterns over a very wide range of observation angles, almost exclusive of the major lobe or close-in minor (Johnson 1963; Long 1960).

From the discussion above, the concept of statistical gain has meaning, if there is a wide range of unknown but likely observation angles. In other words, the likelihood of gain exceeding a given level is a useful means for estimating the susceptibility to interference, especially for narrow-beamwidth antennas. In fact, the statistics of radiation patterns are useful for predicting near- and far-field interference from antennas, at in-band or out of-band frequencies, and from antennas in the presence of interfering objects (Cain and Byers 1969; Cain, Cofer, and Ecker 1970; Cain, Ryan, and Cown 1972; Cain, Weaver, and Duffy 1974).

Figures 9–5 and 9–6 show results of gain measurements on the AN/SPS-10 radar antenna (C-band). From Fig. 9–5, the gain versus angle of the antenna is above isotropic (0 dB) for only about 5.3 degrees. Thus, the probability that the gain is less than isotropic is 0.98, as illustrated in Fig. 9–6. Similarly, one can see from Fig. 9–5 that the gain is less than −10 dB for more than half the angles. This is illustrated in Fig. 9–6, where the probability is 0.74 that the gain is less than −10 dB. Although the peak gain of the antenna is almost 30 dB, the median gain (the gain at which the cumulative probability is 0.5) is only −13 dB. Thus, there is a significant difference between median gain and average gain. (Average gain for a lossless antenna is unity, i.e., 0 dB).

9.2. Far-Zone Pattern Measurements

The measurement of a pattern involves two antennas: the one whose pattern is being measured, and another some distance away. One antenna transmits (radiates) and the

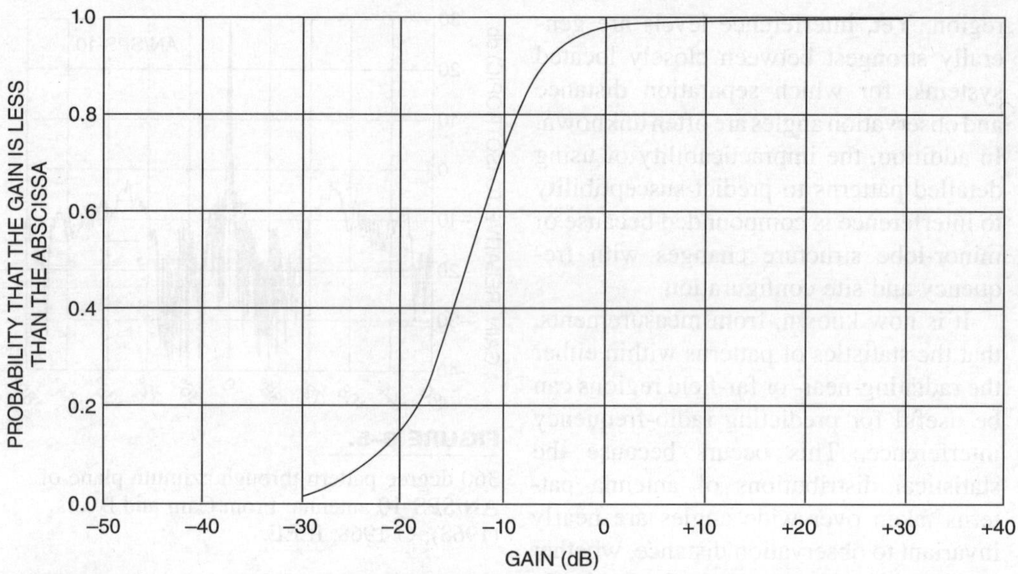

FIGURE 9–6.
Cumulative gain distribution in azimuth plane for AN/SPS-10 antenna. From Cain and Byers (1968); © 1968, IEEE.

other receives. Because of the reciprocity principle, the antenna whose pattern is being measured can be either the transmitting or the receiving member of the pair. The measured pattern will be the same in either case. In the following discussion the antenna whose pattern is being measured will be called the antenna under test (AUT), and the one used as the other terminal of the transmit-receive path will be called the range antenna, regardless of which one transmits and which receives.

It is essential that the range antenna have the same polarization as the AUT antenna. Ideally, the polarization of the range antenna should be controllably variable, so that the pattern of the AUT antenna can be investigated for all polarizations (see Appendix B). This is especially important in applications where very low side lobes are required, because side lobes sometime have polarization different from that of the major lobe.

Typically, antennas transmit or receive electromagnetic waves over long distances. Thus, knowledge of antenna characteristics with antennas in the radiating far-field is needed, which is accomplished by placing the antennas under test in a plane wave of uniform amplitude, phase, and polarization. The traditional method employs a free space range, that is, one for which the separation between the AUT and range antennas meets or exceeds the far-field requirements previously outlined.

The needed separation distances are generally large and often require the measurements be made in out-of-doors environments. Thus, a major concern is the need to suppress unwanted reflections from the ground and nearby surrounding objects, even for narrow-beam antennas. Typical free-space range geometries minimize effects of unwanted reflections by using elevated transmit and receive sites, slanting the propagation path, or by housing the range in an anechoic chamber lined with absorbing material.

Hollis, Lyon, and Clayton (1970) and IEEE (1979) include comprehensive discussions regarding far-zone ranges. Methods that permit smaller separation distances between antennas and thereby permit indoor pattern measurements include compact (sec. 9.3), near-field (sec. 9.4), and scale model (sec. 9.6) ranges.

9.2.1. Low-Frequency Techniques

At the very lowest frequencies, where an electrically short vertical antenna is almost universally used for transmitting (as in AM radio broadcasting), the pattern in the horizontal plane is virtually uniform, and ordinarily it need not to be measured. Occasionally two or more towers may be used in an array to create a null in a certain direction or directions, and broad maxima in other directions. To measure such a low-frequency array, its beam is held fixed in pointing direction, while the range antenna is transported around it in a circular path at a constant distance. The range antenna, if its beam is directional, is kept aimed at the AUT antenna so that only the AUT antenna pattern will affect the result. The mobile antenna may be mounted on a panel truck, a helicopter, or an airplane. Or, if the AUT antenna is on a ship or an island, the range antenna may be located on a ship or boat.

If an absolute field-strength pattern is desired, it may be obtained by measuring the voltage output of the range antenna. This voltage is then compared with the output voltage of a calibrated signal generator to introduce a comparison signal into the receiver, and adjusting its output to give the same voltage as obtained from the range antenna. A similar procedure is used for relative-pattern measurement, except that it is unnecessary to measure the absolute value of the range antenna output voltage. The receiver used in such measurements must be very gain-stable. When the measurements are made over land, the ground conductivity and the presence of nearby reflecting objects will affect the results. Thus, it is customary to make measurements at more positions than would ordinarily be required, to "smooth" the resulting pattern for obtaining an average of the measurements made in approximately the same observation direction.

An important consideration in pattern measurement is to provide adequate separation of the AUT and range antennas, to insure measurement of the far-field pattern. As discussed previously, a rule-of-thumb formula is that the separation must be at least $2D^2/\lambda$ where D is the maximum antenna dimension as viewed from the measurement point and λ is the wavelength. If, however, D is less than 0.707 λ, a minimum permissible separation is the distance of one wavelength. This second requirement is more likely to be applicable to very low-frequency antennas, because their wavelengths are very long.

9.2.2. High-Frequency Techniques

At frequencies above about 100 MHz, an antenna pattern is customarily obtained by rotating the AUT antenna. This may occasionally be done at lower frequencies, and the "low-frequency" procedure may sometimes be used up to considerably higher frequencies. It is then especially important to make the field-strength measurements at points

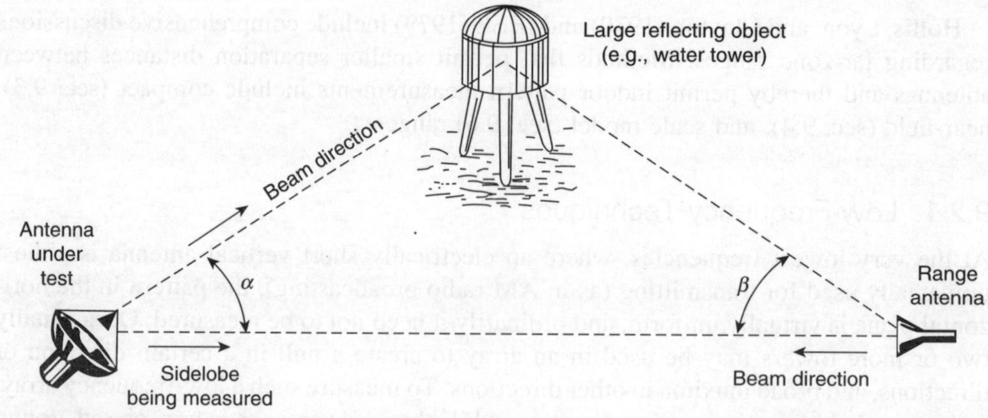

FIGURE 9–7.
Effect of nearby reflecting object on pattern measurement.

that are in the clear—not too close to large buildings or power and telephone lines, for instance.

When the pattern is to be measured by rotating the AUT antenna, both antennas should be located so that they have an unobstructed view of each other, and also have the required separation to insure a far-field measurement. A further requirement is that the area between the antennas be clear of sizable reflecting objects, not only in the direct line between them but for an appreciable distance on both sides. This requirement is important if an accurate measurement of low-amplitude side lobes is to be made. Figure 9–7 illustrates the reason.

The range antenna is indicated to be the transmitting antenna, which is the customary arrangement because it permits all the measurements (direction and signal strength) to be made at a single location, that is, at the AUT antenna. If a large reflecting object, as shown, is illuminated by the range antenna (whose beamwidth is assumed to be greater than 2β), some signal will be reflected toward the AUT antenna, arriving at the angle α off the in-line direction between the two antennas. (The AUT antenna beamwidth is assumed to be less than 2α.) This signal will be considerably less than the in-line signal and will likely not seriously affect the measurement in the main lobe of the AUT antenna, when the reflected signal will be received in the side-lobe portion of the AUT antenna pattern. When the AUT antenna is rotated to allow measurement of its side-lobe pattern at the angle α off axis, however, its main lobe will point directly at the reflecting object, as shown in the diagram. Then the reflected signal received in this way may be comparable to or even in excess of the in-line signal received in the side lobe, so that a considerably erroneous measurement will result.

This effect is minimized by using a range antenna that is fairly directional, with high gain in the direction of the AUT antenna and considerably reduced gain—or perhaps even a null—in the direction of the reflecting object. However, this requires that the range antenna be quite sizable and expensive. If there is just one major reflecting object in a troublesome position, a null of the range antenna may be directed toward the object, if this is possible without too greatly reducing the radiation in the desired direction or giving it an incorrect polarization. As already noted, ideally, the polarization of the range antenna should be controllably variable, so that the pattern of the AUT antenna can be investigated for all polarizations. This is because the side lobes may have different polarization properties than those of the main lobe.

Other possible remedies for the reflecting-object problem exist. One is to interpose absorbing material (available commercially) between the range antenna and the object, or between the object and the AUT antenna. Another is to erect a reflecting barrier that will intercept the radiation going to or from the object and reflect it in some harmless direction. This barrier is usually a flat sheet of solid metal or mesh material set at an angle that will direct the reflected waves away from the AUT antenna.

9.2.3. Far-Field Ranges

When antenna measurements at far-field distances or greater are required on a regular basis, it is customary to set up a *far-field range* for this purpose, consisting of a large clear area with facilities at opposite ends for operating the AUT and range antennas. The separation of the terminals of the range must of course be sufficient to satisfy the far-field criteria, which depend on the aperture sizes and frequencies of the antennas to be measured.

Potential problems and solutions relating to undesirable reflections from objects near the pattern range have already been discussed above. A further problem in pattern measurement is the reflection that occurs from the surface of the ground between the two antennas. Specifically, waves propagate between the range and AUT antennas by two or more paths: directly through the atmosphere and by reflections from various objects, including the earth. Field strength at a point is affected by the interference (complex-vector sum) of the direct and reflected waves. This interference phenomenon is called multipath propagation. Appendix D discusses forward reflections from land and water surfaces and multipath propagation. The discussion there pertains to reflections from surfaces with various rms surface roughnesses, but for which the mean surface at the reflection area is flat. For a perfectly smooth and flat surface, the beamwidths after reflection in both elevation and azimuth are the same as prior to reflection. However, the surface roughness reduces the effective reflection coefficient for forward reflections and it broadens the reflected beamwidths.

The multipath phenomenon results in an interference lobe pattern of the range antenna radiation at the AUT antenna (see Fig. D–5, Appendix D). If this interference pattern is such that there is appreciable variation of the incident field across the vertical aperture of the AUT antenna, its pattern will not be correctly measured. On the other hand, if the resulting interference pattern is such that the variation is slight within the AUT antenna aperture, the resulting error will be insignificant. Effects of multipath may be calculated by the methods described in Appendix D.

A special type of far-zone reflection range is one for which the site geometry permits reflected waves from the ground to add constructively with waves that are propagated directly between antennas. For this case (Hemming and Heaton 1973), the use of horizontal polarization is preferred to vertical because ground reflections are less sensitive to the reflection angle at the air-ground interface.

In general, the mean surface of terrain undulates and consequently there may also be increased beamwidth broadening caused by terrain slope changes at areas of surface reflections. Then, a simple multipath calculation may not be feasible. When adequate terrain flatness is not present, a possible solution to the problem is to set up reflecting "fences" at appropriate points to intercept the waves that would otherwise result in an interference pattern, and reflect them in harmless directions. Or the terrain may be deliberately roughened to such an extent that no appreciable, specular reflection will occur. Another option is to select a site so that a "valley" exists between the antenna locations; then, if the range antenna has a fairly narrow vertical-plane beamwidth, there will be no appreciable reflection from the "floor of the valley." In an industrial or built-up area this effect may be achieved by locating the AUT and range antennas on the roofs of tall buildings separated by relatively clear areas, or on tall towers. In rural areas, two hilltops may be used.

The foregoing discussion has been concerned with horizontal (i.e., azimuth) plane pattern measurement. Elevation-angle patterns are virtually impossible to measure in the presence of a reflection-interference lobe structure. One method of circumventing this difficulty is to turn the AUT antenna on its side so that its "vertical plane" pattern can actually be measured in a horizontal plane. The vertical patterns of antennas that can be tilted upward can be measured from a helicopter or an airplane, if some method of measuring the aircraft direction angle and range can be provided. Use of a precision tracking radar or a global position system (GPS) may be ideal for this purpose.

9.3. Compact Ranges

The *compact range* provides a method of acquiring far-field patterns without a far-field pattern range. In a compact range, patented by Johnson (1967), the test antenna is placed near the aperture of a larger reflector antenna that creates a plane wave (Hess and Johnson 1982; Hickman and Johnson 1972; Johnson, Ecker, and Moore 1969). In this technique, AUT is located in a collimated beam of the radiating near-field (called the quiet zone), thus simulating far-field conditions and permitting a direct measurement of the far-field pattern.

The compact range technique is useful for measurements of small- to medium-size antennas. (In contradiction, Fig. 9–11 shows a huge compact range used for measuring patterns from large and heavy structures). Johnson, Ecker, and Hollis (1973) include in-depth discussions of the advantages and disadvantages. A disadvantage is that the range reflector must be large compared to the antenna under test, and thus the technique is usually impractical for measurements on very large antennas. Moreover, the surface-accuracy required of the range reflector may be critical at frequencies above about 40 GHz. Obviously, basic advantages are that a measurement of the far-field pattern can be made at short distances and indoors, with no more data processing required than for far-field measurements.

Typically, compact ranges are located indoors, where they are not subjected to adverse weather. Traditionally, they are in shielded, absorber-lined rooms that reduce interference from nearby walls and other objects. The shielded chamber also makes the compact range free from outside interfering signals and secure from outside monitoring. Applications include antenna pattern measurements, antenna impedance measurements, gain and polarization comparisons, boresight measurements, radar reflectivity measurements, and illumination of animals and humans for investigations of the biological effects of microwave radiation.

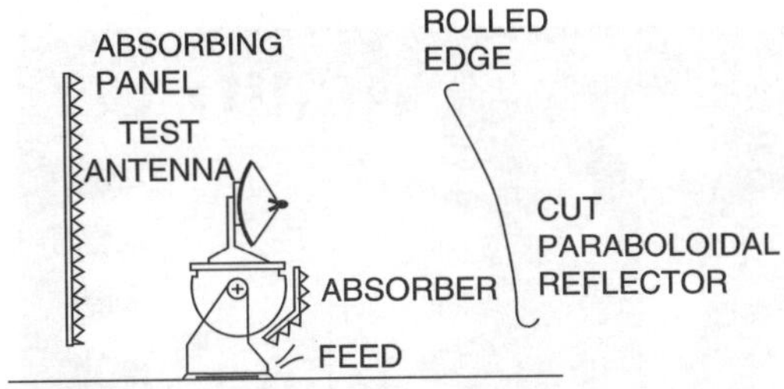

FIGURE 9–8.

Sketch of a point-source compact range. From Johnson, Ecker, and Hollis (1973); © 1973, IEEE.

FIGURE 9–9.

An experimental compact range used to investigate diffraction effects of reflector edges (courtesy of Gerald Hickman).

Figure 9–8 is a sketch of a compact range. One can see that the feed for the paraboloidal reflector is below the turntable on which the test antenna is mounted. The compact range reflector edges were rolled to reduce the intensity of edge diffracted waves toward the test antenna, in an effort to minimize amplitude variations within the quiet zone. Note that the test antenna is necessarily substantially smaller than the compact range reflector. Absorbing material used for reducing interface reflections from the turntable and a nearby wall are also shown.

The reflectors of some compact ranges have been offset parabolic cylinders and others offset paraboloids. Figure 9–9 is a photograph of one of the experimental compact ranges developed by Scientific Atlanta in the 1970s. In this figure one can see the absorbing material along the walls and at the reflector base used to reduce stray reflections near the facility. Also visible is a paraboloidal reflector antenna, which is mounted on a positioner and is being tested. According to Gerald Hickman (now with Electromagnetic Sciences), experience showed that the serrations on the sides controlled edge diffraction; however, the small rolled top and the straight bottom edge did not. Accurate surface tolerances were obtaining by reflector shaping, accomplished with a special milling machine developed for that purpose. Consequently, the compact range reflectors developed later and produced for sale included serrations along all edges.

Figure 9–10 shows a compact range facility, a model currently available through MI Technologies, a company that acquired the antenna instrumentation activities of Scientific

FIGURE 9–10.

A compact range that includes a reflector with serrated edges, and a microwave parabolic antenna on an azimuth-over-elevation positioner (courtesy MI Technologies).

FIGURE 9–11.

Patterns of antennas mounted on an aircraft being measured in a compact range having a 75-foot (approximately 23 m) diameter (courtesy of Henry P. Cotton).

Atlanta. There one can see a large reflector having serrated edges, the surrounding walls and floor covered with absorbing material, and a microwave parabolic antenna with horn feed mounted on an azimuth-over-elevation positioner. Some of the features advertised include frequency coverage from 1 to 110 GHz, unique serrated reflector edges that minimize edge diffraction effects, a precision-machined monolithic reflector surface, and temperature-stable structures.

Figure 9–11 shows a 75-foot (22.9 m) outdoor compact range, located at the U.S. Army Electronic Proving Ground, Ft. Huachuca, Arizona, that was designed and developed by the Georgia Tech Research Institute (Cotton 1988). It was built to measure the patterns of antennas on vehicles, including tanks and aircraft, with dimensions up to 50 feet (15.2 m). This compact range was developed for initial operations from 6 to 40 GHz, but the reflector offers the possibility for extending to even higher frequencies.

The reflector is a section of the upper half of a 150-feet focal-length parabola, and it is positioned so that the parabolic axis is horizontal. The parabola's vertex and focal point (and thus the feed position) are at ground level, which is 2.5 feet below the bottom edge of the reflector. Only five especially designed wide-bandwidth, low-cross-polarization, constant-phase center feed horns are needed to cover the 6- to 40-GHz range of frequencies (Bodnar 1986).

Reflector surface accuracy and edge treatment are two of the principal concerns in compact range design. The reflector surface consists of aluminum panels assembled onto a rigid back structure, and the design specifications include panel surface accuracy of 0.006 inch (about 1.5×10^{-6} m) rms. The reflector faces north, with the backside shielded to minimize thermal distortions caused by the sun. The edge treatment is used to minimize diffraction from the reflector edge for improving the uniformity of the field across the aperture. Shaped serrated reflector edges are used that assisted in providing quiet zone performance suitable for measuring antenna/vehicle radiation with vehicle dimensions up to fifty feet (Joy and Wilson 1987).

Another major design problem for large compact ranges, when the test items are heavy, is the AUT positioner, which is located approximately above the focal point. With a compact range, the item being measured must be within the quiet zone, which is centered roughly 40 feet (12.2 m) above ground. A positioner had to be designed and built, because a suitable one was not available commercially. The positioner, with its base on the ground, is designed to handle weights up to 140,000 pounds (69,300 kg), at heights exceeding 40 feet, and move the test item from –1 to +91 degrees in elevation and continuously in azimuth.

A relatively new electronic timing means appears to have much promise for improving quiet zone performance, by reducing the reflections from the compact range reflector edges and from surrounding objects. The technique is, in essence, a short-pulse-length radar range gating technique (Chang, Liao, and Wu 2004). Although additional electronic instrumentation is required, radar range gating (also called impulse time-domain measurements) may offer improved quiet zone performance as well as simplifications and cost reductions in the traditionally used methods of reflector edge treatment and anechoic chamber construction.

9.4. Near-Field Antenna Measurements*

Conventional far-field antenna measurements are made when the source antenna and the antenna-under-test (AUT) are separated by the far-field criteria, which depend on D, the diameter of the AUT and λ, the wavelength of operation. The required separation can be very large when testing large antennas at short wavelengths. In contrast, near-field antenna measurements can be made with a separation of only a few wavelengths resulting in a significantly smaller measurement facility (Johnson, Ecker, and Hollis 1973; Yaghjian 1986). The reduction in the size of the measurement facility, the high accuracy achieved, and the ability to perform the measurements indoors has led to the popularity of near-field antenna measurements. Near-field measurements require:

a. Use of a probe antenna to measure the phase and amplitude of two vector components of the near-field of the AUT over a surface surrounding the AUT
b. Characterization of the far-field pattern of the probe in phase, amplitude and polarization
c. Application of well defined mathematical techniques to:
   i. Remove the effects of the probe pattern, gain, and polarization from the measured data (called probe correction)
   ii. Transform the corrected near-field data and obtain the far-field of the AUT

* This section contributed by Donald G. Bodnar, MI Technologies, Inc., Atlanta, Georgia.

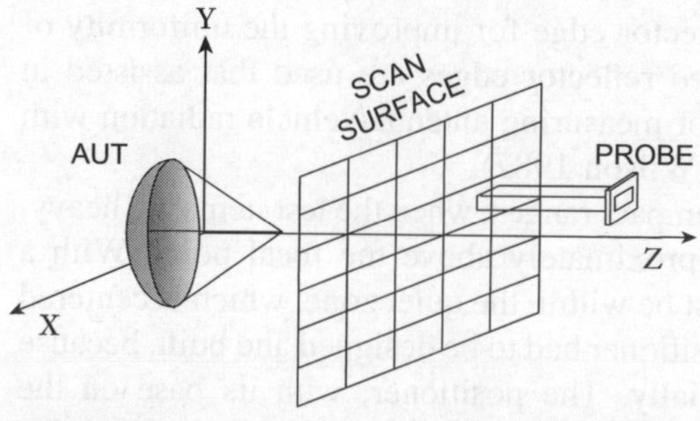

FIGURE 9–12.

Typical planar near-field measured geometry (courtesy MI Technologies).

The near-field to far-field transformation can be accomplished mathematically in three coordinate systems, namely planar, cylindrical, and spherical. Hence, measurement systems for these three geometries have been developed and are discussed next.

9.4.1. Planar Near-Field Measurements

The theory of near-field antenna measurements was first developed by Kerns (1981) for a planar near-field (PNF) geometry that is shown in Figure 9–12. The probe is moved to equally spaced positions in *x* and in *y* on a planar surface located in front of the antenna. The movement of the probe is accomplished using a mechanical positioner under computer control (Joy and Paris 1972). The phase and amplitude of the probe voltage as measured by a microwave receiver is recorded by the computer at each *x*-*y* point. The process is typically repeated for polarization of the probe oriented vertically and again for probe polarization oriented horizontally. In this manner, the tangential component of the electric field on the measurement plane is obtained. However, this measured near-field is distorted by the pattern of the probe and this distortion must be removed to obtain the true near-field of the AUT. The process of removing the probe distortion is called probe correction or probe compensation and involves either mathematically calculating the complete far-field of the probe or measuring its far-field pattern in amplitude, phase, and polarization at the frequency of operation using a separate measurement. The true AUT near-field is obtained from the measured AUT near-field and the probe far-field using the equations of Kerns. Finally, a two-dimensional Fourier transform is performed to obtain the far-field of the AUT from the corrected near-field data.

Planar near-field measurements are especially applicable to narrow-beam antennas since the scan surface must be large enough to collect the majority of the energy radiated by the antenna. Thus, horn antennas and reflector antennas are often measured using a planar near-field scanner. In contrast, a dipole antenna cannot be measured with a planar near-field measurement system since a great deal of energy is radiated in directions other than through the scan surface.

A scanner for moving the probe over a planar surface and sampling the near-field in equal increments, Δx, in x and equal increments, Δy, in y is shown in Figure 9–13. MI Technologies has developed accurate and high-speed planar near-field scanners and the associated high-speed microwave receivers that are needed for measuring phased array antennas, which have many electronically switched beam-pointing directions and many frequencies of operation. High-speed data acquisition is very important in these measurements due to the massive amount of data that must be collected.

9.4.2. Cylindrical Near-Field Measurements

The measurement geometry for cylindrical near-field measurements is shown in Figure 9–14 and the technique is discussed by Leach and Paris (1973). The mathematical formulation employs cylindrical wave modes instead of plane waves as is required in planar near-field measurements. However, the formulation of Kerns (1981) also applies to the cylindrical geometry. Measurements are made in equal increments, Δy, in y, and in equal increments, $\Delta\theta$, in θ measured in the x-z plane. A typical scanner for this geometry is shown in Figure 9–15. Cylindrical measurements systems are well suited for fan beam antennas such as cellular telephone base station antennas as well as pencil beam antennas. The technique is not applicable to antennas that have a great deal of radiation straight up and down since the scanner does not capture this energy. Economical and flexible scanner designs have been developed by MI Technologies, which are required for price sensitive wireless antenna applications (Pearson, Wang, Bodnar, and Tian 2007).

FIGURE 9–13.

Planar near-field (PNF) scanner consisting of a vertical traveling tower over a horizontal slide (courtesy MI Technologies).

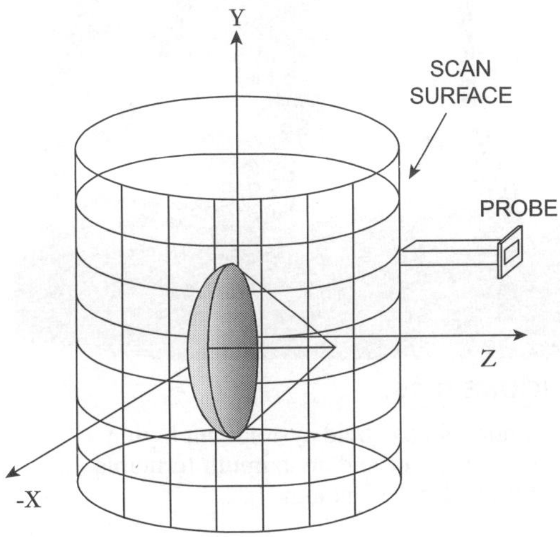

FIGURE 9–14.

Typical cylindrical near-field measured geometry (courtesy MI Technologies).

9.4.3. Spherical Near-Field Measurements

Spherical near-field measurements (Hansen 1988; Leach and Paris 1973) measure the near-field on the surface of a sphere that surrounds the antenna as illustrated in Figure 9–16. Data is collected at equal increments in θ and φ (the standard spherical coordinate angles). This data, is then probe corrected and transformed to the far-field to obtain the far-field of the antenna under test. Any antenna can be measured with a spherical system (e.g., a low-gain, broad-beam antenna as well as fan-beam and pencil-beam antennas) since all of the energy

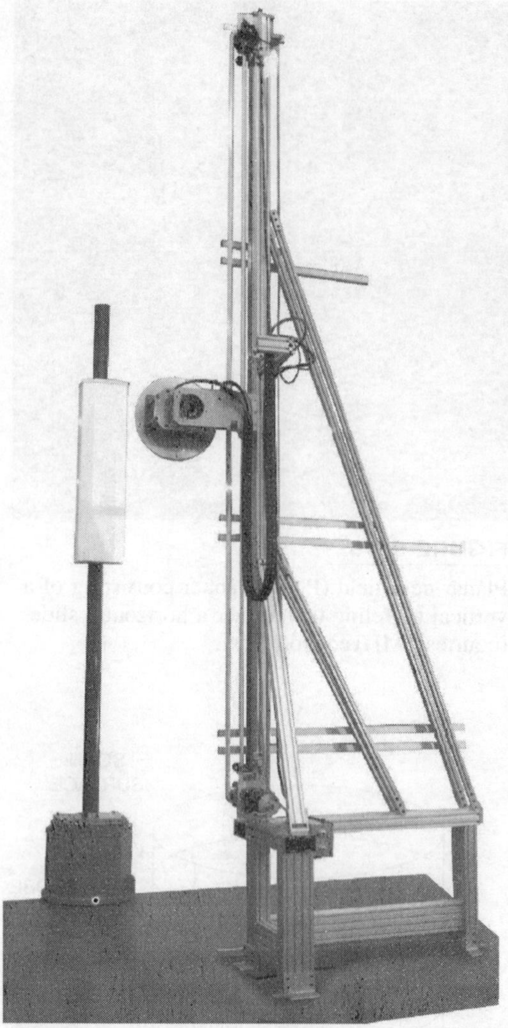

FIGURE 9–15.

Cylindrical near-field system employing a vertical scanner and an azimuth turntable (courtesy MI Technologies).

radiated by the antenna is captured by the measurements (Hansen 1988). A scanner implementation for spherical measurements is shown in Figure 9–17. The azimuth scanner rotates the AUT in azimuth while the arch moves the probe along a circular arc in elevation. This combination of positioners allows near-field measurements over a sphere. Positioner accuracy and positioner alignment are critical issues in spherical near-field measurements especially at microwave and millimeter wavelengths and MI Technologies has developed techniques for handling both of these issues.

9.5. Polarization Measurement

Polarization theory is discussed in Appendix B. The polarization of the radiated field from an antenna may be measured by measuring the received signal voltage with a linearly polarized receiving-range antenna as its polarization is rotated through 360 degrees. If two maxima and two nulls are observed, the field is *linearly polarized* in the direction corresponding to the maxima. (The maxima will be 180 degrees apart, and the nulls will be 90 degrees from the maxima. The direction of the nulls can be measured more accurately than that of the maxima.)

If maxima and *minima* (rather than nulls, or zeros) are observed, the field is *elliptically polarized*, and the ratio of the maximum to the minimum field intensity is called the *polarization ratio* or *ellipticity*. When this quantity is measured along the axis of the main beam of the antenna under test, it is called the *axial ratio*.

When the field intensity is constant as the range antenna polarization is rotated, the field is circularly polarized. (Circular polarization is of course just the special case of elliptical polarization for which the polarization ratio is one.)

Commonly used linearly polarized range antennas include half-wave dipoles and waveguide horns. In fact, any linearly polarized antenna will serve. Polarization measurements may also be made using two fixed receiving antennas linearly polarized at right angles to each other, and measuring the ratio of the intensities received by each. If the field is elliptically polarized, the phase difference of the signals in the two antennas must be measured. For an illustration, see Kraus (1988, p. 838).

9.6. Scale-Model Measurements

Because of the practical difficulties of making measurements on large antennas, and the expense of constructing experimental designs of large size, the scale-model technique is very useful in antenna development and research work. The principle of the scale model is that if two antennas are of exactly the same shape but differ in size by a scale factor S, their electromagnetic behavior will be the same if the smaller antenna is operated at a frequency S times as great as that at which the larger antenna is operated.

This principle is self-evident for simple antennas such as a half-wave dipole, but in fact it holds for all types of antennas. For example, if two paraboloidal reflectors are of exactly the same form (same f/D ratio and same aperture shape) but one is ten times the size of the other, and if they have identically shaped feeds that also differ in size by a 10 : 1 ratio, then if the larger one is operated at 1 GHz and the smaller one at 10 GHz, their operating parameters will be identical. The gains, beamwidths, side-lobe levels, and input impedances will be the same; in fact the patterns will be exactly alike. Also, the percentage bandwidths will be the same. The same would be true of a third antenna five times as large as the larger of the first two, operated at 200 MHz. Thus a large antenna can be scaled down, or modeled, by any desired factor by operating it at a sufficiently high frequency.

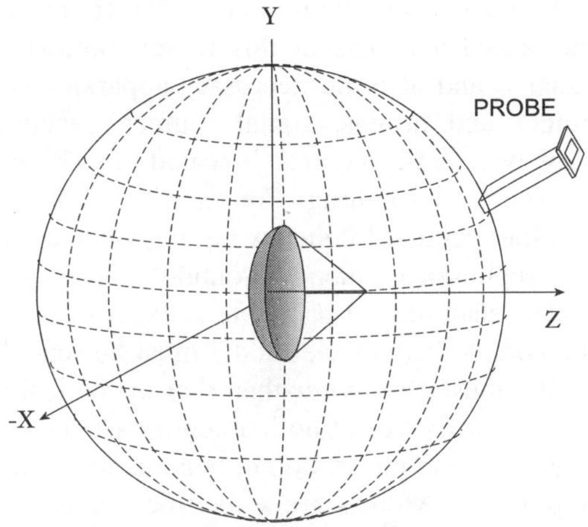

FIGURE 9–16.

Typical spherical near-field measured geometry (courtesy MI Technologies).

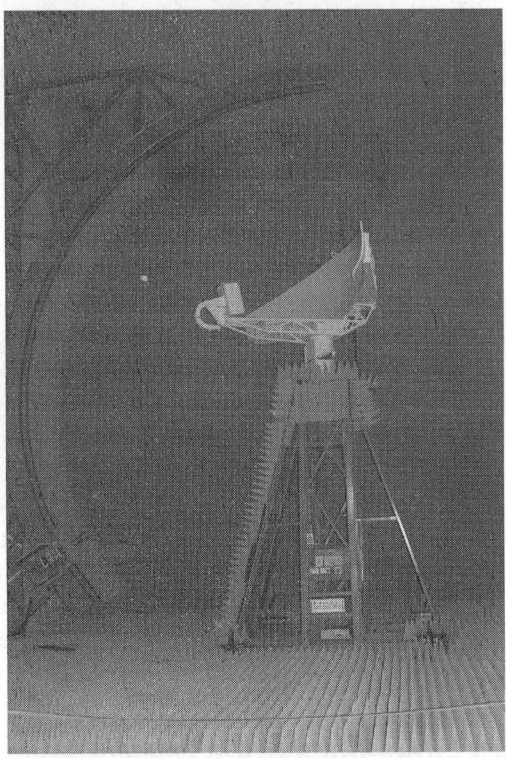

FIGURE 9–17.

Spherical near-field antenna measurement system employing an arch and azimuth turntable (courtesy MI Technologies).

Frequencies in the region of 10 GHz are very popular for scale-model work, because the scaled antennas in this region (known as X-band) are of very manageable size, usually, and also the necessary apparatus is readily available at this frequency: waveguides and fittings, signal sources, receivers, and special measurement equipment. However, some antennas if scaled to so high a frequency would be too tiny and delicate for practical handling. For example, a half-wave dipole is only about 0.6 inch long. Another popular frequency region, when an X-band model would be too small, is S-band (the region of frequency around 3 GHz).

The scale-model principle is exact if the scaling is exact. Not only the size, but also the *conductivity* of the model must be scaled, for exact results. The conductivity of the model must be *greater* than that of the full-sized antenna by the factor S. However, if the conductivities of both antennas are quite high, as is usually the case, and if the conductors of the model do not become too minute, the conductivity scaling is not of much importance. Models are sometimes silver-plated to increase their conductivity. If parts of the antenna involve dielectric or magnetic materials, the *sizes* of these parts *are scaled*, but the *dielectric constants* and *the permeabilities are not*; they should be of the same values in both the model and the full-sized antenna; however, their losses, which often depend on conductivity, must be scaled.

The exactness of scaling of the linear dimensions of the antenna is the most important scaling factor. The scaling requirement applies to *all* dimensions, such as the thickness of the walls of a waveguide horn, the openings of the mesh of a reflector surface, and even the deviations from a true paraboloidal surface—all of these must be smaller in the model by the factor $1/S$, if the results are to be completely accurate. On the other hand, if only approximate results are needed, the scaling need not be applied to some of the details of the antenna, if they are very small compared with the wavelength. Inexact scaling affects the accuracy of impedance measurements more than it does pattern measurements and gain.

An advantage of the use of scale models is that it reduces not only the size of the antenna but also the required size of a pattern range, or separation of AUT and range antennas for any far-field measurements. This can be seen by considering the separation criterion $2D^2/\lambda$. Since D is decreased by the scale factor $1/S$, and λ is reduced by the same factor, the net effect is to reduce the quantity $2D^2/\lambda$ by the factor $1/S$.

Because of this reduction scale-model pattern and gain measurements are sometimes made in an *anechoic chamber*, which is an enclosure whose walls, floors, and ceilings are lined with a special material that absorbs radio waves almost completely. Thus no reflections occur, and the room behaves as if it were free space. To make an enclosure of this type of suitable dimensions for use with full-scale antennas in the VHF and UHF regions would be prohibitively expensive. But for model antennas at S-band or X-band or small full-sized antennas it becomes quite practical. The absorbent material is commercially available.

9.7. Antenna Pattern Measurement Equipment

The basic subsystems of an automatic pattern measuring facility include a signal source, receiver, AUT positioner, and pattern recorder. Figure 9–18 is a block diagram of a

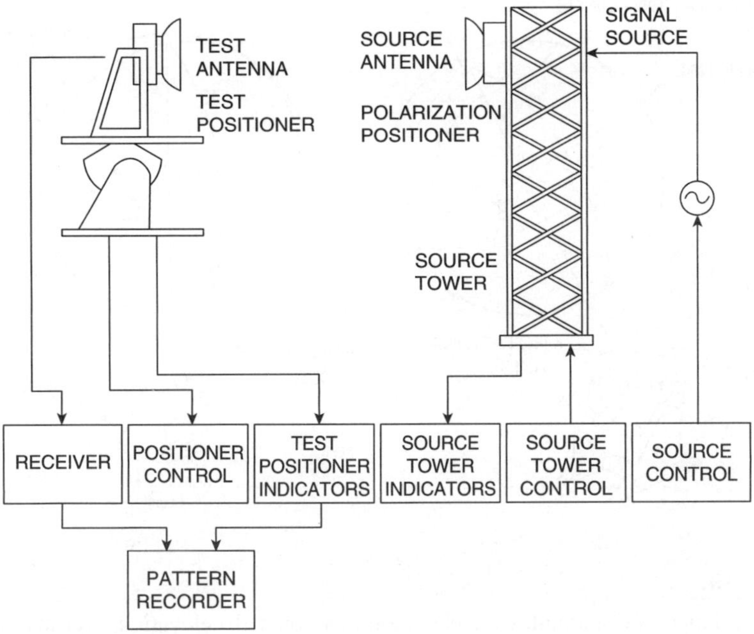

FIGURE 9–18.

Block Diagram of a Typical Antenna Measurement System. Source (IEEE 1979, p. 19); © 1979, IEEE.

simplified antenna measurement system. At major pattern measurement facilities, the subsystems function interoperatively, whereby phase and/or amplitude can be accurately measured and automatically recorded as a function of the coordinate system of the antenna under test (AUT). Usually, a central control system console is employed to allow operator selection of such variables as transmit and receive polarizations, transmit frequency, and range of measured angular coordinates.

For most operating frequencies of interest, most if not all the needed subsystems are available commercially. For example, multiband network analyzers permit coverage over the present practical limits of radio frequencies (tens of kHz to 100 GHz and even higher). A network analyzer (sec. 9.11.2) may be used to provide any or all of the following: signal sources with rapid frequency change over wide ranges of frequencies, receivers for tracking signals from signal sources, rapid phase and amplitude measurements, automatic measurements and computer calculations using the measured results; and multiple visual displays of operating parameters, measured, and calculated results. Additionally, signal sources, receivers, and RF components may be procured separately; and computers with their accessories can provide computations, visual displays, and

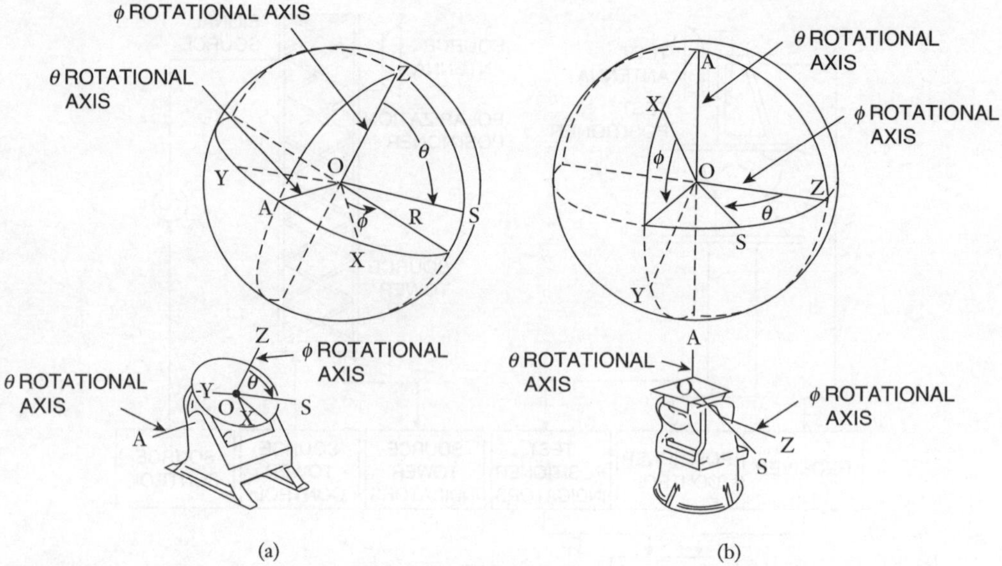

FIGURE 9–19.

Antenna Positioners: (a) azimuth-over-elevation positioner (b) elevation-over-azimuth positioner. Source (IEEE 1979, p. 25); © 1979, IEEE.

printed recordings. Even complete, or near complete, measurement systems that include a central control console may be purchased. Usually, personal computers are used to control the automated measurement system and perform needed calculations.

The AUT positioner, its control system, and its position indicators constitute a key subsystem, which must be selected based on the sizes and weights of the antennas to be measured and on the types of tests to be made. The positioner must of course have the needed movements and yet to be highly stable, handle the requisite weights, and withstand prevalent environmental conditions. Additionally, the position controls and indicators must be accurate and reliable. A wide variety of positioner types, along with their position controls and position indicators, are commercially available. Perhaps the simplest positioners are those that rotate continuously in either azimuth or in elevation. Figure 9–19 includes sketches of two often-used movements, namely azimuth-over-elevation and elevation-over-azimuth.

Positioners are commercially available in various sizes and weight-handling capacities. Figure 9–20 shows a large positioner that includes a bearing having a diameter of 85 inches (about 2.2 m). According to Gerald Hickman, formerly of Scientific Atlanta, this model was used for positioning an F-111 aircraft. Smaller, conceptually similar positioners having platform diameters as small as about 6 inches (15 cm) are also commercially available.

9.8. Directivity and Gain Measurements

FIGURE 9–20.

A large antenna positioner of the type used for positioning an F-111 aircraft (courtesy of Gerald Hickman).

Directivity and gain are discussed in Section 3.3. Directivity D is a measure of an antenna's ability to concentrate radiated power per unit solid angle in a certain direction, and gain takes into account the antenna efficiency as well as its directional properties. In principle, directivity D can also be determined from the numerical integration of a complete far-field pattern, obtained from detailed relative strength measurements. In that case, absolute calibrations are not needed, but gain cannot be determined without knowledge of the antenna losses. The integration method is useful for antennas whose patterns are simple, but it may be of limited use for high-gain antennas with complicated side-lobe or multilobed patterns, because detailed measurement and integration are required over the entire pattern versus θ and ϕ of the antenna. It is interesting to note that these measurements must be performed with high relative accuracy, and directivity measurement does not require an absolute calibration. However, gain that includes antenna losses is generally of greater practical importance.

Gain is the ratio of the radiation intensity, in a given direction, to the radiation intensity that would be obtained if the power accepted by the antenna were radiated by an isotrope. Note that the definition of gain does not include losses resulting from impedance and polarization mismatches. The lossless isotrope is assumed to radiate all of its input power, but some of the power delivered to the actual antenna may be dissipated in ohmic resistance (i.e., converted to heat). Thus, gain takes into account the antenna efficiency as well as its directional properties. Consequently, the efficiency factor k is the ratio of the power radiated by the antenna to the total input power. Therefore, the relationship between gain G and directivity D is

$$G = kD \tag{9–1}$$

where $k \leq 1$ to account for dissipative (I^2R) losses.

If the power input to (i.e., accepted by) the antenna is P_{in},

- the power density $p_{isotrope}$ from the isotrope is $P_{in}/4\pi R^2$ and
- the power density from the antenna $p_{antenna}$ is $E^2/377$, where E is the *rms* value of the electric field strength from the antenna.

Therefore,

$$G = \frac{\dfrac{E^2}{377}}{\dfrac{P_{in}}{4\pi R^2}} = \frac{4\pi R^2 E^2}{377 P_{in}} = \frac{4\pi R^2 p_{antenna}}{P_{in}} \tag{9–2}$$

Efficiency k is P_{out}/P_{in}, and thus from (9–2) the directivity can be expressed as

$$D = \frac{4\pi R^2 E^2}{377 P_{out}} = \frac{4\pi R^2 p_{antenna}}{P_{out}} \tag{9–3}$$

9.8.1. Absolute-Field-Strength Method

A direct method of gain measurement is based on (9–3) above, and it requires an absolute measurement of the antenna input power P_{in}, and the electric field intensity E or power density at distance R from the antenna. The measurement is, of course, made in the direction of maximum radiation. However, if this method is to give the gain of the antenna itself, using (9–3), the measurement must be made under free-space propagation conditions. In other words, the prevailing conditions must not include multipath interference by the earth, or any other factor that may modify the free-space inverse-square law. On the other hand, if the measurement is made using (9–3) with the antenna in its operating location, the gain measured is the effective gain of the antenna in combination with its environment. When earth reflection is involved, this measured gain will depend on the elevation angle of the observation point (as indicated by Fig. 1–15, chapter 1), as well as on the antenna height and the earth's reflection coefficient.

If these factors are known or can be measured, the gain of the antenna by itself (i.e., as would be measured in free space) can be deduced. For example, sometimes there may be enough information available to determine the reflection coefficient of the earth and the propagation factor F, as defined by equation (1–50), chapter 1. Then if a value of field intensity E is actually measured, one could calculate the gain for conditions of free-space propagation. In terms of the factor F, (9–2) can be rewritten as (9–4) so that it expresses the free-space gain of the antenna even if the field intensity E or the power density is *measured under non-free-space conditions*:

$$G = \frac{4\pi R^2 E^2}{377 P_{in} F^2} = \frac{4\pi R^2 p_{antenna}}{P_{in} F^2} \tag{9–4}$$

The absolute field intensity E can be measured at low frequencies by means of a multiturn loop-receiving antenna, as described for small loops in sec. 4.5.1. At higher frequencies at which a "small loop" is impractical, it is more convenient to make the measurement in terms of the received power density p_r. This quantity is related to the receiving-antenna capture cross section (effective receiving area) A_r by the formula

$$p_r = \frac{P_r}{A_r} = \frac{4\pi P_r}{kD_r\lambda^2} = \frac{4\pi P_r}{G_r\lambda^2} \quad (9\text{–}5)$$

where P_r, D_r, and G_r refer to the received power, directivity and gain of the receiving antenna. (For a review of receiving cross section area, see chapter 3, sec. 3.4).

9.8.2. Standard Gain Antennas

A standard gain antenna is one whose gain is accurately known so that it can be used in measurement of other antennas. Certain simple forms of antennas can be constructed to have gain of known amount, based on previous calibrations or calculations. Pyramidal horns (sec. 4.7) are commonly used at microwave frequencies as gain standards.

Alternatively, a standard antenna can be obtained by a gain measurement that does not require an antenna of known gain. This method requires two identical antennas. One is used as a transmitting antenna and the other for receiving. They are separated by a distance R, and aimed at each other. The transmit antenna input power P_{in} and the received power P_r are both measured. Gain in this case can be found easily from the Friis transmission equation of sec. 3.4.2, which, with the two gains equal, becomes

$$P_r = P_{in}\frac{G^2\lambda^2}{(4\pi R)^2}F^2$$

Then, solving for gain one obtains

$$G = \frac{4\pi R}{\lambda F}\sqrt{\frac{P_r}{P_{in}}} \quad (9\text{–}6)$$

This procedure is likely to be most accurate when the propagation factor F is unity, that is, under effectively free-space conditions with minimal earth-reflection interference effects. Equation (9–6) can also be applied successfully under conditions that permit accurate calculation of F, for example, when reflection occurs from a smooth water surface located between the two antennas.

The gain calibration procedure described above, that uses (9–6), is known as the two-antenna method. This method and the three-antenna method, to now be described, are usually performed at a site where the ground and other reflections are negligible, so that F is assumed to be unity. For the three-antenna method, three sets of two-antenna measurements are performed with three antennas that may have different gains, designated here as G_A, G_B, and G_C. Then, by expressing the Friis equation in logarithmic form and setting $F = 1$, three simultaneous linear equations are obtained that follow:

$$10\log G_A + 10\log G_B = 20\log\left(\frac{4\pi R}{\lambda}\right) - 10\log\left(\frac{P_r}{P_{in}}\right)_{AB}$$

$$10\log G_A + 10\log G_C = 20\log\left(\frac{4\pi R}{\lambda}\right) - 10\log\left(\frac{P_r}{P_{in}}\right)_{AC}$$

$$10\log G_B + 10\log G_C = 20\log\left(\frac{4\pi R}{\lambda}\right) - 10\log\left(\frac{P_r}{P_{in}}\right)_{BC}$$

Thus, the three gains may be determined from the above simultaneous equations.

9.8.3. Power-Measurement Methods

Transmitted and received powers can be measured by various methods. A common method of transmitted power measurement is to extract a small fraction of the power in the transmission line by means of a directional coupler and apply it to a power meter. Typically, a power meter consists of a bolometer connected to one arm of a bridge circuit for converting bolometer-resistance changes to indications of power. To obtain the value of the high transmitted power levels, P_t, the power thus measured is corrected for the directional-coupler attenuation and for any additional attenuation that may have been inserted between the coupler and the bridge to reduce the power to the level for which the bridge is calibrated.

Received power is usually measured by a comparison method, using a calibrated signal generator and a receiver with some type of output indicator. The general procedure is to adjust the receiver gain until a useful output indication is obtained; and it should be ascertained that the signal level is high enough so that practically all the indication is due to the signal and not to the background noise. Then the transmitter is turned off, and the calibrated signal generator is turned on. It may either be connected to the receiver in place of the antenna, or the antenna may be left connected and the test signal introduced into the receiver input by way of a directional coupler in the antenna-to-receiver transmission line. The signal generator output is then adjusted until it gives an indication equal to that obtained with the actual received signal. From the signal generator calibration, corrected for attenuation of the directional coupler, the value of the received power, P_r, can be calculated.

9.8.4. Gain Measurement by Comparison

At high frequencies the most common method of gain measurement is by comparison of the signal strengths transmitted or received with the unknown-gain antenna and a standard-gain antenna. This comparison is most conveniently made on a pattern range, with the same general setup of equipment used in pattern measurement and with the range antenna transmitting. The gain of this antenna need not be known, nor does the propagation factor F affect the result as long as F does not vary appreciably over the apertures of the AUT antenna and the gain standard. All that is required of the range antenna and its associated transmitter is that they do not vary the amount or frequency of the radiated power in the direction of the AUT antenna throughout the measurement procedure.

Since the gain of the unknown antenna is ordinarily higher than the gain of the gain standard, the standard antenna is first connected to the receiver (in the manner of an AUT antenna in pattern measurement), and aimed at the range antenna. The receiver gain is adjusted to give a convenient output meter indication (after it is determined that the level of the signal is well above noise level). Then the antenna whose gain is to be measured is connected in place of the standard-gain antenna, and attenuation is introduced into the transmission line between the antenna and receiver until the output indication is the same as it was with the gain-standard antenna. If the attenuation factor, expressed as a power ratio greater than one, is L, the gain of the unknown antenna, G_a, is

$$G_a = LG_s \tag{9–7}$$

where G_s is the standard-antenna gain. Inasmuch as antenna gains and attenuator calibrations are often expressed in decibels, it is frequently convenient to make the calculation in decibels, in which multiplication is replaced by addition:

$$G_{a(dB)} = G_{s(dB)} + L_{dB} \tag{9–8}$$

In the unlikely event that the unknown antenna has a smaller gain than the standard, L in (9–7) is expressed as a number less than one, and the decibel value of L in (9–8) is negative.) The basic set-up for gain measurement by the comparison method is diagrammed in Fig. 9–21. It is essential in this method of gain measurement that both the AUT and the standard antenna are equivalently impedance-matched to the load presented to them by the transmission line. The best way to insure this is to make *VSWR* measurements with each of them connected in turn, and adjust the matching of each for a flat line ($VSWR = 1$). This method basically compares antenna *power gains*, but *directivities* may also be determined if the antenna radiation-efficiency factors are known.

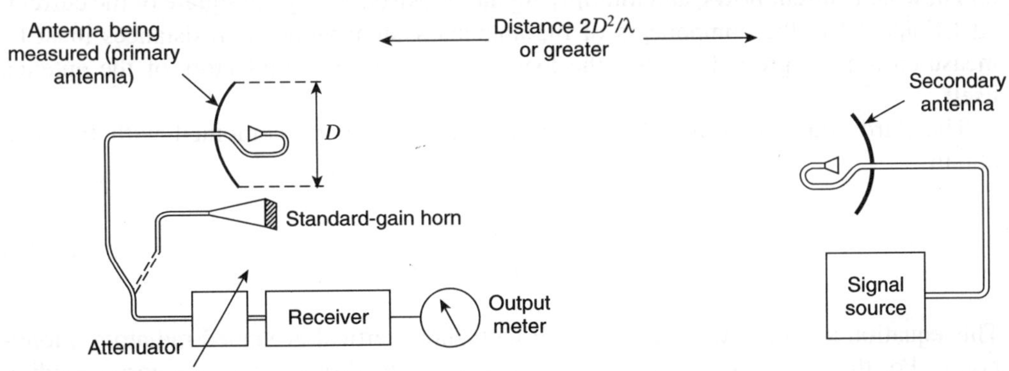

FIGURE 9–21.

Set-up for gain measurement by comparison method.

9.9. Antenna Efficiency

The term *efficiency* has two different connotations in its application to antennas. One is related to the dissipative losses and the other to the ratio of the directivity to the aperture area.

9.9.1. Radiation Efficiency

The *radiation efficiency* k_R, a number between zero and one, expresses the ratio of the power *radiated* P_R to the total power accepted P_{in} by the AUT. The difference of these two quantities is the power *dissipated* P_D in ohmic or dielectric losses. The radiation efficiency is also the factor applied to the directivity D to obtain the gain G. There are in principle several ways of measuring k_R, indicated by the following equations:

$$k_R = \frac{P_R}{P_{in}} \tag{9–9}$$

$$k_R = \frac{P_{in} - P_D}{P_{in}} \tag{9–10}$$

$$k_R = \frac{G}{D} \tag{9–11}$$

The first equation requires direct measurement of the total radiated power, which is possible only in special cases. Measurement of the total input power to the antenna P_{in} is not difficult, since this power flows in the transmission line connecting the transmitter to the antenna.

The second equation requires measurement of the dissipated power P_D. This can sometimes be done, especially at low frequencies, by measuring the resistance of conductors in which current flows, and multiplying these resistances by the square of the current. At LF and VLF, the components of the antenna system whose rf resistances must be measured are the ground system, the loading coil, and the conductors of the antenna itself.

The third equation is not directly useful, but it may be combined with (9–4) to obtain

$$k_R = \frac{4\pi R^2 E^2}{377 P_{in} F^2 D} \tag{9–12}$$

This equation is especially useful at VLF with short vertical grounded radiators (monopoles). For these antennas, D may be taken as twice the directivity of the corresponding short dipole; hence, ordinarily, D is approximately 3. Within line-of-sight distances and over water or moist ground, it can be assumed that $F = 1$. Therefore, if measurements are available of both the total input power to the antenna P_{in} and field strength E at distance R from the antenna, the radiation efficiency can be determined. Since the definition of k_R requires E to be the far-field strength, R must be a distance satisfying the far-field criteria, as discussed in sec. 3.2.5.

9.9.2. Aperture Efficiency

The other connotation of the term "efficiency" relates to the equation for the *directivity* of a large-aperture type antenna—a horn, a large unidirectional planar array, a parabolic reflector, or a lens. From equation (6–13), chapter 6, directivity is expressed in (9–13) as:

$$D = k_A \left(\frac{4\pi A}{\lambda^2} \right) \tag{9–13}$$

where A is the geometric area of the aperture (for antennas that have a physical area such as those listed immediately above) and λ is the wavelength (both expressed in the same system of units). In this context, k_A is called the *aperture efficiency*. If the field intensity over the aperture of an antenna is uniform (no "taper"), with no spillover or leakage, $k_A = 1$. This is the largest value of k_A practically attainable, ruling out "supergain" antennas, which are not feasible except to a limited degree in a few cases. Typical values of k_A range from somewhat less than 0.5 to nearly 1.0. The measurement of k_A is virtually synonymous with measurement of directivity D, since from (9–13):

$$k_A = \frac{D\lambda^2}{4\pi A} \tag{9–14}$$

9.10. Radiation Resistance

The radiation resistance of an antenna is defined by equation (3–28), chapter 3; it is the ratio of the power radiated to the square of the antenna current. As mentioned, it is in a sense a fictitious quantity, since it is referred to an arbitrary point in the antenna and has different values for different reference points. It is conventional to refer it to the current-maximum point, although it may also be referred to the feed point. In many cases the two points are one and the same; an example is the case of a center-fed half-wavelength dipole. When referred to the current-maximum point, it is sometimes known as the loop radiation resistance, since a current maximum is also called a current loop.

If there is no ohmic loss in the antenna—that is, if all the input power is radiated—then the radiation resistance referred to the feed point is equal to the resistive component of the antenna input impedance. In this case, measurement of the antenna input impedance constitutes a measurement of its radiation resistance. If the feed point is not a current-maximum point, the loop radiation resistance may be calculated from the feed-point radiation resistance from the formula:

$$R_{r(\text{loop})} = R_{r(\text{feedpoint})}\left[\frac{I_{\text{feedpoint}}}{I_{\text{maximum}}}\right]^2 \tag{9–15}$$

where I denotes the currents at the points indicated by the subscript notation.

If there is appreciable ohmic loss, so that the antenna radiation efficiency factor k_R is less than one, the radiation resistance is found from equations (3–26) and (3–29) of chapter 3 to be

$$R_r = k_R R_i \tag{9–16}$$

where R_i is the input resistance, that is, the resistive component of the input impedance.

It is apparent that the radiation resistance is sometimes a rather nebulous concept and not always easily measured. In general, it is a useful concept only when it is readily measurable. It has no meaning for antennas in which there is no clearly defined current value to which it can be referred.

9.11. Impedance Measurements

Impedance is defined in terms of the current I that flows if a voltage E is applied between a pair of electrical terminals. According to Ohm's law, impedance Z is $Z = E/I$. Impedance is a complex quantity, having a resistive real part R and a reactive imaginary part X, such that $Z = R + jX$. The algebra of complex numbers is reviewed in Appendix C.

Impedance Z can be determined by measuring the voltage and current at the pair of terminals, and the phase angle between them. At low radio frequencies, voltmeters and ammeters are practical instruments. The direct measurement of the phase angle, however, is not a simple matter, although it can be done. A simple method at low radio frequencies is to apply a small voltage derived from the current I to one deflection axis of an oscilloscope and a sample of the voltage E to the other axis. The resulting pattern will be an ellipse; and the value of the phase angle can be determined from the dimensions of the ellipse. This direct method of impedance measurement may sometimes be useful. However, comparison methods are more commonly employed. The most basic method is the bridge method, which is essentially a sensitive method for measuring an unknown impedance by comparing it with a known impedance.

Prior to the 1970s, before the commercial development of network analyzers, the preferred impedance measurements methods were the impedance bridge and the standing wave method. For measurement of low-frequency antenna impedances, bridges were virtually always employed, and up to frequencies of about 30 MHz they were the method of choice. From 30 MHz to perhaps as high as 1 GHz, the bridge method was used, although the bridge impedance arms might then consist partly of transmission-line elements rather than purely "lumped" capacitances and inductances.

The standing wave method was used for frequencies above a few hundred MHz, whereby the field strength along the transmission line was measured. The so-called slotted line was commercially available for measuring standing wave ratios within coaxial transmission lines or waveguides, up to frequencies of about 100 GHz. As already noted, today the preferred impedance measurement method is the network analyzer, for which multiband designs are commercially available for almost all radio frequencies, from 10 kHz to 100 GHz. The basics of network analyzers are given in sec. 9.11.2. However, the standing wave method is first discussed in sec. 9.11.1, because its principles are basic to the understanding of power transfer to antennas and their related components.

9.11.1. Standing-Wave Method

At frequencies above 30 MHz, a transmission line of sufficient length to exhibit a standing wave, as discussed in secs. 2.1 and 2.2 (see, for example, Fig. 2–5), is not unreasonably long. It then becomes practical to measure the antenna input impedance by determining the *VSWR* (voltage standing wave ratio) on the feed line, and the distance from the antenna terminals to the first voltage *minimum* on the line. Calculation of the antenna impedance by this method is based on equation (2–46) of chapter 2, in conjunction with equations (2–37), (2–47), and (2–48). These equations show how the complex reflection coefficient of the load can be found from measurement of the *VSWR* and distance d from the load to the voltage minimum, and that the load impedance, Z_L, can be calculated when r is known.

The *Smith Chart* is described in sec. 9.12. It can be employed to determine Z_L directly from the values of *VSWR* and d, without going through any calculations, and without the intermediate determination of the reflection coefficient, r. Therefore, the method consists of measuring the quantities *VSWR* and d, and then making use of the Smith Chart.

The quantities to be measured are depicted graphically in Fig. 9–22. (This diagram shows only one of many possible patterns that might be observed.) The *VSWR* is the ratio V_{max}/V_{min}. The wavelength, λ, is twice the separation of the voltage minima. The ratio d/λ, rather than d itself, is the quantity actually used in the calculation.

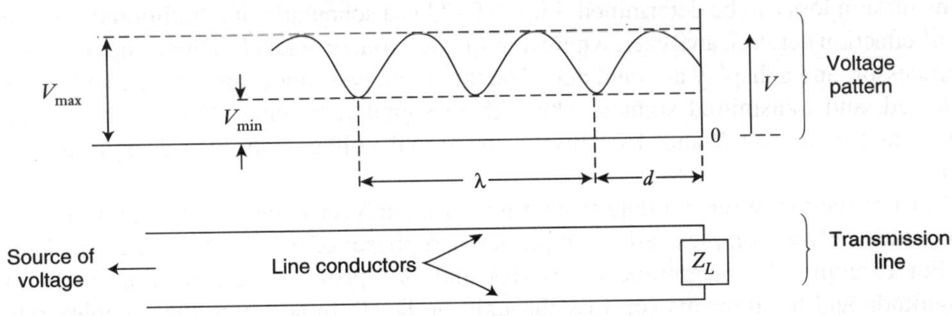

FIGURE 9–22.

Diagram showing quantities to be measured in standing-wave method of impedance determination.

The basic procedure for measuring the position of the voltage minimum, and the *VSWR*, is to move a short sensing probe along a transmission line and find the positions of maximum and minimum field strengths. To meet these requirements, it is possible to employ a special *slotted line*—a horizontal section of coaxial line or waveguide that has a long narrow slot cut into the top of its outer wall, along its length. A short metal pin, the sensing probe, projects through the center of the slot and into the coaxial line or waveguide (without touching the walls). The upper end of the probe connects to a detector (usually a crystal diode). Because the probe is of such small dimensions, it does not disturb the field appreciably, and the detector does not constitute an appreciable load.

Prior to about 1975, slotted lines were commercially available over a wide range of frequencies, but because of the development of highly successful network analyzers, they seem to have become almost extinct. Even so, the slotted section remains a low-cost instrument for making *VSWR* and impedance measurements. For frequencies of several hundred megahertz up to perhaps 3 GHz, coaxial slotted lines of 50-ohm characteristic impedance were standard. At higher frequencies and up to about 100 GHz, slotted waveguides were used. Another method of obtaining *VSWR* is to use a directional coupler, such as the one represented in Fig. 2–19, chapter 2. If the voltage outputs of both ports 2 and 4 of this coupler are separately measured, one measurement will represent the amplitude of the forward-traveling wave in the line, and the other will represent the reflected-wave amplitude. The ratio of the sum of these amplitudes to their difference gives the *VSWR*, in accordance with equation (2–43), chapter 2. A measurement setup that uses a directional coupler in this way is called a reflectometer. If also the phase difference of the two voltages is measured and the distance from the coupler to the load is known, the load impedance can be computed.

9.11.2. Network Analyzers

Traditional network analyzers are used to measure the amplitude and phase characteristics of the transmission and reflection properties of a device under test (DUT). From these measurements, properties such as input impedance, reflection coefficient, and transmission loss can be determined. Figure 9–23 is a schematic of a traditional transmission/reflection network analyzer, where a frequency source, a DUT, a three-input receiver, a processor, and a display are depicted. The three receiver inputs are the incident (input), reflected, and transmitted signals. These three signals are obtained from the couplers designated A, R, and B and, for brevity, the signal voltages are also designated A, R, and B.

Most of the measurement data from a network analyzer is derived from ratios, either magnitude only or complex ratios (amplitude and phase) of the signal voltages A, R, and B. For example, the magnitude ratios R/A and B/A provide the reflection coefficient magnitude and the transmission loss through the DUT. In addition, the complex ratios provide information needed for determining impedance and phase change on transmission through the DUT. From the ratios, the processor also determines such quantities as *VSWR* and input impedance. The display provides the various calculated data, and some

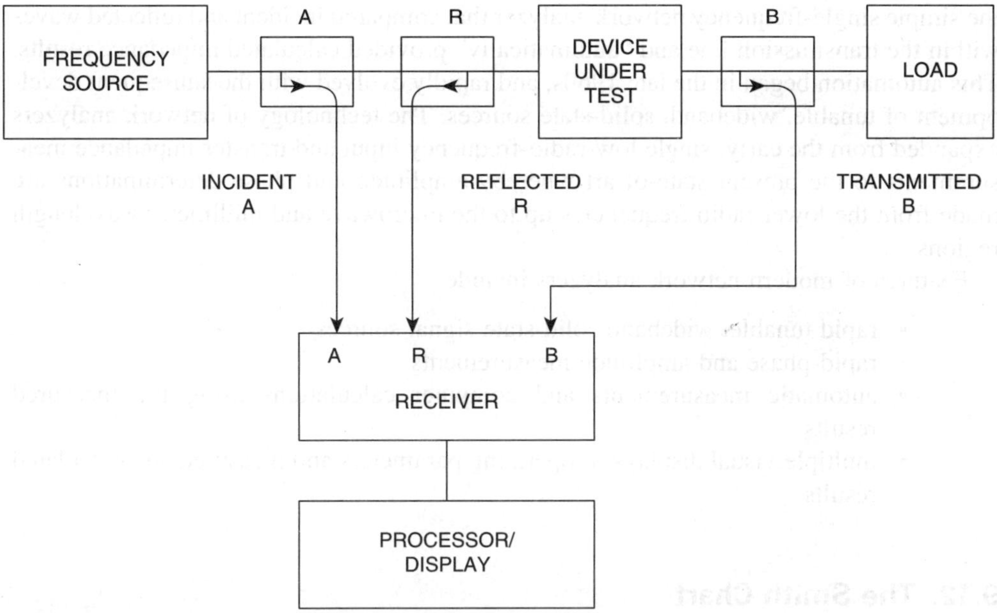

FIGURE 9–23.

Schematic of a basic network analyzer.

commercially available network analyzers even provide such complete information as a Smith Chart (see next section) plot versus frequency.

There are many types of network analyzers that are available commercially, some of advanced design for special applications. As already indicated, frequency sources usually provide a wide range of frequencies, and others have variable output power so that measurements of component linearity may be accomplished. Some analyzers determine features known as the *S*-parameters of a network, which are needed for applications where networks are cascaded into complex configurations. *S*-parameters are determined by two sets of complex (amplitude and phase) ratios: the transmission and reflection ratios (1) at a network input with the output terminated with a matched load and (2) at the network output with the network input terminated with a matched load.

Network analyzers may measure magnitudes only or magnitude and phase, operate manually or automatically, and cover a frequency range continuously or in steps. Modern, commercially available network analyzers permit rapid (virtually simultaneous) phase and amplitude measurements over wide ranges of frequency. Multiband designs are used for very wide frequency coverage, permitting coverage over the present practical limits of radio frequencies (tens of kHz to 100 GHz). Analyzers often allow measurements at two or more ports, thus permitting isolation or cross-polarization measurements versus frequency.

As already described, early UHF, microwave, and millimeter wave impedance measurements used a slotted transmission line, commonly called a slotted line. Next came the simple single-frequency network analyzer that compared incident and reflected waves within the transmission line and "automatically" provided calculated impedance results. This automation began in the late 1960s, and rapidly evolved with the subsequent development of tunable, wideband, solid-state sources. The technology of network analyzers expanded from the early, single low-radio-frequency input and transfer impedance measurements to the present state-of-art whereby amplitude and phase determinations are made from the lower radio frequencies up to the microwave and millimeter wavelength regions.

Features of modern network analyzers include

- rapid tunable, wideband solid-state signal sources
- rapid-phase and amplitude measurements
- automatic measurements and computer calculations using the measured results
- multiple visual displays of operating parameters and measured and calculated results.

9.12. The Smith Chart

When the *VSWR* and the position of a voltage minimum have been measured, calculation of the antenna input impedance can be made from the basic transmission-line equations of chapter 2. The considerable labor of using these equations is usually avoided by using an impedance chart, which is a graphical representation of the impedance relationships expressed by the equations.

A common feature of impedance charts is that they deal with dimensionless ratios, rather than directly with physical quantities. The ratios involved are primarily ratios of impedance, length, and voltage: specifically, the ratio of the load impedance of the line to its characteristic impedance (Z_L/Z_0), the ratio of the distance from the load to a voltage minimum to the wavelength (d/λ), and the ratio of maximum to minimum standing-wave voltages (*VSWR*). Conversions from two of these ratios to the physical quantities Z_L and d, and vice versa, are readily made, since Z_0 and λ are presumed to be known quantities. Because they deal with ratios, the same charts can be used for all characteristic impedances, frequencies, and absolute voltage levels.

The Smith Chart is the most widely used impedance chart, and it became popular shortly after the concept was published by its inventor (Smith 1944). Because of its common usage, it is commercially available in printed form and is in effect a special graph paper made for plotting impedances. The basic plan of the Smith Chart is shown in Fig. 9–24. Within the circular boundary there are two orthogonal families or sets of circles. *Orthogonal* means, roughly, perpendicular, in the sense that the circles of one family intersect those of the other family perpendicularly, that is, at right angles. (Actually it is the tangent lines to the circles at the point of intersection that form right angles.)

There is one point on the chart through which every circle of both families passes; this is the point at the exact bottom of the chart. The circles of one family pass through

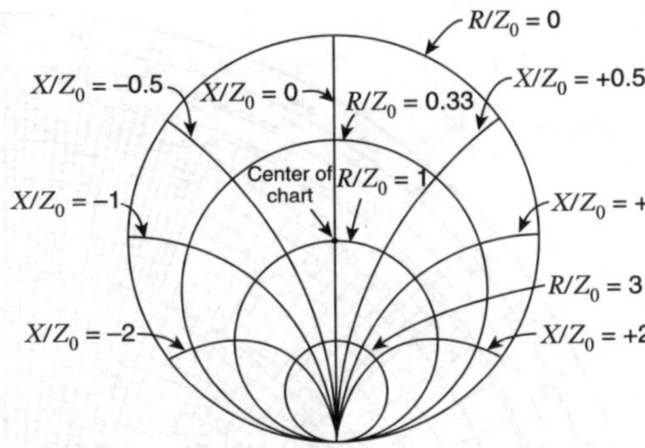

FIGURE 9–24.

Basic construction of the Smith Chart.

this point horizontally; those of the other family go through it vertically. The first of these families of circles represent constant values of the ratio R_L/Z_0, and will be referred to as "*R* circles." The second family of circles corresponds to constant values of X_L/Z_0 and will be referred to as the "*X* circles." R_L and X_L are of course the resistive and reactive components of the load impedance, Z_L. The *X* circles to the left of the center line are negative values of X_L/Z_0, representing *capacitive* reactance, and those on the right are positive, representing *inductive* reactance. The vertical center line is the $X_L = 0$ line. The *R* circle that passes through the exact center of the chart represents $R_L/Z_0 = 1$. Therefore the exact center *point* of the chart corresponds to a load impedance that is a pure resistance of value equal to the characteristic impedance; that is, at this point $R_L = Z_0$ and $X_L = 0$. (This is of course the load value that results in a unity value of *VSWR*.)

These two families of circles are in effect a system of *coordinates*, one coordinate set representing the resistive component and the other set the reactive component of the load impedance. Any particular point on the chart corresponds to a load impedance, Z_L, whose components are given by the two orthogonal *R* and *X* circles that intersect at that point.

In addition to these *R* and *X* coordinates, there is another set of coordinates for the measured quantities, *VSWR* and d/λ. These coordinates are not printed on the chart, since they would result in a hodgepodge of lines and make it difficult to read the chart. Instead, they are to be plotted in by the user for the specific measured values in a particular case. The *VSWR* coordinates are circles whose *centers* are at the center of the Smith Chart—that is, at the $X_L/Z_0 = 0$, $R_L/Z_0 = 1$ point. This point corresponds to $VSWR = 1$, and the circles of increasing size correspond to increasing values of *VSWR*. The largest of these circles forms the outer boundary of the chart and represents an infinite *VSWR* (∞).

The d/λ coordinates are radial lines emanating from the center of the chart. A circular scale of values of d/λ is provided on the outer periphery of the chart. The full circle spans the range from $d/\lambda = 0$, at the top of the chart, through $d/\lambda = 0.25$ at the bottom of the chart, to $d/\lambda = 0.5$ again at the top; thus the complete circle of values corresponds to values of *d* going from zero to $\frac{1}{2}$ wavelength. The values increase counterclockwise, when *d* is the distance from the antenna terminals to the first voltage minimum. This direction on the scale is usually marked "wavelengths toward the load," which refers to the location of the null when the load is short-circuited, with respect to the voltage minimum with the short removed. A complementary scale is also usually provided, marked "wavelengths toward the generator." This scale increases in the opposite direction and corresponds to the distance from the voltage minimum (short removed) to the nearest null (load shorted) in the direction of the generator (signal source).

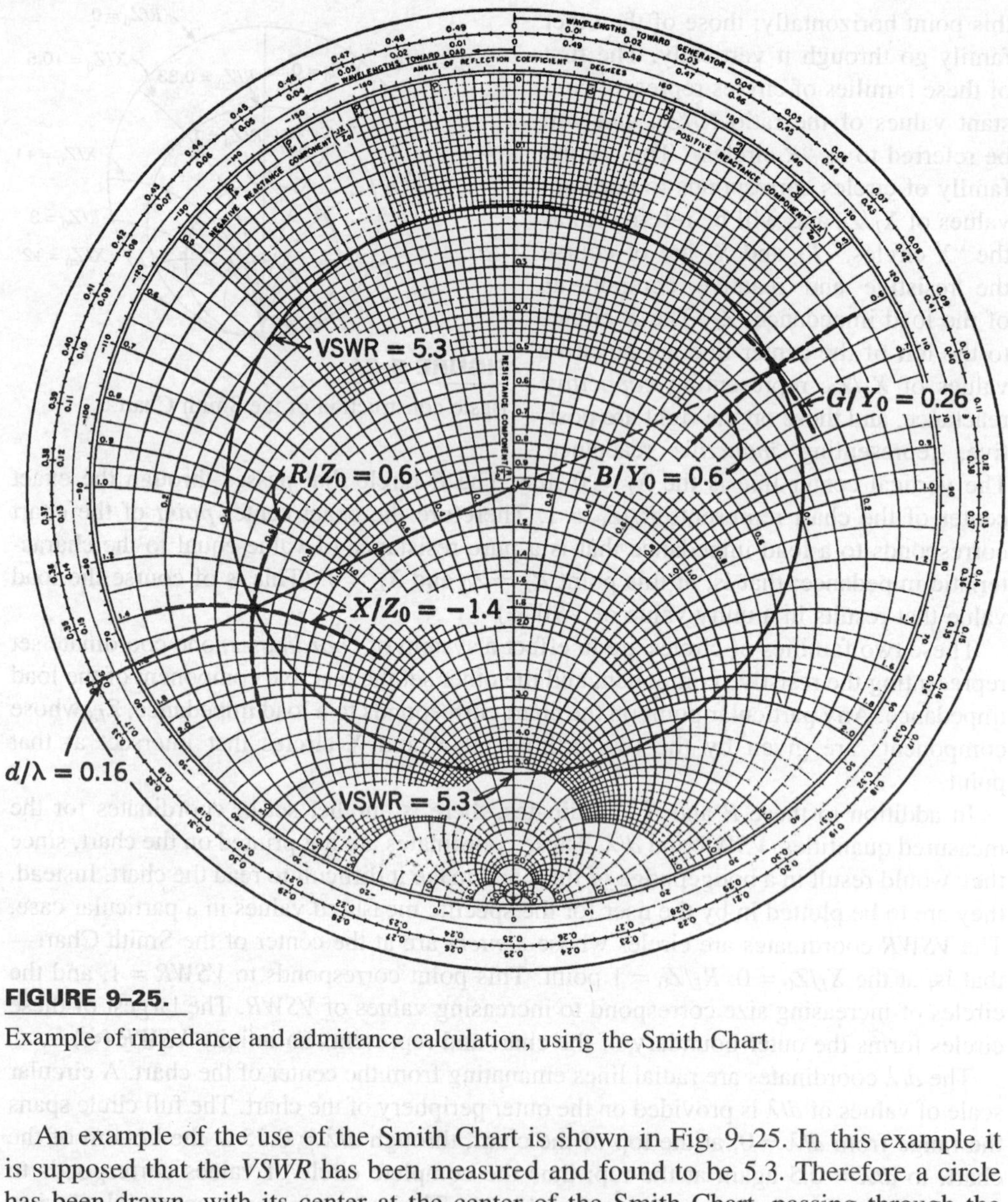

FIGURE 9–25.
Example of impedance and admittance calculation, using the Smith Chart.

An example of the use of the Smith Chart is shown in Fig. 9–25. In this example it is supposed that the *VSWR* has been measured and found to be 5.3. Therefore a circle has been drawn, with its center at the center of the Smith Chart, passing through the *VSWR* = 5.3 point on the vertical center line. The d/λ value has been found to be 0.16, and a radial line has been drawn from the center of the chart to this point on the d/λ scale (the one labeled "wavelengths toward load"). At the intersection of this circle and radial line, a pair of the *R* and *X* circles (shown dashed) also intersect. These are seen to be the ones for $R_L/Z_0 = 0.6$, and $X_L/Z_0 = -1.4$. Therefore, the antenna input impedance in this case consists of a resistive component $R_L = 0.6Z_0$, and a negative (capacitive) reactance component $X_L = -1.4Z_0$. If (for example) the characteristic impedance of the line is

50 ohms, then $R_L = 30$ ohms, and $X_L = -70$ ohms. (Note that X_L here designates "load reactance" and not, as in some cases, "inductive reactance.")

This example illustrates the basic use of the Smith Chart. It can also be used to solve impedance-matching problems. For this purpose it is often convenient to work with admittance, rather than impedance. As discussed in chapter 2 using equations (2–26) through (2–34), admittance Y is the reciprocal of impedance. Its real and imaginary components are called, respectively, conductance G and susceptance B. To find these admittance components, in terms of their ratio to the characteristic admittance of the line Y_0 (= $1/Z_0$), is extremely simple using the Smith Chart. The radial line for the applicable value of d/λ is merely extended (as shown dashed in Fig. 9–25) until it intercepts the opposite side of the *VSWR* circle. The values of G_L/Y_0 and B_L/Y_0 are then read at this point, from the same set of orthogonal circles that represent R_L/Z_0 and X_L/Z_0 at the intersection of the solid radial d/λ line with the *VSWR* circle. In this particular example it is found that $G_L/Y_0 = 0.26$ and $B_L/Y_0 = +0.6$. Since $Y_0 = 1/Z_0$, if $Z_0 = 50$ ohms then $Y_0 = 0.02$ mho. Consequently $G_L = 0.26 \times 0.02 = 0.0052$ mho, and $B_L = +0.6 \times 0.02 = +0.012$ mho, in this example. (Note that whereas capacitive reactance is negative, capacitive susceptance is positive; inductive susceptance is negative.)

9.13. Antenna Noise Measurement

As pointed out in sec. 7.8, the lowest antenna noise is generally present in the frequency region extending from approximately 1 to 10 GHz. Antennas designed for low noise in this region will generally be at least moderately directive, with a well-defined beam, and they will usually be steerable. Low-noise antennas have moderate or narrow beamwidths, low-side-lobe levels, high ohmic efficiency, and impedances are well matched. An example of a low-noise antenna is the earth-based terminal of a space communications system.

9.13.1. Elementary Noise Theory

The noise performance of an antenna is expressed in terms of a *noise temperature* rating. This rating actually expresses the *available noise power* at the antenna output terminals. "Available" in this context means "deliverable to a matched-impedance load." The use of the somewhat fictitious temperature rating stems from the fact that a basic source of noise in electric circuits is the thermal agitation of electrons in resistive circuit components. From Nyquist (1928), it is known that the open-circuit *rms* noise voltage V_n generated in a resistance of value R ohms at an absolute temperature T is

$$V_n = \sqrt{4kTRB} \text{ volts} \tag{9–17}$$

where k is Boltzmann's constant (1.38×10^{-23} watt-second per Kelvin*), and B is the bandwidth in Hertz within which the noise voltage is measured. (The formula is actually

* Parenthetically, absolute temperatures are correctly expressed in Kelvins and not in degrees Kelvin. Following IEEE (1992, p. 320), the Kelvin or absolute temperature scale is related to the Celsuis and Fahrenheit scales by the formula:

$$T_{\text{Kelvin}} = 273.15 + T_{\text{Celsuis}} = 255.37 + (5/9)T_{\text{Fahrenheit}}$$

an approximation that holds for most conditions at frequencies in the radio spectrum. A more exact formula is required at extremely high frequencies and at extremely low temperatures.)

It is well known that the maximum power that can be delivered by a generator or other source having a given internal electromotive force (open-circuit voltage) is obtained when the external load resistance is equal to the internal resistance of the source. (More generally, the external impedance must be equal to the complex conjugate of the source impedance.) From this it readily follows that the thermal noise power deliverable to this optimum *load* by a thermal noise *source* of resistance R at temperature T is

$$P_n = \frac{V_n^2}{4R} = kTB \text{ watts} \tag{9–18}$$

Hence the quantity kTB is the *available noise power*. It does not depend on the particular value of resistance, but only on the absolute temperature T (for a given bandwidth B). Therefore it has become customary to rate a noise source whose available noise power is P_n in terms of its equivalent noise temperature calculated from (9–18)—that is, $T = P_n/kB$. This rating practice is followed even where the noise is not actually of thermal origin, provided it "resembles" thermal noise in statistical and frequency spectrum characteristics.

A thermal-noise voltage is a randomly fluctuating voltage that conforms to a particular statistical law and contains a uniform mixture of all frequencies within the radio spectrum—or, in particular, within any selected band, such as the intermediate frequency (i–f) passband of a receiver. The general appearance of a noise-voltage waveform, as viewed on an oscilloscope connected to the output of a receiver (after detection), is shown in Fig. 9–26. This waveform is the half-wave-rectified "envelope" of the rf noise; the rf cycles have been filtered out. (Such noise is sometimes called "grass.")

Because of their statistically random nature, noise voltages from two different (independent) sources are uncorrelated. Thus, when combined or superimposed in a circuit or as electromagnetic waves in space, they add so that the resultant *rms* voltage (or field intensity) is the square root of the sum of the squares (root-sum-square) of the superimposed voltages (or fields). Consequently, the resultant noise power is the sum of the individual-component noise powers; it is unnecessary to consider whether phase relationships cause addition, cancellation, or some intermediate result. This deduction follows from the fact that the relative phases of uncorrelated noise voltages fluctuate; they do not maintain a constant relationship over time. Therefore, if an antenna receives noise contributions from a number of independent sources, the total noise power (temperature) will be simply the sum of the individual noise powers (temperatures).

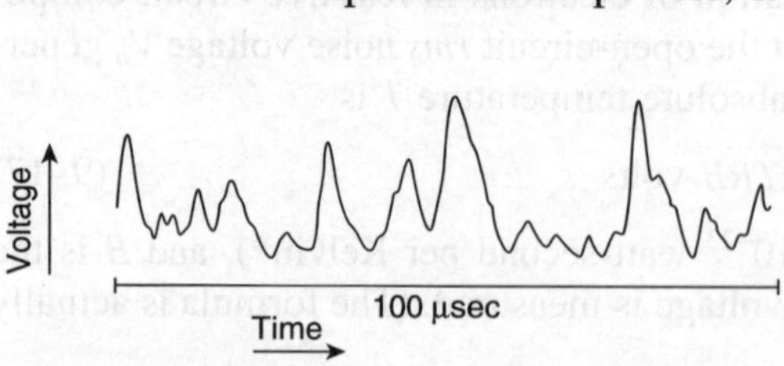

FIGURE 9–26.

Oscillogram of a typical time sample of detected thermal noise; 100-μsec sample, amplifier bandwidth 500 kHz.

The mathematical analysis of noise, the interrelationships of signals and noise, and the physical origins of noise have been intensively investigated, and an extensive literature exists. See, for example, Blake (1986, ch. 4) or Davenport and Root (1987).

9.13.2. Antenna Noise Temperature

As was pointed out in sec. 7.8, antenna noise comes from a number of sources, both external and internal to the antenna. The internal sources are thermal in nature and are due to ohmic losses. The sources of external noise are graphically depicted in Fig. 9–27. The mechanism of generating electromagnetic thermal noise waves in dissipative propagation media, such as the earth, and in the atmosphere at frequencies where it partially absorbs radio waves, is similar to that of thermal noise generation in resistive circuit elements. Noise radiated from some sources, such as the galactic system of which the earth and the sun are members, is not truly thermal in nature, but within limited bandwidths it resembles thermal noise, so that its contribution to total antenna noise may be described in terms of an equivalent noise temperature.

Because some of the external noise is unavoidable, when an antenna noise temperature is measured it is necessary to evaluate the result in relation to the minimum possible noise temperature that could be achieved at the operating frequency. From measurements from many workers on the various noise sources depicted in Fig. 9–27, and by using the principle of addition of noise power from independent sources, it is possible to plot curves of approximate noise temperatures of an ideal antenna as a function of frequency. Figure 9–28 includes such curves.

Calculated noise temperatures for an ideal antenna in the frequency range from 100 MHz to 100 GHz, due to galactic and atmospheric noise are included in Fig. 9–28. In the left-hand region, below 1 GHz, the maximum values will be observed if the antenna is pointing toward the center of the galaxy (the "hottest" part of the sky, in radio-astronomical parlance); whereas the minimum values are observed toward the galactic poles (where the sky is "cold"). In the right-hand region, above 1 GHz, the maximum values are observed with an antenna pointed toward the horizon (elevation angle $\theta = 0°$), looking through the thickest possible section of the atmosphere; whereas the lowest values are observed looking straight up, toward the zenith ($\theta = 0°$). Noise temperature maxima caused by water vapor and oxygen resonances can be seen centered at 22 GHz and 60 GHz, respectively. The values shown in Fig. 9–28 assume that there is no noise due to ohmic losses in the antenna, and none due to ground noise received via minor lobes of the pattern. That is, the antenna is assumed to be lossless and to have no minor lobes. Techniques for minimizing losses and minor lobes are discussed in sec. 7.8.

Experience shows that the noise temperature of a well-designed low-noise antenna in the 1 to 10 GHz range should be less than 60 K, and it may be as low as 4.5 K. This latter value was reported (DeGrasse et al. 1959) from use of a 5.65-GHz horn-reflector antenna of the type described in sec. 7.8 (the same type used in the Telstar satellite communication system). Of the 4.5 K, 2.5 K was attributed to tropospheric noise, and the remaining 2 K to ground noise, via minor lobes.

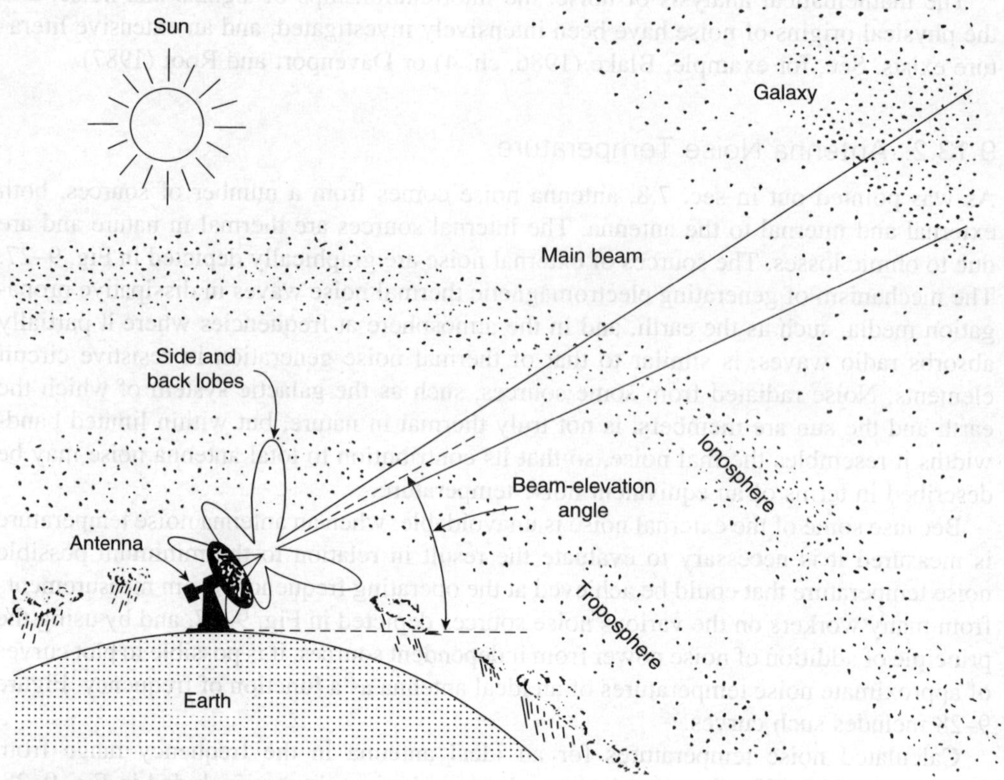

FIGURE 9–27.
External sources of antenna noise.

9.13.3. Measurement Techniques

As in antenna gain measurement, the most convenient technique of measurement of noise temperature is comparison with a source of known (and variable) noise temperature. Figure 9–29 shows the measurement set-up.

The switch in this arrangement must be a high-quality transmission-line switch—a coaxial switch if the line is coaxial, or a waveguide switch when the line is waveguide. It is first set to connect the receiver input to the antenna, and the receiver gain is adjusted to cause the output meter to read a convenient value.

FIGURE 9–28.
Noise temperature of an idealized antenna located on the earth's surface, as a function of frequency and beam elevation angle θ (from Blake 1969).

This reading is noted. The antenna should be pointing straight overhead (zenith direction) when this reading is taken, or at as high an angle as possible. The measurement should be performed in clear weather, with no precipitation or overcast, and at a time when the sun is low in the sky so that it will not be in the main-beam of the antenna pattern. At frequencies below 1 GHz, the approximate galactic temperature should be estimated in the overhead direction, from published sky-noise maps (see, e.g., Ko 1958).

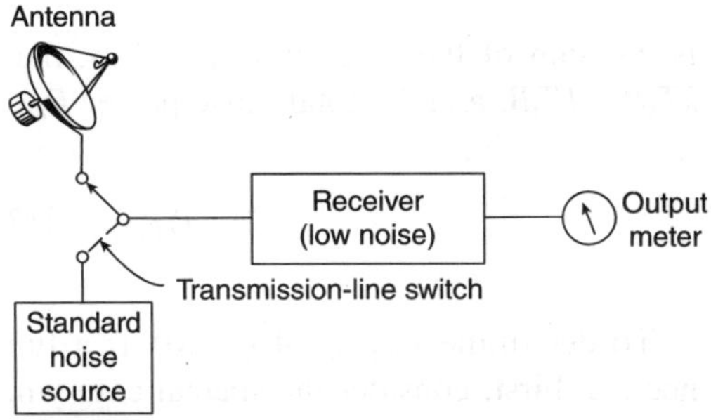

FIGURE 9–29.

Set-up for antenna noise temperature measurement.

Next the switch is connected to the calibrated variable noise source, and its effective temperature (noise power output) is adjusted until the output meter reading is the same as that previously noted. The noise temperature of the calibrated source is then the same as that of the antenna. It is essential that the receiver gain remains constant during the entire measurement procedure. Also, the antenna and the noise source must be equivalently matched to the receiver.

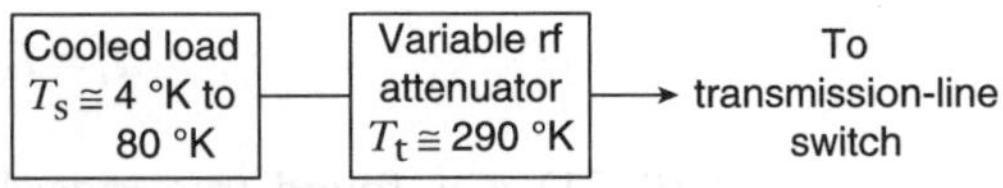

FIGURE 9–30.

Method of obtaining variable noise output from a fixed-temperature source.

A variable-temperature source may be obtained by using a constant-temperature source and an attenuator. The arrangement is shown schematically in Fig. 9–30, where T_s is the temperature of the cooled source and T_t is the temperature of the attenuator. This method is described in a paper by Schuster, Stelzried, and Levy (1962). The attenuator affects the output temperature of the source-attenuator combination in two ways. First, it attenuates the noise from the source. Second, it generates thermal noise itself, since it is a lossy device at a nonzero thermodynamic temperature. Not all the noise thus generated is delivered to the receiver; part of it is coupled back to the source.

Characteristics of an attenuator that influence its output noise are its thermal temperature and its loss factor. The loss factor L is defined as the ratio power input to power output. Therefore, L is the reciprocal of transmission efficiency. Stated differently, $L = 1/G$, where G is power gain (which for an attenuator $G \leq 1$). Thus, that part of the attenuator output noise power P_{source} due exclusively to the input noise source of temperature T_s is

$$P_{source} = kT_sB\left(\frac{1}{L}\right) \tag{9–19}$$

Now let T_i be the equivalent noise temperature, and thus kT_iB the noise power, that reaches the attenuator input. Recall that the available power from separate noise sources is the sum of the noise powers. Thus, the total noise power at the attenuator input is $kT_sB + kT_iB$, and the total noise power $P_{n(total)}$ at the attenuator output is

$$P_{n(total)} = [kT_sB + kT_iB]\frac{1}{L} \tag{9–20}$$

To determine $P_{n(total)}$ of (9–20) as a function of T_s, T_t, and L, an equation for T_i is needed. First, consider the special case when the attenuator thermal temperature T_t and he noise source temperature T_s are equal. Then, $P_{n(total)}$ necessarily equals kT_tB because is the only temperature present. By solving (9–20) when $T_s = T_t$ and $P_{n(total)} = kT_tB$, seen that T_i, the equivalent noise temperature that reaches the attenuator input, nes

$$T_i = T_t(L-1) \tag{9–21}$$

t (9–21) was found true regardless of the magnitudes of either T_s and T_t, nly that $T_s = T_t$. In fact, Dicke et al. (1946) report that noise power lly by an attenuator is always equal to (9–21). Consequently, by replacing th $T_t(L - 1)$, one finds that attenuator output power versus T_s, T_t, and

$$_{tal)} = [kT_sB + kT_t(L-1)B]\frac{1}{L} = kB\left[\frac{T_s}{L} + T_t\left(1-\frac{1}{L}\right)\right] \tag{9–22}$$

nship $P_{n(total)} = kBT_n$ with T_n being the effective noise tempera- ut terminals, one finds

$$T_n = \frac{T_s}{L} + T_t\left(1-\frac{1}{L}\right) \tag{9–23}$$

t can be seen from (9–23) that $T_n = T_t$, whereas if g L effective noise temperatures in the approximate ethod of Fig. 9–29.

cibels, and the decibel attenuation expressed as a s given by

$$\text{og}\left(\frac{A_{dB}}{10}\right) \tag{9–24}$$

measurements is 290 K (IEEE, 1992, p. 8° C (62.3° F). The method (Fig. 9–30) ill yield values that range from T_s up is less than or greater than 290 K.

Ordinarily T_s is less than 290 K, if it is presumed that the antenna noise temperature a low-noise antenna is to be measured.

9.13.4. Low-Noise-Temperature Comparison Sources

To measure a low-antenna noise temperature, a comparison source of noise with a temperature near that of the antenna is required. The ordinary "dummy load" or resistive termination of a transmission line or guide will have a noise temperature equal to its thermal temperature, in accordance with the Nyquist equations (9–17) and (9–18). Since the thermal ambient temperature is ordinarily around 290 K, such a load must be artificially cooled to obtain a low-noise source. This is the method actually employed.

If the load is cooled in a cryostat with liquid nitrogen, a noise temperature of about 80 K will result (–193.2° C, –315.7° F). This is low enough for measurement of moderately low antenna noise temperatures. But for very low-antenna temperatures a lower comparison source is preferred. One may be obtained by using liquid helium in place of the liquid nitrogen. The resulting noise temperature is about 4 K.

These very low values of noise temperature are effective only if the load is connected to the receiver through a very low-loss transmission line. If appreciable loss is present, the effective temperature will be increased in accordance with (9–23). This is the mechanism used for providing increased effective noise temperatures when values higher than those of the cooled load are required.

9.13.5. Measurements Using Ambient Temperature Noise Sources

According to Imbriale (2007, p. 45-21), a variety of noise temperature techniques and measurements are used in connection with the National Aeronautical and Space Administration (NASA) Deep Space Network (DSN) program. The low noise ground-based systems are typically calibrated by injecting a known amount of power into a receiver input. However, it can be difficult to accurately determine the noise temperature of this power when referenced to the receiver input, because of different temperatures and losses of the components and transmission line between the noise source and the receiver.

Also according to Imbriale (2007, p. 45-22), the ambient temperature method described by Stelzried (1971) eliminates the difficulty of calibrating the noise source temperature and it is most often used for low noise (<<300 K) receiving systems in the DSN program. Note that from (9–23) above, with $T_s = T_t$ the output temperature T_n equals T_s and T_t. In other words, with the noise source and its connecting components all at the same ambient temperature, the noise source temperature available is the ambient temperature, independent of the component losses.

The ambient temperature technique is used to determine the receiver operating noise temperature T_{op}, with $T_{op} = T_a + T_e$, T_a = antenna noise temperature, and T_e = receiver effective noise temperature at the receiver input. A measurement is made by alternately connecting the receiver input with a waveguide switch between the antenna and a matched load at ambient temperature load. Thus, the measurement is made by carefully determining the ratio R, where

$$R = \frac{T_p + T_e}{T_a + T_e} = \frac{T_p + T_e}{T_{op}}$$

with

T_p = physical temperature K of ambient termination
T_e = receiver effective noise temperature K at its input
T_a = antenna noise temperature K

The ratio R is determined by means of a precision attenuator located in the receiver IF stage, which is positioned remotely enough that a change in attenuator settings does not influence the effective receiver input temperature T_e. Another readily met requirement is that the receiver response be linear between its input and the attenuator.

The receiving operating noise temperature T_{op} from the equation for R above is

$$T_{op} = \frac{T_p + T_e}{R} \tag{9–25}$$

Then, T_{op} is calculated by using (9–25) with the measured a value of R, measured ambient temperature T_p, and the effective receiver noise temperature T_e that is either measured or estimated. Notice that if $T_e \ll T_p$, T_e may not need to be known accurately.

9.14. System Noise Calculations

As already discussed, noise temperature is a useful measure for the noise level created by components. Often, however, the term "noise figure" is used to quantify the noise levels created by mixers, amplifiers, and even complete receiving systems. Therefore, the term is introduced in sec. 9.14.1, and its relationship with the concept of system noise temperature is discussed in sec. 9.14.2.

9.14.1. Noise Figure

By definition, noise figure is the actual output noise power relative to the output power if the input noise temperature T_0 is 290 K (IEEE 1992). Specifically, noise figure NF is the ratio of actual output power to the output power kT_0BG, if T_0 were 290 K. Therefore,

$$NF = \frac{P_{no}}{kT_0BG} = \frac{kT_0BG + kT_iBG}{kT_0BG} = \frac{kBG(T_0 + T_i)}{kT_0BG} = 1 + \frac{T_i}{T_0} \tag{9–26}$$

Here, as used previously, B is the noise bandwidth, G is the power gain of the device being evaluated, and T_i is the effective noise temperature of its internally generated noise (referred to the device input). Parenthetically, with T_0 being 290 K, the product kT_0 is

4×10^{-21} watt-second; which is easier to remember than Boltzmann's constant (1.38×10^{-23} watt-sec per Kelvin).

Then, from (9–26) and with T_0 being 290 K, one finds

$$T_i = T_0(NF - 1) = 290(NF - 1) \tag{9–27}$$

Thus, (9–27) gives the internally generated noise temperature T_i of a device when referred to its input in terms of its noise figure NF.

An example is now given on determining the output noise power P_{out} of a transistor amplifier having NF of 2 dB ($NF = 1.58$) and an input source with noise temperature T_s of 200 K. Then, from (9–27) T_i is 290(1.58 – 1) or 168.2 K. Thus, the noise temperature, referred to the device input, is $T_i + T_s$ or 368.2 K. Now assume the noise bandwidth B and gain G are one MHz and 30 dB (1,000), respectively. Thus, the average noise power output P_{out} of the transistor amplifier with input source temperature T_s of 200 K becomes

$$P_{out} = k(T_i + T_s)BG = 1.38 \times 10^{-23}(368.2)10^6 \times 10^3 = 5.08 \times 10^{-12} \text{ watt}$$

9.14.2. System Noise Temperature

Sources of noise within a receiving system include the antenna with its externally received noise, the transmission line between the antenna and the receiver, and the receiver itself. For a narrow-beam antenna and a low-noise receiver, effects of antenna pointing may be observed because the sources of external noise include land and sea surfaces, the sun, galactic radiation, and the atmosphere.

Noise may arise anywhere within the receiving system, so that the noise level is different from point to point within the system. Of great importance, of course, is the noise power at the receiver detector (demodulator). However, for the purpose of a signal-to-noise calculation for a complete system, it is convenient and customary to refer the system output noise to the antenna output. Done in this way, system noise temperature T_{sys} is defined such that the system output power N *referenced to the antenna output* is

$$N = kT_{sys}B \tag{9–28}$$

where

k = 1.38×10^{-23} watt-sec/Kelvin (Boltzmann's constant)
T_{sys} = system noise temperature in Kelvins
B = receiver noise bandwidth

Then, if the net available power gain between the antenna output and the receiver output is G, the actual noise-power of the receiver output is $G\, kT_{sys}B$. Thus it is important to state what reference point has been chosen when the concept of system noise temperature is employed.

In general, the effect of a noise source at one point in the system may be referred to another point by properly multiplying or dividing the source noise power by the net power gain of the components between the two points. Then, when both signal and noise powers are referred to the same point in a system, their ratio is the same as the output signal-to-noise ratio, provided that the gain is the same for signal and noise.

Following Blake (1961), the system noise temperature T_{sys} of a system that includes antenna, transmission line, and the receiver is

$$T_{sys} = T_a + T_r(L_r - 1) + L_r T_e \tag{9–29}$$

where

T_a = antenna noise temperature, referenced to the antenna output, which includes the externally received noise plus the thermal noise of the antenna itself

T_r = thermal temperature of the transmission line between the antenna and the receiver

L_r = the transmission line loss factor

$T_r(L_r - 1)$ = noise temperature of the transmission line referenced to its input (antenna output)

T_e = noise temperature of the receiver referenced to its input

$L_r T_e$ = noise temperature of the receiver referenced to the antenna output

It is important to note that in (9–29), T_a, $T_r(L_r - 1)$, and $L_r T_e$ are each equivalent noise temperatures referenced to the antenna output terminals. The reader will recognize that a transmission line is a fixed attenuator. Therefore, the noise temperature created by the transmission line and referenced to its input (antenna output) may be calculated using (9–27) in sec. 9.14.1. The terms T_e and $L_r T_e$ denote the internally generated receiver noise referenced to the receiver input and to the antenna output, respectively. The factor L_r accounts for the transmission line attenuation between the receiver input and the antenna output. In other words, since $L_r \geq 1$, the noise temperature of the receiver referenced to the antenna output $L_r T_e$ exceeds the internally generated receiver noise temperature T_e referenced to the receiver input.

Alternatively, system noise temperature T_{sys} can be expressed in terms of receiver noise figure NF, by substituting (9–27) into (9–29). Then, T_{sys} becomes

$$T_{sys} = T_a + T_r(L_r - 1) + L_r[290(NF - 1)] \tag{9–30}$$

Sometimes the term *system noise figure* NF_{sys} is used to express the performance of an overall receiving system. In that case, the system noise temperature and the system noise figure are related as follows:

$$T_{sys} = 290(NF_{sys} - 1) \tag{9–31}$$

TABLE 9-1 Calculated System Noise Temperatures. (Assumptions include 300 K transmission line temperature, low and moderate transmission line losses and receiver noise figures.)

NF (receiver)	L_r	T_a	$(L_r\text{-}1)T_r$	$L_r 290(NF\text{-}1)$	T_{sys}
1.5 (1.8 dB)	1.047 (0.2 dB)	60 K	14.1 K	152 K	226 K
1.5 (1.8 dB)	1.047 (0.2 dB)	300 K	14.1 K	152 K	466 K
1.5 (1.8 dB)	2.0 (3 dB)	60 K	300 K	290 K	650 K
1.5 (1.8 dB)	2.0 (3 dB)	300 K	300 K	290 K	890 K
4.0 (6.0 dB)	1.047 (0.2 dB)	60 K	14.1 K	911 K	985 K
4.0 (6.0 dB)	1.047 (0.2 dB)	300 K	14.1 K	911 K	1225 K
4.0 (6.0 dB)	2.0 (3 dB)	60 K	300 K	1740 K	2100 K
4.0 (6.0 dB)	2.0 (3 dB)	300 K	300 K	1740 K	2340 K

Table 9-1 below gives calculated noise temperatures when using the assumptions 300 K transmission line thermal temperature, plus low and moderate values of transmission line losses L_r and receiver noise figures NF. Note that signal-to-noise ratio (SNR) is proportional to system noise temperature T_{sys}. Therefore, significant changes in signal detection performance require substantial changes in the ratios of T_{sys}, system noise temperature. Note that changes in the antenna noise temperature T_a will result in significant improvement in signal-to-noise only if both Lr and NF are very small. From Table 9-1, it is apparent that small values of T_{sys} require small values of both L_r and NF. Notice that as L_r is enlarged, the noise contributions from both the transmission line and from the receiver are increased. It is thus doubly important to place the receiver as close to the antenna output as practicable, for minimizing L_r and to thereby improve the system's signal detection performance.

References

Blake, L. V., "Antenna and Receiving System Noise-Temperature Calculation," *Proceedings of IEEE*, vol. 49, October 1961, pp. 1568–69.

Blake, L. V., "A Guide to Basic Pulse-Radar Maximum-Range Calculation," Naval Research Laboratory 6930, December 23, 1969; also see L. V. Blake, ch. 2 in M. I. Skolnik (ed.), *Radar Handbook*, 2nd ed., McGraw-Hill, 1990, p. 2.29.

Blake, L. V., ch. 4, *Radar Range-Performance Analysis*, Artech House, 1986; or ch. 4, Munro Publishing, 1991.

Bodnar, D. G., "Feed Study for USAEPG Compact Range," Final Technical Report, Project A-3922, Georgia Tech Research Institute, August 1986.

Cain, F. L., and K. G. Byers, Jr., "Statistical Gain Characteristics of Radar Antennas at Very Short Fresnel Zone Distances," *IEEE Transactions on Electromagnetic Compatibility, EMC-11*, February 1969; pp. 1–9.

Cain, F. L., and K. G. Byers, Jr., "Relations of Site Effects to Statistical Gain Characteristics of Radar Antennas," *1968 IEEE Electromagnetic Compatibility Symposium Record*, pp. 339–48.

Cain, F. L., J. W. Cofer, and H. A. Ecker, "Prediction Method to Statistically Determine Potential Antenna Interference," *Proceedings of the IEEE International Symposium on Electromagnetic Compatibility*, July 1970, pp. 407–16.

Cain, F. L., C. E. Ryan, and B. J. Cown, "Prediction of Near-Field Antenna Coupling in the Presence of Obstacles," *Proceedings of the IEEE International Symposium on Electromagnetic Compatibility*, July 1972, pp. 310–14.

Cain, F. L., E. E. Weaver, and E. F. Duffy, "Prediction of Near-Field Coupling between Misaligned Antennas," *Proceedings of the IEEE International Symposium on Electromagnetic Compatibility*, July 1974, pp. 1–7.

Chang, D., C. Liao, and C. Wu, "Compact Antenna Test Range without Reflector Edge Treatment and RF Anechoic Chamber," *IEEE Antennas and Propagation Magazine*, August 2004, pp. 27–37.

Cotton, H. P., "Development of an Outdoor Compact Antenna Range," *ITEA Journal of Test and Evaluation*, vol. 9, no. 1, 1988, pp. 28–31.

Cutler, C. C., A. P. King, and W. E. Kock, "Microwave Antenna Measurements," *Proceedings of the IRE*, December 1947, pp. 1462–71.

Davenport, W. B., and W. L. Root, *An Introduction to the Theory of Random Signals and Noise*, Wiley-IEEE Press, 1987.

DeGrasse, R. W., D. C. Hogg, E. A. Ohm, and H. E. D. Scovil, "Ultra low noise measurements using a horn reflector antenna and a traveling wave maser," *Journal of Appied.Physics*, vol. 30, December 1959, p. 2013.

Dicke, R. H., et al., "Atmospheric Absorption Measurements with a Microwave Radiometer," *Physical Review* 70, Sept. 1946, pp. 340–48.

Dyson, J. D., "Measurement of Near Fields of Antennas and Scatterers," *IEEE Transactions on Antennas and Propagation*, vol. AP-21, July 1973, pp. 446–60.

Hansen, J. E., *Spherical Near-Field Antenna Measurements*, Peter Peregrines Press, 1988.

Hemming, L. H., and R. A. Heaton, "Measurement of the Radiation Patterns of Full-Scale HF and VHF Antennas," *IEEE Transactions on Antennas and Propagation*, July 1973, pp. 532–38.

Hess, D. W., and R. C. Johnson, "Compact Ranges Provide Accurate Measurement of Radar Cross Section," *Microwave Systems News*, September 1982, pp. 150–60.

Hickman, T. G., and R. C. Johnson, "Boresight Measurements Utilizing a Compact Range," Abstracts of the 1972 Spring USNC/URSI Meeting, Washington, D.C., April 13–15, 1972, p. 11.

Hollis, J. S., T. J. Lyon, and L. Clayton, *Microwave Antenna Measurements*, Scientific-Atlanta, Inc., 1970. This publication may be available through MI Technologies, Inc. (www.mi-technologies.com).

IEEE, *The New IEEE Standard Dictionary of Electrical and Electronic Terms*, 1992.

IEEE Standard Test Procedures for Antennas, The Institute of Electrical and Electronics Engineers, Inc., IEEE Standard 149, 1979.

Imbriale, W. A., "Earth Station Antennas," ch. 45 in *Antenna Engineering Handbook*, 4th ed., J. L. Volakis (ed.), McGraw-Hill, 2007.

Johnson, R. C., "Mutual Gain of Radar Search Antennas," *Proceedings of the Ninth Tri-Service Conference on Electromagnetic Compatibility*, IIT Research Institute, Chicago, Illinois, October 1963.

Johnson, R. C., "Radar Search Antennas and RFI," *IEEE Transactions on Electromagnetic Compatibility, EMC-6*, July 1964, pp. 1–8.

Johnson, R. C., "Antenna Range for Providing a Plane Wave for Antenna Measurements," U. S. Patent 3,302,205, January 31, 1967.

Johnson, R. C., H. A. Ecker, and J. S. Hollis, "Determination of Far-Field Antenna Patterns from Near-Field Measurements," *Proceedings of the IEEE*, December 1973; pp. 1668–94.

Johnson, R. C., H. A. Ecker, and R. A. Moore, "Compact Range Techniques and Measurements," *IEEE Transactions on Antennas and Propagation*, September 1969, pp. 568–76.

Joy, E. B., and D. T. Paris, "Spatial sampling and filtering in near-field Measurements," *IEEE Transactions on Antennas and Propagation*, vol. AP-20, May 1972, pp. 253–61.

Joy, E. B., and R. E. Wilson, "Shaped Edge Serrations for Improved Compact Range Performance," *Proceedings of the 1987 AMTA Symposium*, Seattle, Washington.

Kerns, D. M., "Plane-Wave Scattering-Matrix Theory of Antennas and Antenna-Antenna Interactions," NBS Monograph 162, National Bureau of Standards, Boulder, CO, June 1981.

Kraus, J. D., *Antennas*, 2nd Edition, McGraw-Hill, 1988.

Ko, H. C., "The Distribution of Cosmic Background Radiation," *Proceedings of the IRE*, 46, No. 1, January 1958, pp. 208–15.

Leach, W. M., Jr., and D. T. Paris, "Probe Compensated Near-Field Measurements on A Cylinder," *IEEE Transactions on Antennas and Propagation*, July 1973; pp. 435–45.

Lee, T. H., and W. D. Burnside, "Performance Trade-Off Between Serrated Edge and Blended Rolled Edge for Compact Range Reflectors," *IEEE Transactions on Antennas and Propagation*, January 1996, pp. 87–96.

Long, M. W., "Wide Angle Radiation Measurements," *Proceedings of the 6th Conference on Radio Interference Reduction and Electronic Compatibility*, IIT Research Institute, Chicago, Illinois, October 1960.

Mahmoud, M. S. A., T. H. Lee, and W. D. Burnside, "Enhanced Compact Range Concept Using an R-Card Fence: Two-Dimensional Case," *IEEE Transactions on Antennas and Propagation*, March 2001, pp. 419–28.

Nyquist, H., "Thermal Agitation of Electric Charge in Conductors," *Physical Review*, vol. 32, July 1928, pp. 110–13.

Pearson, L. W., X. Wang, D. G. Bodnar, and B. Tian, "Spherical Near-Field Scanning Measurements of Base Station Antennas," 2007 Antenna Systems / Short-Range Wireless Conference, Denver, Co, Sept 26, 2007.

Pistorius, C. W., and W. D. Burnside, "An Improved Main Reflector Design for Compact Range Reflectors," *IEEE Transactions on Antennas and Propagation*, March 1987, pp. 342–47.

Schuster, D., C. T. Stelzried, and G. S. Levy, "The Determination of Noise Temperatures of Large Paraboloidal Antennas," *IRE Transactions on Antennas and Propagation*, vol. AP-10, no. 3, May 1962, 286–91.

Smith, P. H., "An Improved Transmission Line Calculator," *Electronics*, vol. 17, January 1944, pp. 130–33.

Stelzried, C. T., "Operating Noise-Temperature Calibrations of Low-Noise Receiving Systems," *Microwave Journal*, vol. 14, June 1971, p. 41.

Volakis, J. L., *Antenna Engineering Handbook*, 4th ed., McGraw-Hill, 2007.

Yaghjian, A. D., "An Overview of Near-Field Antenna Measurements," *IEEE Transactions on Antennas and Propagation*, vol. AP-34, January 1986, pp. 30–45.

Problems and Exercises

1. A paraboloidal-reflector antenna is designed for operation at 3 GHz. Its largest aperture dimension is 20 feet. At what minimum distance should a far-field range antenna be placed for use in measuring the radiation pattern?
2. An electrically short vertical radiator (monopole) at 100 kHz has an input power of 5000 watts. At a distance of 5 km, the field strength is 0.082 volts rms per meter. What is the radiation efficiency of this antenna? (Assume $F = 1$, $D = 3$.)
3. The two terminals of an antenna pattern range are on opposite shores of a lake that is 2 km wide. Two identical paraboloidal antennas are mounted on towers at these terminals and are aimed at each other. One is used as a transmitting antenna with a power input of 10 watts. The other antenna receives a signal whose power level is measured and found to be 1.5 mw at the antenna output terminals. The operating frequency is 100 MHz. It has been determined that the propagation factor, due to the interference of direct waves and reflected waves from the lake surface, is $F = 1.9$. What are the gains of these antennas?
4. A microwave lens has a circular aperture whose diameter is 3 meters. Its directivity at 10 GHz is measured and found to be $D = 59{,}000$. What is the aperture efficiency?
5. A gain-standard horn is known to have a gain $G = 12.5$. It is being used to measure the gain of a large directional antenna by the comparison method. When the antenna being measured is connected to the receiver, it is found to be necessary to insert an attenuator adjusted to attenuate by 23 dB, in order to have the same receiver output that was observed with the horn connected. What is the gain of the large antenna? Express the answer both as a power ratio and in decibels.
6. It is desired to build a scale model of the antenna of Problem 1, with the largest aperture dimension scaled to 18 inches. (a) At what frequency must this model be operated in order to have the same pattern as the full-size antenna? (b) At what minimum distance should a far-field range antenna now be placed for pattern measurement?

7. A dummy antenna connected to a receiver consists of a resistance of proper value to match the receiver input impedance. It is cooled with liquid nitrogen to a temperature of 80 K. The receiver has a power gain factor of 10^{16} (160 dB). Its bandwidth is 100 kHz. If the receiver were ideal, in the sense that it contained no internal noise sources, what would its noise power output be, with this dummy antenna connected to its input terminals?

8. A paraboloidal antenna used for satellite communication is pointed at the zenith sky, and the receiver gain is advanced until a measureable noise output is observed on an output meter. The reading is noted. Then the receiver input is switched to a liquid-helium-cooled load at 4 K whose impedance is identical to that of the paraboloidal antenna. An attenuator, which does not change the impedance presented to receiver, is connected between the load and the receiver. Its actual (thermal) temperature is $T_t = 300$ K. When its attenuation is adjusted so that the loss factor is $L = 1.05$, the noise output meter is observed to have the reading that was noted with the antenna connected. What is the noise temperature of the paraboloidal antenna? (*Note:* At high microwave frequencies, some error may be incurred by using equations based on Nyquist's approximation, equation (9–17), at the very low temperature of liquid helium; but for the purposes of this problem, assume that the equations given in this chapter are valid.)

9. A receiving system has the following properties: noise bandwidth 1.0 MHz, antenna noise temperature 200 K, receiver noise figure 6 dB, transmission line line thermal temperature 20° C, transmission loss 1.0 dB. What is the receiver noise temperature referenced to the antenna output?

10. For the receiving system of Problem 9, show that the system noise temperature is 1,365 K.

11. For the receiving system of Problem 9, find the signal-to-noise ratio expressed in dB, for a received signal level of 10^{-10} watt at the antenna output.

Answers to Problems

Chapter 1

1. 2.59 *v/m*
3. (a) 1.93×10^{-8} w/m^2. (b) 7.16×10^{-6} a/m
5. 15.52°
7. (a) 159 km. (b) 198 km.
9. 1.27×10^{-5} w/m^2

Chapter 2

1. The plotted curve is a sinusoid of unit amplitude, with its negative maximum at x approximately 0.75 m and its positive maximum at x approximately 2.25 m.
3. (a) $I_{rms} = -0.22 - j1.82$ amp; $|I_{rms}| = 1.83$ amp
   (b) $\phi = -96.9°$
5. (a) 215.4 ohms. (b) $L = 3.43 \times 10^{-6}$ henry (3.43 μh)
7. (a) $r = 0.52 + j\,0.3$; $r = |r|e^{j\phi}$ with $|r| = 0.6$ and $\phi = 30°$
   (b) $Z_L = 1198 + j1125$
9. 50 ohms

Chapter 3

1. (a) F; (b) T; (c) T; (d) F; (e) F; (f) F
3. $D = \dfrac{4\pi}{\Omega} = 2.1 \times 10^5$, or 53.2 dB
5. (a) 23.9 m^2 (b) 5.5 m
7. (a) $R_r = 75 - 8 = 67$ ohms (b) $k_r = 67/75 = 0.89$ (c) $G = 1.46$
9. N

Chapter 4

1. The radiation field is ten times the reactive field at distance $r = 10$ m.
3. (a) 12.5a. (b) 2.5a. (c) Zero

5. (a) $n = 3$ ($\theta_{max} = 45°$) (b) NE-SW or NW-SE
7. (a) $\theta_E = 56°$ and $\theta_H = 67°$ (b) 6.5 or 8.1 dB, using Eq. 4–24.
9. Approximately 33 ohms, from Sec. 4–3.

Chapter 5

1. (a) $\alpha = 120°$.

   (b)

ϕ	0°, 180°	30°, 150°	60°, 120°	90°	210°, 330°	240°, 300°	270°
E	0.50	0.71	0.83	0.87	0.26	0.07	0

3. $$E_{A(rel)} = \left| \frac{\sin(2\pi \sin\theta \cdot \sin\phi) \cdot \sin\theta}{4\sin\left(\dfrac{\pi}{2}\sin\theta \cdot \sin\phi\right)} \right|$$
5. (a) $0.45\pi = 1.4$ radians $= 81°$.
   (b) $E(90°) = 0.647$; $E(270°) = 0.159$. Front-to-back electric-intensity ratio: 4.07 (12.2 dB).
7. (a) Area = 20 square meters; side length 4.5 meters approx.
   (b) 361 dipoles.
9. The angle of the V should be 52 degrees (actually 51.7° is the result obtained by doubling the angle calculated from equation (4–14) with $n = 10$).

Chapter 6

1. From Eq. 6–1, $(D/2)^2 = (4)(10)(6.4) = 256$. (a) Therefore, $D_a = 32$ feet. (b) $f/D = 10/32 = 0.3125$.
3. $\cot \beta = 0.6 - 1/2.4 = 0.1833$; $\beta = 79.43°$. Therefore (a) $2\beta = 158.9°$. (b) $\tau_2 = -12(79.43/100)^2 = -7.58$ dB. (c) $\tau_1 = 40 \log \cos \beta/2 = -4.56$ dB. Therefore $\tau_1 + \tau_2 = -12.14$ dB. Hence (from tabulation given on p. 238) sidelobe level is about −26 dB.
5. $l = 2d = 1$ meter = 3.28 feet = 39.36 inches. $D_a = 1.414$ meters = 4.64 feet = 55.68 inches.
7. The reflector antenna is: (i) lighter in weight; (ii) less complicated; (iii) less expensive.
9. $\phi = +/-5.74°$

Chapter 7

1. (a) 535 MHz and 825 MHz ($f_1 = 1.07f_0$ and $f_2 = 1.65f_0$).
   (b) 500 MHz and 875 MHz ($f_1 = 1.00f_0$ and $f_2 = 1.75f_0$).
   (Answers within ± 5 MHz of these figures are acceptable.)
3. 31, 38, 48, 75, 94, 117, 146, 183, 229, and 286 Mz.

5. (i) crossed dipoles; (ii) horns; (iii) helixes.
7. (i) When the larger antenna would have virtually the same pattern (directivity) as the electrically small antenna, and
   (ii) the predominant noise in the receiving system is of external origin—that is, enters by way of the antenna.
9. The required angular speed in azimuth is 3 degrees in 0.1 second, or 30 degrees per second. This is equivalent to 1800 degrees per minute, or 5 rpm.

Chapter 8

1. 1.67 ns
2. Zero degrees
5. 2.6 ns
7. 8 degrees
9. (a) 5, (b) 11.25 degrees and 180 degrees

Chapter 9

1. 743 meters or 2438 feet
3. $G = 54$ or 17.3 dB
5. $G = 2512$ or 34 dB
7. 1.1 watt
9. 1088.9 K
11. 37.3 dB

APPENDIX A

Maxwell's Equations

James Clerk Maxwell (1831–1879) is generally regarded the founder of electromagnetic theory, which he conceived in 1864 (Herrera 1991). His theory began with equations that described all previously known results on both electric and magnetic experiment and theory. From those equations he removed a mathematical inconsistency by adding a term to include a then unknown electrical phenomenon, called displacement current. Displacement current flows even in a perfect dielectric. Consequently, his completed equations contain both the previously known conduction current and the up-until-then unheard of displacement current. Electromagnetic (E-M) wave propagation requires the presence of displacement current, a concept invented by Maxwell.

A brief overview of Maxwell's equations follows. These equations appear in numerous books, yet the details of the information they contain are not expressible solely with a few words. The mathematics of Maxwell's equations is complex and thus, without appropriate knowledge and experience, their overarching meanings are not be fully appreciated. These equations are of tremendous importance, because they summarize all known laws of electromagnetics. In fact, the existence of E-M wave propagation was not recognized until after the development of these equations.

E-M fields are described in terms of four quantities (**E**, **H**, **B**, **D**) written in bold type, to indicate that they are vectors having both magnitude and direction. **E** and **H** are the electric and magnetic intensities, respectively. **D** is the electric displacement and **B** is the magnetic induction. The sources of the E-M fields are electric charge and current, which are in general functions of both time and position. The symbol ρ denotes electric charge, a scalar term having magnitude only; and current is described by current density **J**, a vector.

Discourses on E-M theory often begin with a presentation of the four Maxwell equations, (A–1) through (A–4) below. The International System of Units (abbreviated SI), a modern version of the metric system, is used. These equations employ two commonly used partial differential functions, from vector calculus, called divergence (abbreviated div) and curl, as follow:

$$\textbf{div}\ \mathbf{D} = \nabla \cdot \mathbf{D} = \rho \tag{A–1}$$

$$\textbf{div}\ \mathbf{B} = \nabla \cdot \mathbf{B} = 0 \tag{A–2}$$

$$\textbf{curl}\ \mathbf{E} = \nabla \times \mathbf{E} = \frac{-\partial \mathbf{B}}{\partial t} \tag{A–3}$$

$$\textbf{curl}\ \mathbf{H} = \nabla \times \mathbf{H} = \mathbf{J} + \frac{\partial \mathbf{D}}{\partial t} \tag{A–4}$$

Equations (A–5) and (A–6) that follow include the definitions of divergence and curl in rectangular coordinates.

$$\text{div}\ \mathbf{A} = \nabla \cdot \mathbf{A} = \frac{\partial A_x}{\partial x} + \frac{\partial A_y}{\partial y} + \frac{\partial A_z}{\partial z} \tag{A–5}$$

$$\text{curl}\ \mathbf{A} = \nabla \times \mathbf{A} = \mathbf{i}\left(\frac{\partial A_z}{\partial y} - \frac{\partial A_y}{\partial z}\right) + \mathbf{j}\left(\frac{\partial A_x}{\partial z} - \frac{\partial A_z}{\partial x}\right) + \mathbf{k}\left(\frac{\partial A_y}{\partial x} - \frac{\partial A_x}{\partial y}\right) \tag{A–6}$$

No attempt in made here to provide the mathematics required for a comprehensive understanding of Maxwell's equations. Instead, the equations are included to provide a glimpse into the nature of the Maxwell theory. Equations (A–1) through (A–4) are E-M field equations from which the electric and magnetic fields, produced by charge density ρ and current density **J**, can be determined. The fields also depend on the material medium in which they exist; thus additional fundamental equations are applicable that involve conductivity σ (reciprocal of resistivity), electric permittivity ε, and magnetic permeability μ. Other applicable equations are Ohm's law, expressed as $\mathbf{E} = \mathbf{J}/\sigma$, and the electric and magnetic field relationships $\mathbf{D} = \varepsilon\mathbf{E}$ and $\mathbf{B} = \mu\mathbf{H}$.

A brief mention is now made of the physical meaning of Maxwell's four equations. Equation (A–1) can be interpreted as saying that the **E**-field vector is a direct measure of the total enclosed electric charge ρ. From (A–2), it can be reasoned that no magnetic flux line **B** has a beginning or end. Equation (A–3) is from Faraday's law, which states that electromagnetic force is induced in a circuit by time rate of change in **B**. In (A–1) through (A–3) plus (A–7) below, Maxwell encapsulated mathematically all electrical properties that had been experimentally verified. The development of these equations was truly significant. However, without question, the invention of (A–4) was even more significant, because it contained predictions that had never been observed.

Maxwell's development of (A–4) began with an equation that can be expressed as

$$\text{curl}\ \mathbf{H} = \mathbf{J}, \tag{A–7}$$

that describes previous experimental observations of the magnetic field **H** resulting from a steady current density **J**. However, from vector calculus it is known that div curl **A** is zero. Therefore div $\mathbf{J} = 0$, which means that "the current is always closed and there are no sources or sinks" (Slater and Frank 1947, p. 84). Plates of a capacitor are examples of both a source and a sink. In this regard, consider discharging a capacitor. Current starts at the positive plate, its charge decreases as the current flows to the negative plate, and there the charge is diminished and removed. Thus, one plate serves as a source and the other a sink.

To mathematically include sinks and sources in electrical phenomena, Maxwell invented displacement current density, which is $\partial \mathbf{D}/\partial t$. It is entirely different than conduction current density $\mathbf{J}$ that flows, for example, because of the conductivity of wire. Beliefs pronounced by Maxwell include (a) displacement current only exists in the presence of a varying field, and (b) displacement and conduction currents will produce, separately or collectively, a magnetic field.

Thus, because matter has both conducting and dielectric properties, Maxwell added $\partial \mathbf{D}/\partial t$ to $\mathbf{J}$ in (A–7) to provide his revolutionary equation (A–4). After this change, the divergence of curl $\mathbf{H}$ from (A–4) is zero and the contradiction between mathematics and physical phenomena, as conjectured by Maxwell, is removed. Then, the combination of (A–3) and (A–4) provide the theoretical mechanism whereby $\mathbf{E}$-fields create $\mathbf{H}$-fields, and conversely; thereby creating electromagnetic waves that propagate indefinitely.

A basis for displacement current density having amplitude $\partial \mathbf{D}/\partial t$ follows. Let

v = voltage across two parallel capacitor plates
d = spacing of the plates
A = area of each plate
ε = dielectric constant
$C = \varepsilon A/d$, where C is capacitance
I = current input to a fixed capacitance

From basic circuit analysis, the current I that flows into a fixed capacitance is related to the change in voltage across its capacitor plates as follows:

$$I = C \cdot (\partial v/\partial t) = (\varepsilon A/d) \cdot (\partial v/\partial t) = \varepsilon A \cdot (\partial \mathrm{E}/\partial \mathrm{t}) = A \cdot (\partial \mathrm{D}/\partial \mathrm{t})$$

Then, the current density along the capacitance plates is I/A, that equals $\partial \mathrm{D}/\partial t$. Thus, since a variable voltage applied to a capacitor forms a closed circuit, the displacement "current" density between the plates equals the current density at the capacitor plates. Therefore, total current density $(\mathbf{J} + \partial \mathbf{D}/\partial t)$ is continuous around the circuit.

Maxwell's equations are simplified when considering plane waves in a uniform material having permittivity ε, magnetic permeability μ, zero conductivity σ, and zero electric charge ρ. Even further simplification occurs if we assume the propagation medium is lossless, so that $\sigma = 0$. Then Maxwell's equations, in differential form, become

$$\text{div } \mathbf{E} = \text{div}(\mathbf{D}/\varepsilon) = 0 \qquad \text{(A–8)}$$

$$\text{div } \mathbf{H} = \text{div}(\mathbf{B}/\mu) = 0 \qquad \text{(A–9)}$$

$$\text{curl } \mathbf{E} = -\mu \frac{\partial \mathbf{H}}{\partial t} \tag{A–10}$$

$$\text{curl } \mathbf{H} = \varepsilon \frac{\partial \mathbf{E}}{\partial t} \tag{A–11}$$

Equations (A–8) through (A–11) are much simpler than (A–1) through (A–4). Equations (A–8) and (A–9) differ from (A–1) and (A–2) only because ρ is now zero. Equation (A–10) says a changing magnetic field will produce an electric field, and (A–11) says that a changing electric field will produce a magnetic field. Since conductivity is assumed zero, (A–11) does not include the conduction current term $\mathbf{J} = \sigma\mathbf{E}$ of (A–4), that otherwise also contributes to producing magnetic field. Equations (A–8) through (A–11) can be solved to obtain the plane wave equations (1–2) and (1–3) of chapter 1 (see, e.g., Slater and Frank 1947, pp. 90–93). However, the necessary mathematical detail is not included here. Instead, the effects of (A–10) and (A–11) on producing E-M waves are now discussed.

As noted above, a changing electric field produces a magnetic field and that in turn produces an electric field, and so on. Thus, there is a series of energy transfers started when either an electric or magnetic disturbance occurs. Energy is transferred from the electric to the magnetic field, and back to the electric field, and repeated indefinitely. Therefore, in this process energy is being transferred from one form to the other as it propagates through space, the result within a uniform material is that electromagnetic waves propagates at constant velocity. Then, the effect of an electric or a magnetic disturbance at one location creates an E-M wave that later reaches another location. The resulting time delay depends on separation distance between the two locations, and on ε and μ that control the propagation velocity.

Maxwell was able to calculate the velocity of electromagnetic waves, if they were to exist, in terms of ε and μ. Then, based on his careful electrical measurements on ε and μ in about 1865, he expected that E-M waves travel at the rate of about 3×10^8 m/s. Furthermore, he collected all the best measurements on the speed of light, and he found that the average of those available to him was about the same that he had predicted from his measurements and wave calculations (Skilling 1942, p. 112). Thus, Maxwell hypothesized that light is an electric wave and it appeared to him that he had substantiated his hypothesis. However, many scientists did not accept Maxwell's hypothesis until 1887. This was when Heinrich R. Hertz proved that radio waves and light have similar properties, including the same velocity in a vacuum.

As a wave passes through an imaginary surface in space, there is a flow of power through the surface area. The power density at the surface can be expressed as a vector **P**, called the Poynting vector after a mathematician of the nineteenth century. In addition to the magnitude of power density, the vector **P** gives the direction of power flow, that is, direction of propagation. In terms of vector analysis,

$$\mathbf{P} = \mathbf{E} \times \mathbf{H} \tag{A–12}$$

where **E** and **H** are the electric and magnetic field vectors. The magnitude of the vector cross product $\mathbf{A} \times \mathbf{B}$ is $A \cdot B \sin \gamma$, where γ is the angle between **A** and **B**. Thus, since **E** and **H** are perpendicular, the magnitude of **P** is simply E·H. With E and H denoting effective (rms) amplitudes, the average of the Poynting vector, that is, power density, is $E^2/377$. The direction of the Poynting vector, as with other cross products, is obtained from a right-hand rule. Specifically, if the fingers of the right hand curve from **E** to **H**, the thumb shows the direction of propagation. Thus, from the relative pointing directions of the **E**- and **H**-fields, one can determine the direction of propagation.

In conclusion, experimental optics and ray analyses for light were known before Maxwell conceived and developed his equations, but without them a theoretical explanation for the propagation of light did not exist. After Maxwell developed the equations in 1864, he used them to calculate the propagation velocity of light, and the calculations agreed with previously measured values. Still later, in 1887, Heinrich Hertz demonstrated that the velocities (and other properties) of radio waves and light were the same. Thus, from the use of Maxwell's equations and experimental observations, the theory of E-M waves was established. Today it is known that the phenomenon of E-M radiation covers the entire energy spectrum from very high frequency cosmic rays to low-frequency, long-wavelength radio waves.

References

Herrera, J. C., "Electromagnetic Radiation," in *Encyclopedia of Physics*, 2nd ed., by R. G. Lerner, R. G. and G. L. Trigg, VCH Publishers, 1991, pp. 285–88.

Skilling, H. H., *Fundamentals of Electric Waves*, John Wiley and Sons, 1942, p. 112.

Slater, J. C., and N. H. Frank, *Electromagnetism*, McGraw-Hill, 1947.

APPENDIX B

Polarization Theory

Wave polarization is introduced in sec. 1.1.3 and further discussed in sec. 3.10. Polarization is a property of an electromagnetic wave, which describes the time-varying direction and amplitude of its E-vector. Specifically, polarization describes the figure traced as a function of time of the extremity of the E-vector at a fixed location in space, when observed looking in the direction of propagation. Polarization of an antenna is defined as the polarization of the far-field wave that it radiates. As discussed in secs. 1.1.3 and 3.10, linearly polarized waves are the most commonly used. When the amplitude of E-vector varies and the E-vector points only up and down, the wave is vertically or V polarized. Similarly, if the amplitude and direction of the E-vector varies and its direction is only horizontal, the wave is horizontally or H polarized. Circular polarization (CP) is the next most frequently used polarization. Its E-field has constant magnitude, but its direction rotates (within a plane) continuously through 360° and it completes a cycle in one wave period.

The most general form of a wave polarization is elliptical. The E-vector of an elliptically polarized wave can be regarded from three viewpoints. Namely, it can be considered to be (1) a rotating vector, the end point of which traces out an elliptical helix whose axis lies in the direction of propagation; (2) the resultant of the E-vectors of two linearly polarized waves of the same frequency; or (3) the resultant of the oppositely rotating E-vectors of two circularly polarized waves of the same frequency. Figure B–1 illustrates the E-vector of an elliptically polarized wave at various positions in space, at a fixed instant of time. An ellipse within an x-y plane is shown at the left end of this spiraling wave. The ellipse is created by tracing the end-point (terminus) of the E-vector onto the x-y plane, during the duration of one rf cycle.

B.1. Elliptically Polarized Waves Resolved into Linearly Polarized Components

An elliptically polarized wave can be created by the vector sum of two linearly polarized waves, polarized along the unit vectors $\boldsymbol{1}_x$ and $\boldsymbol{1}_y$ as follows:

$$\boldsymbol{E} = \boldsymbol{1}_x E_x + \boldsymbol{1}_y E_y \tag{B–1}$$

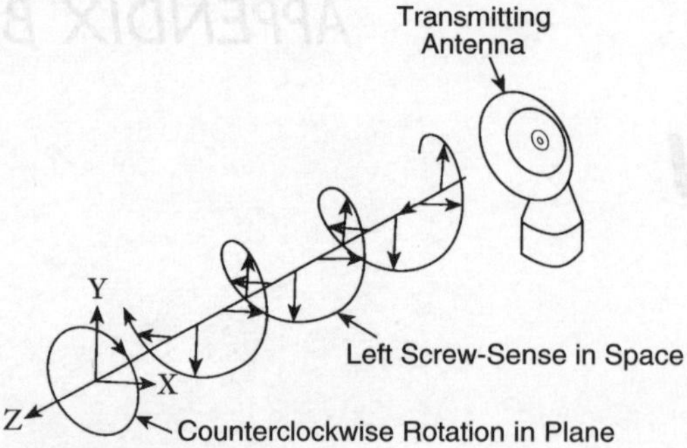

FIGURE B–1.

A left circularly polarized wave exhibits counterclockwise rotation of the E-vector in a plane, when viewed in propagation direction Z. (Adapted from Huynen 1970, p. 10.)

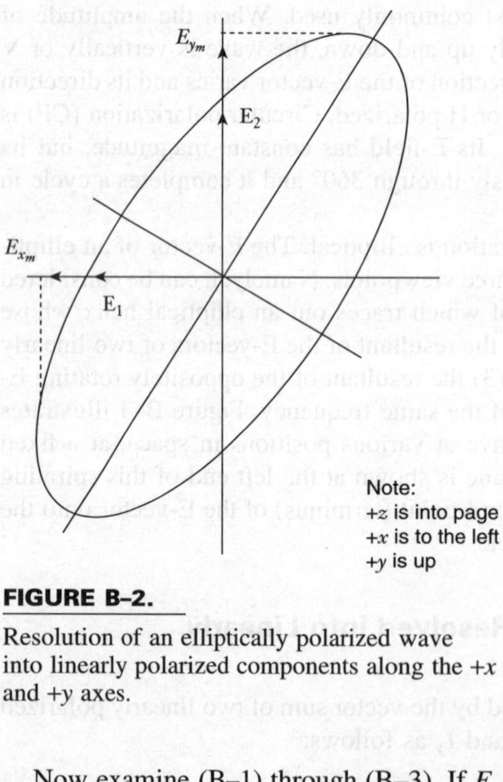

FIGURE B–2.

Resolution of an elliptically polarized wave into linearly polarized components along the +x and +y axes.

where

$$E_x = E_{xm} \sin(\omega t - \gamma z) \qquad \text{(B–2)}$$

and

$$E_y = E_{ym} \sin(\omega t - \gamma z + \delta) \qquad \text{(B–3)}$$

In (B–2) and (B–3), E_{xm} and E_{ym} are the peak amplitudes of the *x*- and *y*-polarized electric fields.

Equations (B–1) through (B–3) describe an elliptically polarized wave of radial frequency ω and with propagation constant γ traveling in the positive *z* direction. There is a phase difference δ between its *x*- and *y*-directed components, which are in space quadrature and which have maximum values E_{xm} and E_{ym}. If viewed in the direction of propagation, the endpoint of the E-vector traces an ellipse on a fixed plane in space, as shown in Fig. B–2. This ellipse is known as a polarization ellipse.

Readers will recognize the similarity of a polarization ellipse and a Lissajous figure. A Lissajous figure is used to determine relative amplitude and relative phase of two equal-frequency sinusoids with an oscilloscope. In the polarization ellipse of Fig. B–2, the E-field is obviously largest when pointed along the major axis and smallest when pointed along the minor axis. Also, notice that the field strengths in Fig. B–2 along the *x*- and *y*-axes are smaller than E_{xm} and E_{ym}, respectively. These properties, as well as major-axis tilt and E-vector rotation direction, depend on the relative phase δ and the ratio E_{xm}/E_{ym}.

Now examine (B–1) through (B–3). If $E_{ym} = 0$, the E-vector varies in magnitude and direction, but it is always along the *x*-axis. Thus, the wave is linearly polarized in the *x* direction. Similarly, if $E_{xm} = 0$, the E-vector is always along the *y*-axis and the wave is linearly polarized in the *y* direction. Now suppose $E_{xm} \neq 0$, $E_{ym} \neq 0$, and $\delta = 0$ or

$\delta = 180°$. Then the amplitudes E_x and E_y are synchronized, being zero and at their maximum amplitudes (E_{xm} and E_{ym}) simultaneously. In this case, however, the tilt angle of the linearly polarized E-field then depends on the ratio E_{xm}/E_{ym}. With $E_{xm} = E_{ym}$ and the special cases $\delta = 0$ or $\delta = 180°$, the linear polarization is oriented at 45° to the X- and the Y-axes.

Other special cases are when $\delta = \pm 90°$. Then, the major axis will lie along the x-axis if $E_{xm} > E_{ym}$ and along the y-axis if $E_{ym} > E_{xm}$. After horizontal and vertical polarizations, circular polarization (CP) is the most frequently used (sec. 7.3). CP is the special case of $\delta = \pm 90°$ and $E_{xm} = E_{ym}$. Using (B–2) and (B–3), let $\delta = 90°$ and $t = z = 0$; then $E_x = 0$ and $E_y = E_{ym}$. Now consider a later time so that $\omega t = 90°$; then $E_x = E_{xm}$ and $E_y = 0$. Thus, **E** rotates from the $+y$ direction to the $+x$ direction during the time that causes ωt to change from zero to 90°. In other words, **E** rotates counter-clockwise when looking *outward* (the direction of propagation); that is, the polarization is left circular. Correspondingly, if $\delta = -90°$ the polarization is right circular.

It should now be apparent that knowledge of the amplitudes of the two orthogonal (perpendicular) linear components and the phase difference between them is sufficient to define a polarization ellipse. Figure B–3 includes the polarization ellipses for selected ratios E_{ym}/E_{xm} and relative phases δ.

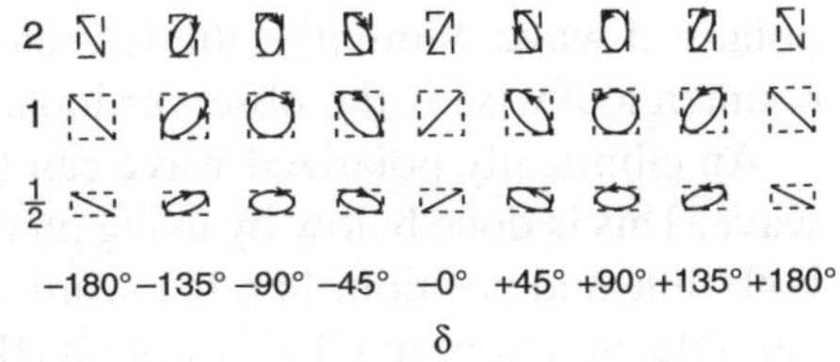

FIGURE B–3.

Polarization ellipses with waves propagating into the page. The polarization is right circular if $\delta = -90°$ and left circular if $\delta = +90°$.

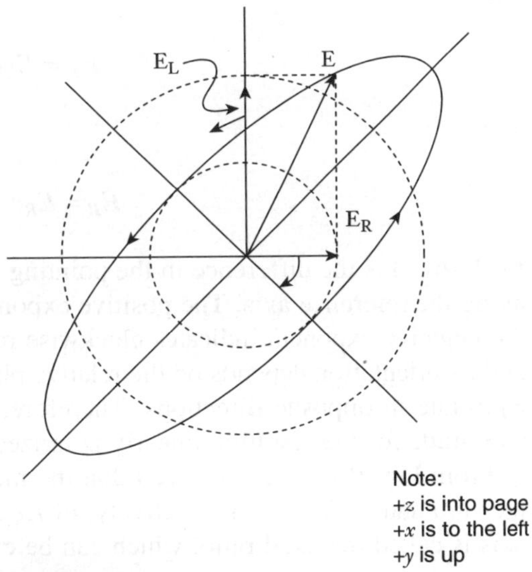

FIGURE B–4.

Resolution of a polarization ellipse into a left-circular E_L and a right-circular E_R polarized wave. Note that the relative phase Δ of E_L and E_R is determined by the orientation of the major axis.

B.2. Elliptically Polarized Waves Resolved into Circularly Polarized Components

The resolution of the rotating E-vector into two circularly polarized components is shown in Fig. B–4, where E_L and E_R are the magnitudes of left circular and right circular waves respectively. A circularly polarized wave which has a clockwise rotation of the E-vector when one looks in the direction of propagation is defined as a right circular, or RC, polarized wave. Similarly, the E-vector of a left circular, or LC, polarized wave rotates counterclockwise if the observer looks in the direction of propagation.

An elliptically polarized wave can be created by the vector sum of an RC and an LC wave. This is done below by using phasor notation to indicate the E-field direction versus both time and position. In other words, the phasor serves the role of a unit vector having variable direction. In (B–4) through (B–6) below, E_L and E_R are the constant amplitudes of the left- and right-circular polarized waves, and bold type indicates a vector having both amplitude and direction.

$$\boldsymbol{E} = \boldsymbol{E_L} + \boldsymbol{E_R} \tag{B–4}$$

where

$$\boldsymbol{E_L} = E_L e^{j(\omega t - \gamma z)} \tag{B–5}$$

and

$$\boldsymbol{E_R} = E_R e^{-j(\omega t - \gamma z + \Delta)} \tag{B–6}$$

In (B–6), Δ is the difference in the pointing *directions* of $\boldsymbol{E_L}$ and $\boldsymbol{E_L}$ when $\boldsymbol{E_L}$ is pointed along the reference axis. The positive exponent indicates counterclockwise rotation and the negative exponent indicates clockwise rotation. If $E_L = E_R$, the polarization is linear and its orientation depends on the relative phase Δ. Note that, at a point in space, $\boldsymbol{E_L}$ and $\boldsymbol{E_L}$ rotate in opposite directions. Therefore, since their amplitudes are equal, the peak amplitude for the resulting linearly polarized wave is $2E_L = 2E_R$.

From Fig. B–4, it can be seen that the major and minor semi-axes of this ellipse are the sum and difference, respectively, of E_R and E_L. The ratio of the major to the minor axis is called the axial ratio, which can be expressed as

$$AR = \frac{E_R + E_L}{|E_R - E_L|} \tag{B–7}$$

From Fig. B–4 it also can be determined that the rotation direction of the E-vector is the same as that of the larger of E_R and E_L. Thus the ratio of the magnitudes of the RC and LC waves determines the direction of rotation, in addition to the axial ratio AR.

B.3. Relationships between Linearly and Circularly Polarized Components

A relationship between the linear and circular resolutions may be obtained by considering the components of the circular waves along the x- and y-axes. The real parts of (B–5) and (B–6) are along the x-axis, and the imaginary parts are along the y-axis. Then the magnitudes of the linearly polarized components are as follows:

$$E_x = E_L \cos(\omega t - \gamma z) + E_R \cos(\omega t - \gamma z + \Delta) \tag{B–8}$$

$$E_y = E_L \sin(\omega t - \gamma z) - E_R \sin(\omega t - \gamma z + \Delta) \tag{B–9}$$

More detailed discussion of the theory of polarized waves can be found in Kraus (1988, pp. 70–80), and in Stutzman (1993, pp. 1–65). Stutzman is also recommended reading on multipolarization antennas, systems, and phenomena. Long (2001) is recommended for reading on the polarization and depolarization properties of radar echoes from land and sea.

The magnitudes of the four polarizations (H, V, RC, LC) may be received simultaneously with four separate antennas. Alternately, the separate signals from two orthogonal linear or two orthogonal circular polarization antennas, when combined appropriately, can be used to obtain simultaneously the magnitudes of the four separately polarized signals. Further, a dual linear or a dual circular polarization feed (coupler) can be employed, thereby allowing the amplitudes of each of the four polarizations to be simultaneously obtained with an appropriately designed antenna.

References

Huynen, J. R., *Phenomenological Theory of Radar Targets*, Drukkerij Bronder-Offset N.V., 1970, p. 10.

Kraus, J, D., *Antennas*, 2nd ed., McGraw-Hill, 1988.

Long, M. W., *Radar Reflectivity of Land and Sea*, 3rd ed., Artech House, 2001.

Stutzman, W. L., *Polarization in Electromagnetic Systems*, Artech House, 1993.

APPENDIX C

Review of Complex-Variable Algebra

Complex variables are (variable) numbers containing the factor j, which is a symbol denoting $\sqrt{-1}$. The notation $\sqrt{-1}$ means "the number that, when squared (multiplied by itself), equals –1." But none of the "real numbers" fits this specification. There is no real number that, when multiplied by itself, equals –1. When any real number, positive or negative, is squared, the result is a positive number. In particular, $(-1)^2 = +1$.

Therefore, the "number" that, when squared, equals –1, represents an extension of the system of real numbers. It is called an "imaginary" number—possibly unfortunate terminology, since it implies something that does not "really" exist. Imaginary numbers exist just as much as do the so-called real numbers. Although j is "imaginary," it need not be mysterious. It is just another way of writing $\sqrt{-1}$. It is a different kind of number from the familiar real numbers, which are 0, ±1, ±2, ±3, etc. Yet obviously it has something in common with them, since the symbol "1," which is part of the quantity $\sqrt{-1}$, is a real number.

When j (or as it is denoted in physics, i) is multiplied by any real number (for example, $j5$ or $-j6$), the resulting product is an imaginary number. Thus the totality of imaginary numbers is obtained by multiplying j by all the real numbers. Another way of writing $j5$ is $5\sqrt{-1}$ or $\sqrt{-25}$. Another way of writing $-j6$ is $-6\sqrt{-1}$ or $-\sqrt{-36}$. (Note that $-\sqrt{-36}$ is not the same thing as $\sqrt{+36}$, which is of course a real number equal to either +6 or –6.)

If two imaginary numbers are multiplied together (for example $j3 \times j5$), the ordinary rules of algebraic multiplication apply. In other words, $j3 \times j5 = j^2 15$. But $j^2 = j \times j = \sqrt{-1} \times \sqrt{-1} = -1$. Therefore, $j3 \times j5 = -15$, which is a real number. Thus *the product of two imaginary numbers is a real number* (further evidence that imaginary numbers are not wholly "unreal").

By the same process of reasoning, all *even powers* of j are real numbers. Thus, $j^2 = -1$ (as was just shown); $j^4 = j^2 \times j^2 = -1 \times -1 = +1$; $j^6 = -1$; $j^8 = +1$; and so on. On the other hand, *odd powers* of j are imaginary: $j^3 = j^2 \times j = -j$; $j^5 = j^4 \times j = +j$; and so forth. The reciprocal of j is equal to $-j$, as can readily be seen by the following argument: $1/j = j/j^2 = j/(-1) = -j$. Reciprocals of odd powers of j may thus be shown equal to minus the value of the odd power; that is: $1/j^3 = -j^3 = +j$, etc. Reciprocals of even powers are equal to the even power: $1/j^2 = j^2$; $1/j^4 = j^4$; etc. Reciprocal quantities are of course also expressible with negative exponents; $1/j = j^{-1}$; $1/j^2 = j^{-2}$; and so on. In short, j may be manipulated algebraically in exactly the same way as any symbol.

A *complex number* is the sum of a real number and an imaginary number. Thus if $z = x + jy$, where both x and y are any real numbers, then z is a complex number. (Actually, since either x or y may have the value zero, in which case z will be either purely imaginary or purely real, the purely real and purely imaginary numbers are both special cases of complex numbers.) The real number x is called the *real part* of z, and the real number y is called the *imaginary part* of z. This statement is sometimes written in the abbreviated form: Re $(z) = x$; Im $(z) = y$. Notice that y is a real number, though it is called the imaginary *part* of z. The imaginary *number* is jy.

Manipulation of complex numbers follows all the rules of ordinary algebra. The symbol j is treated like any other algebraic symbol, although it may at times be convenient to convert expressions like j^2 and j^3 into their equivalent forms, -1 and $-j$, and so on.

As an example, if the two complex numbers $z = x + jy$ and $w = u + jv$ are to be *added*, the result is

$$z + w = (x + u) + j(y + v) \tag{C–1}$$

That is, the real part of the sum is the sum of the real parts of the added complex numbers, and the imaginary part of the sum is the sum of the imaginary parts.

Multiplication of imaginary numbers is performed as follows:

$$zw = (x + jy)(u + jv) = xu + jxv + jxu + j^2yv = (xu - yv) + j(xv + yu) \tag{C–2}$$

(since $j^2 = -1$).

The real numbers are represented as points on a line, with one point designated zero; numbers to the left are "mirror images" of numbers to the right except that those to the left are negative and those on the right are positive. The complex numbers are represented as points in a plane by a cartesian coordinate system. The horizontal coordinate axis is the real-number line just described, and the vertical coordinate axis is an identical imaginary-number line, its zero coinciding with the real-axis zero. This *complex-plane* representation is illustrated in Fig. C–1 for the particular complex numbers $x = 4$, $y = 3$ $(z = 4 + j3)$, and $x = -2$, $y = 5$ $(z = -2 + j5)$.

In this representation the direct or straight-line distance from the origin to the complex-number point is called its *modulus* or absolute value. The modulus is (by definition) a positive real number, regardless of which quadrant of the coordinate plane contains the number point. It is the length of a line. The modulus of z_1 in Fig. C–1 is designated r_1. From the Pythagorean theorem for right triangles it is apparent that $r_1 = \sqrt{x_1^2 + y_1^2} = \sqrt{4^2 + 3^2} = \sqrt{25} = 5$. That is, the modulus of a complex number is the (positive) square root of the sum of the squares of its real and imaginary parts. The modulus is denoted algebraically by the "absolute value" brackets ||; thus:

$$|z| = |x + jy| = \left|\sqrt{x^2 + y^2}\right| \tag{C–3}$$

The angle (θ_1 in Fig. C–1) that the modulus line forms with the real part of the complex number is called the *phase angle*. Its tangent is the ratio of the imaginary part (y_1) to the real part (x_1). Certain physical quantities characterized by phase angles are conveniently represented by a "directed line segment" called a *phasor*, having a length equal to the modulus of a complex number, and a direction given by its phase angle. Accordingly, such a quantity is represented by a complex number. Phasors are very similar in their nature to two-dimensional *vectors*, but the latter term is properly reserved for physical quantities with two rectangular components having mutually perpendicular directions in space. Thus, an electric field intensity is a vector, which may be represented by the vertically and horizontally polarized components. A voltage developed by a current flowing through a resistance and a reactance in series, on the other hand, may be represented as a phasor, of which the real part represents the component of the voltage in phase with the current, and the imaginary part the component 90 degrees out of phase with the current. Similarly an impedance is a phasor whose real part is the resistance and whose imaginary part is the reactance.

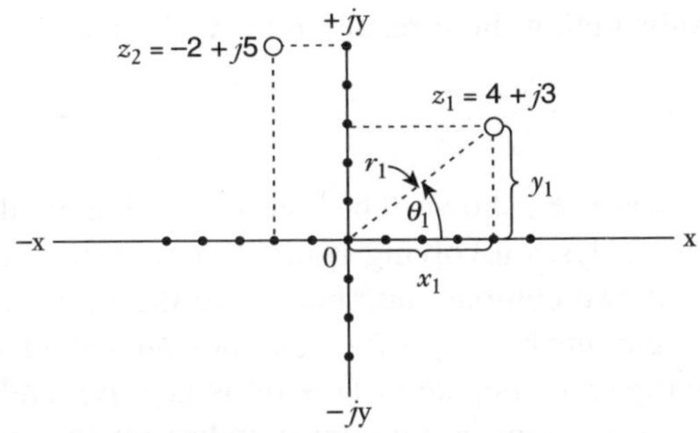

FIGURE C–1.

Complex-plane representation of real and imaginary numbers (z-plane).

Complex numbers may also be represented by a *complex-exponential* notation based on the relationship of the real and imaginary parts to the modulus and the phase angle. In this notation the complex number $z = x + jy$ is written

$$z = |z| e^{j\theta} = re^{j\theta} \tag{C–4}$$

The equivalence of this representation and the original one is based on deMoivre's theorem, which defines the meaning of a complex exponent as follows:

$$e^{j\theta} = \cos\theta + j\sin\theta \tag{C–5}$$

(The proof of this theorem is based on concepts of advanced calculus.) Rewriting (C–4) in terms of deMoivre's theorem gives

$$z = r\cos\theta + jr\sin\theta \tag{C–6}$$

By inspection of the right triangle of Fig. C–1 (in which $z = z_1$, $r = r_1$, etc.) it is apparent that

$$\left.\begin{aligned} x &= r\cos\theta \\ y &= r\sin\theta \end{aligned}\right\} \tag{C–7}$$

Substituting these results into (C–6) gives

$$z = x + jy \tag{C–8}$$

as was to be shown. The complex exponential notation is extremely useful in mathematical analyses involving complex numbers.

If two complex numbers have the *same real parts*, and *imaginary parts of the same magnitude but opposite sign*, they are called *complex conjugates* of each other. Thus the complex conjugate of $(x + jy)$ is $(x - jy)$, and vice versa.

Multiplying a complex number by its conjugate yields the square of the modulus; thus:

$$(x + jy)(x - jy) = x^2 - j^2y^2 = x^2 + y^2 \tag{C–9}$$

In the complex exponential notation the conjugate of $re^{j\theta}$ is $re^{-j\theta}$. This is shown from de Moivre's theorem in the following way:

$$\begin{aligned} e^{-j\theta} = e^{j(-\theta)} &= \cos(-\theta) + j\sin(-\theta) \\ &= \cos\theta - j\sin\theta \end{aligned} \tag{C–10}$$

because $\cos(-\theta) = \cos(+\theta)$ and $\sin(-\theta) = -\sin(+\theta)$. That the product of the complex conjugates yields the square of the modulus is also readily seen from this notation, as follows:

$$\begin{aligned} re^{j\theta} \cdot re^{-j\theta} &= r^2 e^{(j\theta - j\theta)} \\ &= r^2 e^0 = r^2 \end{aligned} \tag{C–11}$$

In algebraic equations involving products and quotients of complex numbers, it is usually required to reduce each side of the equation to separated real and imaginary parts. For products, this is accomplished simply by performing the indicated multiplication, as exemplified by (C–2), and grouping together the real terms and the imaginary terms. For a quotient, the procedure is slightly more complicated, but basically simple. It consists of first multiplying both the numerator and the denominator of the fraction representing the quotient by the complex conjugate of the denominator. This procedure eliminates imaginary terms from the denominator. Then the numerator is separated into real and imaginary parts. For example:

$$\frac{a + jb}{c + jd} = \frac{(a + jb)(c - jd)}{(c + jd)(c - jd)} = \frac{ac + jbc - jad - j^2bd}{c^2 - j^2d^2} = \frac{ac + bd}{c^2 + d^2} + j\left(\frac{bc - ad}{c^2 + d^2}\right) \tag{C–12}$$

An important theorem of complex algebra is that if two complex numbers are equal to each other, their real parts and their imaginary parts are separately equal. This means that every complex equation is equivalent to two real equations. Thus, if

$$x + jy = u + jv \tag{C–13}$$

it necessarily follows that

$$\begin{aligned} x &= u \\ y &= v \end{aligned} \tag{C–14}$$

(two equations). This theorem has many applications. For example, the relationship between impedance and admittance is $Z = 1/Y$, where in general $Z = R + jX$ and $Y = G + jB$. Therefore

$$G + jB = \frac{1}{R + jX} = \frac{R - jX}{R^2 + X^2} = \frac{R}{R^2 + X^2} - j\left(\frac{X}{R^2 + X^2}\right) \tag{C–15}$$

Therefore, applying the theorem, it is found that

$$G = \frac{R}{R^2 + X^2} \tag{C–16}$$

$$B = \frac{-X}{R^2 + X^2} \tag{C–17}$$

as was stated without detailed proof in equations (2–30) and (2–31), chapter 2.

APPENDIX D

Complex Reflection Coefficients and Multipath Effects

Chapter 1 (sec. 1.4.5) includes an introduction to the polarization dependencies of the reflection coefficient for a smooth, flat surface and to the effects of multipath propagation. The present appendix includes equations and example calculations for reflection coefficients of smooth and rough earth surfaces. Furthermore, equations are given for calculating the pattern propagation factor F for both flat earth and spherical earth geometries. In addition, the SM that accompanies this book provides examples using Mathcad for calculating reflection coefficients and the pattern propagation factor F. Therefore, by changing the initial assumptions, the user may readily attain computer calculated solutions to a wide variety of problems involving reflections applicable to either flat earth or spherical earth geometries.

D.1. Fresnel's Equations

Fresnel's equations are basic relationships that give reflection coefficient magnitude and phase as a function of polarization, arrival angle of incoming e-m waves, and complex permittivity. These equations include the cases with electric vector perpendicular to and in the plane of incidence. The two cases are indicated by E_H and E_V in Fig. D–1, and correspond to horizontal and vertical polarizations. Elsewhere, these components are sometimes designated as $E_{parallel}$ and $E_{perpendicular}$, respectively. Note that the direction for vertical polarization is perpendicular to horizontal polarization and to the direction of propagation. Otherwise, it is not precise because the direction of vertical polarization depends on angle Ψ. For calculations involving reflections of an elliptically polarized wave (Appendix B), the Fresnel equations are used to separately determine the reflection coefficients for the horizontally and vertically polarized components.

Now assume that the electromagnetic wave incident on the surface is in free space and the surface material is nonmagnetic, as it is ordinarily for the earth. Then, from Fresnel's equations, the complex (amplitude and phase) reflection coefficients for horizontal and vertical polarizations (Γ_H and Γ_V) follow:

$$\Gamma_H = \frac{\sin\psi - (\varepsilon_r - \cos^2\psi)^{1/2}}{\sin\psi + (\varepsilon_r - \cos^2\psi)^{1/2}} = \rho_H \exp(-j\phi_H) \tag{D–1}$$

$$\Gamma_V = \frac{\varepsilon_r \sin\psi - (\varepsilon_r - \cos^2\psi)^{1/2}}{\varepsilon_r \sin\psi + (\varepsilon_r - \cos^2\psi)^{1/2}} = \rho_V \exp(-j\phi_V) \tag{D–2}$$

The reader will notice that (D–1) and (D–2) contain $-\phi_H$ and $-\phi_v$ terms, meaning that positive ϕ_H and ϕ_v denote phase *delays*. This use of phase delay follows Kerr (1947, pp. 396–97) and is consistent with the fact that the phase of reflected waves for land and sea lags that of the incidence wave. This practice of defining ϕ_H and ϕ_v as phase lags differs from sec. 1.2, where positive ϕ denotes leading phase. As also discussed in sec. D.2, there can be uncertainties regarding the correct phases when using (D–1) and (D–2), because the square root of a complex (real and imagery parts) number has two answers and they are at different angles. Consequently, because of this ambiguity in phase, it is useful to remember that, for land and sea, reflected phase always lags.

As shown in Fig. D–1, the angle ψ is the angle between the incident wave (and the reflected wave) and the tangent to the surface at the point of reflection. The term ε_r is the complex permittivity, relative to permittivity of vacuum, expressed as

$$\varepsilon_r = \varepsilon_r' - j\varepsilon_r'' - \varepsilon_r' - j60\lambda\sigma \tag{D–3}$$

where λ is the free-space wavelength in meters and σ is conductivity in mhos per meter. Example values of ε_r' and ε_r'' for soil and water are given in Table D-1. By definition, $\varepsilon_r = 1$ for a vacuum and it is essentially the same for the earth's atmosphere. In addition, Appendix H includes the electrical properties of some low-loss dielectric materials used for radomes.

For normal incidence ($\psi = 90°$), where E_H and E_V are parallel to the reflecting plane, the H and V reflection mechanisms are necessarily identical. However, from (D–1) and (D–2) Γ_H and Γ_V become

$$\Gamma_H = \frac{1-\varepsilon_r^{1/2}}{1+\varepsilon_r^{1/2}} \tag{D–4}$$

$$\Gamma_V = \frac{\varepsilon_r - \varepsilon_r^{1/2}}{\varepsilon_r + \varepsilon_r^{1/2}} = \left(\frac{\varepsilon^{-1/2}}{\varepsilon^{-1/2}}\right)\left(\frac{\varepsilon_r - \varepsilon_r^{1/2}}{\varepsilon_r + \varepsilon_r^{1/2}}\right) = -\Gamma_H \tag{D–5}$$

The cause for the sign difference between Γ_V and Γ_H is based solely on geometry and without regard to phase change, per se. Note from Fig. D–1 that the direction

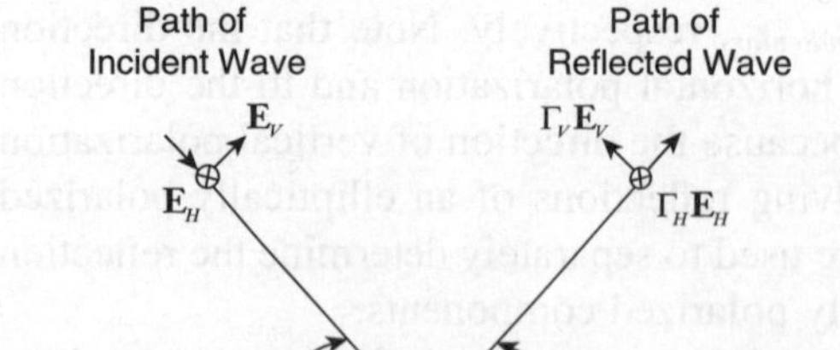

FIGURE D–1.

Reflection from a smooth, flat surface. E_H and E_V are electric vectors for horizontal and vertical polarizations, respectively.

TABLE D-1 Approximate Electrical Properties of Soil and Water Sources: Kerr (1947, p. 398) and Dicaudo (1970, p. 14–30)

Material	λ	σ (mhos/m)	ε_r'	ε_r''
Vacuum (defined)		0	1	0
Ice	3 cm		3.2	25.6×10^{-4}
Snow	3 cm		1.3	6.5×10^{-4}
Seawater	3 m/20 cm	4.3	80	774/52
Freshwater lakes	1 m	$10^{-3}/10^{-2}$	80	0.06/0.60
Moist ground	1 m	10^{-2}	30	0.6
Very dry ground	1 m	10^{-4}	4	0.006
Very wet sandy loam	9 cm	0.06	24	32.4
Very dry sandy loam	9 cm	0.03	2	1.62
Texas, very dry soil	3.2 cm	0.0074	2.8	0.014

Note: $\varepsilon_r'' = j\,60\,\lambda\sigma$, and thus it is highly sensitive to wavelength. The wavelength dependency of ε_r' is much less, and its values given in Table D-1 are typical of the kilohertz to gigahertz frequency range. Note that for ground, ε_r' and ε_r'' each increases with an increase in moisture content.

of the reflected E_V at $\Psi = 90°$ is opposite to its incident direction at $\Psi = 90°$. However, a change in E-field direction does not occur for E_V at $\Psi = 0°$. Furthermore, the change in E-direction does not occur for E_H at either $\Psi = 90°$ or $\Psi = 0°$. Thus at $\psi = 90°$ and with equal phase change upon reflection, Γ_H and Γ_V must differ in sign.

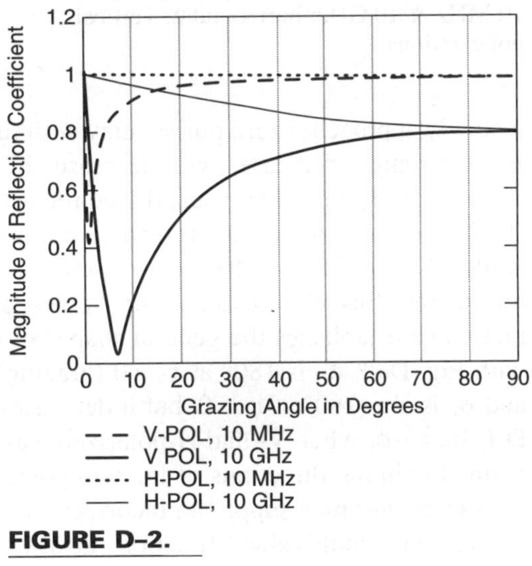

FIGURE D–2.

Magnitude ρ of reflection coefficient for smooth sea surface versus grazing angle Ψ. 10 MHz & 10 GHz; horizontal & vertical polarizations.

D.2. Reflection Coefficients for Smooth Land and Sea

Figures D–2 and D–3 show the general trends in reflection coefficient versus grazing angle ψ and frequency for a flat, smooth seawater surface. Figure D–2 includes reflection coefficient amplitude ρ for both H- and V-polarizations at two frequencies, 10 MHz and 10 GHz, with $\varepsilon_r' = 80$ and $\sigma = 4.3$ mhos/m assumed. Note that ρ is essentially unity at zero grazing angle for each polarization and frequency. The magnitude ρ_H is usually close to unity at all ψ angles, but it drops to as low as 0.8 at the higher frequencies and larger ψ values. Figure D–3 shows examples of phase delay on reflection for H- and V-polarizations at 10 MHz and 10 GHz. For H-polarization, the

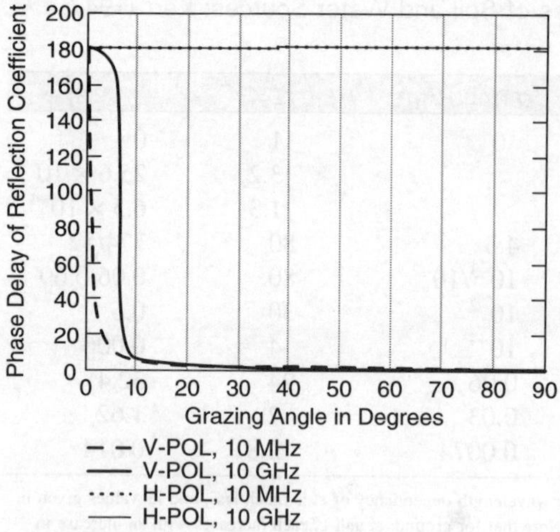

FIGURE D–3.

Phase delay ϕ of reflection coefficient for smooth sea surface versus grazing angle ψ. 10 MHz & 10 GHz; horizontal & vertical polarizations.

phase delay is 180° (or slightly greater) for all grazing angles and the two frequencies.

From Figs. D–2 and D–3, it is seen that ρ_V and ϕ_V are more sensitive to frequency and grazing angle than are ρ_H and ϕ_H. However, Γ_V and Γ_H are both −1 at zero grazing angle (horizon direction) at all frequencies. Note that ρ_V has minimum values at small angles Ψ, and that the particular Ψ for the minimum ρ_V depends on frequency. For a lossless dielectric, the minimum for ρ_V is zero and that angle Ψ is known as Brewster's angle. For imperfect dielectrics such as land and sea, the minimum is not zero and the angle is the pseudo-Brewster angle. From Fig. D–3, it can be seen that, near the pseudo-Brewster angle, the phase delay ϕ_V changes rapidly between 180° and 90° with increases in grazing angle, and then it slowly approaches zero phase delay with further increases in ψ. In addition, the pseudo-Brewster angle decreases with decreases in frequency.

In sec. D.1, the reader is cautioned regarding the correct phases when using (D–1) and (D–2), because the square root of a complex number has two answers with different angles. Kerr (1947, pp. 400–401) discusses how the complex numerators and denominators of the Fresnel equations vary versus ψ; and he thereby resolves the ambiguity in phase and establishes the general shapes of ϕ_H and ϕ_V versus ψ. Namely, in accordance with Fig. D–3, ϕ_H is 180° at $\psi = 0$ (grazing) and increases slightly with increases in ψ; and ϕ_V is also 180° at $\psi = 0$, but it decreases to 0° at $\psi = 90°$. Thus, as discussed in sec. D.1, $\phi_H = -\phi_V$ when V- and H-polarized waves arrive normal to a surface, because of the defined pointing directions of the two polarizations.

A computer may supply an incorrect angle, because software often provides only one answer for a multivalued function. In Mathcad, for example, the answer given for the root of a complex term is the principal value, that is, the smallest positive angle relative to the positive real axis in the complex plane. However, ambiguities regarding signs and magnitudes of ϕ_H and ϕ_V are properly resolved when their general shapes versus ψ are consistent with the paragraph above.

Sections SM 1.1 and 1.2, in the SM that accompanies this book, provide numerical examples using Mathcad for calculating complex reflection coefficients for smooth flat land and sea surfaces. There it can be seen that the shapes of ρ_V, ρ_H, ϕ_V, and ϕ_H versus grazing angle for land are, generally, similar to those of seawater. However, land is a poorer conductor than sea water, the pseudo-Brewster angles are somewhat larger, and at most grazing angles ρ_v and ρ_h are smaller for land than for sea. Furthermore, as the grazing angles approach zero, the complex reflection coefficients for horizontal and vertical polarizations approach −1 for both land and sea.

D.3. Reflection Coefficients for Rough Surfaces

The field scattered by a rough surface is the sum of two components: a specular component and a diffuse component. For specular reflections, the angle of incidence and the angle of reflection are equal. However, diffuse scattering can occur in any direction relative to the incident EM field. A specularly reflected component is a coherent wave, that is, one that has deterministic amplitude and phase and can be described as a function of position. For example, the sum of a specularly reflected field and a coherent "direct" field will produce a periodically varying field, if sampled in the vertical dimension above the flat surface. On the other hand, the amplitude and phase of a diffusely scattered field are unpredictable and are random functions of position. Therefore, a diffusely scattered field added to a coherent field will produce a total field that varies randomly as a function of position.

The Rayleigh criterion is introduced in sec. 1.2, as being a rule-of-thumb for estimating if a semi-rough surface will reflect as if the surface were smooth (specular reflector). There is not a specific, clearly defined specular/nonspecular boundary, because the amount of specularity gradually changes with changes in surface roughness, incidence angle, and wavelength. Note that in Appendix D and the accompanying SM, the grazing angle ψ of Fig. D–1 is used, instead of θ_i of Fig. 1–6, because of its convenience in multipath analyses. Thus, ψ is the complement of θ_i, and $\sin\psi$ replaces $\cos\theta_i$ in equation (1–25).

A useful characterization of surface roughness is σ_h, the standard deviation of the surface height distribution. Mathematically, σ_h equals the rms of heights on the surface, if the average height is the zero reference height. As a guideline for roughness, following Rayleigh's criterion (chapter 1), a surface is considered *not* smooth if

$$\sigma_h \sin\psi \geq \lambda/8 \tag{D–6}$$

Experience indicates that the "significant wave height," the height of a sea wave that most observers guess from a quick observation, exceeds σ_h of sea surfaces by a factor of about four. Thus, the standard deviation is actually substantially smaller than peak-to-trough surface height.

A further refinement in calculating the effects of roughness provides an estimate of the effective value of the magnitude of Γ, as follows:

$$|\Gamma| = \rho_o \exp\left[-2\left(\frac{2\pi\sigma_h \sin\psi}{\lambda}\right)^2\right] \tag{D–7}$$

Here ρ_o is the magnitude of the reflection coefficient for a smooth, flat surface. From (D–7), $|\Gamma|$ is approximately ρ_o if $\sigma_h \sin\psi << \lambda$ and it equals $0.29\rho_o$ if $\sigma_h \sin\psi = \lambda/8$. Thus, as is already known, surface reflections become more specular-like with decreased roughness, decreased grazing angle, and with increased wavelength (decreased frequency).

D.4. Pattern-Propagation Factor *F*

Effects of the earth and its environment on received signal strength are conventionally included by means of the *pattern propagation factor* F (sec 1.4.7). Pattern-propagation factor is, according to the Institute of Electrical and Electronics Engineers (1997), the ratio of the field strength amplitude that is actually present at a point in space to that which would be present if free-space propagation had occurred with the antenna beam directed toward the point in question. Consequently, the power at a point is F^2 times its value if the propagation path were in a vacuum. Therefore, as discussed in sec. 1.4.7, received power P_r for one-way transmission can be expressed as

$$P_r = \frac{P_t G_t G_r \lambda^2}{(4\pi)^2 R^2} F^2 \tag{D–8}$$

where P_t is transmit power, G_t and G_r are transmit and receive antenna gains, and R is distance between transmit and receive antennas.

Figure D–4 shows the basic multipath process that consists of the phasor addition of waves at point P. The shortest path is the direct path and it has length designated as R_d,

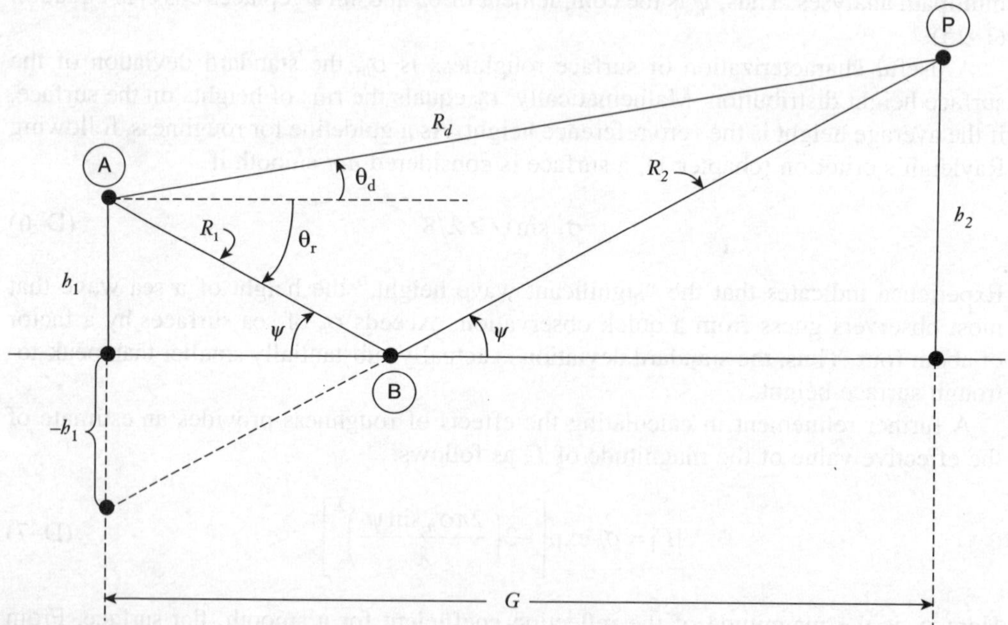

FIGURE D–4.
Geometry for a flat earth, with image of source A located at $-h_2$.

and the other path is the indirect path and has length $R_1 + R_2$. The phase difference of the two waves is affected by three factors: (1) the path-length difference δ which equals $(R_1 + R_2 - R_d)$, (2) the phase change of the reflected wave that occurs upon reflection, and (3) the phase difference, if any, of the fields radiated by the antenna in the direct-ray and reflected-ray directions (θ_d and θ_r, respectively).

The two waves may also have amplitude differences caused by the following factors: (1) each wave is subject to the inverse-square-law power-density reduction, and they travel different distances, (2) the reflected wave undergoes at least some loss of intensity in the process of reflection, and (3) antenna patterns are, in general, not constant in the vertical plane and may therefore have different field intensities in the θ_d and θ_r directions.

In most multipath situations, the path difference δ is small compared to the path lengths of the direct and reflected paths. Therefore, the usual small difference in amplitudes caused by these path length differences δ can be neglected, and the primary effect of δ is on the phase difference between the waves that arrive from the direct and reflected paths.

As already noted, the elevation pattern of the antenna affects the relative strength of the rays in directions θ_d and θ_r, and therefore possible effects of the pattern must be addressed. Often in multipath situations, however, the angles θ_d and θ_r are small enough that the pattern's relative strengths at those angles are insignificant. Then, if both the direct and indirect paths are energized equally, the resultant electric field at point P is

$$E = E_d\left\{1+\Gamma e^{-j(2\pi/\lambda)\delta}\right\} = E_d\left\{1+\rho e^{-j[(2\pi/\lambda)\delta+\phi]}\right\} \tag{D–9}$$

where E_d is the field due to the direct wave, δ is the difference in lengths between the indirect and direct paths, and ϕ is the phase delay created by the reflecting properties of a surface. Therefore, in accordance with (D–9), the propagation factor F is

$$F = \left|E/E_d\right| = \left|1+\rho e^{-j[(2\pi/\lambda)\delta+\phi]}\right| \tag{D–10}$$

Note that F consists of two components, of amplitude one and ρ, separated by angle $(2\pi/\lambda)\delta + \phi$. Thus, from use of the law of cosines, it is seen that (D–10) becomes

$$F^2 = \left(1+\rho^2+2\rho\cos\psi\right) \tag{D–11}$$

where $\Psi = (2\pi/\lambda)\delta + \phi$.

D.5. Flat Earth Geometry

The flat earth approximation is useful for applications involving relatively short ranges and small transmit and receive heights, so that the effects of the earth's curvature are negligible. This section includes the equations applicable to the flat earth approximation and sec. D.7 discusses the spherical earth model. Section 1.4.3, chapter 1, describes a simplified flat earth multipath model based on a number of assumptions, including

- a flat, smooth, and perfectly conducting surface
- direct- and reflected-wave paths that are effectively parallel at the point of observation, and
- horizontal polarization.

Often the antenna height h_1 above the earth is small compared to R_d, the distance between the antenna and the observation point P. Then, it may be true that $R_d >> h_1$ and thus consequently R_2 is effectively parallel to R_d. With these assumptions, there are several simplifications regarding Fig. D–4; namely, $\psi = \theta_d$, $\delta = 2h_1 \sin\theta_d$, and knowledge of h_2 is not required. In general, however, accurate multipath calculations require the use of the more detailed geometrical equations, such as those that follow and those for the spherical earth model included in sec. D.7.

Figure D–4 provides for a more general analysis of the flat earth model, and the following equations are applicable:

$$R_d = \sqrt{(h_2 - h_1)^2 + G^2} = G\sqrt{1 + \left(\frac{h_2 - h_1}{G}\right)^2} \tag{D–12}$$

$$R_1 + R_2 = \sqrt{(h_2 + h_1)^2 + G^2} = G\sqrt{1 + \left(\frac{h_2 + h_1}{G}\right)^2} \tag{D–13}$$

When $G^2 >> (h_1 + h_2)^2$, useful approximations are

$$R_d \approx G\left[1 + \frac{1}{2}\left(\frac{h_2 - h_1}{G}\right)^2\right] \tag{D–14}$$

and

$$R_1 + R_2 \approx G\left[1 + \frac{1}{2}\left(\frac{h_2 + h_1}{G}\right)^2\right]$$

By using the equations (D–14), it can be seen that the difference δ, in the reflected wave path-length $R_1 + R_2$ and the direct wave-path length R_d, may be expressed as

$$\delta = (R_1 + R_2) - R_d \approx \frac{2h_1h_2}{G} \tag{D–15}$$

Equation (D–15) is often a valid approximation for ground communications systems, because usually for those systems $G^2 >> (h_1 + h_2)^2$.

A number of exact equations can be obtained from the geometry of Fig. D–4, and they include the following:

$$\sin\theta_d = \frac{h_2 - h_1}{R_d} \tag{D–16}$$

$$\cos\theta_d = G/R_d \tag{D–17}$$

$$\sin\psi = \frac{h_1 + h_2}{G} \tag{D–18}$$

$$\theta_r = \psi \tag{D–19}$$

Recall that the solution of multipath problems in exact form requires knowledge of ψ versus θ_d. However, the relationship between ψ and θ_d is not available, mathematically, in a simple closed-form. However, accurate multipath solutions can be acquired by computer with step-by-step procedures. For example, to calculate an antenna pattern at distance R_d and with antenna height h_1, let h_1 and R_d be constants. Then, the following are attained: θ_d versus h_2 from (D–16), G versus θ_d from (D–17), ψ versus G from (D–18), and θ_r from (D–19).

D.6. Multipath Dependencies on Frequency, Polarization, and Surface Roughness

The phenomenon of interference between the direct and indirect waves produces polarization sensitive lobes above the reflecting surface. Generally, the positions of the lobes do not coincide for horizontal (H-POL) and vertical (V-POL) polarizations, because of differences in the phases (ϕ_H and ϕ_V) and amplitudes (ρ_H and ρ_V) of the reflection coefficients. Figures D–5 through D–8 that are now discussed were prepared by using the flat earth model.

Examples of field strengths above a flat, smooth sea for H- and V-polarizations at 1 and 4 GHz are given in Fig. D–5. Notice that an advantage of V-polarization, especially at lower frequencies, is that the relative field strength near the surface is larger. Interference between direct and reflected waves also may create maxima and minima in field strength versus range, somewhat analogous to the variation in Fig. D–5 with height at a fixed range.

Some differences in the propagation factor F for vertical and horizontal polarizations versus grazing angle and frequency are shown in Fig. D–6. Here it is assumed that the earth is perfectly smooth and the following are additional assumptions: a non-directive antenna at height 3 m above the earth, frequencies of 1 MHz ($\lambda = 300$ m) and 100 MHz (3 m), and $\varepsilon_r' = 16$ and $\sigma = 10^{-2}$ mho/m. It may be seen that:

- at 1 MHz, because there is 180° phase change for H-POL reflection: (a) V-POL signal always exceeds H-POL signal (i.e., $F_V > F_H$), and (b) at less than 10°, F_V exceeds F_H by at least 30 dB.
- at 100 MHz, because pathlength differences between the direct and indirect paths cause large changes in phase versus grazing angle: (a) H-POL signals can be either smaller or larger than V-POL signals, and (b) H-POL peaks are larger than the V-POL peaks and the H-POL minima are smaller than the V-POL minima because $\rho_H > \rho_V$.

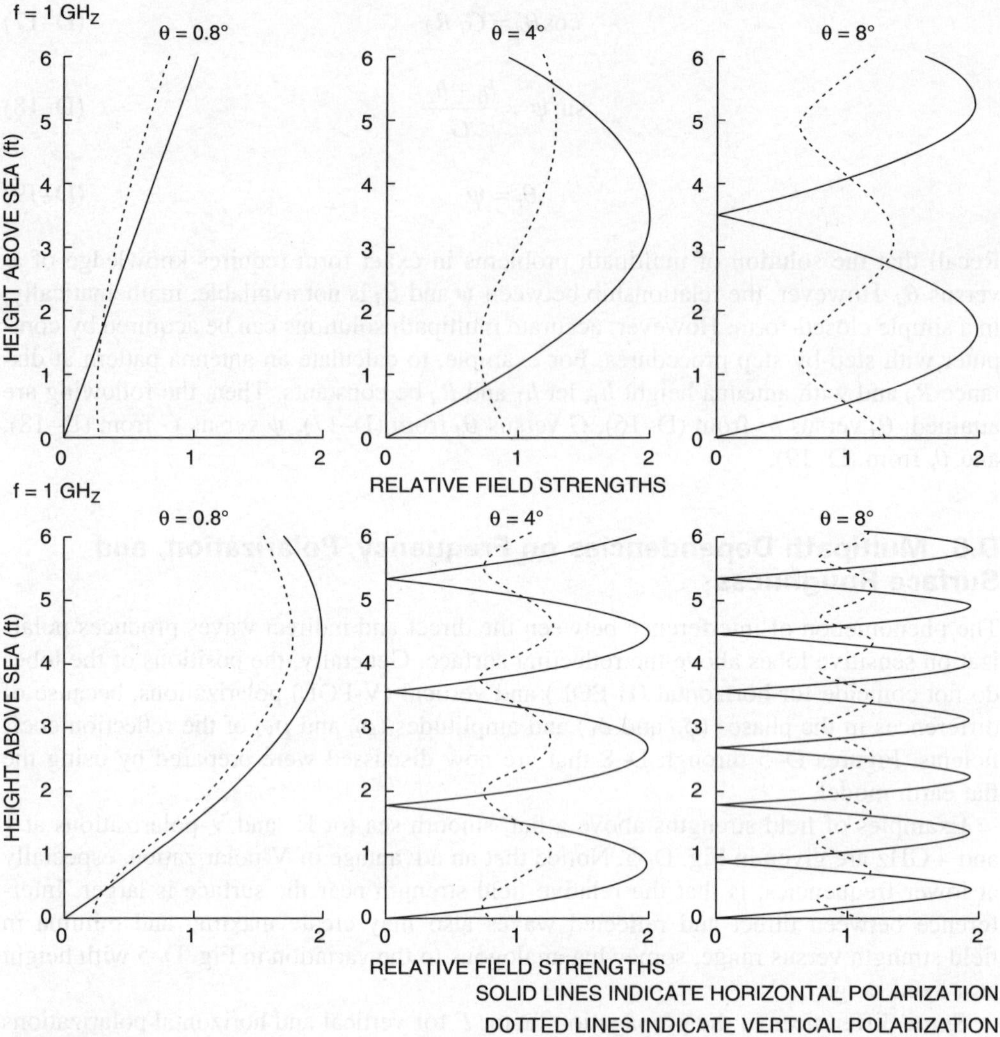

FIGURE D–5.

Electric field amplitude patterns above a smooth sea relative to free-space amplitudes. 1 and 4 GHz, with 0.8°, 4°, and 8° grazing angles. From Long, Wetherington, Edwards, and Abeling (1965).

Figures D–7 and D–8 show the propagation factor F for H-POL with and without surface roughness. The curves were prepared under the following assumptions: $\sigma_h = 0$ (flat, smooth earth) and $\sigma_h = 0.3$ m (representing a recently plowed agricultural field), $\lambda = 3$ m (100 MHz) and 0.3 m (1 GHz), and land with $\varepsilon_r = 16 - j60\lambda\sigma$ and $\sigma = 10^{-2}$ mho/m. In Fig. D–7 for 100 MHz, the surface roughness causes only a slight filling of the minimum at 30°, and there are little effects of surface roughness at smaller grazing angles. Also in Fig. D–7, the effect of surface roughness at 100 MHz is not strong, even for grazing angles up to 70°. In Fig. D–8, for 1 GHz, effects of surface roughness are not apparent for angles less than 3°, and for the rough surface essentially all effects of multipath have disappeared for angles above 10°. Thus, in some applications, the use of higher frequencies may be a useful method of minimizing the effects of multipath interference. There are practical limits, of course, on the use of the higher frequencies (shorter wavelengths) imposed by the general increase in atmospheric attenuation. In summary, the electromagnetic effects of roughness depend on σ_h, θ, and λ through their relationships with the roughness parameter $\sigma_h \sin \psi/\lambda$ and on its effect on the magnitude of reflection co-efficient in accordance with (D–7) of sec. D–3.

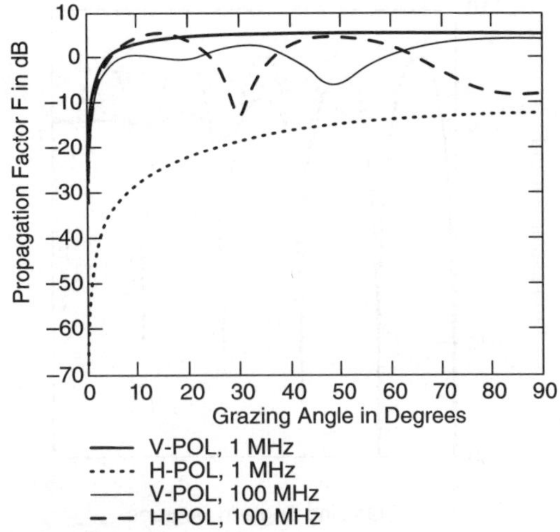

FIGURE D–6.

Propagation factor F in dB versus grazing angle. V- and H-polarizations, 1 and 100 MHz, antenna 3 m above flat smooth land.

D.7. Spherical Earth Geometry

The earth's overall shape is roughly spherical and its curvature decreases the path-length difference δ between the direct and reflected waves. Another effect of the earth's curvature is to decrease the amplitude of reflected waves, caused by them being spread out or diverged by the convex surface of the earth.

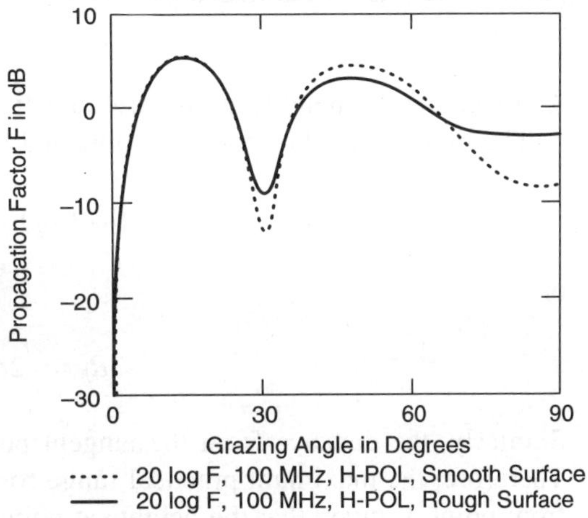

FIGURE D–7.

Propagation factor F versus grazing angle. 100 MHz, horizontal polarization, smooth land and plowed land (standard deviation $\sigma_h = 0.3$ m).

Electromagnetic waves propagating within the earth's atmosphere do not travel in straight lines but bend slightly because of refraction. One effect of refraction is to extend the distance to the horizon, thus increasing radio and radar coverage; another effect is to change the elevation pointing direction of the antenna pattern at long distances. In computations, a commonly used method is to (1) replace the actual earth of radius a by an equivalent earth of radius $a_e = ka$ and (2) replace the actual atmosphere by a vacuum (free space) in which the waves propagate in straight lines. It is customary to use the value $k = 4/3$ for approximating the effects of refraction. Although $k = 4/3$ is typical,

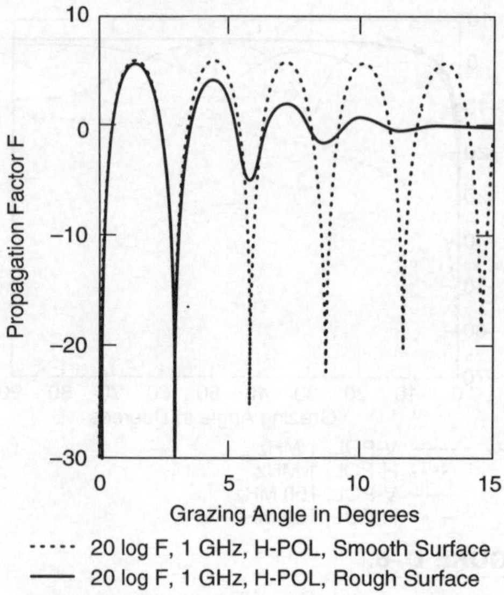

FIGURE D–8.

Propagation factor F versus grazing angle. 1 GHz, horizontal polarization, smooth and plowed land (standard deviation $\sigma_h = 0.3$ m).

measurements may yield larger or smaller values (U.S. Department of Commerce 1966).

Figure D–9 illustrates straight-line propagation in accordance with the spherical earth model. Note that, unlike flat-earth geometry, the horizontals at the two terminals (points A and P) are not parallel. The horizon is located where path R_d is tangent to the earth's surface. Therefore, at the horizon, ray paths R_d and R_1 are parallel, with angle ψ being zero. The range to the horizon R_h is the distance from point A to the point that the tangent ray (for which $\psi = 0$) strikes the earth. Range to the total horizon R_{max} is the range from point A to point P, when R_d exceeds R_h and point P is located along the extension of the tangent ray beyond its tangent point at the earth. According to the spherical earth model, R_{max} is the maximum practical range for detecting an electromagnetic wave emitted from point A, given that the heights at points A and P are h_1 and h_2.

The range to the horizon R_h is obtained from the right triangle relationship

$$(a_e + h_1)^2 = R_h^2 + a_e^2$$

or

$$R_h = \sqrt{2a_e h_1 + h_1^2} \tag{D–20}$$

Similarly, the distance from the tangent point to point P of height h_2 is $\sqrt{2a_e h_2 + h_2^2}$. Therefore, the maximum practical range for detecting an electromagnetic wave emitted from point A, given that the heights at points A and P are h_1 and h_2, is

$$R_{max} = R_h + \sqrt{2h_2 a_e + h_2^2} \tag{D–21}$$

The equations that follow are from Blake (1986, pp. 249–58). They allow the parameters of Fig. D–9 to be computed if the heights h_1 and h_2, the total ground range G, and the equivalent earth radius a_e are given. The first step is to obtain the ground ranges G_1 and G_2, where G is ($G1$ + $G2$). This requires solving for two parameters, p and ξ, that follow:

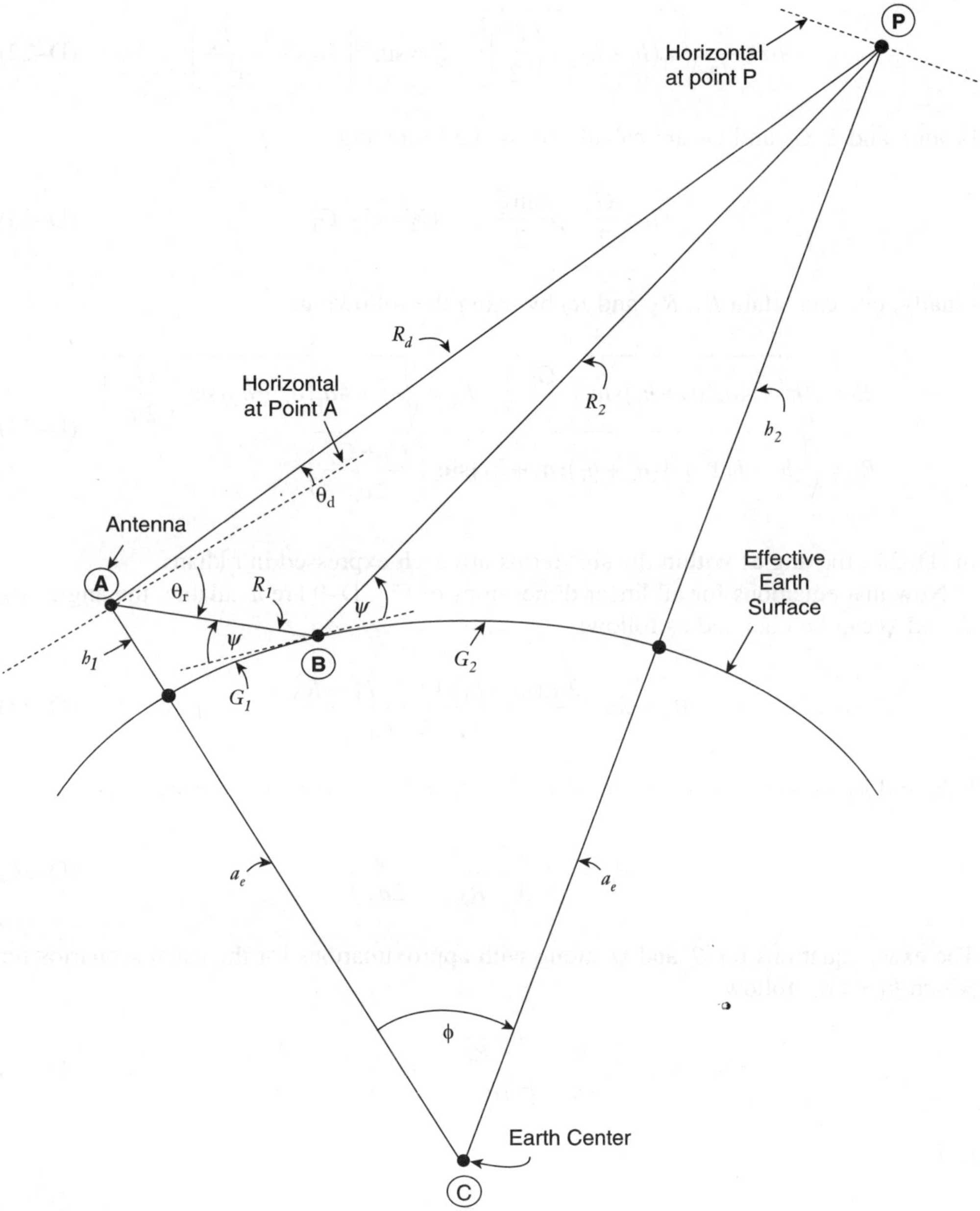

FIGURE D–9.

Geometry for spherical-earth model. (Effective earth has radius a_e, compatible with assumption of straight ray paths A-P and A-B-P). Adapted from Blake (1991, p. 255).

$$p = \frac{2}{\sqrt{3}}\sqrt{a_e(h_1+h_2)+\left(\frac{G}{2}\right)^2} \qquad \xi = \sin^{-1}\left[2a_eG\frac{h_1-h_2}{p^3}\right] \tag{D–22}$$

From p and ξ, G_1 and G_2 are calculated by the following:

$$G_1 = \frac{G}{2} - p\frac{\sin\xi}{3} \qquad G_2 = G - G_1 \tag{D–23}$$

Finally, one can attain R_1, R_2, and R_d by using the following:

$$\begin{aligned} R_1 &= \sqrt{h_1^2 + 4a_e(a_e+h_1)\sin^2\left(\frac{G_1}{2a_e}\right)} \qquad R_2 = \sqrt{h_2^2 + 4a_e(a_e+h_2)\sin^2\left(\frac{G_2}{2a_e}\right)} \\ R_d &= \sqrt{(h_2-h_1)^2 + 4(a_e+h_1)(a_e+h_2)\sin^2\left(\frac{G_1+G_2}{2a_e}\right)} \end{aligned} \tag{D–24}$$

In (D–24), the angles within the $\sin^2$ terms are each expressed in radians.

Now that equations for all linear dimensions of Fig. D–9 are available, the angles θ_d, θ_r and ψ can be obtained as follow:

$$\theta_d = \sin^{-1}\frac{2a_e(h_2-h_1)+h_2^2-h_1^2-R_d^2}{2(a_e+h_1)R_d} \tag{D–25}$$

If h_1 and h_2 are both much smaller than a_e, which is true for most applications,

$$\theta_d \cong \sin^{-1}\left(\frac{h_2-h_1}{R_d} - \frac{R_d}{2a_e}\right) \tag{D–26}$$

The exact equations for θ_r and ψ, along with approximations for the usual scenarios for which $h_1 << a_e$, follow

$$\theta_r = \sin^{-1}\frac{2a_eh_1+h_1^2+R_1^2}{2(a_e+h_1)R_1} \cong \sin^{-1}\left(\frac{h_1}{R_1}+\frac{R_1}{2a_e}\right) \tag{D–27}$$

and

$$\psi = \sin^{-1}\frac{2a_eh_1+h_1^2-R_1^2}{2a_eR_1} \cong \sin^{-1}\left(\frac{h_1}{R_1}-\frac{R_1}{2a_e}\right) \tag{D–28}$$

From Fig. D–9 it can be seen that

θ_d is the elevation angle, relative to the horizontal at point A of the direct ray between points A and P;

θ_r is the depression angle, relative to the horizontal at point *A* of the indirect path ray between point *A* and the earth (point *B*); and

ψ is the angle measured above the horizontal at the earth (point *B*) of the indirect path ray between point *A* and the earth.

For many applications where multpath interference is significant, the elevation (vertical) antenna pattern is sufficiently broad that the pattern strengths at the beam center and at angles θ_d and θ_r are approximately equal. Then, the approximation of (D–9) in sec. D.4 is valid. Otherwise, multipath analyses must include effects of the shape of the elevation pattern.

The pathlength difference δ is, of course, equal to $(R_1 + R_2) - R_d$. Consequently, because this equation involves differences in numbers that are large compared to δ, significant computing errors can occur. Blake (1986, p. 257) uses a more accurate method for calculating δ, which follows:

$$\delta = \frac{4R_1R_2\sin^2\psi}{R_1 + R_2 + R_d} \tag{D–29}$$

Thus, by starting with only the heights h_1 and h_2, the ground range G and an assumed equivalent earth radius a_e, one can make calculations for the various path lengths and angles of Fig. D–9. The accompanying SM includes spherical earth calculations using Mathcad, where the user can choose the initial assumptions in accordance to his or her needs.

D.8. Divergence Factor

For a spherical wavefront incident on a spherical surface, the power density after reflection is reduced by a divergence or spreading of the ray paths. This geometric (not electromagnetic) description causes the calculated reflected field strength to be reduced with decreased grazing angle. However, at grazing angles of about one degree or less, forward propagation from a curved surface is not accurately described by the reflection of rays. Then, instead, its description requires advanced electromagnetic diffraction techniques beyond the scope of this book (Meeks 1982, Ch. 6).

The letter *D* denotes the divergence factor, a power reflection coefficient based entirely on geometry. Specifically, *D* is the calculated fractional reduction in the field strength resulting from geometry that describes rays reflected from a curved surface. Field strength is proportional to the square root of the ray density. Thus, *D* is the square root of the ratio of the beam's solid angles before reflection from a smooth spherical surface divided by the solid angle after reflection. To include effects of divergence, the magnitude of the specular reflection coefficient is expressed as

$$|\Gamma| = \rho_o \exp\left[-2\left(\frac{2\pi\sigma_h \sin\psi}{\lambda}\right)^2\right]D \tag{D–30}$$

where ρ_o is the reflection coefficient magnitude if the surface is smooth and the exponential function is the roughness factor that was introduced in Sec. D.3.

From detailed geometrical analysis, Kerr (1951, p. 406) in his equation (16) provides a general equation for D. This equation, expressed in terms of the parameters of Fig. D–9, was obtained by the present author by using Kerr's equations (11) and (12). That equation that follows Kerr and various approximations for D are included in SM 3.6 of the accompanying SM. To obtain another and yet simpler equation, Kerr uses assumptions that are valid if the effects of divergence are appreciable. These assumptions include small grazing angles, and terminal heights and path lengths small compared to the earth's radius. Kerr's approximation follows:

$$D = \left(1 + \frac{2G_1G_2}{a_e G \sin\psi}\right)^{-1/2} \tag{D–31}$$

A number of other approximations for D appear in the literature (Balanis 1984, 2005; Beckmann and Spizzachino 1963). These approximations and (D–31) are compared in SM 3.6 with both terminal heights (h_1 and h_2) being 20 km, and each gives almost identical calculated values. Consequently, each of the equations will provide acceptably calculated *geometrical* values for D if neither platform height exceeds 20 km. However, an accurate geometrical calculation of D does not necessarily provide a valid electromagnetic result.

The risk of using the calculated divergence factor for very small grazing angles (about one degree or less) is now illustrated. Recall that a small D value implies a small reflected field, and then the total field would approximate the free space field. Contrarily, measurements indicate that the field strength actually becomes smaller as ψ becomes smaller and the horizon is approached. However, because of diffraction from the earth, the pattern propagation factor F is very small, but not actually zero at ranges that exceed the calculated horizon R_{max} (Blake 1991, pp. 271–74). Accordingly, incautious use of a D value can cause the calculated pattern propagation factor F versus range to incorrectly approach the free-space value of unity.

References

Balanis, C. A., R. Hartenstein, and D. DeCarlo, "Multipath Interference for In-Flight Antenna Measurements," *IEEE Trans. on Antennas and Propagation*, January 1984, pp. 100–104.

Balanis, C. A., *Antenna Theory, Analysis and Design*, 3rd ed., Wiley-Interscience, 2005, pp. 208–11.

Beckmann, P., and A. Spizzachino, *The Scattering of Electromagnetic Waves from Rough Surfaces*," The MacMillan Company, 1963, p. 224.

Blake, L.V., *Radar Range-Performance Analysis*, Munro Publishing, 1991; Artech House, 1986.

Dicaudo, V. J., "Radomes," ch. 14 in M. I. Skolnik, *Radar Handbook*, McGraw-Hill, 1970.

Institute of Electrical and Electronics Engineers, *IEEE Standard 686-1997*, 1997.

Kerr, D. E., *Propagation of Short Radio Waves*, McGraw-Hill, 1951.

Long, M. W., R. D. Wetherington, J. L. Edwards, and A. B. Abeling, "Wavelength Dependence of Sea Echo," Engineering Experiment Station, Final Report, Contract N-62269-3019, Georgia Institute of Technology, July 1965.

Meeks, M. L., *Radar Propagation at Low Altitudes*, Artech House, 1982.

Reed, H. R., and C. M. Russell, *Ultra High Frequency Propagation*, 2nd ed., Boston Technical Publishers, 1964, p. 140–41.

U.S. Department of Commerce, *A World Atlas of Atmospheric Radio Refractivity*, ESSA Monograph No. 1, 1966.

APPENDIX E

Radomes

A radome is a dielectric structure that is used to protect an antenna from its environment (wind, rain, ice, salt spray, dust, insects), and it may be used to reduce aerodynamic drag. Radomes serve as feed covers, covers attached to the antenna, or covers within which an antenna moves. Therefore, they have a wide variety of shapes and wall structures (Huddleston and Bassett 1993).

A radome can cause unwanted changes in beam-pointing direction, create energy loss by reflection and absorption, cause gain loss and side-lobe degradation by defocusing, create internal reflections that produce impedance mismatches, increase side-lobe levels, and may also depolarize the radiation. Rulf (1985) discusses electrical design issues for an airborne radome used with a large, very-low side-lobe antenna. The reader should be aware that radome design is a highly specialized subject. For example, the design for a radome with pointed nose for high-speed aircraft may be more complex than the antenna design.

Schrank, Evans, and Davis (1990) discuss a variety of radome types, and descriptions of some of the more common radome wall cross sections are given here and illustrated in Fig. E–1.

Thin wall. A solid dielectric, with thickness usually less than $\lambda/10$ measured in the dielectric. The reflections from the air-radome and radome-air interfaces have opposite phases. Thus, if the radome wall thickness is thin compared to the wavelength within the radome material, the net effect is near-cancellation of the reflections. A thin wall radome has good electrical properties, but it may be weak structurally when designed for frequencies above 1 GHz.

Half wavelength. This is a solid dielectric surface having an electrical thickness near one-half wavelength. A half-wavelength-thick surface is nonreflecting at its design frequency. Because of the half-wavelength requirement, its bandwidth and its useful range of incidence angles are limited.

A-sandwich. A commonly used three-layer wall configuration consisting of two thin dielectric skins separated by a thicker but low-dielectric constant core. The core might be a honeycomb or a foam material. Since the reflections from the two

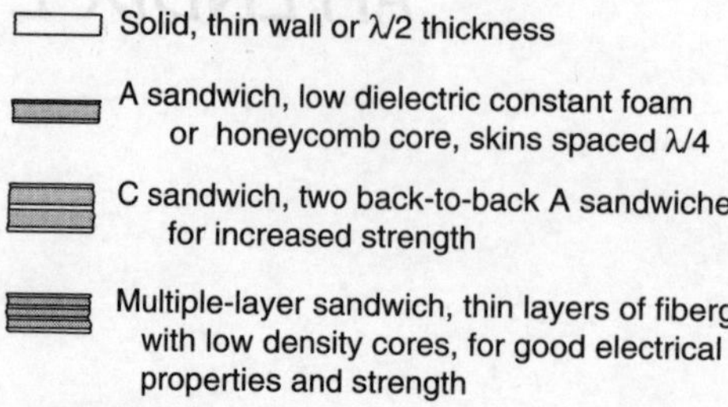

FIGURE E–1.

Commonly used radome wall cross sections.

skins will be roughly equal in amplitude and phase, a quarter-wavelength spacing of the skins will minimize their combined reflections

C-sandwich. Two back-to-back *A*-sandwiches. It can be used when the ordinary *A*-sandwich does not provide sufficient strength.

Multiple-layer sandwich. These include many thin layers of fiberglass with low-density cores for providing great strength and good electrical performance.

Dicaudo (1970) includes numerous useful graphs that show electrical performance versus incidence angle for single-layer, *A*-sandwich, and *C*-sandwich walls; and for polarizations parallel and perpendicular to the plane of incidence formed by the direction of propagation and the normal to the radome surface. These curves show transmission efficiency and insertion phase delay versus the radome-wall thickness-to-wavelength ratio. The data are included for several dielectric materials.

Relative permittivity is the permittivity of a medium relative to its free space value ε_o of 8.85×10^{-12} farads/meter. To account for the ohmic loss of a dielectric material, a complex relative permittivty ε_r is used that follows:

$$\varepsilon_r = \varepsilon_r' - j\varepsilon_r'' = \varepsilon_r' - j60\lambda_0\sigma \tag{E–1}$$

where λ_0 is the free-space wavelength in meters and σ is conductivity of the medium in mhos per meter. The term ε_r' is the conventional relative dielectric constant ordinarily quoted for materials, and it and the index of refraction n of a nonmagnetic material are related as follows

$$(\varepsilon_r')^{1/2} = n = c/v \tag{E–2}$$

where v is wave velocity in the medium and c is wave velocity in free space. Then from $\lambda = v/f$ and the wavelength λ in an open, unbounded (not a waveguide) medium is

$$\lambda = v/f = c/\left[(\varepsilon_r')^{1/2} f\right] = \lambda_0/(\varepsilon_r')^{1/2} \tag{E–3}$$

where λ_0 is the free space wavelength. Thus, for a dielectric constant of 4 (typical of epoxy resin fiberglass radomes), the internal wavelength would be one-half λ_0. Then, for this example, a layer of $\lambda_0/10$ thickness corresponds to $\lambda/20$ internal thickness and would be electrically acceptable as a thin radome or as a thin wall for a layered radome.

The term ε_r'' accounts for a dielectric's ohmic loss, and the ratio $\varepsilon_r''/\varepsilon_r'$ is defined as the loss tangent or tan δ. Although not relevant to antennas and transmission lines, another electrical term is dielectric power factor PF, where $PF = \sin\delta$. Loss tangents for radome

TABLE E-1 Approximate Electrical Properties of Selected Materials at 10 GHz

Material	ε_r'	Loss tangent ($\varepsilon_r''/\varepsilon_r'$)
Vacuum (defined)	1	0
Plexiglas	2.6	1.5×10^{-2}
Polystyrene	2.54	4×10^{-4}
Teflon	2.08	4×10^{-4}
Duroid	2.7	3×10^{-3}
Aluminum oxide	9.2	3×10^{-4}
Fused silica	3.6	2×10^{-4}
Boron nitride	4.4	1×10^{-4}

dielectrics are in the range of 10^{-4} to 10^{-2}. Thus, for these materials loss tangent and power factor are essentially equal.

Table E-1 includes typical electrical properties of some radome materials at 10 GHz. For further details, see Bodnar (2007) and Burks (2007). Although ε_r' varies with frequency, the values given are generally typical for kiloHertz and gigaHertz frequencies. On the other hand, $\varepsilon_r'' = j\ 60\ \lambda\ \sigma$ and thus loss tangent ε_r'' is a strong function of frequency. Electrical properties also depend on fabrication method, material density, and temperature.

The loss per unit length of a dielectric is proportional to loss tangent and is derived theoretically by Ragan (1948, pp. 28–29). The attenuation, expressed in nepers per meter, within the dielectric is

$$A_{Np} = (\pi/\lambda)\tan\delta \quad \text{in nepers per m} \tag{E–4}$$

or

$$A_{Np} = \pi\tan\delta \quad \text{in nepers per } \lambda \text{ within the dielectric} \tag{E–5}$$

By using the relationship between attenuation in nepers A_{Np} and in decibels A_{dB}, namely $A_{Np} = 0.115\ A_{dB}$, we obtain

$$A_{dB} = 27.3\tan\delta \quad \text{in dB per } \lambda \text{ within the dielectric} \tag{E–6}$$

or by using the index of refraction n, that is, $(\varepsilon_r')^{1/2}$, of the dielectric medium,

$$A_{dB} = 27.3n\tan\delta \quad \text{in dB per free space wavelength, } \lambda_0 \tag{E–7}$$

As examples of possible dielectric losses, we now consider radome wall thicknesses of $\lambda/20$ and λ for a dielectric having a relatively high loss tangent of 10^{-2}. Then from (E–6), the attenuations in dB are

$$A_{dB} = 27.3 \cdot 10^{-2} \cdot (1/20) = 1.4 \times 10^{-2} \text{ dB for } \lambda/20 \text{ thickness and } 10^{-2} \text{ loss tangent}$$

and

$$A_{dB} = 27.3 \cdot 10^{-2} \cdot 1 = 0.27 \text{ dB for } \lambda \text{ thickness and } 10^{-2} \text{ loss tangent}$$

Thus it is seen that ohmic loss, when using a relatively high loss material, is insignificant for a thin wall radome. However, the loss can be appreciable if the thickness were one wavelength. Another major concern is the likely negative effect of the radome on antenna focusing. Generally, thin wall radomes do not create significant degradation to antenna gain or side lobes. However, much caution is needed when using the thicker radomes, often needed for structural strength.

References

Bodnar, D. G., "Materials and Design Data," ch. 55, pp. 55–3 through 55–5 in J. L. Volakis, *Antenna Engineering Handbook*, 4th ed., 2007.

Burks, D. G., "Radomes," ch. 53, pp. 53–16 and 53–17 in J. L. Volakis, *Antenna Engineering Handbook*, 4th ed., 2007.

Dicaudo, V. J., "Radomes," ch. 14 in M. I. Skolnik, *Radar Handbook*, McGraw-Hill, 1970.

Huddleston, G. K., and H. L. Bassett, "Radomes," ch. 44 in R. C. Johnson (ed.), *Antenna Engineering Handbook*, 3rd ed., McGraw-Hill, 1993.

Ragan, G. L., *Microwave Transmission Circuits*, vol. 9, M.I.T. Laboratory Series, McGraw-Hill, pp. 28–29, 1948.

Rulf, B., "Problems of Radome Design for Modern Airborne Radar, Part 1," *Microwave Journal*, Jan. 1985, pp. 145–48, 152–53; "Problems of Radome Design for Modern Airborne Radar, Part 2," *Microwave Journal*, May 1985, pp. 265–67, 271.

Schrank, H. E., G. E. Evans, and D. Davis, in ch. 6, "Reflector Antennas," pp. 6.44–6.52 in M. I. Skolnik, *Radar Handbook*, 2nd ed., McGraw-Hill, 1990.

APPENDIX F

Far-Zone Range-Approximation and Phase Error

The far-field region, that is, the far zone, is the region of an antenna field where the antenna radiation pattern is essentially independent of the distance from the antenna. In free space, with the antenna maximum dimension D being large compared to a wavelength, the far-field region is commonly taken to be greater than r_{min}, where

$$r_{min} = 2D^2/\lambda \tag{F–1}$$

λ is wavelength (IEEE Standard 100–1992, p. 482). Greater distances are desirable, especially if accurate measurements are needed for antennas with very low side lobes. The distance criterion (F–1) is based on the phase variation caused by the path-length change δ over a linear aperture of dimension D, resulting from spherically spreading radiation from a point P, as illustrated by Fig. F–1. Sometimes, however, additional criteria are necessary for assurance that a measured pattern replicates a far-field measurement.*

From a right triangle of Fig. F–1 with sides R, $D/2$, and $(\delta + R)$, one attains

$$R^2 + (D/2)^2 = (\delta + R)^2 = \delta^2 + 2\delta R + R^2$$

or

$$(D/2)^2 = \delta^2 + 2\delta R \tag{F–2}$$

Ordinarily $\delta << R$, and then $\delta^2 << 2\,\delta R$. Thus,

$$(D/2)^2 \approx 2\delta R$$

*While reviewing the manuscript, E. B. Joy added two additional criteria: (1) $r_{min} = 20\,\lambda$, that pertains to electrically small antennas and assures that the reactive near-field is negligible at r_{min} and (2) $r_{min} = 20\,D$, that limits the relative down range far-field decrease across the antenna under test to an acceptable value. As with the factor 2 in (F–1), choice of the factors 20 depends on the accuracy of measurement required. According to J. S. Hollis, T. J. Lyon, and L. Clayton, Jr., (1970, sec. 14.2), the relevant effects are usually considered negligible if $r_{min} \geq 10\lambda$ and $r_{min} \geq 10D$.

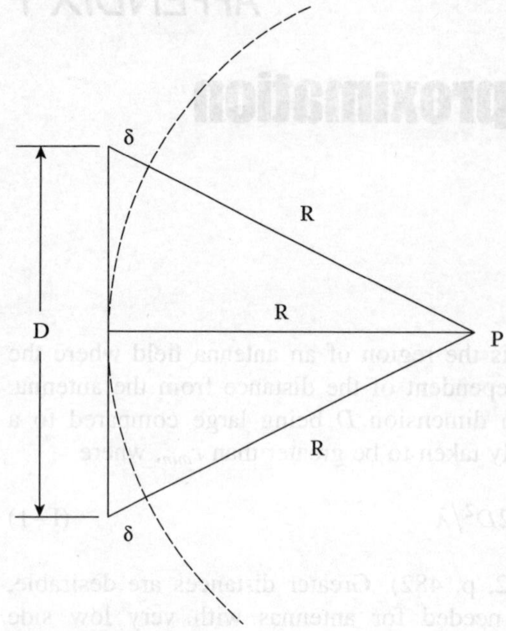

FIGURE F–1.
Path-length difference δ for an aperture dimension D and range R.

or

$$\delta \approx (D/2)^2(1/2R) = D^2/8R \quad \text{(F–3)}$$

We can now find the phase error caused by the path-length difference δ if $r_{min} = 2D^2/\lambda$, with $\delta << 2R$ in accordance with (F–1). Then from (F–3),

$$\delta = D^2/8R = D^2/8\left(2D^2/\lambda\right) = \lambda/16 = 22.5° \quad \text{(F–4)}$$

Therefore, when the separation distance is $2D^2/\lambda$ between an aperture (of maximum dimension D) and the source, the maximum phase error is 22.5° ($\lambda/16$). In addition, it is to be noted that the phase error caused by the pathlength difference δ varies in proportion to D^2, from zero at the aperture center to a maximum at an aperture edge.

A question now to be addressed is the required minimum far-zone distance $2D^2/\lambda$, when δ is not much less than $2R$, the assumption used to get the $\lambda/16$ far-zone criterion of (F–4). Returning to the exact equation (F–2) and letting $\lambda/16$, it may be seen that $D = \lambda/8$ if $R = 0$. Thus, the pathlength difference δ of Fig. F–1 is less than $\lambda/16$ if $D < \lambda/8$. In other words, according to the $\lambda/16$ far-zone criterion, the far zone always exists if the antenna maximum aperture dimension D is less than $\lambda/8$. However, it is to be noted that both reactive and radiative fields surround an antenna (sec. 3.2). Thus, although the $\delta < \lambda/16$ far-field criterion may be satisfied at very short distances from very small antenna aperture, the reactive near-field may exceed the far-field at separation distances less than 20λ (sec. 3.2.5).

References

Hollis, J. S., T. J. Lyon, and L. Clayton, Jr., sec. 14.2 of *Microwave Antenna Measurements*, Scientific-Atlanta, 1970.

The New IEEE Standard Dictionary of Electrical and Electronic Terms, 1992.

APPENDIX G

Radiating Near and Far Fields, and the Obliquity Factor

Appendix G discusses the radiating E- and H-fields that surround an energized antenna, including radiation patterns versus separation distance from an antenna aperture. This material is supplemented by the accompanying website that contains example calculations using Mathcad for radiating near- and far-field patterns, where the Huygens-Kirchhoff formulation is used for the near-aperture radiating field calculations (Good 1990).

G.1. The Radiating Fields

The E- and H-field regions that surround an energized antenna are of three types: the reactive near-field, the radiating near-field, and the radiating far-field. The locations of these fields depend on distance to the observation point, wavelength, and aperture size. The reactive near-zone field decays the most rapidly with distance from the antenna so that, except at relatively close distances, its magnitude is insignificant compared to the magnitudes of the radiating fields. Historically, the closer-in and more distant radiating fields have been called the Fresnel and Fraunhofer regions, but today the terms "radiating near-field" and "radiating far-far field" are preferred (IEEE, 1992). Furthermore, these fields are not located at clearly defined distances, but the "far field" region is where the radiation pattern versus angle is for practical purposes independent of distance. As a rule of thumb, the far-zone distance is said to be at and beyond $2D^2/\lambda$, where D is the largest dimension of the aperture. This and other requirements are given in Appendix F.

Figure G–1 is a depiction of the three regions as given by Johnson, Ecker, and Hollis (1973). It illustrates the propagation paths within the radiating far-field region as if they were emitted radially from the antenna, that is, as if the energy emanates from a specific point (like a radiating point source). Notice that, within the radiating near-field region of this high-directivity antenna in Fig. G–1, propagation is shown as being both along parallel paths from the aperture and transitioning in the diverging directions of the far-field region. Existence of the parallel paths indicates, at least theoretically, that the phase and amplitude are both constant perpendicular to the propagation path. These features permit

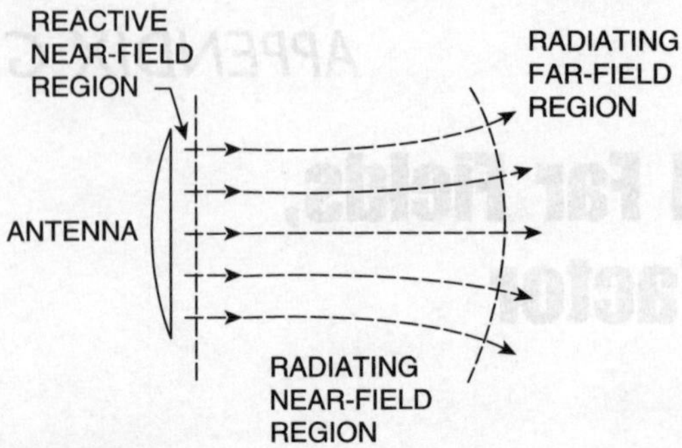

FIGURE G–1.

The three regions surrounding a high directivity antenna. (Johnson, Ecker, and Hollis, © IEEE 1973).

the measurement of accurate far-zone radiation patterns within a compact range (see sec. 9.3), even though the antenna under test is within the radiating near-field of the compact range antenna.

Radiation patterns for aperture antennas are most often calculated based on assumptions called high-frequency scalar approximations. High frequency refers to the aperture being large enough that the effects of radiation from aperture edges are negligible and the distance to the observation point is at least several wavelengths; and scalar refers to the field over the aperture being almost completely linearly polarized, with only a small fraction of the energy being cross-polarized.

Silver (1949, pp. 169–99) published classic equations for the close-in (Fresnel) and the more distant (Fraunhofer) radiation fields, that are now described. Assume an aperture is in the *x-y* plane, in accordance with Fig. G–2. Also assume the amplitude and phase excitation on the surface (the aperture) is described by the term $A(x, y)$, and let each surface point be located a distance $r1$ from observation point P.

Equation (2) of Silver (1949), page 170, is a general diffraction equation developed for continuous aperture dimensions that are large compared to a wavelength. For specificity, let the aperture be rectangular with $\pm a/2$ and $\pm b/2$ being its edges along the x and y directions. With two assumptions, described below, Silver's equation (2) reduces to the Huygens-Kirchhoff diffraction formulation (Lerner and Trigg 1990); for which pattern field amplitudes can be expressed as

$$g(\theta,\phi)=\left|\int_{-a/2}^{a/2}\int_{-b/2}^{b/2}A(x,y)\frac{e^{-j\frac{2\pi}{\lambda}r1}}{r1}\left[\frac{\cos\eta(x,y)+1}{2}\right]dxdy\right| \qquad \text{(G–1)}$$

where $A(x, y)$ is the amplitude and phase distribution over the aperture, $\eta(x, y)$ is the angle between the outward direction of $r1$ and the Z axis at each x,y aperture position. The assumptions include: (1) the $r1$ and R lengths are at least several wavelengths and (2) the phase fluctuations across the aperture are small enough so that the phase distribution is essentially uniform.

Persons familiar with physical optics will recognize (G–1) as being the phasor summation of Huygens' wavelets (Fig. 1–9, chapter 1) that emanate from the aperture x,y positions, with their amplitudes modified based on propagation direction, in accordance with the factor $(1/2)[\cos\eta(x, y) + 1]$. This amplitude multiplier is the Fresnel obliquity factor, which has been verified with mathematical rigor (see, e.g., Slater and Frank 1947). Accordingly, forward propagating wavelets have unity amplitude if $\eta(x, y) = 0°$; and the wavelets have zero amplitude in the backward direction if $\eta(x, y) = 180°$. In general, $\eta(x, y)$ is a complicated function of the aperture coordinates and θ. Fortunately, however, the obliquity is not needed for calculating array patterns, and often it is not needed when calculating radiation from continuous aperture antennas.

Another approximation, valid for the far-field and much of the near radiating field, assumes the lengths $r1$ and R are large compared to the linear aperture dimensions a and b. Now, with this, we neglect the variation of $\cos\eta$ over the aperture and we replace η with θ and $r1$ with R. Then, (G–1) is simplified and becomes (G–2) that follows

$$g(\theta,\phi)=\frac{(\cos\theta+1)}{2R}\left|\int_{-a/2}^{a/2}\int_{-b/2}^{b/2}A(x,y)e^{-j\frac{2\pi}{\lambda}r1}\,dxdy\right| \tag{G–2}$$

In the radiating near-field region described by (G–2), in accordance with Appendix H, the distance $r1$ varies with the observation angle θ, the x and y aperture coordinates, and the distance R between the aperture origin and the observation point P. Thus, the normalized near-fields are functions of R and there are gradual changes versus R from the radiating near-field out to and including the far-field.

It is to be noted that field amplitudes are highly sensitive to the pathlength difference δ between $r1$ and R, and a useful relationship follows:

$$e^{-\frac{2\pi}{\lambda}r1}=e^{-\frac{2\pi}{\lambda}(\delta+R)}=e^{-\frac{2\pi}{\lambda}R}e^{-\frac{2\pi}{\lambda}\delta}$$

To obtain an equation for use only within the radiating far-field, distance $r1$ in (G–2) is replaced by using (H–6) of Appendix H. Then, the integrand of (G–2) is simplified,

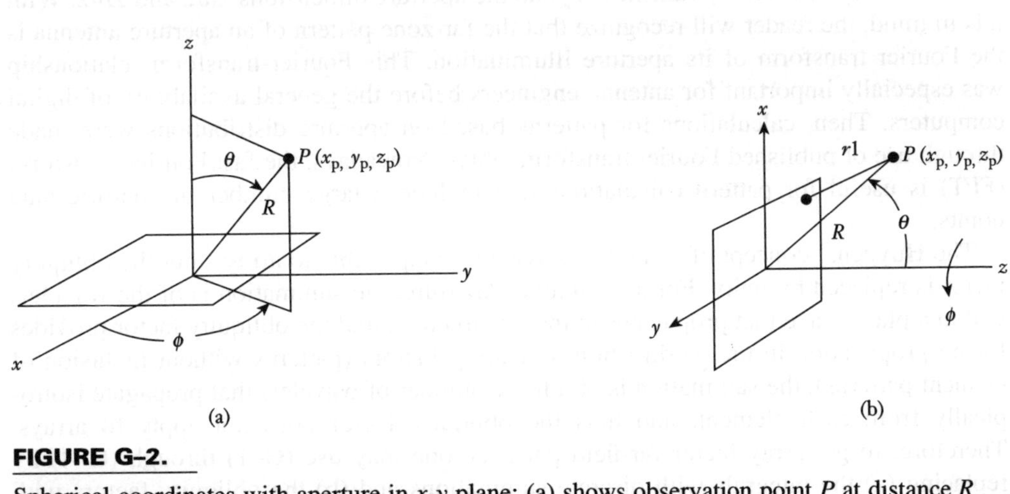

FIGURE G–2.

Spherical coordinates with aperture in x-y plane: (a) shows observation point P at distance R from origin and (b) shows point P at distance R from the origin and distance r_1 from a specific position on the x-y plane.

and the equation for the pattern amplitude in the radiating far-field becomes (G–3) that follows:

$$g(\theta,\phi)=\frac{(\cos\theta+1)}{2R}\left|\int_{-a/2}^{a/2}\int_{-b/2}^{b/2}A(x,y)e^{j\frac{2\pi}{\lambda}\sin\theta(x\cos\phi+y\sin\phi)}dxdy\right| \tag{G–3}$$

Note that, consistent with the definition of far zone, the integral of (G–3) is not a function of R.

Recall that θ is the observation direction and is measured from the normal to the aperture (the z-axis). For θ of 30°, 60°, and 90°, the obliquity factor reduces the calculated E-field amplitude by 0.6, 2.5, and 6 dB, respectively. On the other hand, the beam pointing direction is determined by the phase term within the aperture excitation $A(x, y)$. Often the main beam (major lobe) is pointed along the z-axis ($\theta = 0$). Then, especially for narrow-beam antennas, the θ values of greatest interest are small enough that the obliquity factor is assumed unity. Therefore, the term $(1 + \cos\theta)/2$ in (G–3) is commonly neglected. Furthermore, the equation for $g(\theta, \phi)$ is usually simplified by neglecting the multiplicity factor $1/R$. Then the electric field pattern in the radiating far-field may be expressed as

$$g(\theta,\phi)=\int_{-a/2}^{a/2}\int_{-b/2}^{b/2}A(x,y)e^{j\frac{2\pi}{\lambda}\sin\theta(x\cos\phi+y\sin\phi)}dxdy \tag{G–4}$$

If the limits of integration of (G–4) are replaced by infinity and minus infinity, the integral becomes a Fourier integral of two variables. Then, for practical purposes (G–4) is a Fourier integral, because the aperture illumination $A(x, y)$ is zero outside the aperture. Thus, the integral in (G–4) vanishes beyond the aperture dimensions $\pm a/2$ and $\pm b/2$. With this in mind, the reader will recognize that the far-zone pattern of an aperture antenna is the Fourier transform of its aperture illumination. This Fourier-transform relationship was especially important for antenna engineers before the general availability of digital computers. Then, calculations for patterns based on aperture distributions were made through use of published Fourier transform tables. Nowadays, the fast Fourier transform (FFT) is useful for pattern calculations that include a large number of aperture data points.

The Huygens' concept of summing wavelets is applicable to arrays, but the obliquity factor is replaced by unity. For a continuous aperture, the summation is of the wavelets within a plane wave that propagates in the $+z$ direction, and the obliquity factor provides for no propagation in the $-z$ direction. For array factors (patterns without inclusion of element patterns), the summation is of a finite number of wavelets that propagate isotropically from each element, and thus the obliquity factor does not apply to arrays. Therefore, to get array factor far-field patterns, one may use (G–1) through (G–4) by replacing (a) the integrals with discrete summations and (b) the obliquity factors with the numeral one.

G.2. Principal-Plane Patterns Versus Range

This section discusses x-z plane pattern calculations versus range, for continuous apertures and arrays located on the x-axis. Let us assume that there are N radiating elements with equal phase and with different amplitudes $a(n)$ that are functions of the positions $x(n)$ along the x-axis. Then, the integral can be replaced by discrete summation, where for continuous apertures the elements are infinitesimal and their spacing approaches zero. Then, (G–1) becomes

$$g(\theta)=\left|\sum_{n=1}^{N}a(n)\frac{e^{-j\frac{2\pi}{\lambda}r1}}{r1}\left[\frac{\cos\eta(n)+1}{2}\right]\right| \qquad \text{(G–5)}$$

Ordinarily, $r1$ is large compared to the dimensions of the antenna, and then the bracketed term in (G–5) becomes $(\cos\theta + 1)/2$. However as noted in sec. G–1, for array elements the $(\cos\theta + 1)/2$ term is inapplicable and is replaced by numeral one.

In general, pattern calculations are highly sensitive to $r1$ and the pathlength difference δ, where δ is $r1 - R$. For $r1$, equation (H–4), Appendix H, is exact. Then, with radiating elements located only at positions $x(n)$ on the x-axis, $r1$ becomes

$$r1=R\left[1-2\frac{x(n)}{R}\sin\theta+\left(\frac{x(n)}{R}\right)^{2}\right]^{0.5} \qquad \text{(G–6)}$$

Furthermore, where aperture dimensions are small compared to R, δ is considerably simplified, as determined from equation (H–6), Appendix H. Consequently, for far-field patterns in the x-z plane ($\phi = 0$) and for an aperture with its coordinates $x(n)$ on the x-axis, one obtains

$$\delta=r1-R\approx -x(n)\sin\theta \qquad \text{(G–7)}$$

Now, using (G–6) and (G–7) when R is much larger than $r1$, one obtains (G–8) that follows.

$$g(\theta)=\frac{(\cos\theta+1)}{2R}\left|\sum_{n=1}^{N}a(n)e^{j\frac{2\pi}{\lambda}x(n)\sin\theta}\right| \qquad \text{(G–8)}$$

Equation (G–8) may be used for far-field calculations, provided R is $2D^2/\lambda$ or greater. As in the previous equations, the obliquity factor $(\cos\theta + 1)/2$ for arrays is replaced by numeral one. In addition, this factor is often assumed to be unity for aperture antennas; because major interest is usually near small θ values, where the obliquity factor is essentially one.

Example pattern calculations versus range are included in the accompanying website.

References

Good, Myron L., "Diffraction," in *Encyclopedia of Physics*, 2nd ed., R. Lerner and G. L. Trigg (eds.), 1990, VCH Publishers, p. 252.

Hansen, R. C., "Aperture Theory," in R. C. Hansen (ed.), *Microwave Scanning Antennas*, Academic Press, Inc, New York, 1964.

IEEE Standard 100-1992, *The New IEEE Standard Dictionary of Electrical and Electronic Terms*, 1992.

Johnson, R. C. (ed.), *Antenna Handbook*, 3rd ed., p. 1–10, McGraw-Hill, 1993.

Johnson, R. C., H. A. Ecker, and J. S. Hollis, "Determination of Far-Field Antenna Patterns from Near-Field Measurements," *Proceedings of the IEEE*, December 1973, pp. 1668–94.

Silver, S., *Microwave Antenna Theory and Design*, McGraw-Hill, 1949.

Slater, J. C., and N. H. Frank, *Electromagnetism*, 1947, Mc-Graw-Hill, ch. 13.

APPENDIX H

Path Length Differences from a Planar Aperture

Appendix H includes calculations on the differences in distances from points on a planar surface to a distant point P. The results are used in Appendix G for determining antenna patterns versus range.

Consider the spherical coordinate system of Fig. H–1(a) with point P located at coordinates x_p, y_p, z_p in space and where P is located a distance R from the origin ($x = y = z = 0$). Notice that angle θ is measured from the z-axis, but angle ϕ is measured from the x-axis and it is always in the x-y plane. From standard spherical coordinate relationships,

$$\begin{aligned} x_p &= R\sin\theta\cos\phi \equiv R\alpha \\ y_p &= R\sin\theta\sin\phi \equiv R\beta \\ z_p &= R\cos\theta \end{aligned} \tag{H–1}$$

In (H–1) above, the abbreviations $R\alpha$ and $R\beta$ are used to denote x_p and y_p to simplify equations that follow. Notice that

$$R = \left[(x_p)^2 + (y_p)^2 + (z_p)^2\right]^{1/2} = \left[(R\alpha)^2 + (R\beta)^2 + (R\cos\theta)^2\right]^{1/2} \tag{H–2}$$

Next, referring to Fig. H–1(b), we find the distance $r1$ between points at x_a and y_a on the aperture ($z_a = 0$) and point P is as follows

$$r1 = \left[(x_a - x_p)^2 + (y_a - y_p)^2 + (z_p)^2\right]^{1/2} = \left[(R\alpha - x_a)^2 + (R\beta - y_a)^2 + (R\cos\theta)^2\right]^{1/2} \tag{H–3}$$

After expanding (H–3) and noting from (H–2) that $[(R\alpha)^2 + (R\alpha)^2 + (R\cos\theta)^2] = R^2$, we find

$$r1 = R\left[1 - \frac{2}{R}(\alpha x_a + \beta y_a) + \frac{x_a^2 + y_a^2}{R^2}\right]^{1/2} \tag{H–4}$$

Now assume that the aperture dimensions are small compared to R, that is, $x_a << R$ and $y_a << R$. Then, $r1$ of (H–4) is simplified and becomes (H–5) that follows

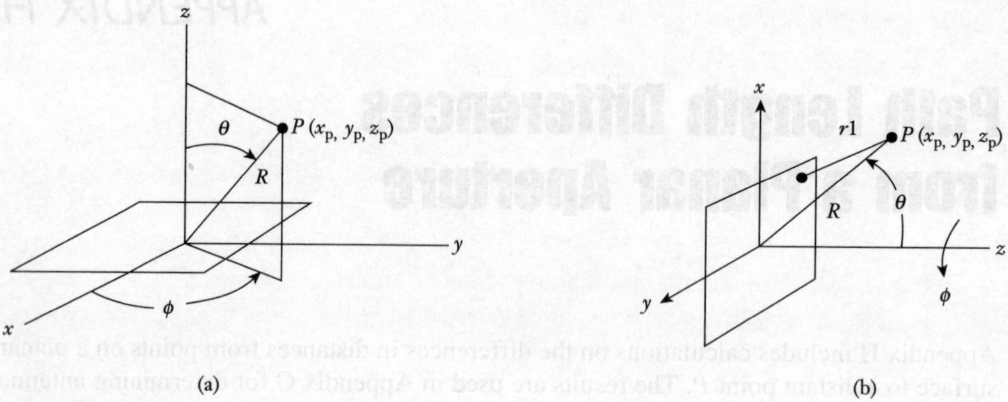

FIGURE H–1.
Spherical coordinates with array elements in *x-y* plane. In (a), point *P* is at distance *R* from origin; in (b), point *P* is at distance *R* from the origin and distance r_1 from a position x_a, y_a on the *x-y* plane.

$$\begin{aligned} r1 &\approx R\left[1-\frac{2}{R}(\alpha x_a+\beta y_a)\right]^{1/2} \approx R\left[1-\frac{1}{R}(\alpha x_a+\beta y_a)\right] \\ &= R - x_a\sin\theta\cos\phi - y_a\sin\theta\sin\phi \end{aligned} \quad \text{(H–5)}$$

Therefore $r1$ exceeds R by an amount δ, where

$$\delta = r1 - R = -\sin\theta(x_a\cos\phi + y_a\sin\phi) \quad \text{(H–6)}$$

Now consider effects on $r1$ and δ with R fixed, and with P only on one of the principal planes, *x-z* or *y-z*. Then, for the *x-z* and *y-z* planes: $\phi = 0$ and $\phi = \pi/2$ (90°), respectively. Thus, from (H–6), with R fixed and P in the *x-z* plane

$$\delta = r1 - R = -x_a\sin\theta \quad (\text{for } \phi = 0) \quad \text{(H–7)}$$

and with P in the *y-z* plane

$$\delta = r1 - R = -y_a\sin\theta \quad (\text{for } \phi = \pi/2) \quad \text{(H–8)}$$

Now assume the x and y axes are vertical and horizontal, respectively, as in Fig. H–1(b). Then from (H–7) and (H–8), which are applicable when $x_a << R$ and $y_a << R$, we see that to close approximations the following are true:

(1) for P on the vertical plane (*x-z*), $r1$ and δ are functions of the x_a (vertical) location on the aperture—not on the y_a (horizon) location; and similarly
(2) for P on the horizontal plane (*y-z*), $r1$ and δ are functions of the y_a (horizontal) location on the aperture—not on the x_a (vertical) location.

Now continuing to refer to Fig. H–1(b), we see that

- the principal plane pattern in azimuth is the θ dependent pattern when $\phi = 90°$; and
- the principal plane pattern in elevation is the θ dependent pattern when $\phi = 0$.

It is to be underscored that all discussion following (H–4) is limited to situations for which the antenna aperture dimensions are small compared to the distance *R*, between antenna origin and the observation point *P*. Therefore, that discussion is applicable only to the far zone. In general, however, radiating near-field pattern calculations must include the exact pathlength difference δ (i.e., $r1 - R$) attainable from (H–4). Patterns versus distance *R* are discussed in Appendix G and relevant calculations are included in the accompanying SM.

APPENDIX I

Effects of Random Aperture Phase Errors

In arrays, aperture phase errors are caused by element misalignment and improper phase excitation, and surface errors are a major source of aperture error for reflector antennas. Section 6.5 includes a general discussion on reflector errors, and the present appendix addresses relatively simple calculations on the effects of random phase errors.

In Fig. I–1, it may be seen that the difference ΔR in the pathlengths aa' and bb' is

$$\Delta R = 2h \sin\alpha \tag{I–1}$$

Thus the phase difference in radians $\Delta\Psi$ caused by the path length difference ΔR between paths aa' and bb' is

$$\Delta\psi = (2\pi/\lambda)\Delta R \tag{I–2}$$

Then, if the height distribution for a random rough surface is designated by Δh, the distribution of phase differences can be expressed as

$$\Delta\psi = (2\pi/\lambda)2\Delta h \sin\alpha \tag{I–3}$$

Experience shows that random surface roughness is well described by surface heights, which can be expressed statistically as a normal (i.e., Gaussian) distribution. Then, in Mathcad, the surface height distribution Δh becomes

$$\Delta h = \text{rnorm}(n, \mu, \sigma) \tag{I–4}$$

where

n = number of data points
μ = average value
σ = standard deviation

If $\mu = 0$, the standard deviation σ equals the rms of the distribution in height.

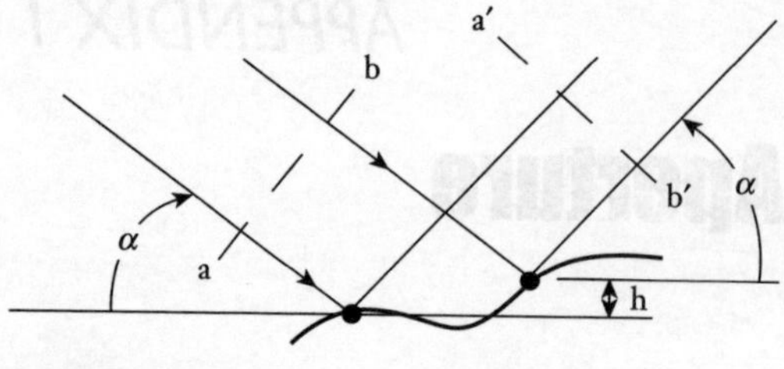

FIGURE I–1.

The difference ΔR in the path lengths of aa' and bb' is $2h \sin\alpha$. Thus the phase difference $\Delta\Psi$ is $(2\pi/\lambda)\ \Delta R = (4\pi/\lambda)h\sin\alpha$ from Long 2001, courtesy Artech House.

When $\Delta\Psi$ of (I–3) is sufficiently small, the relative phases of the rays from the various reflecting points is small and their phases tend to add constructively. Then, the reflections are specular. Otherwise, to account for the phase differences $\Delta\Psi$ caused by rougher surfaces, effects of the terms λ, Δh and $\sin\alpha$ in (I–3) must be included.

If a surface is curved, as for most antenna reflectors, effects of curvature on (I–3) must also be included, as is now discussed. From Fig. I–2, which depicts a ray reflected from a parabolic surface, it can be seen that $2\alpha + \beta = 180°$ or

$$\alpha = (180° - \beta)/2 \qquad \text{(I–5)}$$

Therefore, to include effects of random errors on the parabolic surface, effects of the angle β on $\Delta\Psi$ must be included. Then, for (I–3) to be used with Fig. I–2, $\Delta h = \text{rnorm}(n, \mu, \sigma)$ and $\alpha = (180° - \beta)/2$. Thus, for a curved reflector surface having a uniform surface roughness, the spread in phase error (standard deviation) depends on the angle β and therefore it varies along the aperture x dimension.

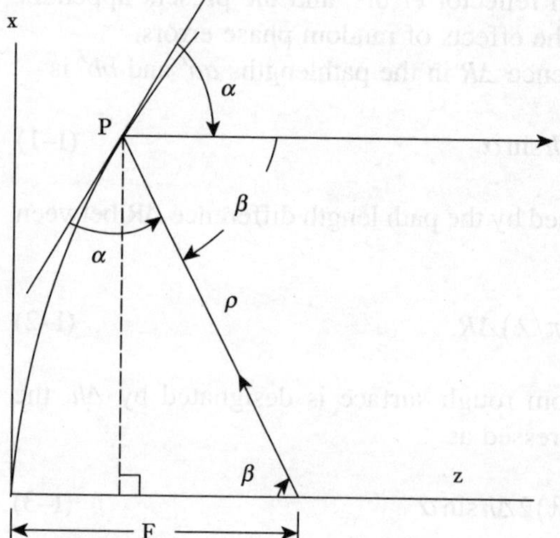

FIGURE I–2.

Geometry showing that $\alpha = (180° - \beta)/2$. Thus, for a uniform surface roughness, since α depends on β, the range of random phases $\Delta\Psi$ varies over the reflector surface.

A cautionary note: up to this point α in Appendix I is used to denote the grazing angle at a reflecting surface. In (I–6) that follows, α_i is the phase of the ith element of an array and it is therefore unrelated to this previous use of α.

The following is an example of the effects of random phase error on the pattern of an array of closely spaced array elements, having a length of 4 meters and located on the x-axis. The pattern calculated is a function of θ and it is in the x-z plane, with $\phi = 0$. It is assumed that $\lambda = 0.1$ m and that a continuous aperture is simulated by sampling at 401 points on the x-axis. Thus, the sample spacing is 0.1 λ. In order for the aperture to be centered at the x-y-z origin, we sum over the index i and define the aperture coordinates as

$$x_i = (i - 200)10^{-2}$$

Then, using the general relationship from array theory for the amplitude of the electric field (sec. 5.5.1), for the far zone we have

$$|E(\theta)| = \left|\sum_{i=0}^{401} a_i \exp\left\{j\left[\alpha_i + \left(\frac{2\pi}{\lambda}\right)x_i \sin\theta\right]\right\}\right| \tag{I–6}$$

where

a_i = the amplitude of the ith element
α_i = phase of the ith element

We now make the following additional assumptions, namely, that (1) amplitude is constant over the aperture with each $a_i = 1$ and (2) the phase is uniformly and normally distributed over the x_i.

Figure I–3 shows results of assuming rms phase errors of $\lambda/16$ and $\lambda/8$ (22.5° and 45°), and comparing those results with zero phase error (for the calculations, see the accompanying SM). Note that the pattern peak levels are reduced with increases in

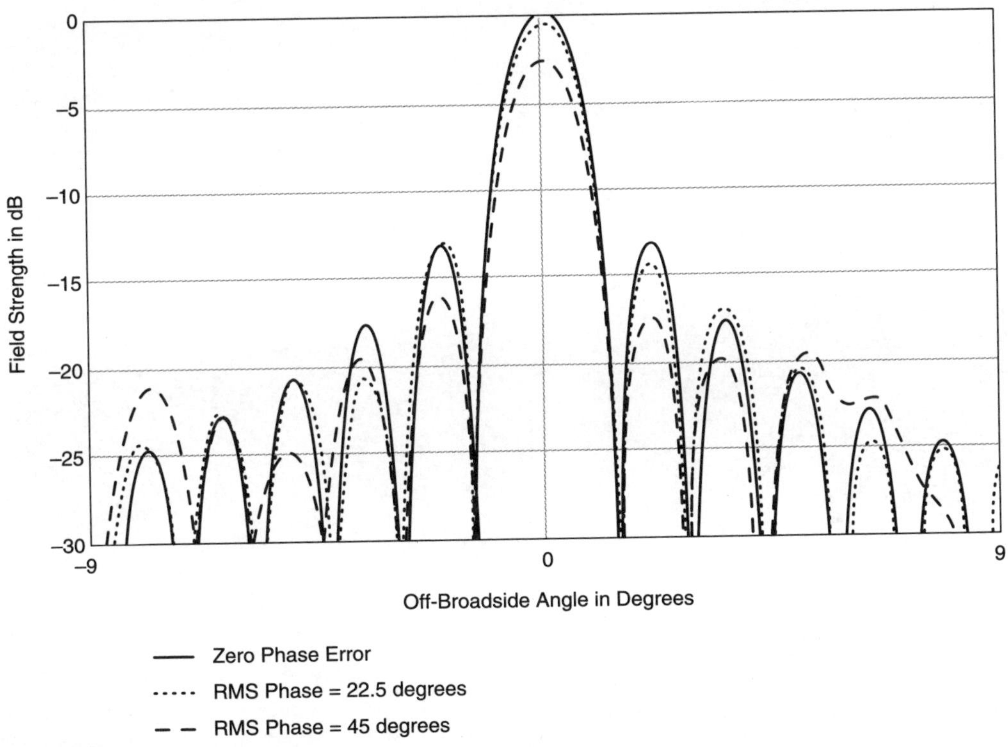

FIGURE I–3.

Antenna patterns from apertures with rms phase errors of 0, $\lambda/16$, and $\lambda/8$.

the rms errors. Additionally, the loss in gain caused by $\lambda/16$ rms phase error is only a fraction of a dB, but it is discernible. On the other hand, because of the randomness in phase error and the resulting randomness in side-lobe levels, the patterns are not symmetrical between the negative and positive angles from the major lobe.

Reference

Long, M. W., *Radar Reflectivity of Land and Sea*, 3rd ed., Artech House, 2001, p. 52.

Index

absorption, attenuation due to, 13
absorption coefficient, 20
active arrays, 354
active ESA antennas (AESAs), 367
active element pattern, 177
adaptive array antennas
  adaptive beam-forming arrays, 360–362, 360 fig., 362 fig.
  advantages of, 365
  background system developments for, 358–360, 359 fig.–360 fig.
  basic components of, 360, 360 fig.
  space-time adaptive processing in, 362–364, 362 fig.
  wireless two-dimensional, 363
adaptive beam-forming (ABF) system, 337, 360–362, 360 fig., 361 fig.
Adcock antenna, 311, 312
Aegis weapon system, 365
AESAs. *see* active ESA antennas
airborne warning and control system (AWACS), 366
aircraft landing systems, antenna patterns for, 314
Alford loop antenna, 147 fig.
amateur (ham) radio, 4
amplitude tapering, *see* tapering
AN/FPS-108 Cobra Dane system, 366, 366 fig.
AN/MPS-29 (XE-1), geodesic lens-scanning antenna for, 317, 318 fig.
AN/SPS-10 radar antenna (C-band), gain measurements on, 378
AN/SPY-1 shipboard multifunction S-band radar, of U.S. Navy, 365–366
AN/TPS-32, 364, 364 fig.
antenna design, 371
antenna measurements
  compact ranges, 382–385, 383 fig., 384 fig.
  directivity and gain, 393
    absolute-field-strength method, 394–395
    gain measurement by comparison, 396–397, 397 fig.
    power-measurement methods, 396
    standard gain antennas, 395–396
  of efficiency, 398–399
  equipment for, 390–392, 391 fig.–393 fig.
  of impedance, 400–404
  near-field, 385–388, 386 fig.–389 fig.
  of noise temperature, 409–414, 411 fig.
antenna patterns, 371–377, 372 fig., 374 fig., 375 fig.
  far-zone pattern measurements, 377–382, 380 fig.
  near- and far-field statistical gain, 376–377, 377 fig., 378 fig.
  positioner for, 392, 393 fig.
  radiating near- and far-fields patterns, 373–376, 374 fig., 375 fig.

antennas
array, 169
broad-band, 285
current and voltage in longer, 132–136, 133 fig.–135 fig.
defined, 1, 87
direction-finding, 310–314, 312 fig., 313 fig.
electrically small, 308–310
with extremely low side lobes, 325–327
fractals, 328–330, 330 fig., 331 fig.
frequency-independent, 293–301, 295 fig., 296 fig., 298 fig.–301 fig.
frequency-scan, 338, 341, 339 fig.
helical, 148–149, 148 fig.
ideal, 87
leaky-wave, 159
loop, 144–148, 144 fig., 147 fig.
low-noise receiving, 320–324, 323 fig.
mechanical scan, 314–321, 316 fig., 318 fig.–320 fig.
microstrip, 157–159
for multiple polarization
for circular polarization, 302–305, 303 fig.
corrugated horn feeds, 307, 307 fig.
dual-mode transducers, 306, 306 fig., 307 fig.
polarizers, 305–307, 307 fig.
nonresonant, 142, 142 fig.
omnidirectional, 307–308
parameters for, 87
aperture dimensions, 113–115
bandwidth, 111–113
beamwidth, 105–107
directivity and gain, 98–103
effective area, 103–105
input impedance, 110–111
minor lobes, 107–108, 108 fig.
polarization, 112
radiation resistance and efficiency, 108–109
patch, 157–159
receiving, 30
resonant, 139
standard gain, 397
structures of, 89–91
surface-wave, 159
synthetic-aperture, 285, 324–325
transmitting *vs.* receiving, 30–31
antennas, long-wire
classification of, 138–139
directivity of, 141
effect of ground on, 143
polarization of, 144–145
radiation patterns of, 138–141, 140 fig., 142, 142 fig.
radiation resistance of, 141, 141 fig.
uses of, 143
antenna-under-test (AUT), 385
aperture, of antenna, 269
circular, 279, 279 fig.
of parabolic aperture, 240
shape of, 233
aperture analysis, 329
continuous line source in, 273–276, 273 fig., 277 fig., 278 table
general, 274
historical note on, 270
pattern calculations for continuous, 269, 271, 273, 275, 277, 279
pattern *vs.* Θ and Φ in, 279, 279 fig.
principal plane patterns in, 279, 278 table
separable x and y distributions in, 275, 277, 277 fig.
aperture dimensions
and beamwidth, 119
interdependent with gain, 113–114, 116
aperture distribution, 151
calculating, 209
defined, 236
Dolph-Chebyschev (D-C) distribution, 203
planar and volume arrays with uniform, 190–191, 193, 191 fig.
for reflector antenna, 251, 255, 255 fig.
Taylor distribution, 239

aperture efficiency, 114, 420
aperture phase errors, effects of random, 480–482, 481 fig.
aperture tapers, 239
Arecibo, Puerto Rico, Arecibo Ionospheric Observatory at, 252
array fill time, 344
array patterns
  broadside linear, 183, 184 fig., 186 fig.
  general equations for, 194, 209, 214
arrays
  electronically steered, 221
  elements of, 169
  horn, 220
  long-wire, 218–219, 219 fig.
  microstrip, 220
  multielement uniform linear, 182–183, 185, 187
  and mutual coupling, 221–222
  parasitically excited endfire, 188–189, 189 fig.
  patch, 220–221
  planar, 209–211, 213–217
  slot, 220, 220 fig.
  with uniform aperture distribution, 190–191, 193, 191 fig.
array tapering. *see also* tapering
  Dolph-Chebyschev patterns, 203, 204 fig.
  for side-lobe reduction, 201, 203
  Taylor distribution for, 206–208
array theory, 169
  element directivity and mutual coupling, 181–182
  input and mutual impedances in, 178–179
  mutual coupling in, 177–178, 181–182
  parallel-dipole two-element array, 173–175, 176 fig.
  pattern *vs.* Θ and Φ, 174
  principle of pattern multiplication in, 179–181, 184
  radiation resistance in, 179
  two-isotropic-element, 170–171, 174, 171 fig., 173 fig.
artificial-dielectric media, 260
atmosphere, absorption attenuation in, 14
atmospheric gases, and propagation on radio, 32
attenuation
  due to absorption, 13, 14
  logarithmic expression of, 12
  for point and line sources, 230
  of transmission lines, 65
attenuation factor, 14
AUT, 392. *see* antenna-under-test
AWACS. *see* airborne warning and control system
AWACS radar antenna, 326
azimuth dimension, interference suppressed in, 367
azimuth scanning, 315

Babinet's principle, 155
baluns, 70
  in broad-band design, 287
  defined, 163
  examples of, 163, 163 fig.
bandwidth
  defined, 112
  impedance, 111, 112
  instantaneous, 112
  pattern, 111
  in phased array, 345
  specification of, 286
  tunable, 112
beam-maximum systems, 312
beam shift, estimates of, 344
beam steering
  effects of, 345, 349
  by feed offset, 269, 270 fig.
beam-steering technology
  effects of element mutual coupling, 350
  effects of phase quantization, 349
  phase shifters, 349–351, 351 fig.
  time delayers, 351

beamwidth
  in aperture analysis, 274 table, 278 table
  and aperture shape, 234
  definition for, 106–107
  half-power, 106, 106 fig.
  for horn antennas, 245, 247
  and line-source feeds, 239
  measurements for, 372
  for planar arrays, 213–216
  practical significance of, 104–105
  principal-plane, 106
  for short dipoles, 125, 123 fig.
  for slot radiators, 155
  Taylor distribution for, 206
Beverage antenna, 143–144
biconical antennas, 289–290, 290 fig.
biconical horn, 154–155, 155 fig.
Blass matrix, 356
Booker's principle, 300
Bootlace lens, 353–354
Brewster angle effect, 40
broad-band antennas, 285
  basic principles of, 286–288
  biconical antennas, 289–290, 290 fig.
  dipoles, 288–289, 288 fig., 289 fig.
  folded dipoles, 291–292, 291 fig., 292 fig.
  miscellaneous dipoles, 292–293, 294 fig.
  monopoles, 290–291, 290 fig.
  superturnstile antenna, 292, 292 fig., 293 fig.
broadside arrays, 174, 185, 185 fig., 186 fig.
  amplitude tapering of, 200–201, 200 table, 202 fig.
  beamwidth and gain of, 213–216
  and continuous aperture antenna, 196–197, 197 fig.
  linear, 181–184, 182 fig., 184 fig.
broadside patterns, of planar arrays, 211
Butler matrix, 355–356, 356 fig.

Cassegrain feed system, 245–246, 244 fig.
  and noise reduction, 323–324

coaxial lines, characteristic impedance for, 72
Cobra Dane (AN/FPS-108) phased array antenna, 366, 366 fig.
coherent side-lobe canceller (CSLC), 358
collimation
  defined, 228
  ray, 281
collinear broadside array, 183, 183 fig.
compact range, 382–385, 384 fig., 385 fig.
complementary antennas, 298
complex-variables, 439–443
conducting materials, of antennas, 90–91
conductors, 90–91
conformal arrays, 377–378
conical scan lobing system, 313
conical scanning, 311–314
conical spiral antenna, 297, 297 fig.
coordinate systems, 92–95, 98 fig.
corner-reflector antennas, 254–255, 254 fig., 255 fig.
corona, considerations in, 91
corrugated horns, 307, 307 fig.
cosmic-ray radiation, 3
coupling devices
  directional couplers, 81–84, 82 fig.–84 fig.
  hybrid couplers, 81–84, 82 fig.–84 fig.
  for transmission-line-to-waveguide coupling, 78–79, 80 fig.
current
  displacement, 122
  and electromagnetic fields, 1
  in long antennas, 131–135, 132 fig.–133 fig.
curtains, 188
Cutler, Maine, U.S. Navy installation in, 131
cutoff frequency, for waveguides, 75
cylindrical lens, 257

decibels, space attenuation in, 13
delta-match feed, 159, 159 fig.

design ratio, for frequency-independent antennas, 295
device under test (DUT), measurements of properties of, 401
dielectric constants, 17, 447 table, 465 table
dielectric lenses, 260–262
dielectric rods, as waveguides, 81
dielectrics, artificial, 258
diffraction, 15, 224
  defined, 25–26, 26 fig.
  at edge of obstacle, 25–26, 27 fig.
  geometric theory of, 326–327
diffuse reflection, 20
digital signal processing (DSP), 322
diode switching, 348–349
dipole antenna, 388
dipole-array patterns, two-element, 172–175
dipoles. *see also* short dipoles
  biconical antennas as, 289
  and broad-band antenna design, 287, 288–289, 288 fig., 289 fig.
  circular polarization with, 302–303, 303 fig.
  folded, 291–292, 291 fig., 292 fig.
  fractal, 329–330
  half-wave, 135–137, 136 fig.
  horizontal-plane patterns of two vertical, 174 fig.
  miscellaneous broad-band, 293–294, 395 fig.
directional couplers, 81–84
direction-finding antennas
  beam-maximum systems, 311
  lobing antennas, 311–313, 311 fig., 312 fig.
  low-frequency null systems, 310–311
directive antenna types, comparison of, 279
directivity
  calculation of, 181, 209
  defined, 98
  and electrically small antenna, 310
  element, 181–182
  of elemental dipole, 125–126
  and Hansen-Woodyard condition, 188, 216
  for helical antenna, 150
  IEEE definition of, 99
  of long-wire antenna, 139, 143
  of long-wire arrays, 219
  and pattern multiplication, 181
  of planar array, 190, 209–213
  and radiation intensity, 99
  of reflector antenna, 249
  for slot radiators, 155, 157
  and solid angle, 99, 100 fig.
discone antenna, 294 fig.
displacement current, 123
divergence, definition of, 428
divergence factor, 459–460
Dolph-Chebyschev (D-C) distribution, 203
Dolph-Chebyschev (D-C) patterns
  simplified calculations for, 205
  and Taylor distribution, 206, 208
dual-mode transducers, 305
ducting, 35
DUT. *see* device under test

E-3A airplane, 326
earth's reflection, and measured gain, 394
earth's reflection coefficient, variations in, 39–40
earth's surface
  effects of, 31–32
  reflection from, 35–39
E-2C aircraft, UHF array on, 216
Echo 1, 34–35
Echo 2, 34–35
edge taper, defined, 236
effective area, 103–105
Effelsberg, Germany, fully steerable radio-telescope antenna at, 252
efficiency, antenna
  aperture efficiency, 399
  radiation efficiency, 398–400

"egg crate" construction, 261
EHF. *see* extremely high frequency
electrically small antennas, 308–310
electric field intensity, geometry of, 123
electrodynamic phenomenon, radiation as, 121
electromagnetic (E-M) wave propagation, 427
electromagnetic (E-M) waves, velocity of, 430
electromagnetic field, 1
  energy transferred in, 123
electromagnetic spectrum, 3
electromagnetic waves, 159
  characteristics of
    absorption, 13–15
    decibel (logarithmic) expression of attenuation, 12–13
    field intensity and power density, 10–12
    frequency and wavelength, 3–4
    polarization, 6–7
    rays and wavefronts, 7–8
    space-time relationships, 4–5
    spherical waves and inverse-square law, 8, 10
    wave velocity, 2
  defined, 2
  environmental wave-propagation effects, 31–44
  origins of, 21
  and radiation requirements, 28–30
electromagnetic wave theory, 1
electronically scanned antennas (ESA), 315
electronically scanned array (ESA), in AWACS, 366
electronically steered arrays (ESAs), 169, 337, 364, *see also* phased arrays
  adaptive array antennas, 358–364
  advancements in, 337
  and beam-steering technology, 347–351
  Butler matrix, 355–356, 356 fig.
  microstrip and printed-circuited technology, 357
  and T/R modules, 354–355, 354 fig.
electronic scanning array
  design of, 169
  use for, 285
elemental dipole, 120, 151
  current and voltage in, 132
  directivity of, 125–126
  pattern of, 123–125, 124 fig.
  total power radiated by, 125
elementary doublet, 120
element directivity, effects of, 181–182
ellipsoidal dipole, 294 fig.
endfire arrays, 175, 186–188, 187 fig.
  feed arrangement for, 185, 187 fig.
  parasitically excited, 188–189
  patterns calculations of, 199–201
  unidirectional, 185
energy conservation, principle of, 8
Engineering Experiment Station (EES), at Georgia Institute of Technology, 271, 315, 319 fig.
environmental wave-propagation effects
  beyond-the-horizon propagation, 32–35, 33 fig.
  and earth environment, 31–32
  radio-transmission equation, 42–44
  and reflection from earth's surface, 35–39
  transionospheric, 41–42
  variations in earth's reflection coefficient, 39–40
  wave nomenclature, 40–41, 41 fig.
equiangular log-periodic antennas, 299–300
equivalent-circuit line representation, of transmission line, 48–49, 49 fig.
extremely high frequency (EHF)
  characteristics of, 3 table
  frequency allocations for, 4
extremely low frequency (ELF), characteristics of, 3 table

Faraday rotation, of polarization of wave, 41–42
Faraday's law, and Maxwell's equations, 428
far field
  and inverse-square law, 10
  minimum permissible distance for, 95
  statistical gain, 376–377
far-field range, for antenna measurements, 381
far zone, defined, 469
far-zone amplitude, measured wide-angle, 373, 374 fig.
far-zone approximation, 467–468, 468 fig.
far-zone measurements, 373, 377–383
  far-field ranges, 381–382
  high-frequency techniques, 379–381, 380 fig.
  low-frequency techniques, 379
fast Fourier transform (FFT), 328, 363, 472
Federal Communications Commission (FCC), 4, 177
the feed, defined, 233
feed design, for reflector or lens, 235–236, 235 fig., 236 fig.
feed lines, 89
feed methods
  basic, 159–164, 159 fig.–163 fig.
  "delta match," 161, 161 fig.
  for Franklin antenna, 185, 185 fig.
  for horn radiator, 150–151, 153, 163, 163 fig.
  for longer antennas, 132–135, 134 fig.
  with quarter-wave transmission-line transformer, 161, 163, 161 fig.
  "Zepp," 161–162, 162 fig.
feed systems
  Cassegrain, 244–245, 244 fig.
  corporate, 351–353, 353 fig.
  for endfire arrays, 186–188, 187 fig.
  line-source, 239–240, 240 fig., 241 fig.
  matrix methods, 355–356, 356 fig.
  for MILORD antenna, 316–317, 316 fig.
  for parabolic reflectors, 228–230, 230 fig.
  for paraboloid, 255
  for phased arrays, 357–358, 359 fig.
  primary, 249
Fermat's principle of least time, 265–266
ferrite phase shifters, 348–349
field-strength pattern, 36–40, 37 fig.
flat earth geometry, 450–453, 450 fig.
Fourier integral computer, development of, 271
Fourier transform, 472
fractal dipole antennas, types of, 330–331, 331 fig.
fractals, 285, 328, 330, 332
Franklin antenna, 185, 185 fig.
Fraunhofer region, 96, 233, 469
free space
  electromagnetic waves in, 2
  plane electromagnetic wave in, 5–6, 6 fig.
  point-source wavefronts and rays in, 9 fig.
  and wave velocity, 3
frequency
  defined, 3
  in electromagnetic spectrum, 3
frequency allocations, in U.S., 4
frequency-independent antennas
  equiangular log-periodic antennas, 299–300, 299 fig.
  and log-periodic principle, 294–297, 295 fig., 296 fig.
  practical log-periodic designs, 297–300, 298 fig.
  properties of, 295–296
  self-complementary antennas, 300–301, 300 fig., 301 fig.
  spiral antennas, 301, 301 fig.
frequency-scan antennas, 341–342, 341 fig.

Fresnel equations, 328–329, 445–447
Fresnel obliquity factor, 469–470
Fresnel region, 96, 233, 469–470
Friis transmission equation, 103–104
Ft. Huachuca, Arizona, U.S. Army
 Electronic Proving Ground at, 384

gain, 42
 in aperture analysis, 274 table, 278 table
 and aperture dimensions, 113–115
 and beamwidth, 105
 defined, 103, 399
 determination of, 107, 106 fig.
 of horn antennas, 242
 IEEE definition of, 99
 for long-wire arrays, 220, 221 fig.
 measurements for, 381
 and pattern multiplication, 181, 184
 and radiation intensity, 99–101
 and solid angle, 99–101, 100 fig.
 specified, 98–99
gain calibration procedures, 395
gain measurement
 absolute-field-strength method, 394
 by comparison, 410–413, 410 fig.
 power-measurement methods, 396
gain standards, 395–397
geodesic lens, 266–268, 266–268 figs.
geometric optics, 22, 233
 collimation, 228–229
 focusing, 228–229, 231, 235
geometric theory of diffraction (GTD), 285, 328–329
geometry
 flat earth, 451–453, 450 fig.
 fractal, 335
 planar near-field, 386–387, 387 fig.
 spherical earth, 455–457, 459, 456 fig., 457 fig.
 spherical near-field measured, 387, 389 fig.
 stripline, 367
Georgia Institute of Technology, Engineering Experiment Station at, 271, 315
global positioning satellite (GPS), frequency allocations for, 4
goniometer, 311–312
GPS. *see* global positioning satellite
GTD. *see* geometric theory of diffraction
grating lobes, 186, 198, 346–347, 349
Green Bank, West Virginia, U.S. National Radio Astronony Observatory at, 252
grounding, 91
ground reflection, and long-wire antennas, 143
ground wave, 40–41
group velocity, 72–74
guy wires, 90, 91

half-wave dipole, 133, 134, 136–139, 141–144, 134 fig., 137 fig., 138 fig.
Hamming function, 209
Hansen-Woodyard, 186, 188, 200, 201
helical antenna, 148–150, 148 fig.
 directivity for, 150–152, 154, 155
 feed method for, 159, 162
 normal mode, 149
 use of, 153, 157
Hertz, Heinrich, 120, 122, 430, 431
Hertzian dipole, 120
high frequency (HF), characteristics of, 1, 2, 3 table
horn antennas, 283
 aperture dimensions for, 113
 feed patterns for, 246, 248, 249
 and shapes of major lobes, 246, 248, 252
 wide-beamwidth patterns for, 247, 252
horn array, 220
horn radiators, 150–153
 biconical horn for, 154, 155, 154 fig.
 circular polarization with, 308

feed methods for, 159, 162, 161 fig.
radiation patterns for, 151, 152, 154, 155, 157
horns, corrugated, 307, 307 fig.
Howells-Applebaum method, of pattern optimization, 360–362
Huygens-Kirchhoff formulation, 469, 470
Huygens' principle, 2, 25–26, 26 fig., 151, 227
Huygens' wavelets, 470, 472
hybrid couplers, 80–82, 82 fig.

IEEE. *see* Institute of Electrical and Electronics Engineers, Inc.
illumination
defined, 236
reflectors, 227, 229–252, 228 fig., 230 fig., 235 fig., 243 fig., 244 fig.
ILS. *see* Instrument Low-Approach System
images, principle of, 21, 21 fig., 22, 129
impedance charts, 404
impedance match
in broad-band design, 285–290, 292, 293, 296
between transmitter and free space, 221, 223
impedance measurements, 401–404
network analyzers for, 391, 400–404, 403 fig.
standing-wave method, 401, 404, 401 fig.
impedances
in array theory, 169, 171
characteristic, 51, 53, 55, 71, 72, 76
mutual, 177
impedance transformation, analysis of, 65, 67, 69
impedance transformer
single-stub, 66, 66 fig.
transmission line as, 54, 55, 64, 65
induction field, 28
infinitesimal dipole, 120
input impedance, 110, 111
of basic folded dipole, 291
calculation of, 414, 415
for electrically small antennas, 308–311
equations for, 59, 62
and feed methods, 159, 162
measurement of, 389–391
of short dipoles, 126–129, 127 fig.
Institute of Electrical and Electronics Engineers (IEEE), 43, 450, 460
Instrument Low-Approach System (ILS), 314, 319
insulators
protection of, 90, 91
uses for, 83
intercontinental ballistic missile (ICBM) detection and analysis, 366
interference, 15, 394
and antenna applications, 20, 23, 25
effects of, 29
problem of, 53
interferometer system, 314
International Telecommunications Union (ITU), 3–4
inverse-square law, 10
and attenuation, 12–14
and power density, 8, 10–12
and radiation process, 28
spherical waves and, 8
ionosphere
and long-distance radio propagation, 33, 34
and radio waves, 2, 40–41
ionospheric scatter, 34
irises, reactance introduced into waveguides by, 77, 77 fig.
Isbell log-periodic dipole array, 299, 230, 305
isotrope, defined, 8
isotropic point source, 169–171, 171 fig.
ITU. *see* International Telecommunications Union

jamming, 7
"J" antenna, 162
Jodrell Bank, radio telescope antenna at, 252

Kirchhoff method, 328
Koch loop antenna, 330, 331, 330 fig.
Kraus, John, 148

Law of Conservation of Energy, 8, 10
leaky-wave antenna, 159
lens
  beamwidth and, 233, 238, 239
  Bootlace, 353
  for low side lobes, 326
  Rotman, 353
  waveguide horns as feeds for, 245–247
  zoned, 259
lens antennas
  beam steering by feed offset with, 269
  compared with reflectors, 275, 281
  dielectric lenses, 264–266
  focusing with dielectric and metal plate lenses, 262
  geodesic Luneberg lenses, 265–268, 268 fig.
  lens refracting media, 260, 262, 268
  low side-lobe design for, 327
  metal plate lenses, 262, 264, 265, 265 fig.
  optical lenses, 257, 258
  surface configurations for, 257–259, 259 fig.
  use of, 257, 266
  variable-index-of-refraction lenses, 261
lens design, 262
light
  free-space velocity of, 73
  Maxwell's hypothesis for, 430
lightning-induced currents, protection against, 91
light waves, reflection of, 19
Lincoln Laboratory, 367
linear arrays
  broadside, 183–186, 186 fig., 190–194, 191 fig.
  element spacing of, 215
  pattern calculations for, 194–199
  synthetic aperture as, 324
linear superposition, principle of, 22
line-source feed, 239–241, 240 fig., 249
line sources, pattern calculations for, 271, 276, 277 fig.
Litz wire, 90
load impedance, determination of, 63
loading coils, and radiation resistance, 309
lobes
  grating, 184, 186, 194, 198, 208, 218, 332, 346–347, 349, 370
  for horn antennas, 245
  phase quantization, 347, 349
lobing antennas, 312–315, 312 fig.
Lockheed Martin, 329, 364 fig.
log-periodic antennas
  equiangular, 299–301, 299 fig.
  problems and exercises, 335
log-periodic principle, 294–297, 295 fig., 296 fig.
long-wire antennas, directional properties of, 218
loop antenna, 87
  Alford, 147 fig.
  circular, 146
  coaxially positioned, 147
  feed methods for, 145
  Koch, 330–331, 330 fig., 331 fig.
  resistance of, 145
  small, 144–145, 144 fig.
lossless infinite line, 50–51
low frequency (LF), characteristics of, 3 table
Luneberg lens, 261–262, 262 fig.
  beam steering by feed offset with, 269
  geodesic, 260, 265–269, 262 fig., 266 fig., 268 fig.

Luneberg lens antenna, rapid-scan, geodesic, 317, 319, 319 fig.

magnetic dipole, oscillating, 120
magnetic field. *see also* electromagnetic field
  generation of, 28
  of short dipoles, 120–123, 121 fig., 122 fig.
Marconi, Guglielmo, 32
masts, 88
matched load condition, 55–56
matching principle, in impedance relations, 65
Mathcad calculations, 39, 97, 445, 459, 469, 479
Mathcad software, 250, 374
Maxwell, James Clerk, 1, 122, 427
Maxwell's equations, 1, 427–431
  for analysis of radiation, 151
  and determination of gain, 105, 106 fig.
  for electric currents and associated fields, 27
  for electromagnetic analysis of element coupling, 178
  Huygens' principle deductible from, 25
  physical meaning of, 428
  plane waves in uniform material in, 429
  on reciprocity, 30
medium frequency (MF), characteristics of, 3 table
metallic-obstacle delay medium, 260
metal-plate lens, 262–265, 264 fig., 265 fig.
metal-plate waveguide refracting medium, 260
metals, as conductors, 89–90
meteor scatter, 34
Method of Moments (MoM), 285, 328–329
microstrip antennas, 157–158, 158 fig.
microstrip array, 220
microwave region, 4
millimeter wavelength region, 4
MILORD antenna, 316–317, 316 fig., 318 fig.
Molnya orbits, 35
Molnya satellites, 35
monopoles, 290–291, 290 fig.
  conical skirt, 294 fig.
  folded, 294 fig.
  horizontal-plane patterns of two vertical, 176 fig.
  uses for, 291
monopulse, 314
monopulse lobing, 314
monopulse operation, 357
multielement array, 178, 182, 184, 182 fig., 184 fig.
multipath analyses, 459
multipath effects
  and flat earth geometry, 451–453
  of pattern propagation factor F, 450
multipath propagation, 381
mutual coupling
  between array elements, 169, 172
  in array pattern analysis, 221
  in beam-steering technology, 347–349
  effects of, 177–178, 181–182
  with planar arrays, 271
mutual impedance, 178–179

narrow-beam antennas, 378, 386
National Aeronautical and Space Administration (NASA)
  Deep Space Network program, 413
  and satellite communications, 34
National Telecommunications and Information Agency, 4
near-field
  radiating, 96, 470–472
  reactive, 96
near-field measurements, 96, 382, 385–386
  cylindrical, 386–387, 387 fig., 388 fig.
  planar, 386–387, 386 fig., 387 fig.
  spherical, 386–389, 389 fig.

near-field statistical gain, 376–377
network analyzer, 391, 400–404, 403 fig.
noise
  atmospheric, 321
  calculated temperatures for, 409, 410 fig.
  comparison source of, 413
  cosmic, 321
  at high frequencies, 29
  measurement techniques, 410–413, 411 fig.
  in radio systems, 321
  system noise temperature, 414–417, 417 table
  theory, 407–408
  using ambient sources of, 413
noise, antenna
  external sources of, 410 fig.
  temperature, 409, 410 fig.
noise figure, 414–417, 417 table
noise measurements, 371, 412
noise theory, 407
nomenclature, wave, 40, 41 fig.
nonresonant antennas, 139, 143
normal mode helical antenna, 149
null-filling effect, due to phase error, 375, 375 fig.
null systems, low-frequency, 311–312

obliquity factor, 469–474
ohmic loss, for thin wall radome, 466
omnidirectionality, 308
optical principles, radio-wave, 15–26
optics
  geometric, 22, 227–234
organ-pipe feed, 267

parabola, geometry of, 228, 229 fig.
parabolic antenna, steps for developing, 251–252
parabolic cylinder, 230, 230 fig.
  aperture of, 232
  attenuation for, 230–231
  line-source feed for, 239
  pattern evaluation for, 251–252, 251 fig.
  stacking, 256
parabolic reflector
  compared with lens antennas, 257–258
  feed-positioning requirements for, 241–244, 243 fig.
paraboloidal reflector
  Cassegrain feed for, 244, 244 fig.
  elliptical-aperture, 237–238
  feed-support for, 242, 243 fig.
  simultaneous-lobing (monopulse) feed for, 312, 312 fig.
paraboloidal reflector antenna, far-zone pattern of, 373, 374 fig.
paraboloids, dual polarized back-to back, 317, 319 fig.
paraboloid surface, 230, 230 fig., 232
parasitic elements, 188
parasitic excitation, 188
Pascal's triangle, 202
patch antennas, 157–159, 158 fig.
  design and development, 158
  with fractal patch, 331, 331 fig.
patch arrays, 220–221
path length differences from aperture, 476–477, 476 fig.
path length differences, from planar aperture, 475–477, 476 fig.
pattern measurements, 377
pattern multiplication, principle of, 179–181, 184
pattern optimization, 361–362
pattern-propagation factor F, 43–44, 450–451, 450 fig.
patterns, endfire array, 199–201, 200 fig.
  see also radiation patterns
pedestals, 88–89
phase-comparison lobing, 314
phased arrays
  alternative configurations, 355
  array bandwidth, 342–343
  array sum and difference patterns, 357

conformal, 357–358
defined, 169
effective aperture *vs.* scan angle, 340
feed system technology for, 351–358, 352 fig.–354 fig., 356 fig.
frequency-scan antennas, 341–342, 341 fig.
grating lobes, 346–347
patterns calculated for, 344–346
and phase shift requirements, 339
principles of, 338
for scanning, 221
subarrays, 355
time delay, 339–340, 339 fig.
phased array technology, 338
phase distribution patterns, of current and voltage, 132–133, 133 fig., 134 fig.
phase error
effects of random aperture on, 479–482, 480 fig.
far-zone range-approximation and, 467–468
phase pattern, 93
phase-phase steered scanning arrays, 364
phase quantization, effects of, 349–350
phasers, *vs.* phasors, 347
phase shifters, 347–349, 349 fig.
phase velocity, 72–73
pillbox antenna, 240 fig.
planar aperture, path length differences from, 475–477, 476 fig.
planar arrays
broadside patterns of, 213
calculations for, 209–210
elements of equal amplitude, 212–213
element spacings for, 210, 210 fig.
equations for patterns of, 213–215
pattern *vs.* Θ and Φ in, 191–192
separable aperture distributions, 211–212
with uniform aperture distribution, 190
plane wave, space-time relationships for, 5–6, 6 fig.
point source feed, 249
polarization
circular, 7, 42, 113, 150, 235, 300, 302–305, 303 fig., 388, 433
defined, 433
effect of Faraday rotation on, 41–42
of electromagnetic waves, 6–7
elliptical, 388, 389
horizontal *vs.* vertical, 39
linear, 7
measurement of, 371, 398
multipath dependencies on, 453–455, 454 fig.–456 fig.
polarization pattern, 93, 113
polarization theory, 433
and circularly polarized components, 435–436, 435 fig.
and linearly polarized components, 433–435, 434 fig., 435 fig.
relationships between linearly and circularly polarized components, 436–437
polarizers, 305–306, 306 fig.
polyrod antenna, 159
positioner, 390–391, 391 fig.
in compact range design, 384
types of, 403
power density
calculation of, 8, 10
defined, 8
of electromagnetic fields, 10–11
and reflection of radio waves, 19
power-density ratio, 12
power dividers, for transmission lines, 67–69, 67 fig., 69 fig.
power transmission coefficient, 19
Poynting vector, 430–431
principal-plane patterns, defined, 93
propagation
beyond-the-horizon, 33, 33 fig.
round-the-world, 34
with spherical earth model, 456, 457 fig.

propagation medium, 2
  isotropic, 10
  with nonlinear properties, 22
  refractive index of, 16
  and wave impedance, 11
pseudo-Brewster angle, 40

quantization lobes, 349
quarter wave plate, 304

radar band designations, 4, 5 table
radar monopulse method of direction finding, 357
radiating far-field, 96, 470–472
radiating near-field, 96, 470–472
radiation
  and electric currents, 27
  and electromagnetic waves, 26
  from electrons in galactic space, 29
  major and minor lobes of, 107
  requirements for, 28, 29 fig.
  from sharp edges, 332
radiation efficiency, 111, 400
radiation field, 28, 124
radiation intensity, determination of, 102
radiation patterns, 95
  absolute and relative, 94
  from aperture analyses, 246
  of array, 171, 177–178
  array factors, 194, 197
  of continuous aperture antennas, 248
  coordinate systems, 91, 92 fig.
  definition of, 93
  and earth-reflection interference, 98
  in free space, 97–98
  of horn antennas, 151, 153, 247
  of long-wire antennas, 139
  near-field and far-field, 95–97
  of nonresonant antennas, 142
  in a plane, 93–94
  of resonant antennas, 139
  for uniform linear arrays, 185
radiation resistance
  in array theory, 181
  calculation of, 108–109
  concept of, 102, 104, 108
  for electrically small antennas, 309
  input impedance and, 177
  of long-wire resonant antenna, 141
  measurement of, 401
  in resonant antennas, 139
  of short dipoles, 125
radiators, 293
  adapted to feeding reflectors, 235
  broad-band dipoles, 292, 303
  half-wave dipole as, 136
  helical antennas, 148–150
  horn, 152–155
  long-wire, 141
  loop antennas, 144–147
  primary, 239
  short dipoles, 121
    beamwidth for, 126, 129
    dipole radiation, 120
    directivity of, 125, 137
    input impedance of, 126, 132
    with nonuniform current distribution, 127, 130
    pattern of, 123–124, 126
    radiation resistance of, 130
    short vertical antenna with ground image, 129
    top-loaded antenna, 130
  slot radiators, 155, 157
  vertical-tower, 138
radio broadcasting, two-element array in, 175
radio frequency identification (RFID), 96
Radio Frequency Spectrum, 3 table
radio-horizon effect, and earth's shadow, 31 fig.
radio propagation, long-distance, 32–34
radio transmission, 1
radio transmission equation, 42
radio transmitter, power delivered by, 65

radio-wave optical principles, 15, 17, 19, 21, 23, 25
  Huygens' principle, 25–26
  interference, 22–23, 25–26
  principle of images, 21, 21 fig.
  reflection, 18–21
  refraction, 15–18
radio waves
  beyond-the-horizon propagation, 32, 33 fig., 35
  and earth environment, 31
  and earth's reflection coefficient, 39
  and reflection from earth's surface, 35–36, 38
  velocity of, 5
radomes
  defined, 469
  electrical properties of materials used for, 465
  problems caused by, 479
  types of, 486
  use for, 103
random phase errors, effects of, 479
range
  compact, 385, 417
  far-zone approximation, 470, 472
  principal-plane patterns *vs.*, 473
range antenna, in far-zone pattern measurements, 388, 396
ray collimation, 281
Rayleigh criterion, 21, 449
rays
  characteristics of, 9
  defined, 5
  point-source, 9 fig.
  in propagation medium, 7
ray-wave front analysis, 227
reactive field, and dipole polarity, 121
reactive near-zone field, 469
reception
  defined, 30
  and polarization, 42
reception patterns, 91
reciprocity
  between conductance and resistance, 58
  defined, 21
  for electrically small antennas, 309
  principle, 31
reflection, 15
  defined, 15–16
  diffuse, 20
  from earth's surface, 35–36, 38, 40
  laws of, 229
  at plane boundary, 19, 19 fig.
  from semi-rough surface, 21, 21 fig.
  specular, 20, 21
  and standing waves, 52, 76
reflection coefficients, 19
  divergence factor, 459–460
  and Fresnel's equations, 445
  pattern-propagation factor, 450
  for rough surfaces, 449
  for smooth and rough earth surfaces, 445
  for smooth land and sea, 447
  variation in earth's, 39–40
  and VSWR, 61, 63
reflector antenna
  advantages of, 284
  and beamwidth, 237–238
  Cassegrain, 245
  compact range, 384, 384 fig., 385
  compared with lenses, 285
  construction of, 253–254
  corner-reflector antennas, 255–256
  design, 251–252
  directivity for, 234
  far-zone amplitude pattern of, 373, 374 fig.
  feed-positioning requirements for, 241
  illumination of, 237–239
  largest, 252–253
  low side-lobe design for, 329
  offset, 245, 252
  parabolic, 232–234, 230 fig., 235 fig.
  parabolic cylinder, 235, 243 fig.
  surface accuracy requirements for, 253
  waveguide horns as feeds for, 248

refraction
  atmospheric, 32
  effects of, 467
  with gradual variation of refractive index, 17–18, 18 fig.
  at plane boundary, 18 fig.
refractive index
  of air, 18
  defined, 16
resonant antennas, 136
  long-wire, 169
  patterns of, 139, 140 fig., 142
resonant circuits, 57–58
RFID. *see* radio frequency identification
rhombic antenna, 219, 219 fig.
rotational lens, 258
Rotman lens, 353
roughness, electromagnetic effects of, 455
rough surfaces, reflection coefficients for, 459–460
round-the-world propagation, 34

SAR. *see* synthetic aperture radar
satellite communications, early, 34
satellites
  geostationary, 35
  low earth orbiting, 35
  Molnya, 35
  turnstile antenna on artificial, 308
scale-model measurements, 389
scan angle, 269
scan antennas, rapid mechanical, 341
scan element pattern (SEP), 177
scan mode of operation, 325
scanning
  conical, 323
  phased arrays for, 221
scanning arrays, phase-phase steered, 364
scatter methods, limitation of, 34
Scientific Atlanta, Inc., 271, 383
sea
  field strengths above smooth, 453, 454 fig.
  reflection coefficients for, 458–460
self-complementary antenna, 300
  example of, 306
  logarithmic-spiral, 301 fig.
  problems and exercises, 335
SEP see scan element pattern, 177
SHF. *see* super high frequency
shielding, principle of, 29
ships, search radar antenna on, 106
short-circuited lines, 60
short dipoles
  beamwidth for, 202, 205
  center-fed, 120
  characteristics of, 111
  circuits of center-fed, 127 fig.
  compared with half-wave dipole, 139, 141
  current and voltage in, 132–133
  current-voltage relationship for, 120
  and dipole radiation, 120
  effective length of, 129
  input impedance of, 126
  isolated, 119
  with nonuniform current distribution, 127, 130
  pattern of, 125–126
  short vertical antenna with ground image, 129, 132
  and spherical coordinate systems, 123
short monopoles, total radiated power of, 131
side-lobe blanker (SLB), 358
side-lobe canceller (SLC) antenna, 358, 359
side-lobe levels, measurements for, 389
sidelobe ratio, 107
side lobes
  in aperture analysis, 274
  and aperture dimensions, 113
  array tapering for reduction of, 201, 203
  of Dolph-Chebyschev patterns, 207
  for elliptical apertures, 237
  extremely low, 326–327
  of reflector antenna, 251–252

signal-to-noise ratio, 320
skin effect, phenomenon of, 50
sky wave, 40–41
slot array, 220
slot radiators
  bandwidth properties of, 293
  impedance properties of, 155
  use for, 203
  waveguide slots for, 157
slotted lines, 402–403
Smith Chart, 63, 66–67, 289, 401
  basic plan of, 404
  example of use of, 415
soil, electrical properties of, 447 table
solid angle, 101, 102
space attenuation, 13, 14
  for paraboloidal reflector, 240
  for point and line sources, 230
space-fed array, 353–354
space shuttle-imaging-radar-B (SIR-B), 324
space-tapering, 208. *see also* tapering
space telemetry applications, for helical antenna, 150
space-time adaptive processing (STAP), 362
space-time relationships
  for electromagnetic waves, 10, 22
  and interference phenomenon, 25
specular reflection, 20, 21
"speed of light," in vacuum, 2
spherical coordinate system, standard, 372 fig.
spherical earth geometry, 455, 457
spherical earth model, to estimate wave-propagation path, 32
spiral antennas, 301
spotlight mode of operation, 325
stacking, for superturnstile TV transmitting antenna, 293, 302
standing-wave, 62–64, 67
standing-wave measurement
  determination of load impedance by, 63
  of impedance, 401 fig., 404, 406 fig., 407
standing-wave pattern, of current and voltage, 132
standing-wave ratio, with attenuation, 62–64
standing-wave voltage patterns, 62
STAP. *see* space-time adaptive processing
static-charge buildup, protection against, 91
static field, and dipole polarity, 121
steady-state lossless line equations, 54
steering angle, 269
stripline geometry, 357
strip lines, 69, 71
stripmap mode of operation, 331
stub transformers, 66
submillimeter, characteristics of, 3 table
super high frequency (SHF)
  characteristics of, 3 table
  frequency allocations for, 4
superposition, principle of, 22–25
superrefraction, 35
superturnstile, 292, 292 fig., 293 fig.
superturnstile antenna, 303
surface roughness
  multipath dependencies on, 453
  reflection coefficients for, 445, 447 table, 448, 449
surface-wave antennas, 159, 188
surface wave propagation, 33
synthetic-aperture antennas, 285, 324–325
synthetic-aperture radar (SAR), 324, 332
system noise temperature, 415–417, 417 table

taper, *see* tapersing
tapering
  amplitude, 191, 191 fig., 192, 194–197, 197 fig., 198–203, 204 fig., 205–206, 206 fig., 207–209
  and Dolph-Chebyschev synthesis, 205, 207
  in low-noise designs, 322

tapering (*cont'd*)
with low-side-lobe array distributions, 208
and mutual coupling, 181
for elliptical apertures, 237
for side-lobe reduction, 353, 355–356
Taylor distribution
aperture, 203, 205–206, 206 fig., 207–209, 211, 213–214, 216–218
optimum illumination, 238
tables, 274, 278
TE. *see* transverse-electric
television, frequency allocations for, 4
Telstar satellite-communication ground terminal, at Andover, Maine, 322–323, 327
TEM. *see* transverse-electric-magnetic
thinning, 210. *see also* tapering
tin-hat lens, 273
TM. *see* transverse-magnetic
top loading
procedure, 131
and radiation resistance, 315
short-monopole antenna, 131 fig.
towers, 88–91
T/R. *see* transmit/receive
transionospheric propagation, 41
transmission equation, 42
transmission line equations
attenuation constant, 64
for determination of load impedance, 63
special line conditions, 55
steady-state lossless line equations, 54
transmission lines
basic concepts, 49–50
in broad-band array design, 287
coupling devices, 77, 80
and feed methods, 158–164
forms of, 69, 71, 70 fig., 75 fig.
impedance matching and power division, 65–71
input impedance of, 59
lossless infinite line, 50
for multiple loads, 71 fig.
parallel branching, 67
power dividers for, 67
reflection and standing waves, 52
reflection coefficient and VSWR, 60
resonant and nonresonant, 143
standing-wave patterns, 62
strip, 69, 70 fig., 71
two-conductor, 69, 76
two-wire, 47, 48 fig.
waveguides as, 47–48, 71–90
transmit and receive (T/R) modules, 362–363, 362 fig. 364
transverse-electric (TE) lines, 75
transverse-electric-magnetic (TEM) lines, 75
transverse-magnetic (TM) lines, 75
trapezoidal tooth antenna, 297, 298 fig., 305
"trapping," 35
traveling wave antennas, 136
traveling waves, 136
triangular dipole, 294
triply folded horn reflector antenna, 324
Tropospheric scatter propagation, 34
tuning inductors, and radiation resistance, 315
tuning screws, reactance introduced into waveguides by, 77
tuning stub, 66
turnstile antenna, 308

UHF. *see* ultra high frequency
ultra high frequency (UHF)
absorption in, 13
characteristics of, 2
frequency allocations for, 4
ultra low frequency (ULF), characteristics of, 3 table
ultra side lobe array, 367 fig.
uniform linear arrays, 182–183
endfire arrays, 186–188
radiation pattern for, 214

vacuum
  electromagnetic propagation in, 2
  electromagnetic waves in, 1
V antenna, 218, 219 fig.
variable-index-of-refraction lenses, 261
velocity
  in transmission lines, 72, 76
  versus refractive index, 16
vertical-tower radiators, 138
very high frequency (VHF)
  absorption in, 13
  characteristics of, 2
very low frequency (VLF)
  characteristics of, 2
  wave-guide-mode propagation, 33
VHF. *see* very high frequency
VLF. *see* very low frequency
voltage
  and electromagnetic fields, 1
  in long antennas, 139, 140 fig.
voltage equation, 54
voltage maximum, 61–62
voltage standing-wave ratio (VSWR), 67
  on impedance charts, 404
  and input impedance, 161
  measurement of, 413
volume arrays
  formation of, 208
  two-element-deep, 193
VSWR. *see* voltage standing-wave ratio

wall cross sections, radome, 463, 464 fig.
water sources, electrical properties of, 447 table
"wave" antenna, 143
wavefronts
  characteristics of, 2
  defined, 5
  in geometric optics, 233
  in isotropic propagation medium, 10
  point-source, 9 fig.
  in propagation medium, 7
  spherical, 8
waveguide horn radiator, 151
waveguides
  circular guides, 78
  coaxial transmission lines as, 80
  cutoff frequency for, 74–76
  forms of, 78, 87
  impedance in, 76
  impedance matching in, 76
  junctions, 78, 80 fig.
  modes of propagation for, 75–76
  phase and group velocities for, 72
  rectangular, 76, 75 fig.
  transmission-line-to-waveguide coupling, 77
wavelength in, 73
wavelength
  antenna size and, 88
  calculation of, 5
  defined, 5
  free-space, 3
wave nomenclature, 40
wave polarization, elliptical, 433. *see also* polarization
waves. *see* electromagnetic waves; radio waves
wave velocity, in transmission lines, 72
weather protection, 90
wind forces, and antenna construction, 255
wind resistance, of superturnstiles, 292
wire, antenna, 90, 330
wireless communications, original, 96
"wireless," first use of, 33
wire-trapezoidal-tooth antenna, 305
wire triangular tooth antenna, 299, 298 fig.

Yagi-Uda antenna, 159
Yagi-Uda array, 147–148
  cross-polarized, 305
  folded dipoles for, 291

"Zepp" feeder, 161
zigzag antenna, 159

About the Author

Maurice Long's interest in antennas and propagation began as a teenager with his amateur radio station W4GPR. Shortly after World War II, he began research work at Georgia Institute of Technology on microwave propagation, and that was followed by antenna developments for microwave and millimeter radar. Activities in multipolarization and rapid scan antennas lead to his being General Chairman of the Department of Defense sponsored 1956 Georgia Tech/SCEL Symposium on Scanning Antennas. Subsequently, much of his work at Georgia Tech focused on antennas, electromagnetic scattering, and microwave and millimeter radar. Later, as a consultant to Lockheed Martin and other companies, he worked in radar design and analysis, including the use of large airborne mechanical and electronic scanning antennas.

At Georgia Tech he held research and academic positions, including Principal Research Engineer, Professor of Electrical Engineering, Associate Graduate Dean for Research, and Director of the Engineering Experiment Station (now Georgia Tech Research Institute). Presently he teaches graduate courses part time at Southern Polytechnic State University in antenna design and radar systems, works as a radar consultant, and maintains an affiliation as a retiree with the Georgia Tech Research Institute.

Dr. Long's previous books include *Radar Reflectivity of Land and Sea*, 3rd ed., Artech House and *Airborne Early Warning System Concepts*, SciTech Publishing. He is a Life Fellow of the Institute of Electrical and Electronics Engineers; and member of Academy of Electromagnetics and Commission F of International Union of Radio Science. Additional personal information is available in *Who's Who in America, Who's Who in Engineering*, *American Men and Women in Science*, *and McGraw-Hill Leaders in Electronics.*